SAMS
# Teach Yourself

# Red Hat®
# Fedora™ 4
## Linux®

Aron Hsiao

**SAMS** 800 East 96th Street, Indianapolis, Indiana, 46240 USA

# Sams Teach Yourself Red Hat® Fedora™ 4 Linux® All in One

International Standard Book Number: 0-672-32707-4

Library of Congress Catalog Card Number: 2004093742

Printed in the United States of America

First Printing: July 2005

08   07   06   05        4   3   2   1

## Trademarks

All terms mentioned in this book that are known to be trademarks or service marks have been appropriately capitalized. Sams Publishing cannot attest to the accuracy of this information. Use of a term in this book should not be regarded as affecting the validity of any trademark or service mark.

Red Hat is a registered trademark of Red Hat, Inc.

## Warning and Disclaimer

## Bulk Sales

Sams Publishing offers excellent discounts on this book when ordered in quantity for bulk purchases or special sales. For more information, please contact

**U.S. Corporate and Government Sales**
**1-800-382-3419**
corpsales@pearsontechgroup.com

For sales outside of the U.S., please contact

**International Sales**
international@pearsoned.com

**Acquisitions Editors**
Linda Bump Harrison
Shelley Johnston

**Development Editor**
Scott Meyers

**Managing Editor**
Charlotte Clapp

**Project Editor**
Dan Knott

**Copy Editor**
Chuck Hutchinson

**Indexer**
Rebecca Solerno

**Proofreader**
Leslie Joseph

**Technical Editor**
Dallas Releford

**Publishing Coordinator**
Vanessa Evans

**Multimedia Developer**
Dan Scherf

**Designer**
Gary Adair

**Page Layout**
Jeff Henn

# Contents at a Glance

## Part V: Advanced Topics

## Appendixes

# Table of Contents

**Sams Teach Yourself Red Hat Fedora 4 Linux All in One**

**Part VI: Appendixes**

# About the Author

**Aron Hsiao** is a longtime Unix and Linux enthusiast with over a decade of experience administering Unix-like operating systems. Over the years, he has worked in network deployment, software development, web development, and Internet advertising. He has also worked as a volunteer in a number of computer-related capacities in his community and served as the About.com guide to Linux from 1997 through 2001. He holds degrees in English and Anthropology from the University of Utah and a master's degree in the Social Sciences from the University of Chicago. He currently works as an editor for military history titles at ABC-CLIO. He is the author of a number of Linux titles, including *The Concise Guide to XFree86 for Linux, Sams Teach Yourself Linux Security Basics in 24 Hours*, and others.

# Dedication

*To all of the people in my life—past, present, and future. Be well.*

# Acknowledgments

Each time I do this, I think the final product gets a little better, but each time the process is also a little harder. There are always stumbling blocks along the way. Without the support of a large cast of people, it would never happen!

The team at Sams Publishing has been the driving force behind the ultimate success of this book. Many thanks are due to Shelley, Linda, Katie, Lorna, Dave, Nancy, Tricia, Dallas, Dan, Chuck, and everyone else who has worked on this title or who has participated in its ongoing development. I owe a special debt of gratitude to Jeff Koch, who got me started writing technical books.

A work like this one could never exist without the support of my immediate and extended family, who have always been willing to contribute time, energy, and other resources. Included in this group of people are Carlos, Tammy, Onyx, and Linda, who provided the physical space in which recent work on this book has taken place. Finally, thanks are also due to Jolinda, who has made this year a year to remember.

# We Want to Hear from You!

As the reader of this book, *you* are our most important critic and commentator. We value your opinion and want to know what we're doing right, what we could do better, what areas you'd like to see us publish in, and any other words of wisdom you're willing to pass our way.

You can email or write me directly to let me know what you did or didn't like about this book—as well as what we can do to make our books stronger.

*Please note that I cannot help you with technical problems related to the topic of this book, and that due to the high volume of mail I receive, I might not be able to reply to every message.*

When you write, please be sure to include this book's title and author as well as your name and phone or email address. I will carefully review your comments and share them with the author and editors who worked on the book.

Email:     opensource@samspublishing.com

Mail:      Mark Taber
           Associate Publisher
           Sams Publishing
           800 East 96th Street
           Indianapolis, IN 46240 USA

# Reader Services

For more information about this book or another Sams Publishing title, visit our website at www.samspublishing.com. Type the ISBN (excluding hyphens) or the title of a book in the Search field to find the page you're looking for.

# Introduction

Welcome to the world of Linux!

You're reading this introduction, so it's likely that you've heard the hype: Linux is a fast, powerful, stable operating system that is used more and more every day, in business, in government, in education, and in homes. Linux powers a large portion of the servers that form the backbone of the World Wide Web and the Internet. Linux can be found operating manufacturing equipment, point of sale equipment, automotive equipment, personal data management equipment, and even a variety of equipment at government agencies like NASA. Vendors, too, are now heavily invested in Linux; large companies such as IBM have adopted Linux as the basis for entire large-scale computing product lines.

This book will help anyone wanting to use the Fedora Core family of Linux operating systems for any of these purposes. Its real target audience, however, is somewhat more accessible: the ever-growing body of daily computer users, business owners, and network administrators who want to use Linux to do everyday work of all kinds. This book assumes that you have no previous experience working with Linux; it presents all the information you need to get acquainted and become productive with Fedora Core 4—right away.

This book is organized into easy-to-digest chapters that are intended to operate as lessons. Each of these lessons begins with a list of topics you'll cover as you work your way through the chapter; each lesson is designed to instruct you in one major topic related to using Fedora Core 4. As you progress through the lessons presented here, you'll learn to install Fedora Core 4 for yourself; to perform everyday tasks, such as Web browsing, word processing, and file management at the command line and on the desktop; and to troubleshoot and administer a Linux PC or small Linux server.

## Fedora Core 4 and Linux

If you have studied Linux at all, you are probably aware that there are a number of popular "distributions" of Linux, each of which is an operating system in its own right. Fedora Core is a community-supported Linux operating system. Fedora Core 4 was designed from the ground up to be a powerful business or personal desktop environment.

Other names in the Linux world might sound familiar to you as well: Debian Linux, SuSE Linux, Linux Mandrake, Connectiva Linux, and Slackware Linux among them. Make no mistake: Each of these products is also *Linux,* built from the same rock-solid code and with many of the same goals in mind. Fedora Core and these other Linux distributions also are largely compatible with one another, both in hardware and software terms. Still, each Linux operating system maintains its own unique focus and personality as well—Debian for free software purists; Mandrake for those seeking ease of use above all else; Slackware for converts from other, more traditional Unix operating systems; and so on.

In the final analysis however, Fedora Core remains one of the most well known and well liked of the Linux operating systems for business and professional deployment. Those responsible for the creation of Fedora Core are largely responsible for bringing Linux from the marketplace of ideas to the marketplace of business and to the halls of government. Fedora Core also offers an excellent balance between power, ease of installation, and ease of administration. If you're thinking of giving Linux a try, you can't go wrong with Fedora Core 4.

# What You'll Learn in This Book

As a set of lessons that build on one another sequentially, this book is written to be studied one chapter at a time, in order, from beginning to end. Early lessons ground you in Linux basics, and later lessons build on the foundations laid by those earlier lessons. Taken together, all of these lessons represent a general introduction to Linux use and to the nuances of the Fedora Core desktop in particular. Again, the information in this book is targeted at readers with no prior experience with Linux or other Unix-like operating systems.

There are five major topic areas to discuss when learning to use a Unix-like operating system; an attempt has been made to present them in logical order in this book's five parts:

- ► Chapters 1–3 cover basic Fedora Core 4 installation and configuration. This topic is important because so few PCs and only a relatively small number of low-end servers come bundled with Linux as a turnkey product, meaning that you'll likely be installing and configuring Linux yourself.

- ► Chapters 4–7 cover the basics of the Fedora Core 4 desktop environment, such as working with icons and menus on your desktop and with application windows. You'll also learn how to find and manage files and folders on your Linux system, first by using your mouse and then by using the Linux command line.

- ► Chapters 8–17 take you more deeply into the world of Fedora Core desktop applications, covering a number of business-oriented and network-oriented applications similar to those found in the Windows and Mac OS worlds. You'll use the Fedora Core 4 desktop environment to create documents, spreadsheets, and presentations; to edit your photos; to browse the Web; and to read and respond to electronic mail, among other tasks.

▶ Chapters 18–25 introduce the powerful, programmable Linux command line and a number of applications that don't require a desktop environment or a mouse to be able to operate. For all the polish you'll find on the Linux desktop, the command line still lies at the center of the Linux universe and provides one of the most flexible rapid application development and scripting environments anywhere in computing.

▶ Chapters 26–35 take you under the hood, to cover system administration and other advanced topics in Linux. The term **system administration** refers loosely to the set of skills necessary to tailor a Linux system to your needs and then to keep it operating securely and robustly—often while providing varied network services to multiple users. Although understanding Linux system administration isn't always necessary to be able to perform everyday tasks such as word processing or Web browsing, system administration remains an essential skill for users hoping to deploy Linux for anything other than purely personal computing. Even casual Linux users are likely to need some system administration skills—for example, the ability to install software or to back up important data to removable storage media.

Users with some Linux experience already might find that they want to study only particular chapters, or to study the chapters in this book in a different order. Each of these chapters should be self-contained enough to make this type of study possible. For those with no previous Linux experience, however, I prefer to repeat the sage advice of Lewis Carroll:

"Begin at the beginning, and go on till you come to the end: then stop."

Enjoy teaching yourself how to use Fedora Core 4!

# Conventions Used in This Book

This book uses the following conventions:

The terms *Fedora Core 4, Fedora Core, Fedora,* and *Linux* are used interchangeably.

Text that you type and text that you see onscreen appear in monospace type:

```
It will look like this.
```

Variables and placeholders (words that stand for what you will actually type) appear in *italic monospace*.

Each chapter ends with questions pertaining to that lesson's subject matter, with answers from the author. Most chapters also include an exercise section and a quiz designed to reinforce that lesson's concepts.

| | |
|---|---|
| A **By the Way** presents interesting information related to the discussion. | **By the** Way |

| | |
|---|---|
| A **Did You Know** offers advice or shows you an easier way of doing something. | **Did you** Know? |

| | |
|---|---|
| A **Watch Out** alerts you to a possible problem and gives you advice on how to avoid it. | **Watch** Out! |

New terms appear in **bold**.

When a line of code is too long to fit on one line of this book, it is broken at a convenient place and continued to the next line. The continuation is preceded by a special code continuation character (➡).

# PART I

# Installing Fedora Core 4

# CHAPTER 1

# Preparing to Install Fedora Core 4

---

## *What You'll Learn in This Chapter:*

▶ How to create a simple hardware inventory

▶ What you might need to upgrade to meet Fedora Core 4's hardware requirements

▶ How to make space on the hard drive by repartitioning

▶ How to launch the installer

Few computer users in the world have ever installed an operating system from scratch. Even today, with Linux enjoying more popularity than ever before, most computers of any kind are delivered with another operating system already installed. As a Fedora Core user, you will probably install Linux yourself. Because the world of PC hardware is diverse, and because it is often helpful to have both Linux and Windows installed at once, preinstallation preparation will help your Linux experience proceed smoothly.

If you are not experienced with PC hardware or installing operating systems, hang in there. The first few chapters might seem challenging, but using Fedora Core 4 gets easier from there.

## Taking a Hardware Inventory

The Fedora Core 4 installer has been designed to automatically detect and support nearly every piece of hardware in a typical personal computer system. Because there are so many variations on the typical computer, though, there is a chance that you will need to know a few basic details about your computer system to be able to help the Fedora Core 4 installer along.

If you are an experienced PC user who is knowledgeable about computer hardware or you already have detailed hardware specifications close at hand, feel free to proceed to the next section; the remainder of this section is designed to help users who aren't extremely familiar with the components in their computer system.

By the Way

**The Many Faces of Windows**

Many of the step-by-step directions in this section instruct you to perform tasks in Windows so that you can learn about your computer system. Because there are several different versions of Windows, each of which behaves differently, you might find that you have to make minor adjustments to some of the steps. For example, Windows XP users might need to click the Switch to Classic View link in the Windows Control Panel to follow along completely.

## Finding Your Memory Capacity

The memory capacity of a computer system is commonly expressed in megabytes (MB) or kilobytes (KB); one megabyte equals 1,024 kilobytes. Common memory capacities in today's PCs range from 128MB (131,072KB) to 512MB (524,288KB), although it is no longer uncommon to see systems with memory capacities as high as 768MB (786,432KB) or more.

If you don't know your system's memory capacity, you probably can determine it by watching your computer system's BIOS (basic input/output system) display; it is generally the first thing you see on your monitor as you power on the computer system. Most PCs today perform a quick memory check before attempting to load an operating system. Look for the appearance of small numbers in multiples of 16 (32, 64, 96, 128), which indicate your memory size in megabytes, or large numbers in multiples of 1,024 (32,768, 65,536, 98,304, 131,072), which indicate your memory size in kilobytes.

A BIOS display containing memory capacity information appears in Figure 1.1.

By the Way

**When BIOS Information Isn't Visible**

Some users might find that their BIOS does not display hardware information as they power on. In such cases, you might need to enter your BIOS setup area to learn about your installed memory capacity and CPU model and speed.

If this is the case, press a designated key as the computer system starts. Often, a message such as the following explains how to do so:

```
Press F1 to enter setup.
```

Common BIOS setup keys include F1, F2, Delete, Insert, End, and Esc. The required keystroke is usually discussed in system or mainboard documentation.

Processor speed

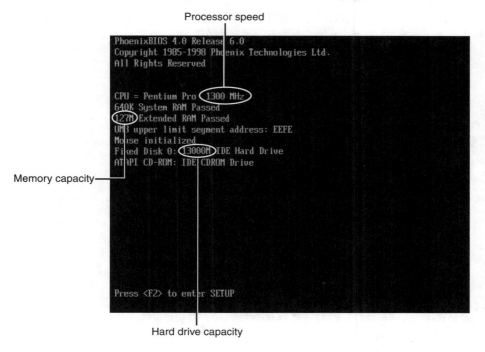

Memory capacity

Hard drive capacity

**FIGURE 1.1**
This BIOS display indicates a machine with a 1.3GHz processor, 127MB memory capacity, and 13,000MB (13GB) hard disk drive.

If your PC has an existing installation of Windows, your system memory capacity is also listed in the System and Device Manager tool. Open it by following these steps:

1. Double-click the My Computer icon on your Windows desktop. The Windows Explorer appears, displaying icons for each storage device in your system plus an icon labeled Control Panel that you can use to launch the Windows Control Panel.

2. Double-click the Control Panel icon in the Windows Explorer. The Windows Control Panel appears, displaying icons for a number of different configuration dialogs.

3. Double-click the System icon in the Windows Control Panel to open the System and Device Manager tool. The System Properties dialog box appears, displaying the amount of memory detected by Windows, as shown in Figure 1.2.

---

### Accessing the Control Panel in Windows XP

If you are using Windows XP, you can open the Windows Control Panel by clicking the Start button and then Control Panel item located in the right column of the Start menu.

**By the Way**

**FIGURE 1.2**
The System
Properties dia-
log box shows
the amount of
memory present
and, in some
versions of
Windows, the
CPU type and
speed.

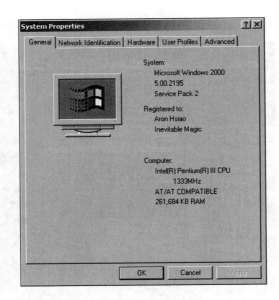

## Finding Your CPU (Processor) Speed

Most PCs today contain a processor made by one of two companies, Intel or
Advanced Micro Devices (AMD). The Intel line of processors includes the Celeron,
Pentium, and Pentium Xeon families, and the AMD line of processors includes the
K6, Duron, and Athlon families. In the end, however, it is the speed of the CPU in
megahertz (MHz) or gigahertz (GHz) that matters most to your ability to run Linux.

One gigahertz is equivalent to 1,000MHz; a 2GHz processor is thus equivalent to a
2,000MHz processor. If you are unsure about the speed and model of your processor,
you should look again at your BIOS display for this information.

### Finding CPU Speed in Windows 2000 or XP

If you are using some versions of Windows 2000 or Windows XP, you may be able
to learn the speed of your CPU in the System and Device Manager tool, in the
same dialog box where you found your system's memory capacity.

## Finding Your Hard Drive Capacity

If you have an existing Windows installation, finding your hard drive capacity and
the amount of unused space on it is a simple task:

1. Double-click the My Computer icon on your Windows desktop. The Windows
   Explorer appears, displaying icons for each storage device in your system. Your

first hard drive is normally drive C, and additional hard drives, if any, might have icons as well.

2. Right-click the icon for the hard drive where you plan to install Fedora Core 4. In the context menu that appears, choose the Properties option.

3. A pie chart appears, showing the capacity of the hard drive in question along with the relative amounts of used and available storage space. Make a note of the amount of free space shown in the chart.

If you do not have an existing installation of Windows, you might also be able to obtain information about your hard drive capacity by watching your BIOS display. Many newer systems display either hard drive capacity or hard drive make and model information as the computer starts. Armed with make and model details, you can visit a hard drive manufacturer on the Web or contact it by telephone to find capacity information.

If you are unable to find any hard drive capacity information using these methods, you might be able to find it later in this chapter in the section on using FIPS, a tool for resizing Windows partitions to make room for Linux.

## Learning About Your Communications Hardware

Nearly every modern PC contains either Ethernet hardware, wireless network hardware, modem hardware, or some combination of the three. As a Fedora Core 4 user, you'll learn to use Internet Linux forums and websites early and often for software and support, so it's important that your communications hardware be compatible with Linux. Nearly any built-in Ethernet controller in a modern PC will work with Linux. The same goes for most brand name wireless networking hardware from the likes of Cisco, Adaptec, Intel, or similar manufacturers. Ethernet capability can be identified by the presence of what looks like a slightly wider than usual telephone jack on the back of your PC, to which a cable or DSL modem (or your company network) is generally connected.

Modems, which connect directly to your telephone line, are a more complex issue:

▶ External serial port (RS-232) and USB modems that comply with the USB Abstract Control Model (ACM) standard are much more likely to be Linux-compatible than other types of modems; they are well supported by Linux and generally require no special drivers or configuration work.

▶ Very old built-in modems that use the Industry Standard Architecture (ISA) also generally work with Linux, although some plug-and-play modems of this type might require additional, somewhat cryptic configuration steps to work properly.

► Built-in modems on newer PCs are unfortunately the most problematic. The manufacturers or designers of these types of modems often refuse to support Linux operating systems like Fedora Core 4. If you have a newer PC with a built-in modem and you find yourself unable to use it after you finish installing Linux, you must purchase another type of modem to use dial-up Internet in Fedora Core 4. External modems (either serial or USB type) are generally compatible with Linux, and are thus the best purchase decisions. (See the following By the Way for additional information.)

*By the Way*

### Identifying and Choosing Modems

The process of identifying the hardware used in a built-in modem can be a long and technical one, and is therefore beyond the scope of this book. Adventurous and determined users with internal modems can visit the website http://linmodems.org for details on using modern built-in modems with Linux.

For most other users, the answer is to use an external modem with Linux, preferably of the traditional serial (USB or traditional 25-pin RS-232) variety. When buying a USB modem for use with Fedora Core 4, confirm that it is compliant with the USB ACM standard. Most USB modems for Apple computers fall into this category; these modems also work with Linux, even on computers that originally came with Windows.

The most complete reference for using modems of various types with Linux is the Linux Modem-HOWTO document, which you can find online at the Linux Documentation Project website at http://www.tldp.org/HOWTO/Modem-HOWTO.html.

# Evaluating Your Hardware

Fedora Core 4 is a very modern Linux operating system with a powerful graphical user interface (GUI) and extensive networking and server capabilities. Although Linux operating systems are modular enough to be run on very minimal or very old computers, such feats are generally better left to experts. If you are new to Linux, you should ensure that your computer meets the list of suggested system requirements for Fedora Core 4, as listed in Table 1.1.

**TABLE 1.1** Suggested Requirements for Running Fedora Core 4

| Hardware Item | Suggested System Requirement |
| --- | --- |
| CPU (processor) | Pentium II, Duron, Athlon, or similar processor running at 300MHz (0.3GHz) or faster. Processors slower than 300MHz might feel sluggish. |

**TABLE 1.1**   Continued

| Hardware Item | Suggested System Requirement |
| --- | --- |
| | 256MB (131,072KB) or more is required if you plan to use the Linux desktop. Server users who do not install the Linux desktop might be able to get by with 128MB, but less memory availability can incur performance penalties. |
| Hard drive space | 4GB (4,000MB) or more of free disk space is the comfortable minimum for standard installations of the type covered in this book. Ideally, at least 6–10GB (6,000–10,000MB) of disk space should be available for serious users. |
| Ethernet or modem | Internet access is really a necessity for the serious Linux user. Most common Ethernet and wireless hardware is supported by Linux, but modems are much more problematic. If you find that your communication hardware will not function after you install Linux, check with the manufacturer for Linux compatibility. If your hardware isn't compatible with Fedora Core, you will need to replace it. |

If your hardware inventory falls short in one or several areas when compared against this list of suggested requirements, as a beginner, you should give serious consideration to upgrading or replacing the computer system in question before installing Linux.

# Making Space for Linux

After you make sure your hardware is suitable for use with Linux, you must ensure that space is available on your hard drive for a Linux installation. Unfortunately, this task is not as simple as it might seem. Merely having unused space on your hard drive is not enough; a proper Linux installation requires unpartitioned space—space that is not being used by another operating system.

**By the Way**

### Already Use Linux? Skip This Part!

If you already have a recent version of Linux installed on your computer, your system is likely to work with Fedora Core 4 as well. . If you are sure that you have enough space for Fedora Core 4 in your existing partitioning scheme, feel free skip to the section near the end of the chapter called "Launching the Fedora Core 4 Installer."

## Understanding Partitions

PC operating systems such as Windows or Linux must be installed on one or more hard drive partitions. A **partition** is an area of the hard drive that has been set aside specifically for one operating system; in a sense, it is space that is "owned" by the operating system in question. A Windows partition therefore belongs, in a sense, to Windows, while a Linux partition belongs to Linux.

Most PCs today ship with Windows preinstalled. The entire hard drive has therefore been given to Windows; such drives contain only one partition that occupies the entire drive and that is owned by Windows.

Because of this, when you plan to install Linux on a system that already contains Windows, you have the following three options:

▶ Delete the Windows partition or partitions that occupy the entire hard drive and allocate the entire hard drive to Linux. This approach has the effect of *removing* Windows from the computer system. The entire computer system and its hard drive are then owned exclusively by Linux. When a computer configured this way is switched on, it starts Linux immediately.

▶ Resize or rebuild the existing Windows partition(s) so that Windows no longer occupies the entire hard drive, and then create new partitions for Linux in the resulting free space. The effect is like dividing a room using a large wooden screen and then declaring one section of the room to be yours and the other section to be your roommate's. One section of a repartitioned hard drive belongs to Windows, and the other section belongs to Linux. When a computer is configured this way, each time you switch on the computer, you can choose to start either Linux or Windows. Both operating systems share the same hard drive, but each has its own space on it. This process is commonly referred to as **dual-booting**.

▶ Install an additional hard drive (or have one installed by a technician) specifically to hold Linux. When a computer is configured this way, each time you switch on the computer, you can choose to start either system, and Linux and Windows will have an entire hard drive to themselves. This is also a form of dual-booting.

Most users interested in building a server-oriented Linux computer choose to replace the Windows partition completely. This gives Linux exclusive control of the computer and all of the hard drive space it contains. If this is what you plan to do, you do not need to worry about repartitioning because the Fedora Core 4 installer can delete existing Windows partitions for you; feel free to skip the rest of this chapter.

If you plan to dual-boot Linux and Windows—that is, to let them share a hard drive and to choose between them each time you switch on your computer—you need to repartition your hard drive to ensure that space is allocated to both systems. Most desktop and laptop computer users who are installing Linux for the first time choose this option.

---

### Using Windows Applications in Linux

Dual-booting is a good choice for the beginner because Windows can then act as a failsafe. If you have trouble installing or configuring Internet access in Linux, for example, you can start Windows and visit Linux help sites for technical support to solve your problem. On the other hand, dual-booting means that less space will be available to Linux, because some of your existing hard drive space (often half or more) has been reserved for Windows.

Some users prefer not to dual-boot but still want the ability to run important Windows applications like Microsoft Office or Adobe Photoshop. Three solutions work very well for such needs: Win4Lin, which you can find at http://www.netra-verse.co; VMWare, which you can find at http://www.vmware.org; and Crossover Office, which you can find at http://www.codeweavers.com.

Windows compatibility options are discussed in detail in Appendix B, "Adding Windows Compatibility to Linux."

---

## Nondestructive Repartitioning

Users of Windows 95, Windows 98, and Windows Me can easily make room for Linux using a utility called FIPS, which is available on the Internet at no charge and is written by the same kinds free software developers that work on Linux. FIPS shrinks an existing Windows partition while preserving the data stored there. You can then create Linux partitions in the resulting unassigned space without losing or having to rearrange any Windows files.

Unfortunately, FIPS does not work with most Windows NT, 2000, or XP systems because FIPS is not capable of rearranging files stored in the way that Windows 2000 or Windows XP stores them. If you are using Windows NT, 2000, or ME and would like to repartition nondestructively, you can determine whether FIPS will work for you by following these steps:

1. Double-click the My Computer icon on your Windows desktop or select My Computer from your Start menu. This will open the Windows Explorer and display icons for each of the storage devices in your system.

2. In the Windows Explorer, right-click the icon representing the hard drive you plan to repartition and choose Properties from the pop-up context menu that appears.

**3.** Look for the phrase File system in the Properties dialog box. If the words FAT or FAT32 are shown, you *can* use FIPS to resize your Windows partition while preserving all your data. If the word NTFS is shown, you *cannot* use FIPS to rearrange your existing Windows files in order to free space for Linux. Figure 1.3 shows a Properties dialog box listing an unresizable NTFS hard drive partition.

**FIGURE 1.3**
If you see the word NTFS in your Properties dialog box, you cannot resize your hard drive partition using FIPS.

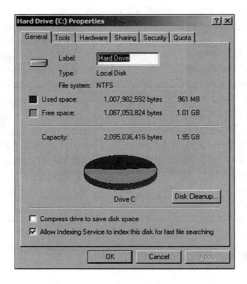

*By the Way*

### Nondestructive Repartitioning with NTFS

Several commercial software vendors sell tools that can nondestructively resize Windows 2000 or XP NTFS partitions with varying degrees of success. Partition Magic is one such tool; for more information, visit http://www.partitionmagic.com. Another similar tool is called BootIt Next Generation; a demo version available from http://www.bootitng.com can help you decide whether BootIt is the right product for you.

## Defragmenting Prior to Using FIPS

Before you actually use FIPS, you must defragment the drive partition. **Defragmentation** is necessary prior to running FIPS because FIPS can shrink a Windows partition only if a continuous area of empty space is available. The defragmentation process rearranges your files so that they are all stored one immediately after another toward the beginning of the partition. This leaves all the unused space near the end empty, where FIPS can trim it away and make it available to other operating systems like Linux.

Launch the Windows defragmentation tool by following these steps:

1. Double-click the My Computer icon on your Windows desktop or select My Computer from your Start menu. This will open the Windows Explorer and display icons for each of the storage devices in your system.

2. Right-click the icon representing the hard drive you want to defragment; choose Properties from the pop-up context menu.

3. Select the Tools tab from the dialog box that appears.

4. Click the Defragment Now button. A progress indicator shows that your hard drive is being defragmented. When Windows indicates that defragmentation has finished, exit the defragmentation tool.

---

**Sometimes There's Just No Room**                                  *By the Way*

Even after you use the Windows defragment tool, the FIPS utility we're about to discuss may in some cases tell you that you don't have much empty room left on your hard drive. If that's the case, your best bet is to add a second hard drive to hold Linux.

---

**Safeguard Your Data While Repartitioning**                        *Watch Out!*

FIPS is a well-tested program that does a remarkably good job of resizing existing partitions while preserving data. But don't forget that *you* are responsible for protecting your data. Be absolutely sure that you back up any important files (copy them to a floppy disk, CD-ROM, flash device, or other storage device) before attempting to resize your Windows partition.

At the very minimum, most users choose to back up their My Documents folder. That way, if a hard drive is accidentally erased, important personal files stored in My Documents are preserved.

---

# Creating a FIPS Floppy and Starting FIPS

The FIPS program can be downloaded at no charge by typing the following address into your Internet Explorer or web browser window:

```
http://www.tux.org/pub/dos/partition-programs/fips/fips-20/fips.exe
```

When prompted, save the file to your Windows desktop. After saving the FIPS program to your desktop, type the following address in your web browser to save the FIPS documentation:

```
http://www.tux.org/pub/dos/partition-programs/fips/fips-20/fips.doc.
```

Be sure to print the fips.doc file before continuing, so that you can refer to it as you use FIPS.

To use FIPS, you must run it from a DOS boot floppy. Such a floppy can be created only on an MS-DOS, Windows 95, Windows 98, or Windows Me system; Windows 2000 and Windows XP do not provide utilities for creating DOS boot floppies. Windows 2000 and XP users not intending to use FIPS can move to the section "Destructive Repartitioning," later in this chapter.

**By the Way**

**Boot Floppies and Windows 2000/XP**

Windows 2000 and Windows XP users need to gain temporary access to an MS-DOS or a Windows 95, 98, or Me computer system to create a boot floppy following the directions given here. If you use Windows 2000 or Windows XP and don't have access to a computer system suitable for creating a boot floppy, destructive repartitioning is the only way to provide space for Linux on an existing Windows hard drive.

To create a DOS boot floppy containing FIPS from within Windows 95, 98, or Me, follow these steps:

1. Insert a blank floppy disk into your PC.

2. Double-click the My Computer icon on your Windows desktop; then right-click the icon representing the floppy drive. A context menu appears.

3. Choose the Format option from the pop-up context menu. A dialog box presents floppy formatting options, as shown in Figure 1.4.

**FIGURE 1.4**
The Format Floppy dialog box allows you to format a DOS boot floppy.

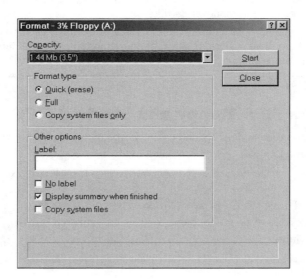

**4.** Select Full as the format type and check the Copy System Files box. Click Start to format the floppy.

**5.** When the format finishes, copy the FIPS program from your desktop (or wherever you saved it after downloading it) to the newly formatted floppy disk.

After you have created your FIPS floppy and printed the `fips.doc` file, switch off your computer. Insert the FIPS floppy disk into the PC and power on again. When you reach the DOS prompt, type **fips** and press Enter. Carefully follow the directions in `fips.doc` to resize partitions according to your needs.

---

### More Details on FIPS, Hard Drives, and Floppy Drives

The following FIPS walk-through assumes that you have only one hard drive in your system. If you will be resizing partitions on a hard drive other than your primary hard drive, consult the FIPS documentation for instructions.

Note also that some personal computers do not have a floppy drive. If you own one of these computers, you need to add a floppy drive before you can use FIPS.

*By the Way*

---

## Using FIPS

When you first start FIPS, you're shown a small amount of general information about the program; press Enter to page through it. You're then shown technical information about your hard drive as FIPS performs a few basic checks to ensure that your existing hard drive partitions are in good condition:

```
Boot sector:

Bytes per sector: 512
Sectors per cluster: 8
Reserved sectors: 32
Number of FATs: 2
Number of rootdirectory entries: 0
Number of sectors (short): 0
Media descriptor byte: F8h
Sectors per FAT: 3993
Sectors per track: 63
Drive heads: 64
Hidden sectors: 63
Number of sectors (long): 8092417
Physical drive number: 80h
Signature: 29h
Checking boot sector .. OK
Checking FAT .. OK
Searching for free space .. OK
```

FIPS then asks whether you want to back up the root and boot sectors of your hard drive:

```
Do you want to make a backup copy of your root and boot sector before
proceeding (y/n)?
```

Choose y. Should FIPS fail to correctly repartition your hard drive, you will need such backups to restore your original partition information and avoid data loss. FIPS then prompts you to insert a bootable floppy disk:

```
Do you have a bootable floppy disk in drive A: as described in the
documentation (y/n)?
```

Answer y to this question as well, since you started FIPS from a bootable floppy. FIPS then creates a root and boot sector backup file on your floppy called rootboot.000. You can use the rootboot floppy to restore some of your hard drive's structure if anything goes wrong and you find that your system no longer boots as expected. (See the FIPS documentation for details on restoring from backups.)

**By the Way**

**Receiving INT 13h Errors with FIPS**

A few manufacturers ship PCs in which the primary hard drive is connected to the second Integrated Drive Electronics (IDE) channel. If FIPS quits unexpectedly after reporting that it can't find an INT 13h hard drive device, you might need to connect your hard drive to the primary IDE channel to use FIPS. This step typically involves opening your PC and altering connections to sensitive components; consult a technician if you are unfamiliar with this process.

After the rootboot.000 backup file is created, FIPS presents you with a simple table that lists the proposed new size for the old partition, a  cylinder boundary (the location on your hard drive where the disk will be divided), and the proposed size for the new partition:

```
Old partition      Cylinder      New partition
  397.7 MB           202            3600.6 MB
```

The old partition size is the amount of disk space that will remain allocated to Windows after the repartitioning process is complete. Remember, this number does not represent the *free* space available to Windows, but rather *all* space allocated to Windows (including space used by existing Windows files and folders). The new partition size is the amount of space that will be unallocated and available to the Fedora Core 4 installer for Linux. Use your left- or right-arrow key to adjust these values; allocate space as desired to the old and new partitions. Remember that for Fedora Core 4 to function properly, you should have at least as much free space as the minimum hard drive size shown in Table 1.1 available to Linux.

When you are satisfied with the numbers that FIPS shows, press Enter to confirm the changes. FIPS performs several more sanity checks and displays a table showing your proposed new partitions, as shown in Figure 1.5.

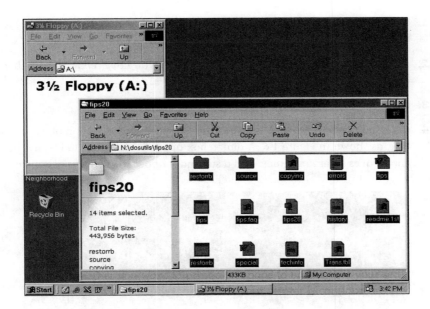

**FIGURE 1.5**
FIPS displays
the new parti-
tion table that
you have pro-
posed. Check
the sizes shown
in the rightmost
column to make
sure they match
the numbers
you intended to
choose.

After displaying the new partition details, FIPS asks whether you want to continue (you have one more chance to abort before changes are saved) or re-edit the partition table:

```
Do you want to continue or reedit the partition table (c/r)?
```

Select r to re-edit if you have changed your mind about the sizes of the partitions you want to create. If you select c to continue, you are shown an updated set of technical details about your hard drive, as it will appear after the changes are saved to the disk. FIPS then asks you one final time to confirm your changes:

```
Ready to write new partition scheme to disk
Do you want to proceed (y/n)?
```

This is your last chance to change your mind, by selecting n at the prompt. If you have not yet backed up your data, you should seriously consider selecting n now, exiting, and backing up your data before running FIPS again. If you are ready to have FIPS save your changes to the disk and resize your Windows partition, select y to proceed.

You should quickly see a success message:

```
Repartitioning complete
With FAT32 partitions, you should now run scandisk on the shortened partition
```

Remove the floppy disk, restart your computer, and immediately perform a file-system integrity check by following these steps:

1. Double-click the My Computer icon on your Windows desktop or choose My Computer from your Start menu.

2. Right-click the icon representing the hard drive you have repartitioned; then choose Properties from the pop-up context menu.

3. Select the Tools tab from the dialog box that appears.

4. Click the Check Now button in the Error-Checking Status section of the dialog box, as shown in Figure 1.6. A dialog box appears; click Start to begin. The check takes several minutes, and a summary appears when it is complete.

**FIGURE 1.6**
Click the Check Now button to begin a file-system check.

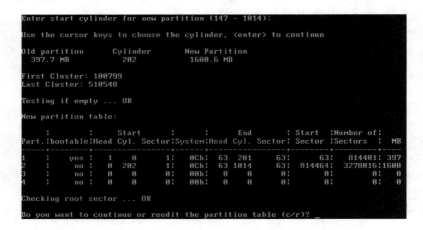

After you run FIPS to make space for Linux and check your newly resized Windows partition for errors, you are ready to launch the Fedora Core 4 installer.

## Destructive Repartitioning

**Destructive repartitioning** works just as it sounds: You will use your Windows 2000 or XP install CD to *erase your hard drive completely and install Windows from scratch,* taking care to specify to the Windows installer that you want Windows to be given only a portion of your hard drive, rather than the entire thing.

### Destructive Repartitioning Erases Data!

Destructive repartitioning lives up to its name: It *erases* all your existing Windows data, including your personal letters, images, and other data. You must therefore copy any data that you want to preserve onto some other storage device such as a floppy, CD-ROM, or flash drive—or you will lose it forever!

Most users choose at least to copy the contents of their My Documents folder to another storage medium. That way, their important data remains intact and can be copied back on to their hard drive after Windows has been installed again.

The process of installing and partitioning Windows varies between releases of the Windows operating system. Full instructions for installing and partitioning the particular version of Windows that you own appear in the installation guide that accompanied your Windows CD-ROM. Most current business and home users are Windows 2000 users, and can destructively repartition using a Windows 2000 install CD by following these steps:

1. Insert the Windows install CD-ROM and turn on your computer. When prompted, press a key to boot from the CD-ROM. A number of drivers will be loaded; this part might take some time. After the drivers load, the Welcome to Setup screen appears.

2. At the Welcome to Setup screen, press Enter to indicate that you want to install Windows 2000. A list of existing partitions appears.

3. Use the up and down arrows to select the partition marked C:, and press the D key to delete the partition. A warning screen opens.

4. Press Enter to confirm that you want to delete the partition. A second warning screen opens. Press L to delete the partition.

5. When the partition list appears once again, use the arrow keys to select the Unpartitioned Space entry, as shown in Figure 1.7. Then press C to create a partition of your own choosing.

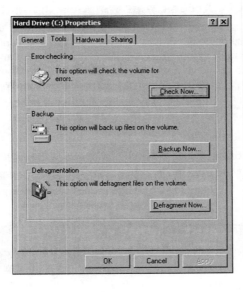

**FIGURE 1.7**
Select the unpartitioned space and then press C to create a new partition for Windows in that space.

6. When the partition sizing screen appears (see Figure 1.8), select a partition size for Windows.

**FIGURE 1.8**
The Windows 2000 installer enables you to allocate only a portion of the drive to Windows. Here 4GB of storage space is being allocated for the Windows 2000 partition. The remaining 6GB is available for Linux.

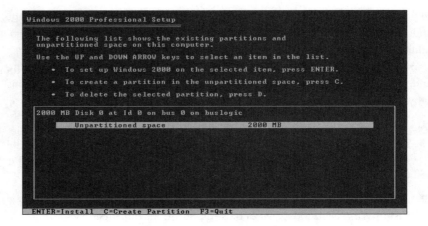

7. After you enter the partition size you want, press Enter to redisplay the partition list. Be sure to create a partition large enough to hold Windows plus any applications that you want to install—usually no smaller than 2,000MB.

8. Select the C: entry in the partition list and press Enter once more to proceed with Windows installation, using your Windows installation guide.

*By the Way*

**Allowing Linux to Access Your Windows Installation**

If you are reinstalling Windows 2000 or Windows XP as part of a destructive repartitioning of your hard drive, be sure to specify that you want Windows installed on a FAT32 partition, rather than on an NTFS partition. This step allows you to use FIPS in the future to resize your Windows partition, should you need to do so; it also allows Linux to access the personal files stored on your Windows partition—something that can't currently be accomplished with an NTFS partition.

After selecting the desired Windows partition size, simply install Windows using the installation instructions that accompany your Windows CD-ROM. After you finish reinstalling Windows to make space for Linux, the destructive repartitioning process is complete and you are ready to launch the Fedora Core 4 installer.

## Avoiding Repartitioning by Adding a Hard Drive

If all this talk of repartitioning makes you more than nervous, you are not alone. Even professionals who have installed Linux many times dread repartitioning. There are so many variables involved in the process that sooner or later you are bound to erase a hard drive by accident and find yourself restoring data from a pile of Zip disks or CD-ROMs. Even when your data has been recently backed up, this process can be both time-consuming and frustrating.

There is an easier way, if you're willing to allow for a modest hardware budget. Most PCs today can accommodate four Enhanced IDE (EIDE) devices such as hard drives, CD-ROM/RW drives, or DVD drives. Most PCs, however, ship with only two drives connected—one hard drive and one removable drive (CD or DVD). This leaves room for up to two more EIDE devices in the typical PC.

Although the actual nuts and bolts of installing an additional hard drive are beyond the scope of this book, many experienced PC and Windows users are capable of adding a second hard drive to a PC system. Most computer retail shops can also install any hard drive that you purchase for a modest labor fee. By adding a second hard drive just for Linux, you gain several advantages:

▶ You can proceed directly to Linux installation without needing to modify your Windows partitions at all.

▶ Your Linux data is kept separate from your Windows data, so bugs in either operating system are less likely to affect data stored by the other.

▶ You don't have to lose space in Windows in order to gain space for Linux.

If you can afford to have an additional hard drive installed, or if you can install one yourself, you should consider doing so, instead of repartitioning.

# Launching the Fedora Core 4 Installer

As the finale to your first chapter, it's time to launch the Linux installer. Insert the Fedora Core 4 install DVD or CD-ROM and restart your computer. You should quickly find yourself face-to-face with the Fedora Core logo and can proceed to the next chapter.

If you see nothing but a blank screen, or if Windows starts just as it always has, your PC isn't currently capable of booting from a DVD or CD-ROM.

If this is the case, it may be possible to start from a DVD or CD-ROM by changing settings in your system's Basic Input/Ouptut System (BIOS) setup. Consult your system documentation or consult with its manufacturer for additional help. You must be able to start from DVD or CD in order to install Fedora Core 4.

# Summary

In this chapter, you took a basic inventory of your computer's hardware and compared it to the suggested minimum system requirements for Fedora Core 4.

You learned how to make space for a Linux installation on a dual-boot system in one of several ways: by repartitioning with FIPS, by destructively repartitioning using a Windows install CD, or by adding an additional hard drive to your computer system.

Finally, you launched the Fedora Core 4 installer.

# Q&A

**Q** *My computer system has a slower processor or less memory than is suggested. I am a patient person. Can't I install Fedora Core 4 anyway, even if it's slow?*

**A** No. A 386 or 486 processor will certainly get there in the end if simple arithmetic is the only task at hand. *However*, an older processor or a limited amount of memory is usually indicative of an entire system full of older, slower components not suitable for modern desktop-oriented tasks such as web browsing.

**Q** *I've heard that Linux can be installed "on top of" a Windows file system, thereby eliminating the need to repartition. Is this true?*

**A** Several Linux operating systems are designed to be installed within a Windows file system. However, there are problems with such installations, not the least of which are poor performance and lack of stability. If you're serious about Linux, you should give Linux its own partitions.

# Workshop

The Workshop is designed to help you anticipate possible questions, review what you've learned, and begin learning how to put your knowledge into practice.

## Quiz

**1.** What is the difference between nondestructive and destructive repartitioning?

**2.** What is the FIPS tool used for?

**3.** Which operating systems might not easily support nondestructive repartitioning?

## Answers

1. Nondestructive repartitioning makes room for Linux without placing Windows data at risk; destructive repartitioning requires a complete erasure of the hard drive and a reinstallation of Windows.

2. The FIPS tool is the most popular tool among Linux users for nondestructive repartitioning.

3. Windows 2000 and Windows XP.

## Activities

1. Find out your computer's CPU type. Also determine its speed, memory, and hard drive capacities.

2. Find out what type of modem is installed in your computer. If it is a built-in modem, visit http://www.linmodems.org and find out whether it's supported by Linux.

# CHAPTER 2

# Installing Fedora Core 4

## What You'll Learn in This Chapter:

▶ How to create new hard drive partitions
▶ What Fedora Core 4 packages you want to install
▶ How to install the packages you select
▶ How to tell Fedora Core 4 about your monitor

In the preceding chapter, you prepared to install Fedora Core 4 on your computer system. It is during this chapter that your Linux adventure truly begins. After you complete this chapter, you should have a bootable installation of Red Hat's Enterprise Linux Desktop operating system on your computer.

## Starting the Fedora Core 4 Installer

At the end of Chapter 1, "Preparing to Install Fedora Core 4," you found yourself looking at the Fedora Core 4 logo and facing a boot prompt after having booted from your first Fedora Core 4 CD or Fedora Core 4 install floppy. To install Linux, you must now boot Linux and start the installer.

Press Enter at the boot prompt to start the installer using the default options, which should work for most users. If Linux is able to locate your hard drive and your CD-ROM or DVD drive, the installer will find your Fedora Core 4 CD-ROM or DVD and ask whether you want to test your install media.

Unless your media is very scratched, feel free to skip the media test. Press the Tab key until the word Skip is highlighted and then press Enter. If all goes as expected, the screen clears, and a Fedora Core 4 logo appears once again as the graphical installer starts.

# Beginning the Installation

After the graphical installer starts, a welcome screen for the Fedora Core 4 installation process appears, as shown in Figure 2.1.

**FIGURE 2.1**
Welcome to the Fedora Core 4 installer.

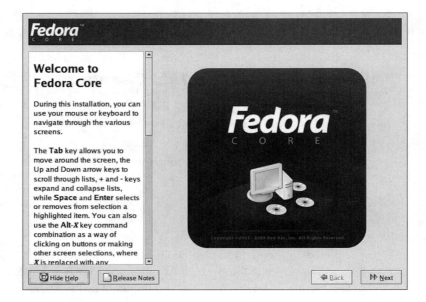

Screens in the default installer contain the following components or areas:

▶ When clicked, the Release Notes button displays a dialog box containing specific additional information about this release of Fedora Core 4.

▶ The Activity Panel is the area of the screen that you, the user, interact with as the installation process progresses.

▶ The Help Panel displays help information about the decisions you are making in the Activity Panel at any given time. You should always read the information in the Help Panel before making any changes in the Activity Panel.

▶ The Next button becomes active when you finish all the necessary configuration in the Activity Panel in this step of the installation; you can then click it to proceed to the next step of the installation.

▶ By clicking the Back button, you can go back to remedy a mistake if you realize that you did something wrong in a previous step of the installation. Note that the Back button will not always be available after you have made permanent changes to your system.

After you have read the information in the first screen's Help Panel and are ready to proceed with installation of Fedora Core 4, click Next to continue to the first step.

## Language Selection

The first step of the installation process is to select the language that the installer itself will use as you proceed.

This is not the language that Fedora Core 4 uses after the operating system is installed on your computer; your choice here applies only to the rest of the installation process. Click Next after you select the language you want to use.

## Keyboard Configuration

On the Keyboard Configuration screen, you are asked to select a national keyboard layout, as shown in Figure 2.2.

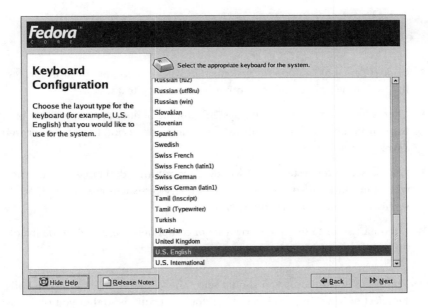

**FIGURE 2.2**
Installing a keyboard layout.

If you will be using a keyboard layout other than the standard U.S. English keyboard, you should select the layout that you want to use now. After you make your selection, click Next to continue.

## Installation Type

After you've selected your keyboard layout, you'll be asked to select the type of installation you want, as shown in Figure 2.3.

**FIGURE 2.3**
Choose the type of Fedora Core 4 system that you want to install. Select Workstation if you plan to follow along with this book.

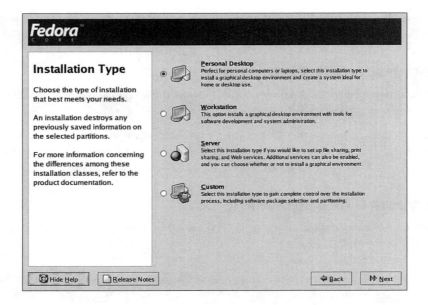

- ▶ Choose Personal Desktop for systems that will be used only for word processing, web browsing, email, and other basic desktop tasks.

- ▶ Choose Workstation to create a system capable of doing multiple kinds of work, from basic desktop applications to network serving to software or web development.

- ▶ Choose Server for systems that will do only minimal desktop work and that will be primarily used to provide network services (such as web, mail, or file services) to other hosts on the network.

- ▶ Choose Custom to select your own set of components and tools to be installed; this option should be selected by experts only.

For the purposes of this book, you should select the Workstation option. This will have the effect of installing a full set of desktop applications so that you can browse the web, work on common types of documents, create pictures, listen to music, and more. It will also install a full complement of command-line tools and a basic set of network service tools, which we'll discuss in later chapters.

Throughout the rest of this book, chapters will assume that you installed Fedora Core using the Workstation option.

After you have selected the type of installation you want, click Next to continue.

# Disk Partitioning Setup

On the Disk Partitioning Setup screen, shown in Figure 2.4, you are asked which method you want to use to allocate disk space to Linux. If you are installing Fedora

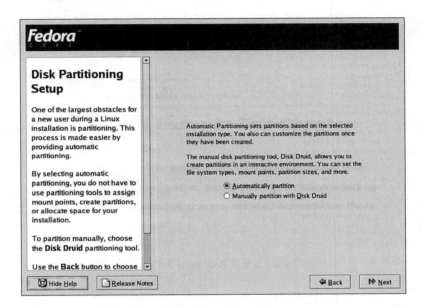

**FIGURE 2.4**
Selecting the partitioning method you want the installer to use.

Core 4 alongside Windows or another operating system, all on a single hard drive, select Manually Partition with Disk Druid and click Next to proceed. Hard drives that have been repartitioned using the FIPS utility (discussed in Chapter 1) are not organized in a way that is suited to the installer's automatic partitioning scheme. Proceed to the next section, "Disk Setup," if this is the option you select.

If you are installing Linux on an empty or newly added hard drive, or if you destructively repartitioned in Chapter 1, select Automatically Partition and click Next to proceed to the Automatic Partitioning screen shown in Figure 2.5.

If you have more than one hard drive in your system, select the drive that should eventually hold Fedora Core 4. Additional hard drives are shown alongside the primary hard drive in the box in Figure 2.5. Then choose among the following options:

▶ Select Remove All Linux Partitions on This System if you have an existing Linux installation on the drive in question and want to overwrite it with Fedora Core 4.

Select partitioning behavior

**FIGURE 2.5**
After you select
Automatic
Partitioning, the
installer asks
you questions
about how it
should proceed.

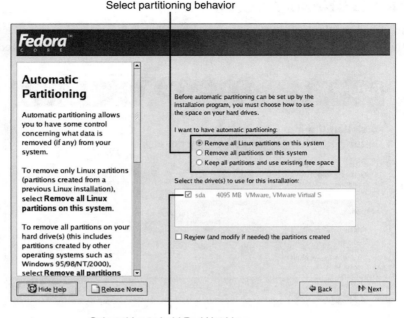

Select drive to hold Red Hat Linux

▶ Select Remove All Partitions on This System if you want to completely erase the selected hard drive, replacing its existing contents with Fedora Core 4.

▶ Select Keep All Partitions and Use Existing Free Space if you performed destructive repartitioning in Chapter 1 or have unused, unpartitioned space on the selected hard drive.

Be sure to check Review (and Modify, If Needed) the Partitions Created so that you can preview the partitioning scheme the installer creates for you. If you have chosen to remove partitions on your system, you will see a warning message that asks whether you want to delete the partitions in question. Click Yes to continue or No to go back and make another selection.

When you are ready to continue, click Next to proceed.

## Disk Setup

Next, you see the Disk Setup screen, which provides an interface to the Disk Druid tool. If you selected Manually Partition with Disk Druid on the Disk Partitioning Setup screen, you see a list of your existing partitions, as shown in Figure 2.6.

Logical volume group

Logical volumes

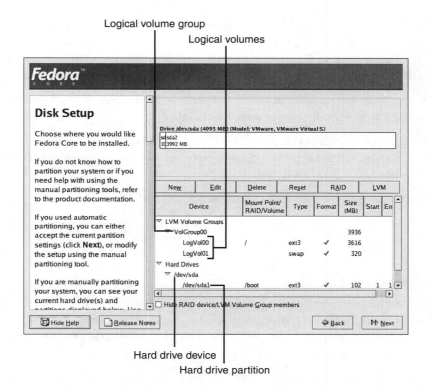

**Disk Setup**

Choose where you would like Fedora Core to be installed.

If you do not know how to partition your system or if you need help with using the manual partitioning tools, refer to the product documentation.

If you used automatic partitioning, you can either accept the current partition settings (click **Next**), or modify the setup using the manual partitioning tool.

If you are manually partitioning your system, you can see your current hard drive(s) and

Hard drive device

Hard drive partition

**FIGURE 2.6**
The Disk Druid tool enables you to review, delete, create, or edit partitions on a hard drive.

**By the Way**

---

## Disk Druid and Automatic Partitioning

If you select Automatically Partition on the Disk Partitioning Setup screen, you see a list of the partitions that Disk Druid has automatically created for you. You don't normally need to change them; this section is intended to direct those who opted to use manual partitioning. You can therefore click Next and proceed to the next section.

You might want to read along with this section anyway, however, to better understand the list of partitions automatically created and to get a feel for the way Disk Druid works, in case you want to edit this list.

---

### Understanding the Partition List

The partition list in the Disk Druid tool has a number of separate columns:

▶ The Device column lists the hard drive or partition in question by Linux device name. (See the following section.) If you have more than one hard drive, be sure to check the device column as you add, remove, or edit partitions in Disk Druid. This step ensures that you are making changes to the correct hard drive!

▶ The Mount Point/RAID/Volume column lists the place in the Linux file system where the data stored on the partition in question appears. For an introduction to the structure of the Linux file system, see the section titled "Understanding the Linux File System" in Chapter 5, "Working with Files on the Desktop."

▶ The Type column lists the type of the partition in question. Existing window partitions generally appear with the vfat type.

▶ The Format column contains a check mark if the partition in question is scheduled to be formatted (erased in preparation for use) as the install process continues.

▶ The Size column shows the size, in megabytes, of the partition.

▶ The Start and End columns show the starting and ending cylinders of the partition in question. Lower numbers are nearer the beginning of the disk.

## Understanding Devices

Most users have only one hard drive containing a relatively short list of partitions. If, however, you have multiple hard drives or a long list of partitions, or you repartitioned using FIPS, you need to be able to decipher the device names in Disk Druid's Device column to partition safely for Linux.

You may see three types of devices listed in Disk Druid:

▶ Devices that begin with /dev/hd represent IDE- or ATA-type hard drives. These are the most common types of hard drives—the types most users will have on their systems. In IDE systems, hda and hdb refer to the master and slave drives on the primary channel, respectively; hdc and hdd similarly refer to the master and slave drives on the secondary channel.

▶ Devices that begin with /dev/sd represent SCSI-type hard drives. In SCSI systems, drives are lettered as they are found—sda being the first SCSI hard drive, sdb the second, and so on.

▶ Devices listed as VolGroup or LogVol are logical volume groups or logical volumes; they are collections of one or more other hard drive partitions that Linux will access as a single storage area.

## Freeing Space Created by FIPS

If you used the FIPS tool to resize an existing Windows partition in Chapter 1, you likely see two partitions in your partition list that begin with /dev/hda and that are followed by a number, like /dev/hda1 or /dev/hda2. One of these is the now smaller Windows partition; the other is an empty partition containing space that can be used by Linux. For Linux to be able to use the space made available by FIPS, however, you must delete the empty partition. Doing so will not harm your Windows partition, but it's always a good idea to have a reliable backup of any critical data before changing partitions on a disk.

The first partition in your partition list—which is shown with vfat as its type and whose size *should match closely* the size of your Windows partition after the resizing you did in Chapter 1—is the place where Windows now resides and should not be deleted.

The second partition—which is shown with Win95 FAT32 as its type and whose size *should match closely* the amount of space freed by FIPS during repartitioning—contains nothing but empty space, which can be used to hold Linux.

To delete the empty partition and make this space available to Fedora Core 4, click its entry in the list and then click the Delete button. When you are presented with a confirmation dialog box, click the Delete button to confirm that you want to delete the free space partition created by FIPS. The partition list is updated to show the change, as shown in Figure 2.7, and the amount of listed free space increases.

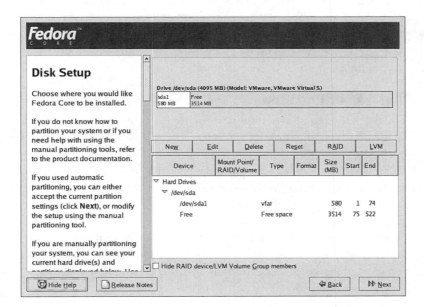

**FIGURE 2.7**
After you delete the space freed by FIPS, you're ready to create new partitions for Linux.

---

## Don't Delete the Wrong Partition

Before deleting either partition, *check the sizes* of the two partitions listed by Disk Druid against the sizes you selected when using FIPS to ensure that you delete the correct partition!

## Calculating Needed Space

If you did not ask the Fedora Core 4 installer to automatically partition for you, you will soon need to create some partitions for Linux to use. You create at least three partitions as follows:

▶ A swap partition of approximately double the size of your computer's memory. If you have 256MB of memory, you need a 512MB swap partition, and so on. The Linux virtual memory subsystem uses this partition to keep memory available to applications as you work.

▶ A root file system partition to hold Fedora Core 4 itself.

▶ A 150MB boot partition to hold the Linux kernel and a few related files.

Before you can create these partitions, you must ensure that you have enough free space for a working Fedora Core 4 installation. You can establish this fact by performing a simple test.

First, calculate the size of your swap partition by doubling the amount of RAM you have installed and then adding 2600 (the minimum root partition size plus the size of a boot partition). For example, if you have 512MB of memory, your total is 3624MB. Now, check to see that you have a free space entry in your Disk Druid partition list of at least this size. If not, you don't have enough space to install Fedora Core 4. You either have to further resize or delete partitions, or you have to add a hard drive.

## Creating a Boot Partition

After you ensure that you have enough free space to install Fedora Core 4, it is time to create the partitions where Linux will reside. The first of these is the /boot partition, which holds the Linux kernel and a number of other files related to the kernel and booting. To create a new /boot partition, click the New button. The Add Partition dialog box appears, as shown in Figure 2.8.

Fill out the dialog box as follows:

▶ Choose /boot from the Mount Point drop-down list to indicate that this partition is mounted on the /boot tree in the Linux file system. For a full explanation of what it means, see the section titled "Understanding the Linux File System" in Chapter 5.

▶ Select ext3 from the File System Type drop-down list to indicate that this partition should be formatted using the Linux ext3 file system.

▶ Enter **150** in the Size entry box to indicate that this partition should be 100MB in size.

▶ Check Fixed Size in the Additional Size Options area.

Mount Point drop-down list

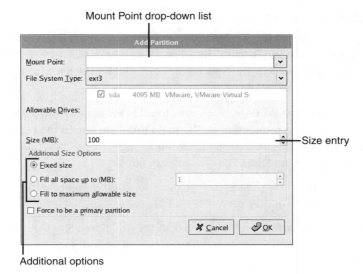

Size entry

Additional options

**FIGURE 2.8**
The Add Partition dialog box enables you to create new partitions for use with Fedora Core 4.

After you fill out the dialog box, click OK to allocate space for the boot partition and return to the main Disk Druid display.

## Creating a Swap Partition

Next, you must create a swap partition to allow the Linux virtual memory system to manage applications even when the system is running low on real memory. To create a new swap partition for Fedora Core 4, click the New button. The Add Partition dialog box opens. Fill out the dialog box as follows:

▶ Choose Swap from the File System Type drop-down list to indicate that this partition is a swap partition.

▶ Enter the desired size of this partition (approximately twice the size of your installed system memory) in the Size entry box.

▶ Check Fixed Size in the Additional Size Options area.

---

### Does More Swap Space Mean Better Performance?

Although the absence of an adequately sized swap partition hurts Linux performance significantly, swap partitions larger than twice the size of system memory do not *increase* system performance either.

*By the Way*

---

After you finish the dialog box and are ready to create the swap partition, click OK to return to the main Disk Druid display.

## Creating a Root Partition

The final partition that you must create to install Fedora Core 4 is the root partition, which holds the bulk of the Fedora Core 4 operating system and all your data. To create the root partition, click the New button. The Add Partition dialog box opens. Fill out the dialog box as follows:

► Choose / (the forward slash) from the Mount Point drop-down list to indicate that this partition is mounted on the root file system tree in the Linux file system. For a full explanation of what this means, see the section titled "Understanding the Linux File System" in Chapter 5.

► Select ext3 from the File System Type drop-down list to indicate that this partition should be formatted using the ext3 file system.

► Check Fill to Maximum Allowable Size in the Additional Size Options area. This option gives all the remaining (contiguous) unpartitioned space on your hard drive to Fedora Core 4.

After you finish the dialog box and are ready to create the root file system partition, click OK to return to the main Disk Druid display.

## Mounting Additional Partitions

If you are installing Fedora Core 4 alongside Windows and want to be able to access your Windows hard drive from inside Linux, you need to specify a mount point for your Windows partition. To do so, click the Windows partition in the partition list and then click the Edit button.

When the Edit Partition dialog box appears, enter **/windows** into the Mount Point entry box, as shown in Figure 2.9. This step causes the files on your Windows hard drive to appear in the /windows directory in your Linux file system and in the My Computer window on your desktop. For a full explanation of what it means, see the section titled "Understanding the Linux File System" in Chapter 5.

**FIGURE 2.9**
Use the Edit Partition dialog box to create a mount point for an existing Windows partition.

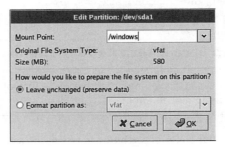

**Be Careful with NTFS Partitions in Linux**

If your Windows partition is listed as an NTFS partition rather than as a VFAT partition, consider leaving it inaccessible to Linux. NTFS support in Linux is currently experimental and in some cases might cause data corruption.

Users of Windows 95, 98, or Me or users who repartitioned with FIPS do not need to worry: Your partitions are VFAT rather than NTFS.

Click OK when you are done to return to the main Disk Druid display and partition list.

**Leave Your Windows Partition Unchanged!**

When editing the Windows partition, be sure to leave the Leave Unchanged (Preserve Data) option checked in the Edit Partition dialog box. Accidentally checking the Format Partition As option instead causes your Windows partition—including all your data and Windows itself—to be erased!

## Checking the Partition List

If you are manually partitioning, at the main Disk Druid display, you should now see at least three new Linux partitions: a swap partition, a /boot partition, and a / (root) partition. If you are installing Linux alongside Windows, you should also still see your vfat-type Windows partition in the first position on your partition list. Figure 2.10 shows one possible Disk Druid display. If you used the installer's automatic partitioning tool, you might see many more Linux partitions in your list and several logical volumes, which is normal.

**Understanding Extended Partitions**

You might notice partitions with the Extended type or small areas of remaining free space in your partition list. You can safely ignore them; extended partitions merely act as placeholders for compatibility with existing hardware and operating systems, and small areas of free space represent areas of the hard drive smaller than a single partition allocation unit. The important thing to understand is that neither of these types of entries represents either a significant amount of wasted space or a problem of any kind.

After you verify that all the necessary partitions appear in the list, check also to ensure that all the sizes are correct, that all the Linux partitions are marked with a check in the Format column, and that any existing Windows partitions are *not* marked with a check in the Format column.

Pre-existing Windows partition

Linux boot partition

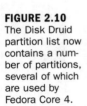

**FIGURE 2.10**
The Disk Druid
partition list now
contains a num-
ber of partitions,
several of which
are used by
Fedora Core 4.

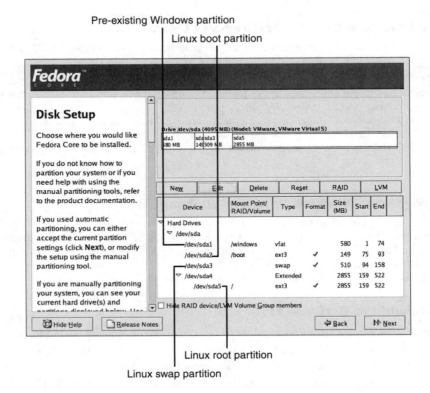

Linux root partition

Linux swap partition

If anything is amiss, select the partition that needs to be fixed and click the Edit button to display the partition dialog box once again, where you can make changes to
the selected partition.

When your list of partitions is correct as described in this section, you are finished
partitioning for Fedora Core 4. Click Next to proceed with the installation process.

# Boot Loader Configuration

After you finalize your partitioning, the Boot Loader Configuration screen appears,
as shown in Figure 2.11.

A **boot loader** is a tool that enables you to choose which operating system you want
to start when you first power on your system. For example, if you install Linux
alongside Windows, a boot loader enables you to choose between Linux and
Windows each time you power on.

If you have more than one bootable partition listed in the bootable partition list,
you need to choose a default partition to boot. Whichever partition is checked as the

List of bootable partitions

Default boot partition check boxes

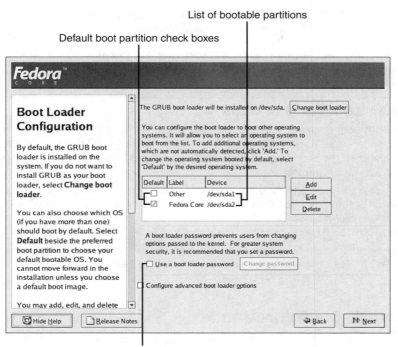

**FIGURE 2.11**
The Boot Loader Configuration screen decides how your system will boot after Fedora Core 4 is installed.

Password check box

default is automatically started at power on if the user fails to make a choice after a given period of time. This choice is a matter of convenience but can also be very useful—for example, in cases involving unattended network servers that have been affected by power outages. To make a partition the default, click in its Default Partition check box.

If your Fedora Core 4 computer will be in a public area such as an office building, you also should select a password to protect your boot loader and to enhance system security. To do so, check the Use a Boot Loader Password box; the Enter Boot Loader Password dialog box appears, as shown in Figure 2.12.

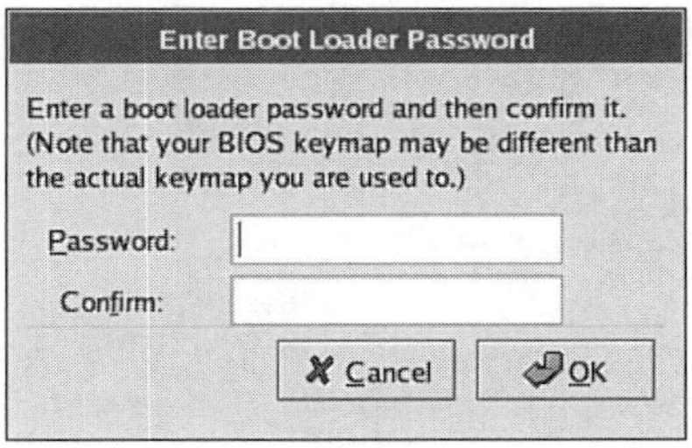

**FIGURE 2.12**
After checking the Use a Boot Loader Password box, you are asked to enter a password.

Enter your password in the upper entry box. Then enter it *again* in the lower entry box to ensure that you typed it correctly. Then click OK to accept your password.

After you finish configuring your boot loader, click Next to proceed with the installation.

### Using LILO Instead of GRUB

The GRUB boot loader is installed on Fedora Core 4 systems by default. However, some experienced users might prefer the classic LILO boot loader over GRUB; other users might already be using a third-party or commercial boot loader that they don't want to replace.

To select LILO as an alternate boot loader or disable the installation of a boot loader altogether, click the Change Boot Loader button at the top of the Boot Loader Configuration screen. You see a simple dialog box that enables you to select GRUB, LILO, or no boot loader at all.

Be sure not to select No Bootloader unless you already have another bootloader you want to use; otherwise, you won't be able to use Linux after it's installed!

## Network Configuration

Next, you see the Fedora Core 4 Network Configuration screen, which applies only to users who will be using Fedora Core 4 on a local area network or with a broadband (usually cable or DSL) Internet service. Figure 2.13 shows the Network Configuration screen.

**FIGURE 2.13**
The Network Configuration screen controls the way in which your Fedora Core 4 computer finds its network identity.

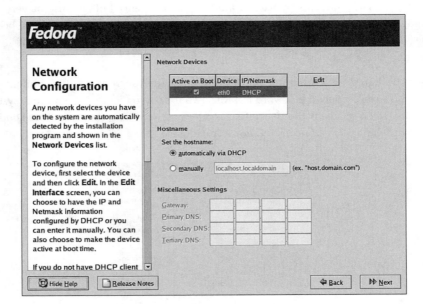

The default configuration specifies that Fedora Core 4 should obtain a network address and identity for your computer each time it starts by using Dynamic Host Configuration Protocol (DHCP). This configuration is the correct configuration for personal computers on most corporate or local area networks. Users who fit into these categories can click Next and proceed to the next section.

Automatic configuration via DHCP is also the correct configuration for most home users on broadband (cable or DSL) networks. In some cases, you need to set your computer's hostname manually for the broadband network to recognize you. If so, click the Set the Hostname Manually option and enter the hostname you've been given into the entry box. Additional Internet configuration, such as the use of Point-to-Point Protocol (PPP) to connect to the Internet, will be covered in Chapter 3, "Booting, Logging In, and Configuring." For now, click Next to proceed to the next section.

If you have been given an Internet Protocol (IP) address and domain name service (DNS) information by your network administrator or broadband provider, or if this Fedora Core 4 machine is a network server, automatic configuration via DHCP is likely not the correct choice for you.

To manually configure your computer for use with a static IP address, follow these steps:

1. Highlight the network interface you want to configure (if you have more than one) and click the Edit button near the top of the display. The Edit Interface dialog box appears.

2. Uncheck the Configure Using DHCP option and enter your assigned IP address and netmask. If you don't know your netmask, enter **255**, **255**, **255**, and **0** in the entry boxes, from left to right, as a guess. Click OK to accept the values you entered.

3. Enter your computer's assigned hostname in the Hostname box.

4. Enter the address for your assigned Internet gateway, primary domain name server, secondary domain name server, and tertiary domain name server (if provided) in the appropriate spaces in the lower half of the screen.

After you configure your network settings according to your needs or the instructions of your network administrator, click Next to proceed to the next step in your Fedora Core 4 installation.

# Firewall Configuration

After your network device configuration is complete, the installer proceeds to the Firewall Configuration screen, shown in Figure 2.14.

**FIGURE 2.14**
Use the Firewall
Configuration
screen to set
network security
parameters.
Change the
SELinux option
to Disabled if
you plan to fol-
low along with
this book.

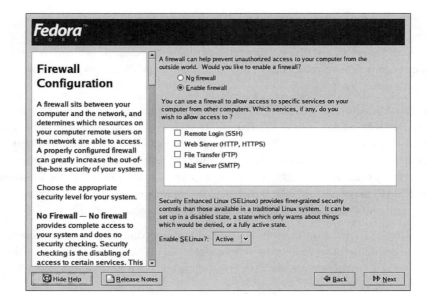

Here, you can configure the basic level of security that Fedora Core 4 will maintain on your computer system. A **firewall** is a software feature that filters incoming network traffic according to your specifications. You can use this filter to discard harmful or potentially harmful network traffic to prevent your system from being attacked by malicious network or Internet users.

By default, the Fedora Core 4 firewall is enabled. It protects your system while still enabling common types of Internet use, such as RealPlayer streaming and various types of chat and messaging. This setting is ideal for personal computing or desktop computing situations.

If you are using your computer as a network server, take care to check the boxes next to any of the listed services that you plan to provide; incoming requests for network services that you do not check now will be blocked by default. For example, if you want to run a web server, you should check the WWW (HTTP) box to indicate that incoming web traffic should not be filtered out.

Near the bottom of the Firewall Configuration screen is an option to configure Security Enhanced Linux (SELinux). Because SELinux can make Linux much more difficult to use for beginners, set the SELinux option to Disabled. The rest of the chapters in this book assume that you have disabled SELinux.

After you finish configuring the firewall to suit your needs, click Next to continue with the Fedora Core 4 installation process.

# Time Zone Selection

The next screen you see contains options related to your time zone. To keep accurate time and communicate about your time with other users on the network and on the Internet (for example, in email headers), Fedora Core 4 needs you to select a time zone. Figure 2.15 shows the Time Zone Selection screen.

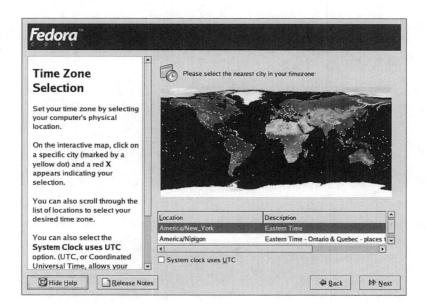

**FIGURE 2.15**
Select your time zone by click-ing the major city nearest to you on the world map.

The easiest way to select your time zone is to use your pointing device to point to the major city nearest to you on the world map that shares your time zone. When the name of the city under the map is the major city nearest to you, click to set the time zone of your computer to match.

If this method is inconvenient for you, choose a location from the scrolling list under the map or click the UTC Offset tab near the top of the screen to select your time zone as an absolute offset from universal time.

After you choose your time zone, click Next to continue with the installation process.

# Set Root Password

For security reasons, the root (administrative) account of any Linux system must be protected by a password. The Set Root Password screen, shown in Figure 2.16, enables you to choose a password for your system's root account.

Because root password selection is mandatory, the installer will display an error message if you try to click Next before you enter a suitable root password.

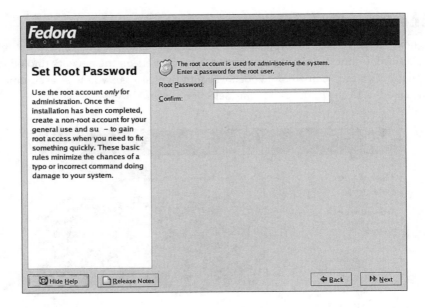

To enter a root password, click in the Root Password entry box and enter the password you want to assign to the root account. Then click in the Confirm entry box and re-enter the password to ensure that you typed it correctly.

If you enter a password that is shorter than six characters, you'll see a message indicating that the root password must be at least six characters long. Choose a longer password and enter it instead. Short passwords are easy to guess and are therefore less secure.

If, after entering the password in both boxes, you see a message stating that the passwords you entered were different, you have mistyped the password in one of the two boxes. Clear both boxes and re-enter the root password you've chosen.

After you enter an acceptable root password, the message Root password accepted appears beneath the entry boxes, and the Next button at the lower-right corner of the screen is activated. Click it to continue with the installation process.

**By the Way**

**Reading Package Information Takes Time**

Depending on the installation options you've selected, at some point over the next few screens, you'll receive a message that says the installer is Reading package information....

This process takes from a few seconds to several minutes, depending on the speed of your computer.

## Package Installation Defaults

Next, the Package Installation Defaults screen appears, as shown in Figure 2.17. It provides a list of the major software components that will be installed by the Fedora Core 4 installer. You are given the option to continue installation with the default set of packages or to customize the list of packages that are to be installed.

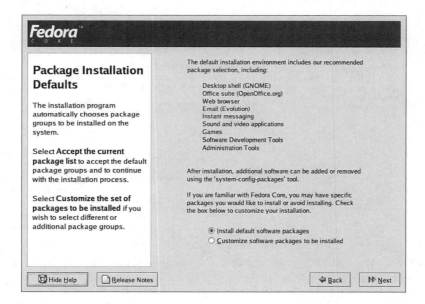

**FIGURE 2.17**
You are given the option to customize the set of packages that will be installed by the Fedora Core 4 installer.

For most users, the correct (and easiest) answer at this point is to opt to use the default set of packages for the time being; if you want to install additional Fedora Core 4 software components later, you can do so by referring to Chapter 31, "Installing Linux Software."

If you want to select the list of packages that will be installed now, click Customize the Set of Packages to Be Installed option before clicking Next to proceed with the installation.

## Package Group Selection

If you choose to customize the set of packages to be installed on the Package Installation Defaults screen, the Package Group Selection screen appears, as shown in Figure 2.18.

Each item in the Package Group Selection screen represents a group of related software packages that can be selected for installation or left out of installation.

Package group selection check boxes

**FIGURE 2.18**
The Package
Group Selection
screen enables
you to choose
which groups of
software pack-
ages you want
to install.

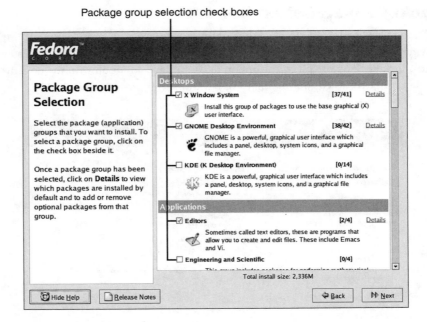

Checking a box enables the installation of a default selection of packages from the package group. Unchecking a box ensures that none of the packages from the group will be installed.

When you check a package group, a Details button appears next to it (refer to Figure 2.18). Clicking the Details button provides a means by which you can individually mark packages from within the group for installation, as shown in Figure 2.19.

**FIGURE 2.19**
Clicking the
Details button
provides a way
to individually
select packages
from a package
group.

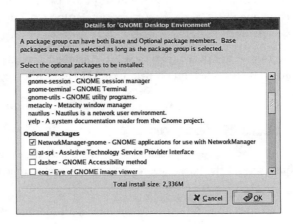

By the Way

### Running Out of Space When Selecting Packages

As you select or deselect packages and package groups for installation, the required space indicator beneath the package group selection list is updated. If this number exceeds the size of your primary Linux partition, you do not have enough space to install the list of packages you have selected. In this case, you must deselect some packages before continuing with the installation process.

By the Way

### So Many Packages, So Little Time

A complete discussion of the contents of each package group is beyond the scope of this book; if you find yourself confused or unsure, consider returning to the Installation Type screen (use the Back button) and selecting either the Personal Desktop or Workstation option for a predefined installation that is adequate for most common computing tasks.

Also, note that it is possible to add and remove software packages later, after Linux has been installed, if you want to adjust the configuration you've chosen.

Before completing package group selection, remember that the default selection of packages for the Workstation installation is assumed for the remainder of this book. If you choose not to install some of the packages that are selected by default, some of the information on day-to-day use of Fedora Core 4 in later chapters might not apply to your installation of Fedora Core 4 because you might not have the necessary operating system components installed.

After you finish selecting the package groups and packages you want to install, click Next to proceed with the installation process.

## About to Install

At this point, you have finished the bulk of the preinstall configuration that must be completed before the Fedora Core 4 installer can begin copying software to your hard drive and the About to Install screen appears.

If you have any uncertainties about whether you really want to install Linux, or if you haven't yet backed up the important files in an existing Windows installation, *now is the time* to think over your decision, boot into Windows and back up your files, or do whatever else might need to be done.

The About to Install screen does not present any options; it simply represents the last chance for you to abort Linux installation before all the requested changes are written to your hard drive.

When you are ready to proceed, click Next to begin creating and formatting partitions and then copying software to your hard drive.

## Installing Packages

The first thing that occurs after installation has begun in earnest is the creation and formatting of the hard drive partitions that will hold Fedora Core 4; a progress bar in the middle of the screen tracks the progress of partition creation and formatting. A few other housekeeping tasks also occur, and their progress is tracked with a progress bar at the center of your screen. If your Linux partitions are very large or your computer is somewhat slow, this part of the installation process might take quite a long time.

After your Linux partitions are created and formatted and the installation image is transferred to your hard drive, the installer begins to install the list of packages you selected for installation, as shown in Figure 2.20.

**FIGURE 2.20**
After creating and formatting Linux partitions, the installer begins to copy software to your hard drive.

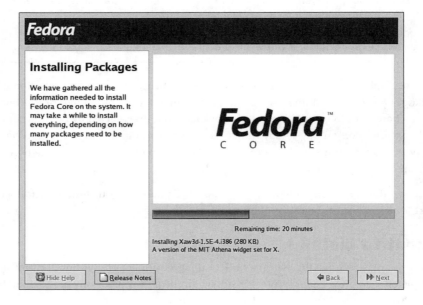

Depending on the speed of your computer and the number of packages you've selected, the installation process might take anywhere from a few minutes to several hours. You can check the time indicator in the Remaining status row (refer to Figure 2.20) for an estimate of the amount of time required for installation to finish at any given moment.

Depending on the packages you've chosen to install, the installer might at some point request that you insert additional Fedora Core 4 CD-ROMs if you are installing from CD. Do so when prompted and click OK to continue.

After package installation is complete, postinstall configuration begins; a progress bar in the center of the display follows the process as Linux performs a number of housekeeping tasks behind the scenes. After postinstall configuration, the installation of packages is complete.

## Congratulations!

The final screen displayed by the graphical installer is the Congratulations screen. Click the Reboot button to end the basic installation process and reboot the computer system. You are now ready to proceed to the next chapter.

# Summary

In this chapter, you installed Red Hat's Enterprise Linux Desktop operating system to your hard drive by following these major steps:

1. You launched the Fedora Core 4 installer.
2. You created new hard drive partitions to hold the Linux operating system.
3. You copied Fedora Core 4 to your hard drive.

Assuming that you installed your boot manager using the default boot manager configuration, the next time you power on your computer, you should find that one of two things will happen:

▶ If your hard drive contains only Linux, Fedora Core 4 will start automatically the next time you power on.

▶ If your hard drive contains both Windows and Linux, you will be offered a choice between starting Windows and starting Fedora Core 4.

In the next chapter, you boot into your new Fedora Core 4 system. The most difficult part of your Linux journey is now complete!

# Q&A

**Q** *I chose to customize my installation. What are the differences between the GNOME and KDE environments, selectable at the Package Group Selection screen?*

**A** In Fedora Core 4, GNOME is simpler, easier to use, and more closely tied to the included Red Hat system administration tools. Using KDE in Fedora Core 4 will require more configuration before you are able to use it comfortably, but it is also more powerful and programmable and offers a wider range of configuration options. If in doubt, you can install both at once; you can then switch between them easily. Note that the content of this book is written with the GNOME desktop in mind.

# Workshop

The Workshop is designed to help you anticipate possible questions, review what you've learned, and begin learning how to put your knowledge into practice.

## Quiz

1. True or False: If you repartitioned using the FIPS command before installing Linux, you have to delete an empty partition to free up space before Linux can be installed.

2. What Linux partitions do you need to create before you can install Linux?

3. How do you calculate the ideal size of the Linux swap partition?

## Answers

1. True.

2. A /boot partition of type ext3, a root (/) partition of type ext3, and a swap partition.

3. The ideal Linux swap partition is approximately double the size of your installed memory.

# CHAPTER 3

# Booting, Logging In, and Configuring

---

## *What You'll Learn in This Chapter:*

- ▶ How to perform preliminary Fedora Core 4 configuration
- ▶ How to shut down or reboot your Fedora Core 4 system
- ▶ How to configure your printer in Fedora Core 4
- ▶ How to configure dial-up in Fedora Core 4

In this chapter, you start your Fedora Core 4 system for the first time. You encounter the GRUB boot loader, which you use to start Linux or Windows. Then, before you can begin to use Linux for everyday tasks, you take care of some preliminary tasks. After you finish this chapter, you'll have a fully functional Fedora Core 4 Linux operating system ready to perform most any common task that a Windows computer can perform.

## Booting Fedora Core 4

If your computer has been a Windows-only computer thus far, you are probably used to switching on your computer and watching Windows load more or less immediately, without any intervention from you. Now that Linux is installed on your computer, things will change a little.

Fedora Core 4 has installed the GRUB boot loader to start your computer system. GRUB can start Linux or Windows; if you have both installed, it offers you a choice between the two each time you start. Switch on your computer now. If you followed along with the installation instructions in Chapter 2, "Installing Fedora Core 4," and installed the GRUB boot loader, within a few moments you should find yourself looking at the GRUB boot display, as shown in Figure 3.1.

**FIGURE 3.1**
The GRUB boot display presents you with the available list of boot options. This computer has both Windows (labeled DOS) and Linux on it.

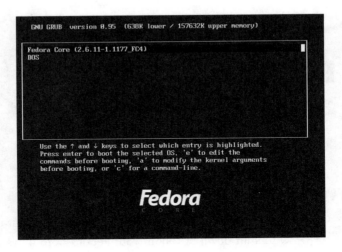

At the GRUB display, you have five seconds to select which operating system you want to start. Use your up- and down-arrow keys to move the selection bar, and press Enter to select and start an operating system in the list.

### Select DOS When You Want Windows

If you have Windows installed alongside Linux, you might find that Windows appears in the list of available operating systems as "DOS." The DOS label is used by Fedora Core 4 to refer to most MS-DOS or Microsoft Windows operating systems. Selecting DOS therefore starts your Windows operating system.

If you do not select an operating system yourself, GRUB automatically starts the selected operating system after five seconds.

When Fedora Core 4 starts, you first see a few lines of text scrolling across your display as Linux examines and adjusts to your CPU, mainboard and memory configuration, and to other hardware. Fedora Core 4 then displays a progress bar in the center of your screen to show its progress as it launches system services and performs other housekeeping tasks (see Figure 3.2). This process might take several minutes the first time you start Linux. On subsequent boots, it will go much more quickly. This process is repeated each time you start Linux. If you didn't choose to install the Workstation configuration in the previous chapter but installed the Server configuration instead, you will see a text display containing more detailed information instead of a progress bar.

After Fedora Core 4 starts all its components, the screen clears and you see the Welcome to Fedora Core banner.

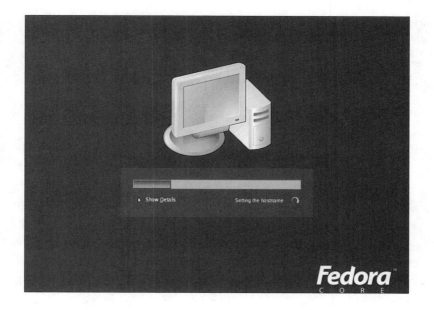

**FIGURE 3.2**
Fedora Core 4
shows a
progress bar as
it starts system
services.

# Welcome to Fedora Core 4!

When your Fedora Core 4 computer system starts for the first time, Fedora Core 4
automatically displays the Welcome to Fedora Core screen. Beginning at this screen,
you are led through a few remaining configuration steps that must be completed
before you can use Fedora Core 4. The following section walks you through these
remaining configuration steps.

## Finishing First-Run Configuration

On the Welcome to Fedora Core screen, click the Next button to proceed to the
License Agreement screen. Here, you are asked to read and agree to the software
license terms set forth for Fedora Core 4 users. After you read the terms and feel that
you agree with them, click Yes, I Agree to the License Agreement and then click Next
to proceed with first-run configuration.

Now you see the Date and Time screen, shown in Figure 3.3. Use this screen to be
sure that your current date and time are set correctly.

You can choose a month and year by using the navigation arrows; after the correct
month and year appear, you can choose a day simply by clicking its number. If
you need to adjust the current time (shown in 24-hour format), enter the correct
values into the Hour, Minute, and Second entry boxes. After you set your date and
time correctly, click Next to proceed to the Display configuration screen shown in

Figure 3.4, where you select the desktop resolution that you plan to use on a day-to-day basis and tell Fedora Core 4 about your monitor.

**FIGURE 3.3**
The Date and
Time screen
allows you to
set your current
date and time.

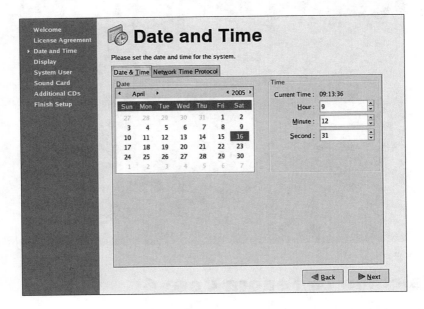

Click to select monitor

**FIGURE 3.4**
At the Display
configuration
screen, you tell
Fedora Core
about your moni-
tor and the size
of the desktop
you want to use.

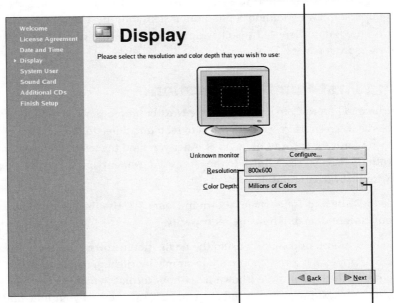

Click to select desktop size    Click to select color depth

If your monitor is listed as "Unknown monitor," you should configure your monitor before selecting a desktop resolution. To do so, click the Configure button to display the dialog box shown in Figure 3.5.

**FIGURE 3.5**
Select the monitor that most closely matches the make and model of your own.

In the Monitor dialog box, you'll see a list of monitor manufacturers. Click the small arrow next to the manufacturer of your monitor; then select the model of your monitor from the list of models. After you've selected your monitor from the list, click OK to save the change.

After configuring your monitor, select the size of the desktop that you prefer from the Resolution drop-down list:

▶ Select 800×600 if you want text and icons to appear larger on your display (while not being able to fit as many items or words onscreen at once).

▶ Select 1024×768 if you want text and icons to appear smaller on your display (while being able to fit more items or words onscreen at once).

▶ Select another value if you know its properties and are sure that it's what you prefer.

Finally, select Millions of Colors from the Color Depth drop-down list if it is available. If Millions of Colors isn't listed, select Thousands of Colors instead.

After you have configured your monitor, desktop resolution, and color depth, click Next to display the System User screen shown in Figure 3.6, where you create a user account with regular privileges on the system for day-to-day use. It is this account that you will use while you follow along with the rest of the chapters in this book. Enter all of the following information:

▶ A username (account name) in the Username box

▶ Your real name in the Full Name box

▶ Your desired password in the Password box

▶ Your desired password a second time in the Confirm Password box

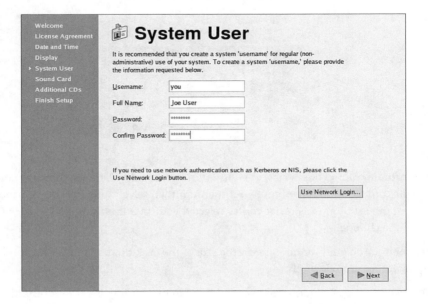

When you are done entering account information, click Next to create your standard user account and proceed with first-run configuration.

If Fedora Core 4 has detected sound-generating hardware in your computer (of the kind that allows you to listen to music or hear other sounds on your PC), the Sound Card screen shown in Figure 3.7 is displayed. On the Sound Card screen, you can ensure that Fedora Core 4 has successfully configured your sound hardware by checking the listed sound hardware against your system configuration and then clicking the Play Test Sound button. If, after clicking the button, you are unable to hear the sample sound, ensure that your sound cabling and speakers are correctly installed and powered on and that your sound card or other sound-generating hardware is supported by Fedora Core 4.

After you finish testing your sound configuration, click Next to proceed to the Additional CDs screen, shown in Figure 3.8.

Because you will learn how to install additional software from Fedora Core 4 CD-ROMs or DVD any time you like in Chapter 31, "Installing Linux Software," we don't spend extra time now installing additional software. Click Next to proceed to the Finish Setup screen, which confirms that your preliminary configuration of Fedora Core 4 is complete.

Click Next one more time to display the Linux desktop login prompt.

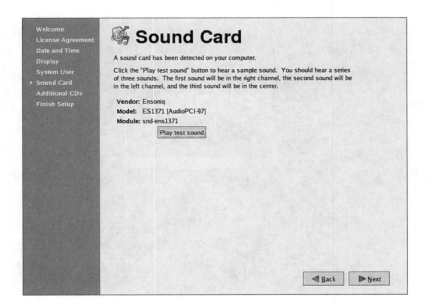

**FIGURE 3.7**
The Sound Card test screen allows you to verify that Fedora Core 4 has correctly configured your sound hard-ware.

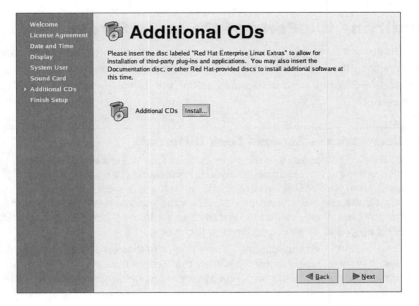

**FIGURE 3.8**
At the Additional CDs screen, Fedora Core 4 gives you the option of installing more software from your CD-ROMs or DVD.

## Logging In for Configuration

After you finish the first-boot configuration discussed in the preceding section, you find yourself looking at the login prompt shown in Figure 3.9. This screen appears every time you start Fedora Core 4.

**FIGURE 3.9**
Every time you start Fedora Core 4 from now on, you will see the Linux login prompt.

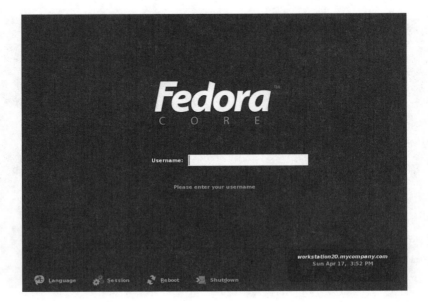

## Identifying the Parts of the Login Screen

The login prompt is primarily designed to enable you to log in to the Fedora Core 4 environment so that you can begin to use your computer. Before you log in for the first time, however, you need to become familiar with a few functional areas of the login screen.

*By the Way*

### For Users Whose Screens Look Different

If, in Chapter 2, you chose to customize your software selection or installed a configuration other than Workstation, and you subsequently did not install the X Window System graphical environment, you will not see a graphical login prompt. Instead, you will see a text login prompt. Study the console-related sections of Chapters 5–7 and then proceed to Chapter 19, "Performing Basic Shell Tasks," for details on logging in to and using Linux in text mode.

If you chose the Workstation install, as was shown in Chapter 2, and you still don't see a graphical login prompt, it's likely that Fedora Core 4 doesn't support your computer's display hardware. Consider upgrading before proceeding with the rest of this book.

If you chose to install more than one language when you installed Linux, clicking the Language button displays a list of languages from which you can select, as shown in Figure 3.10. The language you select is the language used by Fedora Core 4 for communicating with you in the desktop environment. The default language is English.

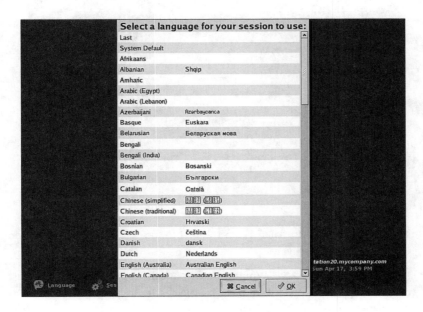

**FIGURE 3.10**
Clicking the Language button enables you to select the language Fedora Core 4 will use in text and dialog boxes.

The Session button on the login screen is used to select the Linux desktop environment you want to use if you have installed more than one desktop environment. Clicking it displays the dialog box shown in Figure 3.11.

The options in the Session dialog box log you in to the desktop in the following ways:

▶ The Last option logs you in to whichever desktop environment you used the last time you logged in, or to the default Fedora Core 4 GNOME (GNU Network Object Model Environment) desktop if this is your first time logging in.

▶ The Default option logs you in to whichever desktop environment is your current default, or to the GNOME environment if this is your first time logging in.

▶ The Failsafe option instructs Fedora Core 4 to log you in to a basic X Window System desktop in an environment called TWM that is discussed in more detail in Chapter 26, "Desktop Power Tools."

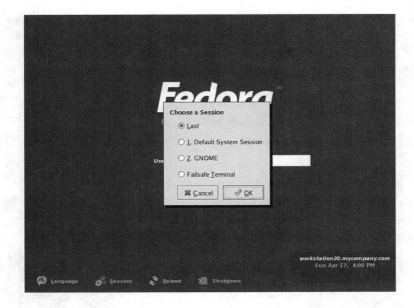

▶ The GNOME option instructs Fedora Core 4 to log you in to the GNOME and KDE desktops, respectively.

▶ If you have installed KDE, Window Maker, or other optional environments, they will appear in this list and can be selected for login as well.

If you installed the Workstation configuration of Fedora Core 4 as was suggested in the previous chapter, the default environment is the GNOME desktop. The GNOME environment is the environment that will be discussed throughout the rest of this book whenever we refer to "the Fedora Core 4 desktop," to "the Linux desktop," or simply to "the desktop." You can learn more about logging in to and using the desktop in Chapter 4, "Introducing the Fedora Core 4 Desktop."

The Reboot and Shutdown buttons near the bottom of the screen are used to restart Fedora Core 4 or to shut down the computer, respectively. Both buttons present a confirmation dialog box when you click them. The confirmation dialog box for the Shutdown button appears in Figure 3.12.

*Did you Know?*

### Always Shut Down Before Powering Off

Before you turn off your Linux computer, you should always remember to return to the Login screen, click the Shutdown button, and choose Shutdown to shut down the system. Although it is *very unlikely*, it is nonetheless *possible* that not shutting down correctly could cause you to lose some of your data.

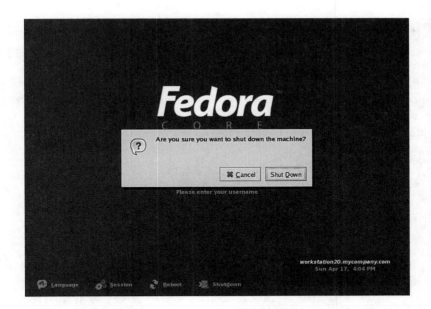

**FIGURE 3.12**
After you click the Shutdown button, a confirmation dialog box appears. To shut down the system, click Shut Down.

# Configuring Your Printer and Internet Service

Before you begin using Linux, you'll likely want to configure both your printer and your dial-up Internet service (if you are a dial-up user) to make your Linux system fully operational.

In order to do this, you must log in to the root (administrative) user's account and use several Fedora Core 4 configuration tools. To log in to the root account, enter the word **root** into the Username box that you see in the center of your screen and press Enter. When the word Password appears in front of the box, enter the root password you selected when installing Linux into the same box and press Enter once more.

---

**New to Desktop Environments?**

In this chapter, we gloss over the ins and outs of the login process and the Linux desktop: We want to dig only deep enough to configure your printer and dial-up Internet service just now. We'll get to details about the Linux desktop in later chapters. If you're not comfortable entering **root** and the root password without knowing why, or if you've never worked with a graphical operating system and would like to learn about using the mouse to manipulate menus and windows before you configure your printer and dial-up Internet service, you might want to skip ahead and read Chapter 4 before continuing with this one.

---

*By the Way*

## Configuring Your Printer

After you enter the word **root** and the root password at the login screen, you find yourself logged in to the root account's desktop environment. To configure your printer, click the word Desktop near the top of your display to open the Desktop menu, then click the System Settings item in the menu, and then click the Printing item in the System Settings menu, as shown in Figure 3.13. After you click the Printing item, the Printer configuration tool opens.

**FIGURE 3.13**
Click Desktop,
System
Settings,
Printing to open
the Printer con-
figuration tool.

Click the New button near the upper-left corner of the Printer configuration tool window now to add a printer to Fedora Core 4's list of available printers. The Add a New Print Queue dialog box appears.

Click the Forward button to display the Queue Name dialog box, which is used to name your printer, as shown in Figure 3.14. In the Name box, enter 1p. You should always name your default printer **1p** because it is what many older Linux and Unix applications expect the default printer to be called. You can also enter a brief human-readable description of the printer in the Short Description box if you choose to do so.

Click the Forward button after you have named your printer to display the Queue Type dialog box, which is used to tell Fedora Core 4 how to communicate with this printer, as shown in Figure 3.15.

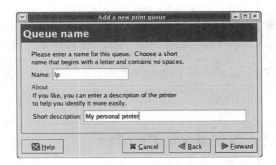

**FIGURE 3.14**
Enter **lp** as the queue name for your default printer. You can also enter a description if you want.

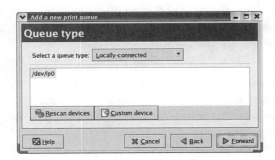

**FIGURE 3.15**
Choose a connection type for this printer. For parallel or USB printer users, the correct queue type option is the Locally-connected option.

If your printer is connected directly to your computer by Universal Serial Bus (USB) or parallel (Printer) port, select Locally-connected from the Select a Queue Type drop-down list.

In the box below the Select a Queue Type drop-down list, choose the port to which your printer is connected. Table 3.1 contains a list of common ports.

**TABLE 3.1    Common Ports to Which Printers Might Be Connected**

| Port | Description |
| --- | --- |
| /dev/lp0 | First parallel (Printer) port, LPT1: or PRN: in MS-DOS |
| /dev/lp1 | Second parallel (Printer) port (if present), LPT2: in MS-DOS |
| /dev/usb/lp0 | First USB printer found by Linux |
| /dev/usb/lp1 | Second USB printer found by Linux |

In the list of ports that Linux has discovered in your computer system, select the port to which your printer is connected.

> **Invisible USB Printers**
>
> If your printer is connected via USB and you don't see any USB printer ports listed, turn your printer off and then back on again, wait a few moments, and then click the Rescan Devices button near the bottom of the Queue Type dialog box. Your USB printer should now appear.

## Configuring a Network Printer

If you need to print to a printer that is on your local area network, click on the Select a Queue Type drop-down list and select the network protocol that is appropriate for your configuration. For users on primarily Unix- or Linux-based networks, the correct choice is usually CUPS or Unix; for users on primarily Windows-based networks, the correct choice is usually either Windows or Novell type networks.

After you select the appropriate type of network connectivity for the printer in question, enter the network address or other related details for the printer in question. If you need assistance with this process or aren't sure what type of network printer you will be using, contact your network administrator.

## Selecting a Printer Make and Model

After you select your printer port (for locally connected printers) or enter your printer's network information (for networked printers), click the Forward button to display the Printer Model dialog box, used to select the type of printer connected to your computer. By selecting a make and model for your printer, you tell Fedora Core 4 what language to use when communicating with your printer.

In the Printer Model dialog box, shown in Figure 3.16, select the make of your printer from the drop-down list near the top of the dialog box. The list of known printers for the make you selected then appears in the bottom half of the dialog box; select your model from the list. Then click the Forward button to display the confirmation dialog box.

> **What If My Printer Isn't Listed?**
>
> If your printer's make (brand) is listed, but the specific model that you own isn't listed, select the model name or number that most closely approximates yours. If this doesn't work, or if your printer's make isn't listed, select HP as your brand and LaserJet as your model—many printers, both old and new, are LaserJet compatible. If you're still unable to get your printer to work, consider upgrading to a printer in the list that is compatible with Linux.

Select printer manufacturer...

...then select printer model

**FIGURE 3.16**
Select your
make from the
drop-down list
and then your
model from the
list in the lower
half of the dia-
log box.

Review the settings listed in the confirmation dialog box; if your make and model are correctly listed, click the Finish button to save your printer configuration. You then are asked whether you want to print a test page to ensure that your settings have been entered correctly. To be certain that your printer is configured correctly, you should choose Yes. If the test page does not print correctly, remove the queue by clicking the Delete button in the Printer configuration tool window and repeat the steps in this section, trying different settings.

After you successfully add a printer, if you want to add more printers, repeat the steps in this section. If you are done adding printers, click the word Action at the upper left of the Printer configuration tool window and then select Quit from the drop-down menu to exit the Printer configuration tool. When prompted, click the Save button to save your new printer configuration.

## Configuring Your Dial-up Internet Service

If you use broadband Internet service like Cable Internet or Digital Subscriber Line (DSL), you most likely need no special network configuration. Simply plug your network cable into the back of your computer system and skip to the next chapter.

If your Internet service requires more than simple Ethernet connectivity—for example, if you use a dial-up modem or your environment requires Virtual Private Network (VPN) capability—you need to perform additional configuration before you can enjoy full network connectivity in Fedora Core 4. To start the Network Configuration tool, click the word Desktop near the top of your screen to display the Desktop menu, then click System Settings, and then Network, as shown in Figure 3.17. The Network Configuration tool starts.

To configure a modem for dial-up Internet use with Fedora Core 4, click the New button in the Network Configuration tool to indicate that you want to create a new connection. Be sure that your modem is powered on (if it is external), then select Modem connection and click the Forward button in the Add New Device Type dialog shown in Figure 3.18 to cause Linux to search for your modem. When your modem is found, the detected settings appear, as shown in Figure 3.19.

**FIGURE 3.17**
Start the Network Configuration tool to configure Fedora Core 4 to connect to your Internet service provider.

**FIGURE 3.18**
Select Modem Connection in the Add New Device Type dialog box and click Forward to have Linux auto-detect your modem.

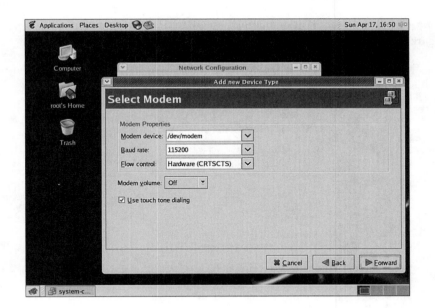

**FIGURE 3.19**
After your modem is detected by Fedora Core 4, the correct settings automatically appear.

### Networking Beyond Dial-Up

If your computer is connected to the Internet using a technology other than dial-up modem service or Dynamic Host Configuration Protocol (DHCP) over Ethernet, contact your network administrator or ISP for help in configuring your LAN service using the Internet Configuration Wizard.

*By the Way*

With the exception of the Modem Volume setting, which you can adjust to suit your dialing volume tastes, you should not change any of the other settings from those detected by Linux. Click the Forward button to display a dialog box that allows you to enter details related to your ISP, as shown in Figure 3.20.

### If Your Modem Isn't Found

If Fedora Core 4 displays a message saying that no modem can be found, check your modem to ensure that it is powered on and connected properly to your computer. If it is, or if your modem is internal and you still receive an error message, your modem is not easily supported by Linux.

Refer to "Communications Hardware" in Chapter 1, "Preparing to Install Fedora Core 4," for details on the types of modems that are compatible with Linux operating systems like Fedora Core 4.

*By the Way*

Enter your dial-up service provider's dialing details, name, login (username), and password into the relevant entry boxes shown in Figure 3.20. When you are done, click the Forward button to display the IP Settings dialog box, as shown in Figure 3.21.

**FIGURE 3.20**
The Network Configuration tool needs details about your ISP to configure your connection.

Enter prefix, area code, and phone number          Enter provider's name

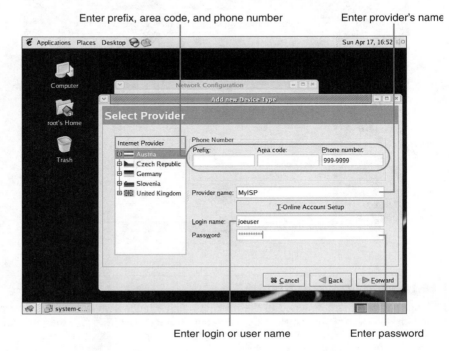

Enter login or user name          Enter password

**FIGURE 3.21**
In the IP Settings dialog box, you can adjust the parameters that Fedora Core 4 will use to establish your Internet connection.

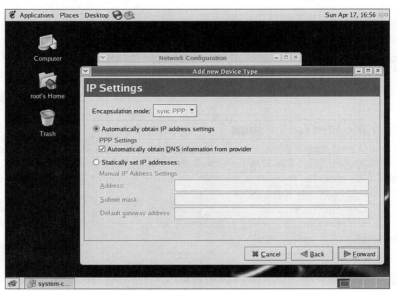

Most users should leave the default choice, Automatically Obtain IP Address Settings, selected. If, on the other hand, your ISP has provided you with a specific set of static IP addresses and settings, select Statically Set IP Address and enter those settings now. When you are done, click the Forward button to display your configuration summary.

After you verify that all the information shown in the summary is correct, click Apply to save your changes and display the Network Configuration tool once again, this time listing the connection that you have just created, as shown in Figure 3.22.

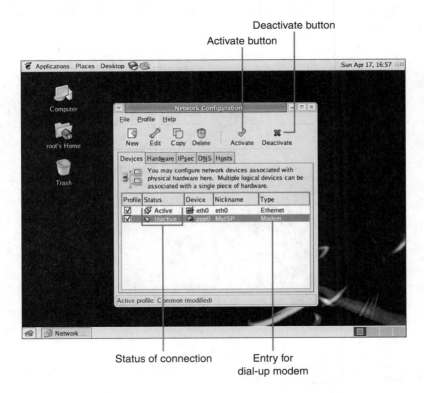

Deactivate button

Activate button

Status of connection

Entry for
dial-up modem

**FIGURE 3.22**
The Network Configuration tool is used to activate (connect) and deactivate (disconnect) your Internet connections.

To connect to your ISP, click your modem's entry in the device list and then click the Activate button near the top of the dialog box. Fedora Core 4 then attempts to connect to your ISP. While you are connected, the word Active appears in the Status column for your dial-up connection. When you click the Deactivate button to disconnect once again, the status returns to Inactive.

Any time you want to connect to the Internet using your dial-up account, restart the Network Configuration tool, select your modem, and click the Activate button.

For additional details on using the Network Configuration tool, refer to "Managing Network Interfaces" in Chapter 29, "Command-Line System Administration."

## Logging Out

After you finish configuring your printer and dial-up Internet service, exit the root desktop account and return to the Linux login screen by clicking the Desktop button near the top of your screen and then selecting the Log Out option, as shown in Figure 3.23. The confirmation dialog box shown in Figure 3.24 is displayed. To confirm that you want to log out and return to the Linux login screen, select Log Out and then click OK.

**FIGURE 3.23**
Click Desktop, Log Out to indicate that you want to log out of the root desktop account and return to the Linux login screen.

**Did you Know?**

### The Save Current Setup Check Box

You might notice the Save Current Setup check box as you log out of the desktop environment. This check box doesn't refer to the configuration changes you've just made; those changes have been saved already. Checking the Save Current Setup box causes Fedora Core 4 to restart any applications that are still running the next time you log in. This option will be discussed in more detail in the next chapter. For now, simply leave the box unchecked.

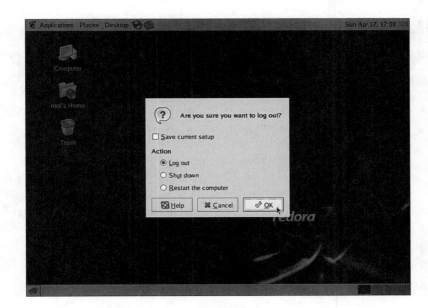

**FIGURE 3.24**
A confirmation dialog box appears to make sure that you really want to log out. Choose Log Out and click OK to return to the login prompt.

# Summary

In this chapter, you booted for the first time into your new Fedora Core 4 Linux computer system. You answered a few final configuration questions posed by Fedora Core 4, and then you did the following:

▶ Learned how to tell Fedora Core 4 to use a language other than English when communicating with you

▶ Learned how to shut down or restart your system

▶ Added a printer to your Fedora Core 4 system

▶ Configured Fedora Core 4 to use your modem to dial your ISP for Internet service

▶ Learned how to connect to and disconnect from your ISP if you are a dial-up user

Your system is now fully configured, and you are ready to begin using and learning about Linux. On to adventure!

# Q&A

**Q** *I followed the directions in Chapter 2 exactly, but when I started Linux for the first time, I saw a text login prompt instead of the graphical login screen. What's wrong?*

**A** If you installed the Workstation configuration of Fedora Core 4 as was suggested in Chapter 2, yet you find yourself at a text login prompt, your graphics hardware is not supported or detected properly by Fedora Core 4. Although you can sometimes get uncooperative display hardware to work in Linux, such techniques are beyond the scope of this book. You still can follow some of the lessons in chapters that deal with the Linux command line, but in order to follow along with the rest of this book, you should upgrade to a supported graphics configuration so that you can use the Linux desktop environment.

**Q** *I can't find my printer in the list of makes and models, and selecting LaserJet also doesn't work with my printer. What should I do?*

**A** If your printer is a PostScript-compatible printer, select Generic from the make drop-down list and then select PostScript Printer from the list of models. If you are unsure, check with your printer's manufacturer to see if your printer is fully compatible with another make and model of printer. If it is, simply select the compatible make and model. If neither of these suggestions applies to you, your only alternatives are to select Text Only Printer from the Generic make list or to invest in a supported printer. Beware that a text-only printer cannot print documents from Linux desktop applications such as OpenOffice or from the LaTeX document system discussed in Chapter 21, "Managing High-Quality Documents at the Command Line."

**Q** *I use America Online as my ISP. Can I run AOL in Fedora Core 4?*

**A** Unfortunately, you cannot yet run AOL in most Linux operating systems.

# Workshop

The Workshop is designed to help you anticipate possible questions, review what you've learned, and begin learning how to put your knowledge into practice.

## Quiz

**1.** How do you shut down your Linux computer from the login screen?

**2.** What are your options if Fedora Core 4 can't find your modem?

**3.** How do you connect to or disconnect from your ISP?

## Answers

1. Click the Shutdown button near the bottom of the login screen and then select Shut Down when the confirmation dialog box appears.

2. Realistically, your only option is to buy a Linux-compatible modem. Details on the types of modems that are compatible with Linux appear in Chapter 1.

3. To connect, start the Network Configuration tool by clicking Desktop, then System Settings, and then Network. In the tool, select your modem and click the Activate button to activate your network connection.

   To disconnect, start the Network Configuration tool, select your modem, and click the Deactivate button.

## Activities

1. If you have a dual-boot system, restart your computer and use GRUB to start Windows in order to familiarize yourself with your dual-boot system.

2. Connect to and disconnect from your ISP several times to familiarize yourself with the process.

# PART II

# Exploring Linux Fundamentals

# CHAPTER 4

# Introducing the Fedora Core 4 Desktop

---

## *What You'll Learn in This Chapter:*

- ▶ How to log in
- ▶ How to use the menubar to launch applications
- ▶ How to move, resize, and close application windows
- ▶ What virtual workspaces are and how to use them
- ▶ How to log out

When you use Fedora Core 4, most of the work you do takes place through a graphical user interface (GUI), a full-color, pictorial way of presenting computing files and processes to the user. By the time you finish this chapter, you will be comfortable enough with the Linux desktop's GUI to perform basic desktop tasks and even to do some exploring on your own.

## Logging In to the Desktop

The Linux security model requires that all users log in to the system before they can use applications, create files, or perform other computing tasks. When you boot Fedora Core 4, you eventually find yourself face to face with the desktop login prompt, shown in Figure 4.1.

To log in, simply enter your username, press Enter, and then enter your password. Note that your password is not displayed as you type it; this prevents others from stealing your password by looking over your shoulder. The username and password that you should enter now are the ones that you created in Chapter 3, "Booting, Logging In, and Configuring." If you enter the information correctly, you are soon greeted by the Fedora Core 4 desktop, as shown in Figure 4.2.

**FIGURE 4.1**
The Fedora Core 4 login prompt appears after you boot the system.

Menubar    Application launchers
Clickable menus

**FIGURE 4.2**
The default Fedora Core 4 desktop holds the tools you need to start working with applications.

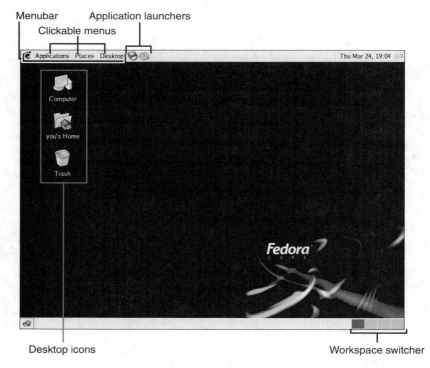

Desktop icons                    Workspace switcher

By the Way

**Usernames and Passwords Are Case Sensitive**

In the world of Unix and Linux, nearly everything is case sensitive—meaning that capital letters and lowercase letters cannot be used interchangeably. This goes for usernames and passwords, too! As you log in, keep in mind that Betsy is not at all the same thing as betsy to a Linux computer!

The components of the Fedora Core desktop shown in Figure 4.2 include the following:

► The menubar lies at the top of the screen and provides menus and icons to launch applications or change the settings that affect the appearance or behavior of your computer system. It also displays the system clock and volume control.

► Clickable menus provide the ability to launch Linux applications, change your computer's settings or your desktop's appearance, or log out of the desktop environment.

► Application launchers are icons in the menubar that start Linux applications when they are clicked.

► Desktop icons provide a graphical way to open storage devices or to manage your files.

► The taskbar lies at the bottom of the screen and displays a visual representation of each already-running application.

► The workspace switcher (which will be discussed later in this chapter) helps you to monitor and move between virtual workspaces—the GUI equivalent of virtual consoles.

Though the list of items on your Fedora Core 4 desktop can at first seem daunting, especially if you are already accustomed to other desktops (such as the Windows desktop), you will soon find the Linux desktop environment to be both intuitive and efficient.

# Navigating the Desktop

If you use Windows, Macintosh, or any other GUI operating system, you should already be at least moderately familiar with the use of the mouse or another pointing device. Feel free, therefore, to follow along and to click at will on desktop items you're curious about.

Across the top of the display is the menubar, containing a number of menus and icons. The menubar is designed to give you immediate access to frequently used applications, storage areas, settings, and information. You will use the menubar to launch programs, access your hard drive or the network, tailor your computing environment to suit your needs, or log out of your desktop before shutting down. Starting at the left, the menubar contains the following features:

- ▶ The Applications menu shows a list of menus and additional applications when clicked; once the menu has been opened, you can launch the currently selected (highlighted) application by clicking again.

- ▶ The Places menu shows a list of virtual "places" that you can interact with as a user. Among these places are storage areas on your hard drive, or on the hard drives of other computers on your network.

- ▶ The Desktop menu provides you with a set of tools that can be used to customize your computing environment's appearance and behavior, along with an option to log out (exit the desktop).

- ▶ The icon marked with a mouse circling earth launches the Web browser.

- ▶ The icon that looks like a stamp and an envelope launches the email program.

- ▶ The area to the far right of the menubar displays the current date and time and a small speaker icon that can be used to change your computer's audio volume.

Across the bottom of the desktop is the taskbar, which consists of three major components, described from left to right:

- ▶ The lone icon at the lower-left corner of the display is the desktop button. Clicking it will cause any open application windows to be temporarily minimized (hidden) so that the desktop and desktop icons are visible.

- ▶ The middle area in the taskbar, empty when you first log in, displays an icon and title for each running application. You can then click on the icon or title to raise an application window that is obscured by other applications, or to restore a minimized (hidden) application window to its previous location.

- ▶ The four squares at the rightmost extreme are part of the workspace switcher, which is used to select among four independent workspaces available to you as a desktop Linux user. You'll learn more about workspaces and the workspace switcher later in this chapter.

Down the left side of the display are the desktop icons. These icons give you double-click access to frequently used tools and folders. You learn how to add your own icons to the desktop later, but the following icons appear there by default:

- ▶ The Computer icon gives you quick access to your hard drive, CD-ROM drive, and other storage devices, as well as to other systems on your network (similar to My Computer in Windows).

▶ The Home icon opens a folder that contains your home directory (similar to My Documents in Windows), in which you will find all the files and folders you create while using Linux.

▶ The Trash icon is a clickable shortcut to a folder that contains all your deleted files. You can drag files and drop them in this folder to delete them.

Icons for any removable media (such as a DVD or CD-ROM) will also appear on your desktop below these icons whenever you insert a DVD or CD.

## Launching Applications

To launch an application, click the Applications menu at the upper left of the display. Here, you find a listing of the most commonly used Linux applications, organized by category. Hover your mouse cursor over any submenu (an item with an arrow next to it) to open it; Figure 4.3 shows the Accessories submenu opened. Clicking the entry for a specific application launches that application in a new window.

**FIGURE 4.3**
The Applications menu is used to launch a wide variety of Linux applications.

Take a moment to familiarize yourself with the contents of the menu and then move the mouse cursor over the Text Editor entry in the Accessories submenu. Click to launch the text editor application.

---

### Navigating Menus Using This Book

**By the Way**

Throughout the rest of the text, when you are to choose a series of menu items or commands, you'll see each choice separated by a comma. So, for example, instructions for clicking the Applications menu, hovering over the Accessories submenu listing to open it, and then clicking the Text Editor listing to open the text editor, would read

Choose Applications, Accessories, Text Editor to start the text editor.

When you click Text Editor item in the Accessories submenu, the text editor opens in a new application window. Figure 4.4 shows the text editor, along with labels showing its window control icons.

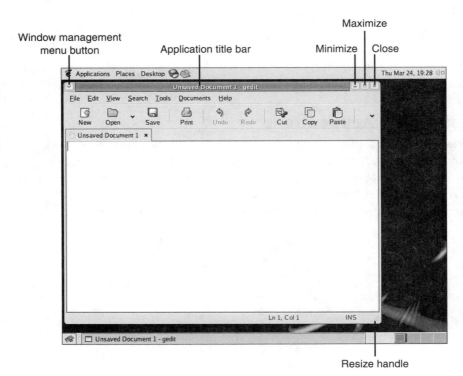

**FIGURE 4.4**
The text editor application, called gedit, opens in its own window, with a toolbar of icons for common text editing tasks, including Cut, Paste, Print, and others.

As previously mentioned, when you open an application in Fedora Core 4, an icon representing that application also appears in the taskbar (in Figure 4.4, this button is labeled Unsaved Document 1 - gedit). You can click buttons in the taskbar to move between open application windows.

## Using Window Controls

The application window of the Fedora Core 4 text editor works much like the application windows you might be accustomed to from other operating systems. The following list identifies the window controls and describes their use:

▶ **The Window Menu button**—Clicking this button displays a list of actions that can be performed on the application window.

▶ **The Application title bar**—This area displays the name of the application and in some cases the file currently opened in the application.

▶ **The Minimize Window button**—Clicking this button hides the application window (clicking the application's taskbar button restores it).

▶ **The Maximize Window button**—Clicking this button expands the application window to fill the desktop.

▶ **The Close Window button**—Clicking this button closes the window and the application.

# Moving, Resizing, Minimizing, and Maximizing Windows

By clicking or clicking and dragging elements of application windows, you can change their size, shape, and position to suit your needs and to enhance your work-flow. This small collection of standard controls helps you to manipulate your work environment to suit your own needs and preferences.

Try these operations on the gedit window you started earlier:

▶ To move the window, click on the application title bar, hold down the mouse button, and drag the window to a new position.

▶ To resize the application window, click and drag the **resize handle**, which can be seen as a pattern of diagonal lines at the lower-right corner of each application window.

▶ To cause a window to fill the entire screen, click the Maximize Window button; the application window fills the screen. After you maximize the window, the Maximize button disappears and is replaced by a Restore Window button.

▶ To restore a maximized window to its original size, click the Restore Window button that appears once a window is maximized.

▶ To minimize (hide) a window, click the Minimize Window button; the window disappears from the desktop, but it still appears in the taskbar. Brackets around the button indicate that the application is open but has been mini-mized (hidden).

▶ To display a minimized application window again, click the application's taskbar button; the window reappears on the desktop and the brackets disap-pear from the window's taskbar button.

▶ To close (quit) an application, click the Close Window button in the upper-right corner of the window. If you've made no changes since last saving the current file, the application closes immediately. If you've made changes since last saving the file, you're asked whether you want to save the changes before the application exits.

**The Window Menu**

Generally speaking, you will find that the Window Menu (the window decoration at the upper left of the application window) simply contains items that perform the tasks performed by the other window decorations, such as minimize, maximize, and close—although one important additional use for this menu—making windows appear in all workspaces—is discussed later this chapter in the context of the workspace switcher.

## Application Menus and Application Toolbar

Another important set of application controls lies near the top of each application window in the application menubar. In gedit, these controls include File, Edit, View, Search, Documents, and Help. Although the items in the application menubar vary between applications, nearly every application has an application menubar that contains functionality helpful for users of that application.

Clicking any item in the application menubar displays a menu of relevant options or controls that can be performed or used in the application. Some menus, such as File and Help, appear in almost all applications. Although you learn how to use the Help menu in Chapter 17, "Getting Help on the Desktop," you might want to take some time now to briefly experiment with this menu and its contents.

Just below the application menubar, you often see an application toolbar that contains small icons and, beneath these, text labels that describe what each icon does. Usually, items on the toolbar are duplicates of the most commonly used functions from the menus in the application's menubar. So, for example, clicking the Save icon in the toolbar performs the same task as choosing File, Save from the menubar—except that clicking a single icon in the toolbar is faster because you don't have to click as many times.

# Working with Multiple Windows

The true power of any graphical desktop environment lies in the fact that users can easily work in several open applications at once. To see this capability in action, you can try launching several applications now.

If you don't already have a gedit (text editor) window running, launch one now by choosing Applications, Accessories, Text Editor. So that you have several applications to work with, also choose Applications, Games, Same GNOME and then Applications, Accessories, Calculator. Each of these applications opens in its own window, and an icon for each appears in the taskbar. All three applications are shown running in Figure 4.5.

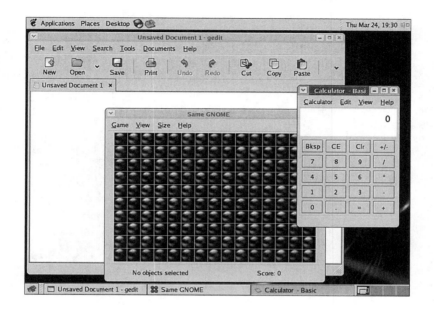

**FIGURE 4.5**
The Linux desktop with three running applications that have been dragged into position for better visibility: the gedit text editor, the Calculator, and the Same GNOME game. The active application is the topmost window (here, the Calculator).

# Changing the Active Application

When you have multiple windows open on the Linux desktop, each window's status is indicated in the appearance of its application title bar and taskbar icon. You can enter commands and perform tasks in an active window; in the Linux world, this window is said to be **focused**. Inactive or **unfocused** windows are idle until you click them or their taskbar icon. An unfocused window has a grayed-out application title bar. A focused window's title bar is in color, and its taskbar button is shaded. When you press a key on your keyboard, only the application that is currently focused responds to your keypress and acts on what you have entered. Applications that do not have focus do not respond and are not aware of your keypresses.

To change focus from one window to another, click the target application's taskbar icon or click in an exposed area of the application's window. When you do so, the window you've selected is raised to the top of the stack of windows on your desktop and becomes the new focused window. Figure 4.6 shows the same set of open applications you saw on the desktop in Figure 4.5, but with a new focused application.

If you want to focus a window that's completely covered on the desktop, you can click the window's taskbar icon; this makes the window active, just as though you had clicked its application title bar.

**FIGURE 4.6**
After the Same GNOME application title bar is clicked, the Same GNOME application window is made active. The other windows are still present, and the applications are open; they are simply not focused.

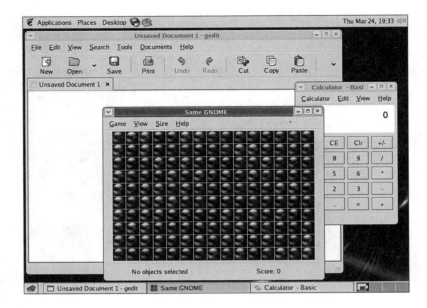

## Minimizing and Restoring with the Taskbar

You can use the taskbar icons to minimize and restore application windows and to switch between active applications. When you click the taskbar icon of the currently active window, the window is minimized, as if you had clicked the Minimize Window button. You can then restore the window by clicking the window's taskbar icon again.

# Understanding Virtual Workspaces

Many of the window management techniques discussed so far likely seem familiar to users of Windows and Mac OS. However, Linux desktops typically offer one function with which users of other operating systems are generally less familiar.

**Virtual workspaces** give you a number of independent workspaces that all share your computer at the same time. Each virtual workspace is a complete Linux desktop all its own, with its own sense of desktop space, its own set of open applications, its own desktop wallpaper, and so on. When you start an application on a Linux desktop, the window for the application you've started appears in the currently active virtual workspace. If you then switch to another virtual workspace, that window is no longer visible on your display, although it is still active and running in Linux; the window doesn't show on your display because the workspace in which it resides is no longer visible on your display.

Virtual workspaces can be used to minimize desktop crowding when you are using many applications at the same time; by starting a few applications in each workspace, you can avoid having to manage a taskbar crammed full of window buttons. Many users also use virtual workspaces to categorize their running applications, for example by starting all the Internet-related applications in one workspace, the word processing applications in another workspace, and so on.

## Knowing Which Workspace Is Active

Earlier in this chapter, you saw a reference to a taskbar element called the workspace switcher; it's the set of four squares that appear at the extreme lower right of your desktop, in the taskbar. The workspace switcher shows which of the virtual workspaces is currently active. The virtual workspaces themselves are laid out side-by-side in a row, just as the workspace switcher shows.

The darkened square in the workspace switcher is the currently active workspace. Each small square in the workspace switcher shows a miniature diagram of the windows currently displayed in that workspace.

## Selecting a New Workspace

To switch between virtual workspaces, click in the workspace switcher on the square representing the workspace that you want to make active (the workspace that you would like to be visible on your display). That workspace is then displayed, and the new active workspace is highlighted in the workspace switcher.

Figure 4.7 shows the Linux desktop with a new workspace selected. All the applications launched earlier are still running and can be seen in the small icon representing the first workspace in the workspace switcher.

## Moving a Running Application to a New Workspace

To move a running application window from its current virtual workspace to the same physical position in a different virtual workspace, use the Window Menu (the button at the extreme upper left of any application window's title bar). At the bottom of the Window Menu, you'll find several functions to help you use virtual workspaces:

▶ Selecting Always on Visible Workspace causes the current window to "travel with you" whenever you switch to a new virtual workspace, staying in the same location on your screen. When an application is set to appear in every workspace, it is said to be **sticky**.

**FIGURE 4.7**
The Linux desk-
top with a fresh
virtual work-
space selected.
The applications
started in the
other virtual
workspace are
all still running
and are repre-
sented by the
open window
images in that
virtual work-
space's quarter
of the work-
space switcher.

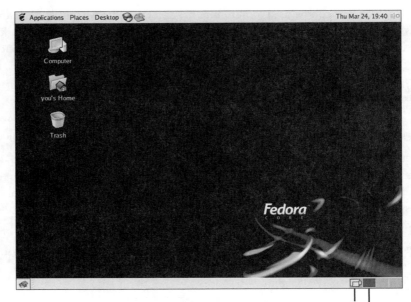

Miniatures of windows on first workspace

Second workspace (visible)

▶ Selecting Move to Workspace Right or Move to Workspace Left moves the application window one workspace to the right or to the left, respectively. Note that either of these options might not appear in the menu, if there are no more workspaces to the right (or to the left) of your current workspace.

▶ Selecting a workspace from the Move to Another Workspace menu causes the application window in question to be moved directly to the workspace that you select. Figure 4.8 shows the Move to Another Workspace menu open, ready to move the Same GNOME application to another workspace.

**FIGURE 4.8**
Use Move to
Another
Workspace, in
the Window
Menu, to put
running applica-
tions on other
workspaces.

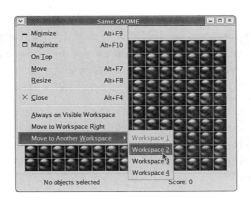

# Logging Out of the Fedora Core 4 Desktop

When you are done using your computer system, you must log out of the Linux desktop before you can shut down. To log out, choose Desktop, Log Out. A dialog box with several options is presented, as shown in Figure 4.9. The default selection, Log Out, returns you to the login prompt. Any running applications are automatically closed for you.

Checking the Save Current Setup option causes Linux to remember the positions of your currently running application windows and to restore them when you next log in. This dialog box also offers two additional options: Click Shut Down to shut Linux down, or choose Restart the Computer to shut Linux down and restart the system.

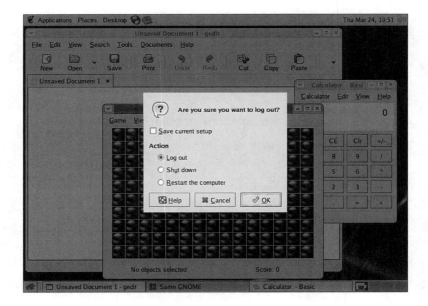

**FIGURE 4.9**
Logging out of the Fedora Core 4 desktop environment. If you check the Save Current Setup box, your application windows will be restored the next time you log in.

# Summary

In this chapter, you logged in to the Linux desktop environment for the first time. You learned to identify and use the components of an application window, including

▶ The application title bar, which indicates focus and provides a convenient way to move or activate a window

▶ The Minimize Window and Maximize Window buttons, which provide ways to hide a window or cause it to fill the entire display

▶ The Close Window button, which enables you to exit an application and remove its window

▶ The resize handles, which appear at the bottom of an application window and enable you to change its size

You also began to use menubar to launch applications and gained some experience using the taskbar and workspace switcher to switch between running applications and virtual workspaces.

Finally, you logged back out again, learning how to save the your application windows and their locations if you want to have them automatically restored the next time you log back in to your Fedora Core 4 desktop.

# Q&A

**Q** *I've heard Linux users talk about KDE and GNOME. Is the Fedora Core Desktop related to either of these?*

**A** The Fedora Core 4 desktop is a GNOME desktop, and is thus similar in appearance and functionality to the Linux systems that offer a GNOME desktop.

Furthermore, some users prefer some of the behavioral quirks of the KDE environment (such as the busy mouse cursor while launching applications) over the GNOME environment.

**Q** *Can I use KDE with Fedora Core 4 if I prefer KDE over GNOME?*

**A** Yes. In fact, your Fedora Core 4 CDs also contain the KDE environment; they are simply not installed by default. For instructions on installing KDE, refer to Chapter 31, "Installing Linux Software."

**Q** *When I launch applications, they appear in different places or at different sizes from those shown in the figures pictured here. Why?*

**A** Most likely, your desktop is set to display at a different screen size or resolution (number of horizontal and vertical pixels) than the desktop that was used to make the illustrations for this book. Application windows in the figures may appear either larger or smaller than those on your own desktop; new application windows may also appear in different positions.

# Workshop

The Workshop is designed to help you anticipate possible questions, review what you've learned, and begin learning how to put your knowledge into practice.

## Quiz

1. Where can the Applications menu be found?

2. When multiple application windows are present, how do you change the active (focused) application window?

3. When a window is minimized (hidden), how can you restore it to its previous position and appearance?

4. How do you log out of the desktop?

## Answers

1. The Applications menu is at the extreme upper left of your Fedora Core 4 desktop, in the menubar.

2. To change the active window, you click a window's title bar or anywhere inside the window to focus it.

3. You can restore a minimized window by clicking its button in the taskbar.

4. You log out by choosing Desktop, Log Out.

## Activities

1. Try starting a number of applications to fill your desktop. Then experiment by moving them around, minimizing them, and focusing them one by one.

2. Put a running application on another virtual desktop. Then switch to that desktop to display it.

3. Start a few applications and then log out, choosing to save your session. Log in again and notice how your applications have been restarted and placed for you.

# CHAPTER 5

# Working with Files on the Desktop

## *What You'll Learn in This Chapter:*

▶ What files and directories are and how they are organized in Linux

▶ How to create and save a new text file with the text editor

▶ How to use the file manager to list files in your home directory

▶ How to open an existing file, edit it, and save the changes

▶ How to navigate through files and directories in your file system using the file manager

▶ How to copy or move file(s) from one directory to another

▶ What the context menu is and how to use it

In the previous chapter, you learned about the Linux desktop; you now know how to access the desktop and open, move, and close application windows. In this chapter, you learn how to use the Linux desktop to work with files and data.

## Creating a File Using the Text Editor

Because you are still new to using Linux, we're going to start slow. One of the most common and basic tasks that you can perform with a computer is to create and edit a file full of text—letters, numbers, and words. So, as your first real Linux task, you're going to launch the text editor, compose a few sentences, and then save those sentences to a file that can be retrieved whenever you want to look at (or edit) those sentences again. You already learned how to launch a text editor window in Chapter 4, "Introducing the Fedora Core 4 Desktop." If you need a refresher, remember to choose Applications, Accessories, Text Editor from the menubar at the top of your desktop. Launch a text editor now and enter several lines of text.

*By the*
*Way*

> ## A Program by Any Other Name...
>
> After you start the text editor, you might notice that the application title bar actually displays the name `gedit`. This is the name of the text editor program as Linux knows it—the name of the actual application that you use to edit text.
>
> For more details on application title bars and what they are used for, refer to Chapter 4.

Even though you've now entered several lines of text in a text editor, the words that you've typed haven't actually been saved anywhere as of yet; if you were to switch your computer off suddenly, you would never see them again. To create a new text file that contains the lines of text you've entered and that can be retrieved hours, days, or even weeks later, you must save the text you've entered to your hard drive. To do so, open the File menu in the text editor's application window and choose the Save option, as shown in Figure 5.1.

**FIGURE 5.1**
Save your work
by choosing
File, Save.

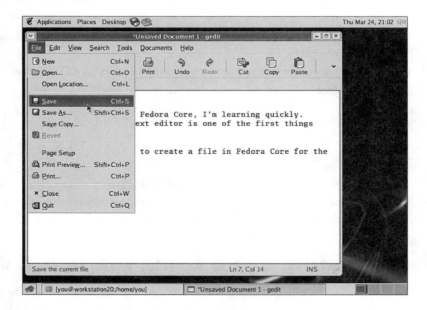

After you click Save, the Save As file dialog box appears, as shown in Figure 5.2. A **file dialog box** is a special dialog box that is used to save or load files in an application by helping you to visually navigate the list of files stored on your Linux computer. You'll use file dialog boxes frequently as you work in Fedora Core 4.

If you're a longtime Windows or Mac OS user, you've likely seen file dialog boxes before and can even make out a few familiar parts of the Fedora Core 4 file dialog box, such as the list of directories on the left or the list of files on the right in

Figure 5.2. But there are important differences between the way Fedora Core 4 manages files and the way files are managed in Windows or Mac OS.

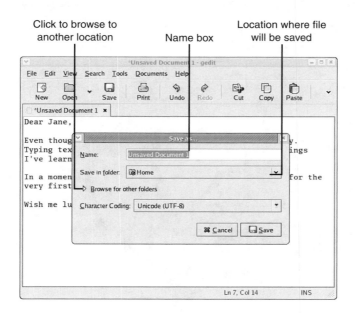

**FIGURE 5.2**
The file dialog box will become familiar to you as you use Fedora Core 4.

# Understanding the Linux File System

To really use Linux effectively, you need to understand the basics of the Linux file system. A **file system** is a collection of files that contain various kinds of data (in some cases, for example, words and sentences) and the collection of organizational details with which the files are stored. These files and the details that organize them are all maintained together inside a computer system, and together they make up a file system. All modern computer operating systems use a file system to organize information, in much the same way that every office has a filing system for its documents. The Linux file system, however, differs in important ways from the file systems you might have used in Windows or Mac OS. To illustrate these differences, we compare the Windows and Linux file systems in the following sections.

## Many Trees, Many Roots: The Windows File System

As a refresher to those who are already familiar with Windows, in Windows the C: drive contains files of various types along with numerous file folders, each of which can contain more files. All these files and file folders are collectively referred to as the file system of the C: drive. Like most operating systems, Windows allows file folders to contain other file folders in addition to data files. This capability creates a structure that commonly is referred to as a **tree**, as shown in Figure 5.3. At the base of the tree—in this case at the C: drive itself—is what you can imagine to be a kind of **root**.

**FIGURE 5.3**
In general, file systems look like a tree; here, in a diagram showing some of a Windows file system, the hard drive itself is the root of the tree.

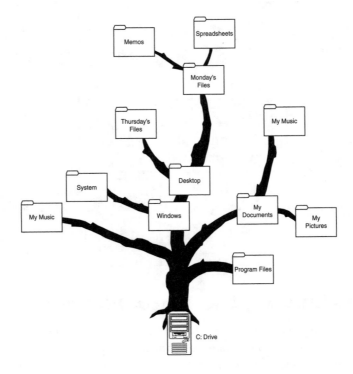

In Windows, each storage device is assigned a drive letter and contains its own set of files and folders. Each drive letter is therefore the root of its own file system and, thus, of its own **file system tree**. Mac OS assigns each storage device in the computer its own file system in much the same manner. An illustration of this concept appears in Figure 5.4.

## One Tree, One Root: The Linux File System

Linux and Unix file systems, on the other hand, aren't organized like Windows or Mac OS file systems. Any Linux computer has only one file system—and thus one tree. The most fundamental location or starting point within the Linux file system is not a hard drive letter like C: or D: but is rather a file folder that contains all other devices, files, and folders—a conceptual storage area known simply as the root of the file system. The Linux file system's root is referenced with a forward slash (/). As is the case in Windows and Mac OS, Linux is capable of using multiple storage devices at the same time; however, in Linux each storage device is positioned within the main file system tree, rather than being the root of a separate, independent file system tree. You can see this system in Figure 5.5. Incorporating a storage device into the main file system tree in Linux is known as **mounting** a device onto the file system tree.

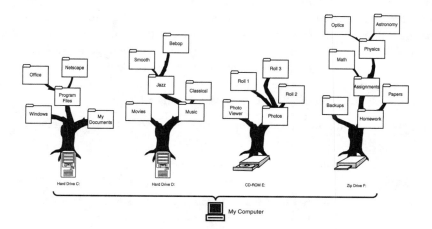

**FIGURE 5.4**
In Windows systems, each storage device has its own file system. The system has many trees and many roots.

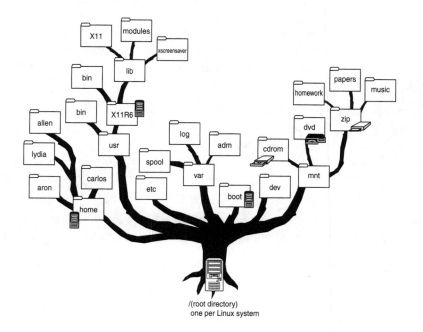

**FIGURE 5.5**
A Linux file system tree with additional storage devices mounted at /usr/X11R6, /home, /boot, /mnt/cdrom, /mnt/dvd, and /mnt/zip. Each device enlarges the single, unified tree, and the system still has only a single root.

## Files, Folders, and Directories

In Linux, as is the case in Windows or Mac OS, the data that you work with is stored on a hard drive somewhere in the file system, in individual data **files**. Each file has a unique name and can be opened by one or sometimes several applications or programs that are designed to access the data inside.

Windows and Mac OS users often use folders to organize these files, and so do Linux users—but in Linux you may also hear them referred to as **directories**. Although the names are different, the concept is precisely the same (throughout this text, we'll use the terms **folder** and **directory** interchangeably). If you've never encountered one before, a folder (or directory) is a kind of container in the file system for holding data files of various types or for holding still more folders (or directories). Folders are used primarily as an organizational tool, just like file folders in an office.

The root of the Linux file system is commonly referred to as the **root directory** because it contains *all* the other files and folders in the file system.

## Paths

Most computer systems that get used on a day-to-day basis will eventually come to hold a large number of data files in their file system(s). In nearly all instances, for organizational purposes some of these files end up being stored inside folders that themselves reside inside other folders (refer again to Figures 5.3 through 5.5 if you need help visualizing this tree-like structure). With such a mishmash of nested files and directories, it's often helpful to be able to describe the precise location of a file within a file system in some kind of shorthand—for example, if you want to tell a friend exactly where in the file system a particular file has been saved.

In Linux, this shorthand is called a **path**, and it's written like this:

```
/directory1/directory2/directoryN/filename.ext
```

This particular path shows that a file called `filename.ext` is stored inside a directory called `directoryN`, which itself is stored inside a directory called `directory2`, that is in turn stored inside `directory1`, which resides in the root directory (`/`).

This kind of shorthand is called a path because, when read from left to right, it provides the path that you need to travel along through the Linux file system in order to reach the file. For example, consider this path:

```
/cities/parks/trees/oaks.txt
```

If you were to begin at the root directory (`/`) of the Linux file system, to be able to find the file `oaks.txt`, you would need to first open the directory called `cities`. Inside `cities`, you would need to find and open another directory called `parks`, and then inside parks, a directory called trees. Only in the list of files contained in the directory called trees would you finally find the file oaks.txt. A few more sample paths and their explanations can be found in Table 5.1.

**TABLE 5.1** Sample Linux Paths

| Path | Explanation |
| --- | --- |
| / | Refers to the root directory |
| /home | Refers to the directory home, which is contained in the root directory |
| /usr/X11R6/lib | Refers to the directory lib in the directory X11R6, in the directory usr, which is itself in the root directory |
| /usr/share/xmms/Skins | Refers to the directory Skins in the directory xmms, in the directory share, in the directory usr, which is itself in the root directory |

## The Home Directory

If the concepts of paths, directories, and files all seem a little fuzzy to you right now, don't worry; you're going to get some hands-on experience in just a moment.

You've already learned about one special directory in Linux called the root directory that contains all other directories and files. Before you're ready to use the text editor's Save As dialog box to save the text you've typed, however, you need to know about one more special directory, called the **home directory**.

When a Linux user creates and saves files, receives email, scans an image on a scanner, or performs any number of other common tasks, any data that the user needs to store in a file on the hard drive is generally placed somewhere in the user's home directory.

Every user account on a Linux system has its own home directory; your home directory usually shares the same account name that you use to log in to your Linux desktop and is stored in /home. So, if you log in as jack, your home directory is located at /home/jack, and any files you save or new directories you create while logged in as jack are generally placed in /home/jack. If you log out and another user subsequently logs in as jill, any files or directories she creates after logging in are usually stored in /home/jill.

### Home Directories and My Documents

You can think of home directories as the My Documents folders of the Linux world. Just as you save your files in My Documents when you use Windows, you save your files in your home directory when you use Linux.

*By the Way*

In this way, Linux allows for the creation of many user accounts, while at the same time keeping all users' files separate from one another. This system of organization also keeps the file system uncluttered by ensuring that most of the day-to-day files that a user creates are stored in one single location that's owned by that user.

# Using File Dialog Boxes in Linux

Now that you know something more about the Linux file system, paths, and home directories, you're ready to master the Save As file dialog box shown in Figure 5.2. Here are the major components that you see in the file dialog box and how each of them is used:

- ▶ The Name box allows you to enter either a filename or full file path by hand for loading or saving. If you know the path to the file you want to access, just typing it into the filename entry box can sometimes be faster than navigating through the file system using the mouse. If you enter only a filename, the file is stored using that name in the current directory.

- ▶ The Save in folder drop-down list begins by showing the current directory—the directory to and from which the application is currently expecting to save or load files. Clicking on this list lets you opt to save or load from other common locations or locations that you've bookmarked (something we'll discuss in a moment), like your Desktop or removable storage devices such as Zip drives or USB memory sticks.

- ▶ The Character coding drop-down list, which won't always be present, is used to save your files using special character sets if, for example, you are working on a document that contains international characters.

- ▶ Click Browse for other folders when you want to store a file in a specific folder that hasn't been bookmarked, and thus isn't listed in the Save in Folder drop-down list. When you click Browse for other folders, the file dialog box expands to provide you with additional navigation tools, as shown in Figure 5.6.

In the expanded file dialog box that's displayed when you click Browse for other folders, you'll see two panes. The left pane contains a list of common "starting" locations, including your Home directory (Home), your desktop (Desktop), the root directory (Filesystem), or removable storage devices like a CD drive (CD-ROM), as well as any locations in the file system that you've bookmarked. In the right pane are the files or folders stored in the current location. A number of navigational tasks can be performed in the expanded file dialog box:

**FIGURE 5.6**
Click Browse for other folders to expand the Save As file dialog box if you want to navigate through the file system.

▶ Double-click on any folder that's listed in the right-hand pane (marked with a folder icon) to "visit" that folder and display its contents in the right-hand pane.

▶ When you locate the file that you are looking for in the right-hand pane, double-click to save the current document using that name (in a save file dialog box) or to load the document (in an open file dialog box).

▶ Click on any path navigation button to visit the directory in question along your current path. For example, if the right-hand pane is currently displaying the files in /usr/X11R6/lib, you will see path navigation buttons labeled usr, X11R6, and lib, each of which will cause the directory in question to be displayed in the right-hand pane.

▶ Use the Add bookmarks button to add a location to the left-hand pane for quick return after you've browsed to it.

▶ Use the Delete bookmarks button to remove a location that you no longer use very often from the left-hand pane.

Using the file dialog box, you can navigate to any location in the Linux file system and ask an application to create a new file there, or to load an existing file that is already stored there.

---

*Did you Know?*

## Practice Using the File Dialog Box

If the file dialog box seems confusing to you, take a few moments to navigate around the file system using the dialog box so that you become comfortable with it. Use the present working directory drop-down to visit the root directory of the Linux file system and then double-click your way back to /home/you using the directory navigation pane.

---

When you feel comfortable with the Save As file dialog box and have navigated back to your home directory, enter a suitable name for the text file you want to create in the filename entry box; for this example, name the file **anotherfile.txt**, as shown in Figure 5.7. After you name the file, click Save to save it and close the Save As dialog box.

**FIGURE 5.7**
Here, text is being saved in a file named anotherfile. txt in the home directory.

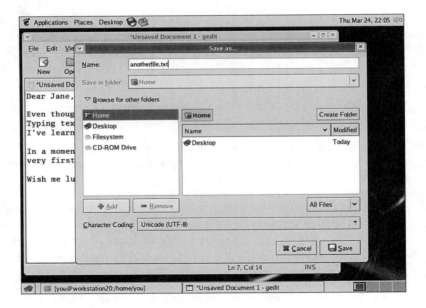

After you save the file under its new name, the new filename appears in the application window's title bar. From now on, choosing File, Save while you work in this file saves your changes in the same place—in anotherfile.txt.

---

*By the Way*

## What's the Difference Between Save and Save As?

You might notice that the text editor's File menu has two save options: Save and Save As. Choosing Save replaces the existing, stored version of your document with the contents of the current application window, including any changes you've made since last accessing the file; choosing Save As opens the Save As dialog box, so that you can save the file under new name or in a different directory. Each time you use Save As and enter a new filename for a file you're working on, a new file is created. This way, you can maintain multiple versions of the same file and access each at will.

After you save `anotherfile.txt`, choose File, Quit to exit the text editor. You should now see an empty desktop once again.

# Using the File Manager

As you use the Fedora Core 4 Desktop, you will often need to navigate the Linux file system to perform housekeeping tasks such as creating, copying, moving, or deleting existing files or directories. These tasks can be performed using a program called a **file manager**. The file manager is used to perform all basic file manipulation tasks in Linux, including

- ▶ Listing the files and directories contained in any directory

- ▶ Moving, renaming, copying, and deleting files

- ▶ Creating new directories

- ▶ Duplicating existing files or directories

- ▶ Deleting files and directories and their contents

All these tasks can be performed with just a few clicks of your mouse on the Fedora Core 4 Desktop.

## Opening a File Manager Window

The file manager is always active as long as you are logged in. Even when you have no open application windows, the icons on your desktop belong to, and are managed by, the file manager.

To use the file manager to create directories, copy files, and perform other file or directory manipulation tasks, however, you must first open a file manager window. Double-click the Home icon at the upper left of your desktop or choose Places, Home Folder to open a file manager window that displays the files and directories in your home directory, as shown in Figure 5.8.

File and directory icons

Name of current folder

**FIGURE 5.8**
A folder icon designates a directory in the file manager window. The other icon in this figure represents a regular (text) file.

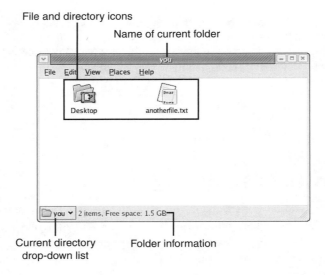

Current directory drop-down list

Folder information

*By the Way*

### Your List of Files Might Be Different

Depending on the amount of work you've already done with your Linux system, you might see a different list of files when you open a file manager window. In any case, the list of files that you see represents the files that are present in your home directory. If you see an empty window, it means that no files are present in your home directory.

## Navigating the Directory Tree

To make use of the file manager, you need to know how to navigate through it to access specific files and directories. A file manager window contains two essential navigation tools: the current directory drop-down list, shown in Figure 5.8, and the file and directory icons themselves that are displayed in each folder. The current directory drop-down list is used to navigate to locations closer to the root of the file system, while the icons in each location are used to navigate into the depths of the file system tree, farther away from its root. Refer again to Figures 5.3 through 5.5 if necessary to try to visualize the difference.

The current directory drop-down list always contains a list of the directories in the path from the root directory to the directory whose contents are currently being displayed. For example, the home directory for the user you is stored at the path /home/you, meaning that the files for the user you are stored in the folder you that is stored inside the folder home that is, in turn, inside the root directory.

The current directory drop-down list in the home directory for the user you therefore contains / (the root directory), home, and you, in that order, as shown in Figure 5.9. Selecting any one of them causes a new file manager window to open, displaying the files and directories in that location.

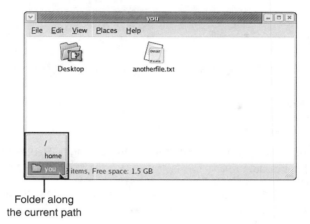

Folder along
the current path

**FIGURE 5.9**
Select from the current directory drop-down list to open a new file manager window for any of the folders along the current path.

Double-click any of the folder icons in a file manager window to display a new file manager window showing the contents of that folder, along with a new current-directory drop-down list that reflects its addition to the current path.

Double-click any file icon to open the file in the application that created it or that is best suited to view or edit it.

# Working with Files and Directories

You've learned to make your way around the file system now; it's time to get to work. To open, copy, cut, move, or otherwise operate on files you see in the file manager, you use the **context menu**—a menu that shows all the things that you can do to the file in question.

To show the context menu for a given file, right-click the file's icon (position your cursor over the icon and click the button on the right of the mouse or trackball). The context menu often changes from file to file because it always displays only the actions that you can perform on the file you clicked; if you right-click a text file, for example, you see options associated with text files and the text editor. To see a context menu in action, right-click anotherfile.txt. This action displays the context menu shown in Figure 5.10.

**FIGURE 5.10**
The context
menu for text
files is dis-
played when
you right-click
the file
anotherfile.
txt.

You can choose any option in a context menu by clicking it. Here's what the options in the context menu do:

▶ The first item in the context menu always opens the file with the application best suited to open it, in this case the text editor.

▶ You may also see additional Open options that open the file with alternate applications that may also be useful for working on the file.

▶ Open with Other Application allows you to specify your own application to use when opening the file. This option is recommended for experts only.

▶ Cut File clips the file from the current directory so that you can move it to another using the Paste Files command.

▶ Copy File creates an imaginary "copy" of the file that the file manager will remember; you can then create a new copy of the original file on disk using the Paste Files command.

▶ Paste Files becomes active after you use the Cut File command to remove an item from a directory or the Copy File command to create an imaginary copy of it. You navigate to a new directory and click Paste Files in its file manager window to place the cut or copied item in the new location.

▶ Make Link creates a symbolic link to the file. Although we haven't discussed symbolic links yet, you can learn more about them by referring to Chapter 7, "Understanding File Properties."

▶ Rename is used to change a file's name.

▶ Move to Trash puts the file in the trash can shown on the desktop, effectively throwing it away. If you later empty the trash can (something you'll learn how to do later in this chapter), the files it contains will be deleted from the disk.

▶ Create Archive is used to create or add the file in question to an archive file of any common type (for example, a ZIP, LZH, or TGZ file, suitable for transmission across the Internet).

▶ Properties displays properties such as file size, date last edited, and so on, for the selected item.

You learn more about using these and other menu options in the sections that follow.

---

**Context Menus Aren't Just for Files and Directories**

Although you work with context menus for files in this chapter, you can access context menus for many items on the Linux desktop. Context menu options provide a quick, intuitive method for managing or manipulating most desktop items in Fedora Core 4.

By the Way

---

## Opening an Existing File

To reopen the file `anotherfile.txt` for editing in the text editor application, simply double-click its icon in the file manager window or right-click its icon and select the first option, Open with Text Editor. The text editor opens, the file is loaded, and you can now edit and save the file again at your discretion.

The Open with Other Application option displays a list of other programs that can be used to open the file. These other programs include the much more powerful OpenOffice applications suite, similar to Microsoft Office in many ways; you learn more about OpenOffice in Chapters 8 through 10.

## Cutting, Copying, and Pasting Files

If you have worked extensively in Word, WordPerfect, or other common word processing programs, you may be familiar with the cut, copy, and paste functions. If not, you won't have any trouble learning to use these functions; they provide a simple way to move text in a document, but you can also use them to move files from one directory or location to another in the Fedora Core 4 file manager.

You can use the Copy File command to copy a file to another directory without removing the file from its original location. To duplicate a file, right-click it to produce the context menu and then choose Copy File. Navigate to the directory where you want the file's duplicate to appear and right-click any empty space in the window. In the context menu that appears, choose Paste Files. A duplicate of the file is created in the currently displayed directory using the same filename as the original.

You also can use the context menu to remove a file from its current location and place it in a new directory. To move a file, right-click its icon and then choose Cut File. The file manager window displays a notice at the bottom of the window indicating that the file will be moved when you select the Paste Files command. Navigate to the directory where you want to place the file, right-click in empty window space, and choose Paste Files from the context menu. The file is copied to the currently displayed directory and then deleted from its original location.

You can also use this functionality to duplicate an existing file. To do so, simply copy it and then paste it again in the same directory. A new copy of the file will be created, as shown in Figure 5.11.

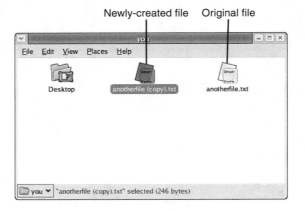

Newly-created file     Original file

## Selecting Multiple Files

Many of the context menu and drag-and-drop operations discussed here can be performed on a number of files simultaneously. Simply use the file manager to select more than one file at a time and then click, drag, or right-click on any one of the selected files to perform the same operation simultaneously on all of them.

There are two ways of selecting multiple files at once. The first and easiest, commonly referred to as using a **rubber band**, is accomplished by clicking the left button on your pointing device in an empty area of the file manager window, dragging the pointer and enlarging the rubber band to enclose a number of files, and then releasing the button. Selected files are highlighted to show that they have been selected. This process is shown in Figure 5.12.

The other way to select multiple files is to hold down the Ctrl key while single-clicking each file you want to select, one by one. Each file you select remains highlighted and is added to the group of selected files, as long as the Ctrl key is held down. This method enables the selection of noncontiguous groups of icons.

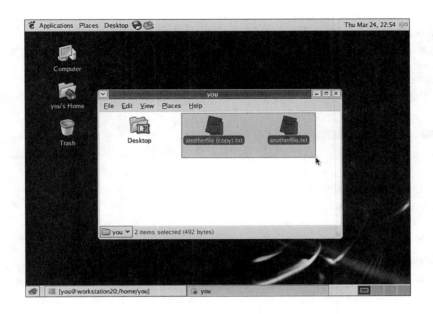

**FIGURE 5.12**
Using the rubber band to select two files simultaneously in /home/you. The selected files are highlighted.

## Renaming an Item

You can use the Rename command in the context menu to change a file's or directory's name. After you choose Rename from the context menu, the icon's filename appears in a text box, as shown in Figure 5.13. You just type a new name for the file and press Enter to save the name and exit the text box.

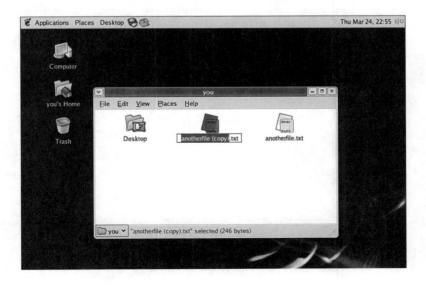

**FIGURE 5.13**
The file anotherfile (copy).txt is ready to be renamed; when the filename text box is active, as shown here, you can type to replace the current name. Press Enter to save the new name.

*By the*
Way

> ### Don't Change the Last Three Letters!
> When renaming a file, be sure not to change the file's three-letter extension, if it has one, because doing so might change the way Linux or other operating systems identify the file's type!

## Deleting Items

To delete a file or directory, choose the Move to Trash option from the context menu. The selected item disappears from the currently displayed directory and is moved to the trash can. Double-click the Trash icon on the Fedora Core 4 Desktop to view, restore, or permanently delete trashed items (see "Working with Trash Contents," later in this chapter).

## Creating a New Directory

To create a new directory in the currently displayed path, right-click an area of empty space within the file manager window. A context menu for the currently displayed path appears.

Choose the Create Folder item from the context menu to create a new directory in the currently displayed directory, as shown in Figure 5.14. The new directory appears with the name untitled folder, in a selected text box; type a new name and press Enter to name your new folder.

**FIGURE 5.14**
The newly created directory is given the name untitled folder. Type a new name to name your folder or simply press Enter to accept the default name.

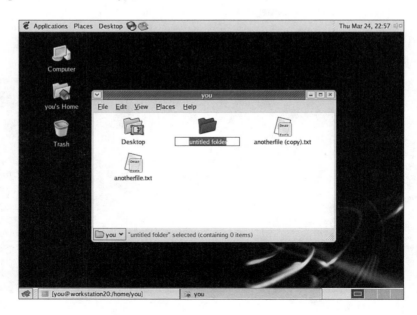

> ## What's the Difference Between a Folder and a Directory?
>
> Remember that you don't need to be confused by the terms *folder* and *directory*: For our purposes, these terms can be used interchangeably. Typically, when accessed from the command line or when discussed in the context of the Linux file system, they are known as **directories**. In many desktop applications, however, and in the file manager, they are called **folders**.

*By the Way*

## Rearranging or Sorting Icons

The icons in the currently displayed directory can be rearranged and re-sorted by right-clicking an empty area of the file manager window to display a context menu and then choosing Arrange Items. The submenu shown in Figure 5.15 is displayed.

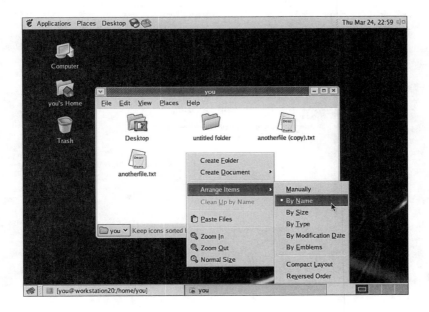

**FIGURE 5.15**
The Arrange Items submenu enables you to dictate the way in which the file manager organizes the display of files and directories in the current directory. A dot is shown next to the current arrangement style.

Depending on how you want the current directory to be displayed, you select from the following:

▶ Manually allows you to position the icons as you choose by dragging them around the window. When this item is selected, the file manager will not attempt to arrange or rearrange icons for you at all.

▶ By Name sorts the files in ascending alphabetical order (from A–Z).

▶ By Size sorts the files in descending order, from largest to smallest, beginning with directories, which are sorted by the number of items each contains.

▶ By Type groups the files by type (usually indicated by a file's three-letter extension), sorting alphabetically (from A–Z) within each type.

▶ By Modification Date sorts the files in order from the files or directories most
recently edited to those least recently edited.

▶ By Emblems groups the files by the emblems that have been assigned to them
by selecting Properties from the file context menu.

▶ Compact Layout causes the icons to be spaced more closely together, as shown
in Figure 5.16.

▶ Reverse Order causes the ordering of the sorting methods listed above to be
reversed.

**FIGURE 5.16**
When Compact
Layout is
enabled, the
icons for the
files in the
directory are
spaced more
closely.

# Manipulating Files Using Drag and Drop

Nearly all the file and directory operations you've learned to perform so far are
accomplished using context menus. Although the context menu is certainly a powerful tool, another technique known as **drag and drop** is often more convenient.

To drag and drop, place your cursor over the icon of the file or directory you want to
move; then click the mouse or trackball button, and hold it down as you drag the
pointer and icon to the new location. Release the button to drop the item into its
new location. The following sections show you how to use drag and drop in some
simple file management tasks.

# Moving a File into a Directory or to the Desktop

For you to be able to perform a drag-and-drop operation, both the file you want to affect and its destination must be visible on the screen. To move a file into a directory using drag and drop, use the left button to drag the file's icon onto the icon or into the file manager window of the directory you want to move the file into. Then release the button to drop the file into its new location.

You also can use drag and drop to move files and directories to the desktop. Using the file manager, navigate until the icon for a file or directory that you want to move is visible; then click it and drag it out of the file manager window and onto the desktop. Release the mouse button to drop the file. Figure 5.17 shows the results of dragging and dropping untitled folder from your home directory to the desktop. You can use the same drag-and-drop process to move files and directories from the desktop back into a file manager window or into directories displayed there.

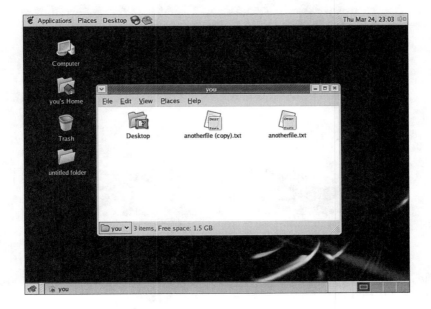

**FIGURE 5.17**
The directory untitled folder has been dragged and dropped onto the desktop. Files can be stored in it as in any other directory.

---

**Can You Delete a File by Dragging It to the Trash Icon?**

Files or directories can also be moved into the Trash (thrown away) using this technique. Simply drag the file you want to throw away onto the Trash icon. When the Trash icon is highlighted, release the button, and the file in question will be placed in the Trash.

*By the Way*

## Using Context Drag and Drop

If you have a three-button mouse or pointing device, you can also use an operation called **context drag** to move, copy, and link files between folders using the file manager. To use this feature, drag and drop using the *middle* pointer button rather than the left one. When you release the middle button after dragging an icon to a new location, a context menu appears for the drag-and-drop operation. You can choose options from this menu to perform several different tasks.

Try the context-drag operation by dragging a file to the desktop using the middle button instead of the left button of your pointing device. When you release the button, a menu similar to the one shown in Figure 5.18 appears.

**FIGURE 5.18**
The context drag has been used between the file anotherfile. txt and the desktop. The context menu enables you to choose the action you want the file manager to perform on the file in question.

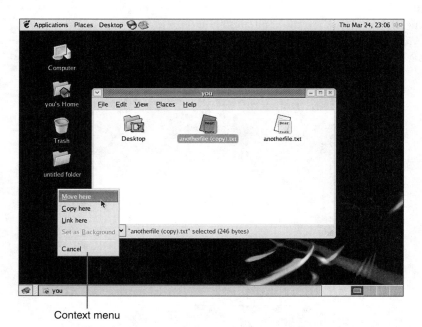

Context menu

When you choose an option in the context menu, the selection action is performed. Here are the choices:

▶ Move Here moves the file or the directory and all its contents from its original location to the location where you released the button.

▶ Copy Here copies the file or the directory and all its contents from its original location to the location where you released the button.

▶ Link Here creates a symbolic link in the location where you released the button pointing to the file's original location. To learn more about symbolic links, see Chapter 7.

▶ Set as Background, available only when dragging image files, causes the image being dragged to be used as the wallpaper (background image) for the desktop or for the file manager window in question.

▶ Cancel voids the operation; the menu will disappear and all will be as if you had never dragged the file icon from its original location.

---

**What If You Don't Have a Middle Mouse Button?**

Although most PC mice these days come with three buttons (or two buttons and a clickable scrollwheel), there are a few two-button-only mice in use as well.

If your mouse has only two buttons, you may be able to emulate the functionality of a middle click by using both the left and right buttons on your mouse at the same time (that is, clicking them together).

*By the Way*

---

# Working with Trash Contents

The Trash icon represents a special directory used to temporarily hold items you have deleted using the file manager. This directory gives your files a second chance—allowing you to be certain that you no longer want to access or edit a deleted item before it is finally removed entirely from your system. After you send an item to the Trash, you can do two things with it: You can restore the item to its original location, or you can permanently delete it. The following sections describe these operations in detail.

## Restoring Files That Have Been Thrown Away

If you decide you want to save an item that you've previously sent to the Trash, you can restore it to the desktop or a directory. To do this, double-click the Trash icon to open a new file manager window listing the Trash contents, as shown in Figure 5.19. Then drag and drop or cut/copy and paste files from the Trash to other storage areas such as your home directory.

## Emptying the Trash

If you know you don't want to save any of the files and directories you've thrown in the Trash, you can permanently delete them from the Trash folder. Emptying the Trash folder removes the deleted items from your hard drive forever. To empty the Trash, follow these steps:

**1.** Right-click the Trash icon on the desktop to produce the context menu.

2. Choose Empty Trash. A dialog box appears, asking you to confirm that you want to empty the Trash.

3. Select the Empty option to permanently delete all items currently in the Trash folder or select Cancel to abort the operation.

**FIGURE 5.19**
Double-click the desktop Trash icon to open a file manager window listing its contents. To restore a file or directory from the Trash, drag and drop or cut/copy and paste items to the location where you want to preserve them.

**By the Way**

**Empty the Trash Only If You're Serious!**
When you empty the Trash, any files or folders it contains are erased forever and cannot be recovered.

# Summary

In this chapter, you learned to use file dialog boxes and the desktop file manager to open, save, move, copy, modify, and delete files and directories. Along the way, you gained practice launching graphical applications and using the desktop context menu. You gained practice with basic cut, copy, and paste procedures, and you learned how to create duplicates and change filenames.

# Q&A

**Q** *I notice that the file manager displays letters or words in some icons but not in others, and they sometimes don't make sense. Why?*

**A** If a file is human-readable (that is, not a program or an image file or some-thing composed mostly of data), the file manager attempts to use the first few letters or words from the document as part of the icon to help you identify files without having to open them.

# Workshop

The Workshop is designed to help you anticipate possible questions, review what you've learned, and begin learning how to put your knowledge into practice.

## Quiz

1. How do you open a file manager window?

2. How do you copy a file from your home directory to your desktop using drag and drop?

3. How do you create a new directory?

4. How do you open an existing file for editing?

## Answers

1. Double-click the home icon on your desktop.

2. Open a file manager window and then use the right button on your pointing device to drag the file's icon to your desktop. When you release the button and the context menu appears, choose Copy Here to copy the file.

3. Right-click inside the file manager window. Choose Create Folder from the context menu that appears.

4. Double-click on the file's icon or select the first Open option from the file's context (right-click) menu.

## Activities

1. Spend some time navigating your file system using the file manager, location bar, and directory icons.

2. Insert a CD-ROM and double-click the CD-ROM icon that appears on your desktop. Spend some time browsing the contents of the CD-ROM using the file manager.

# CHAPTER 6

# Working with Files in the Shell

## What You'll Learn in This Chapter:

▶ How to access the Linux shell (command line) in Fedora Core 4

▶ How to structure commands given to the shell

▶ How to use the `ls` command to list files

▶ How to use the `touch` command to create empty files

▶ How to use the `cd` command to change your current working directory

▶ How to use the `cp` and `mv` commands to copy and move files

▶ How to use the `mkdir` command to make directories

▶ How to use the `rm` and `rmdir` commands to remove files and directories

This chapter introduces you to one of the environments you'll need to master in order to be a fluent user of Linux and other Unix-like systems. At this point, you have installed Linux successfully, have logged in to your desktop, and have learned to perform some basic desktop and file tasks; now it's time to begin to use the more powerful environment for which Linux and Unix are famous.

> **Take It Slow and Easy**
>
> Don't feel as though you need to become comfortable with the Linux command line all at once. Use this chapter and the next one to familiarize yourself with the Linux command line, but don't try to memorize everything you read. Just read through the text and try your hand at some of the commands for now. The details will become clearer as you progress through future chapters, especially the chapters in Part IV, "Using the Linux Command Line," and you'll find what you read in this chapter becoming more and more valuable as you progress through all the remaining content of this book.

# Why Learn to Use the Linux Command Line?

Is it really necessary to learn to use the Linux command line?

Yes, it's necessary. Here's a brief explanation of why that's the case.

Years ago, computer graphics that today's users take for granted—colors, lines, icons, and windows—represented a very rare, expensive, and specialized technology. Most computer systems did not ship with graphics capability because they were intended to perform office, database, and network-related tasks; such tasks involved the manipulation of letters and numbers, not of pictures and colors. Unix systems, which were common long before MS-DOS or Windows systems became established in the marketplace, were among the workhorse systems designed to manage very large amounts of information very efficiently. Developers didn't have graphics, desktops, or personal computers in mind when they built Unix.

A powerful, network-oriented Unix graphics system had been added to Unix by scientists and researchers by the time Linux was developed in the early 1990s. This system was called the X Window System, and it is still in use today. However, the original set of powerful text and information processing paradigms and tools remained of the greatest selling points of Unix, and one of its most unique strengths.

Linux (and, by extension, Fedora Core) uses the X Window System to provide you, the user, with a powerful, friendly graphical user interface that is in many ways like those found in Windows or Mac OS. Unlike Windows or Mac OS, however, Linux and the X Window System are much more complex, flexible, and powerful than just what you see on your desktop.

Furthermore, the nuts and bolts of Linux, too—the configuration details, much of the functional infrastructure, and the primary method of storing and retrieving data—are closely tied to text, text files, and data processing.

After a user masters the command line, the rest of the Unix world, including the desktop, seems to fall magically into place, and a new universe of functionality unmatched by Windows or Mac OS is opened. Only rarely do users master other Unix functions before mastering the command line.

Even though the thought of a "command line" is daunting to many first-time Linux users, this chapter introduces the command line in contexts that you are now already familiar with from Chapter 5, "Working with Files on the Desktop"—tasks related to the manipulation of files and directories. It should therefore be a somewhat approachable introduction to a powerful set of tools.

# Introducing the Shell

A **shell** is any Linux program that allows you to give instructions in some way and that then carries out those instructions using the underlying facilities of the Linux operating system and your computer system. The instructions in question can be anything you might want to do, such as printing a file, starting a program, or opening a network connection. When veteran Linux users talk about using "the shell" in everyday conversation, however, they are usually referring to a command interpreter, a special kind of program that understands words and alphanumeric characters—in short, language, rather than actions like mouse clicks—and that then passes these language-based instructions to Linux.

## Understanding the Shell's Role as Command Interpreter

The term *shell* is a metaphor; you can think of the Linux kernel, which is the core of Linux, as an organism that lives beneath or inside the shell. The Linux kernel is a very technical program that is not user friendly; it manages and coordinates everything that is going on inside your Fedora Core 4 computer system as you use it.

In almost any normal circumstance, talking directly to the Linux kernel is the *hardest* way to accomplish a task, because the Linux kernel is designed to communicate with electronic equipment and with other computers, rather than with humans. At the same time, you must communicate with the Linux kernel *somehow* in order to be able to give Linux instructions. One way to do this is to point and click on your desktop, but this method is somewhat constrained; the realm of possibilities is limited by the space for icons, menus, and other items on your desktop, and only a certain limited amount of information can be conveyed by a mouse click.

As a text-based command interpreter, the shell accepts a wide lexicon of text commands that are designed to make sense to humans and that can be combined with each other in various ways, just like words in human languages, to make new meanings. The shell's job is to interpret the meanings of these human-style instructions and then to pass them on to the Linux kernel in the technical format that the kernel can understand.

*By the*
*Way*

> ### There Are Actually Several Common Shells
>
> You can choose to use one of several command-line shells on most any Linux or Unix system; each is slightly different in terms of behavior and features, although most of the actual commands remain the same. The most common shell by far is the default shell, **bash**, which stands for the Bourne-Again SHell, so named because it is a re-creation (with many new features) of the old Bourne Shell, **sh**, from traditional Unix systems.
>
> From now on in this book, when we talk about the shell, we mean the Bourne-Again Shell (or **bash**) that Linux uses by default.

## Launching a Terminal Window

The easiest way to access the shell from your Linux desktop is to start a **terminal emulator** program. A terminal emulator is an application that provides you and the shell with a text-oriented window in which to communicate. You can type commands to the shell, and the shell can respond by displaying informative text about what it is doing and what Linux is doing.

To start a terminal window in Fedora Core 4, choose Applications, System Tools, Terminal. The terminal application appears, as shown in Figure 6.1.

**FIGURE 6.1**
The terminal application helps you to interact with the Linux command line via the shell.

Command prompt

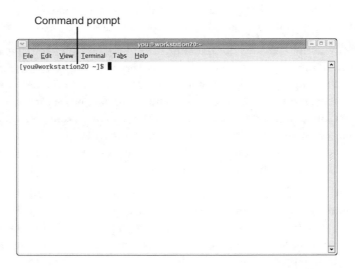

The last line of text in a waiting terminal window is always a command prompt. This command prompt signals you that the shell is ready to accept your commands and translate them into tasks for the Linux kernel to perform. When you use the shell, you type whatever command(s) and option(s) you want to supply at the command prompt and then press Enter, which signals the shell to process and carry out the instructions you've just provided. When the command prompt reappears, your instructions have been carried out.

# Learning Fundamentals of Shell Use

The first thing to notice about the Linux shell is that the command prompt contains useful information about your computing environment. Right now, in your terminal window, you probably see a command prompt something like this:

```
[you@workstation20 ~]$
```

The first part of the prompt, you@workstation20, varies depending on your username and the network name of the machine you are using; its format is *user@machine*. So, for example, if you are logged in as kensmith, and you are using a computer called netstation52, the first part of your prompt would read

```
kensmith@netstation52
```

The second part of the prompt displays the last part of the current path—the directory or folder you and the shell are currently working in. By default, when you start a new shell, this is your home directory. For the user kensmith, this would be /home/kensmith; for the user you, it's /home/you. In either case, the final directory in the path is the default current working directory of the shell.

A special shorthand, the tilde (~) character is used at the Linux command line to represent your home directory. When the shell shows you a tilde, it is referring to your home directory; when you send a tilde to the shell as part of a command, it assumes that you are talking about your home directory.

---

### What Is a Home Directory Again?

If you've forgotten what the term **home directory** means, feel free to review the section called "Understanding the Linux File System" in Chapter 5.

---

*Watch Out!*

The default prompt for the user you, which incorporates the username, the machine name, and the current working directory, is therefore

```
[you@workstation20 ~]$
```

If you're not sure why all these details are useful at the moment, don't worry; we're going to get our hands dirty soon, and you'll begin to see in a more direct way how the command prompt relates to what you are doing with the shell.

## Talking to the Shell

As you work with the shell, you will soon notice that the text of every set of instructions you give it follows the same basic pattern. The following description of the contents of a shell command might seem obtuse at first, but hang in there. As you gain experience with the shell, these details will become less confusing to you.

In general, you type the following when you give an instruction to the shell:

▶ A one-word command chosen from the massive list of available commands on your Linux system, each of which performs some specific task. There are literally thousands of commands.

▶ If needed, an **option** or **flag**, which modifies or directs the command's behavior, and is usually preceded by a dash. Each command has its own list of understood options and flags that are used to alter the behavior of the command to suit your needs.

▶ If needed, **arguments**, which provide additional data that a command needs to function or to employ a specific option or flag.

▶ If needed, additional options and flags or arguments in whatever number is necessary to suitably direct the command's behavior.

This list of elements is common in the Linux and Unix world; you will see it appear each time you read the documentation for a specific command. However, in online documentation, you usually see it written in shorthand or synopsis form, like this:

```
mycommand -opt1 arg1 [-opt2 arg2 ...]
```

This line of text roughly represents what you just learned: that when you type the fictional command mycommand at the shell, you should provide at least one option or flag (-opt1) that the command understands, followed by one argument (arg1). If necessary, you can enter an optional second flag (-opt2), followed by a second argument (arg2), and so on. Although this brief notation seems cryptic at first, it appears everywhere in the command-line world and soon becomes second nature to shell users.

## Entering Your First Command

It's time to introduce your first command. The ls command is the command you use to display the contents of a directory in the Linux file system. It is in many ways akin to opening a directory in the file manager and looking at the icons that it contains. To see what is in your Linux system's root directory, enter the ls command now, supplying the slash (for the root directory) as an argument. The output of this command is shown in Figure 6.2.

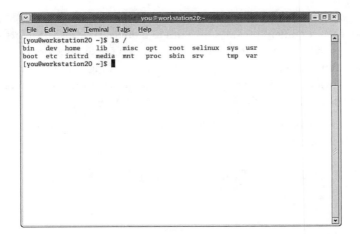

FIGURE 6.2
After you enter
the ls com-
mand and pro-
vide the root
directory (/) as
an argument,
the contents of
the root directo-
ry are listed.

## Colors Indicate File Types

At the Fedora Core 4 command line, the output of the ls command is color-coded
to help you differentiate between files, directories, and other types of data, the
same way that icons help you on the desktop. Though you can't see it in the text,
you can on your screen—directories appear in blue.

By the
Way

Here, the ls command provided you with two lines of output. Each of the names
you see is a directory stored in the root directory of your Linux system. Now list the
contents of the usr directory by using the same command with /usr as an argument, as shown in Figure 6.3.

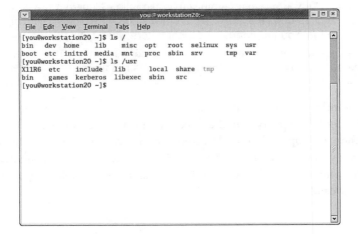

FIGURE 6.3
A second
invocation of
the ls com-
mand displays
the contents of
/usr.

The results of the first command you typed are still visible. When you use the ls command, each argument provides the path to a directory whose contents you want to display. When referring to the specific location of a file or directory (its path) at the Linux command line, you will generally begin with the root directory (/) and proceed to provide a kind of roadmap for arriving at the desired file or directory, separating each step along the way with an additional slash.

Now list the contents of one more directory, /usr/X11R6, just for practice. The results are shown in Figure 6.4.

**FIGURE 6.4**
The results of one more invo-cation of the ls command, this time listing the contents of the path /usr/X11R6.

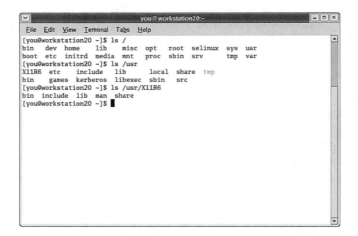

By the Way

**Linux Is Case Sensitive**

Having trouble? If you've been faithfully trying to follow along but are getting error messages such as Command not found or No such file or directory, check to make sure that you are not using capital letters when typing these commands.

Linux, like most Unix-like operating systems, is **case sensitive**. This means that ls is *not* the same as LS to Linux; similarly, x11r6 is not the same as X11R6.

In these commands, you listed the contents of the root directory, the directory called usr inside the root directory, and the directory called X11R6 inside the usr directory. The roadmap you supplied to the ls command in each case is exactly the same kind of **path** you learned about in Chapter 5. If you need a refresher on the struc-ture of the Linux file system and paths in particular, you can refer to Chapter 5 and Table 5.1 for details.

# Using the Current Working Directory

Now that you've seen directories in action at the shell prompt and are already familiar with the root directory and the home directory, it's time to really navigate the Linux file system at the command line. Let's begin by creating a file. You can create an empty text file at the command line using the touch command and giving the filename you want to use as an argument. First, create a file called empty.txt:

```
[you@workstation20 ~]$ touch empty.txt
[you@workstation20 ~]$
```

Linux responds by creating for you an empty text file called empty.txt. To see that the file exists, use the ls command without arguments:

```
[you@workstation20 ~]$ ls
Desktop  anotherfile.txt  empty.txt
[you@workstation20 ~]$
```

If you're wondering exactly where the new file was created in the file system tree, you're an astute reader. Each time you have used the ls command thus far, you have supplied it with an argument—the path to the directory you wanted to list. This time, however, ls lists the contents of a directory without having been told which directory you wanted to see. So what's going on? And in what directory did you just create empty.txt?

As was previously mentioned, the shell always keeps track of something called your **current working directory**. At your request, any directory in the file system can be made your current working directory. Linux created empty.txt in your current working directory because you didn't specify an alternate location. The ls command displays the contents of your current working directory in the preceding example for the same reason. In most cases, if you provide an argument to a command without supplying a path, the command is executed as though you had actually supplied the path of your current working directory. Because you have just started this shell and issued only a few commands, your current working directory is still your home directory, as can be seen by the tilde character (~) in the prompt. Whenever you start a new shell, the default current working directory is your home directory.

From the previous output of ls, you can see that there are three files in this current working directory; if you have been following along with our previous chapters, your list of files might be the same—the file you created in the text editor called anotherfile.txt, a folder or directory called Desktop, and a file called empty.txt that you just created. To ask the shell at any time just what your current working directory is, use the pwd (print working directory) command:

```
[you@workstation20 ~]$ pwd
/home/you
[you@workstation20 ~]$
```

As you can see, your current working directory is indeed your home directory—the directory in /home that belongs to your account and is intended to hold your files. To change your current working directory, you use the cd command, supplying your desired current working directory as an argument. Try changing your current working directory to the root directory now:

```
[you@workstation20 ~]$ cd /
[you@workstation20 /]$
```

Notice that the command prompt has changed to reflect your new current working directory. You can also use pwd to see that the change has taken effect:

```
[you@workstation20 /]$ pwd
/
[you@workstation20 /]$
```

Now, using the ls command without arguments displays the contents of the root directory, rather than the contents of your home directory:

```
[you@workstation20 /]$ ls
bin   dev  home   lib    misc  opt   root  selinux  sys  usr
boot  etc  initrd  media  mnt   proc  sbin  srv      tmp  var
[you@workstation20 /]$
```

Try making /usr/X11R6 your current working directory, using pwd to verify the change and then using ls without arguments to list the contents of the directory:

```
[you@workstation20 /]$ cd /usr/X11R6
[you@workstation20 X11R6]$ pwd
/usr/X11R6
[you@workstation20 X11R6]$ ls
bin  include  lib  man  share
[you@workstation20 X11R6]$
```

Because your home directory is so fundamental to day-to-day use of Linux at the command line, you can always return to it quickly by simply issuing the cd command without arguments:

```
[you@workstation20 X11R6]$ cd
[you@workstation20 ~]$ pwd
/home/you
[you@workstation20 ~]$
```

*By the Way*

**Two Names, One Concept**

In other texts or in Linux-oriented conversation, you might also encounter the term *present working directory* instead of *current working directory*; these terms are identical in meaning.

## Manipulating Files and Directories

Now that you're back in your home directory, assume that you want to make a copy of the file you created earlier called empty.txt. You can do so with the cp command, supplying two arguments—first the name of the source (original) file and second the name of the destination (new) file:

```
[you@workstation20 ~]$ cp empty.txt notfull.txt
[you@workstation20 ~]$ ls
Desktop  anotherfile.txt  empty.txt  notfull.txt
[you@workstation20 ~]$
```

There are now three files in your home directory: anotherfile.txt, empty.txt, and notfull.txt, which is a copy of empty.txt. Suppose, however, that you don't want empty.txt hanging around in your home directory but instead want to put that particular file in its own directory called emptyfiles. To create a directory, use the mkdir command, supplying the name of the directory you want to create as an argument:

```
[you@workstation20 `]$ mkdir emptyfiles
[you@workstation20 ~]$ ls
Desktop  anotherfile.txt  emptyfiles  empty.txt  notfull.txt
[you@workstation20 ~]$
```

You have now created a directory called emptyfiles (which ls shows in blue to indicate that it is a directory) and can move empty.txt into it. You can move Linux files using the mv command, which accepts a space-separated list of the files you want to move as arguments and the destination directory as the last argument. After you are done, you can verify the effects of mv by using the now familiar ls command:

```
[you@workstation20 ~]$ mv empty.txt emptyfiles
[you@workstation20 ~]$ ls
Desktop  anotherfile.txt  emptyfiles  notfull.txt
[you@workstation20 ~]$ ls emptyfiles
empty.txt
[you@workstation20 ~]$
```

Notice that the path arguments in the commands you just entered don't begin with a slash character. These commands were given relative paths, which are discussed in the next section.

## Using Relative Paths

In the series of commands you just entered, you gave ls only a directory name, emptyfiles, as an argument, rather than a full path beginning with a slash. A directory name without a roadmap back to the root directory is called a **relative**

**path**, so called because it doesn't begin with the root directory (/) but instead speci-fies that the argument is *relative to your current working directory*. Linux is smart enough to notice that the path you gave to ls when you displayed the contents of emptyfiles didn't begin at the root directory; it therefore adds the path you sup-plied in your argument to the end of your current working directory, which always begins with a slash. In this case, /home/you (the current working directory) plus emptyfiles (the argument given to ls) causes the contents of /home/you/ emptyfiles to appear on the console, saving you the trouble of entering the entire long path by hand.

To gain more practice with relative paths, try creating one more directory. This time, call it deeperfiles. Place it "deeper" within your home directory by creating it inside the directory you created earlier called emptyfiles. Remember that your cur-rent working directory is still your home directory; you can use pwd to verify this:

```
[you@workstation20 ~]$ pwd
/home/you
[you@workstation20 ~]$ mkdir emptyfiles/deeperfiles
[you@workstation20 ~]$ ls
Desktop  anotherfile.txt  emptyfiles  notfull.txt
[you@workstation20 ~]$ ls emptyfiles
deeperfiles  empty.txt
[you@workstation20 ~]$
```

Now, just for practice, move the file notfull.txt into the deeperfiles directory:

```
[you@workstation20 ~]$ mv notfull.txt emptyfiles/deeperfiles
[you@workstation20 ~]$ ls
Desktop  anotherfile.txt  emptyfiles
[you@workstation20 ~]$ ls emptyfiles
deeperfiles  empty.txt
[you@workstation20 ~]$ ls emptyfiles/deeperfiles
notfull.txt
[you@workstation20 ~]$
```

Before finishing with relative paths, you need to learn about two special relative paths. They are a single period (.) and a double period (..), and you can use them anywhere you would normally use the name of a directory.

The single period is a kind of shorthand that always refers to the current working directory. So, assuming that your current working directory is /home/you, the follow-ing three commands produce identical results:

```
[you@workstation20 ~]$ ls
Desktop  anotherfile.txt  emptyfiles
[you@workstation20 ~]$ ls /home/you
Desktop  anotherfile.txt  emptyfiles
[you@workstation20 ~]$ ls .
Desktop  anotherfile.txt  emptyfiles
[you@workstation20 ~]$
```

The double period always refers to the directory one branch lower (closer to root) in your file system tree, relative to your current working directory. So, assuming that your current working directory is /home/you, the following two commands produce identical results:

```
[you@workstation20 ~]$ ls /home
you
[you@workstation20 ~]$ ls ..
you
[you@workstation20 ~]$
```

You also can use relative paths to modify your current working directory with cd:

```
[you@workstation20 ~]$ cd ..
[you@workstation20 home]$ pwd
/home
[you@workstation20 home]$
```

Because the root directory is at the base of the file system tree and there is no "lower" directory in the Linux file system, in the root directory, the single period and double period are equivalent:

```
[you@workstation20 home]$ cd ..
[you@workstation20 /]$ pwd
/
[you@workstation20 /]$ ls
bin   dev  home   lib    misc  opt   root  selinux  sys  usr
boot  etc  initrd media  mnt   proc  sbin  srv      tmp  var
[you@workstation20 /]$ ls .
bin   dev  home   lib    misc  opt   root  selinux  sys  usr
boot  etc  initrd media  mnt   proc  sbin  srv      tmp  var
[you@workstation20 /]$ ls ..
bin   dev  home   lib    misc  opt   root  selinux  sys  usr
boot  etc  initrd media  mnt   proc  sbin  srv      tmp  var
[you@workstation20 /]$
```

Remember that you can quickly return home by issuing the cd command without arguments:

```
[you@workstation20 /]$ cd
[you@workstation20 ~]$ pwd
/home/you
[you@workstation20 ~]$
```

## Parent and Child Directories

By the Way

The double period (..) is often referred to as the **parent directory**. In the Linux file system, a file's parent directory is the directory that contains it. For example, /home is the parent directory of /home/you. You also will see the term **child directory**. In this example, /home/you is a child directory of /home, sometimes also called a subdirectory.

Although it's difficult to conceive at first how the two special relative paths might be useful, routine applications do arise. For example, you can use them to move empty.txt, notfull.txt, and deeperfiles all back into your home directory:

```
[you@workstation20 ~]$ mv emptyfiles/empty.txt emptyfiles/
➥deeperfiles deeperfiles/notfull.txt .
[you@workstation20 ~]$ ls
Desktop  anotherfile.txt  deeperfiles  emptyfiles  empty.txt  notfull.txt
[you@workstation20 ~]$
```

Get lost? Note that the last argument to mv in the command is the single period (.), causing mv to use the current working directory as the final destination for all the files listed:

▶ The first argument to mv moves the file empty.txt from the emptyfiles directory to . (the current working directory, currently your home directory).

▶ The second argument moves the directory deeperfiles from the emptyfiles directory to the current working directory, illustrating that you can also use mv to move directories.

▶ Finally, because the deeperfiles directory was already moved to the current working directory by the processing of the second argument, the third argument moves the file notfull.txt from the deeperfiles directory to the current working directory.

To illustrate one final use of the mv command before we proceed, let's rename the file notfull.txt to alsoempty.txt and the directory deeperfiles to moreemptyfiles. Linux does not have a "rename" command, but you don't need it because you can use the more powerful mv command to achieve the same result:

```
[you@workstation20 ~]$ mv notfull.txt alsoempty.txt
[you@workstation20 ~]$ mv deeperfiles moreemptyfiles
[you@workstation20 ~]$ ls
Desktop  alsoempty.txt  anotherfile.txt  emptyfiles  empty.txt  moreemptyfiles
[you@workstation20 ~]$
```

You're almost finished learning about basic navigation. But before we go on, let's take a moment to clean up the mess we made in your home directory.

## Deleting Files and Directories

The command to remove files is rm; the command to remove directories is rmdir. With two quick commands and a few arguments, you can get rid of the files and directories you created and left here and there:

```
[you@workstation20 ~]$ rmdir emptyfiles moreemptyfiles
[you@workstation20 ~]$ rm alsoempty.txt empty.txt
```

```
[you@workstation20 ~]$ ls
Desktop    anotherfile.txt
[you@workstation20 ~]$
```

### Removing Lots of Files and Directories at Once

By the Way

You can also use the rm command to delete directories or entire sections of the file system tree. The rm command does this when you supply the -r (recursive) and -f (force) options, commonly shortened to -rf. One of the most commonly typed phrases in Unix is

```
rm -rf somedirectory
```

where *somedirectory* represents a directory full of files and other directories that are no longer needed. Although rmdir will respond with an error message if asked to delete a directory that is not empty, rm -rf will erase the directory and all of its contents (including other directories and the files that they contain) without pause.

Be careful when using rm -rf! Because rm -rf simply removes files and directories (whether or not they are empty) without asking questions, you can easily wipe out vast swaths of your home directory with this command if you're not careful. When you're logged in as the system administrator in later chapters, be doubly careful about using rm -rf, if you are brave enough to do it at all; otherwise, you could end up erasing your entire hard drive with a single command:

```
rm -rf /
```

### Your Files Have Been Alphabetized for You

By the Way

When working in directories with small numbers of files, you might not have noticed that the ls command typically displays the contents of any directory in vertically arranged alphabetical order. This ordering is evident if you use ls to get a listing of the /bin directory.

# Summary

In this chapter, you were introduced for the first time to the Linux command line, and you learned to perform a few basic file management tasks using the shell. You learned to create new files, list the contents of directories, navigate the file system tree, create new directories, and move and delete files and directories.

In the next chapter, you learn about some of the more powerful features of the Linux file system that help to make Linux so flexible and secure. Until then, take a break: you've earned it!

# Q&A

**Q** *You mentioned earlier that there were "literally thousands of commands" in Linux. Where can I learn about them all?*

**A** Because there are so many commands, so many different varieties of Linux operating systems, and because you can always customize your Linux installation, there is no "official" list of all of the thousands of Linux commands you might encounter in Linux.

Several books do a good job of listing many of them, however. One of the very best is *Linux in a Nutshell*, little more than a concise reference of thousands of Linux commands, published by O'Reilly and Associates.

**Q** *I haven't ever created any files or directories in my home directory, yet files or directories are already there, according to the ls command. Why?*

**A** Various Linux applications create files and directories for you when you start them. Depending on the amount of work you had already done with your Fedora Core 4 system before you started this chapter, the files in your home directory might not exactly match those in the examples.

**Q** *What happens when using mv or cp if a file already exists with the same name as the destination I've given to the shell in my argument?*

**A** If the destination file already exists when you use mv or cp, it is *replaced* by the new file. The existing file is deleted before the new file by the same name is created. You should therefore learn to be cautious when using mv or cp in day-to-day work.

# Workshop

The Workshop is designed to help you anticipate possible questions, review what you've learned, and begin learning how to put your knowledge into practice.

## Quiz

1. What command would you use to create an empty text file called friday.txt?

2. What command would you use to rename friday.txt to saturday.txt?

3. What command would you use to remove (delete) saturday.txt?

## Answers

1. `touch friday.txt`

2. `mv friday.txt saturday.txt`

3. `rm saturday.txt`

## Activities

1. Spend some time exploring your Linux file system using `ls` and `cd` to visit directories, beginning with the root directory.

2. Practice creating, moving, and removing files, directories, and symbolic links in your home directory

# CHAPTER 7

# Understanding File Properties

This chapter completes your introduction to the Linux file system and to the day-to-day manipulation and use of files in Linux. After you've familiarized yourself with the information in Chapters 5, "Working with Files on the Desktop," 6, "Working with Files in the Shell," and 7, "Understanding File Properties," you'll be ready to put Linux to work for day-to-day computing tasks in the coming chapters.

This chapter uses a mix of command-line (shell) and file manager examples. Whenever you see text providing command-line examples, feel free to follow along using the terminal application that you learned to use in Chapter 6. Whenever you see examples illustrated using the file manager, feel free to follow along using the file manager on your desktop.

## Understanding Executable Files

So far in your exploration of Linux, you've seen several basic text files and several directories or folders. Now we're going to expand our horizons to include other types of Linux files. For example, the /bin directory in the standard Linux file system contains another type of file, called an **executable** file. Executable files can be programs, commands, or scripts—tools and applications that you tell the computer to run, often from the command line, to get things done.

You can use the ls command to view the contents of the /bin directory:

```
[you@workstation20 ~]$ ls /bin
arch      dnsdomainname    gzip        more      rview         traceroute6
awk       doexec           hostname    mount     sed           true
[...]
df        gtar             mknod       rpm       tracepath6
dmesg     gunzip           mktemp      rvi
[you@workstation20 ~]$
```

The files in this directory are coded in several colors, including blue and a light blue known as cyan. Files listed in blue are executable files. (You learn more about the cyan files, called *symbolic links*, in the next section of this chapter.)

> ### Your Files Have Been Alphabetized for You
>
> You might not have noticed when working in directories with fewer contents, but the ls command typically displays the contents of any directory in vertically arranged alphabetical order. This ordering is evident in the /bin directory.

If you look carefully, you might notice that this particular directory, /bin, contains many of the commands you've been using. The commands cp, ls, mkdir, mv, pwd, rm, rmdir, and touch are all stored in the /bin directory. They are all actually Linux programs that are themselves started by the shell every time you enter them as commands. Linux uses these commands to accomplish the work you've been requesting of the system.

Every program, application, tool, or command that you use in Linux exists as an executable program file stored somewhere in the Linux file system. Every time you use such a program or call such a command, Linux loads the executable file, which contains instructions and program code, and runs it.

# Using Symbolic Links

The cyan files in the /bin listing represent another very common file type in Linux called a **symbolic link**. A symbolic link allows a single given file to appear in many places or under many names at once, without taking up any additional space on your hard drive. A symbolic link is often used to conserve disk space; other times, it's used simply for convenience. When a symbolic link points to an executable file, it enables the command to take on several identities or behaviors at once, depending on whether you type the name of the original command to use it or the name of the symbolic link.

Nearly anything done to a symbolic link also affects the original file, with the notable exception of removal. Using rm to remove a symbolic link does not remove the original file; instead, using rm with a symbolic link removes the link itself. To get a little experience with symbolic links, let's create one now. In your home directory, create a directory called green and an empty file within it called color.txt:

```
[you@workstation20 ~]$ mkdir green
[you@workstation20 ~]$ touch green/color.txt
[you@workstation20 ~]$ ls green
color.txt
[you@workstation20 ~]$
```

Now use the file linking command, ln, to create a symbolic link called blue that points to the green directory. To do this, supply the -s option to ln, followed by the name of the source file as the first argument and the destination link as the second:

```
[you@workstation20 ~]$ ln -s green blue
[you@workstation20 ~]$ ls
Desktop  anotherfile.txt  blue  green
[you@workstation20 ~]$
```

To illustrate how the symbolic link behaves, list the files in each directory, both the original green directory and the symbolic link, blue, which points to it:

```
[you@workstation20 ~]$ ls green
color.txt
[you@workstation20 ~]$ ls blue
color.txt
[you@workstation20 ~]$
```

You can see that the symbolic link, blue, behaves very much as the original directory, green, does. You can even make blue your present working directory:

```
[you@workstation20 ~]$ cd blue
[you@workstation20 blue]$ pwd
/home/you/blue
[you@workstation20 blue]$ ls
color.txt
[you@workstation20 blue]$ cd ..
[you@workstation20 ~]$
```

You can also see and create symbolic links using the file manager. Open a file manager window now, and you should see both the new directory called green and the symbolic link to it called blue in the list of icons, as shown in Figure 7.1.

Symbolic links are shown in the file manager with the same type of icon as the file that they point to, along with a small green arrow overlaying the icon, indicating that the icon represents a symbolic link.

To create a symbolic link in the file manager, simply right-click the icon you would like to create a link to. Right-clicking displays the context menu. Then choose Make Link from the context menu, as shown in Figure 7.2, and a new symbolic link icon appears. You are then free to rename or use this link at your discretion; no matter what you call it or how you choose to use it, it still connects to the original file.

**FIGURE 7.1**
In the new file manager window, you see both the directory you created, called green, and the symbolic link you created, called blue. Note the arrow indicating that blue is a symbolic link.

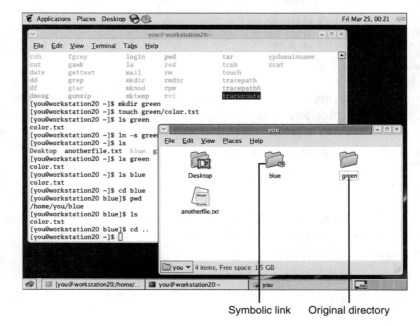

Symbolic link    Original directory

**FIGURE 7.2**
Choose Make Link from the context menu to create a symbolic link using the file manager.

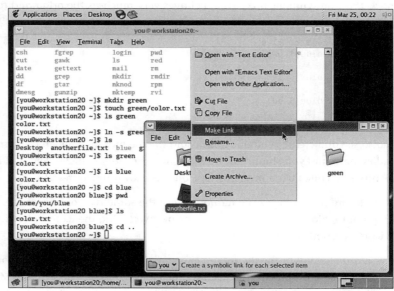

You won't do much more with symbolic links in this book, but they will come up in your day-to-day work with Linux, so you need to be aware of them and how they behave. As a final note, remember that you can also create symbolic links that point to symbolic links:

```
[you@workstation20 ~]$ ln -s blue yellow
[you@workstation20 ~]$ ls
Desktop  anotherfile.txt  blue  green  yellow
[you@workstation20 ~]$ ls yellow
color.txt
[you@workstation20 ~]$ cd yellow
[you@workstation20 yellow]$ pwd
/home/you/yellow
[you@workstation20 yellow]$ cd ..
[you@workstation20 ~]$
```

# Understanding Permissions

Every file and directory in a Linux system is governed by a set of security-related properties. These properties govern the life of the file or directory in two ways:

► Each file or directory must be owned by someone: In Linux, there is no such thing as a file or directory without an owner.

► Each file or directory is associated with a list of the operations that can be performed on it, both by the owners and at times by other users as well. This list is known as the file's **permissions** and it is generally represented in a particular visual format that we discuss in a moment.

Both ownership and permissions are assigned from default values when a file or directory is created; file or directory owners can then change this information as needed.

You should be familiar with these properties when working with files and directories in Linux so that you can control who is allowed to access sensitive data. You also should understand why you might not be able to access data belonging to others. The sections that follow teach you to examine and manipulate a file's ownership and permissions. Let's study some real-world examples.

Up to this point, you've created files only in your home directory because that's the place users are meant to put their files. But can you put your files somewhere else? Let's see. Visit your home directory's parent directory, /home, and try to create a file there called hello.txt:

```
[you@workstation20 ~]$ cd ..
[you@workstation20 home]$ touch hello.txt
touch: cannot touch 'hello.txt': Permission denied
[you@workstation20 home]$
```

You don't have permission to create files in the directory /home. To see why, you need to learn to use the ls command in a new way.

## Long File Listings

So far, you've used the ls command to get a basic listing of the *names* of the files and directories in a given directory. You can use a number of common options, how- ever, to alter the behavior of ls so that it also lists other information, such as the creation date or size of a file or directory. Most used among these options is the -l or long listing option, which causes ls to display a great deal of extra information about each file it lists. Try it now on your root directory:

```
[you@workstation20 home]$ ls -l /
total 20
drwxr-xr-x    2 root root 2344 Mar 23 20:55 bin
drwxr-xr-x    4 root root 1024 Mar 23 20:53 boot
drwxr-xr-x    9 root root 5460 Mar 24 20:48 dev
drwxr-xr-x   75 root root 5912 Mar 24 20:54 etc
[...]
drwxr-xr-x   10 root root    0 Mar 24 15:46 sys
drwxrwxrwt   13 root root  576 Mar 24 20:50 tmp
drwxr-xr-x   14 root root  360 Mar 23 20:52 usr
drwxr-xr-x   22 root root  552 Mar 23 21:25 var
[you@workstation20 home]$
```

The -l option (lowercase *L*, not the number 1) causes ls to display a wealth of new information, including (from left to right)

- The permissions (a string of characters that are enumerated later in this chap- ter) of the file or directory

- The number of hard links to the file or directory

- The **owning user** of the file or directory

- The **owning group** of the file or directory

- The size of the file or directory on the disk in bytes

- The creation date and time if the file or directory was created within the past six months or the creation year and date if the file or directory was created before that

- The name of the file or directory

The date, time, and size information in a long file listing is provided primarily for your convenience as a user. The hard link count provided by the long file listing is not commonly used in the course of day-to-day work and is thus beyond the scope of a book like this one. The owning group, owning user, and permissions are all important for understanding and using Linux permissions and are your focus for the remainder of this chapter.

## Identity and File Ownership

In Linux, the two basic forms of identity are the user account, which you are using right now, and the group membership. At any time, a user account can belong to one (always at least one) or several groups; groups are created by system administrators to manage security and enhance workflow.

Every file and directory in a Linux file system is similarly owned at all times by exactly one primary user and by all the users in exactly one group. The ls command provides this ownership information in columns three and four of a long listing. As you've seen, every item in your system's root directory is owned by the root user and by the root group. For contrast, let's list the files in your home directory:

```
[you@workstation20 home]$ cd
[you@workstation20 ~]$ pwd
/home/you
[you@workstation20 ~]$ ls -l
total 12
drwx------  3 you    you    4096 Mar 23 21:53 Desktop
-rw-rw-r--  1 you    you     324 Mar 23 16:57 anotherfile.txt
lrwxrwxrwx  1 you    you       5 Mar 23 20:41 blue -> green
drwxrwxr-x  2 you    you    4096 Mar 23 20:41 green
lrwxrwxrwx  1 you    you       4 Mar 23 20:48 yellow -> blue
[you@workstation20 ~]$
```

The files in your home directory are owned by the user you. They also belong to the group you. That group was created when your account was created, and you automatically belongs to it.

## Ownership and File Permissions

What do we mean when we say that someone "has permission" to create or delete files in a given directory? In real terms, it means that the person in question owns the directory and that the permissions properties for the directory indicate that the directory's owner should be allowed to change the directory's contents. Referring back to your long listing of the root directory, you might recall the following entry for /home:

```
drwxr-xr-x  3 root    root    4096 Mar 23 04:14 home
```

The ownership of /home is clear; the /home directory is owned by the root user and the root group. The 10-character permissions code at the extreme left determines just what root, members of the group root, or anyone else can do to the /home directory. Each of the 10 positions in the permissions code means something specific. Let's look at this code more closely, with some spaces added to separate the major parts of the code:

d rwx r-x r-x

The character in the leftmost (first) position indicates the type of file /home is. In this case, the d in this position indicates that /home is a directory. Table 7.1 lists the common values for file types.

**TABLE 7.1    Common File Types from Permissions Strings**

| Type | Description |
|------|-------------|
| d | The file in question is a directory. |
| l | The file in question is a symbolic link. |
| - | The file in question is a normal file (text, data, image, and so on). |

A few other file types are available, but we're not going to worry about them in this chapter. Let's look at the code for /home again:

d rwx r-x r-x

Positions 2–4 of this code, rwx in the case of /home, dictate what the owning user of a file, in this case root, can do to it. Table 7.2 shows the precise meanings of the characters in positions 2–4.

**TABLE 7.2    Meanings of the Characters in Positions 2–4**

| Position | Possible Values | Meaning |
|----------|-----------------|---------|
| 2 | r = permission to read/list granted<br>- = permission to read/list denied | In the case of a file, indicates whether the owning user will be allowed to read data from the file. In the case of a directory, indicates whether the owning user will be allowed to list the contents of the directory. |
| 3 | w = permission to write/create/delete granted<br>- = permission to write/create/delete denied | In the case of a file, indicates whether the owning user will be allowed to write data to the file. In the case of a directory, indicates whether the owning user will be allowed to create or delete files in the directory. |

**TABLE 7.2**  Continued

| Position | Possible Values | Meaning |
|---|---|---|
| 4 | x = permission to execute/visit granted<br>- = permission to execute/visit denied | In the case of a file, indicates whether the owning user will be allowed to execute the file—to use it if it is a command or program. In the case of a directory, indicates whether the owning user will be allowed to make the directory his or her present working directory—to "visit" the directory. |

In the case of /home, the owning user is allowed to list the contents of the directory, create and delete files in the directory, and visit the directory. Let's examine that permissions code for /home one more time:

```
d rwx r-x r-x
```

The characters in positions 5–7 (the middle group of three) have the same possible values and meanings as those shown in Table 7.2 but apply to members of the owning group, instead of to the owning user. In the case of /home, people who are not root but who happen to be members of the owning group, also called root, are allowed to list the contents of the directory and visit the directory. They are not, however, allowed to create or delete files within the directory.

Finally, the characters in positions 8–10 (the final group of three) again have the same meanings, but they apply to all other users—users who are neither the owning user nor members of the owning group. In this case, users who are not root and who do not belong to the root group (this includes you) are allowed to list the contents of /home and visit /home but are not allowed to create or delete files in /home. So, when you tried to create a file in /home, Linux returned an error message.

## More Permissions Examples

Because permissions can be a little confusing, going over some examples with brief explanations might be helpful. The following are hypothetical files with owning user, owning group, and permissions codes:

```
-rw-r----- 1 jack   admins   16384 Aug 3 04:14 jacks_peppers.txt
```

The file jacks_peppers.txt is likely a text document containing private information that jack doesn't want anyone to edit. Here is what this long listing tells you:

▶ The file jacks_peppers.txt is owned by the user jack and by members of the group admins.

▶ [-] It is a regular file, not a directory or a symbolic link.

▶ [rw-] The user jack is allowed to read data from the file and write data to the file.

▶ [r--] Members of the group admins are also allowed to read data from the file, but they may not write data to or make changes to the file in any way.

▶ [---] Users who are not jack and who do not belong to admins can't read from the file or write to the file at all.

Here's another example:

```
-rwxr-x---  1 root    wheel    54696 Aug 3 04:14 launchit
```

The file launchit is a program that likely performs an administrative task of some kind because only root and members of wheel can run it. Here is what this long listing tells you:

▶ The file launchit is owned by the user root and by members of the group wheel.

▶ [-] It is a regular file, not a directory or symbolic link.

▶ [rwx] The user root is allowed to read data from the file and write data to the file. The file launchit is likely a program or command because the user root is also allowed to execute it (run it as a program).

▶ [r-x] Members of the group wheel are allowed to read from launchit and execute it, but they may not write to it.

▶ [---] Users who are not root and who do not belong to wheel can't read launchit, write to launchit, or execute launchit at all.

**By the Way**

### Symbolic Links and Permissions

When you look at the permissions of symbolic links, they always seem to grant permission for everything to everyone. A symbolic link uses the permissions of the file that it points *to* rather than its own permissions.

# Changing Permissions

Sometimes, you might want to change the permissions of files you own in your home directory. You might want to allow other users to modify them, for example, or prevent other users from reading them. You can change file permissions with the chmod command.

You can use chmod in two ways: using the symbolic method or the numeric method. The **symbolic** method for changing permissions is easier to understand because it uses the same characters you've seen used for permissions codes. The **numeric** method uses numbers to assign permissions and is more commonly used by system administrators because of its brevity.

Here is the format for using chmod in symbolic mode:

```
chmod permcode file1 [file2 ...]
```

The permcode consists of three parts:

▶ One letter or a combination of these letters:

u (for owning user)

g (for owning group)

o (for "other")

This letter or group of letters indicates whose permissions are to be changed.

▶ Either a plus, minus, or equal sign, depending on whether permissions are to be added, removed, or explicitly assigned, respectively.

▶ One letter or a combination of these letters:

r (for adding/removing/assigning read permission)

w (for adding/removing/assigning write permission)

x (for adding/removing/assigning execute permission)

This letter or group of letters indicates how permissions are to be allocated.

Let's look at some examples to illustrate how chmod works in symbolic mode. Return to your home directory and create a new file called illustration.txt:

```
[you@workstation20 home]$ cd
[you@workstation20 ~]$ touch illustration.txt
[you@workstation20 ~]$ ls -l
total 4
drwx------   3 you    you    4096 Mar 23 21:53 Desktop
-rw-rw-r--   1 you    you     324 Mar 23 16:57 anotherfile.txt
lrwxrwxrwx   1 you    you       5 Mar 23 20:41 blue -> green
```

```
drwxrwxr-x  2 you    you    4096 Mar 23 20:41 green
-rw-rw-r--  1 you    you       0 Mar 23 22:15 illustration.txt
lrwxrwxrwx  1 you    you       4 Mar 23 20:48 yellow -> blue
[you@workstation20 ~]$
```

Notice that in spite of the fact that illustration.txt is *your* file, the entire world (users who are not you and do not belong to your group) can still currently read illustration.txt. Suppose illustration.txt contained private information? You would, of course, want to remove permission for other users to read the file:

```
[you@workstation20 ~]$ chmod o-r illustration.txt
[you@workstation20 ~]$ ls -l illustration.txt
-rw-rw----  1 you    you       0 Mar 23 10:01 illustration.txt
[you@workstation20 ~]$
```

You have now forbidden users who are not you and do not belong to the group you from reading illustration.txt. Other users who try to read the file will get an error message. Now suppose for a moment that you also have a twin, miniyou, who has been made a member of the group you by a system administrator. With the current file permissions of illustration.txt, miniyou would have both read and write access, assuming once again that miniyou was a member of the group you. To prevent this access, you could disable access for all members of the group you:

```
[you@workstation20 ~]$ chmod g-rw illustration.txt
[you@workstation20 ~]$ ls -l illustration.txt
-rw-------  1 you    you       0 Mar 23 10:01 illustration.txt
[you@workstation20 ~]$
```

Now only you have read and write access to illustration.txt. Users who are not you but who are members of the group you have no access. But perhaps you wanted to prevent miniyou only from modifying the file—not necessarily from reading it. No problem—you can restore read permission:

```
[you@workstation20 ~]$ chmod g+r illustration.txt
[you@workstation20 ~]$ ls -l illustration.txt
-rw-r-----  1 you    you       0 Mar 23 10:01 illustration.txt
[you@workstation20 ~]$
```

Now you still have full read and write access; members of the group you (including miniyou) have read-only access. Users who are not you and not members of the group you still have no access at all. Finish by giving full read and write access to everyone in the world, just for fun:

```
[you@workstation20 ~]$ chmod ugo+rw illustration.txt
[you@workstation20 ~]$ ls -l illustration.txt
-rw-rw-rw-  1 you    you       0 Mar 23 10:01 illustration.txt
[you@workstation20 ~]$
```

In practice, you would rarely want to provide this access, because now anyone in any account can read at will and make any changes to illustration.txt.

# Managing Permissions Using the File Manager

You also can view and edit file and directory permissions using the file manager. To view the permissions for a given file or directory using the file manager, right-click the icon for the file or directory in question and choose Properties from the context menu. In the dialog box that appears, select the Permissions tab. This tab displays the permissions for the file in question, as shown in Figure 7.3.

Group ownership selector

Permissions toggles

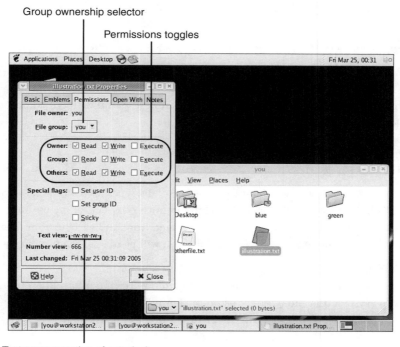

Text representation of permissions

**FIGURE 7.3**
On the Permissions tab of the Properties dialog box, you can view and edit the permissions for the file in question.

The Permissions tab contains a number of options that either display information about the file's ownership and permissions, or allow you to make changes to the file's ownership or permissions using your mouse. These options include

► File Owner, which displays the name of the owning user account.

► File Group, which displays and allows you to change the name of the owning group account.

► Owner, Group, and Others permissions check boxes that allow you to enable or disable read, write, and execute permissions for each of these roles.

▶ Special Flags that allow you to enable or disable certain special file character-
istics that are discussed in detail in Part V, "Advanced Topics."

▶ A Text View of the permissions for the file, just as you would see with `ls -l`.

▶ A Number View of the permissions for the file, used in changing the permissions using `chmod`'s numeric mode, discussed in detail in Chapter 28,
"Command-Line System Administration."

▶ The time and date at which the file was last modified.

To change the permissions or group ownership for a file or directory using the
Properties dialog box, simply check or uncheck the boxes in question, as desired,
and then click Close to save your changes.

For more information on changing ownership and on special file permissions, refer
to Chapter 30, "Security Basics."

# Summary

In this chapter, you learned about two new Linux file types: executable files and
symbolic links. You also learned about Linux permissions—sets of file or directory
properties that enable you to control who can read from and write to your files
while allowing other users to decide whether you will be able to read from or write
to theirs.

Now that you've mastered the basics of saving and retrieving information in the
Linux file system and the basics of using the Linux shell when necessary, you're
ready to put Linux to work for day-to-day tasks! See you next chapter!

# Q&A

**Q** *Is there any way to cause the ls command to display information one page
at a time—for example, when showing a long directory listing?*

**A** You can display information this way by using pipes and the `more` command,
both of which are discussed in Chapter 19, "Performing Basic Shell Tasks." To
pause a long file listing after each page of output, enter

```
ls -l ¦ more
```

When the output pauses, you can press the spacebar to continue to the next
page.

**Q** *What happens if I take away owning user's write permission from a file that I own? Can I still to write to it? Can I still change the file's permissions (for example, to add write permission for myself back again)?*

**A** If you remove owning user's write permission from a file that you own, you cannot save your changes to the file any longer. In a sense, the file is "write protected." You can, however, give yourself write permission once again by using chmod or the file manager, should you decide that you want to be able to make changes to the file once again.

# Workshop

The Workshop is designed to help you anticipate possible questions, review what you've learned, and begin learning how to put your knowledge into practice.

## Quiz

1. What command would you use to find the ownership and permissions associated with saturday.txt?

2. What command would you use to change the permissions for saturday.txt to ensure that all users anywhere could read and write to the file?

3. What command would you use to create a symbolic link to saturday.txt called just_another_saturday.txt?

## Answers

1. ls -l saturday.txt

2. chmod ugo+r saturday.txt

3. ln -s saturday.txt just_another_saturday.txt

## Activities

1. Spend some time creating empty text files and directories, then changing their permissions, and trying to edit, change, copy, or delete them to gain practice with permissions.

2. See what happens when you create a symbolic link using ln -s that refers to a file that doesn't exist. (Hint: The link will still be created, but it might not behave as you would expect.)

# PART III

# Using Fedora Core 4

# CHAPTER 8

# Creating Text Documents with OpenOffice.org Writer

---

## What You'll Learn in This Chapter:

▶ What OpenOffice.org is and what applications are included with it

▶ How to launch the OpenOffice.org Writer application

▶ How to create a new word processing document

▶ How to control basic formatting and layout

▶ How to open, save, and print your Writer documents

In this chapter, you learn to create documents in the Linux desktop environment using OpenOffice.org Writer, a full-featured word processor that is part of the OpenOffice.org applications suite included with Fedora Core 4. By the end of the chapter, you should be able to create, print, and save your own pleasing, professional-quality text documents.

## Previewing the OpenOffice.org Applications

OpenOffice.org is a suite of productivity applications for use with Linux. The OpenOffice.org suite is similar to Microsoft Office, Corel WordPerfect Office, or other "office" suites you might be familiar with. Because OpenOffice.org is open-source software (like Linux itself), it is a favorite among Linux users. OpenOffice.org is also available for use with the Windows OS. Because OpenOffice.org is capable of opening and saving in MS Office file formats, you can exchange files with users of Windows and MS Office using OpenOffice.org.

Like most suites of office productivity applications, OpenOffice.org contains a series of distinct applications, each of which performs a specific task:

▶ OpenOffice.org Writer, a full-featured word processing and document layout application similar to Microsoft Word or Corel WordPerfect. OpenOffice.org Writer enables you to create memos, letters, articles, reports, and books.

▶ OpenOffice.org Calc, a powerful spreadsheet and calculation application similar to Microsoft Excel or Corel Quattro Pro. OpenOffice.org Calc enables you to perform math-oriented tasks, such as budgeting, engineering calculations, physics calculations, and statistics.

▶ OpenOffice.org Impress, a presentations manager similar to Microsoft PowerPoint or Corel Presentations. OpenOffice.org Impress allows you to create visual slide shows with illustrations, charts, and graphs to help you to present information to others.

▶ OpenOffice.org Draw, a drawing and image-manipulation program that allows you to create clean, well-structured sketches and diagrams as well as edit photos and other types of raster graphics.

▶ OpenOffice.org Math, an equation editor, for editing and inserting complex mathematical equations into your documents for output.

*By the Way*

**OpenOffice Versus OpenOffice.org**

If you're thinking that OpenOffice.org sounds more like a website than a set of programs, you're partially correct: OpenOffice.org is the home page for the OpenOffice.org applications. Both the suite of applications and the website that houses them share the same name.

*Did you Know?*

**OpenOffice.org is available for Windows, free!**

OpenOffice.org is also available as a free download for many different operating systems, including Windows. It's a viable alternative to Microsoft Office or similar products, and costs nothing for personal or for business use. Visit OpenOffice.org for details.

In this chapter, you explore the OpenOffice.org Writer, the most commonly used application in the OpenOffice suite.

By the Way

> ## Where Can You Learn More About OpenOffice.org?
>
> For a full treatment of the OpenOffice.org suite, refer to the following books on StarOffice, which is based on OpenOffice technology and virtually identical in most respects:
>
> ▶ *StarOffice 6.0 Office Suite Companion*, by Solveig Haugland and Floyd Jones
> ▶ *Special Editing Using StarOffice 6.0*, by Michael Koch

You can find online documentation for OpenOffice.org and all its features at any time as you work through this chapter and the OpenOffice.org chapters that follow by choosing Help, Contents from any OpenOffice.org application. Every dialog box in OpenOffice.org also contains a Help button; clicking it displays documentation about that dialog in particular.

# Launching OpenOffice Applications

The OpenOffice.org applications can be found by choosing Applications, Office, as shown in Figure 8.1. To launch OpenOffice.org Writer, select the Writer option from the menu.

**FIGURE 8.1**
Choose Applications, Office to access the list of OpenOffice.org applications.

The remainder of this chapter is concerned with the OpenOffice.org Writer application. The Calc and Impress applications are discussed in upcoming Chapters 9,

"Creating Spreadsheets with OpenOffice.org Calc," and 10, "Creating Presentations with OpenOffice.org Impress," respectively.

# Creating and Formatting an OpenOffice.org Writer Document

The OpenOffice.org Writer application enables you to create professional-looking letters, reports, memos, books, and other types of text-based documents that are commonly used in business and academia. In OpenOffice.org Writer, you enter and format lines and paragraphs of text, usually with the eventual goal of outputting them to a printer in an easy-to-read format.

## Launching OpenOffice.org Writer

Click the OpenOffice.org Writer icon to launch the application. Click the taskbar icon; the splash logo appears as the application loads. When the program is loaded, a new Writer application window containing an untitled document appears, as shown in Figure 8.2.

**FIGURE 8.2**
A new OpenOffice.org Writer window. Because no document has been loaded, a new document named Untitled1 appears in the application window.

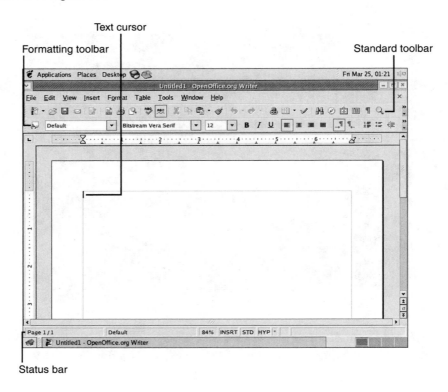

Text cursor

Formatting toolbar

Standard toolbar

Status bar

The following components make up the OpenOffice.org Writer window:

- ▶ The toolbars contain function buttons that, when clicked, perform common tasks, such as saving or printing a file, changing text alignment, or inserting a table.

- ▶ The text body looks like a piece of paper or several pieces of paper and is the place where you enter text as you create documents. This element contains the **text cursor**, a blinking line that indicates where new text appears as you enter it. The faint gray line near the edge of the text body area indicates the position of the text margins.

- ▶ The status bar displays information about the size of your document, the position of your cursor, and other mundane but useful data.

---

**Does Your Writer Window Look Different?**

Your OpenOffice.org Writer window probably looks slightly different from the one shown in Figure 8.2, because the window in Figure 8.2 has been adjusted to display an entire editable page. To do the same thing on your desktop, first maximize the OpenOffice.org Writer window using the Maximize Window button you learned about in Chapter 4, "Introducing the Fedora Core 4 Desktop." Then, right-click on the text "100%" near the bottom of the OpenOffice.org Writer window and select Page Width from the pop-up menu that appears.

*Did you Know?*

---

# Entering Text

To enter text in OpenOffice.org Writer, position the text cursor where you want to enter new text and then begin typing. Any text you type is inserted at that position. Words automatically wrap to the next line when you reach the right margin, so you don't have to press Enter at the end of each line to remain within the right margin and avoid splitting a word across two lines.

Enter a line or two of text now so that you have a nonempty document to work with for the rest of the chapter. The OpenOffice.org Writer application with a few lines of text entered is shown in Figure 8.3.

# Editing Text

One of the greatest advantages inherent in using a word processing application such as OpenOffice.org Writer is that you easily can change text after you've entered it. Here are some of the most common editing techniques:

- ▶ You can remove individual letters or words using Backspace and Delete editing keys. Backspace deletes characters to the left of the insertion point, and Delete deletes characters to the right of the insertion point.

**FIGURE 8.3**
The cursor moves from left to right and from the top of the screen toward the bottom as you type text into OpenOffice.org Writer.

▶ You can edit a block of text by selecting the block and then choosing an editing key or command. Click at the beginning of the block of text you want to edit and then drag your cursor to the end of the text (see Figure 8.4). Selected text appears highlighted onscreen. Click Cut to remove the text from the document. Cut text can remain deleted from the document or moved to a new location (see the steps that follow this list). Click Copy to copy the selected text; then position your cursor where you want to place a copy of the text and click Paste. A copy of the selected text appears at the insertion point.

▶ By selecting blocks of text, you can also type new text to replace existing text. Select a letter or word and then begin typing to replace it with new text.

**By the Way**

## Seeing Squiggly Underlines?

Two of the typed words in Figure 8.3 have squiggly underlines beneath them. You might also notice squiggly red underlines beneath words that you type into OpenOffice.org Writer.

OpenOffice.org Writer places a squiggly line underneath a word when it thinks the word might be misspelled. When you right-click on a squiggly-underlined word, OpenOffice.org Writer displays a pop-up that displays suggested spellings for the word in question. Select the correct spelling from the list, and the word will be fixed for you.

If you're sure that a squiggly-underlined word isn't misspelled, then it simply isn't in the OpenOffice.org Writer dictionary, and you can ignore the underline—it won't appear when you print the document.

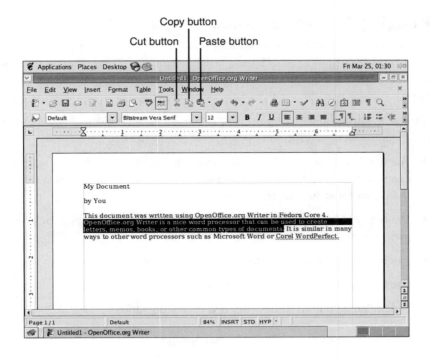

FIGURE 8.4
By selecting blocks of text, you can issue a single editing command to apply changes to the entire block.

To move a selected block of text to another location within a document, follow these steps:

1. Click the Cut button (the scissors icon) to remove the selected text (or choose Edit, Cut); the text disappears from the document.

2. Position the cursor at the location in the document where you want the moved text to appear.

3. Click the Paste icon or choose Edit, Paste; the text appears in the new location.

---

**You Can Select Without a Mouse and Erase Without a Backspace**

You can also select text using your keyboard. Position the text cursor before the block of text you want to select. Press and hold your Shift key as you use the navigation keys to move the text cursor to the end of the block of text you want to select. After you have selected the block of text you want, release the Shift key.

The Insert command key on your keyboard enables you to toggle between Insert and Overwrite mode. In Insert mode, new text you enter pushes text to the right. In Overwrite mode, new text overwrites text to the right of the cursor, letter for letter. Press the key to toggle between the two modes.

*Did you Know?*

## Changing the Appearance of Text

You can apply different font sizes, typefaces, and text effects to change the appearance of text within your OpenOffice.org Writer documents. These changes can make your document look more professional and add emphasis to important words or phrases.

To change the appearance of text in your document, select a block of text and then click one of the following Formatting bar items (see Figure 8.5):

► The typeface drop-down list changes the fundamental style of your text; for example, you might choose to use a sans-serif font such as Helvetica rather than a serif font such as Thorndale.

► The font size drop-down changes the physical size of your text on the printed page; larger numbers indicate larger text.

► The bold button causes text to appear in **boldface**.

► The italic button causes text to appear in *italics*.

► The underline button causes your text to be <u>underlined</u>.

**FIGURE 8.5**
Formatting bar items have been used to change the appearance of the text in the first line of this document. The title text is now in Luxi Sans typeface, 24 point size, boldface.

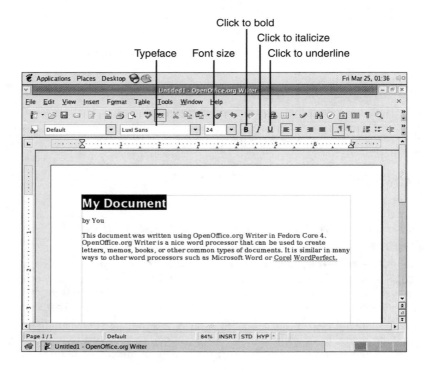

The bold, italic, and underline buttons work as toggles: Click them again to toggle them off.

To apply font styles before you begin typing, position the text cursor where you would like your text to be inserted and then use the font size, bold, italic, and other appearance-editing tools to set your choices. The text you enter reflects your settings.

---

### You Can Choose Many Text Alignment Options

You can align text along the right or left margins, or you can center text on the page. You also can **justify** the text to create straight margins on both the right and left sides. Click in a paragraph and then choose one of the four alignment buttons located to the right of the Underline button in the Formatting bar. Each button face shows the alignment it provides. Select multiple paragraphs and then click a button to align all of them. You also can choose text alignment before you enter text. Choose an alignment option and then type. The text you enter is aligned with that style until you choose another option.

---

*Did you Know?*

## Changing Paragraph Formatting

You can format text in single-spaced, double-spaced, or 1.5-line–spaced paragraphs. You also can indent paragraphs as you type or apply indentation to paragraphs of existing text. You choose line spacing and indentation options within the Indents & Spacing tab of the Paragraph dialog box.

To change the line spacing or indentation properties of an existing block of text, select the block of text you want to modify and then choose Format, Paragraph; the Paragraph dialog box appears, as shown in Figure 8.6.

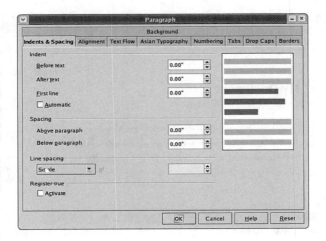

**FIGURE 8.6**
The indentation and spacing values are given in inches. You enter a value or use the arrows to increase or decrease the value. The preview pane on the right shows the effect of your changes.

By changing the values of the settings in this dialog box, you can alter the spacing or margins of a selected block of text or set values for new text before you enter it:

▶ Use the Before Text and After Text settings in the Indent area of the tab to indent paragraphs from the page margins; the higher the values, the greater the indentation.

▶ Use the First Line setting in the Indent area to cause the first line in each selected paragraph to automatically be indented some additional distance relative to the left margin. Check the Automatic check box to make this the default behavior.

▶ Use the Above Paragraph and Below Paragraph spacing settings to force OpenOffice.org Writer to leave some amount of empty space above and/or below each paragraph.

▶ Use the Line Spacing drop-down list to choose single, double, or 1.5 line spacing.

▶ Use the Register-True setting to cause all printed lines in your document to use the same baseline so that you can't see gray smudges between the lines on the current page caused by text lines on the next page.

Figure 8.7 shows the paragraph in the sample document altered to double-spaced and automatically indented from the left margin on the first line.

**FIGURE 8.7**
Double-spacing
and first-line
indent are com-
mon uses for
the Paragraph
dialog box.

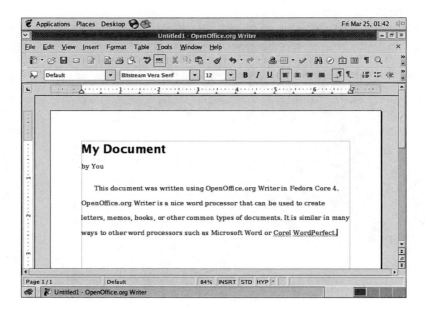

# Changing Margin Size and Page Layout

You can customize the margins of OpenOffice.org Writer documents, and you can change the size and orientation of their printed format. To edit these settings, use the Page tab of the Page Style dialog box, as shown in Figure 8.8. Open this dialog box by choosing Format, Page.

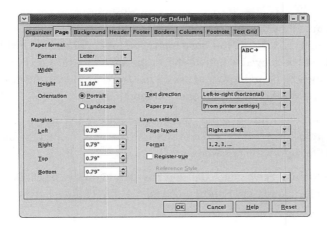

**FIGURE 8.8**
Use the Page Style dialog box to change document page margins, paper size, and paper orientation.

Here's how to use the settings in the Page Style dialog box to change the layout of your document:

▶ Use the settings in the Paper Format area to choose a printed format (such as Letter, Legal, Envelope, and so on), paper size, and orientation. The Text direction setting changes the orientation of text (between vertical and horizontal) for international users. The Paper Tray setting enables you to choose which paper tray the print job should feed from.

▶ The settings in the Margins area enable you to set specific Left, Right, Top, and Bottom margin sizes, as measured in inches. Type in a size or use the arrows to raise or lower the default settings.

▶ The Page Layout setting in the Layout Settings area enables you to apply the current settings to all pages (Right and Left), to only odd pages (Right), to only even pages (Left), or to apply the current settings in anticipation of two-sided printing to allow for easy binding (Mirrored).

▶ The Format setting in the Layout Settings area enables you to specify the type of page numbering that should be used if you have chosen to insert page numbers in your document.

After you make the changes you want, click OK to accept them. The changes you make in the Page Style dialog box affect the entire document you're working on.

## Saving a File

After you finish entering, editing, and formatting a document, you can save the file for later retrieval or use.

Save the document by clicking the Save button (floppy disk icon) in the Function bar (or by choosing File, Save). If you have made changes to or entered text in a file that has not yet been saved, you'll be shown the Save As dialog box you learned about in Chapter 5, "Working With Files on the Desktop." In OpenOffice.org Writer, however, the file dialog has several additional options:

▶ Checking Save with password causes OpenOffice.org Writer to ask you for a password before saving the file. Anyone who wants to open the file must then be able to supply the password.

▶ The Automatic File Name Extension box should always be checked; this allows OpenOffice.org to automatically choose the correct three-letter extension for your file.

▶ To save your file in a format other than the OpenOffice.org Writer format, for example if you want to exchange files with MS Word users, click Browse for Other Folders. This will cause the file type drop-down list shown in Figure 8.9 to be displayed. You can then elect to save your file using a format from this list.

**FIGURE 8.9**
After clicking Browse for Other Folders, the file type drop-down list can be used to save your document for use in other word processing applications.

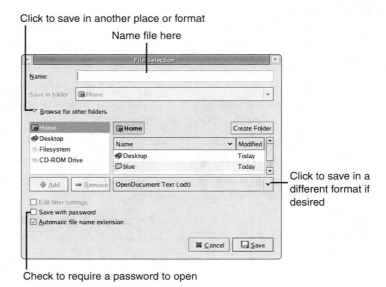

Click to save in another place or format

Name file here

Click to save in a different format if desired

Check to require a password to open

After you choose a filename, format, and directory, click Save to apply your choices and save the file to disk. Each time you save this file in the future, changes will be stored under the same filename.

---

### Need to Save Another Copy?

You can use the Save As option in the File menu to select a new name for an existing document. This option enables you to create a copy of the original file under a new name, so you can make changes to the copy while preserving the original file's content.

# Opening a File

To edit or print an existing saved document, you must first open it. You can open a document by clicking the Open icon (it looks like an open folder) in the Function bar; alternatively, you can choose File, Open from the menu bar.

After either action, the Open file dialog box appears, as shown in Figure 8.10.

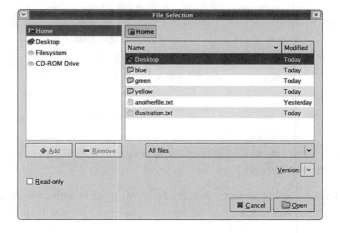

**FIGURE 8.10**
The list box in the Open dialog box lists all the files and directories contained in the current directory (here, the user's home directory). Double-click a file to open it.

Scroll until you see the file you want in the file and directory list box. Double-click the filename to open it.

If your file isn't in the current directory, here's how to use the other controls in the Open file dialog box to find the file:

▶ To list the contents of another directory, double-click the name of the directory in the file and directory list box. You can double-click the Home bookmark in the left-hand panel at any time to return to your home directory.

▶ Use the file type drop-down list to limit the list of displayed files to a certain type of file, if there are too many files to sort through easily.

## Printing a File

Printing a document is a simple process in OpenOffice.org Writer. Begin by opening the document you want to print. If you want to print the entire document, click the Print button (marked with a printer icon) in the Function bar. The document is sent to the printer.

If you want to print only a portion of the document, print multiple copies, or change any of the page layout settings (such as orientation, paper size, and so on), begin the print process by choosing File, Print. The Print dialog box opens, as shown in Figure 8.11.

**FIGURE 8.11**
The Print dialog box allows you to perform special printing tasks, such as printing a specific range of pages or a specific number of copies.

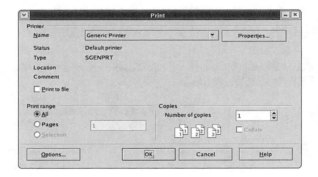

The highlighted controls in the Print dialog box can be used to alter several aspects of the OpenOffice.org Writer printing behavior:

▶ The Number of Copies entry box enables you to determine how many copies of the output OpenOffice.org Writer will cause your printer to generate.

▶ The Print to File check box enables you to output the printer data to a file, rather than to your printer. OpenOffice.org prompts you for the name of the file if you select this option. Because data that would normally have been sent to your printer is in a language suited to printers rather than to humans, you will rarely, if ever, use this option.

▶ If you have chosen to print more than one copy of your file, selecting the Collate option causes the entire document to be printed in sequence multiple times (pages 1, 2, 3, 1, 2, 3). If you do not check the Collate option, each page is output several times in a row (pages 1, 1, 2, 2, 3, 3).

▶ The Print Range options enable you to choose to print only a segment of the document, rather than all of it. To use this feature, enter a page number or range of numbers that you want to print. If you want to print only a paragraph or other block of text from the document, select the block with your mouse, open the Print dialog box, and click the Selection button in the Print Range area.

After you make your choices in the Print dialog box, click OK to begin printing.

# Summary

In this chapter, you learned to use the basic features of the most commonly used OpenOffice.org application, OpenOffice.org Writer—a full-featured word processing application.

In OpenOffice.org Writer, you learned to do the following:

▶ Enter and edit text using your pointing device and the Writer text cursor

▶ Select blocks of text to move them around or copy them within a document

▶ Alter the appearance, size, or style of existing text or newly entered text

▶ Change the alignment of text paragraphs to left alignment, right alignment, center alignment, or full justification

▶ Change the margins, indentation, and spacing properties of paragraphs within your document

You also learned some housekeeping tasks, including how to save your work, load existing files, and print the documents you create.

# Q&A

**Q** *Is there a spell check in OpenOffice Writer?*

**A** Yes. You can access the spell check feature by choosing Tools, Spellcheck. A spell check dialog box appears; as each misspelled word is found, you can replace it with a word from a list of possible corrections or enter a new correction on your own.

**Q** *It distracts me when words are squiggly-underlined because Writer thinks they're misspelled. Is there a way to turn this off?*

**A** Yes. On the Main toolbar across the top of the application window, you'll see a small button containing the letters ABC over a wavy red line. Clicking this button toggles the spell-as-you-go feature.

# Workshop

The Workshop is designed to help you anticipate possible questions, review what you've learned, and begin learning how to put your knowledge into practice.

## Quiz

1. How do you italicize a block of text in Writer?

2. How do you change to double-spacing in Writer?

3. How do you save a text document as a Microsoft Word file instead of as an OpenOffice.org Writer file?

## Answers

1. Select the block of text with your pointing device and then click the italic button in the Formatting bar.

2. Choose Format, Paragraph to open the Paragraph dialog box and then choose Double Spacing from the Line Spacing drop-down list.

3. In the Save As file dialog box, click Browse for Other Folders to display the file type drop-down list, then select one of the Microsoft Word options from the list before clicking the Save button.

## Activities

1. Create a new Writer document, save it, and exit Writer. Then restart Writer and open the document again to become familiar with saving and opening files.

2. Explore the different fonts, sizes, and styles available to you while creating documents in Writer.

# CHAPTER 9

# Creating Spreadsheets with OpenOffice.org Calc

---

## *What You'll Learn in This Chapter:*

► How to create a new electronic spreadsheet
► How to enter text labels and numerical values
► How to change the appearance of spreadsheet contents
► How to perform basic calculations using formulas

In the preceding chapter, you learned how to use the OpenOffice.org Writer application, which is similar in many ways to Microsoft Word. In this chapter, you learn how to use the OpenOffice.org Calc application.

The OpenOffice.org Calc application is an electronic spreadsheet similar in form and function to Microsoft Excel or Corel Quattro Pro. OpenOffice.org Calc can be used to perform mathematical calculations of all kinds. For example, a homeowner can use OpenOffice.org Calc to amortize a loan or maintain a personal budget, an engineer might use OpenOffice.org Calc for load calculations, and a pollster might use OpenOffice.org Calc to maintain lists of statistics or an index of contacts.

By the end of this chapter, you'll be able to put electronic spreadsheets to work for you.

## Understanding Electronic Spreadsheets

Although electronic spreadsheet applications often seem awkward to users at first, they are extremely powerful and commonplace tools in office environments. To use an electronic spreadsheet, you provide lists of numbers or data to OpenOffice.org Calc along with the formulas and calculations that should be used to manipulate them. OpenOffice.org Calc documents consist of rows and columns of **cells**, each of which can contain one of four things:

- ▶ Empty space
- ▶ Text
- ▶ A number
- ▶ A formula that will be used to perform calculations using the text or numbers in one or several other cells

The combination of these four types of data can lead to a surprising breadth and depth of powerful numerical and data management tools. And because OpenOffice.org Calc can read and save files in Microsoft Excel format, OpenOffice.org Calc users can exchange files with Microsoft Office users everywhere.

# Using OpenOffice.org Calc

To start OpenOffice.org Calc, choose Applications, Office, OpenOffice.org Calc, as shown in Figure 9.1.

**FIGURE 9.1**
OpenOffice.org
Calc can be
started by visit-
ing the
Applications
menu.

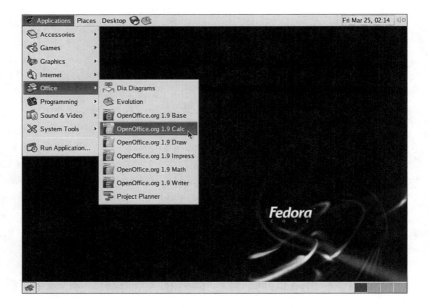

If no other OpenOffice.org applications are running, the splash logo appears while the program loads, and then a new Calc application window opens, containing an untitled electronic spreadsheet (see Figure 9.2).

Selected cell          Input line          Standard toolbar          Formatting toolbar

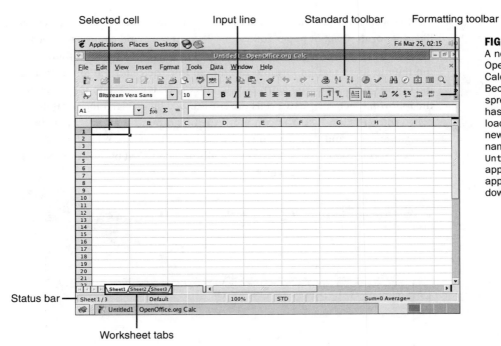

**FIGURE 9.2**
A new
OpenOffice.org
Calc window.
Because no
spreadsheet
has been
loaded yet, a
new document
named
Untitled1
appears in the
application win-
dow.

Before entering any data, familiarize yourself with the parts of the OpenOffice.org
Calc window. The Calc window demonstrates what a rich feature list this application offers. Here's how to use the Calc onscreen tools and components:

▶ Click buttons in the toolbars to perform common tasks, such as saving or
printing a file, changing text alignment, and formatting numeric data within
a cell in a specific way based on the type of data—for example, two decimal
places for currency.

▶ Click a cell within the spreadsheet to make it active and display its contents in
the input line. Cells can contain text and numeric data, as well as formulas
that calculate values in one or more other cells. The currently selected cell is
surrounded by a bold black line that forms the cell boundary.

▶ Use the status bar to find your current cell position in a spreadsheet and perform quick calculations on the right side of the status bar by highlighting
blocks of cells.

▶ Enter cell contents (text, numeric data, formulas) in the input line. The data
you enter here appears in the active or selected cell.

▶ Use the scrollbars to change the viewing area of the spreadsheet display. Cells
are identified by a row number and column letter.

▶ Use the worksheet tabs to switch between open worksheets; each worksheet is like a separate sheet of paper containing its own rows and columns of cells. You add data to a cell by first selecting a cell to make it active and then entering the numbers, text, or formula for the cell into the cell input text box at the top of the Calc screen. You learn how to enter each type of data into cells in the following sections. Active cells are surrounded by a thick black outline, called the **selection box**. You can move the box around the spreadsheet by using the arrow and Page Up/Page Down keys, or by positioning the text cursor over a cell and clicking the mouse. Cells are identified by row number and column letter; in Figure 9.3, cell H14 is selected.

**FIGURE 9.3**
Each cell in a spreadsheet can be referenced with a unique combination of letters and numbers. Here, cell H14 is selected.

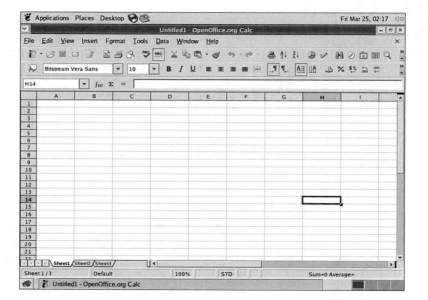

Although you're now visually familiar with Calc, the best way to learn to use a spreadsheet is to start a spreadsheet application and create one. We step through that process in the sections that follow.

## Entering Text Labels

For our sample spreadsheet, let's create a simple sheet that helps keep track of the amount of money you've found lying around while walking down the street lately. Although this scenario is a little wishful thinking, it helps illustrate the use of spreadsheets. We start with some text labels to show what the spreadsheet is to be used for.

Text labels are essential in an electronic spreadsheet because they enable those readers studying the spreadsheet to understand what the numeric data represents. For example, by entering the words Race Times next to a list of race results or Monthly Income next to a series of numbers representing income on a month-by-month basis, you make the spreadsheet easier for readers to understand. In the sample spreadsheet, we create a title for the sheet, along with enough labels for days and weeks to represent one month of money-finding.

To enter a text label in a cell, select the cell where the text label should start and begin typing. The text you enter appears both in the cell and on the input line, as shown in Figure 9.4. When you are done, press Enter to accept the text label you entered.

You can change the appearance of the text label's text to differentiate it from other entries in the worksheet. You can use a different typeface; alter the font size; apply bold, italic, and underlining; and change the color of the text. To change the

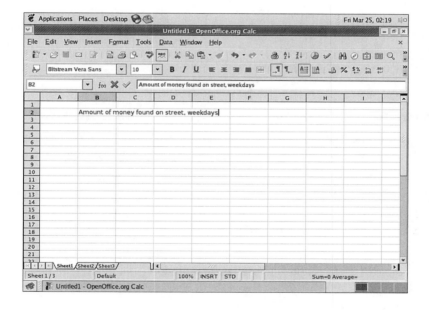

**FIGURE 9.4**
Entering a text label is easy; select the cell where the label should start and begin typing. Here, a label has been entered in B2, although it is allowed to flow over other cells because it is several words long.

appearance of a text label, select the cell containing the label and then use the tools and selection boxes in the Formatting bar to apply changes. All these tools appear in the roughly the same place in OpenOffice.org Calc that they did in OpenOffice.org Writer; once you have become familiar with one, you should be able to quickly find the same buttons in the other.

Row size is automatically adjusted for the size of text contained within the cells in a given row. Figure 9.5 shows the same text label as in Figure 9.4, now enlarged slightly and made boldface. A number of additional text labels have been entered as well, in anticipation of the numeric data that is to be entered next.

**FIGURE 9.5**
The title of the
spreadsheet
has been made
large and bold-
faced; addition-
al text labels
have been
entered in B4
through H4 and
A5 through A10.

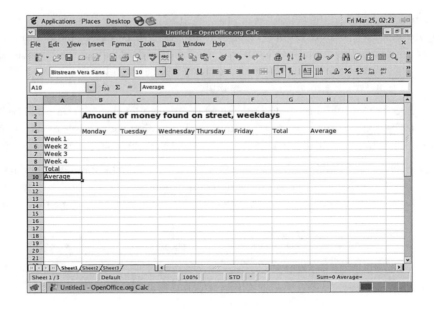

## Entering and Formatting Numeric Data in Cells

To enter numeric data in the spreadsheet, navigate to the cell you want and type in the numbers. After you finish entering a number, press Enter to accept the numeric data as the value for the cell.

Figure 9.6 shows the spreadsheet from Figures 9.4 and 9.5 with numeric data filled in. The numeric values in Figure 9.6 are clearly intended to be currency; however, OpenOffice.org Calc has dropped trailing zeros in decimals in some cells (C5, F5, D6, E6, and D8).

An electronic spreadsheet provides structured formatting of numeric data to display numbers as a dollar value, percentage, or with a specific number of decimal places. The default numeric format in OpenOffice.org is the Standard format, in which trailing zeros after a decimal point are dropped and numbers are otherwise displayed as they were entered. The following are the most common other numeric formats:

▶ Currency format, which displays numbers with the assumption that they are dollar values—with a leading currency symbol and two digits of precision after the decimal point

▶ Percentage format, which displays numbers multiplied by 100, with two digits of precision after the decimal point and a trailing percent sign

▶ Fixed-precision formats, which display numbers with a fixed number of digits of precision after the decimal point

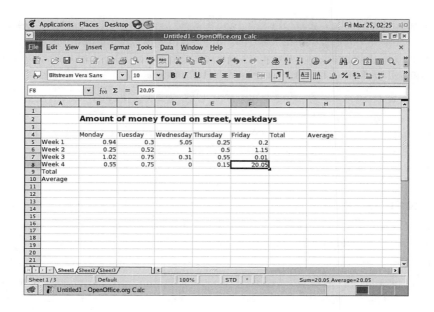

**FIGURE 9.6**
The numeric data for this spreadsheet has been filled in by hand, from B5 through F8.

All these types of numeric formats can be applied using the Formatting bar buttons shown in Figure 9.7.

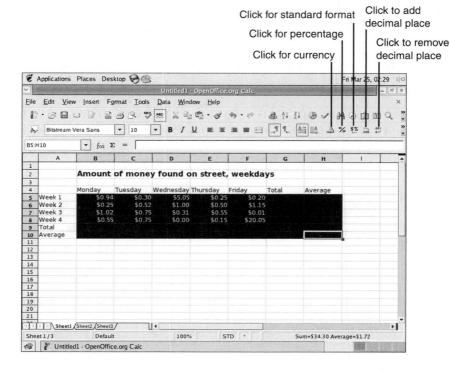

**FIGURE 9.7**
The Formatting bar buttons for numeric formatting have been used to alter the appearance of the data in the cells in B5 through H10.

To format a single cell, select the cell and click the appropriate Formatting bar button. To format a group of cells, click the upper-left cell with your pointing device and drag to the lower-left cell before releasing. This action selects an entire range of cells. Then click the appropriate Formatting bar button.

Figure 9.7 shows the sample worksheet with a large range of cells selected and formatting applied. The Formatting bar button for currency format has already been clicked; all the numeric data has been reformatted to appear as currency. Any numeric data that later appears in the empty selected cells will also appear as currency.

## Entering Formulas

Formulas are the essence of the electronic spreadsheet. Although formulas may be as simple as an addition or subtraction expression, they may also be extremely complex.

Typical uses for formulas in spreadsheets include finding sums or averages of long lists of numbers or calculating percentages based on known quantities, such as the number of respondents in a survey. Users with more specific needs can perform physics, engineering, or calculus computations in a spreadsheet.

In our sample worksheet, formulas must be used in several places. A number of cells have been reserved to hold column or row totals; these totals will be calculated using formulas. The same is true for the cells left for averages. For example, the total findings for week one are to be displayed in G5. Thus, the number that should eventually appear in G5 should be the result of B5 plus C5 plus D5 plus E5 plus F5.

To enter a formula that performs a series of simple calculations, select the cell in which the result should be displayed. Then follow these steps:

1. Type an equal sign (=) to indicate to OpenOffice.org Calc that you are about to enter a formula.

2. Enter a formula consisting of cell references (the letter and number that refer to a cell) and operators such as +, -, /, and *. You can enter a cell reference either by typing the letter and number of a cell or by clicking the cell in question.

3. After you type the complete formula, press Enter to accept the formula and calculate the result.

The process of entering a simple formula to perform a basic calculation is shown in Figure 9.8.

Press enter to display formula result

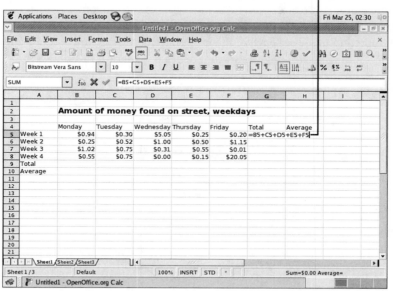

**FIGURE 9.8**
Entering a formula. G5 will display the result of this calculation, rather than the formula, after you press Enter.

---

## The Formula Is Still There!

*By the Way*

Although the formula entered in G5 is no longer visible in the cell on the spreadsheet after you press Enter, you can still view and edit the formula. When you select G5, the formula appears in the Input line.

Even though hidden, formulas are always active. If you change the numeric data in a cell used in a formula calculation, the displayed result of the formula calculation is automatically updated to reflect the new numeric data you've entered.

---

# Using Functions in Formulas

Although the formula in G5 produces the desired result, the method of entering cell references one at a time can become clunky when many cells are involved in a calculation. For many types of common calculations, predefined **functions** built in to OpenOffice.org Calc can operate on ranges of cells. For example, there is a simpler way to sum several cells and display the result. This simpler formula uses the sum() function, which totals the values in a range of cells. Some functions also provide the ability to perform calculations that have no operator like + or -; the trigonometric functions are examples of these: sin() represents the trigonometric Sine function; cos(), the cosine function; sinh(), the hyperbolic sine; and cosh(), the hyperbolic cosine.

A spreadsheet program such as OpenOffice.org Calc includes hundreds of functions that can be used to perform many different types of calculations in user formulas. You can get a listing of the available functions in OpenOffice.org Calc and some information on how to use each of them by choosing Insert, Function List and then choosing All from the drop-down list that appears, as shown in Figure 9.9.

**FIGURE 9.9**
The Functions sidebar enables you to search through and find descriptions of each function in the list of OpenOffice.org functions. Click the small right-arrow icon or choose Insert, Function List again to hide the sidebar.

Select All to display all functions

Select function

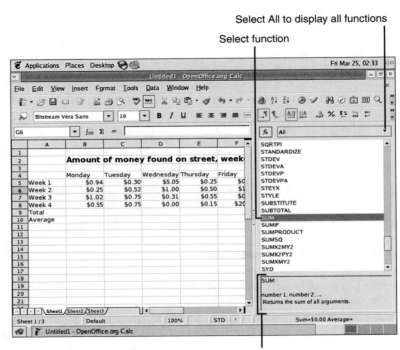

Function description shown here

To use a function such as sum() within a formula, follow these steps:

1. Type an equal sign (=) to indicate to OpenOffice.org Calc that you are about to enter a formula.

2. Enter the name of the function and a left parenthesis. Then select a cell or a range of cells upon which the function is to act by clicking or clicking and dragging, as shown in Figure 9.10.

3. Close the function by entering a closing parenthesis.

4. After you type the complete formula, press Enter to accept the formula and calculate the result.

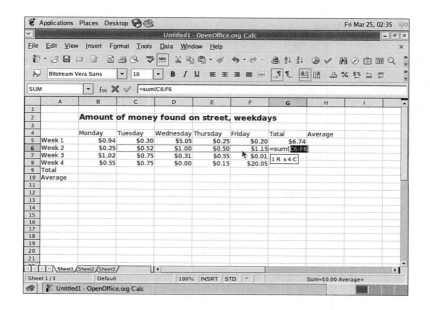

**FIGURE 9.10**
Entering a function as part of a formula. Enter the name of the function, in this case, sum(, and then select a range of cells using the pointing device.

Our sample spreadsheet also includes a number of cells that are designed to hold an average of the amount of found money for a specific day of the week or a specific week of the month. The average() function, which calculates an average over a range of cells, can be used to fill these cells. Figure 9.11 shows the spreadsheet with a few more formulas entered. Remember that because these cells were previously formatted for currency, all the values now appear in dollars and cents.

## Copying Formulas

It is quite common for a single formula to be used over and over, needing to be adjusted only to account for differences in the position of its cell in the spreadsheet. This is the case in our sample spreadsheet: Most of the total and average cells use the same basic calculations (sum or average) over and over again. In cases like this, you can copy a formula from one cell to another, and OpenOffice.org Calc automatically adjusts the cell references to compensate.

In our sample spreadsheet, for example, the formula in C9 is essentially the same formula used in B9, except that Calc adds values in column C instead of column B. This is an ideal candidate for formula copying.

To copy a formula, follow these steps:

**1.** Select the cell containing the formula you want to copy.

**2.** Choose Edit, Copy to copy the selected formula.

**FIGURE 9.11**
The sample spreadsheet with a few more formulas filled in.

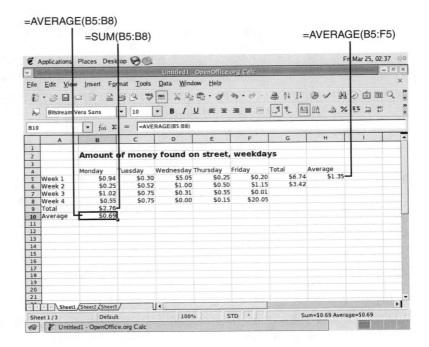

**3.** Select the cell or range of cells where you would like to use the same formula.

**4.** Choose Edit, Paste to copy the formula to the cells; the same formula appears in each destination cell, but with adjustments for position in the spreadsheet.

Figure 9.12 shows the result of copying the formula in B9 and pasting it into a selected range of cells from C9 through F9. Each cell contains the correct calculation for its column.

Figure 9.13 shows the sample spreadsheet completed, by following these steps:

**1.** The average formula in B10 was copied to the range of cells from C10 through F10.

**2.** The total formula in G6 was copied to the range of cells from G7 through G8.

**3.** The average formula in H5 was copied to the range of cells from H6 through H8.

# Printing, Saving, and Opening Spreadsheets

The steps involved in printing, saving, and loading spreadsheets in OpenOffice.org Calc are nearly identical to the steps involved in printing, saving, and loading word processing documents in OpenOffice.org Writer.

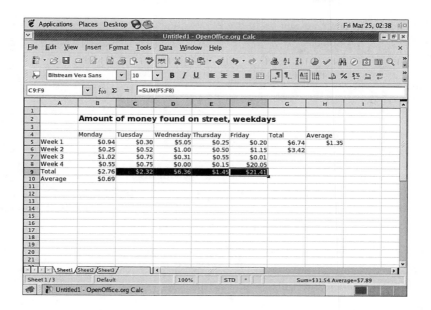

**FIGURE 9.12**
The formula from B9 has been copied to cells C9 through F9.

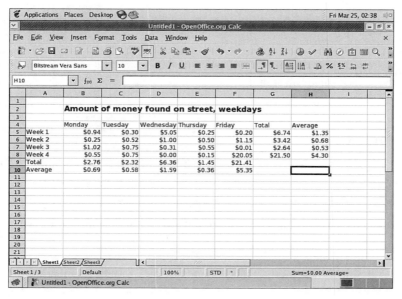

**FIGURE 9.13**
The sample spreadsheet is now complete; average money findings and total money findings have been computed by day and by week.

To print a spreadsheet, choose File, Print and click OK in the Print dialog box.

To print only a range of cells that you select, follow these steps:

**1.** Select the range of cells that you want to print.

**2.** Choose File, Print to display the Print dialog box.

**3.** Choose the Selection option in the Print Range area of the dialog box.

**4.** Click OK to print your selection.

To save a spreadsheet, follow these steps:

**1.** Choose File, Save.

**2.** When the Save As dialog box is displayed, select a location and enter a name for your file.

**3.** If you want to be able to exchange the file with users of MS Office, be sure to select one of the Microsoft Excel formats from the File Type drop-down list, visible when you select Browse for Other Folders. If you want to protect your file with a password, check the Save With password box.

**4.** Click the Save button to save your file.

To load a saved spreadsheet, follow these steps:

**1.** Choose File, Open.

**2.** When the Open dialog box is displayed, browse to the location of the file that you want to open.

**3.** Double-click the file's name. A new OpenOffice.org Calc window appears with the loaded spreadsheet in it.

# Summary

In this chapter, you learned to use the basic features of another commonly used OpenOffice.org application, OpenOffice.org Calc—a full-featured and powerful electronic spreadsheet. You have now learned to do the following:

▶ Navigate an electronic spreadsheet and identify and select specific cells

▶ Enter text labels into cells and adjust their appearance

▶ Enter numeric values into cells and change their format for more attractive output

▶ Enter formulas to perform calculations based on numeric data in other cells in the spreadsheet

▶ Find and use functions within your formulas

▶ Copy formulas from one cell to another cell or a range of cells to save time and effort

You have also learned to save your work in OpenOffice.org Calc, load existing OpenOffice.org Calc files, and print the documents you created using OpenOffice.org Calc.

# Q&A

**Q** *Can I mix numbers, cell references, operators like + and -, and functions in a single formula in Calc?*

**A** Yes. In formulas, you can mix numeric elements, operators, and functions in any order. For example, the following formula is valid and works as expected:

```
=sin(F26/100+G26*1.1)+10
```

**Q** *I've been told that electronic spreadsheets can also be used to perform some database functions. How can I learn more about this?*

**A** If you're familiar with database concepts, you can use a spreadsheet like OpenOffice Calc to manage tables of data for you. In database terms, each row is a record, and each column in a given row is a field in the record. Data can then be sorted or filtered for display based on the values of fields. For more information, choose Help, OpenOffice.org Help to open the help system, then read about the Sort and Filter functions in the Data menu.

# Workshop

The Workshop is designed to help you anticipate possible questions, review what you've learned, and begin learning how to put your knowledge into practice.

## Quiz

**1.** How do you begin a formula in Calc?

**2.** How do you format a range of numeric data cells as currency in Calc?

**3.** How do you use a simple function such as sum() or average() within a formula in Calc?

## Answers

**1.** Click the cell you want and then type the equal sign.

**2.** Select the range of cells with your pointing device and then click the currency format button in the Formatting bar.

3. Enter the name of the function by hand followed by the left parenthesis. Then select the range of cells to include in the function's calculation using your pointing device. Finally, close the function by entering a right parenthesis.

## Activities

1. Try using Calc for a practical calculation of some sort, such as creating a budget or balancing a checkbook.

2. See what happens when negative numbers are entered into Calc cells.

# CHAPTER 10

# Creating Presentations with OpenOffice.org Impress

## What You'll Learn in This Chapter:

▶ How to launch the OpenOffice.org Impress application
▶ How to create a new presentation
▶ How to include various types of data in your slides
▶ How to play back a slide show

In this chapter, you learn to create informative and colorful presentations using the OpenOffice.org Impress application, a presentations manager similar to Microsoft PowerPoint.

## Understanding Electronic Presentations

Whiteboard, blackboard, poster, and slide presentations have been mainstays in the business and education worlds for decades, if not longer. The presentation of various kinds of data as a series of easy-to-read, visual summaries and diagrams remains an excellent way to share information with an audience.

In the computer era, applications called presentation managers have been developed to facilitate just this kind of educational presentation. Presentation managers include applications like OpenOffice.org Impress and Microsoft PowerPoint. By providing simple tools for creating visually appealing presentations, these applications help you to create a series of slides (similar in concept to slides in a slide show of photographs) that can be shown to an audience in order to convey important information.

Slides can contain information of various kinds, including bullet lists, images and photos, charts and graphs, and numeric data. After you create and title a series of slides, you can use your PC to play back this "slide show" in front of an audience.

Because you can control the order in which the slides are shown, the content of each slide, and the transitions between slides, presentations created with applications like OpenOffice.org Impress can be seen as ideal supplements for use in public speaking engagements or any engagement at which you need to present information visually and efficiently to an audience.

# Launching OpenOffice.org Impress

To start OpenOffice.org Impress, choose Applications, Office, OpenOffice.org Impress, as shown in Figure 10.1.

**FIGURE 10.1**
You can start OpenOffice.org Impress by visiting the Applications menu.

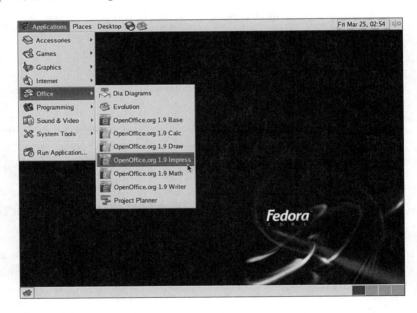

If no other OpenOffice.org applications are running, the splash logo appears while the program loads, and then the Presentation Wizard window opens, as shown in Figure 10.2.

Because the goal of this chapter is to learn how to use OpenOffice.org Impress to create a new presentation from scratch, you should select Empty Presentation in the Presentation Wizard and click the Create button to indicate that you want to create a new presentation. The main Impress window opens, as shown in Figure 10.3.

Select for an empty presentation

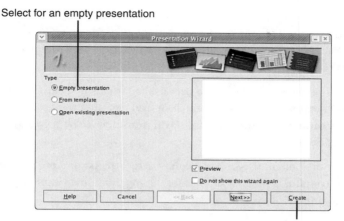

Click to create new presentation

**FIGURE 10.2**
Impress asks whether you want to begin with an empty presentation, start from a template, or open an existing presentation. Select Empty presentation and click Create to create a new presentation.

List of slides          Current slide          Slide types

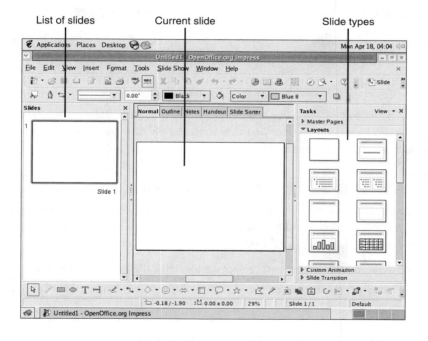

**FIGURE 10.3**
The main Impress window displays three panels of information: a list of slides on the left, the current slide in the middle, and slide types on the right.

You should become familiar with a number of tools and elements in the OpenOffice.org Impress window as you create presentations:

▶ The current slide is the large white area shown in the center of the window. Each slide is like a small canvas that you can fill with text, images, graphs, and other types of data, using the tools around the edges of the application window and the tools in the application menus.

▶ A slide index is shown just to the right of the current slide area. As you add slides to your presentation, each slide you add will be shown in the slide index. You can make any slide in your presentation your current slide by clicking on it.

▶ The Tasks panel, which displays a list of slide formats by default, is used to change the properties of the current slide. You can alter things like a slide's basic appearance and the way that it will transition to the next slide in the presentation when told to do so.

▶ The drawing toolbar, shown horizontally across the bottom of the application window, contains a number of tools for adding diagrams, graphics, charts, and text to the slides you create.

# Creating Your First Presentation

The easiest way to learn about OpenOffice.org Impress is to create a simple presentation. In the following sections, you create a simple four-slide presentation with one bullet list, one graphic, one pie chart, and one slide that combines all these elements. You then learn how to play back the slide show for an audience.

Because the OpenOffice.org Impress application begins with a blank slide, you are ready to begin working on your first slide immediately after you launch the OpenOffice.org Impress application.

## Selecting a Slide Layout and Design

Your first slide begins as a blank white canvas, ready to be filled. Plain white is a little boring, though. Before adding any text or graphics to a slide, you usually begin by selecting a basic design for it from a list of visually pleasing templates.

To select a design for the currently selected slide, click the Master Pages option in the Tasks pane. A number of potential slide designs are displayed, as shown in Figure 10.4.

*By the Way*

> ### Does Your Impress Window Look Different?
> If the Slides pane, the Tasks pane, or any other element of your Impress window looks different from the one shown in Figure 10.3, click on the View menu and ensure that the Normal, Task Pane, Slide Pane, and Status Bar items are checked, and that the rest of the items aren't.

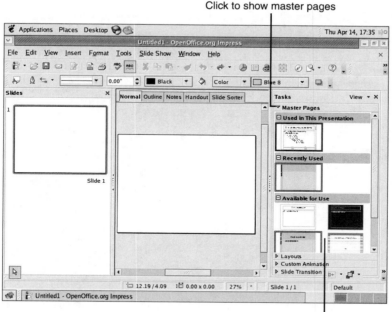

Click to show master pages

Select a master page

**FIGURE 10.4**
The Master Pages list is used to choose the basic visual appearance for slides in this presentation.

You'll see three sections in the Master Pages list:

► The section titled Used in This Presentation shows the master page currently used for your slides.

► The section titled Recently Used shows master pages that you have most recently chosen.

► The section titled Available for Use lists the master pages that you can select.

Click on one of the master pages from the Available for Use section to indicate that slides in this presentation should have the same basic visual appearance. The view of the current slide will change to show the new appearance you've selected, as shown in Figure 10.5.

Now that you have selected a design for your slide, it's time to select a layout to help structure and organize the information that your slide will contain. To select a layout, click on Layouts in the Task pane. A list of common slide layouts is displayed, as shown in Figure 10.6.

**FIGURE 10.5**
After you click on the master page of your choice, the slide takes on the appearance you've selected.

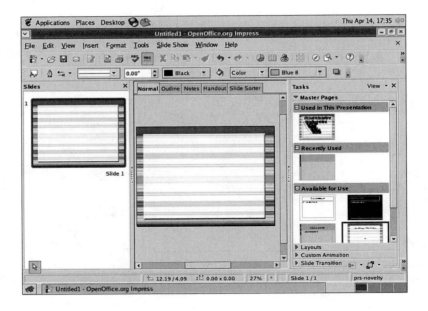

Click to show layouts ⌐ ⌐Select a slide layout

**FIGURE 10.6**
After clicking Layouts in the Task pane, you can select a layout for the information that your slide will contain.

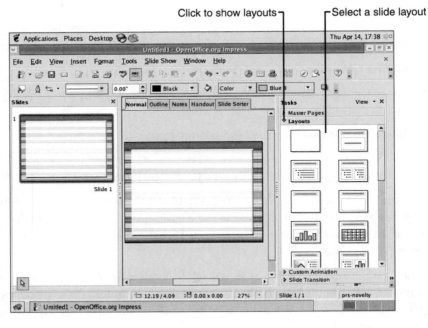

Our first slide is going to be an informative bullet list—mostly text with a title at the top—so for this slide, click the layout that looks like a bullet list with a text title at the top. The resulting layout is applied to the current slide, as shown in Figure 10.7.

Click to work on an outline ┐    ┌ Click to enter a title

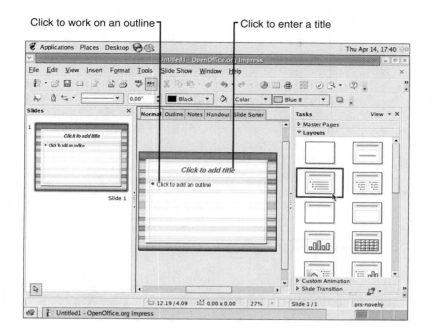

**FIGURE 10.7**
When you click on a layout, it is applied to the current slide. You can then begin to add information.

Notice that the slide now has two general parts: a title area with the text `Click to add title` in large, bold letters suitable for a slide title, and a body area with the text `Click to add an outline` in a smaller font, next to a bullet graphic. Your slide is now ready for use.

## Filling Text Areas in Slides

It's time to add text to both of the text areas on the slide. Begin by clicking the text `Click to add title`. A highlight box is immediately displayed around the area, and the words `Click to add title` disappear, replaced by a blinking cursor. Type **My First Slideshow**, as shown in Figure 10.8.

Notice the squares around the edge of the text box shown in Figure 10.8 (they appear green onscreen). These squares are resize handles, similar in function to the resize handles on application windows that you learned about in Chapter 4, "Introducing the Fedora Core 4 Desktop." By clicking resize handles and dragging them, you can resize and reshape the text and graphic boxes—such as this title text box—that you encounter in OpenOffice.org Impress.

After typing a title for the slide, click anywhere on the slide outside the text box to confirm your new title. The text box outline disappears, leaving the new title you've typed in place.

Text box

**FIGURE 10.8**
After you click
Click to add
title, a text
box and blinking
cursor are
displayed so
that you can
type your own
title for the
slide.

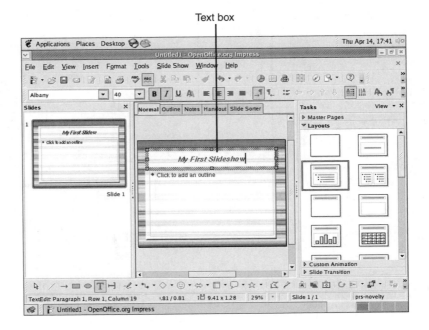

**By the Way**

## Seeing Squiggly Lines?

If you're following along, you may have seen a squiggly line appear underneath the word Slideshow. As was the case with OpenOffice.org Writer, Impress will underline words that it thinks may be misspelled.

If, as is the case in this example, the word isn't actually misspelled, simply ignore the underline; it won't appear when you present your slideshow—it's only visible while you're editing your slides.

Now it's time to add text to the bullet list that forms the body of the slide. Click Click to add an outline to display a text box for the body of the slide, as shown in Figure 10.9.

Because this new text box is an outline or bullet list, the cursor is placed next to a bullet graphic. Each time you press Enter as you enter text, the cursor moves to a new line and a new bullet is added to the list.

To increase the indent level of a new bullet, press your Tab key. To decrease the indent level of a new, indented bullet, hold down your Shift key and press the Tab key. Impress will automatically size and position your text in the most visually pleasing way possible.

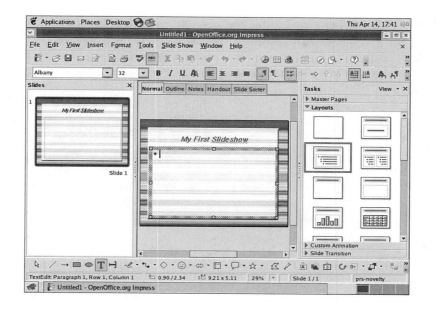

**FIGURE 10.9**
After you click
`Click to add
an outline`,
another text box
is displayed,
this time for
the body of
the slide.

Add the text shown in Figure 10.10 now. Remember to use the Tab and Shift+Tab keys as appropriate to match the indentation in the figure as well.

Press Shift-Tab to unindent

Press Tab to indent

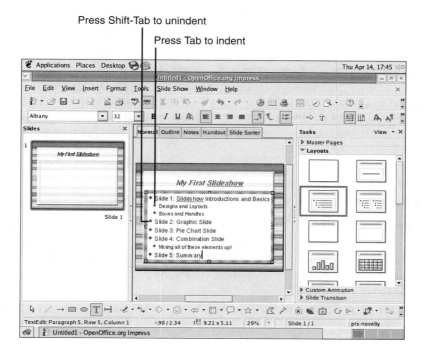

**FIGURE 10.10**
Adding text to
the outline is
easy! Press
Enter to start a
new bullet, Tab
to indent a
bullet after
you've created
it, or Shift+Tab
to unindent
once again.

After you finish entering the text shown in Figure 10.10, click anywhere in the slide outside the active text box to accept the changes (new text) you just entered. The finished slide, without a surrounding text box, is shown in Figure 10.11. This is a miniature sample of what the slide will look like when you use it in your presentation.

**FIGURE 10.11**
Your first slide is now complete; you have added both your own title and your own text content.

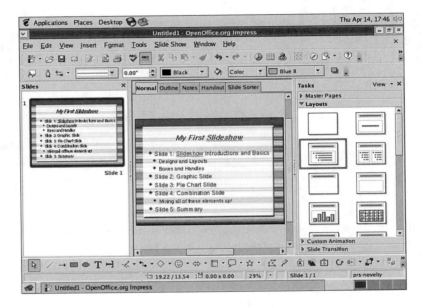

**By the Way**

### What If You Want to Edit the Text Again?

Even though no text boxes are visible in Figure 10.11 and no Click to insert... text can be seen either, you can still edit the text you've entered if you want to make changes to a slide. Simply click the text you want to change, and the text box editing cursor reappears. You can then make changes to the text you've already entered in a slide.

## Adding a Slide to Your Presentation

With the first slide in your presentation complete, it's time to add another blank canvas so that you can begin work on your second slide. To add another slide to your presentation, right-click in an empty area of the Slides pane and select New Slide from the context menu that appears. A new slide will be created and added to the slide index in the Slides pane, and the slide itself will be shown in the center of the Impress window, as shown in Figure 10.12.

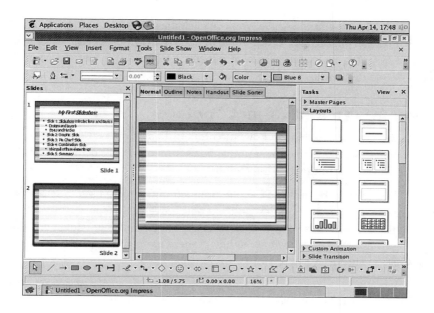

**FIGURE 10.12**
After you right-click in the Slide pane and select New Slide from the context menu, a new slide is created.

Though you now see a new slide, no layout is shown for it. Select a new layout for the slide by clicking on the Title Only layout, as shown in Figure 10.13.

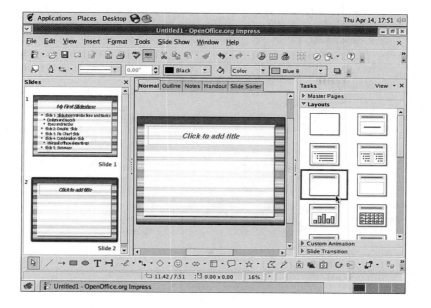

**FIGURE 10.13**
Click on the Title Only layout type (the type that shows a title and nothing else) to make the new slide a title-only slide.

Just as you did with your first slide, you can click the `Click to add title` text to display a text box and cursor where you can add your own title to the slide. Title this slide **Impress Supports Images** and then click outside the text box to save your new title to the slide.

## Using Image and Object Tools

Now it's time to start adding your own decorations to an Impress slide. For this presentation, it's enough to draw a simple figure using the tools across the bottom of the Impress window in the drawing toolbar.

The first six icons in the drawing toolbar, from left to right, are used to select tools to draw lines, arrows, circles, squares, and text, respectively (see Figure 10.14). The next eight icons in the drawing toolbar represent small groups of related drawing tools. Click on the down arrow next to any of them to open a submenu showing those tools, as shown in Figure 10.14.

**FIGURE 10.14**
Click on the icons to the left to select a simple drawing tool, or click on the small down arrows to select from a list of related drawing tools.

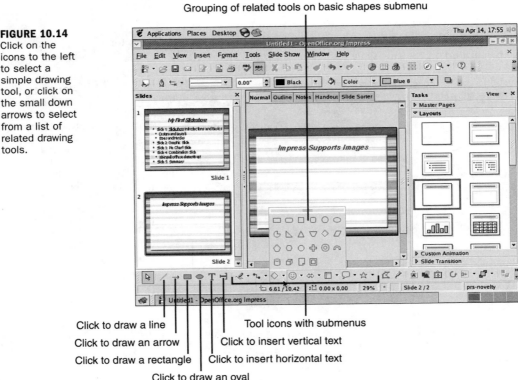

Grouping of related tools on basic shapes submenu

Click to draw a line
Click to draw an arrow
Click to draw a rectangle
Click to draw an oval
Tool icons with submenus
Click to insert vertical text
Click to insert horizontal text

## Want to Know What Each Icon Does?

You can find out what each icon on the drawing toolbar does, and what the icons in each of the drawing toolbar submenus do, simply by letting your mouse hover over them. When you let your mouse hover over an icon without clicking on it, a description of the tool will appear in a little box next to your mouse pointer.

Each icon in a tool submenu is a visual representation of the type of object that can be drawn using the tool in question. For the purposes of this introduction to Impress, let's draw a little house. Begin by clicking the down arrow next to the submenu icon that looks like a diamond to display the list of basic shapes (shown in Figure 10.14). In this submenu, select the icon that looks like a square; then select the color Orange 4 from the Color drop-down list, as shown in Figure 10.15.

Click to select square tool

Click to select color

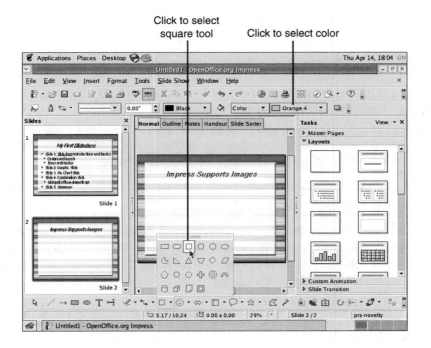

**FIGURE 10.15**
Select the square from the basic shapes submenu. Afterward, select Orange 4 from the Color drop-down list.

Click and hold your mouse button over the slide and drag your pointer to display a box that indicates where the resulting square will be placed. When you have positioned the box where you want the resulting shape to appear, release the mouse button to display the shape you've drawn, as shown in Figure 10.16.

**FIGURE 10.16**
If you are unsatisfied with your shape, adjust its size by clicking and dragging any of the resize handles; adjust the placement of your shape simply by clicking and dragging it.

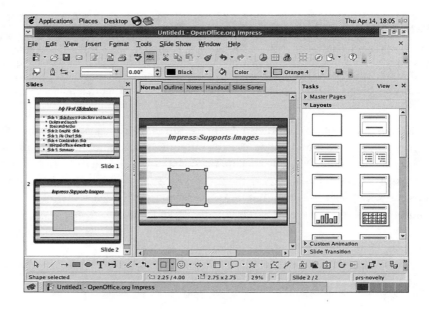

*By the Way*

## What If You Just Want to Try Again?

If you're not quite happy with your cube but just want to try creating it again rather than editing it using the resize handles, simply choose Edit, Undo from the menu bar near the top of the Impress window. After the cube disappears, you can give it another shot.

Now that you have the base of your house looking just the way you want it, it's time to create a roof for it. Select the isosceles triangle tool icon (just to the lower right of the square tool shown in Figure 10.16) and use the tool to draw a little triangle over the top of the cube. You might need to use the resize handles to move your triangle around a little bit before your drawing begins to look like a house, as shown in Figure 10.17.

Finally, use some of the other tools from the basic shapes menu and other colors from the Color drop-down list to add a front door, sun, and front lawn to the house to complete the illustration for Slide 2. Follow these steps to arrive at the house image shown in Figure 10.18:

▶ To draw a sun, use circle tool from the basic shapes submenu; then select the color Pale yellow.

▶ To draw a front door, use the rectangle tool from the basic shapes submenu; then select the color Bordeaux.

▶ To draw a patch of lawn, use the parallelogram tool from the basic shapes submenu; then select the color Green 8.

Use resize handles to resize

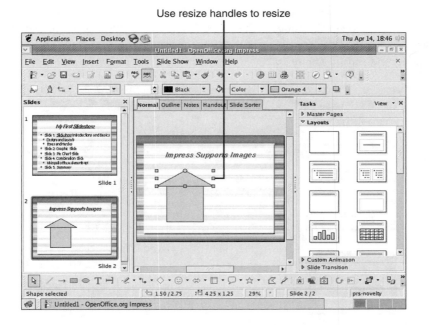

**FIGURE 10.17**
After you add a triangle with the isosceles triangle tool and size and place it carefully, an illustration of a house begins to take shape.

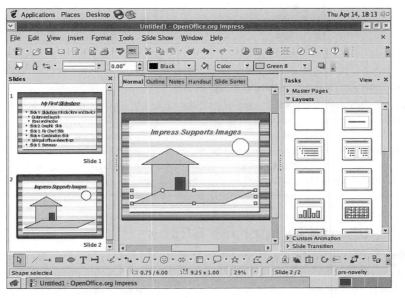

**FIGURE 10.18**
Using the circle tool, the rectangle tool, and the parallelogram tool, you can add a sun, a front door, and a patch of lawn to the house illustration.

Now, to make the lawn look nice, you need to make the house sit on top of the lawn, and not vice versa. To lower the new parallelogram so that it is obscured by the house, instead of the house being obscured by it, right-click it. In the context menu that appears, select Arrange, Send to Back, as shown in Figure 10.19. Afterward, be sure to click outside the shape anywhere on the slide to remove the resize handles. You can see the results of these operations and the final appearance of the second slide in Figure 10.20.

**FIGURE 10.19**
Select Arrange from the context menu to lower or raise objects on your slide in relation to one another.

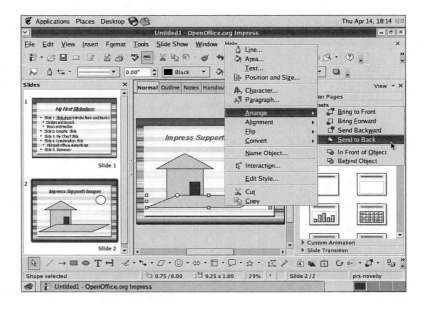

## You Can Edit Any Object, Any Time

*Did you Know?*

If you decide that you want to edit any object on a slide, you can do so at will, even if you've added several objects since then.

To edit an object other than the current one, click the Select tool (the icon that looks like a white arrow near the top of the main toolbar) and then click the object that you want to edit. Resize handles appear. You can then resize, move, raise, lower, or change other properties of the object at will.

# Using Charts in Impress Slides

It's time to create the third slide, a simple chart that Impress will draw for you. To make an empty slide to hold our new chart, right-click the Slide pane somewhere after the second slide and select New Slide from the context menu. Then choose the Title, Chart layout from the list of available layouts, as shown in Figure 10.21.

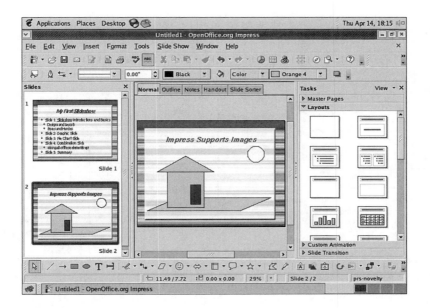

**FIGURE 10.20**
The image in
the completed
Slide 2 was
created entirely
by using the
drawing tools
in Impress.

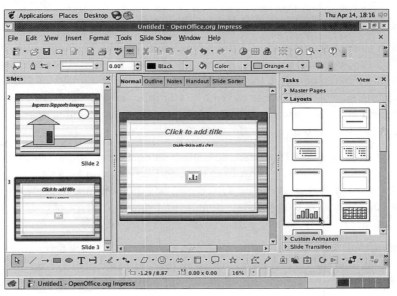

**FIGURE 10.21**
For our third
slide, select
the layout that
contains a title
and a chart.

Click the `Click to add title` text and enter the title **and charts** in the text box.
When you are done, click outside the text box to save your changes to the slide, as
shown in Figure 10.22.

FIGURE 10.22
The new slide
has been titled;
you can now
add a chart by
double-clicking
the area
beneath the
title labeled
Double-click
to add a
chart.

Double-click to add a chart

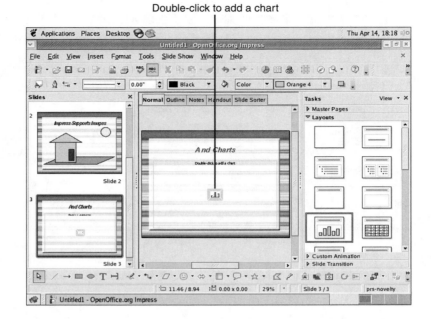

To add a chart to the third slide in this presentation, double-click in the area with the text Double-click to add a chart. A premade chart appears in the space, containing meaningless data (depending on the size of your display, the Slide and Tasks panes may be temporarily hidden). To edit the chart to reflect your own data and desired format, right-click the chart to display a context menu of operations that can be performed on it (see Figure 10.23).

Begin by selecting Chart Type from the context menu. For this slide, create a pie chart. To do so, select the Pies type from the Chart Type box and the Offset 1 variant from the Variants box in the Chart Type dialog box that appears, as shown in Figure 10.24. Click OK to apply your changes and change the type of chart to a pie chart.

Now that your chart appears in the slide as a pie chart, right-click again and select Chart Data from the context menu to display the Chart Data dialog box, which looks like a little Calc spreadsheet, as shown in Figure 10.25.

As you create and edit your own charts using your own data, you need to adjust the size of the spreadsheets in rows and columns. Across the top of the Chart Data dialog box is a row of icons that allow you to manipulate the chart as you enter data. The first four icons are the most important. From left to right, they are

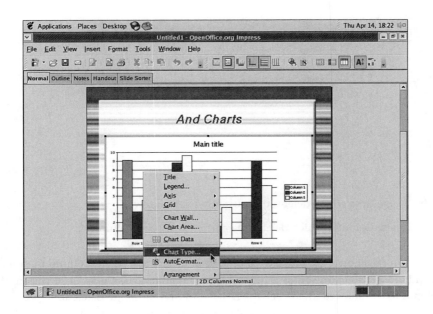

**FIGURE 10.23**
The chart that is inserted by default contains meaningless data. By right-clicking the chart, you can access a context menu that allows you to customize it.

Select chart type

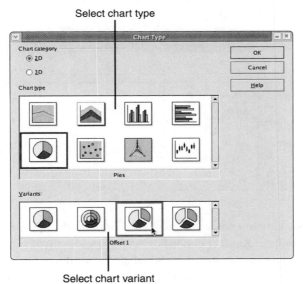

Select chart variant

**FIGURE 10.24**
Right-click the chart and select Chart Type from the context menu to display the Chart Type dialog box. Then select Pies as a type and Offset 1 as a variant.

▶ Insert Row, which inserts an empty row before the currently selected row

▶ Insert Column, which inserts an empty column before the currently selected column

**FIGURE 10.25**
Select Chart
Data from the
chart's context
menu to display
the Chart Data
dialog box,
which looks
like a little
spreadsheet.

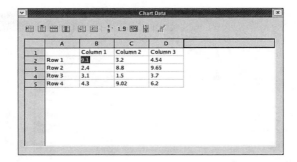

▶ Delete Row, which deletes the currently selected row

▶ Delete Column, which deletes the currently selected column

Because a pie chart uses only one column of data, use the Delete Column button to get rid of the two extra columns in the Chart Data dialog box now. First, click in the column to be removed; then click the Delete Column button to delete it. Repeat the process until there is only one data column (column containing numbers) left. Then enter the numeric and label data shown in Figure 10.26.

**FIGURE 10.26**
Adjust the num-
ber of rows and
columns to suit
your dataset;
then change
the labels for
each row and
column and
enter your data
as necessary.

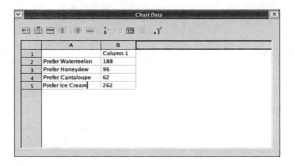

After you're done entering data, click the Close button in the upper right to close the Chart Data dialog box. Another dialog box is displayed, notifying you that new chart data has been entered and asking whether you want to apply this new data to the chart you've created. Click Yes to do so now, and the chart on Slide 3 is rebuilt to reflect the new data you've entered. Finally, double-click Main Title in the chart and enter a more appropriate title, as shown in Figure 10.27. When you're done, click the slide outside the chart area to finalize it and restore the Slide and Task panes if they were hidden.

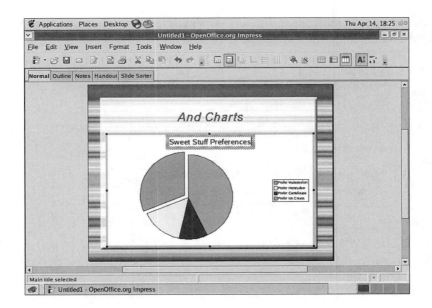

**FIGURE 10.27**
After you apply the new data, double-click the chart's title area to enter a more appropriate title.

## Using Combination Slides

For the final slide in this presentation, it's time to mix all the earlier elements you've learned to use together into a single, mixed slide. Create another new slide by scrolling to the bottom of the slides list in the Slide pane, right-clicking, and selecting New Slide. When the new slide appears, select 2 Objects, Text layout from the Task pane, as shown in Figure 10.28.

Using the knowledge you've gained in creating earlier slides, edit the title and text in the slide's text box so that the slide appears similar to what you see in Figure 10.29.

Now double-click in the top object box, where you see Double-click to add an object. When the Insert OLE Object dialog box appears, select OpenOffice.org Chart and click OK. A new chart appears in the box. Because you already know how to fill charts with your own data and labels, we won't bother to edit this chart any further. Click outside the box to restore the slide view and add additional objects.

Finally, single-click in the lower object box so that green resize handles appear around it. Then press the Backspace key or choose Edit, Cut from the menu bar near the top of the application window to remove the object box, leaving empty space behind in its place. Spend a few moments using the drawing tools in the main toolbar to fill this empty space with any sketch you feel like creating. See Figure 10.30 for one example of a completed final slide.

**FIGURE 10.28**
Create a fourth new slide at the end of the slides list; then choose the 2 Objects, Text layout for it.

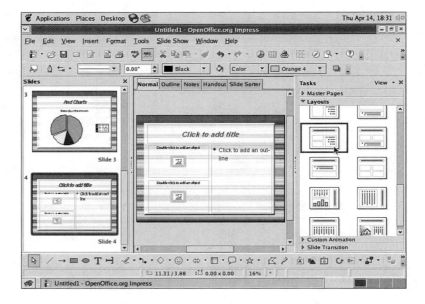

**FIGURE 10.29**
An informative title and additional text have been added to the final slide.

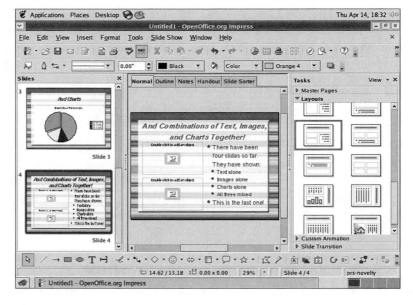

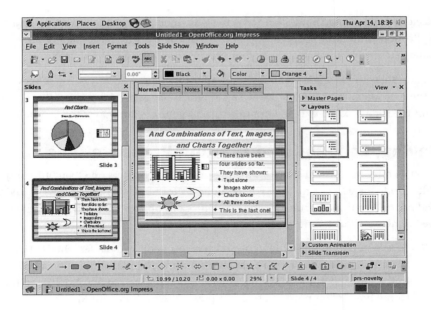

**FIGURE 10.30**
The final slide mixes several different types of information together in a nice layout.

---

### What If You Created Slides in the Wrong Order?

If you want to change the order in which your slides will ultimately play, you can easily arrange them by choosing View, Slide Sorter from the menu bar near the top of the Impress application window.

The Slides View shows all your slides in miniature in a grid, in order from left to right and top to bottom. You can then drag and drop your slides into place in any order you desire using your mouse.

After you're done rearranging your slides, select View, Normal to return and edit more slides.

*By the Way*

# Working with Your Presentation

Now that you have finished creating your first presentation, it's time to learn how to play it back one slide at a time as a slide show, save it for future use, load a presentation that you've saved so that you can use it, and print a presentation.

## Playing a Presentation as a Slide Show

To play back a presentation as a slide show, select Slide 1 in the Slide pane or select the slide where you would like the show to start (remember to use the arrow buttons to scroll the tabs if you can't see the tab you want). Then, when the first slide is selected, choose Slide Show, Slide Show from the menu bar at the top of the Impress application window or press your F5 key. When you start the slide show, your display clears and the first slide of your presentation fills the entire screen.

In Slide Show mode, click the mouse button or press the right-arrow key to proceed to the next slide. Press the left-arrow key to return to the previous slide. When you want the slide show to end or want to return to your desktop, press the Escape key.

## Saving, Loading, and Printing Presentations

If you've already finished studying the preceding two chapters on OpenOffice.org Writer and OpenOffice.org Calc, you're probably familiar with the process of saving, loading, and printing documents in OpenOffice.org applications. Just in case you need it, here's a quick refresher:

▶ To save a presentation after you finish creating all your slides, choose File, Save As from the menu bar near the top of the Impress application window. In the dialog box that appears, enter a name for the presentation file in the Name box. If you need to use an Impress presentation with Microsoft PowerPoint later, be sure to click Browse for other folders and then select a Microsoft PowerPoint format from the file type drop-down list before saving.

▶ To load a presentation that you've previously saved, choose File, Open from the menu bar near the top of the Impress application window. Use the file dialog box to locate the presentation you want to load; then double-click it. After the presentation is loaded, you can play it back as a slide show by choosing Slide Show, Slide Show from the menu bar or pressing the F5 key.

▶ To print the slides from an Impress presentation, choose File, Print from the menu bar near the top of the Impress application window. Click OK to print all the slides in the presentation. To print only certain slides, select Pages from the Print Range area and enter a list of comma-separated (for individual pages) or dash-separated (for page ranges) slide numbers into the entry box. For example, entering **3-5,8,10** would print the slides currently in positions 3, 4, 5, 8, and 10.

## Summary

In this chapter, you learned to use the basic features of OpenOffice.org Impress to create a presentation. You learned to

▶ Apply designs and layouts to slides in a presentation

▶ Create slides that contain text and outlines

▶ Create slides that contain drawings and images

▶ Create slides that contain charts for which you've supplied numerical data

▶ Create slides that contain some combination of these elements

▶ Re-order slides in a presentation

You also learned to save your work, load existing files, and print slides from the presentations you created.

# Q&A

**Q** *Is there a way to add existing images (for example, GIF or JPEG images) to a slide?*

**A** Yes. In the Normal view, with a slide selected, choose Insert, Picture, From File from the menu bar near the top of the Impress application window. In the file dialog box that appears, you can insert most common image formats. The image appears on the slide surrounded by resize handles, which you can then use to move and resize the image to fit your needs for the slide.

**Q** *Can I make slide shows that have fun and interesting transitions between slides, such as fades and wipes?*

**A** Yes. You can display a list of selectable slide transitions for the current slide by clicking Slide Transition near the bottom of the Tasks pane in the Normal view.

**Q** *How do I delete a slide?*

**A** Right-click on the slide that you want to delete in the Slide pane; then choose Delete from the context menu.

**Q** *Is there a way to make a self-executing slide show using Impress in Linux— that is, a slide show that can run without needing to be loaded into the Impress application first?*

**A** Unfortunately, no, although you can export your slide show to an Adobe Acrobat (PDF) or World Wide Web (HTML) document by choosing File, Export from the menu bar.

# Workshop

The Workshop is designed to help you anticipate possible questions, review what you've learned, and begin learning how to put your knowledge into practice.

## Quiz

1. How do you change the size or position of an object in a slide?

2. How do you change the order of the slides in the presentation?

3. How do you start the slide show, and how do you navigate in it?

## Answers

1. Click the Select tool (the white arrow icon) near the absolute left of the drawing toolbar across the bottom of the Impress window. Then single-click on the object you want to edit. When the green resize handles appear, you can use them to resize the object, or you can click the object and drag it to reposition it.

2. The easiest way to change slide order is to choose View, Slide Sorter from the menu bar. Choosing this option shows you all your slides in miniature in a grid, where you can drag them around into whatever order you prefer. When you're done, select View, Normal to return to the editor.

3. To start a slide show, select Slide Show, Slide Show from the menu bar or press the F5 key. In the slide show, click your mouse button or press the right-arrow key to proceed to the next slide. Press the left-arrow key to return to the previous slide. Press the Escape key to leave the slide show and return to Impress.

## Activities

1. Explore more of the drawing tools in the main toolbar to familiarize yourself with the task of creating illustrations in Impress.

2. Add a few more slides to the show you created in this chapter using some of the layouts you didn't use, just to experiment.

3. Rearrange the order of your slides or change some of the transitions between them (see the Q&A item earlier); then play back the slide show to see how it changes.

# CHAPTER 11

# Browsing the Web with Firefox

---

## *What You'll Learn in This Chapter:*

▶ How to launch the Firefox Web browser
▶ How to visit websites using their web address or URL
▶ How to bookmark your favorite websites for easy retrieval
▶ How to organize your collection of bookmarks

This chapter is designed to help you become proficient in accessing the World Wide Web on the Linux desktop.

If you are already familiar with use of the Firefox web browser, either with Linux or another platform such as Windows or Mac OS, you will find that you already know most of what is presented here. If this is true in your case, feel free to skip this chapter and move on to Chapter 12, "Managing Email with Evolution."

## Introducing Firefox

By far, the most visible use for computer networking technology worldwide is for access to the many sites and pages of the World Wide Web. It is widely known that the most common platform for accessing the Web is the Internet Explorer web browser. Although Internet Explorer is available for both Windows and Mac OS, Microsoft has chosen not to produce a version of Internet Explorer for Linux.

Linux web users have always been supported instead by Netscape Corporation and the Netscape web browser. In 1998, Netscape Corporation made the Netscape web browser an open-source product, and the Mozilla project was born. Firefox is a modern, feature-full, standards-compliant web browser created by the Mozilla project, and is now the primary platform for browsing the Web on the Linux desktop.

## Launching the Firefox Browser

To launch the Firefox web browser, choose Applications, Internet, Firefox Web Browser or click the web browser icon on the menubar. The icon appears as a picture of a computer mouse circling the globe.

# Browsing the Web with Firefox

After the Firefox web browser is loaded, a new Firefox browser application window appears on your desktop showing the default Fedora Core information page, as shown in Figure 11.1.

**FIGURE 11.1**
Clicking the web browser icon opens the Firefox web browser on the desktop.

Each item shown in Figure 11.1 performs an important function while you are using Firefox:

▶ The URL bar shows the address of the currently displayed website and enables you to enter addresses for new websites that are to be displayed.

▶ The Status bar shows the progress Firefox is making in loading a new web page.

▶ The Personal toolbar contains a list of folders and bookmarks to enable you to more easily collect and visit your favorite websites.

▶ The currently displayed web page is the large area of the application window in which you can interact with the site you're currently visiting.

## Visiting a Website

To visit a new website, move your pointer so that it is inside the URL bar and double-click. The currently displayed URL address is highlighted. After the current URL is highlighted, begin typing the URL you want to visit; the original URL disappears as you enter the new address. Press Enter when you finish typing the URL. Figure 11.2 shows Firefox displaying the URL http://www.yahoo.com/, otherwise known as Yahoo!, one of the most popular destinations on the Web.

**FIGURE 11.2**
After you enter the new URL, http://www.yahoo.com/, Firefox loads and displays the page.

---

**By the Way**

## What Is a URL?

*URL* stands for **uniform resource locator**; a URL is more commonly known simply as an **address**. You know an Internet address or URL because it begins with a word followed by a colon and two slashes, like http:// for websites or ftp:// for file transfer protocol archives that hold downloadable files.

> **Increase the Screen Area Used by Your Browser**
>
> The browser window in Figure 11.2 has been maximized so that it occupies the entire screen. To maximize your browser window, click the Maximize Window button near the upper right of the window's title bar.

Like most websites, the opening Yahoo! page is too long to be displayed within a single screen of information. You can scroll upward and downward by clicking and dragging on the scrollbar at the right edge of the Firefox window or by turning the scroll wheel on your pointing device (if it has one). For pages that are also too wide to fit into the Firefox window horizontally, you can scroll left and right by clicking and dragging on the scrollbar at the bottom edge of the Firefox window.

## Navigating Websites

Browsing the Web is not simply a matter of entering new URLs into the URL bar; central to the life of the World Wide Web is the **hyperlink**, a word or image displayed in the browser window that, when clicked, automatically loads and displays a new URL. As you move your mouse pointer around the browser window, you know that you have encountered a hyperlink when the appearance of the mouse pointer changes from an arrow to a hand.

Figure 11.3 shows the result of clicking the word Health shown in Figure 11.2. Notice that the URL in the URL bar is updated to reflect the address of the page that is now being displayed.

After you view at least two sites in succession, either by entering new URLs yourself or by clicking hyperlinks, the Back button becomes active. The Back button enables you to return to the URL you were viewing immediately before the URL currently being displayed.

Similarly, after you click the Back button, the Forward button becomes active. After you click the Back button to return to an earlier URL, you can use the Forward button to return again to the later URL. Both the Back and Forward buttons are shown clearly in Figure 11.3.

> **Sometimes You Want to Go Further Back**
>
> Sometimes it is helpful to be able to return to a URL you visited several sites ago. Rather than clicking the Back button repeatedly, try clicking the small downward arrow to the right of the Back button. Clicking this arrow displays a drop-down list containing your **history**—a list of the most recent few URLs you have loaded—and you can then choose to return to any of them by clicking its entry in the list.
>
> The small downward arrow to the right of the Forward button provides similar functionality but moves you forward through the list instead.

Back button

Forward button

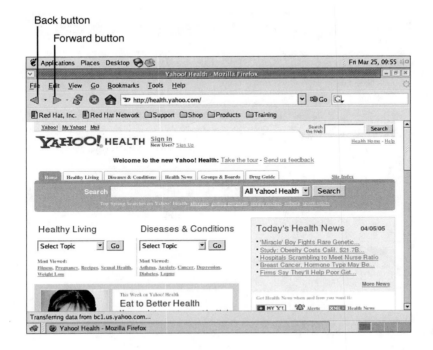

**FIGURE 11.3**
Clicking a hyperlink at http://www.yahoo.com/ causes this site, http://health.yahoo.com/, to be displayed. The new URL is reflected in the URL bar. The Back button also becomes active.

# Remembering URLs You Like

Sometimes as you're clicking hyperlinks, visiting page after page on the Web, you encounter a web page whose address you would like to save so that you can return directly to it at some later time. Instead of trying to remember the URL displayed in the URL bar or writing down the URL somewhere, you can use the Firefox **bookmarks** function to remember the address for you.

A browser bookmark functions in much the same way that a real bookmark does. It saves your place so that you can return to the same location later without a lot of extra searching or legwork. Remembering a URL this way is known as **bookmarking** it.

To bookmark any site you are currently viewing, choose Bookmarks, Bookmark This Page, as shown in Figure 11.4. A dialog box will appear to confirm that you want to bookmark the page. Click the Add button to confirm your bookmark.

Bookmarks that you create this way are added as clickable options to the bottom of the Bookmarks menu. Figure 11.5 shows the new bookmark just added in Figure 11.4. After you create a bookmark, you can reload the page at any time by choosing Bookmarks and then the entry for the URL you want to visit.

**FIGURE 11.4**
Choosing to bookmark the current page causes its address to be remembered for easy access later.

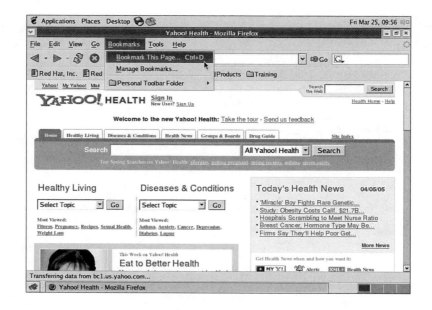

Newly-added bookmark

**FIGURE 11.5**
New bookmarks are added to the bottom of the Book-marks menu for later use.

# Organizing Your Bookmarked URLs

When you begin to browse the Web extensively using Fedora Core 4 and Firefox, you're likely to collect more and more bookmarks over time. As your list of bookmarked URLs becomes longer and longer, having newly bookmarked URLs added to the end of the Bookmarks menu will become more inconvenient. The menu will eventually grow longer than your screen!

To help battle this problem, Firefox contains a Bookmark Manager, which you can use to categorize your bookmarks into submenus. To start the Bookmark Manager, choose Bookmarks, Manage Bookmarks from the Firefox toolbar. The Bookmark Manager appears, as shown in Figure 11.6.

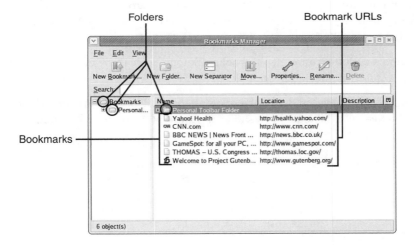

**FIGURE 11.6**
The Bookmark Manager is used to categorize your bookmarks. To open the Bookmark Manager, choose Bookmarks, Manage Bookmarks.

The Bookmark Manager displays bookmarks in a tree view, with the following properties:

▶ All folders in the tree view have a small plus (+) or minus (–) icon next to them. To show the contents of a folder, click the plus icon; the contents are displayed and the plus is replaced by a minus. To hide the contents of the folder again, click the minus.

▶ All folders in the tree can contain both bookmarks and additional folders, which can in turn contain their own bookmarks and additional folders.

▶ Each folder represents a menu or submenu. For example, if you were to create a folder called Politics in the Bookmark Manager, its contents would show up as a submenu called Politics in the Bookmarks menu.

▶ The Bookmarks folder in the Bookmark Manager contains all other book-marks and folders and represents the Bookmarks menu itself.

▶ You can create new folders by selecting the location where you want them to appear in the tree and then clicking New Folder in the Bookmark Manager toolbar.

▶ You can move bookmarks and folders around the tree and move them in and out of folders in the tree simply by clicking and dragging and then dropping them into your desired location.

Because the tree view of the Bookmark Manager can be a little confusing to new users, an illustration will help. Notice the list of bookmarks shown in Figure 11.6. By following these steps, you can move the two news sites, CNN and BBC News, into their own folder called News Web Sites (shown later in Figure 11.8):

1. Single-click the Yahoo Health bookmark to indicate that you want to place the new folder immediately before it.

2. Click New Folder on the Bookmark Manager toolbar. A new folder appears in the tree, and the dialog box shown in Figure 11.7 asks for a new folder name.

Enter name for new folder

**FIGURE 11.7**
When adding a new folder, you need to supply a name.

3. After entering the name News Web Sites for the folder and clicking OK to dis-miss the dialog box, click and drag the bookmarks for the CNN and BBC News websites over the new folder, releasing your mouse button when its name is highlighted. This will place the bookmark being dragged into the folder. The results, after clicking the plus icon to display its updated contents, are shown in Figure 11.8.

New folder

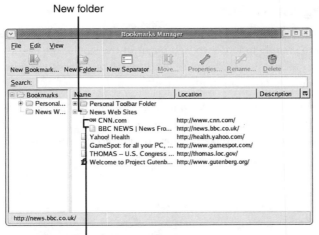

Bookmarks placed in new folder

FIGURE 11.8
The results of creating a new folder called News Web Sites and moving the CNN and BBC News bookmarks into it.

Whenever you make changes to your bookmarks using the Bookmark Manager, the contents of your Bookmarks menu also change. When you are done editing your bookmarks, simply close the Bookmark Manager by clicking the Close button on the application window or by choosing File, Close from the Bookmark Manager's menu bar. Figure 11.9 shows the updated Bookmarks menu in Firefox, with the News Web Sites submenu open.

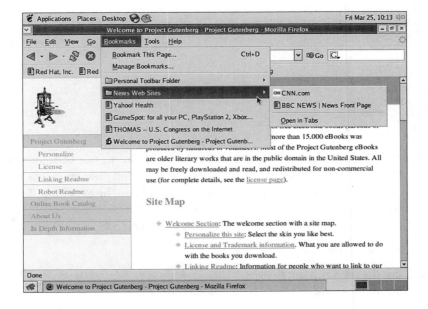

FIGURE 11.9
After you close the Bookmark Manager, the new Bookmarks menu contains the News Web Sites submenu.

## Browsing with Tabs

Whether for the purpose of comparing two websites or for some other reason, it is often helpful to be able to load two web pages at the same time and then switch between them quickly. Rather than use two browser windows to accomplish this task, Firefox offers another solution: tabbed browsing.

**Tabbed browsing** is a method of keeping two or more web pages loaded at the same time and allowing you to switch between them with a single click. To create a new tab, press Ctrl+T. A tab index appears, and a second tab is created, as shown in Figure 11.10.

**FIGURE 11.10**
A new tab is created; it is currently blank because no URL has been entered yet. The original web page is still in Firefox's memory; you can display it by clicking its tab.

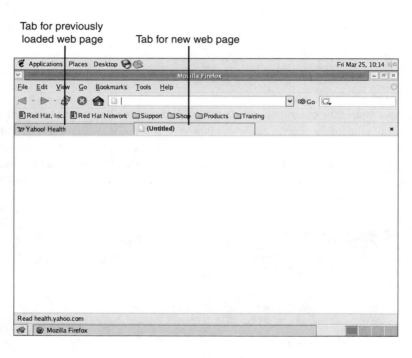

Each tab can hold its own web page. To load a web page into a tab, click the tab you want to use, enter the desired URL into the URL box, and press Enter. The title of the web page loaded into a given tab is always displayed on the tab's label. Each time you want to create an additional tab, press Ctrl+T or choose File, New, Navigator Tab from the Firefox application window's menu bar.

To delete a tab, follow these steps:

**1.** Click the tab you want to delete. This activates the tab, and the content it contains is displayed.

2. After the tab you want to delete is displayed, either click the X to the extreme right of the tabs index, or right-click the tab in question and choose Close Tab from the pop-up context menu that appears.

# Disabling Pop-Up Windows and Window Scripts

Firefox is flexible and powerful enough to help you avoid common annoyances on the Web. By default, Firefox is configured to prevent the appearance of various types of pop-up windows. Sometimes this kind of functionality is desirable—for example, when a site opens a window that contains specific functionality or information in response to your click. Most pop-up windows and most scripts that resize or hide windows, however, are not terribly helpful and are not related to content that you actually want to see; most users find these types of Web advertisements and scripts to be annoying.

To enable or disable nonrequested pop-up windows or prevent websites from manipulating your existing windows, choose Edit, Preferences to display the Firefox Preferences dialog box.

In the list of categories on the left, click the Web Features icon. Check the box labeled Block Popup Windows, as shown in Figure 11.11, to prevent websites you visit from displaying unrequested popup windows. Leave the box unchecked if you want to allow all popup windows

Check to block popup windows

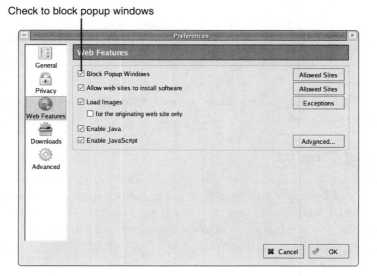

**FIGURE 11.11**
Access the popup window controls by choosing Edit, Preferences, Web Features. Check the box labeled Block Popup Windows to prevent popups.

### Want to Allow Only Certain Popups?

You can also elect to allow popup windows only from a limited list of predetermined sites. To do so, check the Block Popup Windows box, then click the Allowed Sites button. A dialog will appear asking you to enter the URLs of sites that should be allowed to open popup windows on your computer system.

Uncheck the box labeled Allow web sites to install software, shown in Figure 11.12, to prevent websites you visit from installing unwanted software on your computer system.

Uncheck to prevent installation
of unauthorized software

**FIGURE 11.12**
Uncheck the box labeled Allow web sites to install software if you don't want websites to be able to install software on your computer system.

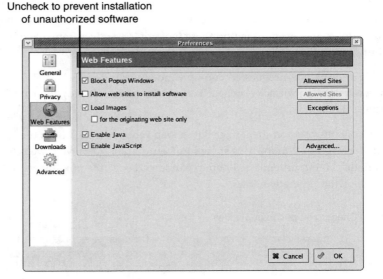

After you make the necessary changes, click OK to save them and close the Preferences dialog box.

## Exiting Firefox

To exit Firefox at any time, choose File, Quit or click the Close button at the extreme upper right of the application window. If you are browsing with multiple open browser tabs, take care when you close Firefox to ensure that you have bookmarked any sites that you want to return to in the future and that you have finished using the content in any of the open browser tabs.

# Summary

In this chapter, you learned to use the open-source Firefox web browser to browse the Web and manage a list of your favorite websites.

You learned to perform each of the following tasks:

- ▶ Load and display a new web page

- ▶ Save your favorite websites as bookmarks

- ▶ Organize your list of bookmarks and the Bookmarks menu

- ▶ Create tabs to hold multiple web pages and delete tabs

- ▶ Disable pop-up ads and scripts that manipulate your browser windows while browsing the Web

Because of the importance of the World Wide Web in day-to-day work, these tasks are likely to become some of the most familiar to you as you use Fedora Core 4.

# Q&A

**Q** *Doesn't the Firefox application also contain an email client?*

**A** No. The other major browsers based on the Mozilla project, namely the Mozilla web browser and the Netscape web browser, both include an email application. Firefox, however, does not. In Fedora Core 4, email functionality is handled by Evolution, which is covered in Chapter 12, "Managing Email with Evolution."

**Q** *Is there any way to browse my files or windows workgroups or domains from inside Firefox?*

**A** You can browse your file system in Firefox by using URLs that begin with file: and that contain the path you want to browse; for example, `file:/home/you` would display your home directory. Firefox is not, however, a file manager like Internet Explorer is; you can't use Firefox to copy files to other locations on your hard drive or to browse shared volumes on a Windows network. For file manager functionality, refer to Chapter 5, "Working with Files on the Desktop." For Windows networking functionality, refer to Chapter 13, "Using Other Network Tools."

# Workshop

The Workshop is designed to help you anticipate possible questions, review what you've learned, and begin learning how to put your knowledge into practice.

## Quiz

1. How do you visit a website whose address you already know using the Firefox web browser?

2. How do you save a favorite website for easy viewing later?

3. What tool do you use to categorize and organize your bookmarks?

## Answers

1. Click in the URL bar near the top of the Firefox application window, replace its contents with the address of the site you want to visit, and press your Enter key.

2. Choose Bookmarks, Bookmark This Page from the toolbar near the top of the Firefox application window.

3. To categorize or organize bookmarks, start the Bookmark Manager by choosing Bookmarks, Manage Bookmarks from the toolbar near the top of the Firefox application window.

## Activities

1. Browse to all your favorite websites in the Firefox web browser and add them to your list of bookmarks.

2. Open five browser tabs and load a different, favorite website into each one.

3. Go to a site whose pop-up windows have annoyed you in the past and enjoy the fact that those windows no longer appear in Fedora Core 4 while you're using Firefox.

# CHAPTER 12

# Managing Email with Evolution

---

## *What You'll Learn in This Chapter:*

▶ How to launch and configure the Evolution email client

▶ How to send and receive email messages with Evolution

▶ How to create and open file attachments in email messages

This chapter is designed to help you start using the Evolution email application that ships with Fedora Core 4. If you are a Webmail-only user (that is, if you access your email through a web browser using a "dot-com" service like Hotmail, Yahoo! Mail, Mac.com or GMail), you can safely skip this chapter. The material presented here applies only to users who usually need to use a standalone email client application such as Microsoft Outlook or Eudora to get mail from a dedicated mail server.

## Reading and Writing Email with Evolution

Many Internet users read and respond to their email using web-based email services. If you access your mail this way, the preceding chapter on web browsing with Mozilla provided you with the necessary skills to access your email within Linux.

If, on the other hand, you are accustomed to accessing your mail with a standalone mail program such as Microsoft Outlook, or your Internet service provider (ISP) or company has given you a so-called POPmail or IMAP email account that you need to use, this chapter helps you get email up and running.

In Fedora Core 4, dedicated email tools are provided by a full-featured mail and calendar program called Evolution that is in many ways similar to the Microsoft Outlook application popular in many corporate environments.

### We're Going to Ignore the Calendar

Evolution has a number of features and capabilities that we won't discuss here—among them, calendaring features similar to those found in Microsoft Outlook. If you would like to use Evolution as a full replacement for Microsoft Outlook, including calendaring and directory features, visit the Ximian home page at http://www.ximian.com.

## Launching Evolution

To launch Evolution, choose Applications, Internet, Email or click the icon that looks like a postage stamp hovering above an envelope in the menubar.

## Configuring Evolution

When you start Evolution for the first time, you see the Evolution Setup Assistant dialog box, containing a greeting message. Click the Forward button to continue with Evolution configuration. The Identity configuration dialog box is displayed, as shown in Figure 12.1.

**FIGURE 12.1**
In the Identity configuration dialog box, you enter your full name, your email address, an optional organization name, and a reply-to address (if you have another address where replies to your messages should go).

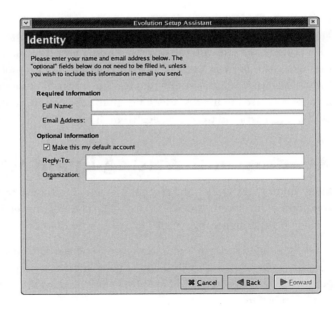

Enter your full name as you want it to appear to others and your email address as supplied by your ISP or network administrator. If you want to associate yourself with a particular organization (often your company name), enter that information in the Organization box.

Click Forward after you finish entering information in the Identity dialog box. The Receiving Mail dialog box is displayed, containing a drop-down list used to choose an email server type. The type of server you select depends on how your mail delivery is configured and the type of service you use to access the Internet:

▶ Select POP if you connect to the Internet through an ISP that uses a POP server or your mail is delivered to a host that employs a POP server. Most dial-up Internet users choose this option.

▶ Select IMAP if you connect to the Internet through an ISP that uses an IMAP server or your mail is delivered to a host that employs an IMAP server. Most corporate network users choose this option.

▶ Select Local delivery if your computer is a server or workstation connected directly to the Internet with its own domain name that is also your email address. Also select this option if you plan to use the fetchmail program to retrieve your mail from POP or IMAP servers, as described in Chapter 23, "Using the Network at the Command Line."

▶ The other options, Standard Unix mbox spools, Maildir-format mail directories, and None, are for unusual situations and should not normally be used.

If you select Local delivery, a text box is displayed, into which you should enter the local mail spool path /var/spool/mail/you (replace you with your own login name). This is the location where incoming network mail is stored. Click Forward to continue with configuration.

If you select POP or IMAP, the Receiving Email dialog box changes to include a series of entry boxes designed to enable you to enter details about the mail server from which your mail should be collected, as shown in Figure 12.2.

Enter the name of your POP or IMAP server into the box labeled Host and the name of your login account on that server into the box labeled Username. This information should have been provided to you by your ISP, network administrator, or hosting company. Unless you are certain that your mail host does not support secure connections, select Whenever Possible from the Use Secure Connection (SSL) drop-down list.

Leave the authentication type set to Password unless your network administrator, mail host, or ISP instructed you to do otherwise. If you want Evolution to remember your password rather than ask you for a password each time you read your mail, check the Remember password box.

After you enter the necessary information about your IMAP or POP server, click the Forward button to continue with configuration. Whether you select Local Delivery, POP, or IMAP as your delivery type, after clicking Forward, you should see a second

**FIGURE 12.2**
When POP or
IMAP delivery is
selected, you
are asked to
provide informa-
tion about the
mail server that
hosts your
email.

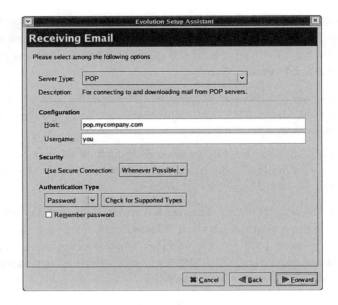

Receiving Mail dialog box containing additional options, as shown in Figures 12.3
and 12.4.

**FIGURE 12.3**
The second
Receiving Mail
dialog box in
the Evolution
Setup Assistant
for users who
select POP
delivery.

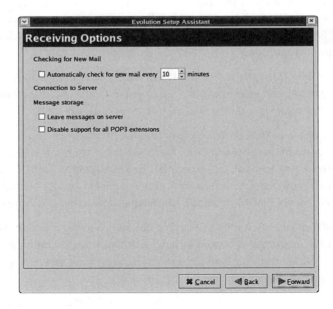

If you want Evolution to automatically check your email on a periodic basis whenever
it is running, check Automatically check for new mail and adjust the timer to reflect

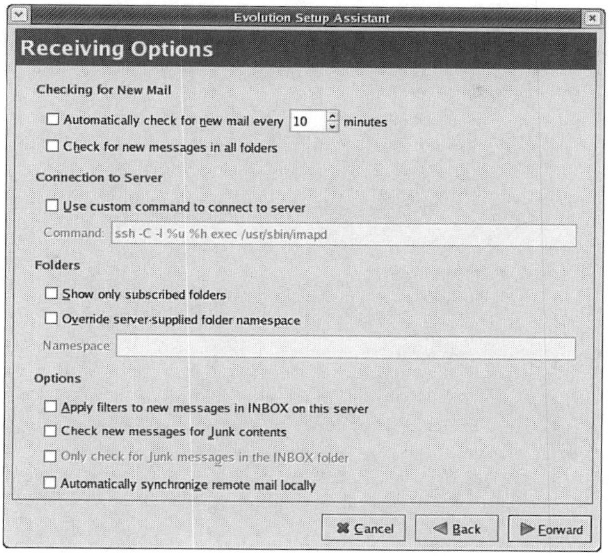

**FIGURE 12.4**
The second
Receiving Mail
dialog box in
the Evolution
Setup Assistant
for users who
select IMAP
delivery.

the number of minutes you would like Evolution to wait between each mail query. Be sure not to check too often, or you might use more than your fair share of network resources, thereby annoying the administrators responsible for your mail server.

If you use IMAP delivery and want to apply mail filters you create to messages on the server, check the Apply Filters to New Messages box. (If you don't know what filters are or don't plan to use them, leave this setting as it is.)

Unless your network administrator, ISP, or mail host has instructed you to do otherwise, leave any other settings on the second Receiving Mail dialog box as they appear by default. After you adjust the options in the second Receiving Mail dialog box to suit your needs, click Forward to proceed to the Sending Mail configuration dialog box shown in Figure 12.5.

If your ISP or network administrator has not provided you with the name of an outbound mail server, select Sendmail as your server type now. The Sendmail option generally works well, but because of the increase in SPAM email (unsolicited commercial email) over the past few years, you might find that some companies and service providers now refuse to accept mail from private systems that were sent using Sendmail. There are no additional options to configure for Sendmail delivery.

If your ISP or network administrator has provided you with the name of an outbound mail server, select SMTP as your server type and adjust the items in the rest of the Sending Email dialog box to match the outbound mail server information you've been given:

**FIGURE 12.5**
The Sending Mail dialog box is used to configure outbound mail service according to your needs.

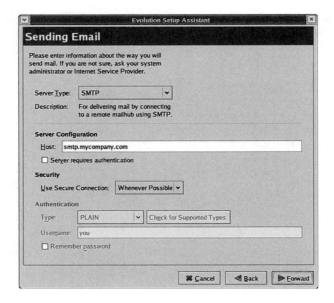

▶ Enter the domain name of the outbound mail server in the Host box.

▶ Unless you are positive that your outbound mail server doesn't support secure connections, select Whenever Possible from the Use Secure Connection (SSL) drop-down list.

▶ If you have been assigned an account and password to use with your outbound mail server, check the Server Requires Authentication box and enter the name of your account in the Username box. Unless you have been told to do otherwise, leave the authentication type set to PLAIN.

▶ If you have been assigned an account and password to use with your outbound mail server and want the password to be remembered rather than having to type a password each time you send an email, check Remember This Password.

After you finish configuring the items in the Sending Mail dialog box, click Forward. The Account Management dialog box is displayed. You should not change the options on the Account Management dialog box if this is your first time using Evolution. Click Forward to proceed to the Timezone configuration dialog box shown in Figure 12.6.

The Timezone configuration dialog box contains a number of small pink dots. As you move your mouse pointer over each dot, the name of the city or location the dot

**FIGURE 12.6**
The Timezone dialog is used to select your time zone so that outgoing email messages show the correct date and time when they reach their destination.

represents is displayed at the bottom of the dialog box. Click the dot closest to the geographical area where your computer resides to select the correct time zone. If none of the dots represents a location you know to be in your time zone, the drop-down list at the bottom of the display contains a much longer list of place names. Select one that shares your time zone.

After you choose your time zone, click Forward. The Evolution Setup Assistant displays a message indicating that you have successfully configured Evolution. Click Apply to launch and begin using the main Evolution application now.

## Visiting Your Mailbox

Now that you have launched and configured Evolution, you'll likely want to go directly to your mailbox to see if you have any email messages. Click on the Mail button on the left side of the Evolution window, then on the Inbox item in the folders list to display your inbox, as shown in Figure 12.7.

**Need to Download Your Mail?**

If you download your email—if you retrieve your mail from a POP server, for example—you need to click the Send/Receive button near the top of the Evolution window in order to download any mail that you have waiting. Only then will it appear in your Evolution mailbox.

*By the Way*

Click to compose new email

**FIGURE 12.7**
Click the Mail
button, and
then on your
Inbox, to display
your mailbox
and the mail it
contains.

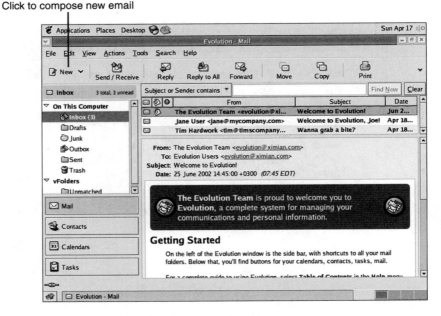

The main Evolution Mail window has a number of components:

▶ The folders list shows the mailboxes you have created in Evolution. By default, only one incoming mailbox, Inbox, is configured. Click on a mailbox in the list to display its contents in the message list.

▶ The message list occupies the upper-right portion of the Evolution application window. It lists all of the messages stored in the currently selected mailbox. Click on a message to display it.

▶ The currently selected message is shown below the message list. The first message in your new Evolution inbox is titled "Welcome to Evolution!" and is from the Evolution development team. If you have any other incoming messages, they are listed below it in the message list.

## Sending a Message in Evolution

Before you begin to read your mail, you should learn how to send a message in Evolution so that you'll be able to reply to messages that you receive. To begin a new message in Evolution, click the New button near the upper left of the Evolution email application. The message composer is displayed, as shown in Figure 12.8.

Enter the email address of the person for whom this message is destined in the To: box and a subject for this email message in the Subject: box.

After you fill out the header (destination and subject) of your message, click in the message entry area. In the message entry area, you can type the body of your message. Whatever you type here will be read by the other party when you send your message.

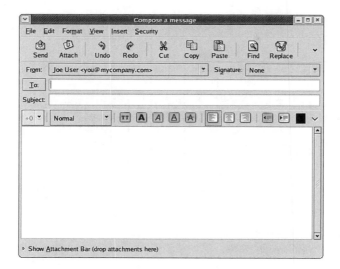

**FIGURE 12.8**
Using the Evolution message composer window, you can create and send new email messages.

# Using HTML Formatting in Your Message

If you want to enable HTML (web-style) formatting for the message you're writing, choose Format, HTML from the message composer window's menu bar. The text editing toolbar, shown in Figure 12.9, is activated. This feature enables you to alter the appearance, size, or alignment of parts of your message to suit your tastes.

The buttons in the text editing toolbar work very much like the formatting buttons you encountered in OpenOffice.org Writer in Chapter 8, "Creating Text Documents with OpenOffice.org Writer." Either select text you want to alter and click buttons to perform the alterations you want to make, or position your cursor, click a button, and enter new text with the property you've selected.

---

**Not Everyone Appreciates HTML Mail!**

Although most users at web-based mail services such as Yahoo! mail or Hotmail are able to receive HTML formatting in their email, many other email users across the Internet are not able (or don't want) to receive HTML-formatted messages.

Because not everyone is prepared to receive HTML-formatted messages, some people consider it annoying to receive them. Before you send these specially formatted messages, make sure your intended recipient does not object to receiving HTML mail.

*Watch Out!*

---

**You Can Send Smiley Faces to Your Friends**

While using HTML mode, you can insert emoticons (smiling, frowning, or other small faces) into your message by choosing Insert, Smiley, and then choosing the face you want from the pop-up smiley menu.

*By the Way*

---

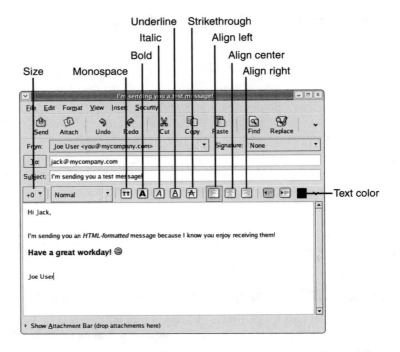

**FIGURE 12.9**
Using the buttons in the text editing toolbar, you can change the appearance, size, or alignment of your text.

## Attaching a File to Your Message

It is often helpful to be able to attach files to your messages to share your work with others across the Internet. To attach a file to an outbound message in the Evolution message composer, click the Attach button. The Attach File(s) dialog box appears, as shown in Figure 12.10.

**FIGURE 12.10**
When you click Attach in the composer window, the Attach File(s) dialog box appears to enable you to select a file to attach to your email message.

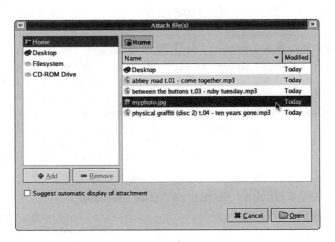

Browse to the file you want to attach, click the file's name in the files list, and click OK. The file is attached to the email message and a notice is displayed giving the number of files that have been attached to the message, as shown in Figure 12.11.

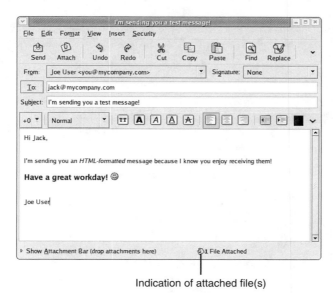

Indication of attached file(s)

**FIGURE 12.11**
The composer window lists the number of files that have been attached to the message.

---

### Can an Attached File Be Removed?

If you change your mind about a file you've attached and want to remove it again, click on Show Attachment Bar. When the attachments are displayed (each attachment will be displayed with its own icon) right-click the file's icon and choose Remove from the pop-up context menu that appears. The file and the icon that represents it are removed from your message.

*Did you Know?*

---

# Sending Your Message

After you've finished composing your message, addressed it, given it a subject, and attached any files you want to send along with it, you are ready to send the message across the network to your intended recipient.

To send your message, click the Send button at the upper left of the composer window. After a brief (sometimes imperceptible) pause, the composer window disappears. Your message is away! The recipient should be able to access your message immediately, should he or she choose to do so.

## Viewing, Replying To, and Forwarding Messages

To view or read a message shown in the message list, simply click on it. The message will be displayed in the area below the message list, as shown in Figure 12.12.

**FIGURE 12.12**
Click on a message in the message list to display it.

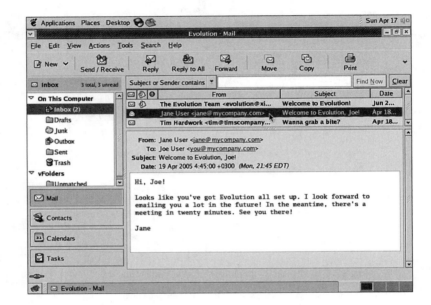

To reply to a message you're viewing, click the Reply button at the top of the Evolution mail window. A new message composer window is opened with the To: and Subject: boxes already filled out to reflect the fact that you are sending a reply.

Enter your message just as you did when composing a new email. Click the Send button in the composer window when you are ready to send your reply.

To forward a message you're viewing to another user, click the Forward button at the top of the Evolution mail window. A new message composer window is opened containing the contents of the message and a small header indicating that it's been forwarded. Enter a destination address in the To: box and click the Send button in the composer window to send your reply.

## Accessing an Attachment

Incoming messages with attached files are marked with a paper clip icon in their index entry. At the bottom of the displayed message, an attachment icon and the attached file's name also appear, as shown in Figure 12.13.

Paper clip icon

Attached file

**FIGURE 12.13**
Attachments in
email messages
are indicated in
the index by a
paper clip icon
and in the mes-
sage body by an
icon and file-
name at the
bottom of the
message.

To access the attachment, click the down arrow next to the attached file icon. A pop-up menu appears asking whether you want to save the file or open it in one of several applications.

If you want to save the file to your account, click Save As. Use the file dialog that appears to name and save the file as desired.

The other actions listed in the pop-up menu include various applications that can be used to open the attached file for viewing or for editing. If you select one of these options, the application you select is launched, and the attached file is automatically loaded for you.

# Printing and Deleting

To print a message, click the Print button, which looks like a printer and is located near the right side of the Evolution toolbar. The Print Message dialog box appears, with options to preview what Evolution will print or to print several copies of the message. Click the Print button in the dialog box to send the message to the printer.

To delete a message, right click on its entry in the message list and choose Delete from the context menu that appears. The message is marked for deletion, removed from view in the message list, and placed in a separate folder called Trash that holds all deleted messages. To purge (irreversibly erase) messages that have been marked for deletion and stored in the Trash folder, choose Actions, Empty Trash. A warning is displayed asking you to confirm your request before the messages in the Trash folder are deleted forever.

If you have marked a message for deletion but want to restore it so that it won't be deleted next time you empty the Trash folder, click the Trash in the folders list. A view of the Trash folder containing recently deleted messages appears, as shown in Figure 12.14. In the Trash folder, right-click any message and choose Undelete to restore it to the Inbox.

**FIGURE 12.14**
Deleted messages are kept in the Trash folder until you empty it.

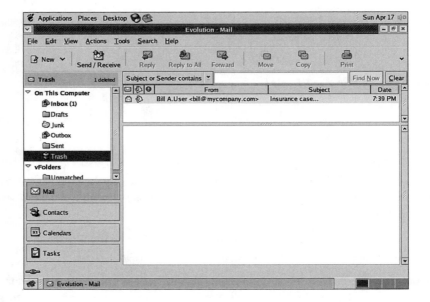

## Exiting Evolution

To exit Evolution, choose File, Quit or click the Close button at the extreme upper right of the application window.

# Summary

In this chapter, you learned to configure and use the Evolution email application that comes with Fedora Core 4. In addition to configuring Evolution to access your host's or company's mail servers, you also learned to perform the following tasks in Evolution:

▶ Create a new email message

▶ Enable HTML formatting when desired in a new email message

▶ Download email from a remote host to your Inbox

▶ Create and receive file attachments in email

You should now be able to function as an active member of your email community while using Fedora Core 4!

# Q&A

**Q** *How do I configure Evolution for multiple email accounts?*

**A** To add additional incoming email spools or additional email boxes to Evolution, choose Edit, Preferences from the Evolution application menu bar. In the Evolution Settings dialog box that appears, look for an area called Mail Accounts. Here, you can add as many email accounts as you need.

# Workshop

The Workshop is designed to help you anticipate possible questions, review what you've learned, and begin learning how to put your knowledge into practice.

## Quiz

**1.** How do you restore a deleted message in Evolution?

**2.** How do you enable the HTML editing mode in the Evolution message composer?

**3.** How do you respond to a message that someone has sent you?

## Answers

**1.** Visit the Trash folder, right-click on the message that you want to restore, and choose Undelete from the pop-up context menu that appears.

**2.** In the message composer, choose Format, HTML.

**3.** After you open the message, click the Reply button near the top center of the Evolution application window. A new message composer window opens, and you can type and send a response.

## Activities

1. Try sending an email message to yourself, to see whether you get it.

2. Spend some time exploring the other features and areas of the Evolution email and calendar client.

3. Send an email to a friend using Evolution and ask him or her to send a reply with an attachment so that you can test your hand at opening file attachments.

# CHAPTER 13

# Using Other Network Tools

---

## What You'll Learn in This Chapter:

▶ How to use the Fedora Core 4 instant messaging application

▶ How to browse and access shares on a Windows host

▶ How to use desktop File Transfer Protocol (FTP) to transfer files between network hosts

This chapter is designed to help you use Fedora Core 4 for a number of networking tasks, including instant messaging (using services such as AIM, MSN, or Yahoo! Messenger), browsing Windows networks, and transferring files between Linux computers across a network. If you don't use instant messaging or have no need for the ability to browse Windows hosts or transfer files across a network, feel free to move on to Chapter 14, "Editing Images and Photos."

# Instant Messaging in Fedora Core 4

As the Internet email system has become more and more clogged with spam and other kinds of junk mail, and as more and more employees and home computer users routinely have Internet access all day long, instant messaging has grown from a niche Internet application into one of the most popular means of online communication.

Although there are a number of very popular instant messaging services, including AOL Instant Messenger (AIM), MSN Messenger, and Yahoo! Messenger, they all share a very basic core functionality: They allow two users on the Internet to chat in real time simply by typing messages back and forth to one another.

Fedora Core 4, too, provides instant messenger functionality that is compatible with most of the popular instant messaging services, including AIM, MSN, Yahoo! Messenger, GroupWise, and Napster messaging.

To start the Fedora Core 4 instant messenger application, choose Applications, Internet, IM. Within a few seconds, the Fedora Core 4 instant messenger application, GAIM, appears, as shown in Figure 13.1.

**FIGURE 13.1**
The GAIM application provides Fedora Core 4's broadly compatible instant messaging functionality.

## Adding an IM Account

Before you can use GAIM, you must enter the details of your instant messenger account so that GAIM can log on to the AIM network for you. To do so, click the Accounts button near the lower left of the GAIM window. The Accounts dialog box is displayed, as shown in Figure 13.2.

**FIGURE 13.2**
In the Accounts dialog box, you can enter the details of your instant messenger accounts.

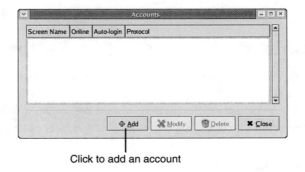

Click to add an account

To add an account, follow these steps:

1. Click the Add button to show the Add Account dialog box, shown in Figure 13.3.

2. Select the messaging service you normally use from the Protocol drop-down list. AIM users should select AIM, MSN users should select MSN, and so on.

3. Enter your IM login and password in the boxes labeled Screen Name and Password, respectively.

4. Check Remember Password if you don't want to have to enter your password by hand each time you log on.

5. Check Auto-login if you want GAIM to log you on to the messaging service automatically when you start it from the Applications, Internet menu.

6. Click Save to save the IM account that you have just created.

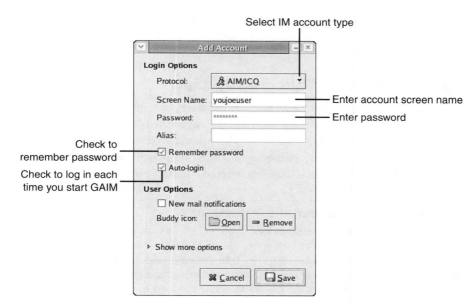

**FIGURE 13.3**
The Add Account dialog box is used to tell GAIM about instant messaging accounts that you use.

After you click the Save button in the Add Account dialog box, the account you've just added to GAIM is shown in the Accounts dialog box. Click Close when you are done adding your instant messaging accounts to GAIM.

## Logging In to AIM in Fedora Core 4

To log in to AIM using Fedora Core 4, choose the screen name you'd like to use from the Accounts drop-down list. If you have chosen not to have GAIM remember your password, be sure to enter your password in the Password box. Then click the Sign On button. You are logged on to the messaging network by GAIM and should soon see the Buddy List window, as shown in Figure 13.4.

Once you are logged on, you will also see a small icon on the far right side of the menubar indicating that you are ready to receive messages.

FIGURE 13.4
After you are
logged in, you
see the Buddy
List window.

## Adding Users to Your Buddy List

If you haven't yet used instant messaging extensively, your Buddy List window is probably empty because you don't have any online buddies. Instant messaging buddies are somewhat similar to web browsing bookmarks: You can easily reach a certain other party using the instant messaging application, without having to type in the name of the addressee each time you want to communicate.

**By the Way**

### Completely New to Instant Messaging?

If you have never used instant messaging before and do not have an account with any of the popular IM services, you need to create an account before you can begin to use the instant messenger client. To create a new account with the free AIM service, go to http://www.aim.com and fill out the signup form that you find there. You can then use the details that you supplied at signup to log on with GAIM.

If you know the account names of co-workers or friends you're likely to want to communicate with using instant messaging, you can add them to your buddy list by choosing Buddies, Add Buddy from the GAIM application menubar. When you do this, the Add Buddy dialog box is displayed, as shown in Figure 13.5.

Type the name of the other person's account into the Screen Name box and select either Co-Workers or Buddies from the Group drop-down list, depending on whether the other user is a co-worker or just a friend (this distinction is just to help categorize your buddies for you in the buddy list and doesn't affect instant messaging functionality at all).

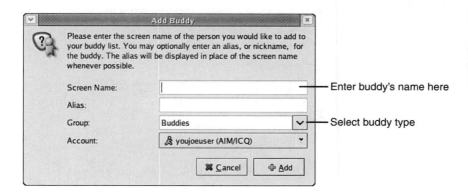

Enter buddy's name here

Select buddy type

**FIGURE 13.5**
The Add Buddy
dialog box helps
you to add bud-
dies to your
instant messag-
ing buddy list.

After you add a buddy, if that person happens to be online, he or she appears in the Buddy List window, as shown in Figure 13.6.

Newly-added buddy

**FIGURE 13.6**
After you add a
buddy, that per-
son's account
appears in your
buddy list if he
or she is online.

# Showing Offline Buddies

If you have entered a number of buddies but still don't see any of them in your Buddy List window, it is likely that none of them are online at the moment.

You still might want to be able to see which buddies are on your list at all times— even those who aren't currently online. To show all buddies whether they are online or offline at the moment, choose Buddies, Show Offline Buddies from the GAIM application menubar. All your buddies now appear in the Buddy List window, as shown in Figure 13.7. When all buddies are visible, the names of those who are online are shown in color, whereas the names of those who aren't online are shown in grayscale (black and white).

**FIGURE 13.7**
Choosing
Buddies, Show
Offline Buddies
causes all bud-
dies to be
displayed,
whether they
are online or
not. Online bud-
dies are in
color; offline
buddies are
in grayscale.

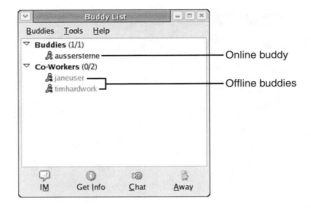

## Sending a Message and Having a Conversation

To start a conversation with an online buddy, send him or her a message. To do so, simply double-click the icon of an online buddy in your buddy list. A dialog box appears with the name of the other user as its title; this is the box (shown in Figure 13.8) that you use to carry on a conversation with the user.

**FIGURE 13.8**
After double-
clicking the
name of an
online buddy,
you can carry
on a conversa-
tion with him in
the window that
appears.

To begin your conversation, simply type a message into the lower box and press your Enter key. Because this buddy is online, whatever you type pops up on his or her computer screen, wherever he or she is. Your buddy is then given a chance to respond.

# Carrying on a Conversation

As you carry on a conversation in the instant messenger application, look for these visual cues that help you to communicate:

▶ All messages appear in chronological order; as new messages are sent out or come in, they simply appear at the bottom of the list. You can scroll back up through the list of previous communication by clicking and dragging the scrollbar.

▶ Each message begins with the time at which the message was sent and the name of the user who sent it, in bold text. These items appear in blue for messages that are from you or in red for messages that are from your buddies to you.

▶ Although all messages appear in the top pane once sent or received, all messages that you type appear in the bottom pane as you type them, and are invisible to the remote user until you press your Enter key, at which time the message is sent to your buddy (see Figure 13.9).

Outbound messages in blue

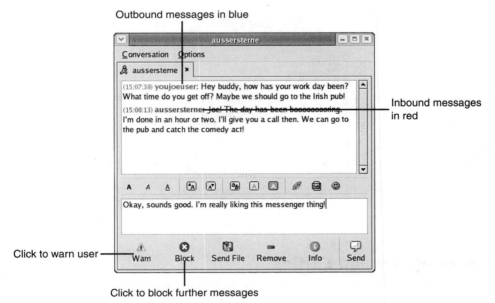

Inbound messages in red

Click to warn user

Click to block further messages

**FIGURE 13.9**
Your entire communication is shown in this conversation window. Received and sent messages are in the upper pane; an unsent message appears in the lower pane.

Each time you get a new message, you hear a tone through your speakers letting you know that a communication has arrived. Two buttons, the Warn and Block buttons near the bottom of the conversation window, also deserve attention.

Click Warn to warn a user who is communicating inappropriately that you don't want to receive ongoing communication that you find bothersome or offensive; click Block to block a remote user from sending any further messages.

## Saving a Conversation

If you decide that a conversation you've been having is important enough to be saved for later review, you can save it to a file on your disk by choosing Conversation, Save As from the menubar near the top of the conversation window. When you do this, a file dialog box appears, allowing you to save your conversation for later retrieval.

## Removing Buddies from the Buddy List

From time to time, you will want to remove buddies from your buddy list. To do this, right-click the buddy in question in the Buddy List window and choose Remove from the context menu, as shown in Figure 13.10. The buddy is removed from your list until or unless you add him or her back again.

**FIGURE 13.10**
To remove a buddy from the buddy list, right-click the buddy in question and choose Remove from the context menu.

## Signing Off and Exiting

To sign off instant messenger (so that you're unavailable for further communication), choose File, Signoff. If you want to sign on again later, you can do so by choosing File, Signon.

To exit the instant messenger, simply click the Close button at the upper right of the application window. Note that if you haven't first signed off, you'll remain online and the instant messenger will appear again if someone sends you an instant message. To sign off once you have closed the main GAIM application window, right-click on the GAIM icon at the upper right of the menubar and choose Signoff, as shown in Figure 13.11. The icon will now show a red circle with a line through it to indicate that you are no longer online.

**FIGURE 13.11**
Right-click on the GAIM icon in the menubar and choose Signoff if you want to sign off after you've closed the main GAIM window.

# Accessing Windows Networks

There are a couple of other tasks that you might want to perform with Fedora Core 4, in addition to using the Web, email, and instant messaging. One of them is accessing files on your local area network.

Most local area networks today are Windows networks. To be useful, a Linux workstation must be able to access files and directories on Windows servers around the local area network.

Fedora Core 4 does not ship with a My Network Places or Network Neighborhood icon. However, using the desktop file manager, you can access files and folders across the local Windows network.

## Accessing Files on Windows Machines

To access the files on a Windows host on the local network using the file manager, follow these steps:

1. Choose Places, Connect to Server.

2. When the Connect to Server dialog box shown in Figure 13.12 appears, select Windows Share from the Service Type drop-down list.

3. Enter the name of the Windows host you want to exchange files with in the Server box.

4. Click Connect.

**FIGURE 13.12**
To connect to and exchange files with a Windows host, select Windows Share from the Service Type drop-down list; then enter the name of the computer in question.

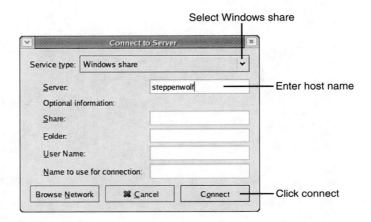

Select Windows share

Enter host name

Click connect

If Linux is able to connect to the Windows host, an icon for the host will appear on your desktop. Double-click it to open a file manager window showing the list of shares available on the Windows host in question, as shown in Figure 13.13.

**FIGURE 13.13**
Double-click on the new icon on your desktop to open the list of shares on the Windows host.

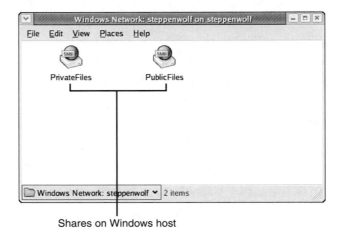

Shares on Windows host

While browsing a Windows host using the file manager, you can navigate the remote file system just as you would local files in the file manager window; you can also perform file copy, paste, delete, and move operations between the remote host and your Linux file system.

## Unmounting Windows Hosts

When you're done with a Windows host and you no longer want its icon to appear on your desktop, close all of the file manager windows that display files on the remote host; then right-click on the host's desktop icon and choose Unmount from the context menu that appears.

# Using File Transfer Protocol on the Desktop

Many networks continue to use File Transfer Protocol (FTP) to distribute files internally, and many of the best download sites on the Internet still use FTP as their primary method of file exchange.

To access an FTP site or archive from the Fedora Core 4 desktop, follow these steps:

1. Choose Places, Connect to Server to open the Connect to Server dialog box.

2. If the FTP server you want to exchange files with requires a password for login, select FTP (with login) from the Service Type drop-down list. Otherwise, select Public FTP from the list.

3. If you selected FTP (with login) in step 2, enter your FTP login in the User Name box, as shown in Figure 13.14. If you've been instructed to do so, enter the connection port and the initial path in Port and Folder, respectively. If you haven't been instructed to use a unique port or an initial folder, leave these extra boxes blank.

4. Click Connect to connect to the FTP site.

After you connect to the FTP site, a new icon for the FTP site will appear on your desktop. To access it, just double-click on the icon to display a file manager window listing the files and folders on the FTP site, as shown in Figure 13.15.

**FIGURE 13.14**
To connect to a private FTP site, select FTP (with login) from the Service Type list; then enter your login in the User Name box.

Select FTP option

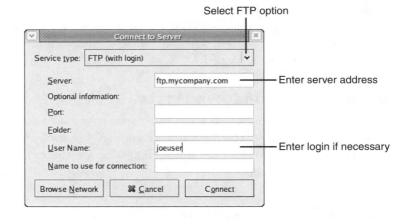

Enter server address

Enter login if necessary

**FIGURE 13.15**
Double-clicking the desktop icon for the FTP site displays the site's contents in a file manager window.

Icon on desktop for FTP server

Files and folders on FTP server

If you're trying to access a private FTP site, the Authentication Required dialog box will appear, asking you to supply a password for the connection, as shown in Figure 13.16. Enter your password and click OK to open the list of files at the site.

Once you have opened a file manager window displaying files or folders on an FTP site, you can copy to or from the site by copying files just as you normally would using the file manager.

FIGURE 13.16
When opening
files on a pri-
vate FTP site,
you'll be asked
to supply a
password.

**You Can Save Your Password!**

*By the Way*

If you're connecting to a private FTP site and would like Linux to remember your password for you until you log out of your desktop, check the box labeled Remember Password for This Session when the Authentication Required dialog box is displayed.

If you would like Linux to remember the password for this FTP site from now on, check the box labeled Save Password in Keyring.

## Closing an FTP Connection

When you're done with an FTP session and you no longer want its icon to appear on your desktop, close all of the file manager windows that display files on the FTP site; then right-click on the FTP site's desktop icon and choose Unmount from the context menu that appears.

# Summary

In this chapter, you learned to use several desktop networking tools to accomplish common networking tasks in Fedora Core 4.

Among other things, you learned how to

- ▶ Log in to your AIM, MSN, Yahoo!, or other instant messenger account in Fedora Core 4
- ▶ Add users to and remove users from your buddy list
- ▶ Access files on a Windows host on your local area network
- ▶ Transfer files between your computer and public or private FTP sites

With the things you've learned in Chapters 11 through 13, your Fedora Core 4 network use skills are complete.

# Q&A

**Q** *I have IM accounts on lots of different services. In the past, I had to run the AIM, MSN, and Yahoo! programs at the same time if I wanted to be logged in to all of them at once. Can GAIM keep me logged in to all of my accounts at the same time?*

**A** Yes. To keep multiple accounts open in GAIM, just add each of the accounts you use in the Accounts dialog box; then check the Online box next to each account.

To open the Accounts dialog box while you're already using GAIM, right-click on the GAIM icon at the upper right of the desktop menubar; then select Accounts from the context menu that appears.

**Q** *Is there any way to browse windows workgroups or domains, similar to what happens when I double-click Network Neighborhood or My Network Places on a Windows host?*

**A** Yes. Choose Places, Network Servers to browse the entire Windows network for hosts.

# Workshop

The Workshop is designed to help you anticipate possible questions, review what you've learned, and begin learning how to put your knowledge into practice.

## Quiz

1. How do you start a conversation with a buddy using the instant messenger?
2. How do you list the volumes on a Windows host called `winstation10` using the Linux file manager?

## Answers

1. Just double-click an online buddy's icon in your Buddy List window to open a conversation window.

2. Choose Places, Connect to Server at the desktop. Then, in the Connect to Server dialog box, select Windows Share from the Service Type drop-down list and enter the name of the computer you want to browse in the Server box. Then click Connect.

## Activities

1. Add all your AIM buddies to your Fedora Core 4 buddy list.

2. Try browsing a few nearby Windows hosts using your file manager.

# CHAPTER 14

# Editing Images and Photos

---

## What You'll Learn in This Chapter:

▶ How to download images from a digital camera

▶ How to fix color and contrast problems

▶ How to make an image black-and-white

▶ How to sharpen, crop, or resize an image

▶ How to load, save, and print an image

This chapter introduces you to one of the most powerful software applications included in Fedora Core 4, called The GIMP. GIMP is short for GNU Image Manipulation Program, and The GIMP is indeed used primarily to manipulate images such as photos taken with digital cameras or scans of other images.

---

**Photoshop Users Have a Head Start**                        *By the Way*

Users who are familiar with programs such as Adobe Photoshop or Corel Photo Paint on other operating systems will find many of the features of The GIMP to be familiar, even if the layout of the windows and buttons is a little unfamiliar. In most cases, if you are looking for a feature from Photoshop or Photo Paint in GIMP it'll be there, although there are some notable exceptions—color profile support, CMYK, and LAB color spaces chief among them.

---

# Downloading Images From Your Digital Camera

There are many different types and sources of images that you're likely to encounter as you use Fedora Core 4 in the future. Without a doubt, however, digital cameras are the most common source of images in personal computing today. No longer a novelty or a professional-level tool costing thousands, digital cameras have become as popular as film cameras once were.

Unfortunately, there is currently no universally accepted communications standard for digital cameras, so no single application can support all digital cameras in existence. To make matters more complicated, most digital camera vendors don't release drivers for Linux systems like Fedora Core 4. Because of this, it might be more difficult to download images from digital cameras into Fedora Core 4 than it is to download images into Windows.

## Downloading from USB Cameras

If your digital camera can be connected to your PC through a USB port, you might be able to use your camera like any other removable storage device in Linux. Simply set your camera to playback mode, plug it in to your computer's USB port, and turn it on to see if it appears on your desktop as a removable storage device, as shown in Figure 14.1.

**FIGURE 14.1**
If you have a USB digital camera, you might be able to simply plug it in and access it like any other storage device.

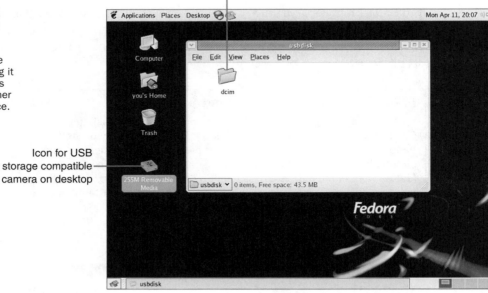

Navigate through folders, if necessary, to find images

Icon for USB storage compatible camera on desktop

If a USB storage device appears on your desktop after you plug your camera into your computer's USB port, you can access it like a hard drive or any other storage device:

► Double-click on the desktop icon to open the camera's storage area and show the file(s) that it contains.

► You might need to navigate through a number of folders in order to access the actual image files, which will usually be stored in JPEG or TIFF format.

► Don't double-click on or edit the images directly in the folders stored in your camera; instead, use the file manager to create a folder on your hard drive, then copy the images from the folder stored on your camera to a folder stored on your hard drive

---

### Having Trouble Accessing Your Camera?

Many digital cameras can actually communicate over USB in several different languages. If your camera fails to appear as a storage device on your desktop when you plug it in, search your owners manual to see if you can place the camera into "Mass Storage Mode," "Hard Disk Mode," or "Storage Mode." Then try again.

*By the Way*

---

## Downloading Images from Non-USB or Incompatible Cameras

If you're unable to download your images directly from the camera, either because it's not a USB camera or because it doesn't appear as an icon on your desktop when you plug it in, you can still download your images in Linux. To do so, you will need to purchase a flash-card or memory-card reading device that can be plugged into your USB port.

Be sure to pay attention to the following when selecting a digital media card reader:

► Make sure that the reader you select uses the same type of digital storage that your camera uses; common types include CompactFlash, SmartMedia, SecureDigital/xD, and Memory Stick.

► If possible, buy a reader that claims to need no additional drivers in order to be used—this usually indicates that it behaves as a standard USB storage device.

► Be sure that the device is returnable, in case it turns out not to be Linux compatible.

Once you have obtained a compatible digital media reader, using it is easy; simply remove the memory card from your camera (follow the instructions with which it came for details), plug the memory card into the reader device, then plug the reader into your USB port.

If it is Linux-compatible, your camera's memory card will now appear as a standard storage device just as was shown in Figure 14.1, and you can access it in the same way.

*By the Way*

### Have a Laptop or Notebook Computer?

If you have a laptop or notebook computer, you are not limited to using USB-based card reader devices; nearly all PCMCIA-type card readers are also compatible with Linux.

Note that most parallel port card readers are **not** compatible with Linux or are difficult to use with Linux. They are also much slower than USB or PCMCIA card readers. For these reasons, most Fedora Core 4 users should steer clear of parallel port digital media readers.

# Using The GIMP for Basic Photo Editing

Downloading images from your digital camera to your computer is only half the battle; once you've saved your images, you'll also probably want to improve them—to edit or fix color and contrast problems, to sharpen, lighten, or darken them, at the very least.

The GNU Image Manipulation Program (GIMP) is designed to do precisely this kind of heavy lifting in graphics work. To start The GIMP now, choose Applications, Graphics, The GIMP or right-click on the image that you want to edit in a file manager window and choose Open with "The GIMP" from the context menu that appears.

Because this is the first time you've started The GIMP, the GIMP User Installation dialog box appears, as shown in Figure 14.2. Click the Continue button on each of the several pages of the dialog box without changing any settings until you see the GIMP startup message shown in Figure 14.3.

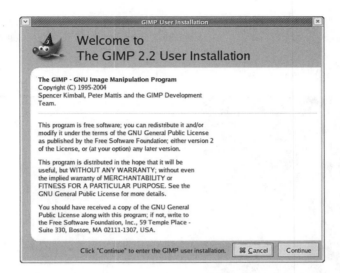

**FIGURE 14.2**
Clicking the Continue button moves you to the next page of The GIMP User Installation agent.

**FIGURE 14.3**
When you see The GIMP's startup message, you know that The GIMP has successfully been installed in your account.

After The GIMP finishes loading, the startup message disappears and the various components of The GIMP appear on your desktop, along with the GIMP Tip of the Day, as shown in Figure 14.4.

**FIGURE 14.4**
Multiple windows providing various aspects of The GIMP's functionality.

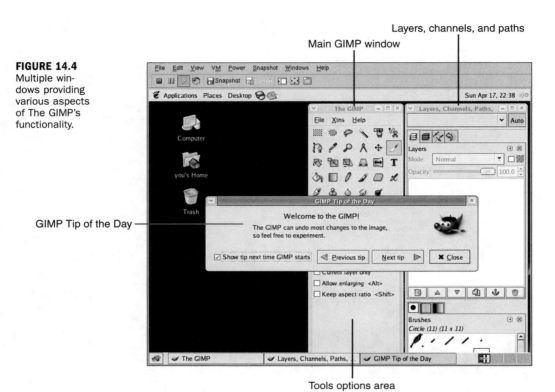

Main GIMP window

Layers, channels, and paths

GIMP Tip of the Day

Tools options area

Now that you have successfully installed and started The GIMP in your account, it's time to begin editing images!

## Loading an Image

To load an image into The GIMP, choose File, Open in the main GIMP window. A standard file dialog box of the sort you've become accustomed to appears. This file dialog box differs from other file dialog boxes you've encountered in one respect: It includes a Preview area. When you single-click on an image file in the file dialog, a preview of the selected image is shown, as shown in Figure 14.5.

After you decide which image you want to load and edit, double-click its filename to load it into The GIMP. The image you've loaded appears in its own window, as shown in Figure 14.6.

Preview is displayed

Image is clicked

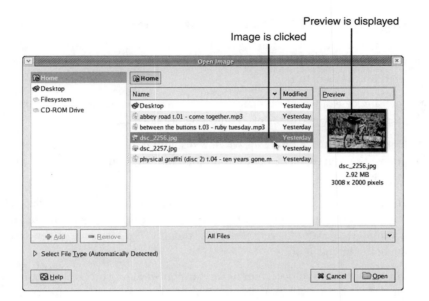

**FIGURE 14.5**
When you select an image file, a small preview of the selected image is shown in the Preview area.

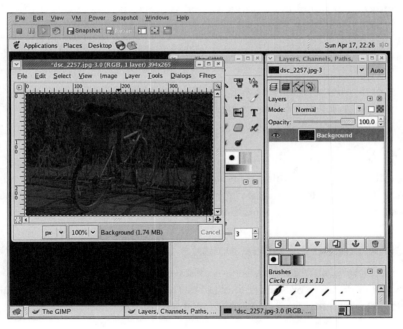

**FIGURE 14.6**
Loaded images appear in their own separate application window.

## Finding Your Way Around The GIMP

Because The GIMP often has so many application and image windows open at a single time, navigating can be somewhat confusing. It is, however, much easier if you keep a list of basics in mind:

▶ Each image window has a menubar of its own that contains many menus also found in applications like Photoshop or Photopaint.

▶ Right-clicking inside an image window displays a context menu for that image; the context menu contains all the functions and tools found in the menubar.

▶ The plus (+) and minus (–) keys on your keyboard zoom in or zoom out of the image, respectively (remember to hold down your shift key when hitting plus). Zooming in is useful for very fine work; zooming out helps you to get a feel for the entire image at once.

▶ When an image is bigger than its application window, you see scrollbars on the right side and bottom of the window. Use them to scroll around images larger than will fit in the window or on your screen.

▶ Near the bottom of the window are units and magnification drop-down lists that you can use to select the units shown in the rulers around the image and the magnification at which the image is shown, respectively.

▶ If at any point you are unsatisfied with a change you've made to an image, you can right-click in the image and then choose Edit, Undo to undo the unwanted or unliked change.

There is, of course, a lot more to navigating the many menus and dialog boxes of The GIMP, but this information is enough to get you started. If you're really hungry for more in-depth detail about navigation in The GIMP, visit http://www.gimp.org and consult the online documentation.

## Automatically Fixing Image Color and Contrast

The image shown in Figure 14.6 is both somewhat flat and uninteresting, and also somewhat dark. Using one automatic tool in The GIMP, you can give it an entirely new look! Many images can be fixed simply by using The GIMP's automatic levels tool.

To access the automatic levels tool choose Layer, Colors, Auto, Stretch HSV, as shown in Figure 14.7. A few moments later, the result, shown in Figure 14.8, is a much more dramatic, pleasing image.

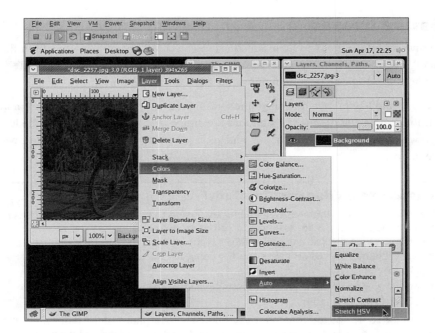

**FIGURE 14.7**
To automatically try to fix color and contrast in an image, right-click and then choose Layer, Colors, Auto, Stretch HSV.

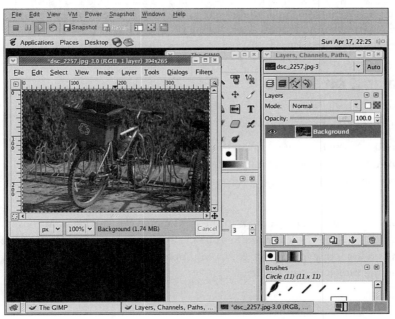

**FIGURE 14.8**
The results are often much more visibly pleasing and eye-catching than the original.

## Saving Images

To save an image that you have edited using The GIMP, choose File, Save from the GIMP menubar. The image is saved using the same image format and same filename as the original; the original is replaced in the process.

If you would like to save an edited image using a new name or to a different image format, choose File, Save As. A standard file dialog box appears. Browse to the location where you want to save the file and enter a new name. Then click OK to save the image.

### Choose Your Filename Carefully!

The GIMP uses the three-letter filename extension that you type to determine how to save the image. So, for example, if you enter `myhouse.jpg` as the filename, The GIMP saves the file using the JPEG (`.jpg`) format. If you enter `myhouse.png` as the filename, The GIMP saves the file using the Portable Network Graphics (`.png`) format.

The GIMP supports many image formats, including GIF, JPG, PNG, TIF, BMP, PCX, PIX, TGA, PNM, and more.

Note that some image formats require additional user input—for example, details about the quality level at which images should be saved. When you save using a format that requires additional information, you see a second dialog box (that varies from format to format) after clicking OK in the Save As dialog box.

## Printing an Image

To print an image in The GIMP, choose File, Print from the context menu. The GIMP Print dialog box appears, opened to the Printer Settings, as shown in Figure 14.9.

A second tab, the Image/Output Settings tab shown in Figure 14.10, contains options related to color and black-and-white printing so that you can adjust halftone or grayscale settings (if you use a black-and-white or laser printer) or color settings.

For most users, the default settings in the Print dialog box are ideal. At most, an adjustment to the Scale slider to fine-tune the size of the image may be required. When you are ready to print, click the Print button at the bottom of the dialog box to send the image to your printer.

Image/Output Settings tab

Printer Settings tab

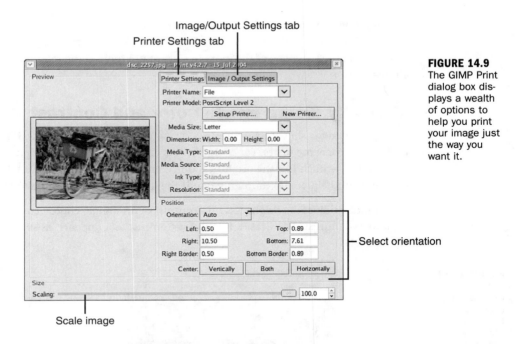

**FIGURE 14.9**
The GIMP Print dialog box displays a wealth of options to help you print your image just the way you want it.

Select orientation

Scale image

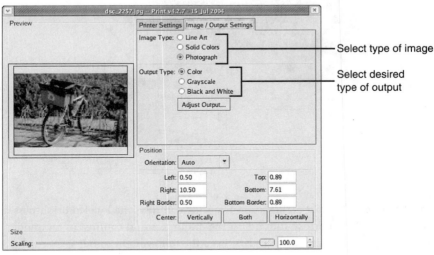

**FIGURE 14.10**
The Image/Output Settings tab contains adjustments for image type and output type.

Select type of image

Select desired type of output

# Using More Advanced GIMP Tools

Although the automatic image adjustment tool offered by The GIMP is enough to repair most images, sometimes additional work is required, or at least desired, before an image is complete and ready for production.

Manual tools are the realm in which The GIMP really shines; adjustments, tweaks, and manipulations are provided for just about any aspect of an image that you can think of. We discuss a few of the more basic manual tools in the remainder of this chapter.

## Manually Fixing Image Color and Contrast

Though the image shown in Figure 14.8 is very dramatic and contrasty, it may be a bit too dark for some tastes. For cases like this one, The GIMP has a brightness and contrast tool—much like the brightness and contrast control found on a television set—that can help you to manually adjust the look of an image for best viewing.

To manually adjust the brightness and contrast of an image, choose Layer, Colors, Brightness-Contrast. The GIMP's Brightness-Contrast tool appears, as shown in Figure 14.11.

**FIGURE 14.11**
The Brightness-Contrast tool contains two sliders with which you can increase or decrease the brightness or contrast of an image.

The Brightness-Contrast tool features two slide controls, one labeled Brightness and the other labeled Contrast, that adjust the brightness and contrast of an image, respectively. When using these sliders, keep the following in mind:

▶ To increase brightness or contrast, move the slider in question to the right.

▶ To decrease brightness or contrast, move the slider in question to the left.

▶ The number over each slider indicates the relative adjustment of the brightness or contrast. Zero (0) means that the slider in question is in its original position. A positive number means that you have increased brightness or contrast, whereas a negative number means that you have decreased brightness or contrast.

When the image appears exactly as you want it to with respect to brightness and contrast, click the OK button to accept your changes. If at some point you find that you want to start over with your original settings, click the Reset button. Figure 14.12 shows the same image as Figure 14.11, but with brightness and contrast both significantly increased.

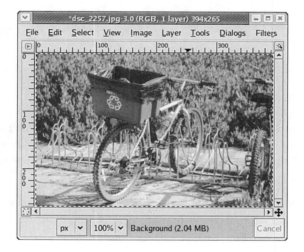

**FIGURE 14.12**
After you use the Brightness-Contrast tool, the image is much easier on the eyes.

## Adjusting Image Color Balance

Sometimes the lightness or darkness of an image isn't all that's wrong with it. Color casts, in particular, are one common kind of image defect that are often easy to spot and hard to remove. The GIMP provides a tool that can help you to change or lessen the color cast of an image.

To make these sorts of changes to an image, Layer, Colors, Color Balance. The Color Balance dialog box appears, as shown in Figure 14.13.

The Color Balance dialog box requires some experimentation and experience to use well, but the basics can be described with just a few points:

▶ Three sliders are available, one for each of three color balance spectrums: cyan versus red, magenta versus green, and yellow versus blue.

▶ The strength of the color you slide toward is increased in your image, whereas the color you slide away from is decreased in your image.

**FIGURE 14.13**
In the Color
Balance dialog
box, you can
warm up a pic-
ture, cool down
a picture, or
change its color
cast.

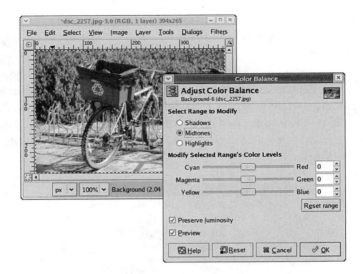

▶ At any given time, the adjustments you make on the sliders affect the shadows (darkest areas), midtones, or highlights (lightest areas) of the image. You
can click Shadows, Midtones, or Highlights to move back and forth through
these adjustments.

▶ Once again, the Reset button resets the current brightness area (Shadows,
Midtones, or Highlights) to its original color balance.

If using this tool sounds a bit complex, don't be intimidated. Just experiment with
the Color Balance dialog box on a few of your favorite images, and you'll soon
come to an understanding of how it works.

**By the Way**

### Warmer Images Are More Pleasing

One of the most popular image adjustments that can be made using the Color
Balance dialog box is toward Yellow and toward Red in the shadow and, to a lesser extent, midtone areas of an image. This adjustment has the effect of "warming
up" the image without the change being too conspicuous. Don't go overboard,
though—too much warming could give your image an unnatural glow!

## Making Images Black-and-White

Even though color printers are the norm nowadays, and nearly all digital cameras
are designed from the word *go* to capture vibrant color, sometimes you just want a
good, old-fashioned black-and-white image.

The GIMP can help with this, too. To convert an image from color to black-and-white, choose Image, Mode, Greyscale from the context menu.

All color information is immediately removed from the image. Note that the Brightness-Contrast control discussed earlier works just as well on black-and-white images as it does on color images!

## Sharpening Images

Sharpening is another common operation that users of The GIMP perform on their images. Sharpening an image enhances the viewer's ability to differentiate between fine details. One tool commonly used in The GIMP to sharpen images is called the Sharpen filter.

To use the Sharpen filter, choose Filters, Enhance, Sharpen. The Sharpen filter is displayed, as shown in Figure 14.14.

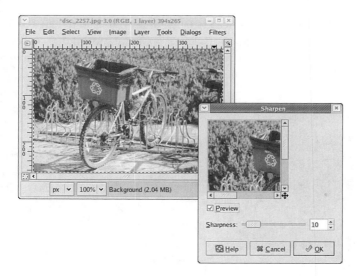

**FIGURE 14.14**
The Sharpen filter can be used to enhance the visibility of fine detail in an image.

In the Sharpen filter, you see a preview area containing a very magnified area of your image and a slider that can be used to increase or decrease the relative amount of sharpening that is to be applied to the image. Use the scrollbars in the preview area to examine critical areas of your image as you increase or decrease sharpening. When you're satisfied with the level of sharpening you've selected, click OK to apply your changes.

By the
Way

**There Are Two Sharpening Filters in The GIMP**

Another sharpening filter, called Unsharp Mask, also has the capability to sharpen images in The GIMP and can often produce superior results. The Unsharp Mask filter is, however, somewhat difficult to use. You can find tutorials for using Unsharp Mask filters by searching for the term *unsharp mask* in Google or another search engine on the Web.

To access the Unsharp Mask filter, right-click in the image where you want to apply it and then choose Filter, Enhance, Unsharp Mask from the context menu that appears.

## Cropping and Resizing Images

The final operations we're going to describe in this chapter are the crop and resize operations, often useful when sending an image to someone else (a photo lab, for example) for printing.

Most commonly, digital images need to be enlarged (have data added to them) before they are large enough for professional photo labs to enlarge. To resize an image, choose Image, Scale Image from the context menu. The Scale Image dialog box is displayed, as shown in Figure 14.15.

**FIGURE 14.15**
Using the Scale Image dialog box, you can enlarge (add data to) or shrink (remove data from) an image before printing.

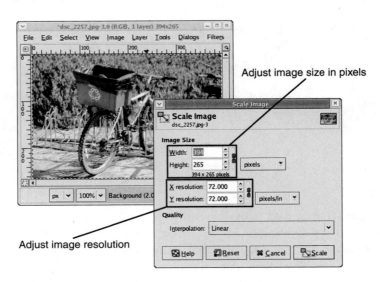

Adjust image size in pixels

Adjust image resolution

To use the Scale Image dialog box, you should generally know the output resolution in dots per inch (dpi) or lines per inch (lpi) that is required by your printer or lab. Enter the numbers for horizontal and vertical resolution (usually, they will be the same) into the Resolution X and Resolution Y boxes. Then adjust the New Width or New Height values until the size in inches matches your desired size. Click OK after you set the desired values to resize the image for printing.

Sometimes simply resizing an image isn't enough; for example, when your image is shaped like a rectangle, but the paper to which you'll be printing is shaped like a square—or when you just don't like the edges of an image and want to use only the center.

When this type of situation occurs, you can use the Crop tool to chop away parts of the image perimeter. The resulting image is smaller (it is minus the parts that you've removed) but contains only what you want it to contain and is shaped in exactly the way you want it shaped. To use the Crop tool, click the icon that looks like a surgical knife in the main GIMP window, as shown in Figure 14.16.

**FIGURE 14.16**
Select the Crop tool, the icon that looks like a surgical knife, when you want to cut away portions of an image's perimeter.

After selecting the Crop tool, notice that your mouse pointer changes to a cross-hair when it is placed over the image you're editing. Click and drag to draw a box that selects the area you want to keep; everything outside the box will be cut away. When the box is shaped just like you want it to be, click the Crop button, as shown in Figure 14.17. The outer portion of the image is cut away, and the new, smaller image remains.

---

**The Crop Rectangle Is Adjustable!**

Instead of spending time drawing the cropping rectangle over and over again trying to get it just right, you can simply use the little squares (like resize handles) in the corners of the rectangle to adjust it. The lower-left and upper-right handles move the rectangle around, and the upper-left and lower-right handles resize it.

*Did you Know?*

**FIGURE 14.17**
When the
rectangle shows
the portion of
the image that
you want to
keep, click the
Crop button to
cut the rest
away.

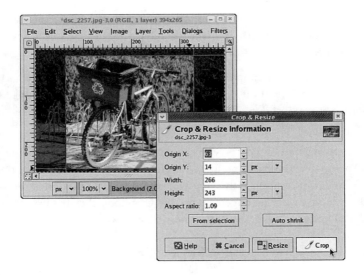

# Summary

In this chapter, you learned how to perform the most common types of image-manipulation tasks on what are currently the most common types of images. Specifically, you learned to

▶ Download images from your digital camera

▶ Fix color and contrast problems in images

▶ Make images black-and-white

▶ Sharpen images

▶ Crop and resize images

▶ Print images

▶ Load and save images

You now have the skills to take, make, and print great images using Fedora Core 4. Even so, in this chapter we haven't really even begun to scratch the surface of what The GIMP can accomplish with your photos and images. For more details about using The GIMP, see the tutorials and other documentation at http://www.gimp.org.

# Q&A

**Q**  *My digital camera connects via a USB port, but the `gtkam` application didn't find it. What gives?*

**A**  A few USB cameras do not speak to Linux like a camera at all, but rather like a hard drive—a hard drive containing all the images you've taken. To see whether your camera is one of these, open a Terminal window and enter the following command:

```
cat /proc/scsi/scsi
```

This command lists all the SCSI and USB storage devices on your system. If you see your digital camera in this list, it is acting as a SCSI hard drive and contains a `vfat` file system. For details on how to mount and access files stored on external SCSI devices of this type, refer to the section called "Managing File Systems" in Chapter 29, "Command-Line System Administration."

**Q**  *My camera has several different USB transfer modes. Which one should I use with Linux?*

**A**  If several modes are available on your camera, select the Mass Storage (USB Storage or Hard Drive) mode to work with Linux.

**Q**  *I don't have a digital camera, but I have a scanner and some photos I'd like to scan. Does Fedora Core 4 support these?*

**A**  If you have a USB or SCSI scanner, then yes, it's likely that Fedora Core 4 supports your scanner. Though we don't have enough room for a complete discussion of scanning here, The GIMP includes scanning software that works like most typical scanner software packages; you can access The GIMP's scanning system by choosing File, Acquire, Xsane from the main GIMP window.

**Q**  *Is it possible to edit out blotches and other blemishes seamlessly using The GIMP?*

**A**  Yes. Although a complete discussion of photo retouching is beyond the scope of a book like this one, you can begin to experiment with your retouching skills using the Clone tool, which has an icon like a rubber stamp down the left side of The GIMP's main window. After selecting the tool, hold down Ctrl and click your mouse button anywhere on your image that you want to paint *from*; then release Ctrl and click anywhere on your image that you want to paint *to*. Getting used to the tool will take some time, but experimentation will yield results.

**Q** *Do any of The GIMP's tools have options like the tools in Photoshop do? Things like feathering or constraining?*

**A** Yes. Options for the currently selected tool appear in the lower half of the main GIMP window. If you don't see tool options in the lower half of the window, double-click on a tool to restore the tool options dialog.

# Workshop

The Workshop is designed to help you anticipate possible questions, review what you've learned, and begin learning how to put your knowledge into practice.

## Quiz

1. How do you access the context menu for a GIMP image?

2. How do you perform an automatic image-level adjustment in The GIMP?

3. How do you open the Sharpen filter in The GIMP?

## Answers

1. Right-click anywhere in a GIMP image to access the context menu for the image.

2. Choose Layer, Colors, Auto, Stretch HSV from the image menubar.

3. Choose Filters, Enhance, Sharpen from the image menubar.

## Activities

1. Take a few pictures with your digital camera and download them to your Fedora Core 4 system.

2. Open the image with the least pleasing color and contrast and run The GIMP's auto levels adjustment on it to see whether it improves.

3. Print the image.

# CHAPTER 15

# Playing and Recording Sound and Music

---

## *What You'll Learn in This Chapter:*

▶ How to adjust volume settings for your sound hardware
▶ How to play audio CDs in your CD or DVD drive
▶ How to play MP3 files and make playlists
▶ How to record and play back your own sounds
▶ How to burn your own data CDs or DVDs

In the preceding chapter, you learned how to become visually creative with images and photos. In this chapter, you learn to enjoy CD and MP3 music and get creative by recording and playing back your own sounds.

## Using the Volume Control

Before you play or record any sound at all, it's important for you to become familiar with the volume controls in Fedora Core 4. To start the volume controls, either right-click the speaker icon at the far right of the menubar and choose Open Volume Control, or choose Applications, Sound & Video, Volume Control. The Volume Control application appears, as shown in Figure 15.1.

You'll notice that the Volume Control application has two tabs, Playback and Capture. The Playback tab contains volume adjustments for sound output, such as your speakers or your computer's audio (wave) generator, while the Capture tab, shown in Figure 15.2, contains volume adjustments for sound sources, such as microphones or CD players.

**FIGURE 15.1**
The Volume Control application's Playback tab contains sliders that adjust volume settings for your sound hardware.

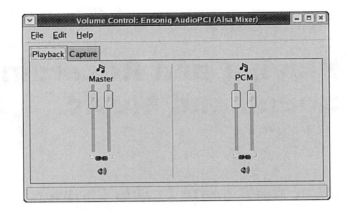

**FIGURE 15.2**
The Capture tab contains sliders that adjust volume settings for sound sources.

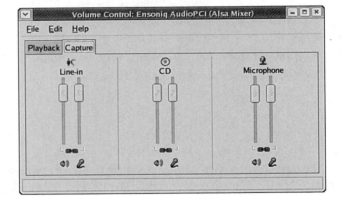

### Not All Sound Hardware Is the Same

Because different makes and models of PC sound hardware often enjoy different capabilities, your Volume Control application might not quite match the appearance of the Volume Control application shown in Figures 15.1 and 15.2. This is normal, and you shouldn't worry too much about it; we deal only with the master volume (Master), wave output (PCM), and microphone (Microphone) adjustments in this chapter anyway.

The Volume Control application contains a number of different sliders related to various capabilities and features of your sound hardware. For the purposes of this chapter, we're interested in only three of them:

▶ The master volume (Master) control on the Playback tab adjusts the output volume of all the sounds processed and output by your sound card. This control is not to be confused with the volume knob on your computer's speakers, if they have one; the volume slider adjusts the level of the signal that your computer sends to your speakers or earphones. You can turn it up or down as needed, but you should never turn it all the way up, or your sound quality will degrade and you may risk damaging your speakers or earphones.

▶ The wave output (PCM) control on the Capture tab adjusts the volume of only the portion of the card that generates sound from digital data supplied by programs or stored on your hard drive. This volume control does not affect audio stored on regular audio CDs, but rather audio from MP3 files, videos, or Internet audio. This volume control is secondary to the master volume control; that is, if the master volume is all the way down, no wave output is audible, no matter how high the wave output volume is set.

▶ The microphone (Microphone) control on the Capture tab adjusts the input volume of microphone devices plugged into your computer's mic jack. A volume set too high lowers the quality of recorded sound, whereas a volume set too low might make recorded sound difficult to hear.

You will probably need to spend some time adjusting all three of these volume control sliders as you progress through this chapter. Because adjusting volume is not a science but a modest form of art, and sound hardware varies from computer to computer, you simply need to employ a trial-and-error process in adjusting volume until your computer's audio sounds the way that you want it to.

Feel free to leave the Volume Control application open on your desktop so that you can return to it if necessary as you work through this chapter.

**Look for the Red X**

If you find that parts of this chapter don't work for you (in particular, that you don't hear sound when you believe you should), look for red X marks over the icons near the bottom of your Volume Control application. These red X marks indicate that the volume control in question is muted. Click on the X to unmute the control.

# Playing Audio CDs

To play an audio CD in Fedora Core 4, simply insert the audio CD that you want to listen to and shut your CD or DVD drive. Within a few moments, you hear the first track on the CD and see the CD player application on your desktop, as shown in Figure 15.3.

**FIGURE 15.3**
The CD player application starts automatically whenever you insert an audio CD. Note the display of the artist, album, and track names.

If you are connected to the Internet, whether through a local area network, dial-up Internet access, or cable/DSL, the CD player application identifies your CD and then automatically obtains the artist, album name, and tracks list from an online database. You then see the artist name, album name, and name of the currently playing track in the CD application's display at all times.

As you can see in Figure 15.3, the CD player application contains a number of controls that you can operate with your mouse or pointing device. On the bottom row, they include the following buttons, from left to right:

▶ Previous Track, which skips to the previous track if the current track has just started, or skips to the beginning of the current track if the current track has been playing for some time

▶ Rewind, which audibly rewinds the current track for as long as you hold down your mouse button

▶ Pause/Play, which either pauses CD playback (without stopping the CD spinning in the CD/DVD drive) if the CD is currently playing, or plays the CD if playback is currently paused

▶ Stop, which stops playback of the CD and stops the CD spinning in the CD/DVD drive

▶ Fast Forward, which audibly increases the speed at which the current track is playing for as long as you hold down your mouse button

▶ Next Track, which skips the rest of the current track and begins playing at the start of the next track

▶ Eject, which causes the CD to stop spinning in the CD/DVD drive and then causes the CD/DVD drive to eject the CD

**Too Many Buttons to Remember?**

One easy way to remember what each control in the CD player application does is to let your mouse pointer hover over the buttons in the application.

Each time you let your mouse pointer hover over the button for a few seconds, a little tooltip appears listing what the button is used for.

*By the Way*

Just above the bottom row of buttons is the CD tracks drop-down list, which you can use to play any track on the CD. To use it, follow these steps:

1. Click the CD tracks drop-down list. The drop-down list displays all the tracks on the CD by number and name.

2. Select the number and name of the track that you want to play from the list. The track you select immediately begins to play.

## Editing Album and Track Information

Sometimes you may find that the information the CD player obtains from the Internet about the album you're playing is inaccurate. Sometimes the artist, album name, or tracks list is incorrect; at other times, you may find that the CD player is unable to find your album at all in online databases, in which case the artist, album name, and all tracks show up as "Unknown." You also see this result if you are not connected to the Internet when you begin playing a new CD.

*To edit the CD player's knowledge of the artist, album name, and tracks list for a particular CD while it is playing, click the Open Track Editor button shown in Figure 15.3 to open the CDDB Track Editor.*

You can make three kinds of changes using the CDDB Track Editor:

- To change the name of the artist for the CD in question, click in the Artist entry box and enter any changes you want to make.

- To change the name of the album for the CD in question, click in the Disc Title entry box and enter any changes you want to make.

- To change the name of any of the tracks on the CD in question, double-click the text name of the track in question; a cursor appears in the title, and you then can enter any changes you want to make. After you are done editing the information for the CD, click the Save button to save your changes. Afterward, whenever you insert the CD in question, the new, updated information will be displayed by the CD player application.

# Playing MP3 Digital Music Files

As computers have become more and more popular (and powerful), many music consumers have begun to choose digital MP3 files as their preferred medium of choice, rather than older formats such as audio CDs or cassette tapes. Although you can play MP3 files in Fedora Core 4, a little bit of work on your part is required.

## Restoring MP3 Support to Fedora Core 4

Because of the legal issue surrounding the MP3 music format, Red Hat has chosen to remove support for MP3 music from Fedora Core 4. You can restore this functionality to Fedora Core 4, however, by installing the X MultiMedia System (XMMS) application. To do so, follow these steps:

1. Open your web browser by clicking on the globe icon on the menubar. Enter the address http://www.xmms.org/download.php in the URL bar. Scroll down the page until you find the Fedora Core section, as shown in Figure 15.4. For details on using the Firefox web browser, refer to Chapter 11, "Browsing the Web with Firefox."

Click to download MP3 player

**FIGURE 15.4**
Start Mozilla and visit http://www.xmms.org/download.php to download a complete version of the XMMS application, including MP3 support.

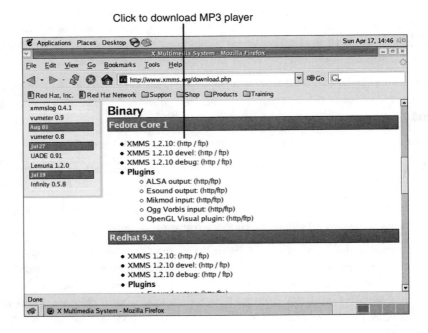

2. Right-click the http link next to the text XMMS 1.x.x (where x.x are version numbers), but be sure not to mistakenly right-click the links next to the "devel" or "debug" versions. In the context menu that appears, choose Save Link Target As. The file dialog box shown in Figure 15.5 appears.

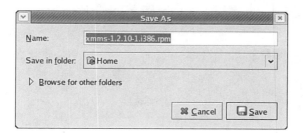

**FIGURE 15.5**
Using this file dialog box, save the XMMS file to your home directory.

---

**Is This the Right Version for Fedora Core 4?**

When you visit xmms.org, you'll find that there might not be a current version of XMMS for Fedora Core 4—the most recent version of XMMS might be intended for an older version of Fedora Core.

Not to worry. Software written for older versions of Fedora Core is generally compatible with Fedora Core 4. This is the case with XMMS as well, so just download and install the most recent version, whatever it is.

*By the Way*

---

3. Be sure that you are saving the file to your home directory, or if not, navigate to your home directory in the file dialog box. In your home directory, click Save to save the file. For more details on using the Linux file system, including information about concepts such as home directories and file dialog boxes, refer to Chapter 5, "Working with Files on the Desktop."

4. The Download Manager shown in Figure 15.6 appears, displaying a bar graph that shows Mozilla's progress in downloading the XMMS application. After the download is complete, exit Firefox or minimize your Firefox window.

5. Open a file manager, either by double-clicking the Home icon on your desktop or by choosing Places, Home Folder. In your home directory, locate the XMMS file; it appears as an icon of a box being opened, as shown in Figure 15.7.

6. Double-click the icon for the XMMS file's icon. Fedora Core 4 briefly shows a bar graph as it prepares to install your new software.

7. When the Completed System Preparation dialog box shown in Figure 15.8 is displayed, click Continue to install the updated XMMS software with MP3 support.

**FIGURE 15.6**
Mozilla displays a bar graph in the Download Manager to indicate download progress.

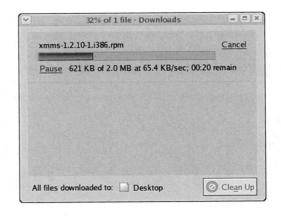

**FIGURE 15.7**
In the file manager, find the icon of the XMMS application that looks like a box being opened and double-click it.

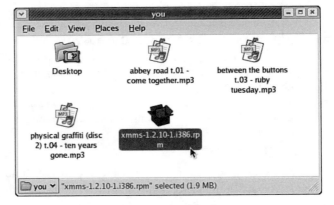

**FIGURE 15.8**
When system preparation is complete, click Continue to install the new XMMS software.

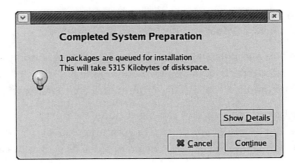

8. Now that the XMMS software is installed, you must tell Fedora Core 4 to use it to play MP3 files. To do this, right-click on an MP3 file and choose Properties. In the Properties dialog, select the Open With tab, shown in Figure 15.9.

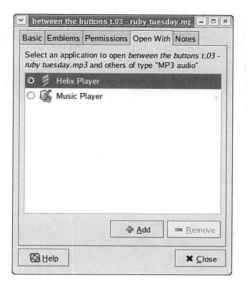

**FIGURE 15.9**
Right-click on an MP3 file, choose Properties, and then select the Open With tab in the Properties dialog.

9. Click the Add button near the bottom of the Properties dialog to display the Add Application dialog shown in Figure 15.10. In the Add Application dialog, choose Use a Custom Command (near the bottom of the dialog), then type xmms into the box. Click Add to save your changes.

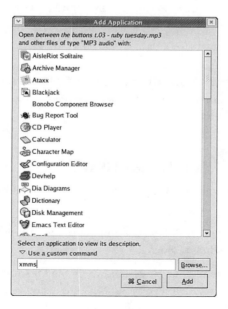

**FIGURE 15.10**
Enter xmms to use the xmms application you've just downloaded to play MP3 files.

10. In the Open With tab of the Properties dialog, you should now see xmms listed as an option, as shown in Figure 15.11. Select it and click Close to save your changes.

**FIGURE 15.11**
Select xmms in the Open With tab to tell Fedora Core to open MP3 files with XMMS. Then click Close to save your changes.

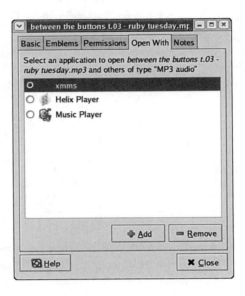

After you install the new software, you can drag the XMMS software's icon to the trash if you want; the software is now installed, and the installer file is no longer needed.

*By the Way*

> **Want More Information on Installing Software?**
>
> For more details on how to install software in Fedora Core 4, refer to Chapter 31, "Installing Linux Software."

## Playing MP3 Files Using XMMS

Now that you have restored MP3 support to Fedora Core 4, playing MP3 files is easy. Just follow these steps:

1. Start a file manager by double-clicking the Home icon on your desktop or by choosing Places, Home Folder.

2. Browse to the area in your file system where the MP3 files are stored, if necessary. You'll know when you've found MP3 files using your file manager because they are displayed with an icon that looks like a musical note.

3. Double-click the music file to start the XMMS application and play the MP3 music file. The XMMS application is shown in Figure 15.12.

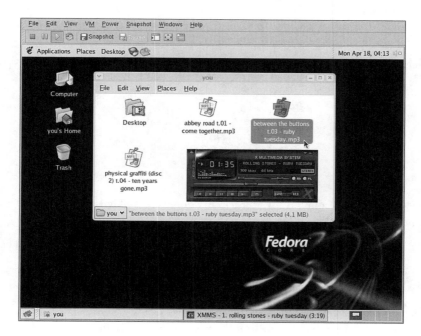

**FIGURE 15.12**
The XMMS application plays MP3 files in Red Hat Desktop.

---

**What If I Don't Hear Any Music?**

If you don't hear any music, yet the XMMS display seems to indicate that music is playing (the audio graph is moving and the minutes:seconds display is counting), try the following steps to rectify your problem and hear the music:

1. Right-click anywhere in the XMMS application and choose Options, Preferences from the context menu.

2. In the Preferences dialog box that appears, select OSS Driver from the Output Plugin drop-down list near the bottom of the dialog box.

3. Click OK to save your changes, exit XMMS by clicking the Close Window button, and then try to play the MP3 track again by double-clicking it. You should now hear sound.

## Using the XMMS Playlist and Controls

Like most MP3 player applications, XMMS can be used to create lists of MP3 files from your hard drive that you want to play all as a batch. It also provides a number of controls to affect how the files are played back.

To open the Playlist editor in XMMS, right-click anywhere in the XMMS window and choose Playlist Editor from the context menu. The Playlist window appears, as shown in Figure 15.13.

**FIGURE 15.13**
The Playlist editor helps you to create and manage your playlists in XMMS.

The Playlist editor displays a list of tracks in your current playlist. The basics of navigating the Playlist editor are as follows:

▶ To add a track to your current playlist, click the Add button. A file dialog box is displayed; use it to select the track(s) that you want to add to the playlist.

▶ To remove a track from your current playlist, right-click the track in question and then choose Remove, Selected from the context menu.

▶ To randomize a playlist (so that the tracks are in random order), right-click in the Playlist editor window and choose Sort, Randomize List from the context menu.

▶ To save a playlist when you're happy with it, right-click in the Playlist editor window and choose Playlist, Save List. A file dialog box appears asking you to name your playlist.

▶ To load a playlist you've saved, right-click in the Playlist editor window and choose Playlist, Load List. A file dialog box appears allowing you to select a list from the file system and load it.

▶ To begin a new playlist, right-click in the Playlist editor window and choose Playlist, New List.

After you finish creating a playlist and are ready to begin playing it back, select the track in the playlist where you want playing to begin; then click the Play button in the main window of the XMMS application (refer to Figure 15.11 for details).

While a playlist is playing, you can also choose two helpful *toggles* in XMMS that affect the way in which a playlist is played:

▶ To enable shuffle play (playing tracks from a playlist in random order), right-click in the main XMMS window and then choose Options, Shuffle.

▶ To enable repeat play (starting over and continuing play with the first track again after all tracks in the list have been played), right-click in the main XMMS window and then choose Options, Repeat.

---

**What's a Toggle?**

A toggle is a kind of option in a program that is on if you select it once, then off if you select it again, then on if you select it a third time, and so on. Each time you select a toggle setting, it changes to its opposite.

In the case of the shuffle and repeat play options in XMMS, selecting once turns shuffle or repeat on; selecting the same option again turns it back off.

---

**What About All the Rest Of XMMS?**

If you use the XMMS application for anything more than a few seconds, you'll realize that there's a lot more to it than we can cover in a chapter like this one. For a more complete rundown of the features of XMMS and how to use them, visit the XMMS support web page at http://www.xmms.org/support.php.

*By the Way*

# Recording and Playing Back Sound

From time to time, you may have the need to record sound from a microphone and save it to a digital file in Fedora Core 4 that you'll be able to play back later. Naturally, to start, you need to have a microphone plugged into the microphone jack of your computer. When you have a microphone handy and plugged in, recording sound is easy.

To start the sound recorder application in Fedora Core 4, choose GNOME Menu, Sound & Video, Sound Recorder. The Sound Recorder application starts, as shown in Figure 15.14.

To record and save a sound, simply follow these steps:

**1.** Select your desired quality level using the Record As drop-down list. The CD quality options produce much better sound quality, but also use more space on disk for your recordings. The Voice option produces less clear sound, but uses much less space.

**FIGURE 15.14**
The Sound
Recorder appli-
cation records
sound from a
microphone to
a digital file
that can be
replayed later.

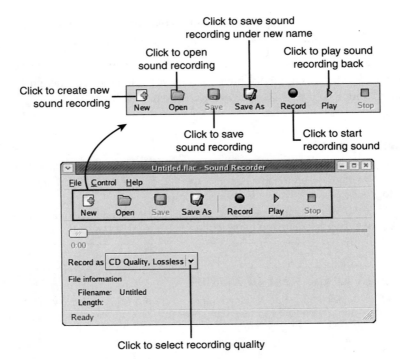

Click to save sound
recording under new name

Click to open
sound recording

Click to play sound
recording back

Click to create new
sound recording

Click to save
sound recording

Click to start
recording sound

Click to select recording quality

2. Click the Record button to begin recording. You see a timer near the bottom of the application window begin to count; it shows the recording time.

3. When you're done recording, click the Stop button.

4. Click the Save As button to display a file dialog box that allows you to save the sound to a digital wave (.WAV) file.

After you make a recording, playing it back is easy and can be done in two ways:

▶ If you have just made the recording and are still in the Sound Recorder appli-cation, simply click the Play button to play back your recording.

▶ If you want to play back a recording that you made some time ago, open a file manager and browse to the location of the recording. Double-click the digital file to which you saved your recording, and the recording is played back.

# Burning Your Own CDs

If you have a CD or DVD recordable or rewritable drive, from time to time you may want to record your own CDs or DVDs containing data or MP3 music. To do this, simply insert a blank CD or DVD recordable disc into your CD or DVD drive or select Places, CD/DVD Creator in any open file manager window. An empty file manager appears showing the title CD/DVD Creator, as shown in Figure 15.15.

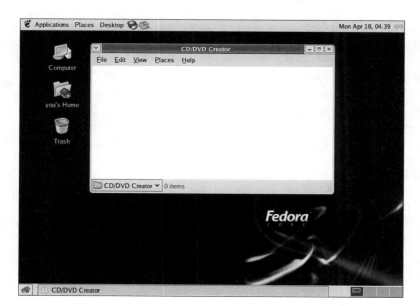

**FIGURE 15.15**
The CD/DVD Creator is a special file manager window that can be used to fill a CD or DVD with files.

To create a CD or DVD, simply drag and drop files and folders into the CD/DVD Creator window just as you would into any other file manager window; refer to Chapter 5 if you have forgotten how to manage files using file manager windows.

When all the files and folders you want to store on the CD or DVD are listed in the CD/DVD Creator window, choose File, Write to Disc. When the confirmation dialog appears, click Write to save the files you've chosen onto the blank CD or DVD. A progress bar is displayed as the contents are "burned" onto the disk. After the burn is complete, you can use the new CD or DVD like any other data CD or DVD.

*By the* *Way*

**Can I Burn Audio CDs or Movie DVDs This Way?**

Unfortunately, the file manager is capable of burning only data CDs or DVDs. They can be useful for storing audio MP3 files or digital movie files, but CDs and DVDs created this way can be accessed only by computer—not by using a standard audio CD player or a standard DVD player connected to a television.

The creation of audio CDs and movie DVDs is beyond the scope of this book because such tasks require that you download or buy, and subsequently install, additional Fedora Core 4 applications. However, you might find the following web URLs for Linux CD/DVD recording software helpful if you are interested in performing more advanced multimedia creation tasks using Fedora Core 4:

http://www.xcdroast.com

http://www.gearsoftware.com

http://www.gnometoaster.rulez.org

# Summary

In this chapter, you learned how to perform a number of tasks related to digital audio and CD and DVD media in Fedora Core 4:

- ▶ Play CD and digital audio MP3 music

- ▶ Make playlists and play them back in several ways

- ▶ Record and play back your own digital recordings

- ▶ Burn data CDs and DVDs using the file manager

With the skills you've just learned, you can listen to your favorite tunes while you work through the rest of the chapters in this book!

# Q&A

**Q** *Can XMMS play music in other digital formats?*

**A** Yes, XMMS can play .WAV files natively, and many other file formats are supported through plug-ins. For more details, visit http://www.xmms.org.

**Q** *What about playing DVD movies in Linux?*

**A** Because a number of complex legal issues surround the playback of commercial DVDs, the use of DVD-playing software in Fedora Core 4 may or may not be legal where you live. Software for DVD playback therefore is not included in Fedora Core 4. To download DVD playback software for Linux, visit one of the following URLs:

http://www.videolan.org

http://www.dtek.chalmers.se/groups/dvd/

**Q** *Can I use Fedora Core to make my own MP3 files from CDs I have?*

**A** Yes. However, because of the legal issues involved, Fedora Core 4 doesn't *include* the software necessary to do so. The process for making MP3 files is therefore beyond the scope of this book. For more information on making MP3 files in Linux, visit the LAME project at:

http://lame.sourceforge.net

Fedora Core 4 *is* capable of changing your music CDs into other music formats such as .WAV, though we won't discuss the process in this book. To start the application used to do this, choose Applications, Sound & Video, Sound Juicer CD Ripper.

# Workshop

The Workshop is designed to help you anticipate possible questions, review what you've learned, and begin learning how to put your knowledge into practice.

## Quiz

1.  How do you begin playing back an audio CD or DVD?

2.  How to you open the Playlist editor window in XMMS?

3.  How do you open the burn window in the file manager?

## Answers

1.  Just insert an audio CD or DVD to automatically launch the CD player application and begin playback.

2.  To open the Playlist editor in the XMMS application, right-click anywhere in the application window and choose Playlist Editor from the context menu.

3. To open a file manager window for burning a CD or DVD, simply insert a blank CD or DVD recordable disc into the recording device or choose Places, CD/DVD Creator in any open file manager window. Drag and drop the files that you want to burn to this window and then choose File, Write to Disc to begin recording.

## Activities

1. Create a playlist of your favorite MP3 files and play them on shuffle play with repeat.

2. Burn some of your favorite MP3 files to a CD for safe-keeping.

3. Make a recording of yourself singing one of your favorite tunes and play it back for a co-worker or a friend.

# CHAPTER 16

# Customizing the Desktop

## What You'll Learn in This Chapter:

▶ How to adjust the sensitivity of your mouse or pointer
▶ How to change the color and appearance of Linux applications
▶ How to change your desktop wallpaper and screensaver
▶ How to create new application launcher icons

You already learned to find your way around the Linux desktop in day-to-day work. In this chapter, you learn how to modify your Linux desktop's behavior and appearance to suit your needs, preferences, and working habits. Making these kinds of changes can enhance your productivity and comfort at the desktop significantly. Furthermore, customizing your desktop can also be fun!

## Using the Desktop Preferences

The Desktop menu is your primary tool for customizing the appearance and behavior of the Fedora Core 4 desktop environment. By choosing Desktop, Preferences, you'll find a collection of tools that can be used to change your desktop settings; each of these settings has some effect on desktop behavior or appearance.

The Desktop, Preferences menu is shown in Figure 16.1.

## Changing Mouse Behavior

Depending on the type of pointing device you're using and whether you're left-handed or right-handed, you might find that you're not comfortable with the speed of the pointer on your display or the configuration of click and double-click behavior.

**FIGURE 16.1**
The Desktop,
Preferences
menu contains
a number of
configuration-
related tools.

To launch the Mouse Preferences dialog box used to configure mouse behavior, choose Desktop, Preferences, Mouse. The Mouse Preferences dialog box appears, as shown in Figure 16.2.

**FIGURE 16.2**
Using the
Mouse
Preferences
dialog box, you
can change the
behavioral prop-
erties of the
mouse. The
default view is
shown here.

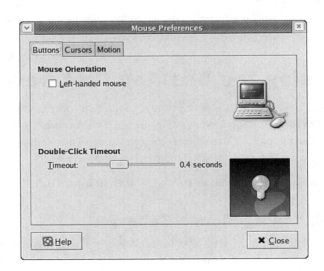

By the
Way

> ## What About Trackball, Touchpad, or Trackpoint Users?
> You use the Mouse Properties dialog box to configure your pointing device even if you use a trackball, touchpad, trackpoint, or similar device instead of a mouse.

The default view in the Mouse Preferences dialog box, shown in Figure 16.2, is of the Buttons tab, which contains the following options:

▶ Mouse Orientation reverses the order of the buttons on your pointing devices. Left-handed users should check the Left-handed mouse box to cause the button under their index finger to act as the first mouse button.

▶ Double-Click Timeout changes the speed at which you must double-click in order for the double-click to be recognized by the Linux desktop. If you often find that the Linux desktop ignores your double-clicks, you should click the slider and increase the allowable delay between clicks.

You can display the second view in the Mouse Preferences dialog box by clicking the Cursors tab, as shown in Figure 16.3.

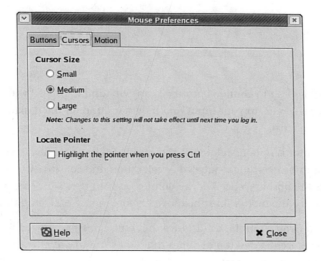

**FIGURE 16.3**
The Cursors tab contains options related to the appearance of the mouse pointer on the screen.

This view enables you to change the appearance of the mouse pointer, or cursor, on the screen. Select Small, Medium, or Large to cause the mouse pointer to appear in a size that is visually most helpful to you.

Check Highlight the Pointer When You Press Ctrl to make it easier to find a lost mouse pointer on the desktop by animating the mouse pointer prominently when you hold down the Ctrl key. If you often find yourself searching for the mouse pointer, consider enabling this option.

You can display the third and final view in the Mouse Preferences dialog box by clicking the Motion tab, as shown in Figure 16.4.

**FIGURE 16.4**
The Motion tab contains options related to the speed of the mouse pointer on your desktop while moving the mouse.

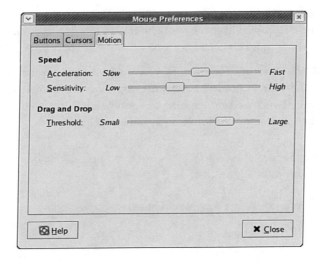

This view enables you to change both the sensitivity and the speed with which the mouse pointer responds to your input and moves around on the desktop. It contains the following options:

▶ Speed contains options related to the speed of the mouse on the desktop. This area contains two sliders, labeled Acceleration and Sensitivity. Acceleration controls the absolute speed of the pointer on your desktop. Sensitivity controls the distance the mouse must be moved before mouse acceleration takes effect.

▶ Drag and Drop controls the distance the mouse must be moved while clicking an icon before the desktop assumes that you want to drag the icon, rather than click it. If you sometimes have unsteady hands, increasing the Drag and Drop value can make desktop use easier.

After you configure the options in the Mouse Properties dialog box to suit your needs, click Close to close the dialog box.

# Changing Window Appearance

If you find the default appearance of the application windows in Fedora Core 4 to be distasteful or difficult to use, you can alter the colors and decorations used to draw application windows by using the Theme Preferences dialog box.

To launch the Theme Preferences dialog box, choose Desktop, Preferences, Theme. The Theme Preferences dialog box appears, as shown in Figure 16.5.

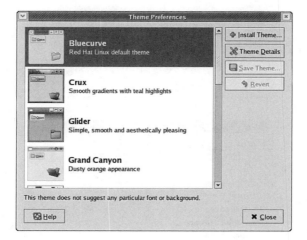

**FIGURE 16.5**
Using the Theme Preferences dialog box, you can change the physical appearance and colors of application windows.

In the Theme Preferences dialog box, icons represent a number of miniature application windows, each containing a menu title and an icon so that you can see how window decorations, menus, and graphics appear in a given theme. By default, Fedora Core 4's own Bluecurve theme is selected.

To change the appearance of application windows to that of an alternate theme, click the icon representing the theme that you want to use. The border, title bar, and window decorations of all running applications change immediately to reflect your new theme selection, as shown in Figure 16.6. If you decide that you don't like your new theme, click Revert to return to your previous setting. Otherwise, to accept the new theme, click Close.

More advanced users may also want to create themes for individual components of the desktop—for example, the widgets (controls) from one theme, the window border and decorations from a second theme, and the set of icons from a third. To find controls that allow you this type of flexibility, click the Details button in the Theme Preferences dialog box. The Theme Details dialog box appears, as shown in Figure 16.7.

**FIGURE 16.6**
Selecting a
theme causes
the appearance
of the desktop
to change
immediately.
This is the
Grand Canyon
theme.

**FIGURE 16.7**
In the Theme
Details dialog
box, you can
select widget,
window deco-
ration, and
icon themes
independently of
one another.

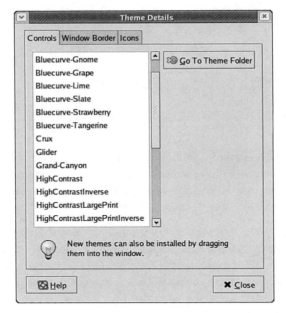

In the Theme Details dialog box, use the three tabs to set the three aspects of application appearance, respectively—controls (widgets), window border, and icons. By
combining elements from disparate themes, you can achieve unique desktop effects.

---

**You Can Install Your Own Desktop Themes**

Ambitious users can download and install their own themes from the website http://themes.freshmeat.net. To download and install a theme, follow the directions on the website to save the theme you want to use to your home directory. Then open a file manager window and drag the icon of the theme package into the Theme Preferences dialog box. The theme you downloaded then appears in the themes list and can be selected like any other theme.

Remember that any theme you want to download and install must be intended for Fedora Core 4; otherwise, it is not likely to work correctly.

---

# Changing Your Desktop Wallpaper

Desktop wallpaper is an image or pattern that appears on the desktop beneath icons and application windows. To change your desktop wallpaper, choose Desktop, Preferences, Desktop Background. The Desktop Background Preferences dialog box appears, as shown in Figure 16.8.

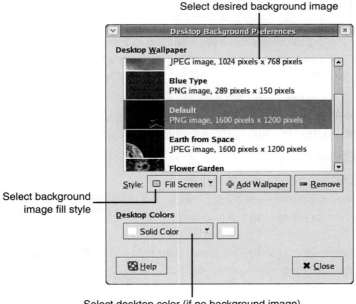

Select desired background image

Select background image fill style

Select desktop color (if no background image)

**FIGURE 16.8**
Using the Desktop Background Preferences dialog box, you can change your desktop wallpaper image.

To change the picture used as your desktop wallpaper, click on any of the images in the Desktop Wallpaper list. If you'd like to use one of your own image files as your desktop wallpaper, click Add Wallpaper. A standard file dialog box appears so that you can select the image file you'd like to use.

For any wallpaper image, you have several choices for how the image is shown on the desktop, accessible via the Style drop-down list. The following options are available:

▶ Centered causes the image to be centered with respect to the desktop. If the image is smaller than the desktop, the edges of the display show a solid color. If the image is larger than the desktop, some of the image's edges may be cut off.

▶ Fill Screen causes the image to be enlarged or shrunk, changing the shape of the image as necessary to fit the size of your desktop exactly from edge to edge, both horizontally and vertically.

▶ Scaled causes the image to be enlarged or shrunk as necessary to fit the size of your desktop as closely as possible without changing the shape of the image.

▶ Tiled should be used if the image is smaller than your desktop to cause the image to be tiled over and over again across your display.

If you don't want to use a picture as your desktop wallpaper image, but instead would prefer a solid color or blend of colors, select No Wallpaper from the top of the Desktop Wallpaper list. Then select one of the following styles from the Desktop Colors drop-down list:

▶ Solid Color uses only one color that you select by clicking the button to the right of the drop-down list. This color then paints the entire desktop.

▶ Horizontal Gradient displays a second color button and then blends the two colors that you select together from left to right.

▶ Vertical Gradient displays a second color button and then blends the two colors that you select together from top to bottom.

After you configure your desktop wallpaper to suit your tastes, click the Close button in the Desktop Background Preferences box to close it.

## Changing Your Screensaver

A **screensaver** is a popular kind of program that takes over your computer display when you haven't used your computer for several minutes. The screensaver paints patterns or animations on the screen until you return and press a key or move the mouse. By default, no screensavers are installed in the Workstation installation described in Chapter 2, "Installing Fedora Core 4."

To change your screensaver, choose Desktop, Preferences, Screensaver. The Screensaver Preferences dialog box appears, as shown in Figure 16.9.

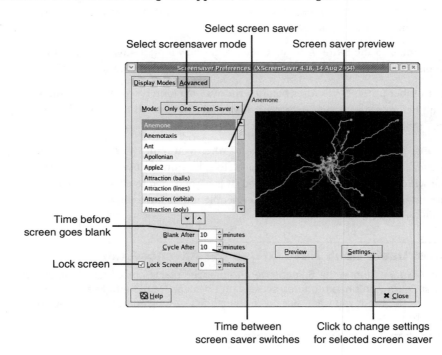

Select screen saver

Select screensaver mode

Screen saver preview

Time before screen goes blank

Lock screen

Time between screen saver switches

Click to change settings for selected screen saver

**FIGURE 16.9**
Using the Screensaver Preferences dialog box, you can choose a screensaver and alter its behavior.

To select the way in which screensavers are used on your system, use the Mode drop-down box. There, you can choose among the following options:

▶ Disable Screen Saver turns off the screensaver feature. Your desktop remains visible no matter how long it has been inactive.

▶ Blank Screen Only causes the screen to go black after a period of inactivity instead of displaying graphics or animations for your amusement.

▶ Only One Screen Saver causes the screensaver that has been selected in the selection box to become active after a period of inactivity.

▶ Random Screen Saver causes the desktop to cycle through the list of screen-savers at random, displaying one after another in turn, after a period of inactivity.

You can click any of the screensavers in the screensaver selection box to see a preview of the screensaver on the right side of the window. If you select the Only One Screen Saver mode, this also selects the screensaver that is used after a period of inactivity.

After you select a screensaver, you can alter its settings (such as color and speed of animation) by clicking the Settings button.

The number in the Blank After box determines how long a screensaver is allowed to run on an inactive system before the screen goes completely blank.

The number in the Cycle After box determines how long a screensaver is allowed to run before a new screensaver starts if you have selected the Random Screen Saver mode.

To cause the system to request a password when you return from a period of inactivity, check the Lock Screen After box and select the number of minutes of inactivity after which a password is to be required. It is a good idea to check this option if you work in an environment in which other people might have physical access to your computer system.

*By the Way*

> **Most Users Don't Need to Use the Advanced Tab**
>
> The Advanced tab in the Screensaver Preferences dialog box contains options that most users won't need to alter, so we won't discuss them here. Feel free to explore the tab if you want, but don't change any settings unless you know what you are doing!

After you configure your screensaver according to your own preferences, click the Close button to close the Screensaver Preferences dialog box.

## Changing Desktop Resolution

Sometimes it can be helpful to adjust the amount of information that you can see on your Linux desktop at any time, either by shrinking everything on the desktop (so that you can fit more things on it) or expanding everything on the desktop (so that you can see the things that *are* on it more clearly).

This change can be made by adjusting your desktop resolution. To do so, choose Desktop, Preferences, Screen Resolution. The Screen Resolution Preferences dialog box is shown (see Figure 16.10). To adjust your screen resolution, choose your preferred setting from the Resolution drop-down list. Some common settings are described here:

▶ 640×480—Displays everything on your desktop as large as is possible, at the expense of being able to fit fewer things onto your screen at once

▶ 800×600—Displays things at a nominally large size, while fitting more on your screen than the 640×480 setting; ideal for 14-inch and some 15-inch displays

▶ 1024×768—Fits more on your desktop still, with the drawback of shrinking text and icons smaller than is comfortable for most 14-inch display users; ideal for most 15-inch and 17-inch displays

▶ 1280×960 or higher—Use these high-resolution settings to squeeze as many items onto your desktop as is possible, by making icons and text as small as possible; ideal for some 17-inch and most 19-inch or larger displays

Select desired desktop size

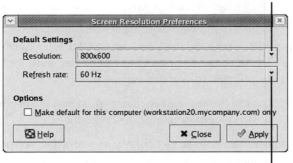

**FIGURE 16.10**
Use the Screen Resolution Preferences dialog box to adjust the size of your desktop and the items on it.

Select desired refresh rate

Once you have selected your preferred desktop resolution, you should also select a refresh rate. In general, you should choose the highest number available to you in the Refresh Rate drop-down list, *after* you consult your monitor or display's documentation to ensure that the refresh rate is supported. The higher the refresh rate you are able to use, the less flicker and eyestrain you'll experience as you use your desktop.

---

**Have a Monitor More Than a Year or Two Old?**

If your computer's display is more than a year or two old, check your manual very carefully before adjusting your resolution or refresh rate.

Newer monitors tell Linux about the resolutions and refresh rates that they can operate at, and Linux is careful to present to you only choices that your monitor can support.

Older monitors, however, do not have this capability, and Linux may therefore present you with choices that could harm your monitor, if your monitor's manual or user documentation doesn't list them as supported modes.

## Changing Other Desktop Preferences

Because of the limited amount of space in a book like this one, we can explore only the most commonly changed desktop preferences—preferences related to mouse movement, application window appearance, desktop wallpaper, screensavers, and desktop resolution. Many other aspects of the desktop can be altered through the Preferences menu, however:

▶ Choose Password to change your password and personal information available to other Fedora Core 4 users on your computer system.

▶ Choose Accessibility to change various aspects of desktop behavior to better suit disabled or differently abled individuals.

▶ Choose More Preferences, Preferred Applications to change programs used by the desktop to handle various types of files and tasks in day-to-day use.

▶ Choose Font to fine-tune the fonts used by GNOME to be as clear and visible as possible on your computer system. Special options exist for laptop computers or for those who find the default fonts to be too fuzzy.

▶ Choose Keyboard to change the key repeat speed and the default text cursor's appearance, and to enable or disable the keyboard bell.

▶ Choose Keyboard Shortcuts to tie Ctrl, Alt, and Function keystrokes of your choosing to various common GNOME functions, such as closing or maximizing windows.

▶ Choose Menus & Toolbars to show or hide text beneath toolbar icons and to show or hide icons in application drop-down menus.

▶ Choose Sound to change the sounds you hear when performing common tasks, such as hiding or closing windows, or to disable sound altogether.

▶ Choose Windows to change how windows are selected; choose either the default mode in which you must click a window to make it active or an alternate mode in which any window the mouse is pointing to will become active.

Feel free to explore the rest of the preferences until your desktop behaves exactly as you would like it to.

# Configuring the Menubar

In addition to changing the simple look, feel, and mouse behavior of your desktop environment, you need to be able to change the way in which you access the applications you most commonly use.

Specifically, you should be able to launch the applications you most commonly use by clicking icons on the menubar, where you can access them easily without having to look for them in several levels of menus.

## Adding an Icon to the Menubar

To add an icon to the menubar, right-click in an empty area of the menubar and choose Add to Panel. The Add to Panel dialog box is launched, as shown in Figure 16.11.

Click to add launcher

Click Add to proceed

**FIGURE 16.11**
Select Application Launcher to add an application icon to the menubar.

To add an application from the Applications menu, select Application Launcher and click Forward. You'll see a facsimile of the Applications menu, as shown in Figure 16.12. Browse through this list of applications to find the application whose icon you want to add to the menubar. Click the small triangle next to each category of applications to display the applications from that submenu of the Applications menu in the menubar. When you find the button that you want to add, double-click its icon. Instead of launching the application, the new application icon appears on your taskbar. Clicking the new icon launches the related application, as expected.

**FIGURE 16.12**
After you select
Application
Launcher in the
Add to Panel
dialog box,
choose the
application
you'd like
to add.

*By the*
*Way*

### Why Can't You Find the Add to Panel Option?

If you right-click the menubar but don't see the Add to Panel option in the context
menu, the menubar probably thinks you right-clicked one of the existing icons.

It can be tricky to find an empty area in the menubar where you can right-click
without hitting an existing launcher. Perhaps the best place is just to the right of
and slightly above the rightmost existing application icon.

## Moving an Icon on the Menubar

To move an icon to the left or right on the menubar, right-click the icon you would
like to move and choose Move from the pop-up context menu that appears. After
you choose Move from the context menu, your mouse pointer changes in appearance to indicate that you are moving an icon, and moving your pointing device to
the left or right causes the icon on the taskbar to move to the left or right, displacing
existing icons as necessary. When you position the icon where you want it, click
any mouse button to release the icon; it remains in that position unless you move
it again.

## Removing an Icon from the Menubar

To remove an item from the menubar, right-click the icon you would like to remove
and choose Remove from Panel from the pop-up context menu that appears. After
you choose Remove from the context menu, the icon is removed from the menubar
permanently or until you decide to add it again.

## Additional Menubar Configuration

There are additional types of menubar configuration in the Add to Panel dialog box that can be fun to explore, although we won't cover them in detail here.

Among the additions that can be made to the taskbar this way are the following:

▶ Applets are small programs that perform useful tasks, such as clocks, system monitors, and volume controls. You can generally move and remove them in the same manner as taskbar icons—by right-clicking them and choosing either Move or Remove.

▶ Custom application launchers can be used to create icons for applications that don't appear in the Applications menu. This technique is discussed in detail in Chapter 31, "Installing Linux Software."

More help on using the GNOME menubar can be found in the User Guide using the help browser discussed in Chapter 17, "Getting Help on the Desktop."

# Summary

In this chapter, you learned how to change the most commonly modified desktop properties in Fedora Core 4 using the Desktop, Preferences menu. Among the desktop properties you learned to change are the behavior of your mouse (including suitability for left- or right-handed use), the color and appearance of application windows, and your desktop wallpaper and screensaver.

You also learned to add icons for your favorite applications to the menubar so that you can launch them without having to access lengthy menus. Finally, you learned to move around items on your menubar so that they appear in convenient logical order for you and to remove items from your menubar that you no longer want to appear there.

# Q&A

**Q** *This chapter explained how to install new themes. I can't find too many themes for Fedora Core 4. Is it really necessary that the themes I download be designed for Fedora Core 4?*

**A** Yes. The themes that you download must be designed either for Fedora Core 4 or for GNOME 3.0, the version of the GNOME desktop environment used by Fedora Core.

# Workshop

The Workshop is designed to help you anticipate possible questions, review what you've learned, and begin learning how to put your knowledge into practice.

## Quiz

1. How do you access the desktop preferences?

2. What is a gradient? How do you enable a gradient?

3. How do you move an icon on the menubar?

4. How do you remove an icon from the menubar?

## Answers

1. You can access desktop preferences by choosing Desktop, Preferences, and then selecting the item that you want to change.

2. A gradient is a gradual blending from one color to another color. To enable a gradient, disable the use of wallpaper images and then select your colors and gradient from the Desktop Background Preferences dialog box.

3. Right-click the icon you want to move and choose Move from the context menu.

4. Right-click the icon you want to remove and choose Remove from the context menu.

## Activities

1. Explore some of the items on the Preferences menu that we didn't discuss. See what the settings do.

2. Change the appearance and colors of your desktop applications and wallpaper to suit your tastes.

3. Add a few application icons to your menubar and arrange them as you prefer them to appear.

# CHAPTER 17

# Getting Help on the Desktop

## What You'll Learn in This Chapter:

▶ How to get help for common desktop applications

▶ How to use the help browser for more detailed help

▶ How to read the online manuals for shell commands using the desktop help browser

As you've already learned, as you work in Linux, you always have a number of help tools and resources available to you. The Linux desktop offers its own help resources in addition to the Linux man and info pages. You can access systemwide help through menus in common desktop applications. In this chapter, you learn how to use desktop tools to find these and other help and documentation materials for assistance with applications and commands commonly used in Linux systems.

After you learn these techniques for finding and using desktop help, you will have gained the skill to locate nearly any kind of online documentation available on a Linux computer system.

## Using Application Help

The most natural place to find help or documentation information for any application is within the application itself. Nearly every desktop application you use in Linux includes some form of online help that you can open from within the application.

Documentation of this sort is often the most useful type of help because it is written by the authors of the application in question. Furthermore, this kind of documentation typically assumes that readers are actually *using* the application while reading the help information. As a result, you should be able to use the in-application documentation to work through your problem step by step, often with alternative suggestions and other information to assist you with snags you might encounter.

## Finding and Launching Application Help

When an application includes its own online help or documentation file(s), it is generally accessible through the Help menu located in the application menubar (by convention, the Help menu is the rightmost menu on the menubar).

In any application, the Help menu contains a list of help and documentation-related options, including the Contents option, which launches application documentation, and the About option, which displays the application version, copyright, authors, and other miscellaneous information.

A typical application Help menu is shown in Figure 17.1.

**FIGURE 17.1**
Opening the Help menu in an application generally reveals at least a Contents option and an About option.

## Using the About Option in Help Menus

When you need to learn licensing, version, or other information about your application, choose Help, About to open the About information dialog box, shown in Figure 17.2. Licensing information provides details about the ways in which you are allowed to use and distribute the application. Version information can be helpful to the application's author if you need to submit a bug report, and can be useful to know in cases in which separate applications are meant to work together, but only in certain version combinations.

The About information includes email addresses for the program's authors (click the Credits button to see it). If you have a bug report, feature request, or specific question about an application not covered in the application's online documentation, you can use the email contact information in the About dialog boxes to write the authors of the application and ask them directly. When submitting a bug report about an application or asking a question about an application of the application's author, be sure to include the following information:

▶ The version of the Linux operating system you're using (Fedora Core 4)

▶ The name of the application in question

▶ The version of the application in which you've encountered a problem or about which you have a question

▶ A complete, in-depth description of the problem you're experiencing or the question you need answered, including details about what other applications are typically running and the circumstances surrounding the incident

After you finish using the About information, click the OK button to close the About dialog box.

### Application Authors Are Busy People!

Be sure to check the other types of online documentation that you learn about in this chapter before you contact an application's author with questions about using the application; application authors don't like to receive questions they've already answered in online documentation.

If you're familiar with search services like Google, try also searching for some terms related to your problem there before you email application authors. For example, try "adjusting sharpness in gimp" or "saving files in openoffice." You may find user communities and documentation websites that are helpful to you.

## Viewing Help Contents

In most applications, you can display the application manual or other use-oriented documentation by choosing Help, Contents. The help browser opens and displays the table of contents for the available application help; in Figure 17.3, help displays the table of contents for gedit version 2.8 help.

**FIGURE 17.3**
Choosing the Contents option from the Help menu displays the table of contents for the application's help. Click a section listing to view that section's contents.

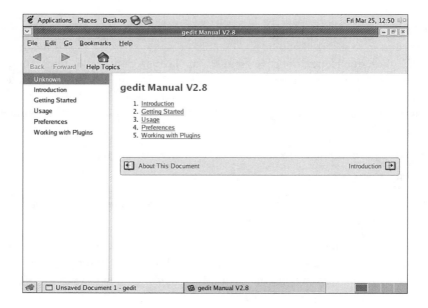

To read any section of the Help contents, click its title in the table of contents, as shown in Figure 17.4. Use the left and right arrow icons in Figure 17.3 that look like open books, located at the bottom of each section, to move through Help contents pages.

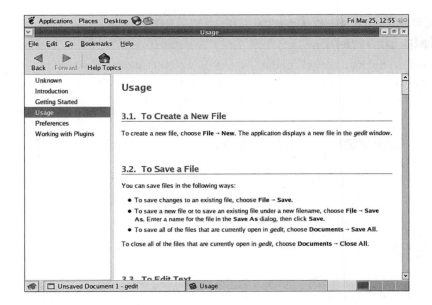

**FIGURE 17.4**
Click on a topic in the left panel of the help browser to display that section of the manual in the right panel.

Choose File, Close or click the application's Close button (X in the upper-right corner) to close the online help.

# Viewing Systemwide Help in the Help Browser

Although application-specific manuals or handbooks are certainly useful for understanding how to use a particular application, often you need more general help for the desktop environment you're using. The Fedora Core 4 desktop provides a general help system that documents the fundamentals of the desktop environment and the aspects of operation that lie outside the bounds of any particular application.

In this help system, you're likely to find FAQs (frequently asked questions), fundamentals on using the desktop, some discussion of the desktop environment's philosophy for use, and some idea about the basic structure of the desktop and the way in which its components work together to provide you with a friendly computing experience.

## Launching and Using the Systemwide Help Browser

To launch the help browser from the desktop, choose Desktop, Help from the menubar. The help browser window opens to display the Help Topics categories for the Fedora Core 4 desktop environment, as shown in Figure 17.5.

**FIGURE 17.5**
The help browser gives you access to help documentation for applications, utilities, graphics, and game packages, as well as system commands, man pages, and info pages.

Each main link in the Help Topics categories leads you to a list of documents for that category; each document within a category represents an online manual. For example, clicking the Desktop link leads to the list of documents and online manuals shown in Figure 17.6.

Documents in the Desktop help section are likely to be especially helpful when you're new to Linux or the GNOME environment that the Fedora Core 4 desktop uses. Scroll to the bottom of the list for a link to the GNOME User Guide, which covers configuration techniques; basic methods of using the mouse to accomplish file and window management tasks; and efficient use of the file manager, taskbar, and desktop. The Desktop section also includes the following documents that may be helpful to new Linux users:

▶ Applets, which discusses several small applications that can be launched to reside in the taskbar

▶ The Accessibility Guide, which gives details on making the desktop more accessible or friendly to users with various physical limitations

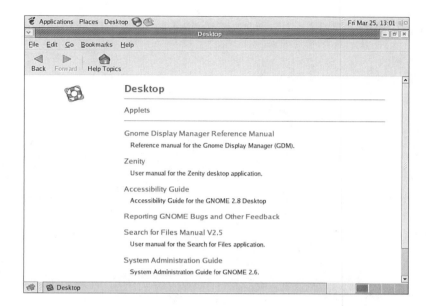

**FIGURE 17.6**
The list of
documents in
the Desktop
section of the
systemwide
help docu-
mentation.

▶ The Search for Files Manual, which describes how to use the desktop's file
search functionality to locate files that have gone astray

▶ The System Administration Guide, which gives more advanced configuration
details on the GNOME desktop environment used by Fedora Core 4, so that
power users can more easily customize the environment to suit their needs

# Browsing Application Manuals in the Help Browser

The help browser also provides a user-friendly way to browse through manuals for
most of the desktop applications you'll find in the Applications menu in the
menubar. To access manuals for desktop applications, click on the Applications
link at the main list of categories shown in Figure 17.5. You'll be shown the list of
Applications categories shown in Figure 17.7.

The Applications page links to a number of different groups of desktop application
manuals:

▶ Clicking Accessibility shows you the list of available manuals for applications
that enhance computing accessibility for users with physical limitations.

▶ Clicking Accessories shows you the list of available manuals for simple desktop tools, like the dictionary and the calculator.

**FIGURE 17.7**
Click on
Applications
in the help
browser's main
category list to
browse through
manuals for
desktop
applications.

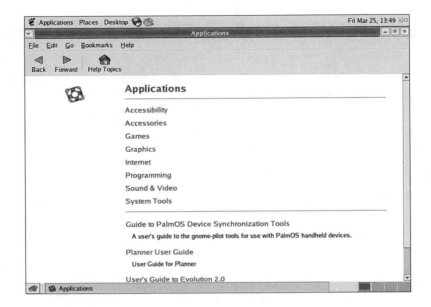

- ▶ Clicking Games shows you the list of available playing instructions for the games you'll find in the Applications, Games menu in the menubar.

- ▶ Clicking Graphics or Internet gives you a list of available manuals for graphics or networking-related applications, respectively.

- ▶ Clicking Programming gives you the list of available manuals related to applications to aid in developing software for the Linux desktop, using the tools that are installed on your Fedora Core 4 system.

- ▶ Clicking Sound & Video gives you the list of available manuals for applications that can record and play back sound or video.

- ▶ Clicking System Tools gives you the list of available manuals for applications related to the management of your computer, like archiving tools and the terminal application.

# Reading Other Documentation on the Desktop

In earlier chapters, you learned to use a few basic Linux commands to manage your files from the command line. All Linux systems include the shell commands you already learned and many, many more as well—far too many for any one person to be familiar with. Each command also offers the user a long list of options that can be used to affect its behavior. You'll learn more about how to use a number of these commands in Part IV, "Using the Linux Command Line," but in the meantime, you can begin to familiarize yourself with them by exploring their online documentation. Nearly every command in a Linux or Unix system offers online documentation via documents called man pages.

---

**Why Are They Called** man **Pages?**

The types of documentation being discussed in this section are called man pages after the shell command, man (short for manual), that is used to access them at the command line. You learn more about using the man command and its relative, info, to access online documentation in Chapter 18, "Becoming Familiar with Shell Environments."

*By the Way*

---

Though man pages can be quickly accessed from the command line, they're also easily accessed on your Linux desktop using the help browser, which provides a fast, more user-friendly way of reading them.

## Reading man **Pages Using the Help Browser**

As you learned in "Launching and Using the Systemwide Help Browser," there are a number of major categories of systemwide help. To access the online manuals for Linux commands, click on the Man Pages link shown in Figure 17.5. Clicking the Man Pages link leads to a list of the manual page sections—categories of commands that you can read about in online documentation. Manual pages are available in these sections (the related man command sections are shown in parentheses):

- ▶ Applications (man command section 1)
- ▶ Configuration Files (man command section 5)
- ▶ Development (man command sections 2 and 3)
- ▶ Games (man command section 6)
- ▶ Hardware Devices (man command section 4)
- ▶ Overviews (man command section 7)
- ▶ System Administration (man command section 8)

More information on the division of system manual pages into sections and the meanings of each section number can be found in "Understanding Manual Page Sections" in Chapter 18.

326 CHAPTER 17: Getting Help on the Desktop

Click any section in the list to open a list of manual pages offered for that section; Figure 17.8 shows a portion of the list of man pages available in the Applications section.

**FIGURE 17.8**
The alphabetical list of manual pages in each section is quite long.

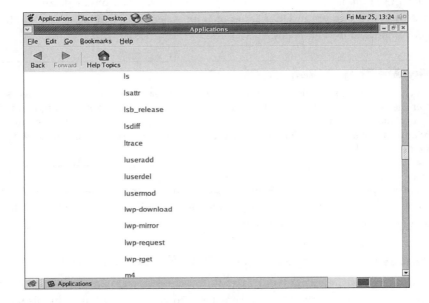

When you locate the manual page you want to read, click its link to display it, as shown in Figure 17.9.

Manual pages you read in the GNOME help browser are formatted according to the same guidelines used by the man command. Each manual page contains the following information:

▶ The man command section from which the manual page has been taken

▶ The name of the command, file, or device being documented and a brief (one-line) summary of its purpose

▶ A synopsis of how to use the command, file, or device

▶ A longer description in paragraph form, which provides more detailed information about the nature of the command, file, or device and the situations in which you might want to use it

▶ A summary of options and arguments that can be provided to alter the behavior of the command or a summary of the format of the configuration file in question

▶ Author, bug reporting, and copyright information

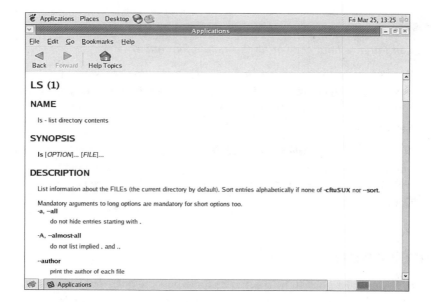

**FIGURE 17.9**
Displaying the manual page for the ls command.

## Exiting the Help Browser

Once you're done reading online manuals or documentation, you can choose File, Close Window from any display or manual to close the help browser application and return to your desktop.

# Summary

In this chapter, you learned to access several types of help and documentation at the Linux desktop by employing different techniques and tools.

You learned to access application-specific manuals and World Wide Web and email contact information by using the About option in the application's Help menu.

You also learned to access a more general, systemwide set of documents and tutorial information using the help browser, by launching it from the Desktop menu. This documentation is intended for users new to the Fedora Core 4 desktop environment, and covers basic topics that apply to all applications. Also included are manuals for many desktop applications, games, and utilities.

Finally, you learned to read shell command man pages, useful for learning to use the vast body of powerful commands available at the Linux command prompt.

# Q&A

**Q** *Can I print a hard copy of all this help information?*

**A** Unfortunately, the help browser does not support an easy way to print. If you have a compelling need to print help information from man pages, use the man command you'll learn about in Chapter 18 in the following way:

```
man mycommand ¦ lpr
```

For more details on the man and lpr commands, as well as on the use of the Linux command line in general, refer to Chapters 18, "Becoming Familiar with Shell Environments," and 21, "Managing High-Quality Documents at the Command Line."

# Workshop

The Workshop is designed to help you anticipate possible questions, review what you've learned, and begin learning how to put your knowledge into practice.

## Quiz

1. How do you open the user manual for a running application?

2. How do you launch the systemwide help application?

3. How do you read a shell command's man page using the help browser?

4. What information should be submitted with an application bug report?

## Answers

1. Choose Help, Contents in the application window.

2. Choose Desktop, Help from the menubar.

3. To read a manual page in the help browser, click Man Pages in its main category list, select a section in the page that follows, and then click the link to the manual page you want to view.

4. You should always include the name of the application, the version of the application, the specific problem you encountered, a list of other applications that were running at the time, and a detailed description of the context in which the problem occurred—what you did to cause the problem, what you were trying to accomplish, and so on.

# Activities

1. Read some of the introductory material about the Fedora Core 4 desktop environment from the User Guide.

2. Try launching a few applications in the desktop of your choice and browsing the related manual or handbook.

3. Read the man pages for the commands you remember from Chapters 6, "Working with Files in the Shell," and 7, "Understanding File Properties."

# PART IV

# Using the Linux Command Line

# CHAPTER 18

# Becoming Familiar with Shell Environments

## What You'll Learn in This Chapter:

▶ How to switch between the desktop display and virtual consoles
▶ How to log in to and use virtual consoles
▶ How to reuse and edit commands that you have already entered
▶ How to use man and info pages to get command-line help

This chapter begins Part IV of this book, which focuses on using the Linux command line. To get a real feel for the command line, in this chapter, you learn about virtual consoles, man pages, and info pages. You also learn a little bit more about the Terminal application introduced in Chapter 6, "Working with Files in the Shell," that lets you use the Linux command line in a window on your desktop.

By the time you've finished this chapter, you'll be well prepared to tackle the coming chapters on the Linux command line with style and grace.

## Why Learn to Use the Linux Command Line?

You've already had some preliminary experience working with the Linux command line in Chapters 6, "Working with Files in the Shell," and 7, "Understanding File Properties," so you may be tempted to skip some of the chapters in Part IV.

Don't!

The Linux command line is much more powerful than most users from outside the Unix world imagine—even after having gained some basic experience with it. One of the goals of this book, and of Part IV in particular, is to show you enough about the Linux command line to give you a taste of what a remarkable computing platform it can actually be, when in skilled hands.

After you master the command line, the rest of the Unix world, including the desktop, seems to fall magically into place; the system becomes a magical, powerful playground where only your ingenuity limits the amount or variety of work that you can accomplish or the number of complex tasks you can automate. Only rarely do users master other Unix functions or services before they master the command line.

# Understanding Virtual Consoles

The term **console** refers to the combination of one input device and one output device designed to enable you to interact with your computer. In real terms, this means a keyboard and a monitor. If you have ever used an MS-DOS–only computer, you should already be familiar with computer use at a console.

In Linux, you also find the term **virtual console** in common use. This term alludes to the fact that in Linux, several **sessions** of interactive console work can be active at any time. Each session is referred to as a virtual console; you can switch between these sessions (or virtual consoles) by using special key combinations. This way, you can launch numerous full-screen applications simultaneously and switch between them easily. For example, you might want to have an editor active on one console and a web browser active on another console. In a way, this functionality is similar to the functionality provided by a windowing system, although each virtual console occupies the entire display.

By default, when you install and boot Linux, seven virtual consoles are configured and active. When you begin to use the Linux desktop, as you did in Part III, "Using Linux on the Desktop," you normally see only the seventh virtual console; it is the one on which the X Window System (the engine of the Linux desktop) runs. Consoles one through six do not, by default, run graphical applications or environments but are instead configured to allow you to log in and perform text-based command-line work.

## Switching Between Consoles

To display a specific console in Linux, hold down the Ctrl and Alt keys simultaneously with one hand, and with your other hand, press F1 through F7, depending on the console you would like to view. F1 displays console one; F2, console two; and so forth. At the moment, the first six consoles should all be identical. Holding down Ctrl and Alt and pressing F7 displays console seven and the Linux desktop once again.

# Logging In at a Virtual Console

To log in to a text-based console, switch to one of the first six virtual consoles by holding down Ctrl and Alt and then pressing the matching function key. When the console appears, you see a banner displaying the operating system name and version and a login prompt, as shown in Figure 18.1.

**FIGURE 18.1**
After switching to one of the first six virtual consoles, you see a text-based Linux login prompt.

To log in, enter your username—the same username you routinely use to log in at the desktop login prompt—and press Enter. Do not use the root account to log in; you should use the root account only for administration, never for day-to-day computing. When the Password: prompt appears, type your password and press Enter. As a security measure, the password characters you type will not appear on the screen. After you correctly enter your password, you are logged in, as shown in Figure 18.2.

**FIGURE 18.2**
After you log in, a command prompt is displayed. You can use this command line in all the same ways that you used the command line in the Terminal application in Chapter 6.

The last line displayed, the line ending with a dollar sign ($), is the **command prompt**, as you learned in Chapter 6. The command prompt in a virtual console provides all the same functionality. Whenever it appears in a virtual console followed by a blinking underline called the **cursor**, the shell is ready to accept your commands.

To log out from a virtual console, type logout at any command prompt. The screen clears, and the login prompt is displayed once again.

# Becoming Comfortable at the Command Line

You're already familiar with a few file management commands from Chapters 6 and 7, such as ls, mv, cp, and rm. Feel free to try out a few of them now, just to get a feel for the way virtual consoles interact. For example, try getting a long directory listing of the /bin directory. Recall that you obtain long directory listings by appending the -1 argument to the ls command, so the command to get a long listing of the /bin directory is

```
[you@workstation20 ~]$ ls -1 /bin
```

The results of this command are shown in Figure 18.3.

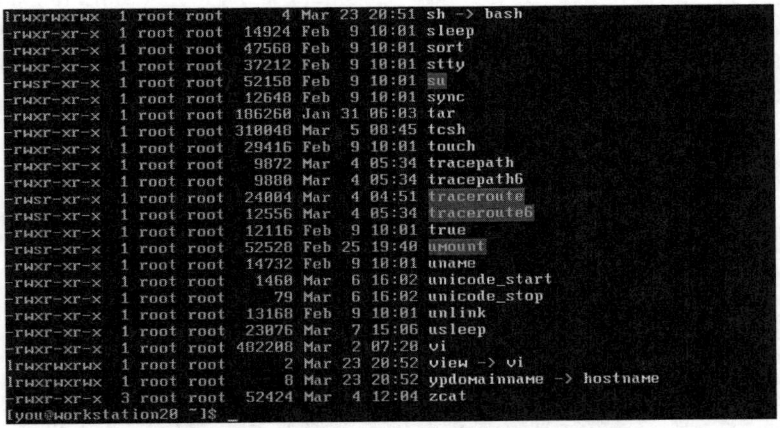

**FIGURE 18.3**
The long directory listing of the /bin directory, generated by typing
**ls -1 /bin**.

Feel free to try out a few more commands now. For example, get a directory listing of your home directory or navigate the file system a little bit using the tools you gained in Chapter 6. Feel free to experiment.

## Scrolling Content in Virtual Consoles

As you viewed the tail end of the directory listing shown in Figure 18.3, you saw some familiar things: executable files, symbolic links, and file permissions flags. You probably also noticed, however, that most of the directory listing had scrolled past the top of the console.

While using a virtual console, you'll often find yourself wishing you could see what commands or what outputs have scrolled past the top of the screen. As you might imagine, there is a way to do just that:

▶ To scroll up (to see progressively older commands and output) at a virtual console, hold down your Shift key and repeatedly press the Page Up (PgUp) key.

▶ To scroll down (to see progressively more recent commands and output) at a virtual console, hold down your Shift key and repeatedly press the Page Down (PgDn) key.

Note that if you have scrolled up by pressing Shift+PgUp repeatedly, you don't need to return to the command prompt by pressing Shift+PgDn repeatedly before you can enter a new command. Just begin typing a new command, and the display automatically returns to the most recent command prompt.

## Using Command History

As you begin to have longer sessions at the command line, performing more complex tasks and in greater quantities, you will begin to find yourself wanting to repeat commands that you entered earlier or to recall a previously entered command that gave the results you wanted.

A feature called the **command history** allows you to do just that. To view the command history for a Terminal or virtual console session you're working in, just type the word history at the command prompt. The history command displays a chronological list of the commands you've entered and associates each one with a number. Sample output from the history command in a virtual console is shown in Figure 18.4.

As you can see, the output of the history command gives you a concise list of all the commands you've recently run. Notice, too, that each command is prefaced by a number. After using the history command to see the list of recently run commands, you can repeat any of them simply by entering an exclamation point followed by the number of the command in question. For example, Figure 18.4 shows the command

```
ls -l ~/sharedjackfiles
```

FIGURE 18.4
The output from
the history
command lists
entered com-
mands in
chronological
order, from old-
est to newest.
Note that the
history com-
mand itself
appears in the
list, too.

```
68  touch myfile.txt
69  touch yourfile.txt
70  ln -s myfile.txt myfile-link.txt
71  ln -s yourfile.txt yourfile-link.txt
72  mkdir ourfiles
73  mv myfile.txt myfile-link.txt ourfiles
74  mv yourfile.txt yourfile-link.txt ourfiles
75  cp ourfiles/myfile.txt /home/jack/sharedfiles
76  cp ourfiles/myfile.txt /home/jill/sharedfiles
77  cp ourfiles/yourfile.txt /home/jack/sharedfiles
78  cp ourfiles/yourfile.txt /home/jack/sharedfiles
79  ls -l /home/jack/sharedfiles
80  ls -l /home/jill/sharedfiles
81  ls -l ourfiles
82  ln -s /home/jack/sharedfiles ~/sharedjackfiles
83  ln -s /home/jill/sharedfiles ~/sharedjillfiles
84  ls -l ~/sharedjackfiles
85  ls -l ~/sharedjillfiles
86  cp monthlyreport.txt ~/sharedjackfiles
87  cp weeklyreport.txt addendums.txt ~/sharedjackfiles
88  cp telephoneindex.txt ~/sharedjackfiles
89  cp policylist.txt ~/sharedjillfiles
90  ln -s /home/jill/sharedfiles /home/jack/sharedfiles/jillsfiles
91  ln -s /home/jack/sharedfiles /home/jill/sharedfiles/jacksfiles
[you@workstation20 ~]$ _
```

Assuming you're the user of the virtual console shown in Figure 18.4, to repeat this command, you need only type

```
[you@workstation20 ~]$ !84
```

to repeat the command once again just as if you had typed it at the command prompt.

**Watch Out!**

## Be Alert When Using the Command History!

Sometimes using a command from the command history can have unintended consequences if the circumstances surrounding the command are different. In particular, reusing potentially destructive file management commands such as rm, rmdir, or mv can have unwanted effects if your current working directory has been changed since the first time you used them.

Whenever you reuse a command from your command history, be sure to check your current working directory first and think carefully through the effects of reusing the command!

In addition to the history command, there is another way to access your command history that is often even more convenient. At any command prompt, simply press your up-arrow key to display the last command you entered, just as if you had typed it at the command prompt; you can then press Enter to reuse the command. (You may need to try pressing your own up-arrow key now to understand the effect.)

Pressing the up-arrow key repeatedly "steps back" through the commands in your history, showing earlier and earlier commands as if you had just entered them. Pressing Enter at any time executes the command as if you had typed it yourself.

Similarly, pressing the down-arrow key "steps forward" through the list of commands in your history if you have already pressed the up-arrow key a number of times.

---

**Repeated Commands Become Part of History, Too**

When you repeat a command from your command history, whether by entering an exclamation mark or by using your up-arrow key, the command that you repeated appears again as the newest command in your command history, just as if you had typed the command by hand.

*By the Way*

---

## Using Command-Line Editing Features

As you progress through the following few chapters, you'll also find yourself typing progressively longer commands. Because commands at the command line invariably involve punctuation keys, and because you're not yet terribly experienced with the command line, sometimes you might want to make changes to what you've already typed without having to retype the whole line.

Fortunately, the shell understands a number of basic editing keystrokes to help you edit your commands as you type them. These keystrokes are shown in Table 18.1.

**TABLE 18.1  Command-Line Editing Keystrokes**

| Key | Action |
|---|---|
| Left arrow | Moves the cursor closer to the command prompt without erasing any of the characters you've typed |
| Right arrow | Moves the cursor closer to the end of the command without erasing any of the characters you've typed |
| Backspace | Deletes the character immediately to the left of the cursor |
| Delete | Deletes the character under the cursor |

As you read through Table 18.1, note that any text you type when the cursor is not at the end of the command will be inserted wherever the cursor is. If you are familiar with nearly any word processor or text editor, the keys shown in Table 18.1 are probably familiar to you, and you'll use them often to edit complex commands as you enter them.

Note also that commands from your history can be edited this way, too. This capability provides a convenient way to use a command you've previously entered as a starting point for a new, slightly different command. To edit your command history, follow these steps:

1. Step back through your command history by pressing the up-arrow key until you find the command that you want to reuse.

2. When the command you want to reuse is visible on the command line, edit it as necessary using the editing keys.

3. After you edit the command as desired, press Enter to execute it.

Keep in mind that the new, edited command will then show up as the most recent command in your command history; you can then re-execute or reuse the new command, too, for later commands.

*By the*
*Way*

---

**These Techniques Work in the Terminal, Too!**

Even though the figures in this chapter show commands and keystrokes being used in virtual consoles, keep in mind that techniques like the command history and command editing work identically when you are using the command line in the Terminal application on the Linux desktop. These features of the shell apply in either environment!

---

# Getting Help at the Command Line

As you progress through the chapters in Part IV, you'll likely find yourself wanting to know more about some of the commands and topics covered.

Unlike desktop applications, commands that you type at the command line don't have a Help menu within obvious reach. Don't worry, though; nearly every command in Linux is thoroughly documented using one of the two documentation systems briefly mentioned in the preceding chapter. These documentation systems are manual (man) pages and info pages.

## Using Manual Pages: The Basics

The **manual page** is one of the most fundamental command-line tools in any Linux or Unix system. Manual pages are brief, yet complete, online documents that describe how to use a specific command or system facility.

Linux and Unix operating systems ship with an extensive library of online manual pages. You will find that few commands or system files in a Fedora file system do not have an associated manual page.

You can display manual pages for a given command or facility by using the man command and supplying the name of the manual page you want to read as an argument. To read the manual page for the ls command, for example, type **man ls** at the command prompt. The manual page for the command appears, as shown in Figure 18.5.

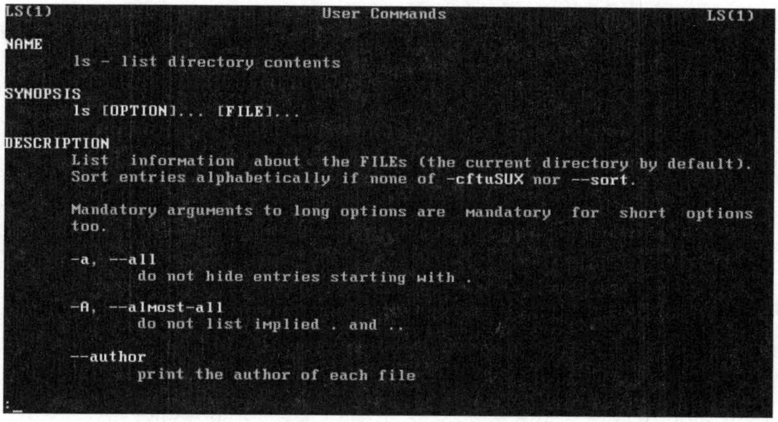

**FIGURE 18.5**
After typing **man ls**, you can see the beginning of the manual page for the ls command.

Each manual page begins with the name of the command, a "manual page section" to which it belongs, and a brief summary of the proper method for calling the command or using the facility in question. The body of the manual page, which contains detailed information, then begins.

The man command always displays a manual page using a **pager**, a command that displays one screen of text or data at a time. After reading each screen of information, you press the spacebar to proceed to the next screen of information. This way, you can read a manual page slowly, without losing information as it scrolls past the top of the display.

The pager used by the man command is called less. Practice bringing up manual pages for some of the commands you've already learned. To help you navigate manual pages more effectively, Table 18.2 shows some keystrokes understood by the less pager.

**TABLE 18.2**   Simple less Navigation for Reading Manual Pages

| Key | Action |
| --- | --- |
| Spacebar | Displays the next screen full of information |
| b | Displays the previous screen full of information (moves "backward" one page) |
| /text | Searches for the next occurrence of text in the manual page you are viewing |
| q | Quits (closes) this manual page and returns you to the command prompt |

**Manual Pages Provide a Deeper Look**

Command manual pages contain useful information. As you read man pages with `less`, pay special attention to the many options for altering or enhancing the behavior of most of the commands.

## Understanding Manual Page Sections

A typical Linux system holds a large number of manual pages that cover a variety of topics, from common commands to system file formats to various types of system programming information. Because of the number and diversity of manual pages, it is not uncommon to find that a term you're trying to look up might represent more than one kind of item and, hence, more than one manual page. For example, the word passwd represents both a command and a common file format; manual pages exist for both items.

Because a single word can lead to multiple manual pages, the canon of Linux manual pages is divided into numbered sections, somewhat akin to chapters, to help you to differentiate between manual pages of different types. When you use the man command, you have the option of telling man to display pages from a specific section. Table 18.3 shows the manual page sections.

**TABLE 18.3   The Linux Manual Page Sections**

| Section | Title | Description |
| --- | --- | --- |
| 1 | User Commands | Commands and applications that users commonly call from the Linux command line |
| 2 | System Calls | Functions used by programmers to access or control various Linux system facilities |
| 3 | Subroutines | Routines used by programmers to access various types of Linux functionality |
| 4 | Devices | Information about using various devices and device drivers of which Linux is aware |
| 5 | File Formats | Information about the formats of many of the numerous system configuration files in /etc and elsewhere that control the behavior and operation of the Linux operating system |
| 6 | Games | Manuals for installed games and entertainment-related commands |
| 7 | Miscellaneous | Documentation for various topics that don't appear to easily fit into any of the other sections |

**TABLE 18.3**    Continued

| Section | Title | Description |
|---|---|---|
| 8 | Administration | Information about commands and concepts related specifically to Linux system administration |
| L | Local | Documentation that is unique to this Linux system or this version of Linux in particular |
| N | New | Documentation for additional user-selected, recently installed, or as yet uncategorized commands, files, and concepts |

As you might be able to see already, the sections can overlap to some extent, meaning that a command, concept, or file format might appear in a section that you don't initially expect. Each time you use the man command to display documentation, the section from which you are reading appears in the manual page header. For example, examine the first line of output from man ls:

```
LS(1)                 User Commands              LS(1)
```

The (1) in the first line of the manual page indicates that this manual page for ls has been taken from Section 1, User Commands.

The man command normally displays only the first manual page it finds for a given topic. If a topic you want to study occurs in several sections—for example, once in user commands and once in file formats—you see only one of them. If you want to read *all* the manual pages for a given topic in succession, you must use the -a option:

```
[you@workstation20 ~]$ man -a passwd
```

As typed, this command lists all the manual pages on file for passwd, in every section. After you press q to exit the first manual page, the second manual page is displayed, and so on.

If you happen to know from past experience or by looking at the section descriptions that you want only the manual page from a particular section, you can specify the section from which you want to read as an argument to man:

```
[you@workstation20 ~]$ man 5 passwd
```

This command reads only the passwd manual page that resides in Section 5, File Formats.

| | **Read the Manual Page for** man |
|---|---|
| | If you want to learn more about using the man command, you can also read its manual page by typing **man man** at the command prompt. |

## Locating Manual Pages Through Topic-Based Searches

Our discussion of manual pages thus far assumes that you know which manual pages you want to consult for help. In the real world, this is often not the case: It is common to know that you want help with a particular *topic* but to find that there is no specific manual page anywhere under that name.

Usually, when this scenario occurs, documentation for the topic in question still exists; it is simply filed under another name or treated as a subtopic in a larger manual page. The apropos command can help you locate manual pages relevant to your topic at the command line.

For example, suppose you want to find manual pages that deal in detail with the concept of Linux directories. You can use the apropos command to help:

```
[you@workstation20 ~]$ apropos permissions
WWW::RobotRules      (3pm)  - database of robots.txt-derived permissions
access               (2)   - check user's permissions for a file
acl_clear_perms      (3)   - clear all permissions from an ACL permission set
chmod                (1)   - change file access permissions
chmod                (2)   - change permissions of a file
console.perms [console] (5)  - permissions control file for users at the
➥system console
fchmod [chmod]       (2)   - change permissions of a file
ioperm               (2)   - set port input/output permissions
pam_console          (8)   - control permissions for users at the system console
pam_console_apply    (8)   - set or revoke permissions for users at the system
➥console
[you@workstation20 ~]$
```

As you can see, apropos supplies a list of manual pages related to the topic of directories, including manual pages for several commands you might already recognize. In the second column, apropos also provides the manual section in which the pages appear, to help you to decide whether the manual page in question will be useful to you. Each manual page is also briefly summarized with a one-line description.

| | **Finding Out What Things Are** |
|---|---|
| | A similar command to apropos, whatis might also be useful. Try typing **whatis** followed by the name of any command or system file in the /etc directory. If a manual page exists for that command or file, details about that page appear. |

# Using the GNU `info` **System**

Although the `man` system has been a staple in the Unix world for ages, another documentation system called `info` has gained some popularity in the Linux world as well. Sometimes you can find `info` pages for commands that have no associated (or no adequate) manual page. If you need more information about a command, it's a good idea to look for an `info` page.

The `info` system works in some ways like the Web. The core of the `info` system is the `info` browser. When called without arguments or options, the `info` browser opens to an index page listing all the topics for which you can obtain `info`-based help. Try starting the browser now by typing **info** at the command line:

```
[you@workstation20 ~]$ info
```

Figure 18.6 shows the `info` display.

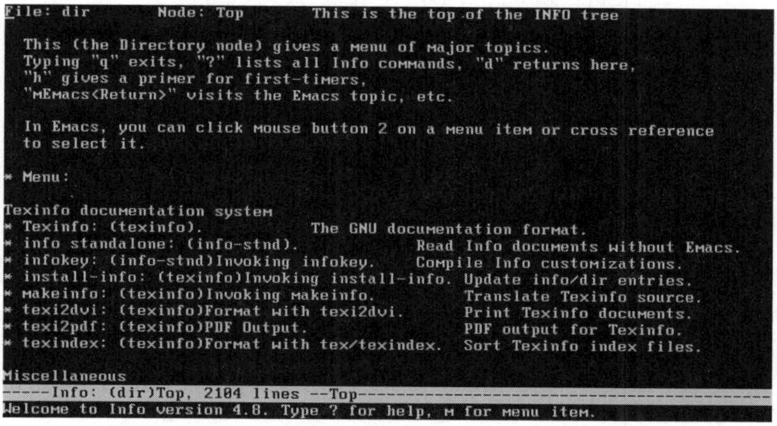

File: dir          Node: Top          This is the top of the INFO tree

   This (the Directory node) gives a menu of major topics.
   Typing "q" exits, "?" lists all Info commands, "d" returns here,
   "h" gives a primer for first-timers,
   "mEmacs<Return>" visits the Emacs topic, etc.

   In Emacs, you can click mouse button 2 on a menu item or cross reference
   to select it.

* Menu:

Texinfo documentation system
* Texinfo: (texinfo).          The GNU documentation format.
* info standalone: (info-stnd).          Read Info documents without Emacs.
* infokey: (info-stnd)Invoking infokey.  Compile Info customizations.
* install-info: (texinfo)Invoking install-info. Update info/dir entries.
* makeinfo: (texinfo)Invoking makeinfo.  Translate Texinfo source.
* texi2dvi: (texinfo)Format with texi2dvi.  Print Texinfo documents.
* texi2pdf: (texinfo)PDF Output.          PDF output for Texinfo.
* texindex: (texinfo)Format with tex/texindex.  Sort Texinfo index files.

Miscellaneous
-----Info: (dir)Top, 2104 lines --Top------------------------------------
Welcome to Info version 4.8. Type ? for help, m for menu item.

**FIGURE 18.6**
When you first launch `info`, you are greeted by a screen full of index information.

Although the `info` system might seem clumsy to navigate at first, it contains a wealth of information, often in greater depth than you can find in the `man` pages.

## Navigating the `info` **System**

Navigating inside `info` can be a little tricky, especially for beginners.

As in a web browser, the `info` pages contain words that link to further information, such as `info` indexes or documents. Most of these words are followed by single or double colon characters (: or ::). To follow one of these links or open such a document, use the arrow keys to place the cursor over the linking word and then press Enter to select it.

In info, the **node** represents the fundamental unit of documentation. Usually, when you are viewing a screen full of information, you are looking at a particular info node. Many nodes contain further links to next and previous nodes, which typically represent related information to the screen you're currently viewing, arranged in some kind of logical order. Table 18.4 provides the basic keystrokes for navigating info.

**TABLE 18.4    Basic Keystrokes for Navigating info**

| Key | Description |
| --- | --- |
| Up arrow | Move cursor up |
| Down arrow | Move cursor down |
| Left arrow | Move cursor left |
| Right arrow | Move cursor right. |
| Enter | Follow the link under the cursor to the indicated node (screen full of information) |
| n | Proceed to the "next" logical node after this one |
| p | Proceed to the "previous" logical node before this one |
| u | Return "up" one node in the index, usually to the location that led you to your current node |
| t | Return to the "top" node or info index page |
| q | Quit the info system |
| Spacebar | Display the next screen full of information in the current node |

> **info and emacs Are Very Similar**
>
> The info system is built using the emacs editor engine. Thus, you can use many of the common emacs commands you'll learn in future chapters, including buffer-oriented and screen-splitting commands, while browsing info.
>
> For more information on using emacs, refer to Chapter 20, "Creating, Editing, and Saving Text Files."

## Using info **Efficiently**

Although the main index page of the info system is useful to those not familiar with the documentation available through info, it can be time-consuming and bothersome to navigate for those who have used info.

When you are familiar with info, you can call it in much the same way you use the man command, supplying the name of the info document that you want to read as an argument to the command. For example, to read the info page for the ls command, you enter

`[you@workstation20 ~]$ info ls`

Used this way, info functions very much like man; you page through the displayed document using the spacebar and then press q when you are ready to quit.

# Getting Help from the Commands Themselves

There is one more common and useful method for obtaining help or documentation about a specific Linux command. Nearly every command supports either -h, -help, or --help as a special option that causes the command to print a brief help message and exit. Listing 18.1 shows one such help message.

**LISTING 18.1    Output of the rm --help Command**

```
Usage: rm [OPTION]... FILE...
Remove (unlink) the FILE(s).

  -d, --directory       unlink FILE, even if it is a non-empty directory
                          (super-user only; this works only if your system
                          supports `unlink' for nonempty directories)
  -f, --force           ignore nonexistent files, never prompt
  -i, --interactive     prompt before any removal
      --no-preserve-root do not treat `/' specially (the default)
      --preserve-root    fail to operate recursively on `/'
  -r, -R, --recursive   remove the contents of directories recursively
  -v, --verbose         explain what is being done
      --help        display this help and exit
      --version     output version information and exit

To remove a file whose name starts with a `-', for example `-foo',
use one of these commands:
  rm -- -foo

  rm ./-foo

Note that if you use rm to remove a file, it is usually possible to recover
the contents of that file.  If you want more assurance that the contents are
truly unrecoverable, consider using shred.

Report bugs to <bug-coreutils@gnu.org>.
```

Help obtained this way is often very brief, filling less than one screen and providing only the most commonly used options and arguments for a given command. Although the man or info page is almost always more exhaustive, you might find that the -h, -help, or --help options are more readily accessible in day-to-day use.

*By the*
*Way*

**How Do You Know Whether to Use** -h, -help, **or** --help**?**

Generally, try the options in this order: --help, -h, and -help. If none of these options seems to provide a help listing for a specific command, consult the man or info page for the command instead.

# Summary

In this chapter, we covered a lot of ground to give you a good foundation for the chapters that follow, in which you learn how to use the command line to perform a variety of more complex tasks. Among the things you learned in this chapter are

▶ What virtual consoles are and how to use them

▶ How to use the command history

▶ How to edit commands as you're typing them

▶ How to use man and info pages to get help on the commands you'll encounter in following chapters

If all this information about command lines seems complex and confusing to you, don't despair. As we work together through the next few chapters, the shell will begin to seem both familiar and helpful to you.

# Q&A

**Q** *I've noticed that when reading* man *pages with* less, *many other keystrokes (in addition to the ones listed in Table 18.2) seem to have some effect. Is there help inside* less *about the available keystrokes?*

**A** Press h while reading a man page or using the less pager to get a list of the available keystrokes and commands.

**Q** *Why do some commands seem to have both* man *and* info *documentation available? Isn't this redundant?*

**A** Yes and no. Generally speaking, when both man and info documentation for a specific command is available, the info documentation is more complete; the man page has been provided simply to ensure that users who aren't familiar with info can still find documentation.

# Workshop

The Workshop is designed to help you anticipate possible questions, review what you've learned, and begin learning how to put your knowledge into practice.

## Quiz

1. What command lets you list all the commands you've already run?

2. How do you reuse one of these commands?

3. When both man and info show documentation for a particular command, which documentation is likely to be more complete?

4. Why are there multiple man sections?

5. How do you call the man command with reference to a specific section?

## Answers

1. The history command lists all the commands you've already run, from oldest to newest.

2. To reuse a command that appears in your history, enter an exclamation mark (!) followed by the number of the command in your history.

3. The info documentation is usually more complete when both man and info cover a specific topic.

4. A single topic word might refer to several different commands or facilities in Linux. Multiple sections enable manual pages to be grouped logically according to function—commands with other commands, file formats with other file formats, and so on.

5. Include the number of the section you want to reference before the topic word or command. For example, to see the section 5 manual page for passwd, you use **man 5 passwd**.

## Activities

1. To familiarize yourself with virtual consoles, log in to several of them at once, without logging out of any of them. Type the ls command in each one, just for fun. Then switch to each one in turn and log out before finally returning to your desktop.

2. Spend some time looking at the manual pages for the commands you learned about in Chapters 6 and 7.

3. Start the info browser and try navigating through some of the info documentation to familiarize yourself with info navigation and with the types of information available.

4. Try using the apropos command with a few interesting words you've encountered while learning Linux, just to see whether any manual pages discuss them.

# CHAPTER 19

# Performing Basic Shell Tasks

---

## What You'll Learn in This Chapter:

▶ How to manage files in groups

▶ How to save the output of commands to a file

▶ How to locate specific files with quick searches

▶ How to use one command's output as arguments to another command

▶ How to start and switch between a lot of programs running simultaneously in a shell

In this chapter, you gain experience with concepts that will be more useful to you the longer you use Linux. You begin the chapter by learning ways to make your life at the command line easier.

As was the case in Chapters 6, 7, and 18, this chapter helps you become familiar with the shell and shell commands and techniques instead of making you an instant pro. Try to follow along and understand what is happening, even if you don't think you can remember all of it later.

To begin this chapter, you should already be logged in to your account at a virtual console or have a Terminal window open on your desktop so that you are ready to give commands at the shell prompt.

## Grouping Files for Efficient File Management

As you begin working with larger numbers of applications and files on a regular basis, you build a library of data, reports, and files-in-progress.

Commands you've already learned such as mv, cp, rm, and ls are certainly helpful for organizing files. As your workload in Linux increases, however, you will need the additional tools provided by the shell and a few more powerful commands to help you navigate your growing file collection. You can group files to make finding and accessing them faster and more efficient. The following sections explain how to group files in Linux for more efficient file management.

## Grouping Files on the Command Line

In Chapter 6, "Working with Files in the Shell," you learned to perform a number of common file management tasks by entering commands and filenames, one or two at a time, at the shell prompt. Sometimes it is helpful to be able to refer to many files at once at the shell prompt, without having to type all their names. The shell provides a tool for grouping similar filenames to save you the trouble of having to type them one by one.

To illustrate, consider the following problem. Suppose you want to create three new empty files called myfirstfile.txt, mysecondfile.txt, and mythirdfile.txt and then move them into a new directory called firstfiles. Using the skills you learned in Chapter 6, you first create the files with touch, the directory firstfiles with mkdir, and then you use mv to move the files by name:

```
[you@workstation20 ~]$ touch myfirstfile.txt mysecondfile.txt mythirdfile.txt
[you@workstation20 ~]$ mkdir firstfiles
[you@workstation20 ~]$ mv myfirstfile.txt mysecondfile.txt mythirdfile.txt
Âfirstfiles
[you@workstation20 ~]$
```

But that's a lot of typing just to move three text files to a more convenient location. It seems as though there should be an easier way, a way to simply tell the shell to move all the text files that begin with my and end with .txt into the new directory—and there is. When used at the shell prompt, the asterisk (*) is one of a special group of characters that you can use for **filename expansion**—a way of grouping files logically so that you don't have to type all their names to manipulate all of them at once. Filename expansion is as much an art as a science; to use it, you employ specific pattern-matching tools to try to collect files into a group and then pass that group on to the shell.

This procedure sounds complicated, but it's actually simple and powerful. Here's an example of using filename expansion to perform the task you just saw demonstrated. Try using the following mv command instead of the longer mv command used previously:

```
[you@workstation20 ~]$ mv my*.txt firstfiles
```

Let's make sure that the command had the desired effect:

```
[you@workstation20 ~]$ ls firstfiles
myfirstfile.txt  mysecondfile.txt  mythirdfile.txt
[you@workstation20 ~]$
```

Obviously, the new, simplified command produced the desired result. The phrase my*.txt has grouped together all files that begin with the two letters my and end with the four characters .txt.

We'll go over other examples, but first, take a look at Table 19.1, which lists the patterns commonly used for filename expansion.

**TABLE 19.1**   Common Pattern-Matching Characters and Their Effects

| Pattern | Matching Effects |
| --- | --- |
| * | Matches all characters in any quantity, including no characters at all |
| ? | Matches any single character |
| [a-b] (range) | Matches a single character in the range of characters between a and b; for example, [A-Z] would match the letter X or the letter P, but not the number 9 or the letter a |
| [AaBbCc] (list) | Matches a single character from the list of characters provided |

> ### Ranges Don't Always Work as Expected
>
> Because letters in a computer are represented internally using a special code called ASCII that doesn't function as humans do, some range patterns might not have the effect you expected.
>
> For example, [a-Z] will match nothing, whereas [A-z] will match a number of characters that are not uppercase or lowercase letters. For this reason, in the interest of clarity, you should use ranges for which both characters are uppercase, both characters are lowercase, or both characters are numbers.

**By the Way**

Working through a few examples can help you better understand what these patterns mean and how they can help you work with groups of files in Linux. Let's create a table of examples. Suppose you were going to use rm on a group of files in your home directory. Table 19.2 shows some sample rm arguments and files that each would (or wouldn't) match.

**TABLE 19.2**  Sample Commands Using Expansion and Their Effects

| Command | Effects |
| --- | --- |
| `rm *.txt` | Would remove any file with a .txt extension—for example, a.txt, b.txt, hello.txt, or everybody_is_cool.txt but not bicycle.gif, car_bills.xls, or myoldtxt. |
| `rm a*jpg` | Would remove any file beginning with the letter a and ending with the three letters jpg—for example, a.jpg, apple.jpg, answermachine.jpg, and anastasiajpg but not boat.jpg, file.txt, monkeys.gif, or macaroni_list. |
| `rm k*n.?if` | Would remove kitchen.gif, kluckchicken.tif, kn.zif, and korn.weekday..if but not korean.if, kasino.gif, or fountain.tif. |
| `rm l[eou]g.*` | Would remove leg.gif, log.txt, lug.jpg, log.my.hours.please, leg.gomyeg.go.txt, and lug.this but not lag.gif, leglover.txt, or log. |
| `rm [a-f]*` | Would remove apple.txt, bacon.jpg, cradle.song, dog.walking.schedule, everybody.mp3, and fanatics_favorites but not goose.txt, xylophone.jpg, or Barbie.gif. |
| `rm *` | Would remove every file in the present working directory. Adding the -rf options would remove every file *and* every directory in the present working directory. (Remember the -r and -f options from Chapter 6?) |

**By the Way**

**Be Careful When Using Patterns**

Be careful when grouping files using filename expansion; constructing your patterns carelessly can have unintended consequences. For example, when you remove files using the methods shown in Table 19.2, Linux does not caution you or ask whether you are sure before removing *all* the files that match the pattern you supplied.

You can use filename expansion in most circumstances to make your life at the console easier by reducing the amount of reading and typing you have to do when managing large numbers of files.

## Preventing Filename Expansion

Sometimes you don't want the shell to perform filename expansion—for example, when you want to use special pattern-matching characters such as the asterisk or question mark in a file's name or as an argument to a command.

Suppose, for example, that you want to create an additional directory called `*txt*` in your new `firstfiles` directory, to hold some interesting text files you've been working on. There is nothing illegal in Linux about having the asterisk in a file or directory name. However, if you try to create such a directory while files that end in .txt are present, the operation doesn't work:

```
[you@workstation20 ~]$ cd firstfiles
[you@workstation20 firstfiles]$ mkdir *txt*
mkdir: 'myfirstfile.txt' exists but is not a directory
mkdir: 'mysecondfile.txt' exists but is not a directory
mkdir: 'mythirdfile.txt' exists but is not a directory
[you@workstation20 firstfiles]$
```

Here, the shell has interpreted `*txt*` as a pattern and tried to match it against the files in your current working directory. As luck would have it, there is indeed a match—the pattern `*txt*` matches the filenames `myfirstfile.txt`, `mysecondfile.txt`, and `mythirdfile.txt`, so the shell behaved as though you had entered this:

```
mkdir myfirstfile.txt mysecondfile.txt mythirdfile.txt
```

At such times, you want the shell to treat the phrase you've entered as normal text, rather than as a pattern. To do this, you need to **quote** the text. You can do so with either single or double quotation marks. (There is a difference, which we discuss in later chapters.) For now, use single quotation marks to create the directory `*txt*` in your current working directory:

```
[you@workstation20 firstfiles]$ mkdir '*txt*'
[you@workstation20 firstfiles]$ ls
myfirstfile.txt  mysecondfile.txt  mythirdfile.txt  *txt*
[you@workstation20 firstfiles]$
```

You have now successfully created a directory called `*txt*` in your current working directory by quoting what could otherwise have been a pattern for filename expansion.

# Searching Files and Directories Quickly

You've learned how to list files with the `ls` command and change your working directory with the `cd` command. To find a specific file using only `ls` and `cd`, however, you must navigate slowly through directory trees, listing each directory, directories inside those directories, and so on, until you find the file you want. Searching with `ls` and `cd` is fine for a collection of two or three files, but how about a collection of a hundred files? A thousand? Eventually, all those filenames will begin to look the same.

Rather than search all day by hand, you can use the `find` and `locate` commands to find the location of your stray files more quickly.

## Searching for Files with `find`

You can use the `find` command to search an entire directory tree or list of directory trees for specific filenames or for filenames that match a specific pattern. The syntax for using `find` this way is

```
find tree1 [tree2 ...] -name filename -print
```

Calling `find` this way searches the supplied directory trees for a specific filename. For example, you can search your home directory for `myfirstfile.txt`:

```
[you@workstation20 firstfiles]$ find ~ -name myfirstfile.txt -print
/home/you/firstfiles/myfirstfile.txt
[you@workstation20 firstfiles]$
```

By the Way

**The Tilde Character Takes You Home**

Remember that the tilde character (~) represents the equivalent of /home/you to the shell.

The `find` command quickly locates `myfirstfile.txt` for you. It is stored in `/home/you/firstfiles`. Similarly, you can search your home directory for all files ending in `.txt` by supplying a pattern to find similar to the kind of pattern used for filename expansion. You need to quote the pattern you supply, however, or the shell will match the pattern to the text files in your home directory before `find` gets to see it:

```
[you@workstation20 firstfiles]$ find /home/you -name '*.txt' -print
/home/you/green/color.txt
/home/you/anotherfile.txt
/home/you/BusinessPlan.txt
/home/you/evolution/RDF-urls.txt
/home/you/firstfiles/myfirstfile.txt
/home/you/firstfiles/mysecondfile.txt
/home/you/firstfiles/mythirdfile.txt
/home/you/illustration.txt
[you@workstation20 firstfiles]$
```

The `find` command has searched your home directory and found three files whose names end with `.txt`. The full paths to these files have been printed for you. (Don't worry if your list of files doesn't look exactly the same; the list of files you see depends on what files actually exist on your computer!)

## Searching the Entire File System with `locate`

Sometimes you want to search the *entire* Linux file system for a specific file. When you want to search the entire file system, `locate` is often a better choice than `find` because `locate` is able to search through a much longer list of files much more quickly. You already know how to use find to run a file-system–wide search; suppose you want to find all the JPEG pictures in your Linux file system. You can do so by issuing a command like

```
find / -name '*.jpg'
```

However, you would soon find that this kind of a search can be time-consuming because find crawls to every corner of your hard drive, directory by directory, looking for filenames that end with .jpg. You would also find your screen filling with error messages as find encountered place after place in the Linux file system that you, logged in as a normal user, don't have permission to access. (For a refresher on permissions, return to Chapter 7, "Understanding File Properties.")

For large filename searches across the entire Linux file system, the locate command can often be more efficient because locate consults a large database that indexes every file in your Linux system. Using locate is simple—just supply the text you want to search for as an argument:

```
[you@workstation20 firstfiles]$ locate '*.jpg'
/usr/lib/pygtk/2.0/demos/images/background.jpg
/usr/lib/mozilla-1.7.6/res/samples/bg.jpg
/usr/lib/mozilla-1.7.6/res/samples/raptor.jpg
/usr/lib/openoffice.org1.9.83/share/gallery/www-back/structure_green.jpg
/usr/lib/openoffice.org1.9.83/share/gallery/www-back/lino-green.jpg
[...]
/usr/share/nautilus/patterns/chalk.jpg
/usr/share/nautilus/patterns/burlap.jpg
/usr/share/emacs/site-lisp/emacspeak/etc/emacspeak.jpg
/usr/share/gtk-2.0/demo/background.jpg
/usr/share/pixmaps/gnect/bg_nightfall.jpg
you@workstation20 firstfiles]$
```

---

## You Can Pause the Output of Commands

*By the Way*

The output of the locate command will likely scroll off your screen. You can pause the output of locate or other commands by appending the text ¦more or ¦less to the end of the command:

```
locate '*.jpg' ¦more
```

This command displays the output of the locate command one page at a time, waiting after each screenful of information for you to press the spacebar before continuing. It passes the output from the locate command to a pager like less so that you can read it in chunks.

This technique, known as **piping**, is discussed later this chapter, in the section titled "Using Pipes to Link Commands."

---

**By the Way**

> **Is `locate` Giving You Error Messages?**
>
> If the `locate` command tells you that it is unable to open the database, your system hasn't yet been indexed by the nightly Linux indexing process. To rectify this situation, either wait a day before trying `locate` again or log out, log back in using the `root` account, and run the `updatedb` command without arguments at a shell prompt before trying `locate` again.

Although the actual list of image files you see will vary depending on whether you customized your Fedora Core 4 installation in Chapter 2, "Installing Fedora Core 4," and what sorts of files you've created in your home directory since then, you can receive a long list of `.jpg` files via `locate` almost instantly.

The database used by `locate` is rebuilt once daily when the system runs the `updatedb` command. The data displayed by `locate` might at times not be current with respect to the work you've done in the past few hours. However, it enables `locate` to find large numbers of files across the entire disk rapidly.

## Saving a List of Found Files

Sometimes saving the output of a search command is helpful. The shell can help you save the output of commands like `find` and `locate` by *redirecting* their output to a file. You can then load such a text file into any editor for editing, perusal, or printing. To redirect the **standard output** of a command (the information it prints to the console to fulfill your request), use the greater-than symbol (>), followed by the name of the destination file. Return to your home directory and save the list of JPEG files on your system to a file called `myjpegs.txt`:

```
[you@workstation20 firstfiles]$ cd
[you@workstation20 ~]$ locate '*.jpg' > myjpegs.txt
[you@workstation20 ~]$ ls -l myjpegs.txt
-rw-rw-r-- 1 you    you     25214 Mar 25 21:12 myjpegs.txt
[you@workstation20 ~]$
```

As you can see, there is now a text file of decent size in your home directory called `myjpegs.txt`. This file contains the list of JPEG files in your Linux file system, as reported by the `locate` command. If you want to view the file, feel free to read it with a pager like `less` or to load it into a text editor.

You can redirect the output of nearly every command available at the command prompt. It is also possible to append the standard output of a command to an existing file by using a double greater-than symbol (>>). For example, to add a list of all GIF images on your system to `myjpegs.txt`, use

```
[you@workstation20 ~]$ locate '*.gif' >> myjpegs.txt
[you@workstation20 ~]$
```

> **Be Careful When Redirecting Output**
>
> To avoid accidentally overwriting important contents, always be cautious when
> appending command output to an existing file. When you use the single greater-
> than symbol (>) to redirect the output of a command to a file that already exists,
> the content of the original file is overwritten by the new data. You therefore must
> be careful to use double greater-than symbols (>>) when redirecting data so that
> you don't overwrite important files.

## Searching Text Files for Word Patterns

You've now created a rather lengthy text file in your home directory called
myjpegs.txt, which contains a list of all the JPEG images and all the GIF images
stored in your Linux file system. But suppose you want to narrow down your list a
bit further: Suppose you want to find only pictures of outer space.

You could load myjpegs.txt into a text editor or browse it with a pager to visually
search for files that match your criteria, but you can find what you want more
quickly by using the grep command to search myjpegs.txt. The grep command's
sole purpose is to search text files for words or patterns that you supply. You call the
grep command like this:

```
grep pattern file1 [file2 ...]
```

Here, *pattern* is the text string or pattern to search for, and *file1*, *file2*, and so
on are the files that grep is to search. Lines from these files that contain the text
string or match the pattern will be displayed on standard output (that is, to the console). Try searching for pictures of space now:

```
[you@workstation20 ~]$ grep space myjpegs.txt
/usr/share/nautilus/patterns/chalk.jpg
/usr/share/nautilus/patterns/burlap.jpg
/usr/share/emacs/site-lisp/emacspeak/etc/emacspeak.jpg
/usr/share/gtk-2.0/demo/background.jpg
/usr/share/pixmaps/gnect/bg_nightfall.jpg
/usr/share/pixmaps/gnect/bg_grotty.jpg
[...]
/usr/share/backgrounds/images/space/hst_antennae_9734a.jpg
/usr/share/backgrounds/images/space/hst_mars060.jpg
/usr/share/backgrounds/images/space/apollo08_earthrise.jpg
/usr/share/backgrounds/images/earth_from_space.jpg
/usr/lib/python2.4/site-packages/Ft/Share/Demos/images/Cards/Cribbage/
➥spacer-border.gif
/usr/share/doc/openjade-1.3.2/jadedoc/images/space.gif
[you@workstation20 ~]$
```

The grep command has found a number of pathnames in myjpegs.txt that contain
the word space. Used this way, grep is a great tool for mining data from long lists.

> ### You Can Use grep to Find Files, Too
>
> You can also use grep to help you find files that contain a certain word. When you search for a word using grep and the -l argument, grep simply prints the names of the files that contain the word in question. For example, if you want to know which files in your home directory contain the text jpg, you can issue the following command to search for jpg in all files in your home directory:
>
> ```
> [you@workstation20 ~]$ grep -l jpg ~/*
> myjpegs.txt
> [you@workstation20 ~]$
> ```

> ### Be Careful About Capitalization
>
> When you use grep, you perform a case-sensitive search; the capitalization of the word you're searching for must mirror the capitalization of your search term so that grep can find a match.
>
> To cause grep to perform a case-insensitive search, use the -i argument:
>
> ```
> grep -il jpg ~/*
> ```

# Using Command Output for Complex Tasks

One of the greatest advantages of the Linux command line is that it enables you to tie multiple commands and their output together in a wide variety of ways. By tying commands, you can perform complex tasks that involve multiple steps; the output can be further refined at each step, to fulfill your needs in the most unusual of situations.

The two most important techniques for tying multiple commands are the use of pipes—which enable the output of one command to act as the input for another command—and command substitution—which enables the output of one command to alter the behavior of another command.

## Using Pipes to Link Commands

Sometimes it is convenient to use the output of one command as the input of another. You can use **pipes**, which you create with the vertical bar (¦), to cause the shell to do this.

For example, you have seen the list of JPEG and GIF images of space on your system; you created this list by redirecting the output of two locate commands to a file called myjpegs.txt and then searching this file with grep for the word space.

Suppose you now want to learn whether any images of space in your Linux file system are stored in the `.png` or `.tif` graphics formats. Wouldn't it be helpful to send the output of the `locate` command directly to `grep` so that `grep` could search the data on the fly, without having to keep saving data to the file `myjpegs.txt`?

You can do this with the help of the pipe (¦) in a command like this one:

```
locate '*.gif' '*.jpg' '*.tif' '*.png' ¦ grep space
```

This command generates a list of all the image pathnames that contain the word space across your entire Linux file system. The output of the `locate` command (to which you supplied four arguments) is sent directly to `grep`, which searches the data it received for the word space.

A more mundane, but no less useful, application of pipes is the paging of command output. For example, try entering the following command:

```
ls -l /usr/bin
```

The listing that this command generates is very long; the vast majority of it will scroll past the top of your console before you get a chance to see it. However, by sending the output of this command through a pipe to another command called `less`, you can remedy the situation. As you've already learned, the `less` command is a pager: It displays a file or input data one page at a time, pausing and requiring you to press the spacebar to continue between each screen of information. Try piping the output of `ls` through `less` now with this command:

```
ls -l /usr/bin ¦ less
```

The listing still contains a great deal of information, but you are now able to see *all* of it at your leisure. Don't worry if the range of applications for pipes seems murky to you now; you'll grow more accustomed to pipe use as we continue to work with the shell.

## Using One Command's Answers as Another's Arguments

Another essential shell tool is known as **command substitution**. Command substitution allows the output of one command to be used as a set of command-line arguments for another command. This process enables the results of a first command to alter the behavior of a second command, thereby affecting its output and *customizing* the second command for the situation at hand.

Suppose you want to create a directory called `spacejpegs` and gather into it every JPEG image on your system whose pathname contains the word space, for easy indexing and access to space images. You already know how to use `locate` to find all the pathnames that contain the word space and end in `.jpg` in the Linux file system. With this output, you can use command substitution to gather these files into one place:

```
[you@workstation20 ~]$ mkdir spacejpegs
[you@workstation20 ~]$ ln -s $(locate '*space*.jpg') spacejpegs
[you@workstation20 ~]$
```

Enclosing the command `locate '*space*.jpg'` in parentheses preceded by a dollar sign ($) caused the output filenames from the `locate` command to be treated as though you had typed them in one by one on the command line as arguments to `ln -s`, which is the command to create symbolic links. The net effect was as if you had typed a command something like this:

```
ln -s /path/to/file1.jpg /path/to/file2.jpg /path/to/file3.jpg [...] jpegfiles
```

*By the Way*

### What Are Symbolic Links Again?

Symbolic links and the `ln -s` command are discussed in Chapter 7.

Use the `ls` command to get a long listing of the `spacejpegs` directory. You'll find that a symbolic link has been created to every file containing the word space in its pathname and ending in `.jpg` on the entire system; all the space-oriented JPEG images have been collected in one place for easy access.

*By the Way*

### Two Ways to Substitute Commands

Command substitution in the bash shell can occur in two ways; the one shown here is to enclose the substituted command in parentheses preceded by a dollar sign:

```
$(locate myfile)
```

An alternate, more traditional way of using command substitution is to enclose the substituted command in backquotes (also known as backticks or simply ticks):

```
`locate myfile`
```

The less traditional method is used in this book because backquotes are often difficult to differentiate from forward single quotation marks and can thus lead to confusion.

As was the case with pipes, the wide range of applications for command substitution is not likely to be immediately obvious to the beginner. Don't worry, though; you'll see them again as we continue to work with the shell.

# Summary

In this chapter, you added to your collection of shell skills that will ultimately help you to become productive at the Linux command line. You learned to group files for issuing commands and otherwise working with them efficiently. You also learned commands for finding files, file types, and specific words or word patterns in files quickly and easily. You learned two ways to hook commands together to save time, effort, and disk space.

Along the way, you learned the following new commands, keystrokes, and special characters for use at the shell prompt:

- ▶ > redirects standard output to a new file.

- ▶ >> appends standard output to an existing file.

- ▶ find searches for files in real time.

- ▶ grep searches a file for a particular piece of text or pattern in a plaintext file or searches a set of files for a particular piece of text or pattern and returns their filenames if they contain it.

- ▶ locate searches an often-updated database of files for the file you seek.

You've now had all the shell, command, and console education you really need to begin doing real work. Until the advanced shell topics in Chapter 25, "Harnessing the Power of the Shell," you won't explore this many nuts-and-bolts type topics again; instead, it's time to proceed to using some powerful shell-based applications.

# Q&A

**Q** *When I redirect the output of some commands to a file using the greater-than symbol as described, some messages are still sent to the console. Why?*

**A** You're seeing standard error messages, rather than standard output messages. Standard error messages are meant to inform you that something out of the ordinary has happened. To redirect standard error messages, append a 2> to the end of the command, followed by the name of the file that should hold the error messages.

**Q** *Is there any way to simply throw away the standard output or standard error messages—for instance, if I want a command to behave "silently"?*

**A** Yes, redirect one or both to the special device file /dev/null, which is commonly known as the **bit bucket**. All data sent to the file /dev/null is discarded by the system.

# Workshop

The Workshop is designed to help you anticipate possible questions, review what you've learned, and begin learning how to put your knowledge into practice.

## Quiz

1. What pattern would you use with the `rm` command to remove the files `houseprices.txt`, `priceless.gif`, and `car.myprice`?

2. How would you search the file `shoecolors.txt` for lines containing the word red?

3. How would you *quickly* search your entire file system for a file called `FedoraNotes.txt`?

## Answers

1. `*price*`

2. `grep red shoecolors.txt`

3. `locate FedoraNotes.txt`

## Activities

1. Use `locate` and `less` to get a listing of all the files of the following types on your system, displayed one page at a time: `.txt`, `.gif`, `.jpg`, and `.gz`.

2. Using the techniques learned in this chapter, create a directory called `~/images` that contains symbolic links to all `.jpg`, `.gif`, `.tif`, `.png`, and `.xpm` files on your system. Then open a file manager window and browse through them!

## CHAPTER 20

# Creating, Editing, and Saving Text Files

---

## *What You'll Learn in This Chapter:*

- ▶ How to use the `vi` text editor
- ▶ How to use the `emacs` text editor
- ▶ How to suspend a running application at the command line
- ▶ How to resume a suspended application at the command line
- ▶ How to use tools for managing running and suspended applications at the command line

In this chapter, you gain experience with two editors that will be useful to you as you read through the rest of the chapters in Part IV; you use them to create text documents and scripts as you work at the command line. Toward the end of the chapter, you also learn about tools that help you to manage multiple running shell applications.

To begin this chapter, you should already be logged in to your account at a virtual console or have a Terminal window started on your desktop so that you are ready to give commands at the shell prompt.

## Using Common Command-Line Editors

In the preceding chapter, you created a few text files using the `touch` command, but they were all *empty* text files—unlikely to be of much use for any common purpose. Most of the time if you're creating a text file, you need it to contain specific text that you enter yourself.

At the Linux command line, two major editors are commonly used to create text files— and they are polar opposites. The first is a small, classic Unix tool called `vi`; the second is a large, extensible data processor called `emacs`. You can use either editor to create the kinds of documents you want to create at the Linux command line. The vi editor is generally preferred by users who want a minimal, fast, no-frills editing experience, and the emacs editor is generally preferred by power users. The editor you choose to use on a daily basis is ultimately a matter of personal preference and little more; some Linux administration tools integrate the vi editor as part of their functionality, however, so you should at least become moderately familiar with vi.

**Text Editor Versus Word Processor**

Although most computer users are familiar with the term **word processor**, the term **text editor** is less widely known.

A word processor includes features designed for desktop publishing, such as typeface selection, layout controls, and formatting options for the printed page. A text editor is designed to edit letters and numbers only; a text editor does not offer features for controlling the appearance or layout of text in printed output.

## Using vi to Create or Edit Text Files

The vi editor is popular because, unlike emacs, it's nearly always present, even on the most minimal system. It's also popular because, unlike emacs, vi is small and fast.

Begin work on an empty document now by typing the vi command followed by the name of the file you want to create as an argument. Call this file myvifile.txt:

```
[you@workstation20 ~]$ vi myvifile.txt
```

**If the File Exists, It Will Be Loaded**

Starting vi does not always *create* a file. If you supply the name of an already existing file as the argument to vi, that file is loaded into vi so that you can edit it.

You always know you're working in vi when you see the line of tilde (~) characters stretching down the left side of your console. These characters indicate that there is no text yet on any of these lines. Don't actually try to type anything yet; you won't be able to. The vi editor is line-oriented and has two modes. When you first start vi, you are in a mode not designed to allow text entry.

You are looking at the **command mode** right now. Anything you type, including normal alphabetic text, will not appear in the document; rather, it will be interpreted by vi as an attempt to demand action. In command mode, you can save your file, move your cursor around, delete phrases or lines of text, and so on.

The **insert mode** is the only mode in which you can directly enter text, and while vi is in the insert mode, text entry is nearly the only thing you *can* do. This two-mode system inevitably confuses new vi users at first, but after a little practice, most people become comfortable with it.

Let's insert some text.

## Inserting Text in vi

To begin inserting text in the vi file you're working on, myvifile.txt, press the i key. Notice that the word INSERT appears at the bottom of the display, as shown in Figure 20.1.

-- INSERT --                                            0,1              All

Enter a few lines of text now. Follow along with the examples here or enter your own text. Note that there is no word wrap in vi; when you come to the end of a line, you must press Enter to start a new line of text:

```
The vi editor is ubiquitous in Unix. Because of this, it is important
that all aspiring Unix users understand how to interact with vi.
```

---

### There Is No Word Wrap in vi

If you choose not to press Enter before you reach the right side of your display, the text on your screen wraps around to the left side of the display in mid-word. Understand, however, that the text in vi's memory buffer does not. If you manage to fill the entire screen full of text without ever pressing Enter, the file you save is stored as *one long line* of text.

Having just one long line of text can have unexpected consequences when you're printing, emailing, or even editing text files.

**By the Way**

When you finish entering text, press the Esc key to exit the insert mode and return to command mode. When you do so, notice that the word INSERT disappears from the status line at the bottom of the screen.

Now you've inserted some text. But what if you want to change what you've typed so far? In vi, the methods for making changes aren't always obvious.

## Editing Text in vi

You use keystroke commands to navigate and edit text in vi. Table 20.1 shows some of the most common keystrokes.

**TABLE 20.1    Common Keystroke Commands for Editing and Navigating in vi**

| Keystroke | Action |
| --- | --- |
| l | Move cursor one character to the right. |
| h | Move cursor one character to the left. |
| j | Move cursor down one *text* line (not one display line). |
| k | Move cursor up one *text* line (not one display line). |
| x | Delete the character immediately under the cursor. |
| d#<Space> | Delete # characters immediately under and to the right of the cursor. |
| dd | Delete the current line. |
| i | Insert: Return to insert mode, inserting immediately under the cursor at its current position. |
| a | Append: Return to insert mode, inserting immediately to the right of the cursor at its current position. |
| A | Append: Return to insert mode, inserting at the end of the current *text* line (not display line). |
| Esc | Return to command mode. |

Try using the movement and editing keys in command mode to alter the text you just entered, to delete a line or a few characters of text, or to insert or append some text to the file. If you get confused, the keyboard stops responding, or keys don't work as you expect them to while you are editing, you have likely keyed incorrectly; press Esc several times to ensure that you return to the command mode.

## You Can Use the Arrow Keys in `vi`

If you've been following along and experimenting with `vi`, you've likely discovered that it's actually easier than we've made it out to be. Fedora Core 4 uses an enhanced version of `vi` called `vim`. In this enhanced `vi` editor, you can use your arrow keys to navigate through the text, even in insert mode, as long as your terminal is properly configured (as is the case at the Linux console).

This enhanced version of `vi` isn't present on most Unix systems, however, or even on all Linux systems—and `vim` might not be included in future versions of Fedora Core 4. Furthermore, some administration situations can limit you to traditional `vi` keys even while using Fedora Core 4. You should become familiar with the traditional `vi` keys and behaviors, in case you find yourself working in a traditional `vi` editor in the future.

*By the Way*

Experiment with `vi` for a while and try to become familiar with it; you'll encounter it often enough in Linux to make it worth your time.

## Saving and Quitting

Let's save the file you just created by entering what may seem like a very cryptic command. Type a colon (`:`) now. Notice that a colon appears at the lower left of the display and that the cursor has moved there; `vi` is now waiting for you to enter a more complex command. Type a lowercase **w** and press Enter. The `vi` editor responds with a status update at the lower left of the display:

```
"myvifile.txt" [New] 2L, 135C written
```

First, `vi` indicates the name of the file that has just been saved; you called this file `myvifile.txt`. Next, `vi` gives the number of lines in the file (2), followed by the number of individual characters in the file (135). You have now saved your first `vi` file.

A Save As function is also available in `vi`. To save your text again, this time as a new file, type a colon, and then enter **w** followed by a space and the name **mynewvifile.txt**. The `vi` editor responds with

```
"mynewvifile.txt" i[New] 2L, 135C written
```

You now have two copies of the file in your home directory: `myvifile.txt` and `mynewvifile.txt`. That's enough of `vi` for this book. To exit `vi`, type a colon and then type **q**. This command quits `vi` and returns you to the command prompt.

**If You Haven't Saved,** vi **Will Let You Know**

If you try to exit vi without first saving the file you've been working on, vi interrupts you with an error message indicating that your file has not been saved; it then returns to command mode.

If you really want to exit anyway, use :q! (with the exclamation mark added) instead of simply :q to exit; vi then complies.

vi is powerful and worthy of some study, both because of the number of efficiency-oriented editing features it provides and because you will so often encounter it while using Linux or Unix computers at the command line. If you're feeling adventurous, you can explore the bulky online help system in Fedora Core 4's version of the vi editor by restarting vi and entering **:help** while in command mode. The resulting title page appears in Figure 20.2.

**FIGURE 20.2**
The title screen for the vi (vim) online help system. The help is reasonably extensive, and you can become quite a vi expert simply by reading these documents.

```
*help.txt*      For Vim version 6.3.  Last change: 2004 May 04

                          VIM - main help file
                                                                    k
          Move around:  Use the cursor keys, or "h" to go left.    h   l
                        "j" to go down, "k" to go up, "l" to go right.    j
    Close this window:  Use ":q<Enter>".
      Get out of Vim:  Use ":qa!<Enter>" (careful, all changes are lost!).

    Jump to a subject:  Position the cursor on a tag between |bars| and hit CTRL-].
        With the mouse:  ":set mouse=a" to enable the mouse (in xterm or GUI).
                        Double-click the left mouse button on a tag between |bars|.
            Jump back:  Type CTRL-T or CTRL-O (repeat to go further back).

    Get specific help:  It is possible to go directly to whatever you want help
                        on, by giving an argument to the ":help" command |:help|.
                        It is possible to further specify the context:
                                                      *help-context*
                           WHAT                  PREPEND   EXAMPLE
                        Normal mode commands     (nothing)  :help x
help.txt [help][RO]                                        1,1           Top

myvifile.txt                                               0,0-1         All
```

**More Detailed** vi **Information Is Available**

You can find a more complete vi tutorial in *Sams Teach Yourself Unix in 24 Hours*, by Dave Taylor.

# Using emacs **to Create Text Files**

If you found vi to be too minimal for your taste, you'll likely feel better about emacs, although emacs also has its quirks. Whereas vi's focus is on minimalism, basic functionality, and speed, emacs is extensible and programmable and has over the years grown into a monster of a system. Very few people on Earth know everything that can be known about emacs; there are hundreds of modes and commands and an entire programming language (Emacs LISP) to master.

For our purposes, however, emacs is going to seem friendly and simple compared to vi. You can start emacs the same way you started vi: Type the emacs command followed by the name of the file you want to open or create as an argument. Use the filename myemacsfile.txt:

```
[you@workstation20 ~]$ emacs myemacsfile.txt
```

Depending on your system configuration, loading emacs might take somewhat longer than loading vi. emacs is a much larger and more complex editor than vi. After emacs loads, you find yourself looking at the screen shown in Figure 20.3 if you started emacs in a virtual console, or at the new application window shown in Figure 20.4 if you started emacs from a desktop Terminal.

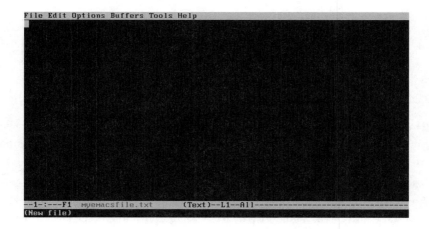

FIGURE 20.3
The emacs editor clearly has a more accessible look than vi and is designed to function in some ways that Windows users are more accustomed to.

Starting emacs from a desktop Terminal opens a new window, complete with point-and-click menus. You should still learn the keystrokes in this chapter, though! Inserting text into the emacs editor is easy: Just type. The arrow keys, Backspace and Delete keys, Page Up and Page Down keys, and Home and End keys all behave as you expect them to.

When you reach the end of the first line, you'll soon find out that, like vi, emacs does not normally automatically word wrap. Remember to press Enter at the end of each line because emacs is a line-oriented editor. If you don't press Enter at the end of each line, only one very long line of text is written when you save your file.

## Using the emacs **Menu System**

If you are using emacs on the desktop, a familiar and relatively user-friendly menu bar appears across the top of the application window; you can navigate through it just as you normally would using your mouse.

**FIGURE 20.4**
If you start emacs from the Terminal application on your desktop, it looks like and responds to mouse clicks just like any other application.

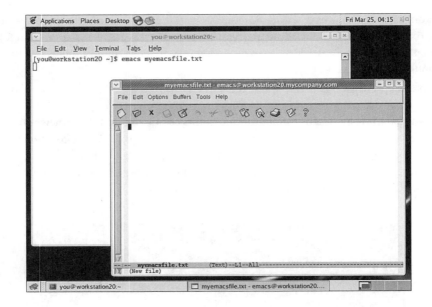

Although the top of the emacs display in a virtual console might appear to have a menu bar as well, this isn't really the case. There is no way to visually activate drop-down menus at the console.

You can, however, access the fairly intuitive emacs menu in a virtual console by pressing the F10 key at almost any time. When you press F10, your display is split in two, and the lower half of your display fills with options that you can activate with a single keypress (see Figure 20.5).

**FIGURE 20.5**
When you bring up the emacs menu system at the console, you can activate each item by pressing its respective key.

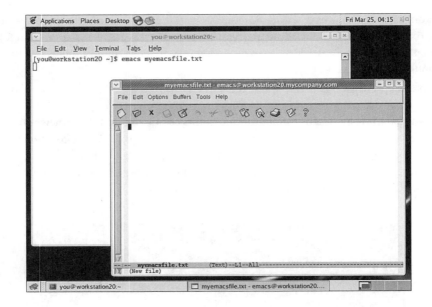

To save the file you have been working on, press f to open the File menu and then s to save it after the File menu appears. emacs displays a message in the small area at the bottom of the screen, known as the **minibuffer**, to let you know that the file has been saved:

```
wrote /home/you/myemacsfile.txt
```

You can use the F10 menu system in emacs to perform most basic editing, saving, and loading functions at the command line. For most users, the F10 menu and simpler editing style make emacs the editor of choice over vi.

## Using Essential emacs Keystrokes

If you aren't too ham-handed, you might be able to use emacs and the F10 menu for months or even years without getting into trouble. However, an accidental keystroke that leaves emacs expecting additional commands may leave you sitting in front of a beeping emacs editor printing cryptic error messages or demands in the minibuffer.

The essential keystroke to know at such times is written in the emacs documentation as C-g (hold down Ctrl and press g). This combination is the emacs abort keystroke. The emacs editor is large enough and complex enough that there will be many opportunities, after mis-keying, to find yourself in an unknown state with respect to emacs' expectations; most of the time, repeatedly pressing C-g until things return to normal is the solution to this type of confusion.

Table 20.2 lists a few other interesting emacs keystrokes—some accessible from the menu system, some not. To understand this table, you must first become familiar with the format of emacs keystrokes:

- ▶ C-x, where x is a letter, means hold down the Ctrl key and press the letter.
- ▶ C-xy, where both x and y are letters, means hold down the Ctrl key, press the first letter, release both the Ctrl key and the first letter, and then press the second letter alone.
- ▶ M-x, where x is a letter, means hold down the Alt key and press the letter.
- ▶ C-x C-y, where both x and y are letters, means hold down the Ctrl key, press the first letter, and then, without releasing the Ctrl key, press the second letter.

Note that the letters in these Control key combinations are case sensitive, so be careful to press the keys indicated, rather than their uppercase or lowercase counterparts.

**TABLE 20.2**    Useful emacs Keystrokes

| Keystroke | Explanation |
| --- | --- |
| C-ht | Launch the emacs tutorial, in which many more keystrokes are documented. |
| C-x C-f | Find (open or create) a file in the current editing pane; you are prompted in the minibuffer for a filename or path. |
| C-x C-s | Save the file you are currently working on. |
| C-x2 | Split the current editing pane vertically. |
| C-x3 | Split the current editing pane horizontally. |
| C-x1 | Cause the current editing pane to fill the entire screen (hide/remove other panes). |
| C-xo | Select the next editing pane. |
| C-xk | Close (without saving) the file or buffer you are currently working in. For example, use this keystroke after you've opened the emacs tutorial to exit it again. |
| C-xb | Switch to another buffer; you are prompted in the minibuffer for a buffer name. If you are unsure about the names of open buffers, press Tab for a complete list. |
| C-xi *file* | Insert a file at the current cursor position. You are prompted 1for the name of the file in the minibuffer. |
| C-x C-c | Exit emacs completely. |
| C-g | Abort the current emacs process. |

One final keystroke before we finish our discussion of emacs takes you well on your way to becoming an emacs guru. To see a list of available commands in emacs, press M-x and then the Tab key. A buffer containing a list of emacs commands appears. Press C-xo until your cursor appears in that pane; you can then use Page Up and Page Down to browse through the available commands. If you see one you would like to try, type it into the minibuffer and press Enter.

The various emacs commands include the following:

▶ M-x dunnet starts a text-based adventure game.

▶ M-x auto-fill turns on word wrap.

▶ M-x calendar opens a new pane containing a three-month calendar.

▶ M-x shell opens a shell in the current pane. Be sure to use C-x2 or C-x3 before running this one so that you can edit a file and work with the shell at the same time, switching between panes with C-xo, as shown in Figure 20.6.

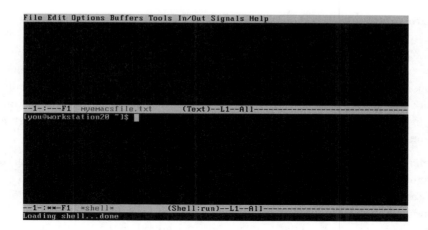

**FIGURE 20.6**
An emacs editor
that has been
split horizontally
with C-x2. A
shell is started
in the lower
pane with C-xo
followed by M-x
shell. You
switch between
the panes with
C-xo.

---

### emacs **Makes Backups of Your Files**

If you become an emacs user, you will soon find that, from time to time, files appear in your working directory with names similar to those you've been working on, but with slight additions. For example, if you've been working on a file called myfile.txt, you might also find #myfile.txt# or myfile.txt~ in the same directory.

emacs creates these "safety" files in the interest of preserving your data.

When you exit without saving a file, emacs saves the file anyway, under the same name but with hash marks (#) at the front and back, in case you want to recover the changes you made later.

When you make changes to an existing file and save them, emacs preserves the original (unmodified) file under the same name, but with a tilde character (~) at the end, in case you want to return to the original file later.

If you don't want to preserve the autosave or backup files, remove them with rm, although you might want to load them into emacs first to make sure that they don't contain data that you want to save.

*By the Way*

# Keeping Your Shell Programs Under Control

In upcoming chapters we're going to be running fairly involved applications at the console, and you'll be using editors like vi and emacs to work on documents and write shell scripts (small shell programs). Before we reach that point, it's important that you know about shell-based job control.

You can log in to several virtual consoles simultaneously to run more than one full-screen application at a time—for example, an emacs on console one and a vi on console two. Switching back and forth between virtual consoles, however, can be both confusing and clumsy. And you may have noticed that even if you start emacs from a Terminal window, you can't actually use the command line in that terminal window until after you exit emacs once again. More to the point, after you learn to log in to Linux systems remotely via telnet or ssh, you need to be able to use the command line without the luxury of multiple virtual consoles.

To maximize your ability to use the command line even while other applications are running these types of situations, you can use shell-based control techniques to pause and resume multiple tasks or applications, like vi or emacs, from a single command prompt. By using these techniques, you can switch between running applications, move jobs to the foreground or background, and end tasks that are no longer needed. The following sections teach you how to use these and other techniques to comfortably multitask at the Linux console.

## Moving Between Multiple Open Applications

Assume for illustrative purposes that you need to be able to start and then switch back and forth between emacs and vi without losing your place in either application. Perhaps you are working on an article comparing the two, or perhaps you are simply editing a file in vi but taking breaks every hour or so to play the dunnet game mentioned earlier when you learned about emacs.

You can use the Ctrl+Z keystroke in a virtual console or in the Terminal window to suspend work on an open application so that you can open another application. You can use the jobs command to list all open applications.

Take a moment to load the myvifile.txt file created earlier in this chapter back into the vi editor:

```
[you@workstation20 ~]$ vi myvifile.txt
```

When the vi editor appears on the screen, the command prompt is hidden, unavailable to you. You can now begin to edit the file, making changes as necessary. But what happens when it's time to take a dunnet break?

You can suspend the vi process by pressing Ctrl+Z:

```
[1]+  Stopped          vim myvifile.txt
[you@workstation20 ~]$
```

The vi process has now been suspended. Note the number 1 in brackets; this is the **job number** of the interrupted vi process. Feel free to start emacs and enter M-x dunnet inside the application to load the dunnet game if you want.

You can play the game for a while, but eventually you must return to your document in vi because you can't play forever. However, to do so, you don't have to exit emacs and lose your place in the game. You can suspend the emacs process in the same way you suspended the vi process earlier—by pressing Ctrl+Z:

```
[2]+ Stopped         emacs
[you@workstation20 ~]$
```

You now have two text editors in your job list that are suspended. To see a list of your current jobs at any time, enter the jobs command:

```
[you@workstation20 ~]$ jobs
[1]- Stopped         vim myvifile.txt
[2]+ Stopped         emacs
[you@workstation20 ~]$
```

Jobs can remain suspended indefinitely without harm; you can continue to work with the shell to perform other tasks, and vi and emacs will be ready to pick up exactly where they left off.

---

**Quitting a Running Job**

You can sometimes use Ctrl+C to simply quit a running job if you don't want merely to suspend it. However, Ctrl+C doesn't always work. For example, it doesn't work in emacs or vi, although it does work during the output of a particularly lengthy locate job.

*By the Way*

---

## Resuming a Job with fg

To return to your editing work in vi, you can use the fg command, passing the percent sign (%) and the correct job number as arguments:

```
[you@workstation20 ~]$ fg %1
```

As was reported by the jobs command, the vi process is shell job number 1; after you enter the fg (foreground) command supplying %1 as an argument, vi returns your editing display to exactly the same state it was in when you suspended it.

You can repeat this suspend and resume process as needed, suspending and resuming applications in any combination or order.

## Running a Job in the Background with bg

Some commands in Linux can take a long time to run, especially on older systems. At such times, the shell can provide an ideal solution. Commands that do not require user intervention to finish can be run as **background tasks**. You can use the bg command to run jobs in the background. This command then frees you up to return to work in other open applications.

Again for purposes of illustration, assume that while you are editing with vi and playing with emacs, you decide that you also need to generate a list of all the files in your Linux file system that locate can tell you about. To save a list of this sort to a file called fileslist.txt, you must suspend whatever editor you are working in by using the Ctrl+Z keystroke and enter a command to create such a list for you:

```
[you@workstation20 ~]$ locate '*' > fileslist.txt
```

The locate command is given a pattern that will match every file in its database. The output has been redirected to the file fileslist.txt. Simple enough in concept, but this job will take quite awhile to finish on most PCs. Let's pause this job and then make it a background task. Press Ctrl+Z to interrupt the command in progress:

```
[3]+ Stopped            locate '*' >fileslist.txt
[you@workstation20 ~]$
```

Notice that the command is assigned a job number of 3 and the command prompt has returned. The command is now suspended; unless it is at some point resumed, it will never finish. To resume it in the background, use the bg (background) command:

```
[you@workstation20 ~]$ bg %3
[3]+ locate '*' > fileslist.txt &
[you@workstation20 ~]$
```

The command is now running in the background; Linux will continue to work on the task until it is complete. In the meantime, you are free to return to your editor or to your dunnet game by using the fg command. To see the updated list of jobs first, use the jobs command:

```
[you@workstation20 ~]$ jobs
[1]- Stopped            vim myvifile.txt
[2]+ Stopped            emacs
[3]  Running            locate '*' >fileslist.txt &
[you@workstation20 ~]$
```

As you continue to work with the shell, you will at some point receive a message that your background process has finished:

```
[3]  Done               locate '*' >fileslist.txt &
```

After a process has finished, it will no longer appear in the jobs list along with the other running or suspended jobs.

## Killing and Starting Background Jobs

There are two more commands related to job control that you can use to feel at home on the command line. The first is kill. You can use the kill command with a job number to forcibly terminate a job that you don't want any longer:

```
[you@workstation20 ~]$ kill %2
[2]+ Stopped          emacs
[1]- Stopped          vim myvifile.txt
[2]+ Terminated       emacs
[you@workstation20 ~]$
```

Although kill aids in destroying jobs, the ampersand (&) aids in creating them. Instead of using Ctrl+Z and then the bg command, if you want to start a job that can run in the background from the beginning, simply follow it on the command line with an ampersand. For example, earlier you could have used

```
[you@workstation20 ~]$ locate '*' > fileslist.txt &
[2] 10413
[you@workstation20 ~]$
```

The first number returned after starting a job in the background is the job number, with which you are now familiar. The second number is the system process number; you learn more about using the system process table in Chapter 28, "Command-Line System Administration."

# Summary

In this chapter, you learned how to use your first two full-fledged command-line applications in Linux, vi and emacs. Among other things, you learned

- ▶ How to start vi and emacs and create a new file

- ▶ How to navigate in vi and use the insert mode

- ▶ How to use a number of common emacs keystrokes

- ▶ How to use job control keystrokes, including Ctrl+Z to suspend a running process

- ▶ How to use the bg, fg, and jobs commands, which resume a job in the background, resume a job in the foreground, and list all currently existing jobs

In the next chapter, you put your new knowledge of command-line editors to work as you begin to create professional-quality documents at the command line!

## Q&A

**Q** *Are there any advantages to using* vi *or* emacs *in the desktop environment, rather than the editor accessible through the GNOME Menu?*

**A** Yes, there are, but there is a learning curve. Both vi and emacs have powerful features that are well suited to writing structured documents such as HTML (Web) pages or programs in various computer languages. Topics like this are beyond the scope of this book, however; for more information, consult any of the numerous books detailing the vi and emacs editors.

**Q** *What is the maximum number of jobs that I can suspend or run in the background?*

**A** Although there are theoretical numerical limits on the number of processes that can run simultaneously on a Linux system, these limits are so large that in practice you will never run into them, even when starting many thousands of processes simultaneously. Feel free to start as many shell jobs or applications as your system resources permit.

## Workshop

The Workshop is designed to help you anticipate possible questions, review what you've learned, and begin learning how to put your knowledge into practice.

### Quiz

1. How do you save the file that you're working on in vi? In emacs?

2. What keystroke opens the menu in emacs when you're working at a virtual console?

3. How would you output a list of currently running emacs jobs? (*Hint*: Use a pipe and a command learned in Chapter 19, "Performing Basic Shell Tasks.")

### Answers

1. In vi, press Esc. Then, when the colon (:) appears, type **w** and press Enter. In emacs, press Ctrl-X followed by Ctrl-S—or in emacs terms, use the keystroke C-x C-s.

2. Press the F10 key to open the emacs menu in a virtual console.

3. `jobs ¦ grep emacs`

## Activities

1. Take some time to study both the emacs and vi tutorials and to familiarize yourself with the capabilities of each.

2. Start a long list of jobs, suspending each of them one by one until the output of the jobs command fills the entire screen. Then exit or kill each of them one by one.

3. Start emacs and play a game of dunnet.

# CHAPTER 21

# Managing High-Quality Documents at the Command Line

---

## What You'll Learn in This Chapter:

▶ How to print from the command line

▶ How to create professional-quality documents using LaTeX-2e

▶ How to format documents you've created with LaTeX-2e for your printer

Over the past few chapters, you learned to use the command line to perform basic file manipulation and data housekeeping tasks and use two popular command-line text editors. You also learned how to get command and application documentation when you need it. In this chapter, you learn to format and print professional-quality documents using a powerful application called LaTeX-2e.

---

### You May Need to Install LaTeX First!

If you didn't choose the Workstation installation of Fedora Core 4 in Chapter 2, "Installing Fedora Core 4," you don't yet have LaTeX installed on your system. If this is true in your case, you should install LaTeX before proceeding with this chapter.

Refer to Chapter 31, "Installing Linux Software," for help installing additional Linux software from your CDs. To follow along with this chapter, you need to install the "Authoring and Publishing" package ground.

*By the Way*

# Printing at the Command Line

While learning to work at the command line, you may have wished on several occasions that you could print the output generated by your commands. Users new to Unix-like operating systems are often surprised to learn that nearly any kind of information can be sent to the printer directly from the command line. In fact, managing printing from the command line is quite easy after a printer has been properly configured. For details on configuring your printer, refer to Chapter 3, "Booting, Logging In, and Configuring."

Printing any kind of information in Linux requires the creation of a print job. When a print job is created, the data to be printed is queued in a list of pending jobs. The print job at the top of the list is the one currently being printed; when it finishes, the system removes it from the queue in a process called **dequeueing**. The next job moves to the top of the queue, is printed, and so on, until all pending jobs have been printed.

This system enables many users to simultaneously use a Linux system for printing text and data; everyone simply waits his or her turn.

## Creating Print Jobs

You create print jobs with the lpr command. To print an existing text file, simply supply it to lpr as an argument:

```
[you@workstation20 ~]$ lpr myfile.txt
[you@workstation20 ~]$
```

This command creates a print job containing the data from the file myfile.txt; when the job reaches the front of the queue, the file myfile.txt is printed. Data can also be queued using the lpr command in conjunction with pipes, which you learned about in "Using Pipes to Link Commands" in Chapter 19, "Performing Basic Shell Tasks." For example, to print a long listing of the contents of the /etc directory, you pipe the output of the ls command to the lpr command:

```
[you@workstation20 ~]$ ls -l /etc | lpr
[you@workstation20 ~]$
```

Print jobs created with pipes behave in exactly the same manner as print jobs created from plaintext files.

## Listing Print Jobs

In a system in which many print jobs can be queued for printing, users sometimes want to check the list of jobs currently in the queue and their print order. You can use the lpq command to get a list of print jobs. To get a listing of current jobs, enter lpq without arguments on the command line:

```
[you@workstation20 ~]$ lpq
lp is ready and printing
Rank   Owner   Job    File(s)           Total Size
active you     3      (stdin)            1024 bytes
1st    you     4      (stdin)          102400 bytes
2nd    you     5      syslog.conf         693 bytes
[you@workstation20 ~]$
```

In this instance, three print jobs are in the queue, all started by you. The first two jobs contain output from commands that were piped to lpr. This is indicated by the word stdin (for *standard input*) appearing in the Files column, meaning that the lpr command is receiving the file to print through a pipe. The last job contains the text in the file syslog.conf.

# Dequeueing Print Jobs

If you decide that you no longer want to print a job that's in the print queue, you can dequeue it. The system won't print a job that has been removed from the queue. To dequeue a print job, use the lprm command; the number of the print job from the Job column of lpq's output must be supplied as an argument. For example, if you want to remove the middle print job from the previous example, the correct command is

```
[you@workstation20 ~]$ lprm 4
[you@workstation20 ~]$
```

Only the root user or the user who created a job can dequeue it. The root user is able to dequeue all jobs.

---

**Printing to Another Printer**

On systems with multiple printers, calling lpr, lpq, and lprm as described here affects only the default printer, usually named lp. However, all three of these commands accept an option, -P, which you can use to specify a different printer.

For example, if you have a second printer named lp2 and want to print myfile.txt to it instead of to lp, add the -P argument followed by lp2:

```
[you@workstation20 ~]$ lpr -Plp2 myfile.txt
[you@workstation20 ~]$
```

The identical option also can be used to affect the respective behaviors of lpq and lprm.

*By the Way*

# Creating High-Quality Documents at the Command Line

Knowing how to send data to the printer is only half the battle; being able to produce professional-quality output is also essential in the modern world. At the command line, the process of producing high-quality output occurs in two steps: **text editing**, in which the textual content of your document is entered, and **text formatting**, in which the content is arranged in a pleasing manner for printing.

This method for creating documents stands in contrast to the **WYSIWYG** method with which most users are familiar. WYSIWYG is an acronym that stands for *What You See Is What You Get*. This refers to the fact that in most word processors, which are usually graphics based, you see fonts, styles, and document layout on the screen as they appear when printed on paper.

The WYSIWYG method of document editing has not always been the norm, however, and it has its limitations. Chief among them is the fact that it forces the user to be aware of formatting consistency at all times; you must keep track of the font size, style, spacing, and indentation of each piece of text yourself, which can interfere with your stream of thought as you write. When using a text formatter, on the other hand, you only need to specify that a certain piece of text is a chapter or a title, for example, and the text formatter will take care of the details of layout and appearance for you. For many types of documents—especially lengthier ones—the text editing/formatting method of creating documents is more powerful and convenient.

In Linux, you can use a simple text editor such as vi or emacs to create text documents, as you learned in Chapter 20, "Creating, Editing, and Saving Text Files." To use these editors, you input text in free form, without worrying too much about text formatting or consistency issues, such as centering, indentation, or typefaces. To control the appearance and layout of your text, you write the document to include **formatting codes** that will be used by a special formatting program to control the quality and layout of the output.

Although using text editors sounds complex, with practice you can learn to use them to enter and format text quickly and easily. This document-editing paradigm is a powerful one that can be used to create professional-looking layouts for large-scale documents, such as books or manuals.

## Introducing the LaTeX-2e Formatter

Several formatting systems are present on a typical Linux system, including the classic Unix formatter, troff. The most modern and widely used formatter today, however, is LaTeX-2e, which uses the TeX formatting engine as its core.

Using LaTeX-2e, you can quickly produce high-quality output through a laser print-er using a text editor such as vi or emacs. In fact, many professional writers, self-publishers, and educators swear by LaTeX rather than more common and widely understood WYSIWYG word processors, largely because LaTeX makes the production of high-quality output so easy.

---

**How Is It *Really* Pronounced?**

For reasons that have faded into the obscurity of history, TeX and LaTeX are most correctly pronounced "teck" and "layteck," respectively, not "tecks" and "laytecks," although in the past few years, this distinction has become less important.

*By the Way*

---

## Understanding LaTeX Basics

Creating a LaTeX document is easy: Start your editor of choice (usually vi or emacs) and enter text. All LaTeX documents begin as simple text files. Here are some of the important basics about the text you enter into a LaTeX document:

- *Some characters are reserved for use as formatting codes.* The backslash character (\) is reserved in LaTeX because it marks the beginning of a command; it does not show up in formatted output.

  Other special characters include the hash (#), dollar sign ($), percent sign (%), caret (^), ampersand (&), underscore (_), left and right braces ({}), and tilde (~). To insert any of these characters in your final document, you must prefix them with a backslash, or they will not appear properly. For example, to insert the text "50% of $35.00," you type `50\% of \$35.00` in your text editor docu-ment.

- *LaTeX automatically formats spacing.* LaTex always inserts a single space between words, a given amount of space between paragraphs, and so on. This means that unneeded extra spaces between words or multiple blank lines don't appear in final output unless you tell LaTeX explicitly to include them.

- *LaTeX commands begin with a backslash and then are typically followed by a single word of text.* The following is an example:

  ```
  \command
  ```

  Some commands require options or arguments, and in such cases you might see commands with more complex structures, usually using brackets or braces:

  ```
  \command[option]
  \command[option]{argument}
  ```

Remember, the command and the options or arguments passed to it will not appear in the final output of the document; LaTeX uses the command instead to change some aspect of the document's text layout, such as a typeface or page style.

▶ *LaTeX commands are case sensitive.* Uppercase and lowercase letters matter.

Now it's time to begin your first LaTeX document.

By the Way

### Identifying a LaTeX File

In the computer world, identifying a file's type using a three-letter extension to the filename has become common. For example, .gif denotes a Graphical Interchange Format file, and .doc indicates a Microsoft Word file.

When you save a LaTeX document in vi or emacs, convention says that you should name it with a .tex extension to indicate that it contains TeX/LaTeX formatting commands.

## Creating an Empty LaTeX Document

Any basic LaTeX document contains at least three commands: \documentclass{}, which tells LaTeX what sort of page layout you want to use, and then \begin{} and \end{}, which demarcate the beginning and end of the text body, in that order.

Listing 21.1 is a simple article-style document for letter-size paper containing only one line of text. Start a text editor now and enter the listing yourself.

### LISTING 21.1　A Short, Simple LaTeX Article Document

```
\documentclass[letterpaper,12pt]{article}
\begin{document}
This is a very short document. Here is my one line of text.
\end{document}
```

The first line of this document, which calls the \documentclass command, contains information about the class to which this document belongs. The information on the right in the braces specifies that this example belongs to a class of documents called article. LaTeX uses classes to determine basic formatting, such as setting margins and indenting for new paragraphs. You assign a class to every LaTeX document you create. Table 21.1 lists the basic LaTeX document classes.

**TABLE 21.1**   Basic LaTeX-2e Document Classes

| Class | Description |
|---|---|
| article | This is the smallest, most basic document type and performs formatting appropriate to articles and papers just a few pages in length. |
| report | This is a slightly more detailed, structured document class intended to be used for papers and reports that might contain sections or chapters. |
| book | This is the most structured document class, intended to be used for works that will be broken into multiple chapters and might need a table of contents or index generation. |

### How Do You Preview a Font or Class?

To preview the appearance of any font or other LaTeX item, type and print a small amount of text. Doing so saves you the trouble of finding that you prefer another choice after you've printed your entire final document.

*By the Way*

For most day-to-day uses—such as creating memos, small presentations, personal or business letters, and so forth—the article class is the best choice.

In addition to selecting a class for each LaTeX document, you may also specify several class options inside an optional pair of brackets to control additional aspects of formatting, such as paper size and column-based layouts for the entire document.

Inside the brackets that follow the \documentclass command, you can specify multiple options by separating them with commas. Table 21.2 lists the common class options.

**TABLE 21.2**   Common LaTeX-2e Class Options

| Option | Description |
|---|---|
| a4paper | Formats output for printing on A4-sized paper |
| b5paper | Formats output for printing on B5-sized paper |
| letterpaper | Formats output for printing on letter-sized paper |
| legalpaper | Formats output for printing on legal-sized paper |
| onecolumn | Specifies that the document should be formatted into a single column as wide as the page (default) |
| twocolumn | Specifies that the document should be formatted into two vertical columns |

**TABLE 21.2**    Continued

| Option | Description |
| --- | --- |
| oneside | Specifies that margins should be set assuming that only one side of each printed page will be used |
| twoside | Specifies that margins should be set assuming that two sides of each printed page will be used (different margins for even and odd pages) |
| openright | Specifies that for two-sided output, chapters should begin on right-side pages only |
| openany | Specifies that for two-sided output, chapters may begin either on left-side or right-side pages |
| $n$pt | Specifies that the basic font size for text in the document should be set to $n$ points (the default is 10) |

By carefully choosing a document class and document class options to suit your output medium and formatting needs, you enable LaTeX to manage automatically nearly all formatting concerns. That leaves you free to concentrate on typing your document into your favorite text editor. Here are some sample uses of options, with descriptions:

▶ `\documentclass[a4paper,twocolumn,12pt]{article}`—Your document will be formatted as an article for A4-size paper. The text will be arranged into two vertical columns on each page. The body of the text will appear in a 12-point font.

▶ `\documentclass[letterpaper,twoside]{article}`—Your document will be formatted as an article for letter-size paper. The formatter will assume that you are printing on both sides of the page; the margins for even- and odd-numbered pages will therefore be different to enable easy binding at one edge of each page.

▶ `\documentclass[legalpaper,14pt]{book}`—Your document will be formatted as a book for legal-size paper. The body of the text will appear in a 14-point font.

## Formatting and Printing Your First Document

Printing a LaTeX document is a two-step process. You first must format the document and save the formatted text in a new file. Then you print the formatted text file. To format an existing document, you call the `latex` command, supplying the name of the LaTeX source file as an argument. Assuming that you've typed in the short document in Listing 21.1 and saved it as `myfile.tex`, you can cause LaTeX to read and format the document for printing by calling the `latex` command this way at the command line:

```
[you@workstation20 ~]$ latex myfile.tex
This is pdfeTeX, Version 3.141592-1.21a-2.2 (Web2C 7.5.4)
entering extended mode
(./myfile.tex
LaTeX2e <2003/12/01>
Babel <v3.8d> and hyphenation patterns for american, french, german, ngerman, b
ahasa, basque, bulgarian, catalan, croatian, czech, danish, dutch, esperanto, e
stonian, finnish, greek, icelandic, irish, italian, latin, magyar, norsk, polis
h, portuges, romanian, russian, serbian, slovak, slovene, spanish, swedish, tur
kish, ukrainian, nohyphenation, loaded.
(/usr/share/texmf/tex/latex/base/article.cls
Document Class: article 2004/02/16 v1.4f Standard LaTeX document class
(/usr/share/texmf/tex/latex/base/size12.clo)) (./myfile.aux) [1] (./myfile.aux)
)
Output written on myfile.dvi (1 page, 288 bytes).
Transcript written on myfile.log.
[you@workstation20 ~]$
```

---

### Why Do You Get an Error When You Run LaTeX?

If you receive a command not found error when trying to run the `latex` command, LaTeX has not been installed on your computer system. As noted earlier, refer to Chapter 31 for instructions on how to install the "Authoring and Publishing" package group that is needed to use LaTeX.

*By the Way*

---

After processing the file and displaying some notes related to formatting, the `latex` command creates a file called `myfile.dvi` and then exits. The new file is called a **device-independent** file and contains the formatted output for `myfile.txt`. A device-independent file contains all the information necessary to create good-looking document output on any type of printing device.

To print a device-independent file such as `myfile.dvi`, you must convert it into the correct type of file for the printing device you plan to use. For consumer-class laser or inkjet printers, you should use the `dvips` program for this conversion, supplying the name of the device-independent file as an argument:

```
[you@workstation20 ~]$ dvips myfile.dvi
```

The `dvips` command converts a device-independent file into Adobe PostScript data, which can then be used to create nicely printed output on a consumer-class printer. The `dvips` command generates varying amounts of output on the console display as it runs. Then `dvips` creates a print job for the formatted output and sends it to the print queue. Your printer then prints the document.

> **Now You Can Create Your Own PDF Documents**
>
> You can also use a LaTeX file to generate your own Acrobat (.pdf) documents by using the `pdflatex` command instead of the `latex` command.

## Selecting a Page Style

Now that you have printed a simple one-line document, it is time to begin creating more useful documents. Obviously, most documents contain more than a single line; generally, a great deal of content exists between the `\begin{}` and `\end{}` commands in a LaTeX document.

LaTex uses **page styles** to determine the use and placement of page and chapter numbers on the printed page. Table 21.3 lists the three common page style options. The default LaTeX page style is `plain`. You can use the `\pagestyle{}` command to choose an alternate page style.

**TABLE 21.3** Common Page Styles in LaTeX-2e

| Style | Description |
| --- | --- |
| empty | LaTeX will not decorate pages at all; even page numbers will be omitted. |
| plain | LaTeX will print the page number at the bottom center of each page. |
| headings | LaTeX will decorate the top of each page with the page number and current chapter name. |

## Creating Title and Author Information

LaTeX provides an easy way to print an attractive title page for your documents: You supply title, author, and date information in your source document and then use the `\maketitle` command. To define the title and author information of your document, you include several title-specific commands after the `\documentclass{}` command and before `\begin{}`. These commands are

- `\title{text}` to specify *text* as the title of the document you are creating

- `\author{text}` to name yourself as the author of the document you are creating

- `\date{text}` to specify *text* as the creation date of the document (optional)

After you supply a title, author, and optional date, you can insert a title page in your document at any time by issuing the `\maketitle` command in the text.

# Controlling LaTeX Paragraphs, Line Breaks, and Pages

In LaTeX, paragraph formatting (indentation, blank space between paragraphs, and so on) is handled automatically. The only task left to the writer is to indicate when a new paragraph should begin. You do this by inserting a blank line in the LaTeX source file using your text editor's Enter key.

The following text illustrates this technique:

```
\documentclass[letterpaper,12pt]{article}
\begin{document}
\pagestyle{empty}
This is some text in a latex document.
This is some text in the same paragraph.
This text will also appear in the first paragraph.

But this text will begin a new paragraph, because there is a
blank line before it.
\end{document}
```

Each time a blank line appears in the text file, LaTeX assumes that a new paragraph should begin. Within paragraphs, LaTeX automatically reflows text to fit the margins for the current page style. This means that the first paragraph in the example does not necessarily represent three lines of text in the final printed output; instead, LaTeX reformats and word wraps the text in these three lines as though they were typed without pressing the Enter key.

Sometimes it is the writer's intent to insert a line break. You can think of a line break as being like pressing the Enter key in the middle of a paragraph in a plain-text file; the cursor moves to a new line without beginning a new paragraph, indenting, or leaving empty vertical spaces after the previous line.

To move to a new line without beginning a new paragraph, add the \newline command where you want the break to occur:

```
\documentclass[letterpaper,12pt]{article}
\begin{document}
\pagestyle{empty}
This is the first sentence in a paragraph.
This is the second sentence in the paragraph, and it doesn't
begin on a new line but is instead reflowed with the first
sentence.\newline
This sentence, however, begins on a new line.\newline
And this one.\newline And so does
this one, illustrating that commands can appear at any place
within the text.

And this is a new paragraph, of course.
\end{document}
```

One sample of output generated by this source file is shown in Figure 21.1.

> This is the first sentence in a paragraph. This is the second sentence in the paragraph, and it doesn't begin on a new line but is instead reflowed with the first sentence.
> This sentence, however, begins on a new line.
> And this one.
> And so does this one, illustrating that commands can appear at any place within the text.
>     And this is a new paragraph, of course.

If it's unclear to you just how the final printed output is affected by the \newline command and blank lines for new paragraphs, experiment by printing some LaTeX text files of your own.

## Organizing Larger Texts

To create a longer document with sections, section headers, a table of contents, or other similar structural elements, you use LaTeX sectioning commands. You insert these commands just like the other LaTeX commands you've encountered so far—by preceding them with a backslash character anywhere in the body of your text. They are used to delineate blocks of text of the sorts you find in most larger documents.

Table 21.4 lists the LaTex sectioning commands.

**TABLE 21.4**    **Common LaTeX Sectioning Commands**

| Command | Description |
|---|---|
| \section{text} | Creates a new section using the title text as a section header and table of contents entry |
| \subsection{text} | Creates a new subsection using the title text as a sub-section header and table of contents entry |
| \subsubsection{text} | Creates a new sub-subsection using the title text as a sub-subsection header and table of contents entry |
| \chapter{text} | Starts a new chapter, using the title text as a chapter title and table of contents entry (report and book document classes only) |
| \part{text} | Starts a new part, using the title text as a part title and table of contents entry (report and book document classes only) |
| \appendix | Starts a new appendix using lettering rather than numbering for sequence, and makes the necessary table of contents entry |

**TABLE 21.4**  Continued

| Command | Description |
|---|---|
| \tableofcontents | Inserts a nicely formatted table of contents at the place in the text where the command appears; the table of contents is generated automatically from information supplied by using the other commands in this table |

---

**Is Your Table of Contents Empty?**

Current versions of LaTeX contain a small bug that affects the table of contents functionality. If you find that you format a .tex file only to end up with an empty table of contents, simply run LaTeX on the file a second time, and the table of contents will be generated correctly.

*By the Way*

---

When you use these basic sectioning commands, it is a simple matter to create a well-structured document with an accurate table of contents just by adding a few extra commands. Consider the following excerpt from a LaTeX source file:

```
\documentclass[letterpaper,12pt]{article}
\begin{document}
\pagestyle{empty}
\section{Learning About Frogs}
This is the first paragraph in a section about frogs. We will have
two subsections, one about frog legs and one about frog sounds.
\subsection{Frog Legs}
Frogs often have legs. These are used for jumping, walking, and
other types of amphibian fun. Often, frog legs are green. That
is all you need to know about frog legs.
\subsection{Frog Sounds}
Frogs also make sounds. These sounds are often characterized as
'ribbits' but this word can sometimes sound silly, so we won't
talk about them any more. That is all you need to know about
frog sounds.
\section{Learning About Birds}
This is the first paragraph in a section about birds. Birds are
really not very much like frogs at all.
\end{document}
```

One sample of output generated by this source file is shown in Figure 21.2.

Notice in Figure 21.2 that LaTeX has automatically numbered the sections and subsections for you. If you insert a \tableofcontents command before the first \section command, LaTeX prints a nice table of contents on the first page containing the sections and subsections and the pages on which they appear.

## 1    Learning About Frogs

This is the first paragraph in a section about frogs. We will have two subsections, one about frog legs and one about frog sounds.

### 1.1    Frog Legs

Frogs often have legs. These are used for jumping, walking, and other types of amphibian fun. Often, frog legs are green. That is all you need to know about frog legs.

### 1.2    Frog Sounds

Frogs also make sounds. These sounds are often characterized as 'ribbits' but this word can sometimes sound silly, so we won't talk about them any more. That is all you need to know about frog sounds.

## 2    Learning About Birds

This is the first paragraph in a section about birds. Birds are really not very much like frogs at all.

# Formatting the Body of Your Text

Sometimes simple page and document structure is not enough to effectively communicate in written text. In many documents, you need to emphasize certain words or format them in a special font or size to indicate their use or meaning. LaTeX uses a number of commands to center text, emphasize text, insert text in quotations, and add other formatting to printed text. You enter these commands immediately before or on either side of the text you want to format.

Here are some of the most common LaTeX text formatting commands and some examples of their use:

▶ To emphasize a particular piece of text, usually in italics, use the \emph{} command:

```
Inserting \emph{emphasized text} with LaTeX is quite easy, especially
In the middle of a paragraph like this one, which was designed for
\emph{your} enjoyment.
```

▶ To insert a footnote to a particular piece of text, use the \footnote{} command:

```
I played football\footnote{Football is a physical contact sport and
should only be played by well-qualified personnel with the proper
equipment.}
yesterday.
```

► To center text, use the `\begin{center}` and `\end{center}` commands:

```
\begin{center}This is centered text.\end{center}
```

► To insert a quoted passage, indenting from right and left on both sides, use the `\begin{quote}` and `\end{quote}` commands:

```
\begin{quote}Ladies and gentlemen, start your engines. I shall
not warn you again; the race is about to begin! If you don't pull
toward the line now, you will miss the gun!\end{quote}
```

► To create ordered (numbered) or unordered (bulleted) lists in your text, use the `\begin{enumerate}` and `\end{enumerate}` or `\begin{itemize}` and `\end{itemize}` commands, respectively, along with `\item` to mark the beginning of each new item:

```
\begin{enumerate}
\item This is the first numbered item.
\item This is the second numbered item.
\item This is the third numbered item.
\end{enumerate}
\begin{itemize}
\item This is an un-numbered, bulleted item.
\item This is another un-numbered, bulleted item.
\end{itemize}
```

Figure 21.3 shows the output generated by all the commands we've just discussed.

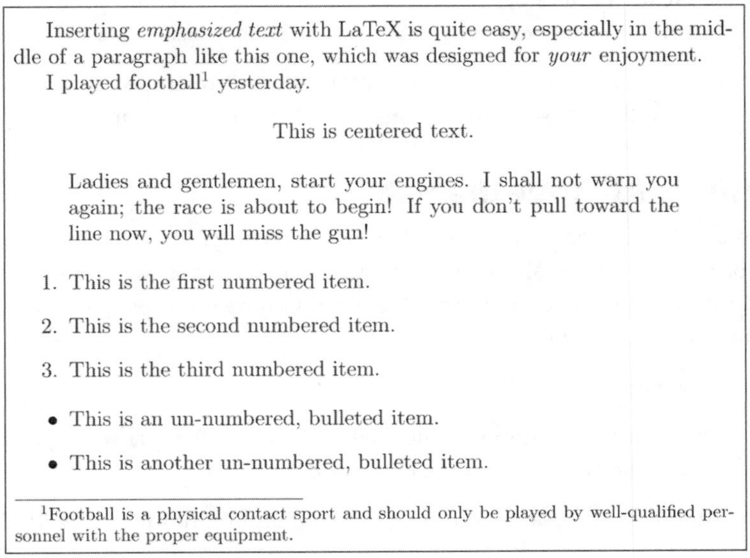

> Inserting *emphasized text* with LaTeX is quite easy, especially in the middle of a paragraph like this one, which was designed for *your* enjoyment.
> I played football[1] yesterday.
>
> This is centered text.
>
> Ladies and gentlemen, start your engines. I shall not warn you again; the race is about to begin! If you don't pull toward the line now, you will miss the gun!
>
> 1. This is the first numbered item.
>
> 2. This is the second numbered item.
>
> 3. This is the third numbered item.
>
> • This is an un-numbered, bulleted item.
>
> • This is another un-numbered, bulleted item.
>
> ---
> [1]Football is a physical contact sport and should only be played by well-qualified personnel with the proper equipment.

**FIGURE 21.3**
Using a simple selection of commands in a plaintext editor, you can add structure to printed documents using LaTeX.

Although a wealth of other formatting commands exist, these are enough to produce most common types of documents using LaTeX. You can learn more about many of these commands by visiting the links provided in the section called "More Information About LaTeX" later in this chapter.

## Inserting Special Characters

People who work in the publishing industry are familiar with the special characters used in printing and typesetting to insert symbols such as dashes and ellipses into text. These symbols usually can't be entered directly from a keyboard. Luckily, they can be generated in LaTeX using commands or special strings.

The most common among these characters are shown in Table 21.5.

**TABLE 21.5    Commonly Used Special Characters in LaTeX**

| Command or Sequence | Description |
| --- | --- |
| \ldots | Inserts a properly spaced ellipsis |
| -- | Inserts an en dash |
| --- | Inserts an em dash |
| `` | Inserts an opening quotation mark |
| '' | Inserts a closing quotation mark |

To illustrate the use of these special characters, consider the following source line:I went to the store---the bookstore, and I was there for hours\ldots

The printed output from this line would contain the indicated special characters instead: I went to the store—the bookstore, and I was there for hours...

## Putting It All Together

With the LaTeX commands you've just learned, you can produce a professional-quality printing of a novel from text written with a text editor such as emacs or vi. Listing 21.2 shows the text and formatting for a document that employs several of the commands presented in this chapter.

In Listing 21.2, you do the following:

▶ Create a new book document intended for letter-sized paper with a 12-point font, using the \documentclass command.

▶ Output a nice title page containing title and author information with the \maketitle command.

▶ Output a table of contents with the \tableofcontents command.

- ▶ Begin chapters called "Beginning My Novel" and "Ending My Novel" using the \chapter command.

- ▶ Create a bulleted shopping list using the \begin{itemize} and \end{itemize} commands, marking each item in the list with the \item command.

**LISTING 21.2**   **A LaTeX Document Using Numerous Commands**

```
\documentclass[letterpaper,openany,12pt]{book}
\title{My Novel}
\author{Aron Hsiao}
\begin{document}
\pagestyle{headings}
\maketitle
\chapter{Beginning My Novel}
It is in \emph{this} chapter that I begin my novel. Unfortunately,
this chapter is only two paragraphs long. Still, it promises to be
a wonderful novel, because it illustrates the formatting prowess
of LaTeX.

Furthermore, it is the first of these paragraphs which is the longest,
but not by much. Still, longest is longest, and to the victor go the
spoils---at least, that is what my history teacher used to tell me.
\chapter{Ending My Novel}
My novel only consists of two chapters\footnote{Though a third
is in the works} right now. The second chapter is just a mysterious
shopping list\ldots

\begin{itemize}
\item Cabbages
\item Red socks with yellow stripes
\item A green rubber washbasin
\item The latest issue of \emph{Time Magazine}
\end{itemize}

Perhaps someday, all of the items in this shopping list will be
explained. But then I suppose we will leave that bit of mystery for the
sequel.
\end{document}
```

Although this document is relatively short, you will find that if you type it, format it with the latex command, and print it with the dvips command, the final result is quite impressive, as shown in Figure 21.4.

*Did you Know?*

**Don't Forget How to Format and Print**

Remember how to format and print? The commands, in order, are

```
latex myfile.txt
dvips myfile.dvi
```

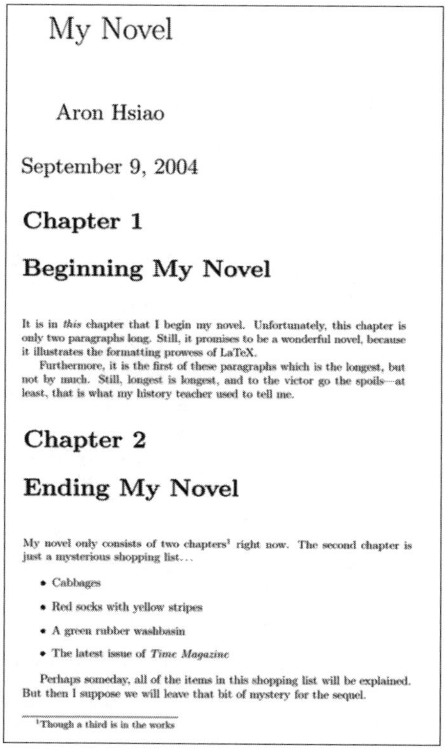

**FIGURE 21.4**
Our final
impressive sam-
ple document,
created and
sent to the
printer using the
LaTeX text for-
matter.

# More Information About LaTeX

We only scratched the surface of LaTeX and its capabilities in this brief introduction. To learn more about LaTeX or use LaTeX on serious projects, you should consult more in-depth documentation.

These sources of online documentation are a good place to start:

▶ http://www.giss.nasa.gov/latex/ contains a hypertext guide to using the LaTeX formatter written by Sheldon Green.

▶ http://www.maths.tcd.ie/~dwilkins/LaTeXPrimer/Index.html contains a hypertext primer for using the LaTeX formatter written by David R. Wilkins.

▶ A nice, printable guide called *The Not So Short Introduction to LaTeX 2e* in portable document (.pdf) format can be downloaded from http://people.ee.ethz.ch/~oetiker/lshort/lshort.pdf.

▶ More reference material of various kinds can be found at the catchall LaTeX website at http://www.latex-project.org.

# Summary

In this chapter, you learned to use the command line in everyday workflow, to produce professionally formatted, multipart documents. The primary tool you used in this chapter, LaTeX, is much more powerful than you might realize when you first begin using it. If you feel as though LaTeX might be useful to you for larger projects such as book publishing, take time to consult the referenced documentation for more extensive instruction.

# Q&A

**Q** *Can I somehow add page numbers to text files that I create in emacs or vi without having to use a full-fledged document formatting system, such as LaTeX?*

**A** Yes. You can use the pr command to accomplish very simple formatting tasks on basic text files and then pipe the output to lpr for printing. To find out more about pr, including the options and arguments it accepts, check out the man page for pr.

**Q** *When I try to run LaTeX, I get an error message and a prompt that looks like a question mark, from which I can't seem to exit. What's wrong?*

**A** This message typically means you have miskeyed a LaTeX command somewhere, and LaTeX has been stumped by it. Look closely at the error message; it usually displays the offending malformed command. Enter exit at the question mark prompt, and your file will be loaded into a vi editor for you, where you can fix the problem.

**Q** *Is LaTeX a Linux- or Unix-only tool? Is it available for Windows or for Mac OS?*

**A** Both Windows and Mac OS users can avail themselves of the features of the LaTeX typesetting engine. There are many versions of LaTeX for the PC, but the easiest to install and use is PCTeX, which can be found at http://www.pctex.com. Information on using LaTeX with Mac OS can be found at http://www.esm.psu.edu/mac-tex/.

# Workshop

The Workshop is designed to help you anticipate possible questions, review what you've learned, and begin learning how to put your knowledge into practice.

## Quiz

1. How do you send a file called `myfile.txt` to your printer?

2. How do you send a file called `myfile.tex` to your printer?

3. What three commands occur in every LaTeX file?

## Answers

1. `lpr myfile.txt`

2. `latex myfile.tex`

   `dvips myfile.dvi`

3. `\documentclass{}`, `\begin{}`, and `\end{}`

## Activities

1. Try writing a letter to someone you know using LaTeX.

2. Print out this document and send it to your friend.

# CHAPTER 22

# Performing Simple Math and Database Tasks at the Command Line

---

## What You'll Learn in This Chapter:

▶ How to perform numeric tasks with the binary calculator

▶ How to sort and query formatted lists of text data

You've now learned how to create and edit text files at the command line and how to turn them into high-quality structured documents.

A large part of the work you do with computers probably involves other types of data, however—numbers and lists of data chief among them. This type of information, too, can be efficiently handled by command-line tools. You learn about a few of these tools in this chapter.

## Performing Math Tasks Using the Binary Calculator

Mathematics and calculation are common daily productivity fare in any office containing computer systems. Many offices use graphic spreadsheet programs, such as Microsoft Excel or Corel Quattro Pro.

As you might have predicted, the Linux command line gives you access to a more primitive—but also more programmable—form of calculation. Using a programmable calculator like bc, you can automate long calculation procedures and have Linux prompt you for inputs, so that you don't miss steps or make mistakes. You can also call the binary calculator from shell applications of the kind you'll learn to develop in Chapter 25, "Harnessing the Power of the Shell."

Although it's a powerful performer, you need relatively little training to use the Linux binary calculator, called bc.

## Starting bc and Performing Basic Calculations

To start the binary calculator, enter bc at the command line without arguments. When you do, you are dropped into the bc command mode:

```
[you@workstation20 you]$ bc
bc 1.06
Copyright 1991-1994, 1997, 1998, 2000 Free Software Foundation, Inc.
This is free software with ABSOLUTELY NO WARRANTY.
For details type 'warranty'.
```

There is no bc prompt, but nevertheless bc patiently awaits your orders. To perform a basic calculation, just enter it naturally. For example, add a few numbers by entering digits and the plus operator as necessary, followed by pressing the Enter key:

```
216 + 45 + 36
297
```

Notice that bc instantly prints the result. You can use other mathematical operators by typing just the characters you would expect to type. Use parentheses to specify the order of operations, as in this example, which specifies $20 + 20$ as the first calculation:

```
( 1200 / ( 20 + 20 ) ) * 6
180
```

Again, the answer is instantly calculated and displayed.

You use a decimal point to indicate a fractional amount, as in this example:

```
10.44 * 3.623
37.824
```

You can exit bc at any time by entering the special command quit on an empty line:

```
quit
[you@workstation20 you]$
```

The capability to perform these types of small calculations quickly, easily, and with arbitrary precision (to any number of decimal places) makes the binary calculator extremely useful.

## Using Variables

Sometimes remembering the results of calculations or storing numbers for later use is helpful. This can be done in bc as well. To make bc remember the results of calculations or numbers you want to use later, you can assign values or the results of calculated expressions to variables:

```
a=10.1
b=6.3
c=a*b
c
63.6
```

Here, you assign the value 10.1 to the variable a, the value 6.3 to the variable b, and the result of multiplying a by b to variable c. You then display the contents of variable c by entering the name of the variable alone.

The results of division might at times be calculated to arbitrary levels of precision without reaching a conclusion. You can use the special variable scale to determine the number of decimal places that will be calculated when dividing:

```
scale=10
3/7
.4285714285
```

Using variables and the operators shown in these examples, you can perform a relatively long and complex series of calculations with ease and accuracy.

## Automating Calculations in bc

Suppose you often perform a series of calculations over and over again. Rather than type the calculations repeatedly into bc using new numbers each time, you can write script to automate these types of calculations in bc. Here is an example:

1. Using vi or emacs, create a file called addthree.bc, which contains the following text:

   ```
   "Number to add? "; y=read()"Adding 3 to "; y
   "produces "; y+3
   quit
   ```

2. Call bc from the command line and supply addthree.bc as an argument.

3. When bc prompts for a number, type a number and press Enter.

   The value of the number you enter is then stored by bc in the variable y and the number 3 is added to it. The result is then displayed:

   ```
   [you@workstation20 you]$ bc addthree.bc
   bc 1.06
   Copyright 1991-1994, 1997, 1998, 2000 Free Software Foundation, Inc.
   This is free software with ABSOLUTELY NO WARRANTY.
   For details type `warranty'.
   Number to add? 7
   Adding 3 to 7
   produces 10
   [you@workstation20 you]$
   ```

The read() command is used in a bc script to get a number from the user and store that number in a variable. You can prompt for any number of variables using the read() command, as shown previously. Text enclosed in quotation marks is output to the user as a prompt. Using these simple tools, you can automate relatively long and complex types of calculations.

## Controlling Script Flow in bc

Scripting of any kind is infinitely more powerful if flow control (if/then statements or while statements) can be used. Flow control allows sections of your script (usually certain calculations) to be repeated over and over again until conditions that you specify are met. For example, if you are working on a calculus problem, you might repeat a calculation involving one variable over and over again until the value of that variable approaches zero, stopping afterward to output the number of times the calculation was performed.

Those familiar with the C computer programming language will find the flow control structures of the binary calculator familiar. Flow control allows you to enclose a list of calculations within a set of opening and closing braces ({}). Depending on the results of a comparison between two values, the calculations you've placed within the braces either are performed or are ignored.

Let's look at the two basic kinds of flow control and then examine them in more detail:

▶ A calculation or set of calculations can be repeated using the while() {} flow control structure:

```
while( y < 3 ) {
    x = x + 1
    y = x / 4

}
```

In this case, as long as the value of the variable y continues to be less than 3, the value of the variable x will be increased by 1, and the new value of x divided by 4 will be assigned to y.

▶ An operation or set of operations can be executed conditionally using the if() {} structure:

```
if( x == z ) {
    "The two sums are equal. Input a new estimate? "; w=read()
    y = x + w
}
```

In this case, if the values of the variables x and z are equal, a new value for the variable w will be obtained from the user, added to the value for the variable x, and the results of the calculation will be stored in y.

Flow control operations can be nested inside one another to enhance functionality, as in the C language.

Notice that whether you're using while or if to determine whether the calculations inside the braces should be performed, the test itself goes in parentheses. The types of tests that can be performed inside the parentheses are shown in Table 22.1.

**TABLE 22.1    Types of Flow Control Tests**

| Test | Explanation |
|---|---|
| value1 == value2 | Calculations inside the braces will be performed if value1 and value2 are equal. |
| value1 < value2 | Calculations inside the braces will be performed if value1 is less than value2. |
| value1 > value2 | Calculations inside the braces will be performed if value1 is greater than value2. |
| value1 <= value2 | Calculations inside the braces will be performed if value1 is less than or equal to value2. |
| value1 >= value2 | Calculations inside the braces will be performed if value1 is greater than or equal to value2. |

To illustrate the use of flow control, let's consider an example. Suppose you want to write a bc script that asks you for the number of rooms in a house, then asks you for the dimension of each room, and finally outputs the total number of square feet in the house as an answer. Listing 22.1 is just such a script. Start a text editor now, type it in, and save it as squarefeet.bc.

**LISTING 22.1    The squarefeet.bc Script**

```
1    "Enter the number of rooms in the house: " ; r = read()
2    c = 1
3    s = 0
4    while( c <= r ) {
5        "ROOM " ; c
6        "Enter length (in feet): " ; l = read()
7        "Enter width (in feet): " ; w = read()
8        s = s + ( l * w )
9        c = c + 1
10   }
11   "Total square footage is " ; s
12   quit
```

_By the_
Way

### Indentation Makes Code More Readable

You may notice that some of the lines have been indented in Listing 22.1. It is common practice to indent blocks of calculations between braces ({}) to help in visualizing the structure of a bc script.

Before you exit your editor to return to the command line, let's study the way the script works:

▶ Line 1 asks the user to enter the number of rooms in the house. This value is stored in the variable r.

▶ Line 2 creates a variable, c, that will be used as a counter. Each time the script asks for the dimensions of another room, the value of c will be increased by 1. When the value of c matches the value of r (the number of rooms in the house), all rooms are accounted for, so the total is displayed and the script exits.

▶ Line 3 creates a variable, s, that will hold the total square footage of the house so far, as the dimensions for each new room are entered.

▶ Lines 4–10 are a while flow control element; the calculations inside the braces ({}) will be performed as long as the value in the variable c (the counter) is less than or equal to the variable r (the number of rooms).

▶ Line 5 displays the current room number just before the script asks for room dimensions.

▶ Lines 6–7 ask for the length and width of the room, respectively.

▶ Line 8 multiples the length and width the user just entered to calculate the total number of square feet in the current room and then adds this value to s, the total number of square feet overall.

▶ Line 9 adds 1 to the counter, c, to indicate that you have added one more room to the total.

▶ Line 11 displays the total, after you have been asked for the measurements of each room.

▶ Line 12 quits the binary calculator after the total is displayed.

Now that you have seen how the script works, exit your text editor and try calling bc at the command line using the script file named squarefeet.bc as an argument. Assume that you've measured a small house with five rooms, measuring 14×10, 12×10, 10×10, 11×8, and 6×5, respectively. The bc session follows:

```
[you@workstation20 you]$ bc squarefeet.bc
bc 1.06
Copyright 1991-1994, 1997, 1998, 2000 Free Software Foundation, Inc.
This is free software with ABSOLUTELY NO WARRANTY.
For details type `warranty'.
Enter the number of rooms in the house: 5
ROOM 1
Enter length (in feet): 14
Enter width (in feet): 10
ROOM 2
Enter length (in feet): 12
Enter width (in feet): 10
ROOM 3
Enter length (in feet): 10
Enter width (in feet): 10
ROOM 4
Enter length (in feet): 11
Enter width (in feet): 8
ROOM 5
Enter length (in feet): 6
Enter width (in feet): 5
Total square footage is 478
[you@workstation20 you]$
```

You can see from the output of bc that the room-based square footage of this tiny house is 478 square feet. Many typical types of mathematical tasks can be automated in this way using the binary calculator. Many shell users and small businesses rely on a library of bc scripts that perform long, in-depth calculations that they routinely have to make. With bc scripts, these calculations are less error prone and completed more quickly.

---

**By the Way**

**There's a Lot More to** bc

The binary calculator supports a large number of additional functions, operators, and comparisons that we haven't discussed here. It is possible to create relatively complex calculation procedures using bc. For an exhaustive discussion of the capabilities of bc, with examples, see the man page for bc.

---

# Creating and Sorting Lists of Data

Database-like storage and search-oriented retrieval functions are also common day-to-day productivity uses for personal workstations. From the command line, you can accomplish these types of tasks using editors such as vi and emacs, plaintext files, and a set of two simple commands: sort, which is used to sort plaintext data into alphanumeric order, and grep, which is used to search text data for a specific word or phrase.

## Creating Searchable or Sortable Lists

The art of creating useful plaintext databases with vi or emacs revolves mainly around the ability to use spaces or tabs effectively to organize information into single lines broken into multiple single-word columns. To create a plaintext database, start your favorite text editor and follow these steps:

1. Logically (that is, in your imagination) separate the information you would like to organize into fields a single word long. For example, for a company-wide list of phone numbers, your fields might be last name, first name, area code, phone number, and department.

2. Enter your first record on a single text line, one field at a time, inserting tabs between them.

3. Enter the rest of your records the same way, one on each line, until all your records are represented in the file.

To continue with the phone number list example, imagine a list of phone numbers in a file called phones.txt, as shown in Listing 22.2.

**LISTING 22.2**    **A Simple Text-Based Database of Phone Numbers**

```
Rasmussen    Jake    800    111-1111    Heating
Larsen       Eve     800    222-2222    Heating
Amberson     Laura   888    111-9999    Cooling
Swenson      Celia   800    666-6666    Operations
Wagoner      Shane   888    232-2323    Cooling
Filipanteng  Lee     800    696-9696    Heating
```

Following the format we imagined earlier, this list of phone numbers has five columns: last name, first name, area code, phone number, and department, in that order. The names aren't in any particular order; they've just been entered into the plaintext file phones.txt using a text editor as each new person joined the company.

As simple as this file appears, it's already a database. Let's examine the ways in which this data can be used.

## Displaying Specific Entries

In Chapter 19, "Performing Basic Shell Tasks," you learned how to use the grep command to search for various kinds of text; grep is also useful for finding and displaying a specific item in a plaintext database. Suppose you want a listing of all the people in the company phone list who work in the Cooling department. To do that, you call the grep command, supplying the word Cooling and the name of the database file as arguments:

```
[you@workstation20 you]$ grep Cooling phones.txt
Amberson     Laura  888  111-9999    Cooling
Wagoner      Shane  888  232-2323    Cooling
[you@workstation20 you]$
```

As you can see, you easily take care of this request. Suppose, on the other hand, that you want to find the phone number for Eve Larsen and the department where she works. To search for Eve's last name, Larsen, call the grep command, supplying the word Larsen and the name of the database file as arguments:

```
[you@workstation20 you]$ grep Larsen phones.txt
Larsen       Eve    800  222-2222    Heating
[you@workstation20 you]$
```

You also accomplish this request easily. Searches of this kind might not be impressive to you on a short list of six phone numbers; the same technique will work equally well, however, on a plaintext database that is several thousand entries long.

## Sorting List Data

Sometimes being able to sort data in a list is helpful. The sort command is designed for just such an occasion; sort simply accepts a plaintext listing and rearranges the lines into alphanumeric order. The simplest way to call sort is to use the name of a text file to sort as an argument on the command line. Here, you sort the phone number list from previous examples:

```
[you@workstation20 you]$ sort phones.txt
Amberson     Laura  888  111-9999    Cooling
Filipanteng  Lee    800  696-9696    Heating
Larsen       Eve    800  222-2222    Heating
Rasmussen    Jake   800  111-1111    Heating
Swenson      Celia  800  666-6666    Operations
Wagoner      Shane  888  232-2323    Cooling
[you@workstation20 you]$
```

Because the surname of each individual is in the first column in your list, you now have a list displayed in alphabetical order by last name. In fact, if you were going to print a long list of phone numbers formatted this way as a phone book, the command to generate the output would be as simple as

```
[you@workstation20 you]$ sort phones.txt ¦ lpr
```

Let's assume for a moment, however, that you want to sort based on first names, rather than last names. The sort command enables you to alter the sorting criteria—or more specifically, the column—on which it will operate by using the -k option. To use the -k option, follow the call to sort with the –k option and the number of the column you want to use as the basis for your sort. Here, you sort the list of phone numbers based on the second column of information—the first names of the employees in the list:

```
[you@workstation20 you]$ sort -k 2 phones.txt
Swenson        Celia  800   666-6666     Operations
Larsen         Eve    800   222-2222     Heating
Rasmussen      Jake   800   111-1111     Heating
Amberson       Laura  888   111-9999     Cooling
Filipanteng    Lee    800   696-9696     Heating
Wagoner        Shane  888   232-2323     Cooling
[you@workstation20 you]$
```

Suppose you want to group employees by department or by area code. To do that, you type the sort command, the –k option, and the number of the column that holds department names, or the area codes, followed by the name of the file to be sorted:

```
[you@workstation20 you]$ sort -k 5 phones.txt
Amberson       Laura  888   111-9999     Cooling
Wagoner        Shane  888   232-2323     Cooling
Filipanteng    Lee    800   696-9696     Heating
Larsen         Eve    800   222-2222     Heating
Rasmussen      Jake   800   111-1111     Heating
Swenson        Celia  800   666-6666     Operations
[you@workstation20 you]$ sort -k 3 phones.txt
Rasmussen      Jake   800   111-1111     Heating
Larsen         Eve    800   222-2222     Heating
Swenson        Celia  800   666-6666     Operations
Filipanteng    Lee    800   696-9696     Heating
Amberson       Laura  888   111-9999     Cooling
Wagoner        Shane  888   232-2323     Cooling
[you@workstation20 you]$
```

As a final example, you can get a listing of only those employees who work in Heating, sort the list alphabetically by first name, and then send the listing to the printer. This can be done by calling grep to search the file phones.txt for the word Heating, sending that output through a pipe to the sort command with an option to sort based on the second column, and then sending that output through a pipe to the lpr command, which prints the data:

```
[you@workstation20 you]$ grep Heating phones.txt ¦ sort -k 2 ¦ lpr
[you@workstation20 you]$
```

More information on the sort command can be found in the man page for sort.

# Summary

In this chapter, you learned to use the command line to perform routine calculation tasks and to manage and retrieve formatted data stored in simple text files. Although the examples here were brief and simple, as you become more familiar with the command line (and study the manual pages for the commands you're learning about), your ability to exploit these tools to their fullest potential will grow, and may find that your quick-and-dirty text databases and work-saving bc scripts will grow at the same rate.

# Q&A

**Q** *I have a much more complicated dataset that I would like to manage as text files from the command line. What alternatives do I have to* sort *and* grep*?*

**A** Several. As you learn more commands (in particular, in Chapter 25, "Harnessing the Power of the Shell"), you'll find that you can link them together to perform more and more powerful tasks. Several full-fledged text-oriented languages are also accessible from the shell, but you'll probably want to refer to other texts (not just their manual pages) to learn how to use them. Still, for introductions to two of these tools, see the manual pages for awk and perl.

# Workshop

The Workshop is designed to help you anticipate possible questions, review what you've learned, and begin learning how to put your knowledge into practice.

## Quiz

**1.** How do you start the binary calculator in interactive mode?

**2.** How would you return all matches for the word Johnson from a text list called mylist.txt, sorted based on the second column, in reverse alphabetical order, and print the output?

## Answers

**1.** Type bc at the command prompt and press Enter.

**2.** The command would be

```
grep Johnson mylist.txt ¦ sort -k 2 -r ¦ lpr
```

## Activities

1. Try writing a bc script to calculate the area of a circle, after prompting the user for the necessary numbers.

2. Use your favorite editor to create a text database containing your personal phone number list and perform some searches and sorts on it.

# CHAPTER 23

# Using the Network at the Command Line

## What You'll Learn in This Chapter:

▶ How to browse the Web using the `elinks` browser
▶ How to use `fetchmail` to download your mail from a remote client
▶ How to download and install the Pine mailer
▶ How to read and respond to email with Pine

So far, you've learned how to do many things at the command line, including basic file management and housekeeping, high-quality document creation, mathematics, and simple database management. But, of course, the real order of the day in computing is networking, especially email and web browsing.

In this chapter, you learn how to use Linux and the command line to accomplish the web browsing and email tasks that are necessary to function in any office or productivity environment. As has been the case with the other chapters in Part IV, you can follow along either in a virtual console or in a Terminal application on the desktop.

Note that to make any use of this chapter, you must have your Linux system connected to a network or have dial-up access activated and ready for use (refer to Chapter 3, "Booting, Logging In, and Configuring," if you need help activating dial-up).

> **Before Starting This Chapter...**
>
> If you didn't choose the Workstation installation of Fedora Core 4 in Chapter 2, "Installing Fedora Core 4," you might not yet have the `elinks` web browser that this chapter discusses installed on your system. If this is true in your case, you should install elinks before proceeding with this chapter.
>
> Refer to Chapter 31, "Installing Linux Software," for help installing additional Linux software from your CDs. To follow along with this chapter, you need to install the "Text-based Internet" package ground.

# Browsing the Web at the Command Line

To many Internet users, networking seems to be an inherently graphics-centric process, largely because the World Wide Web is the primary network medium to which they've been exposed. But even the Web wasn't always so visual; in the early days of the Web, full-featured browsers such as NCSA Mosaic had only rudimentary graphics capability, and *text* files on Unix systems were still the primary medium from which the World Wide Web was built.

Even today, although many sites are difficult to interpret without graphics, many more remain informative and useful without displaying their graphics. When you browse the Web at the command line, the text appears and is laid out more or less as the site designers intended; the graphics are simply omitted or replaced with text to indicate what the image would otherwise have contained.

Though for most users, graphics-based browsing will remain the preferred method for using the World Wide Web, access to a command-line browser can be helpful if you are working a console and need to quickly reference information on a Web site without having to switch back to a desktop, or if you decide to use Fedora Core 4 as a server and want to leave desktop components out of the system, without losing the ability to browse the Web and download files, if it becomes necessary to do so.

## Starting the `elinks` Web Browser

Fedora Core 4 comes with a very nice text-mode web browser called `elinks`. To start `elinks`, simply type the word **elinks** at the command line. You are greeted by a welcome screen, as shown in Figure 23.1.

## Using the elinks Web Browser

Before doing anything else, let's load a web page using `elinks` because that is what you'll do most often while using it. The keystroke to go to a new URL is, not surpris-

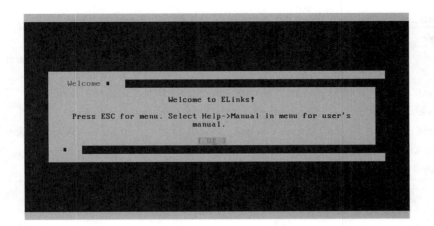

**FIGURE 23.1**
The Welcome
screen for the
elinks browser
included with
Fedora Core 4
informs you that
you can press
the Esc key in
elinks to
access the
menu.

ingly, g. When you press the g key, a Go to URL dialog box appears. Enter the URL
you want to visitand then press Enter.

A visit to http://www.yahoo.com displays the page shown in Figure 23.2. The
elinks browser can render most web pages satisfactorily, although rarely you will
encounter a page that is rendered so poorly that it's unusable; generally, this occurs
when the page in question depends heavily on clickable graphics or on Shockwave,
Flash, or Java applets, none of which are supported at the console.

```
                                                         Yahoo! (1/6)
                             Yahoo!
      Yahoo! Travel - Flights, Hotels, Cars, Vacations, Last-Minute Getaways,
   August Cruise Sale

     Search  _____    [on the Web_____]  * Advanced
     for:    [ Yahoo! Search ]                                       * Preferences

   New!      Movie Trailer - Brosnan and                                  Sign In
             Hayek in 'After the Sunset'       Personal Assistant
   Shop      Auctions, Autos, Classifieds,
             Real Estate, Shopping, Travel        Yahoo! Mail - with more storage.
   Find      HotJobs, Maps, People Search,        Sign up for a free account now.
             Personals, Yellow Pages
   Connect   Chat, GeoCities, Greetings,
             Groups, Mail, Messenger,          In The News
             Mobile
   Organize  Addresses, Briefcase,             * Hurricane survivors wait for
             Calendar, My Yahoo!,                water, gas
             PayDirect, Photos                 * Delegates Urge al-Sadr to leave
   Fun       Games, Horoscopes, Kids,            Najaf shrine
             Movies, Music, Radio, TV          * Bush, Kerry press for women's
   Usemap http://www.yahoo.com/_ylh=X3oDMTB1c2ZmZzF2BF9TAzI3MTYxNDkEdGVzdAMwBHRtcG
```

**FIGURE 23.2**
The very popu-
lar Yahoo! front
page, as ren-
dered by
elinks.

The easiest way to use the features of elinks is to access them through the menu
bar. To display the elinks menu bar, press the Esc key. A bar appears across the top
of the screen showing the words File, View, Link, Setup, Downloads, and Help. You
can navigate the menu system using the keystrokes shown in Table 23.1.

**TABLE 23.1**   Keys for Using the elinks Menu System

| Key | Action |
|-----|--------|
| Esc | Display (or hide, if pressed a second time) the elinks menu bar |
| Down arrow | Move down through options in the selected menu |
| Up arrow | Move up through options in the selected menu |
| Right arrow | Open the menu to the right of the currently selected menu |
| Left arrow | Open the menu to the left of the currently selected menu |
| Enter | Select an item from the menu |

In addition to navigating elinks using the user-friendly menu system, you can use a number of other keystrokes when browsing the Web in elinks. These keystrokes and their actions are shown in Table 23.2.

**TABLE 23.2**   Common elinks Keystrokes and Their Actions

| Key | Action |
|-----|--------|
| g | Go to a new URL (site) |
| Up arrow | Select the previous link (the highlighted link indicates a selected link) |
| Down arrow | Select the next link |
| Right arrow or Enter | Follow (click) the selected link |
| Left arrow | Return (go back) to the previously displayed page |
| Page Down | Display the next screenful (scroll down) |
| Page Up | Display the previous screenful (scroll up) |
| Home or Ctrl+A | Display the top of the current page or document |
| End or Ctrl+E | Display the bottom of the current page or document |
| / | Search for text within the currently displayed page |
| a | Add a bookmark for the currently displayed page |
| s | Open the Bookmark Manager to display a list of bookmarked pages |
| Ctrl+R | Reload the currently displayed page |
| o | Display the elinks options menuTable 23.2 describes just some of the keystroke commands you can use while browsing the Web with elinks; for further documentation on these keystrokes, visit the elinks help system by pressing the Esc key and then choosing Help, Users Manual from the elinks menu. |

## Managing Bookmarks in `elinks`

One of the most important functions in any web browser is the bookmark function. Using it, you can store the addresses of specific pages or sites that were useful to you and return to them later without having to enter a complete URL by hand.

Thanks to Table 23.2, you already know that adding a bookmark in `elinks` is as simple as pressing the a key. When you do so, the Add Bookmark dialog box appears, as shown in Figure 23.3, containing both the title and the URL of the page you are attempting to bookmark.

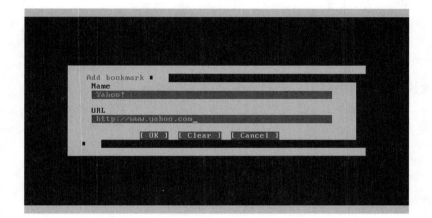

**FIGURE 23.3**
After you press the a key while viewing a web page, the Add Bookmark dialog box is displayed.

Confirm that the information (page title and URL) that you are attempting to bookmark is correct; then press Enter to save your bookmark.

To view your bookmarks, use the s key. The Bookmark Manager is displayed, as shown in Figure 23.4. Use the up- and down-arrow keys to navigate the list of bookmarks and the Enter or right-arrow key to visit a bookmarked link.

Several keystrokes will be essential to you as you navigate the Bookmark Manager. These keystrokes are elaborated in Table 23.3.

**TABLE 23.3**  Commonly Used Keys for Using the `elinks` Bookmark Manager

| Key | Action |
| --- | --- |
| Up arrow | Highlight the previous bookmark |
| Down arrow | Highlight the next bookmark |
| g | Go to (visit) the URL of the highlighted bookmark |
| d | Delete the highlighted bookmark |
| s | Search bookmarks |

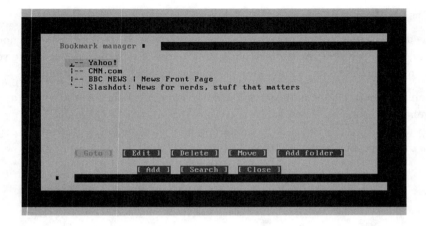

## Exiting the elinks Web Browser

To exit the elinks web browser at any time, press your Esc key until no menus and
dialog boxes are displayed; then press the q key. A dialog box appears, asking you
to confirm that you really want to exit elinks. Use the arrow keys to select the Yes
option and then press Enter to return to the command prompt.

# Managing Email at the Console

Although the Web drives the Internet economy, emailing remains the Internet's
most-used function. It is therefore important that email be fully manageable from
the Linux console—and it is. The Pine program provides console users with powerful
email management capabilities. To use Pine at the console, however, most users
need to configure Linux to retrieve mail from a remote mail server.

## Fetching Post Office Protocol 3 or Internet
## Message Access Protocol Mail

For most people who use a dial-up ISP and many who don't, managing email at the
console begins with the process of bringing mail across from a Simple Mail Transfer
Protocol (SMTP) capable mail server (used by most Internet service providers) to the
local workstation where their mail is saved.

Two major protocol families exist for transferring mail from an SMTP host to a local
host: IMAP (Internet Message Access Protocol) and POP3 (Post Office Protocol). The
Linux program best used to fetch mail from either kind of server is called fetchmail
and is installed by Fedora Core 4 in all basic configurations.

To use fetchmail, you create a configuration file called ~/.fetchmailrc (a file called .fetchmailrc stored in your home directory) that instructs fetchmail where to find your mail and how to go about getting it. After you create this configuration file, you call fetchmail from the command line to download all your mail from your mail server to the local host (your computer), where you can use a console-based mail program to access it. The following sections walk you through each of these processes.

## Creating the .fetchmailrc File

The .fetchmailrc file is a plaintext file, and you can create it using either vi or emacs with methods you've already learned. The format of the file when used merely for downloading mail is relatively simple. You enter one line into the file for each mail server you want to download mail from. The format of this line is as follows:

poll *server* protocol *protocol* username *username* password *password*

Change the values for *server*, *protocol*, *username*, and *password* to the Internet address (domain name) of your mail server, the protocol (usually auto to automatically detect either POP3 or IMAP), your login, and your password, respectively. This information must be obtained from your network administrator, Internet service provider, hosting company, or web-based email provider, depending on which you use.

---

### Files and Directories Beginning with Dots

*Did you Know?*

You will find, after you create a ~/.fetchmailrc file, that it does not appear in the output of the ls command. The reason is that files or directories whose names begin with dots are not normally displayed by ls.

To cause ls to include files and directories beginning with dots in its output, supply the -a argument to the ls command.

---

For example, consider the following entry from a .fetchmailrc file:

poll mail.mycompany.com protocol auto username jackhenry password 3cheesesI8

This line causes fetchmail to download mail from a server located at mail.mycompany.com; fetchmail attempts to automatically detect the protocol that should be used. In this example, fetchmail attempts to log in to the mail server as jackhenry using the password 3cheesesI8. If you have only one mail server account, you need only one line in your .fetchmailrc file; more lines should be added depending on the number of servers you will be downloading mail from.

> ## What to Do When Fetchmail Won't Fetch
>
> If you have trouble getting `fetchmail` to download mail from your server, try explicitly specifying one of the many protocols supported by `fetchmail` rather than using the `auto` protocol. The list of supported protocols can be found in the man page for `fetchmail`. Work with your network administrator, Internet service provider, hosting company, or web-based email provider's technical support system until you find one that works.

After you create a `.fetchmailrc` file, you *must* remove from it all permissions for group owner and for other users; otherwise, `fetchmail` will refuse to use the file. More importantly, if you don't protect your `.fetchmailrc` file by changing its permissions, your password will be vulnerable to theft. To make this change, use the `chmod` command and remove read, write, and execute permissions from group and other users (leaving them only for the owning user):

```
[you@workstation20 ~]$ chmod og-rwx .fetchmailrc
[you@workstation20 ~]$ ls -l .fetchmailrc
-rwx------  1 you   you       259 Oct 23 2004 .fetchmailrc
[you@workstation20 ~]$
```

Now you can test your new `fetchmail` configuration simply by entering the `fetchmail` command alone:

```
[you@workstation20 ~]$ fetchmail
2 messages for jackhenry at mail.mycompany.com (1889 octets).
reading message 1 of 2 (933 octets) flushed
reading message 2 of 2 (956 octets) flushed
[you@workstation20 ~]$
```

In this case, two messages are waiting to be downloaded from the mail server. They have now been downloaded and are stored on the local system where console-based mail clients can get to them.

Each time you want to check the mail server for new mail, enter the command `fetchmail`. In Chapter 28, "Command-Line System Administration," you learn how to use the `cron` system to automate tasks of this kind so that `fetchmail` can be called regularly in the background.

# Using Pine to Manage Email from the Console

One of the most widely used console-based email programs—and perhaps the most user-friendly—is Pine, based on a classic interactive mailer called Elm. Pine provides the user with a wealth of powerful email features, including support for filters, address books, and MIME attachments. Although there are several ways to read and reply to email at the command line, we focus on Pine here because it is menu driven and familiar to many Unix users.

## Downloading and Installing Pine

Because Pine is not included by default with Fedora Core 4, you need to download the Pine application from Red Hat and install it yourself. Follow these steps exactly to do so:

1. Log in to the root account, either at the desktop or in a virtual console. If you log in at the desktop, start a Terminal window so that you have command-line access.

2. Enter the following command to download the Pine application from Red Hat (you see a download progress indicator as you receive it). Because of the length of the command, it is shown on two lines here, but you should type it on a single, unbroken line before pressing Enter:

```
wget http://dag.wieers.com/packages/pine/pine-4.62-
1.2.el4.rf.i386.rpm
```

3. After the download is complete, enter the following command:

```
rpm -i pine-4.62-1.2.el4.rf.i386.rpm
```

You should now have Pine 4.62 installed and available to you on your Fedora Core 4 system. The two commands used here need a little bit of explaining:

▶ The wget command is used to quickly get a file from a remote host; it's therefore very useful when you want to download a single file (like a program) at the command line, and you already know its URL. For more information, see the manual page for wget.

▶ The rpm command, which works only when you are logged in to the root account, is used to install Linux software. We cover the rpm command (and its easier-to-use desktop counterparts) in full in Chapter 31, but feel free to skip ahead or to consult the rpm manual page if you want more details now.

## Starting Pine

To start Pine after you have installed it, type **pine** at the the command line. The first time you run Pine, you are greeted by the Pine welcome screen (titled Greeting Text), which contains some information about the program, as shown in Figure 23.5.

Notice that a number of keys and their meanings are listed at the bottom of the display. While you are working inside Pine, the most common keystrokes used at a given screen are always displayed at the bottom for your convenience.

**FIGURE 23.5**
The Pine welcome screen is displayed the first time you start Pine.

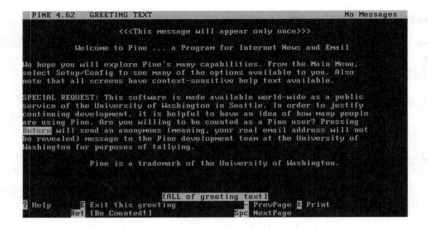

Pressing Enter at the Pine welcome screen sends an email to the Pine maintainers notifying them that another Pine user has gone online. You are then taken to the Pine Main Menu, which you will see whenever you start Pine, as shown in Figure 23.6.

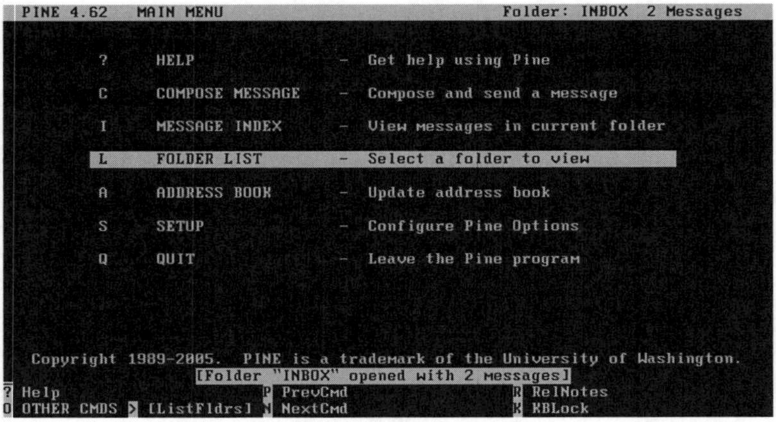

**FIGURE 23.6**
The Pine Main Menu is easy to navigate; the number of messages in your INBOX is displayed at the bottom of the screen.

You can navigate the Pine Main Menu by using the keystrokes listed at the bottom of the display, or by pressing the arrow keys to select an item from the menu and Enter to select the item you want to activate.

# Setting Pine Preferences

Before using Pine for sending and receiving mail, you should take a moment to configure Pine's behavior with regard to message sorting, reply quoting, and so on.

To enter Pine setup from the Main Menu, either press the s key, or use the arrow keys to navigate to the Setup option and then press Enter. The general Setup screen is shown in Figure 23.7.

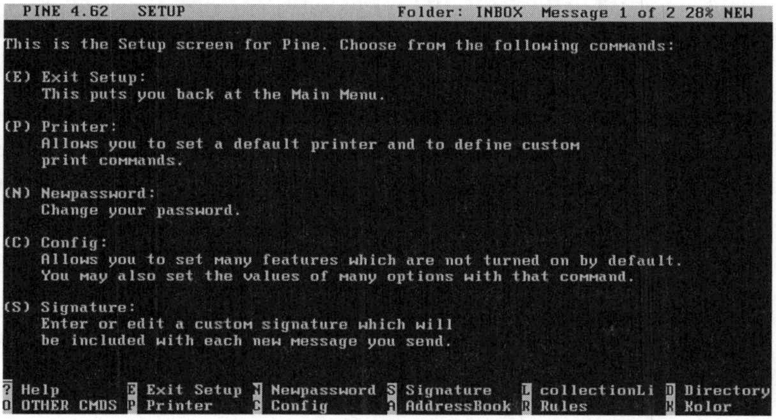

```
  PINE 4.62   SETUP                    Folder: INBOX  Message 1 of 2 28% NEW
This is the Setup screen for Pine. Choose from the following commands:

(E) Exit Setup:
    This puts you back at the Main Menu.

(P) Printer:
    Allows you to set a default printer and to define custom
    print commands.

(N) Newpassword:
    Change your password.

(C) Config:
    Allows you to set many features which are not turned on by default.
    You may also set the values of many options with that command.

(S) Signature:
    Enter or edit a custom signature which will
    be included with each new message you send.

? Help          E Exit Setup N Newpassword S Signature   L collectionLi D Directory
O OTHER CMDS P Printer       C Config       A AddressBook R Rules       K Kolor
```

**FIGURE 23.7**
The general Setup screen for Pine holds commands for setting printing, password, configuration, and signature preferences.

New Pine users need only focus on the options in the Configuration area. You can enter this area by pressing the c key at the Setup screen. The Setup Configuration area appears, as shown in Figure 23.8.

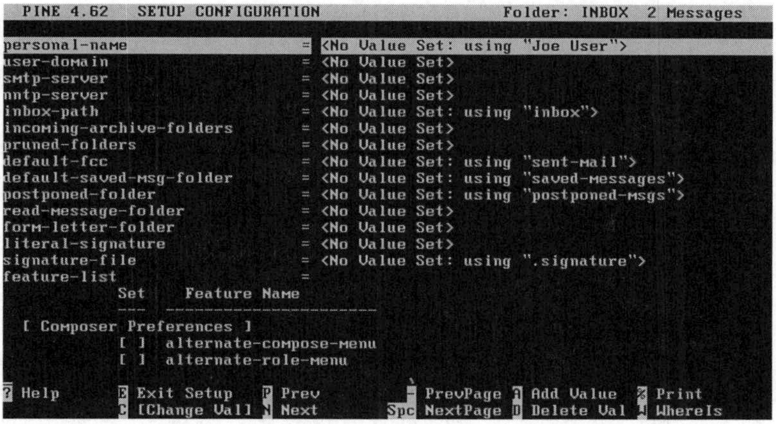

```
  PINE 4.62   SETUP CONFIGURATION             Folder: INBOX  2 Messages
personal-name                = <No Value Set: using "Joe User">
user-domain                  = <No Value Set>
smtp-server                  = <No Value Set>
nntp-server                  = <No Value Set>
inbox-path                   = <No Value Set: using "inbox">
incoming-archive-folders     = <No Value Set>
pruned-folders               = <No Value Set>
default-fcc                  = <No Value Set: using "sent-mail">
default-saved-msg-folder     = <No Value Set: using "saved-messages">
postponed-folder             = <No Value Set: using "postponed-msgs">
read-message-folder          = <No Value Set>
form-letter-folder           = <No Value Set>
literal-signature            = <No Value Set>
signature-file               = <No Value Set: using ".signature">
feature-list                 =
            Set    Feature Name
            ---    ------------
  [ Composer Preferences ]
            [ ]    alternate-compose-menu
            [ ]    alternate-role-menu

? Help         E Exit Setup P Prev        PrevPage A Add Value  % Print
               C [Change Val] N Next  Spc NextPage D Delete Val W WhereIs
```

**FIGURE 23.8**
The Pine Setup Configuration area contains a ponderous number of configuration options. You should leave most of them alone.

To change individual configuration options, use the up- and down-arrow keys to select an option you want to change and then press Enter to select or unselect that option. Watch the lines at the bottom of the screen carefully; it is in this area that you are prompted for input when necessary. You change one option in this chapter; leave the rest of them alone for now.

## Specifying a From Address in Pine

One option in Pine is important for users of the POP or IMAP family of protocols. Because your email address is typically not hosted on your local workstation, but rather on a mail server at a separate host, you need to explicitly tell Pine to use an email address other than the default (which is constructed using your login name and your workstation's hostname).

To specify your email address, use your arrow keys to scroll nearly all the way to the bottom of the Setup Configuration area to the option called `customized-hdrs` and select it by pressing Enter. At the prompt, enter a complete `From:` header in the following form:

From: *My Name <myaddr@myserver.com>*

For example, if your name is Jack Henry and your email address is jackhenry@mycompany.com, you enter the following in the `customized-hdrs` option:

From: Jack Henry <jackhenry@mycompany.com>

After you exit setup, saving your changes, Pine uses this address as the default From address for email until it is changed.

## Composing Mail Using Pine

To compose a new message from Pine's Main Menu, press the c key, or use the arrow keys to navigate to Compose Message and then press Enter (refer to Figure 23.6). You can also press c in the Message Index or Text screens discussed in the following sections to compose a new message. A new Compose Message screen is displayed, as shown in Figure 23.9.

**FIGURE 23.9**
Use the up- and down-arrow keys to navigate between the address and subject fields at the top of the Pine Compose Message screen.

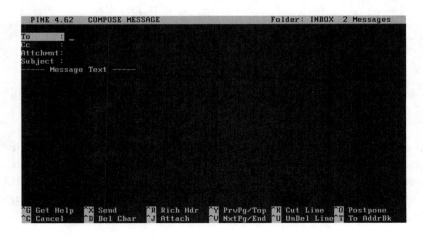

At the top of the Compose Message screen are four fields: To:, Cc:, Attchmnt:, and Subject:. Fill in each field, using the up- and down-arrow keys to switch between them. If you would like to supply multiple recipients in the To: or Cc: fields, separate their email addresses with a comma. After you finish filling the fields, press the down arrow repeatedly to move the cursor into the message editor area of the screen.

---

**Expanding Keystroke Commands**

You can find an expanded listing of keystroke commands in almost every screen in Pine by pressing the o key repeatedly.

*Did you Know?*

---

You are now in the pico editor, a subcomponent of Pine that works like a simple text editor. Notice that pico automatically word-wraps your text and supports user-friendly arrow-key movement and editing keys, such as Backspace and Delete. Also, notice that several editing keystrokes are listed along the bottom of the screen; the caret (^) means that you invoke the keystroke by holding down the Ctrl key and pressing the letter indicated (refer to Figure 23.9).

After you finish editing a message and are ready to send it, use the ^X keystroke (Ctrl+X) to actually send the message out across the network. To cancel a message, use the ^C (Ctrl+C) keystroke.

## Reading Mail Using Pine

To use Pine to read mail from your default mailbox (the one fetchmail services), select the Folder List screen at the Main Menu by pressing l, or by scrolling down to the Folder List option and pressing Enter. Then select INBOX and press Enter again. The Message Index screen then appears, as shown in Figure 23.10.

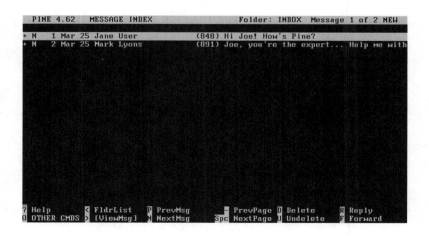

**FIGURE 23.10**
The Pine Message Index screen lists messages contained in the default INBOX folder, and it displays a list of keystroke commands you can use in this screen.

You can navigate within this list of messages using the arrow keys to select individual messages and the Enter key to display them. Other available keys are shown at the bottom of the display (refer to Figure 23.10). Pressing the o key shows still more available keystrokes. Messages marked with the letter N on the far left are messages that you haven't yet viewed.

After a message is displayed, as shown in Figure 23.11, you have a number of choices for dealing with the message. The most common keystrokes used at the Message Text screen are shown in Table 23.4.

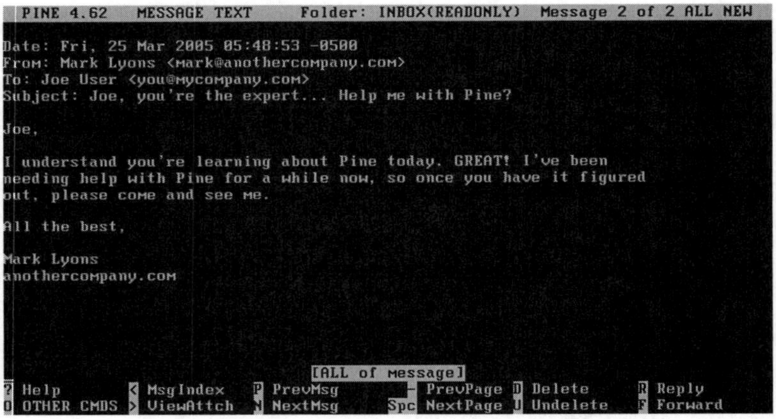

**FIGURE 23.11**
The Pine message viewer, the Message Text screen, is quite user-friendly.

```
   PINE 4.62    MESSAGE TEXT     Folder: INBOX(READONLY)  Message 2 of 2 ALL NEW

Date: Fri, 25 Mar 2005 05:48:53 -0500
From: Mark Lyons <mark@anothercompany.com>
To: Joe User <you@mycompany.com>
Subject: Joe, you're the expert... Help me with Pine?

Joe,

I understand you're learning about Pine today. GREAT! I've been
needing help with Pine for a while now, so once you have it figured
out, please come and see me.

All the best,

Mark Lyons
anothercompany.com

                          [ALL of message]
? Help        < MsgIndex   P PrevMsg       - PrevPage  D Delete     R Reply
O OTHER CMDS  > ViewAttch  N NextMsg      Spc NextPage  U Undelete   F Forward
```

**TABLE 23.4**    Common Keystrokes at the Pine Message Text Screen

| Key | Meaning |
| --- | --- |
| n | Display the next message in the message list |
| d | Mark the currently displayed message for deletion (the marked test will be purged when you exit Pine) |
| r | Reply to the current message (launches the message composer with either an empty body or a body containing a quoted message, depending on your configuration) |
| f | Forward the current message (launches the message composer with a message body containing the current message and a forward note) |

Other keystrokes are listed at the bottom of the Message Text screen; you can find still more keystrokes by repeatedly pressing the o key.

## Getting Help and Quitting Pine

You can access a nice online Pine manual by returning to the Main Menu (use the m key from anywhere but inside the Compose Message screen) and pressing the ? key. Alternatively, you can select the Help menu option at the Main Menu and press Enter.

When you are ready to exit Pine, press the q key from either the Main Menu, the Message Index screen, or the Message Text screen. Pine prompts you to confirm that you want to exit and then returns you to the command line after purging all messages marked for deletion.

---

**Learn Pine by Using** elinks

To read more about using Pine after you install it, see the Pine documentation in the /usr/share/doc/pine-4.62 folder. Some of it is in HTML (Web) format. In fact, you can use elinks to read the documentation for Pine. To do so, enter the following command:

```
[you@workstation20 ~]$ elinks /usr/share/doc/pine-4.62/index.html
```

---

# Summary

In this chapter, you learned to make your way around email and the Web from the Linux command line. You learned to use both the elinks command-line web browser and the Pine command-line email client.

Having finished this chapter, you should feel comfortable doing any of the following things from the command line:

▶ Visiting a web page

▶ Bookmarking a web page

▶ Downloading and reading your email

▶ Sending email to a friend

In the next chapter, you further enhance your knowledge of Linux networking basics at the command line.

# Q&A

**Q** *Are there any reasons for preferring the* elinks *command-line web browser over the more widely known Lynx command-line Web browser?*

**A** The most important reason that elinks is covered here rather than Lynx is that Fedora Core 4 includes the former rather than the latter. In practice, both are powerful text-mode web browsers that should serve you well.

**Q** *Rather than using Pine, I'd like to use the* mutt *command-line email program that comes with Fedora Core 4. Can you give me any pointers?*

**A** Although mutt is a powerful and flexible email client in its own right, it isn't nearly as user-friendly as Pine; details about mutt are therefore beyond the scope of this book. You may, however, wish to consult the manual pages for mutt and muttrc and also the URL to the official mutt home page, http://www.mutt.org.

# Workshop

The Workshop is designed to help you anticipate possible questions, review what you've learned, and begin learning how to put your knowledge into practice.

## Quiz

1. What must you do to your ~/.fetchmailrc file for security reasons before you can use it to collect your email?

2. How do you display the Bookmark Manager in elinks?

3. What does the caret (^) symbol mean in the Pine keystroke menus?

## Answers

1. You must use chmod og-rwx to remove read, write, and execute permissions for everyone but you, the file's owner.

2. Press s to display the Bookmark Manager in elinks.

3. The caret (^) character means that you should hold down the Ctrl key while pressing the matching letter key. For example, when Pine lists ^X in a help menu, it means that you should hold down your Ctrl key and then, while still holding it down, press the x key.

## Activities

1. Visit and bookmark five of your favorite web pages using the `elinks` browser.

2. Use Pine to send an email message to yourself; then read and reply to the message.

# CHAPTER 24

# Using Other Systems Remotely at the Command Line

---

## *What You'll Learn in This Chapter:*

▶ How to connect to and work on remote Linux or Unix systems

▶ How to transfer files from Linux to Linux or Linux to Unix

▶ How to transfer files between Linux and Windows

▶ How to print to network printers

So far, you've learned how to do many things at the command line, including basic file management and housekeeping, high-quality document creation, mathematics, simple database management, web browsing, and email. In this chapter, you begin to learn how to use Linux and the console to accomplish the networking tasks that really set Unix and Linux systems apart from most more consumer-oriented systems: their ability to be used to their fullest as network machines. Chapter 27, "Using Desktop Applications Remotely," might be seen as a companion to this chapter. With the skills you learn here and in Chapter 27, you will be able to truly enter the virtual world, where the geographical location of your computer is completely irrelevant to any computing task in any corner of the globe, so long as it is connected to a network.

# Logging In to a Remote Linux or Unix System

**Remote logins** are a way of accessing the command line, processor, storage, and network resources of one computer, using another computer from somewhere else on a network.

They are one of the most powerful features of Unix-like operating systems, and one of the most important reasons for being able to use Linux at the console. After you master the command line, you will not only be able to use workstations or servers in the same room as you without need for graphics, but you will also be able to connect to and fully use nearly any machine worldwide that is running a Unix-like operating system, even on relatively slow dial-up connections, provided you have access to log in.

To illustrate, suppose you live in Chicago but are responsible for a Linux computer system on your company's network in San Francisco. The machine in San Francisco is in an old office building and is only connected via an ancient 14.4k modem to the Internet. In the past, this system was just a secretary's desktop computer, but the boss wants this computer system to be turned into a web server that dishes out a simple list of inventory numbers to a few other locations around the world.

Using remote logins of the type you're about to learn, you could connect to the computer in San Francisco, install a full-featured web server program such as Apache, edit its configuration files using vi or emacs, create web content for the server to display, remove the old password and data files used by the secretary, and place the system online to serve web pages to the few fellow employees around the world who have the correct password to access the data in question—all without ever leaving the Chicago office and all without needing the remote system to have broadband, ISDN, or a T1 connection, much less a human assistant with a telephone on the other end.

Remote logins generally involve two systems:

- ▶ A **client** system from which the connection originates, and on which you will be running either the telnet or the ssh command.

- ▶ A **server** system, on which a telnet or secure shell (ssh) server program accepts the incoming connection and provides the remote user with a command prompt. The telnet and ssh servers are the software systems that actually manage remote logins, providing remote login service to the connecting user.

Both telnet and ssh provide similar functionality. However, because telnet is not entirely secure, it is generally a good idea to use telnet only between two systems that lie behind the same corporate or personal firewall (that is, on the same local network), or when you absolutely must log in remotely to an older system on which ssh is unavailable. The ssh system is newer than telnet, and it encrypts its communications for much better security. You will sometimes find that older systems do not accept ssh requests, however, because they support only telnet.

# Logging In to Remote Unix Systems Using `telnet`

Although the `telnet` command is less secure, it is the oldest, most widely supported method of logging in remotely to Unix-like operating systems. Nearly any Linux system, Unix system, or Unix-like system connected to a network is capable of offering remote logins using the `telnet` command, provided the network administrators haven't disabled it for security reasons. Unfortunately, `telnet` does not encrypt the data it sends over the network, so anything you do or anything you type (including your password) could conceivably be intercepted by a malicious user. Because of this, you should use `telnet` only behind a firewall, on a private network, or in cases where `ssh` (discussed in the next section) is absolutely unavailable.

To log in to a remote system using `telnet`, enter the `telnet` command supplying the domain name of the system you want to log in to as an argument. For example, to log in to a computer called workstation8.mycompany.com, you enter the following command:

```
[you@workstation20 ~]$ telnet workstation8.mycompany.com
Trying 192.168.242.36...
Connected to 192.168.242.36.
Escape character is '^]'.

SunOS 4.1.3_U1

workstation8 login:
```

Note that after the connection is made to the remote system in question, a very familiar `login:` prompt appears. The process of logging in after connecting with `telnet` is exactly the same as the process of logging in at the console of your local workstation, provided you have an account on the remote machine.

---

**By the Way**

### Fedora Core Turns Off `telnet` by Default

If you are following along with the chapter, using `telnet` to access a remote system, but the remote system in question is a Fedora Core 4 computer, you'll find that you get a message like this one:

```
Trying whateverhost.com...
telnet: connect to whateverhost.com: Connection refused
telnet: Unable to connect to remote host: Connection refused
```

The reason is that Fedora Core turns off the `telnet` server by default, due to its relatively insecure nature. When connecting to Fedora Core 4 hosts or any other newer host, use the `ssh` command discussed the next section. Only when `ssh` is unavailable, or when you are using older Unix systems, will you need to use `telnet`.

After you log in to the remote machine, any commands you execute affect *only that machine* rather than the machine you are logged in *from* (that is, the machine sitting in front of you). The range of commands available to you on the remote system will often seem familiar to you, given what you know about Linux so far; in many cases, they are the same commands and techniques you have been learning so far. On the other hand, you might at times find that you have logged in to a system whose commands do not seem familiar to you. In such cases, you need documentation for the operating system on the *remote* computer to be able to use it.

To log out of the remote machine again, use the `logout` command:

```
SunOS:you@workstation8$ logout
Connection closed by foreign host.
[you@workstation20 ~]$
```

While you are working with remote logins, pay special attention to command prompts; the hostname of the machine you are currently working on is usually displayed in your command prompt. Though this is not the case for all remote systems (especially if the remote systems in question are not running one of Red Hat's Linux operating systems or command prompts have been specially altered), by watching the changes in command prompts, you can often determine whether you are working on your local system or on a remote system at any given moment. If you can't tell from the command prompt, you can use the `hostname` command (with no arguments) to print the name of the host on which you're working.

*By the Way*

### What to Do If Your Session Hangs

Sometimes when you are logged on to a remote system, something goes awry: You get caught in a runaway process or task that cannot be aborted, for example. In cases such as this, use the escape keystroke, ^] (Ctrl+]), to bring up a `telnet>` prompt. At this prompt, you can then type **close** to close the connection followed by **quit** to exit `telnet`.

## Logging In Remotely Using ssh

For logins that occur using the public Internet and are great physical distances apart, the `ssh` or **secure shell** client is a better choice, if it is offered on the system to which you must connect, because `ssh` encrypts all exchanged data (including passwords). You should use `ssh` whenever possible in place of `telnet`.

To log in to a remote host using `ssh`, use the following command syntax:

```
ssh -l login host
```

Here, *login* represents the name of your login account on the remote system, and *host* indicates the domain name or IP address of the remote system. For example, if you have an account called jackhenry on a remote host at pc4.faraway.com, you log in with the following:

```
[you@workstation20 ~]$ ssh -l jackhenry pc4.faraway.com
```

Note that ssh tries to uniquely identify each remote host by keeping track of private identification information. If this is your first time logging in to a particular remote host with ssh, you get a message stating that the remote host's identity can't be verified:

```
The authenticity of host 'pc4.faraway.com (10.4.3.3)' can't be established.
RSA key fingerprint is 48:f5:8b:d2:87:50:53:43:df:e3:10:52:17:d6:14:26.
Are you sure you want to continue connecting (yes/no)?
```

Answering **yes** to this question adds the remote host to the list of known identities and you are prompted for your password:

```
Are you sure you want to continue connecting (yes/no)? yes
Warning: Permanently added '10.4.3.3' (RSA) to the list of known hosts.
jackhenry@10.4.3.3's password:
```

After you enter your password, you are logged in and have access to the command prompt on the remote system. To log out again, you can use the logout command by typing **logout** at the command prompt and pressing Enter.

---

### ssh **Notifies You of Security Risks**

If a remote system to which you have previously connected via ssh suddenly causes ssh to display an error message, stating that the identity information on file doesn't match, you know that either the remote host or the connection has been compromised—hijacked by malicious users to steal your data.

In such cases, always contact the network administrator of the remote system for further instruction before logging in.

*Watch Out!*

---

### **Not Everyone Supports** ssh**, but Everyone Should**

Not all hosts support ssh logins. If you find that ssh doesn't work for logging in to a host where you are supposed to have a remotely accessible account, you need to fall back to the telnet command, which should work for most hosts that accept remote logins and yet do not accept ssh logins. Even better, ask the network administrator of the remote host to add support for ssh, which is far more secure than telnet.

*By the Way*

# Exchanging Files with Linux/Unix Hosts Using ftp

Sometimes you need to transfer files over the network between two computer systems. The command traditionally used to transfer files between two Linux or Unix systems is ftp, which stands for **file transfer protocol**.

As with remote logins, you can use an ftp client only with systems that allow incoming ftp connections with an ftp server. If you find, while following the instructions in this section, that your connect attempts fail with an error message, it is likely that the remote system does not accept file transfer protocol connections.

## Starting ftp and Logging In

Full use of the ftp command also requires that you connect to a remote system and then log in with an account and password; you thus have to be known on the remote system before you can connect via ftp.

To connect to a remote system with ftp, enter the ftp command at the command prompt supplying the domain name of the system you want to connect to as an argument. You are then prompted for your account and password before being delivered to the file transfer prompt. In this example, a connection is made with a system having the hostname archive3.mycompany.com:

```
[you@workstation20 ~]$ ftp archive3.mycompany.com
Connected to archive3.mycompany.com (10.6.2.2).
220 archive3 FTP server (Version wu-2.6.1-20) ready.
Name (10.6.2.2:you): jackhenry
331 Password required for jackhenry.
Password:
230-Please read the file README.TXT
230- it was last modified on Fri Aug 2 15:43:13 2002
230 User jackhenry logged in.
Remote system type is UNIX.
Using binary mode to transfer files.
ftp>
```

After you log in, you are sitting at the ftp> transfer prompt, from which ftp commands can be entered to list, upload, or download files.

*Did you Know?*

> ## Use sftp Whenever Possible Instead of ftp
>
> Like telnet, ftp does not encrypt data as it is sent, meaning that ftp is best used behind a firewall.
>
> An enhanced alternative command, sftp, works the same way but provides encryption just as ssh does. Remote systems that support ssh also usually support sftp. Consider using sftp under these circumstances.

# Navigating an ftp Login

You will find that being logged in to a remote system via ftp is not unlike sitting at a remote system's command prompt in some ways. As is the case with a "normal" command prompt, you can display a present working directory with pwd. You can list files and directories with ls, and you can use the cd command to navigate to other directories that you have permission to visit.

There is, however, one major difference between using the ftp screen and a remote system command prompt. When logged in to ftp, you have not *one* present working directory, but *two*—the one on the local system and the one on the remote system. These dual working directories facilitate the transfer of files between the two systems; files are normally copied between the local and remote present working directories. The process of transferring files therefore involves the following steps (see the commands to implement them in Table 24.1 and a sample session in the next section):

1. Set the remote present working directory to the location where the source file lies or where the destination file is to be created.

2. Set the local present working directory to the location where the source file lies or where the destination file is to be created.

3. Copy the file from one system to another using get (to copy from the remote present working directory to the local one) or put (to copy from the local present working directory to the remote one).

Some of the more fundamental commands that you can use in an ftp session are shown in Table 24.1.

**TABLE 24.1**   Common ftp Commands

| Command | Meaning |
| --- | --- |
| ls | List files in the remote present working directory. |
| !ls | List files in the local present working directory. |
| pwd | Print the remote present working directory. |
| !pwd | Print the local present working directory. |
| cd *path* | Change the remote present working directory to *path* (may be an absolute path or a relative path). |
| lcd *path* | Change the local present working directory to *path* (may be an absolute path or a relative path; note the l rather than the exclamation mark!). |

**TABLE 24.1** Continued

| Command | Meaning |
|---------|---------|
| get *file* | Transfer *file* from the remote present working directory to the local present working directory. |
| put *file* | Transfer *file* from the local present working directory to the remote present working directory. |
| close | Close the current connection to the remote server. |
| open *server* | If no connection currently exists, open a new connection to *server*. |
| quit | If no connection currently exists, exit ftp and return to the command prompt. |

Because this process and command set can seem much more complicated than it actually is, you may find a sample session helpful for illustration purposes.

## Working Through a Sample ftp Session

Suppose you have just successfully logged in to your account on a remote ftp server. In most cases, your local present working directory is the same present working directory you were using when you started ftp. At the same time, your remote present working directory often begins as /home/youraccount on the remote system (in this case, /home/jackhenry).

In this session, the goal is to copy files as follows:

▶ /home/you/basicfile.txt (local) to /home/jackhenry/basicfile.txt (remote)

▶ /home/you/textfiles/mypaper.tex (local) to /home/jackhenry/documents/mypaper.tex (remote)

▶ /home/jackhenry/images/mypicture.gif (remote) to /home/you/mypicture.gif (local)

Because the first source file is located in the home directory of the local system and is to be copied to your home directory on the remote system, no changes in the present working directory need to be made. Simply use the put command to copy the first file:

```
ftp> put basicfile.txt
local: basicfile.txt remote: basicfile.txt
227 Entering Passive Mode (10,6,2,2,225,31)
150 Opening BINARY mode data connection for basicfile.txt.
226 Transfer complete.
115 bytes sent in 0.00075 secs (1.5e+02 Kbytes/sec)
ftp>
```

The first file has now been copied from the local system to the remote system. The next file resides in the textfiles directory on the local system and will be put into the documents directory on the remote system, so some changes to present working directories are required:

```
ftp> lcd textfiles
Local directory now /home/you/textfiles
ftp> !pwd
/home/you/textfiles
ftp> cd documents
250 CWD command successful.
ftp> pwd
257 "/home/jackhenry/documents" is current directory.
ftp>
```

Now that both present working directories are correct (as has been verified with !pwd and pwd), you can use put to copy the file:

```
ftp> put mypaper.tex
local: mypaper.tex remote: mypaper.tex
227 Entering Passive Mode (10,6,2,2,120,95)
150 Opening BINARY mode data connection for mypaper.tex.
226 Transfer complete.
101842 bytes sent in 0.014 secs (7.1e+03 Kbytes/sec)
ftp>
```

Finally, you must retrieve a file called mypicture.gif from a remote directory and store it in the local home directory:

```
ftp> lcd /home/you
Local directory now /home/you
ftp> !pwd
/home/you
ftp> cd ../images
250 CWD command successful.
ftp> pwd
257 "/home/jackhenry/images" is current directory.
ftp> get mypicture.gif
227 Entering Passive Mode (10,6,2,2,232,161)
150 Opening BINARY mode data connection for mypicture.gif (220376 bytes).
226 Transfer complete.
220376 bytes received in 0.179 secs (1.2e+03 Kbytes/sec)
ftp>
```

All the files in the list have now been transferred; you can close the connection:

```
ftp> close
221-You have transferred 322333 bytes in 3 files.
221-Total traffic for this session was 323337 bytes in 3 transfers.
221 Thank you for using the FTP service on archive3.
ftp> quit
[you@workstation20 ~]$
```

**Are Your Files Becoming Corrupted in Transit?**

If you find yourself transferring files that seem broken or corrupted afterward, you are likely not transferring in binary mode. To switch to binary mode after connecting to a server, enter the word **binary** at the ftp> prompt.

If you find that the rather verbose debugging output of the ftp client program bothers you, you can switch it off by entering the word **verbose** at the ftp> prompt.

For a list of additional ftp commands, enter **help** at the ftp> prompt; for a brief description of each command, enter **help command** at the ftp> prompt. For example, typing **help binary** displays the following output:

```
binary      set binary transfer type
```

# Exchanging Files with Windows Hosts Using smbclient

You can browse and exchange files with Windows hosts from the Linux command line relatively easily, provided you are somewhat familiar with the process of copying files from computer to computer on Windows networks and the use of the ftp command on Linux or Unix networks.

The command used for exchanging files with Windows hosts is called smbclient. Although smbclient isn't hard to use, you at least need to know the name of the Windows host with which you want to exchange files. If you don't know the name of the Windows host with which you want to communicate, ask your network administrator or consult the Network Neighborhood or My Network Places icons on a Windows desktop computer on your network.

**Can't Find smbclient on Your System?**

If you didn't choose the Workstation installation of Fedora Core 4 in Chapter 2, "Installing Fedora Core 4," you might not have smbclient installed on your system. If this is true in your case, you should install smbclient before proceeding with the rest of this chapter.

Refer to Chapter 31, "Installing Linux Software," for help installing additional Linux software from your CDs. To follow along with remainder of this chapter, you need to install the "Windows File Server" application group. Doing so installs the smbclient command on your Linux system.

## Listing the Shares on a Windows Host

A **share** is a hard drive or storage area on a Windows host that has been made available to other network users. To list the shares on a Windows host using smbclient, call smbclient from the command line with the -L option and the name of the host as an argument. You are prompted for a password. If no password is required to list the shares on a given host, press Enter. A sample result is shown in Listing 24.1.

**LISTING 24.1**   Sample smbclient Output

```
 1:  [you@workstation20 ~]$ smbclient -L newton
 2:  added interface ip=192.168.1.24 bcast=192.168.1.255 nmask=255.255.255.0
 3:  Got a positive name query response from 192.168.1.52 ( 192.168.1.52 )
 4:  Password:
 5:
 6:      Sharename    Type    Comment
 7:      ---------    ----    -------
 8:      WinSpace1    Disk    9GB General-purpose
 9:      WinSpace2    Disk    9GB General-purpose
10:      MediaDrive1  Disk     30GB Fast video storage
11:      MediaDrive2  Disk     45GB Fast video storage
12:      Optical      Disk     1.3GB Pinnacle Sierra Optical Drive
13:      lp           Printer
14:
15:      Server          Comment
16:      ------          -------
17:      NEWTON          Primary video workstation
18:
19:      Workgroup       Master
20:      ---------       ------
21:      WORKGROUP       SUPERSERV
22:  [you@workstation20 ~]$
```

Listing 24.1 shows that the Windows host called NEWTON (line 17) in the workgroup called WORKGROUP (line 21) is sharing a number of hard drives, an optical drive, and a printer (lines 8–14). When you know the name of the share you want to access, you can connect to that share directly using smbclient.

## Connecting to a Windows Share

To connect to a Windows share using smbclient, supply the full name of the share you want to connect to (including host) as an argument to smbclient in the traditional format, enclosed in quotation marks or single quotes. You are prompted for a password. If no password is required to access the share, press Enter:

```
[you@workstation20 ~]$ smbclient '\\newton\mediadrive1'
added interface ip=192.168.1.24 bcast=192.168.1.255 nmask=255.255.255.0
Got a positive name query response from 192.168.1.52 ( 192.168.1.52 )
Password:
smb: \>
```

After you connect and enter the correct password, if necessary, you are at the smbclient prompt.

## Navigating and Copying Files with smbclient

When you are familiar with ftp, you will find that using smbclient is easy; the commands are largely the same, as is the method of use.

To get a listing of smbclient commands, type **help** at the smb: \> prompt. As was the case with ftp, you can access a description of each command by typing **help command** at the prompt.

After you transfer files to and from the Windows host as necessary, you can close the connection simply by typing **quit** at the smb: \> prompt. After typing the quit command, you are returned to the Linux command line.

# Summary

In this chapter, you logged in to and accessed files on remote systems around your local area network and around the larger Internet.

Having finished this chapter, you should feel comfortable performing any of the following tasks from the command line:

- ▶ Logging in to another Unix or Linux system and running several commands from its command line via telnet

- ▶ Logging in to another Unix or Linux system and running several commands from its command line via ssh

- ▶ Copying files to and from remote Unix or Linux hosts

- ▶ Copying files from a Windows host to your Linux workstation using the network

After completing this chapter and the preceding chapters, you should be familiar with the methods needed to accomplish most basic housekeeping, productivity, and network tasks from the command line. In the next two chapters, you deal with advanced command-line tasks and scripting as you finish your lessons at the Linux command line.

# Q&A

**Q** *I have been instructed to log in to a machine anonymously using* ftp. *What does this mean?*

**A** An anonymous login can best be thought of as a guest login for public use; when you log in to a remote system anonymously, you have access only to certain restricted files and directories that the system administrator wants to make public. To log in anonymously, use either anonymous or ftp as your login name (they are functionally identical) and enter your email address as a password. Then log in and use ftp as usual.

**Q** *When I use* telnet *or* ssh *to connect to a remote system, I am sometimes disconnected for no apparent reason if I am inactive for a little while. Why?*

**A** To protect remote login sessions from being hijacked by malicious users, many system administrators implement a default remote login timeout—a period after which you are automatically disconnected if you haven't pressed a key.

# Workshop

The Workshop is designed to help you anticipate possible questions, review what you've learned, and begin learning how to put your knowledge into practice.

## Quiz

1. When should you use the telnet command for remote logins? When should you use ssh?

2. What is the difference between cd and lcd, pwd and !pwd, and ls and !ls?

## Answers

1. You should use telnet only when ssh connection attempts are not answered by the remote system. When this is the case, you should consider asking the administrator of the remote system to add support for ssh.

2. In each case, the former command (cd, pwd, ls) operates on the local system in an ftp session, and the latter command (lcd, !pwd, !ls) operates on the remote system.

## Activities

1. Try using either the ssh or telnet command to log in to another Linux or Unix system on the network on which you have an account.

2. Try using the smbclient command to access the public files on a nearby Windows system.

# CHAPTER 25

# Harnessing the Power of the Shell

---

## What You'll Learn in This Chapter:

▶ How to manipulate text and numbers from the command line
▶ How to organize shell commands into a shell script
▶ How to use variables inside a shell script to perform complex tasks
▶ How to turn shell scripts into executable commands that accept arguments
▶ How to control the flow of the shell script based on user input

This chapter represents the last of our Linux command-line training lessons. In it, you learn many of the more advanced techniques for interacting with the shell. This chapter is not exhaustive by any means; the focus is on basic skills and on whetting your appetite for more, in hopes that you'll study more man pages or even read a more in-depth book about the very powerful Linux shell.

Because this chapter is all about shell scripts, be prepared to spend a lot of time working inside a text editor, such as vi or emacs. If you've forgotten how these editors work or don't feel familiar with them any longer, you might want to review Chapter 20, "Creating, Editing, and Saving Text Files," before continuing.

## Adding to Your Command Repertoire

**Shell scripting** is a way of building new, custom-made commands for yourself out of existing Linux tools and commands. Using shell scripts, you can shorten tasks that normally involve many steps into just one step—which you design.

Before you begin shell scripting, it will be helpful to become familiar with a few Linux commands that you haven't learned about in previous chapters of this book. Each of these commands can make your life easier when you're shell scripting.

Memorizing this information isn't important. Just become familiar enough with it that you have a general idea about which commands you can use for specific tasks in Linux.

## Sending Text to Standard Output with echo

The echo command is simple; this command takes anything you supply as an argument and echoes it by printing it to standard output. echo is one of the commands that appears most often in shell scripts, largely because it enables a shell script to have output—that is, to provide information to the user. Examples seem almost silly:

```
[you@workstation20 you]$ echo "Hello, how are you?"
Hello, how are you?
[you@workstation20 you]$
```

You'll often use echo to allow commands (scripts) you create to ask questions of the user or to display the results of a calculation or operation. Enclosing the text you want to echo in quotation marks, as shown here, is always a good idea so that the shell doesn't try to interpret special characters, such as the asterisk (*) or question mark (?), for pattern matching.

## Performing Simple Calculations with expr

The expr command provides a way of evaluating arithmetic expressions from the command line. Although expr doesn't do floating-point (fractional) math, it is nonetheless a simple, useful command. You supply the numeric and operational parts of the expression as arguments:

```
[you@workstation20 you]$ expr 3 + 4
7
[you@workstation20 you]$ expr 144 + 13666 / 10
1510
[you@workstation20 you]$ expr 10 - 10
0
[you@workstation20 you]$
```

*Did you Know?*

### Be Careful When Using Asterisks

The common operator for multiplication on a computer is the asterisk (*). Recall that at the command prompt, this character also performs filename expansion. Because you want to provide expr with mathematical operators and not a list of matching filenames, always remember to enclose the asterisk in quotation marks when using expr:

```
[you@workstation20 you]$ expr 3 '*' 36
108
[you@workstation20 you]$
```

Because each number and operator in the computation is a separate argument, you should always take care to separate the numbers and operators with spaces.

## Displaying Text File Beginnings and Endings with `head` **and** `tail`

Sometimes it is useful to be able to display only the first few lines or only the last few lines of a text file. You can use the `head` and `tail` commands to accomplish this task. Usually, `head` and `tail` are used with one option, a dash followed by the number of lines to display:

```
[you@workstation20 you]$ head -4 myfile.txt
This is line 1 in a file called myfile.txt that is 16 lines long.
This is line 2 in a file called myfile.txt that is 16 lines long.
This is line 3 in a file called myfile.txt that is 16 lines long.
This is line 4 in a file called myfile.txt that is 16 lines long.
[you@workstation20 you]$ tail -2 myfile.txt
This is line 15 in a file called myfile.txt that is 16 lines long.
This is line 16 in a file called myfile.txt that is 16 lines long.
[you@workstation20 you]$
```

For example, suppose you want to find the document class details of a LaTeX file called `mylatexfile.tex`. Instead of loading the entire file into an editor such as `vi` or `emacs`, you could use the `head` command to display the first line of the file:

```
[you@workstation20 you]$ head -1 mylatexfile.tex
\documentclass[letterpaper,12pt]{article}
[you@workstation20 you]$
```

## Editing Streams of Data with `sed`

Sometimes you might want to edit streams of data on-the-fly before outputting them. The command you use to do this is the **stream editor**, `sed`, one of the most widely used commands in the Unix world.

The most common way to use `sed` is to have it accept a stream of data through a pipe (a vertical bar), providing as an argument a command that determines how the data `sed` receives should be changed. Although there are many `sed` commands, only one of them, the most common one, is covered in this chapter. It is the s (substitute) command, and it works in either of two ways:

```
sed 's/search/replace/'
```

```
sed 's/search/replace/g'
```

In both cases, *search* is a string of text that is to be searched for, and *replace* is the text that should replace it. If you append a g to the end of the argument, all occurrences of *search* are replaced with the text in *replace*; if you do not use g, only the first occurrence on each line is replaced. Note that nearly any character can be substituted for the slash (/) if necessary (allowing you to use the slash in the *search* or *replace* strings when you need to do so). Note that you also can provide multiple commands to sed by separating them with semicolons inside the quotes.

Here are some examples of sed used in combination with head, which provides input to sed through a pipe:

```
[you@workstation20 you]$ head -4 myfile.txt ¦ sed 's/file/jolly file/'
This is line 1 in a jolly file called myfile.txt that is 16 lines long.
This is line 2 in a jolly file called myfile.txt that is 16 lines long.
This is line 3 in a jolly file called myfile.txt that is 16 lines long.
This is line 4 in a jolly file called myfile.txt that is 16 lines long.
[you@workstation20 you]$ head -4 myfile.txt ¦ sed 's/file/silly file/g'
This is line 1 in a silly file called mysilly file.txt that is 16 lines long.
This is line 2 in a silly file called mysilly file.txt that is 16 lines long.
This is line 3 in a silly file called mysilly file.txt that is 16 lines long.
This is line 4 in a silly file called mysilly file.txt that is 16 lines long.
[you@workstation20 you]$ head -4 myfile.txt ¦ sed 's!line 2!line 2 2/3!'
This is line 1 in a file called myfile.txt that is 16 lines long.
This is line 2 2/3 in a file called myfile.txt that is 16 lines long.
This is line 3 in a file called myfile.txt that is 16 lines long.
This is line 4 in a file called myfile.txt that is 16 lines long.
[you@workstation20 you]$ head -4 myfile.txt ¦ sed 's/e 2/e 5/;s/e 4/e 7/'
This is line 1 in a file called myfile.txt that is 16 lines long.
This is line 5 in a file called myfile.txt that is 16 lines long.
This is line 3 in a file called myfile.txt that is 16 lines long.
This is line 7 in a file called myfile.txt that is 16 lines long.
[you@workstation20 you]$
```

In the last example, two commands were used: Data was piped through sed to change the number 2 to the number 5 in the first command (before the semicolon), and the number 4 to the number 7 in the second command (after the semicolon).

For a more real-world example, consider what most people would call a search-and-replace function. Suppose you used LaTeX to write a long novel in which you had named the main character *Evan*—and now you want to change his name to *Sebastian*. Rather than load the long LaTeX file into a text editor and use the search-and-replace functionality, you could simply use sed and output redirection:

```
[you@workstation20 you]$ sed 's/Evan/Sebastian/g' MyNovel.tex > MyNewNovel.tex
[you@workstation20 you]$
```

Just like that, you have created a new copy of your novel, MyNewNovel.tex, in which the main character's name appears as Sebastian—no additional work needed.

## Matching the Beginnings or Endings of Lines

You can use the dollar sign ($) and caret (^) in a sed command to match the end or beginning of a line, respectively. For example, to substitute the text goodbye with farewall *only when* goodbye *occurs at the end of a line*, use the following sed command:

```
's/goodbye$/farewell/'
```

Similarly, to substitute the text Hello with Greetings *only when* Hello *occurs at the beginning of a line*, use the following sed command:

```
's/^Hello/Greetings/'
```

The sed command is a staple in the Unix world because it is much more powerful than the few examples here have demonstrated. sed is especially powerful when its pattern-matching capabilities are used.

To learn more about sed, take time to study the sed manual page at your leisure; it will likely prove helpful to you as you use the shell on an ongoing basis.

# Using Shell Variables and Quoting

Before you begin to create scripts, let's look at two concepts that will become increasingly important as you deal with the complexity of the tasks at hand. These concepts are shell variables (and variable substitution) and quoting.

**Variables** are special words that, when expanded, are replaced by values that you've assigned to them. The shell provides a built-in process for creating and keeping track of variables, known as **variable substitution**. Variable substitution enables you to generalize commands that are included in shell scripts, making it possible for you to change the way a script acts (for example, the files it will affect) simply by changing the values of the variables it uses.

The use of variables in shell scripts involves two basic steps:

1. The creation of a variable, usually by simply assigning a value to a word using the equal sign.

   Usually, this also involves using quotation marks to enclose the assigned value, to ensure that it is not misinterpreted by the shell.

2. Later in your script, indicating to the shell that you want the value of the variable to be substituted for the variable's name exactly where it appears. You do this by prefixing the name of your variable with a dollar sign ($).

For example, through the use of variables, you can write a script that performs a specific set of operations on a file without having to explicitly name the file in the script, thus allowing the *user* to name the file that should be affected each time the script is run.

# Creating and Substituting Variables

To understand how to create variables, assume that in your work on a day-to-day basis, you often encounter people stopping by your desk to request printouts of the documents named newempl.txt, hours.txt, and phonebook.txt, all of which are stored in /home/you/textfiles. The command you know to print these files from any present working directory is

```
[you@workstation20 you]$ lpr /home/you/textfiles/newempl.txt
/home/you/textfiles/
➥hours.txt /home/you/textfiles/phonebook.txt
[you@workstation20 you]$
```

One way to reduce the amount of typing you have to do is to use a variable. You can create a variable to hold the names and paths of the files you need to repeatedly print, saving yourself the trouble of typing all the names and path information:

```
[you@workstation20 you]$ PRINTFILES="/home/you/textfiles/newempl.txt /home/you/
➥textfiles/hours.txt /home/you/textfiles/phonebook.txt"
[you@workstation20 you]$
```

You have now created a variable called PRINTFILES, which holds the list of filenames you so often need to print. To use the variable, substitute it for the file and pathname information in a command line. From now on, whenever you want to print these three files from this shell session, you can simply type

```
[you@workstation20 you]$ lpr $PRINTFILES
[you@workstation20 you]$
```

This command is much shorter! But how does it work? The shell replaces the word PRINTFILES with the contents of the variable PRINTFILES. To see this effect with a command that makes it more clearly visible, try using the echo command to display the value of PRINTFILES:

```
[you@workstation20 you]$ echo $PRINTFILES
/home/you/textfiles/newempl.txt /home/you/textfiles/hours.txt /home/you/➥
textfiles/phonebook.txt
[you@workstation20 you]$
```

Because the shell replaced PRINTFILES with the value you assigned to it before calling the echo command, echo outputs the value you assigned to PRINTFILES.

After you create a variable, you can substitute the value of the variable anywhere at the command line or in a script by preceding the name of the variable with a dollar sign ($).

## Be Specific When Using Variable Substitution

When variable names are ambiguous, you can also enclose the name of a variable in braces ({ }) to indicate to the shell exactly where the variable name begins and ends.

For example, assume that you want to use the contents of the variable WORD immediately before the number 2000 in a script. The shell might mistakenly assume that you are referring to a variable called WORD2000:

```
[you@workstation20 you]$ WORD=YEAR
[you@workstation20 you]$ echo $WORD2000

[you@workstation20 you]$ echo ${WORD}2000
YEAR2000
[you@workstation20 you]$
```

By enclosing the name of your variable, WORD, in braces, you show the shell which variable name should be expanded—WORD, the variable you created, rather than a variable called WORD2000 that you did not intend to create.

# Quoting Carefully

When you create variables, it is usually a good idea to enclose the value you want to assign in quotation marks. They tell the shell that you want to assign *exactly* the value inside the quotes, rather than expand patterns or other variables or treat values separated by spaces as arguments or commands. Several types of quoting can be done at the command line; variables can be created or assigned using any of them:

VARIABLE=*value*

VARIABLE="*value*"

VARIABLE='*value*'

Each of these commands is subtly different. The first method (no quoting) is the simplest. However, because the shell normally uses a number of characters in special ways, such as the space to separate arguments or the vertical bar (¦) to create a pipe, quoting is necessary if you want to assign these characters to a variable:

```
[you@workstation20 you]$ MYNAME=Horace Walpole
bash: Walpole: command not found
[you@workstation20 you]$ MYNAME="Horace Walpole"
[you@workstation20 you]$
```

In this case, quoting is needed to prevent the shell from using the space as a separation value. Among the other characters that must be enclosed in quotation marks if assigned to variables are parentheses (( )), braces ({ }), and brackets ([ ]). There is also a difference between the result of enclosing data in single quotation marks and the result of enclosing data in double quotation marks. In double quotation marks, although most special characters are ignored, command and variable substitution are still performed; in single quotation marks, they are not. This difference is subtle and perhaps best illustrated by example. Consider the following sequence:

```
[you@workstation20 you]$ QUOTEA="My name is $MYNAME."
[you@workstation20 you]$ QUOTEB='My name is $MYNAME.'
[you@workstation20 you]$ echo $QUOTEA
My name is Horace Walpole.
[you@workstation20 you]$ echo $QUOTEB
My name is $MYNAME.
[you@workstation20 you]$
```

As you can see here, when a phrase is placed within single quotation marks, the dollar sign ($) ceases to be a special character. When a phrase is placed within double quotation marks, the dollar sign retains its special meaning and variables are substituted as necessary, although other special characters lose their unique functionality. This example using the date command and command substitution simply prints the current date to standard output:

```
[you@workstation20 you]$ date
Thu Aug 26 14:34:02 MDT 2004
[you@workstation20 you]$ TIMEA="The time right now is $(date)."
[you@workstation20 you]$ TIMEB='The time right now is $(date).'
[you@workstation20 you]$ echo $TIMEA
The time right now is Thu Aug 26 14:34:14 MDT 2004.
[you@workstation20 you]$ echo $TIMEB
The time right now is $(date).
[you@workstation20 you]$
```

Because quoting can so radically affect the behavior of shell variable substitution and shell command substitution, you need to gain an understanding of the way it works. Feel free to experiment a little longer with variables and quoting until you feel comfortable using them.

## Understanding Environment Variables

Before we finish looking at variables and quoting, it is important to learn about a special class of variables known as **environment variables**. These variables tell the shell how to behave as you work at the command line or in scripts; changing the value of these variables changes some behavioral aspect of the shell.

The single most important environment variable is PATH. The PATH variable contains a list of all the directories that are known to hold commands. When you type a command at the command line, the shell searches through all the directories listed in PATH until it finds a program by that name. The shell loads and runs the program (in reality, a command) and passes on to it any arguments you have supplied. Try printing the contents of PATH now:

```
[you@workstation20 you]$ echo $PATH
/usr/local/bin:/bin:/usr/bin:/usr/X11R6/bin:/home/you/bin
[you@workstation20 you]$
```

In this case, the shell searches for commands in /usr/local/bin, /bin, /usr/bin, /usr/X11R6/bin, and /home/you/bin, in that order. To see where the shell eventually finds any given command, you can use the which command:

```
[you@workstation20 you]$ which emacs
/usr/bin/emacs
[you@workstation20 you]$
```

This means that when you type **emacs** at the command line, the shell uses the PATH variable to search in /usr/local/bin and /bin before finally finding emacs in /usr/bin. If you add to the PATH variable, you can cause the shell to search in more places:

```
[you@workstation20 you]$ PATH="/usr/sbin:$PATH"
[you@workstation20 you]$ echo $PATH
/usr/sbin:/usr/local/bin:/bin:/usr/bin:/usr/X11R6/bin:/home/you/bin
[you@workstation20 you]$
```

You have now added an additional directory, /usr/sbin, to the PATH; /usr/sbin will be searched first for the remainder of this shell session whenever a command is entered.

Perhaps the most important thing to notice about the default value of PATH in Linux is the fact that /home/you/bin appears in it. This means that as you create shell scripts throughout the rest of this chapter, you will be able to place them in the bin directory in your home directory and then use them like any other command.

For more information on the available environment variables and their functions, see the manual page for bash.

# Creating Your Own Commands Using Shell Scripting

Now that you've acquired a sizable amount of experience using the console and the shell; have learned a number of common commands; and are familiar with concepts such as pipes, command substitution, variable substitution, and quoting, it's time to begin creating shell scripts.

A shell script is really a way of automating complex tasks or repetitive sequences of commands that you often carry out at the shell so that you don't have to type these commands over and over each time you want to repeat the task. Often, the sequences of commands in shell scripts are complex enough that your shell scripts really become new commands, tailor-made to your productivity needs.

Structurally, a shell script is a plaintext file that contains normal commands just as you might type them at the command line, in the order in which you want them to be executed when the script is run. In more complex shell scripts, you might also find various special control statements that are interpreted and acted upon by the shell. They can cause the shell to call extra commands or to ignore some commands in the script, depending on user input or testable environmental conditions—such as the existence (or nonexistence) of a particular file or directory.

## Beginning a Shell Script

To create a shell script, launch your favorite editor (generally vi or emacs) and create a new file called myscript. On the first line of this file, enter the following:

```
#!/bin/sh
```

This line indicates to Linux that the file you are creating is a shell script. When you call myscript from the command line, Linux checks the first line of the file, realizes that it is a shell script, and then calls the shell, /bin/sh, to execute your list of commands.

## Processing Command-Line Arguments

The simplest use of shell scripting is to automate a series of commands you often use, to avoid always having to type them.

Recall that in Chapter 21, "Managing High-Quality Documents at the Command Line," you learned that printing a LaTeX file in Linux is a two-step process. First, you must run your input file through the formatter with the latex command to produce a dvi file. Then you must use dvips to print the file. You can use shell scripting to create a command that automates this process. The goal for our first script is to create a command that enables the user to pass one argument—the name of a .tex file—and have the file both formatted and printed without needing to enter further commands.

You create this command using a special set of variables that hold command-line arguments. Within a shell script, the shell creates a special set of variables called 1, 2, 3, and so on to hold the command-line arguments entered by the user when the shell script was called. Using $1, $2, $3, and so on therefore substitutes the value(s) of the argument(s) the user provided.

Consider the script in Listing 25.1. This script creates a variable named LATEXFILE and assigns to it the value of the special variable $1. That means that the first argument passed to myscript will end up in the variable LATEXFILE as the script is running.

---

### Why Put Quotation Marks Around Filenames?

Notice that nearly everything in myscript is enclosed in double quotation marks. In Linux, filenames may contain spaces. To access filenames that contain spaces at the command line, the filename must be quoted. By quoting every place where a file is accessed in myscript, you guarantee that the script will work if it is ever called with a filename containing one or more spaces as an argument.

---

**LISTING 25.1** A Shell Script Called myscript

```
#!/bin/sh

LATEXFILE="$1"
DVIFILE="$(echo "$LATEXFILE" | sed 's/tex$/dvi/')"
latex "$LATEXFILE"
dvips "$DVIFILE"
```

The second variable assignment in myscript is considerably more involved than the first, but it is manageable. The entire value of the variable is enclosed in $( ), meaning that the value of DVIFILE will be obtained through command substitution; in other words, the output of the commands inside the parentheses becomes the value of DVIFILE.

Inside the parentheses, two things occur. First, the echo command echoes the value of LATEXFILE. Remember that this value is the name of a .tex file that was passed to your script by the user. The vertical bar then pipes the output of echo to the sed command, which replaces .tex with .dvi. Thus, if the value of LATEXFILE is myfile.tex, the assigned value of DVIFILE is myfile.dvi. If you want to see this at work outside a script, try typing it at the command line:

```
[you@workstation20 you]$ echo myfile.tex | sed 's/tex$/dvi/'
myfile.dvi
[you@workstation20 you]$
```

The rest of the script in Listing 25.1 is simply a list of commands the shell is to execute. The script calls LaTeX with the name of the .tex file supplied by the user. You already know that when LaTeX formats this .tex file, the result is a .dvi file by the same name in the same directory as the original file.

Because a .dvi file can be printed with the dvips command, your script then performs this second step, calling dvips and supplying as an argument the .dvi file by the same name. This command prints the file.

## Making myscript Easily Executable

After saving myscript, you have a file called myscript in /home/you, which contains all the commands necessary to allow the shell to automate the printing of .tex files for you. Naturally, you should try out the script to see whether it works. However, you can't do that just yet.

Recall that the shell maintains an environment variable called PATH that contains the list of directories in which commands are found. Before this script can be used like other commands, you must move it into one of the directories listed in the PATH variable so that the shell can find it and then give it executable permissions so that the shell can execute it. Because /home/you/bin appears in the PATH environment variable, you can prepare the script for execution by making sure that /home/you/bin exists (using mkdir to create it if it doesn't) and then using mv to move the script there and chmod to set executable permissions:

```
[you@workstation20 you]$ mkdir ~/bin
[you@workstation20 you]$ mv myscript ~/bin
[you@workstation20 you]$ chmod u+x ~/bin/myscript
[you@workstation20 you]$ ls -l ~/bin
total 4
-rwxrw-r--  1 you     you       115 Oct 1 13:52 myscript
[you@workstation20 you]$
```

Now try it out:

```
[you@workstation20 you]$ myscript myfile.tex
[...loads of output...]
```

If you tried this experiment on a real LaTeX file, you should have enjoyed success; the file was formatted and printed. You have created a new command! The name myscript is a little generic, so rename it:

```
[you@workstation20 you]$ mv ~/bin/myscript ~/bin/lxprint
[you@workstation20 you]$
```

The new command myscript has now been renamed lxprint, and its calling syntax is as follows:

```
lxprint filename.tex
```

Here, *filename.tex* represents the name of the .tex file that should be printed.

## Using Conditional Statements

Sometimes in a shell script it is helpful to execute part of the script if some condition is true or a variable holds some specific value. Perhaps you want a particular script to generate printed output only if the user calls the script with the -print option, or perhaps you want a script to create a new file only if a file by the same name doesn't already exist. This technique of omitting or including certain parts or behaviors of a script depending on current circumstances or user input is called **conditional execution**.

The most basic form of conditional execution in shell scripts is used with the following syntax. Here, the first set of commands is executed only if *test expression* is true. The optional word else precedes a second set of commands that will be executed only if *test expression* is not true:

```
if [ test expression ]; then
command
command
  ...
else
command
command
  ...
fi
```

The term **test expression** refers to one of a number of different kinds of tests and comparisons that can be performed. The most common of these expressions are shown in Table 25.1; many more can be found in the manual page for test.

**TABLE 25.1**   Common Test Expressions

| Expression | Meaning |
| --- | --- |
| *val1* = *val2* | True if the word or quoted text item *val1* is identical to the word or quoted text item *val2* |
| *val1* != *val2* | True if the word or quoted text item *val1* is not identical to the word or quoted text item *val2* |
| *val1* -gt *val2* | True if the numeric value of item *val1* is greater than the numeric value of item *val2* |
| *val1* -lt *val2* | True if the numeric value of item *val1* is less than the numeric value of item *val2* |
| *val1* -eq *val2* | True if the numeric value of item *val1* and the numeric value of item *val2* are equal |
| -e *file* | True if *file* is the name of an existing file of any kind |
| -f *file* | True if *file* is the name of an existing regular file (not a device or a directory) |
| -d *directory* | True if *directory* is the name of an existing directory |
| -x *command* | True if *command* is the name of an existing file that is marked as executable |

To illustrate conditional execution, let's modify `lxprint` in two ways. First, let's add a few lines so that if the user supplies the classic `--help` as an option, `lxprint` prints a help message. Then let's force `lxprint` to verify that a file actually exists before it tries to call `latex` or `dvips`. If the file doesn't exist, `lxprint` should display an error message.

The new and improved `lxprint` is shown in Listing 25.2.

**LISTING 25.2**   The New and Improved `lxprint`

```
 1:    #!/bin/sh
 2:
 3:    if [ "$1" = --help ]; then
 4:        echo "Use lxprint to print out LaTeX files in one easy step."
 5:        echo "Just supply the name of a .tex file as an argument!"
 6:        exit 0
 7:    fi
 8:
 9:    LATEXFILE="$1"
10:
11:    if [ -f "$LATEXFILE" ]; then
12:        DVIFILE="$(echo "$LATEXFILE" | sed 's/tex$/dvi/')"
13:
14:        latex "$LATEXFILE"
15:        dvips "$DVIFILE"
16:    else
17:        echo "There doesn't seem to be a file called $LATEXFILE."
18:        exit 1
19:    fi
```

This listing includes two conditional statements. The first one, which begins on line 3 and ends on line 7, checks to see whether the argument supplied by the user is actually the word `--help`. If it is, a help message is displayed. The second conditional statement, which begins on line 11 and continues through line 19, checks for the existence of the file the user has asked to be formatted and printed. If the file exists, formatting and printing commence. If the file does not exist, an error message is printed.

**By the Way**

### Why Are Some Lines Indented?

Indenting four spaces for each new level of nesting in a script is traditional. Indenting commands within `if...then` conditional statements is not mandatory. However, in complex scripts in which `if...then` statements can occur within other `if...then` statements, indentation can make it much easier to visually understand how a script works.

Notice that one final command has also been introduced here. The `exit` command can be used to exit a shell script and return to the command prompt. It accepts one argument, the exit status, which should be zero if the script has exited normally or nonzero if the script is exiting because it has encountered a problem.

Let's try the two new conditional chunks of the script, first by calling lxprint with the argument --help and then by calling it with a nonexisting filename:

```
[you@workstation20 you]$ lxprint --help
Use lxprint to print out LaTeX files in one easy step.
Just supply the name of a .tex file as an argument!
[you@workstation20 you]$ lxprint nosuchfile.tex
There doesn't seem to be a file called nosuchfile.tex.
[you@workstation20 you]$
```

The changes are functional, and the lxprint command has been further improved.

## Testing Over and Over Again

The types of tests shown in Table 25.1 aren't only for use with if...then statements. They can also be used with another type of statement, known as the while...do statement, which follows this format:

```
while [ test expression ]; do
command
command
  ...
done
```

The difference between if...then and while...do is that in the former case, commands are executed a single time if the test condition is true, and in the latter case, they are executed again and again and again as fast as the computer can execute them until the condition is false.

Let's continue to use lxprint as our test case. When you're working with publishing projects involving multiple documents, having multiple source files isn't uncommon. For example, a large project called 02projections might be split across several files ending in sequence numbers:

```
02projections1.tex
02projections2.tex
02projectison3.tex
```

It would be nice if lxprint could accept a base name like 02projections and then be smart enough to print all the files in the set in sequence. Using a while loop and some more conditional statements, you can do this easily. The result is shown in Listing 25.3. This script includes comments—lines that begin with a hash mark (#)—and are inserted for the benefit of humans only. The shell ignores comments.

**LISTING 25.3**   The New `lxprint` Command Incorporating Sequence
Printing

```
 1:  #!/bin/sh
 2:
 3:  # If the user uses '--help' as an argument,
 4:  # we want to display a help message.
 5:
 6:  if [ "$1" = --help ]; then
 7:      echo "Use lxprint to print out LaTeX files in one easy step."
 8:      echo "Just supply the name of a .tex file as an argument!"
 9:      echo " * or the base name of a numbered sequence of .tex files"
10:      echo "  to print them all!"
11:      exit 0
12:  fi
13:
14:  LATEXFILE="$1"
15:
16:  # If the filename supplied as an argument exists,
17:  # then print it out.
18:  if [ -f "$LATEXFILE" ]; then
19:      DVIFILE="$(echo "$LATEXFILE" | sed 's/tex$/dvi/')"
20:
21:      latex "$LATEXFILE"
22:      dvips "$DVIFILE"
23:  else
24:
25:      # If the filename doesn't exist as supplied, see if
26:      # it's a base filename-- for example, if the user
27:      # supplied '02projections' as an argument and the file
28:      # '02projections1.tex' exists, then the user wants to
29:      # print the entire sequence.
30:
31:      if [ -f "${LATEXFILE}1.tex" ]; then
32:          # The variable COUNTER will hold the current number
33:          # in the sequence we're printing. We'll start at
34:          # 1 and use expr to add one to it each time we
35:          # print another file.
36:
37:          COUNTER=1
38:
39:          while [ -f "$LATEXFILE$COUNTER.tex" ]; do
40:            echo "Printing $LATESFILE$COUNTER.tex"
41:            latex "$LATEXFILE$COUNTER.tex"
42:            dvips "$LATEXFILE$COUNTER.dvi"
43:            COUNTER=$(expr $COUNTER + 1)
44:          done
45:
46:      else
47:
48:          echo "There doesn't seem to be a file called $LATEXFILE."
49:          exit 1
50:
51:      fi
52:  fi
```

The execution of `lxprint` is gradually getting more complex. Now when `lxprint`
starts, it first checks to see whether the user has sent `--help` as an argument in lines

6–12. If this isn't the case, it checks to see whether the user has supplied a valid filename in line 18; if the user has, the file is formatted and printed in lines 19–22. If the argument isn't a valid filename, `lxprint` checks to see whether it might be a base filename by adding a number and the `.tex` extension to it in line 31. If it is, `lxprint` formats and prints all the files in the set, in sequence, by using a `while..do` loop and the `COUNTER` variable, which holds the number of times the commands in the loop have been executed so far; this happens in lines 37–44. As long as another file in the sequence seems to exist, the loop is executed again and the value of `COUNTER` increases by 1.

Take a moment to study the script, the use of expr, and command and variable substitution as they appear here. Because of the size and complexity of the script, it might seem daunting at first, but you will eventually be able to follow the flow of the script as it is written.

## Repeatedly Executing for a Predefined Set

Although the `if..then` and `while..do` statements both work by performing a test and making a decision based on the result, another statement, the `for..do` statement, simply executes a set of commands for every element in a list. For example, the `for..do` loop provides ideal functionality for performing the same set of operations on each file in a long list of files. The syntax is

```
for var in item1 item2 item3 ...; do
command
command
  ...
done
```

The `for..do` statement first assigns the value *item1* to the shell variable *var* and then executes the commands inside the statement. After it reaches done, it assigns the value *item2* to the shell variable *var* and executes the commands inside the statement again. This process continues until there are no more *items*.

Let's examine the use of the `for..do` loop by giving the `lxprint` command one more capability—to print *every* `.tex` file in a user's current working directory if the user supplies `--all` as an argument or option. You can easily do this with a well-placed `for..do` statement. The updated and final `lxprint` is shown in Listing 25.4.

**LISTING 25.4**  The `lxprint` Command with the `--all` Capability Added

```
1:    #! /bin/sh
2:
3:    # If the user uses '--help' as an argument,
4:    # we want to display a help message.
5:
```

**LISTING 25.4**    Continued

```
 6:     if [ "$1" = --help ]; then
 7:         echo "Use lxprint to print out LaTeX files in one easy step."
 8:         echo "Just supply the name of a .tex file as an argument!"
 9:         echo " * or the base name of a numbered sequence of .tex files"
10:         echo "   to print them all!"
11:         echo " * or --all to print every .tex file in the pwd!"
12:         exit 0
13:     fi
14:
15:     # If the user supplies '--all' as an argument, then use
16:     # filename expansion and a for..do statement to print
17:     # every .tex file in the present working directory, one
18:     # by one. Then exit.
19:
20:     if [ "$1" = --all ]; then
21:         for LATEXFILE in *.tex; do
22:             echo "Printing $LATEXFILE"
23:             DVIFILE="$(echo "$LATEXFILE" | sed 's/tex$/dvi/')"
24:
25:             latex "$LATEXFILE"
26:             dvips "$DVIFILE"
27:         done
28:         exit 0
29:     fi
30:
31:     LATEXFILE="$1"
32:
33:     # If the filename supplied as an argument exists,
34:     # then print it out.
35:     if [ -f "$LATEXFILE" ]; then
36:         DVIFILE="$(echo "$LATEXFILE" | sed 's/tex$/dvi/')"
37:
38:         latex "$LATEXFILE"
39:         dvips "$DVIFILE"
40:     else
41:
42:         # If the filename doesn't exist as supplied, see if
43:         # it's a base filename -- for example, if the user
44:         # supplied '02projections' as an argument and the file
45:         # '02projections1.tex' exists, then the user wants to
46:         # print the entire sequence.
47:
48:         if [ -f "${LATEXFILE}1.tex" ]; then
49:
50:             # The variable COUNTER will hold the current number
51:             # in the sequence we're printing. We'll start at
52:             # 1 and use expr to add one to it each time we
53:             # print another file.
54:
55:             COUNTER=1
56:
57:             while [ -f "$LATEXFILE$COUNTER.tex" ]; do
58:                 echo "Printing $LATEXFILE$COUNTER.tex"
59:                 latex "$LATEXFILE$COUNTER.tex"
60:                 dvips "$LATEXFILE$COUNTER.dvi"
61:                 COUNTER=$(expr $COUNTER + 1)
62:             done
```

**LISTING 25.4**   Continued

```
63:
64:      else
65:
66:          echo "There doesn't seem to be a file called $LATEXFILE."
67:          exit 1
68:
69:      fi
70:   fi
```

The change in Listing 25.4 is relatively small, but potentially confusing because
*.tex looks like a single item. Remember, though, that the shell uses the * if it is
not enclosed in quotation marks to expand to a list of matching filenames. So, in
this case, *.tex is replaced by a space-separated list of .tex files, as if you had
typed them yourself. The for..do statement then uses this list as the basis for the
value of the LATEXFILE variable as it executes the commands between the do and
the done in lines 21–27. At the end of the for..do statement, exit in line 28
returns the user to the command prompt.

## Going Beyond Shell Scripting

Believe it or not, all the techniques we've documented so far in this chapter can be
used directly at the command line as well as from within shell script files. Although
if..then has limited utility when entered directly at the command line, while..do
and especially for..do can have incredible utility on a day-to-day basis.

To use one of these structures at the command line, enter it as you would in a script.
After you begin a loop or conditional statement, the shell prompt changes and
remains altered in appearance until you reach the closing fi or done; then the commands in the loop are executed. For example, you can use a similar for..do loop
to the one in Listing 25.4 to print all the .txt files in your home directory to the
printer. Just use the *.txt pattern as your for..do list and the lpr command inside
the loop:

```
[you@workstation20 you]$ for GONNAPRINT in *.txt; do
> lpr "$GONNAPRINT"
> done
[you@workstation20 you]$
```

Notice how the prompt changed after you entered the for..do line and remained
different until you entered the word done. After you enter done, the shell sends every
file ending with .txt in the current working directory to the printer with the lpr
command. Over time, you'll find unexpected uses for for..do and, to a lesser
extent, while..do and if..then everywhere you look—sometimes when you least
expect them.

Shell scripting is a very powerful application development tool; the shell offers several techniques, statements, structures, commands, and facilities that are not discussed in this book. For more in-depth information on shell scripting and shell programming, I recommend the following books, which cover shell scripting and the bash shell commonly used with Linux in detail:

▶ *Sams Teach Yourself Shell Programming in 24 Hours* by Sriranga Veeraraghaven

▶ *Linux Shell Scripting with Bash* by Ken O. Burtch

▶ *Wicked Cool Shell Scripts* by Dave Taylor

▶ *Learning the bash Shell* by Cameron Newham and Bill Rosenblatt

# Summary

In this chapter, you learned to harness the power of the Linux shell to create your own powerful, functional commands in just a few minutes using shell scripting. Specific topics you learned about in this chapter include

▶ Creating, assigning values to, and substituting variables

▶ Using the different types of quoting for variable and command substitution

▶ Using the PATH environment variable as it applies to commands and shell scripts

▶ Assigning execute permissions to your script and moving it to a directory listed in PATH so that it can be easily called

▶ Using the if..then conditional statement structure

▶ Using the while..do conditional statement structure

▶ Using the for..do conditional statement structure

After you've spent some time practicing the techniques you learned in this chapter, you will be able to use techniques such as command substitution and filename expansion, along with the wide variety of shell commands you learned earlier to employ the shell efficiently.

Although use of the console and the shell prompt might seem like a blur to you after these few short chapters, as you refer back to them while using Linux, you'll gradually become more familiar with the command-line personality of Linux and other Unix-like operating systems. In time, you'll come to feel at home on the command line to the same extent that you do at a graphical desktop.

# Q&A

**Q** *I'm trying to write a long shell script, and it's not working as I expect it to. Are there any tools to help me see exactly what the shell is doing when my script is running?*

**A** Yes. Inserting the special command `set -x` into your shell script causes the shell to display everything it does afterward, one line at a time, as your script is running. Inserting the special command `set +x` later in your script turns this debugging feature off again.

**Q** *When I try to use quotes at the command line, I often end up trapped by a strange prompt that doesn't seem to accept any commands. Why?*

**A** If you're stuck at a prompt that looks like a greater-than symbol, it means you've used unbalanced quotes somewhere in your command. They can take the form of mismatched quotation marks (one single and one double) or an uneven number of quotation marks (meaning that you've forgotten to close a set of quotes somewhere), as can be seen in the examples of mismatched quotes below:

```
"This text is in mismatched quotes'
And so is this word, because there is no closing quote: 'Hi!
```

When you are stuck at a prompt that looks like a greater-than symbol, the shell is waiting for a matching close quote for an opening quote that you've entered. Try entering a single quotation mark or a double quotation mark; one of these should return you to the command prompt.

**Q** *I'm trying to experiment with shell scripts, but my script `test` doesn't seem to do anything at all, no matter what I put in it! Why?*

**A** This is because running a `test` command that actually exists at `/usr/bin/test`—so it never finds your `test` script because `/usr/bin/test` is being executed instead. The easiest solution is to rename your script to something else using the `mv` command.

# Workshop

The Workshop is designed to help you anticipate possible questions, review what you've learned, and begin learning how to put your knowledge into practice.

## Quiz

**1.** What is the functional difference between single quotation marks and double quotation marks when assigning values to variables?

2. What special character causes the value of a variable to be substituted?

3. How do you test for the existence of a directory in an `if..then` statement?

4. In the statement `for MYVAR in a b c d e; do`, which begins a `for..do` loop, what values will the variable `MYVAR` hold?

5. What do the caret (^) and dollar sign ($) characters do when used in a `sed` command?

## Answers

1. When a value is assigned in single quotation marks (' '), variable and command substitution are not performed even if a dollar sign ($) appears in the value. When a value is assigned in double quotation marks (" "), variable and command substitution are performed before the value is assigned the variable.

2. The dollar sign ($).

3. `if [ -d directory ];` then, where *directory* is the name or path of the directory you want to test for.

4. The commands inside the loop will be executed five times. The values of `MYVAR` each time through the loop will be `"a"`, `"b"`, `"c"`, `"d"`, and `"e"`, in that order.

5. The caret matches the beginning of a line; the dollar sign matches the end of a line.

## Activities

1. Experiment with quoting and assigning values to variables and then expand them using the `echo` command. Do this until you feel familiar with the way variable assignment and substitution work.

2. Study the final listing of the `lxprint` command until you feel confident that you understand how every line in it works.

3. Try modifying the `lxprint` script to make sure that when the user passes a filename as an argument, it is a `.tex` file and not some other kind of file. (*Hint:* There are at least two ways to modify the script, both using command substitution and an `if..then` statement; one uses the `grep` command and the other uses `sed`.)

# PART V

# Advanced Topics

# CHAPTER 26

# Desktop Power Tools

---

## What You'll Learn in This Chapter:

▶ How to launch graphical applications using the terminal
▶ How to write shell scripts that interact with users through dialog boxes
▶ How to write scripts for the Nautilus file manager

In previous chapters, you learned the ins and outs of using Linux at the command line, and you learned to launch the Terminal application to access the command line from the desktop. You also learned how to use the most popular applications on the desktop. In this chapter, you learn to integrate the two—to launch desktop applications directly from the command line and to write shell scripts that can take advantage of the desktop environment. By combining the power of the command line with the productivity enhancements of the desktop, you can increase both your workflow and the complexity of tasks you are able to accomplish using Linux.

## Additional Features of the Terminal Application

You've already gained some experience with the Terminal application, which allows you to access the command line from the Linux desktop. Before we proceed with the other topics in this chapter, there are a few extra tips about the Terminal application that you might find useful.

## Using Multiple Tabs in the Terminal Application

You might remember that while you're using the command line at the console, multiple virtual consoles are provided so that you can enjoy the benefits of running many command-line applications at once. You can enjoy similar benefits by launching multiple instances of the terminal application at once *or* by creating multiple **tabs** inside the terminal application, each of which contains a command line of its own. You can open a new command line in a new tab by choosing File, New Tab, Default. A terminal window with three running command prompts, each in its own tab, is shown in Figure 26.1.

Tab for command prompt #2

Tab for command prompt #1  Tab for command prompt #3

**FIGURE 26.1**
The terminal application with three running command prompts, each in its own tab.

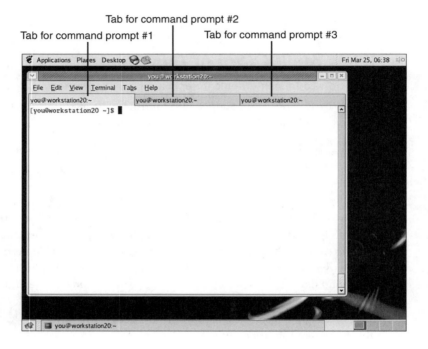

In the KDE's terminal application, you can open a new tab by choosing Session, New Shell.

The command lines in each tab are completely autonomous; each has its own current working directory and its own list of jobs, and all can be busy simultaneously if you run particularly involved commands that take some time to complete.

To close a tab and exit the command line (shell) that is running in it, click the tab to make it active and enter the word **exit** at the command line. The tab disappears.

## Launching Desktop Applications with the Terminal

Launching desktop applications from the command line in a terminal window is both possible and common. Although the menus and icons on the menubar are usually more convenient ways to launch desktop applications, sometimes being able to type the name of an application at the command line to start it is useful—for example, if you want to be able to supply a command-line argument, as you'll shortly see.

To use the command line to launch an application whose name you already know, enter its name at the command line. For example, recall the gedit text editor that you learned to use in Chapter 5, "Working with Files on the Desktop." To launch gedit from a terminal window, enter **gedit** at the command prompt:

[you@workstation20 ~]$ **gedit**

In fact, you can also supply the name of the file you want to edit as an argument to the command, as is the case with command-line editors such as emacs and vi. For example, to load the file myfile.tex into the gedit text editor, type **gedit** followed by the name of the file you want to load into the editor:

[you@workstation20 ~]$ **gedit myfile.tex**

Entering a command like this one causes the gedit editor to start and load the file you have supplied as an argument. If the file does not already exist, gedit opens with an empty file using the name you supplied, as shown in Figure 26.2.

**FIGURE 26.2**
The gedit editor was launched at the command line in the terminal window; myfile.tex was given as an argument.

Although a list of the number of applications that can be started from the command line is beyond the scope of a book like this one (there are hundreds, even thousands of them), you can explore Linux desktop applications yourself from the command line by getting directory listings (using ls) of many of the desktop application commands in the following paths:

- ▶ /usr/X11R6/bin
- ▶ /usr/bin/g*
- ▶ /usr/bin/k*

Note that not all the commands in these listings are desktop applications; many, however, are. Note also that any desktop application you start via a menu can also be started via the command line if you know the name of the application in the file system. One way to find this information is to use the process list (like the one generated by the ps command) discussed in Chapters 28, "Command-Line System Administration," and 29, "Desktop System Administration."

## Using Job Control Techniques at the Terminal Command Line

You might notice that as you start application windows like gedit using the command line in this way, you are unable to enter further commands in the terminal window. The reason is that gedit acts as the foreground job in the terminal window. Only after you exit gedit does the command prompt return.

*Did you Know?*

### Did You Forget Some Command-Line Techniques?

For a command-line refresher, including such concepts as foreground jobs and background jobs, return to Chapter 5, "Working with Files on the Desktop," Chapter 19, "Performing Basic Shell Tasks," and Chapter 20, "Creating, Editing, and Saving Text Files."

In fact, you can start an application like gedit in the background, so that you instantly have access to the command line again when gedit starts, by appending the ampersand (&) to the end of the command:

```
[you@workstation20 ~]$ gedit myfile.tex &
[1] 9779
[you@workstation20 ~]$
```

Calling gedit as a background job this way instantly displays a job number (in this case, 1) and a process id number (in this case, 9779) and then returns you to the command prompt. Although the gedit window opens and you can edit `myfile.tex`, you also have access to the command line in the terminal window because `gedit` is running in the background.

All the command-line job control techniques that you learned in "Keeping Your Shell Programs Under Control" in Chapter 20, "Creating, Editing, and Saving Text Files," can be used from a command line in a terminal window as well, including the following:

▶ The Ctrl+Z keystroke in the terminal window from which the application was started to suspend the foreground job and restore the command prompt

▶ The `bg` and `fg` commands in the terminal window from which the application window was started to move existing jobs to the foreground or background

▶ The `kill` command in the terminal window to end a running job

▶ The ampersand (&) at the end of a command to start the command in the background, keeping the command prompt available for additional work while the command you have called runs and finishes

The only difference between job control at the command line in a terminal window and job control at a console command line is that in a terminal window, many of your running jobs can be application windows, meaning that you can interact with them even while they are in the background by clicking your mouse pointer within their borders.

# Using `nohup` to Keep Jobs Running

If you start a number of jobs in a terminal window and then close the window or exit the shell, all the jobs in that shell exit as well. This can be an undesired side effect. Often when you start a desktop application in the background, you want the desktop application to remain even if the shell where it was started exits.

Using the `nohup` command, you can indicate that a command should not exit if the shell in which it was started exits or is closed. For example, to launch a `gedit` window in the background, which remains open even if you close the terminal window used to start it, enter the following:

```
[you@workstation20 ~]$ nohup gedit &
```

When you use `nohup`, a file called `nohup.out` is created in your home directory. This plaintext file displays any error messages or warnings that the application normally displays to the terminal window from which it was started. You can safely delete this file after your applications have been closed.

## Accessing Desktop Files from the Command Line

Because some users find themselves storing or copying the documents they often work with to the actual desktop, it is helpful to know how to access those files using the command line as well. Specifically, it is important to know the path to files that are stored on the desktop.

Files on the desktop are stored in ~/Desktop. For example, to create an empty file called emptyfile.txt on your desktop using the touch command you learned in Chapter 6, "Working with Files in the Shell," enter the following at a command line:

```
[you@workstation20 ~]$ touch ~/Desktop/emptyfile.txt
[you@workstation20 ~]$
```

Entering this command creates a file called emptyfile.txt on your desktop, as shown in Figure 26.3.

Command creates empty file in desktop folder

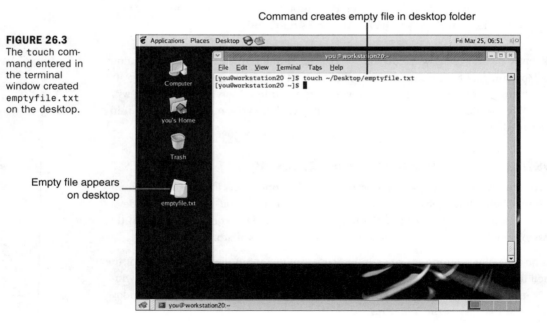

**FIGURE 26.3**
The touch command entered in the terminal window created emptyfile.txt on the desktop.

Empty file appears on desktop

Files and directories that are stored on the desktop can be accessed using any of the command-line file management techniques you learned in earlier chapters.

# Using Basic X Window System Applications

The desktop applications that are included with Fedora Core 4 are always easily accessible from the menus on the menubar; however, Fedora Core 4 also installs a set of desktop applications that are not accessible via the menus and must be launched via the command line. These applications are with a part of the X Window System itself, the underlying technology that forms the basis of the Fedora Core 4 desktop environment.

X Window System applications have wider compatibility; they can usually be found on any Linux or Unix computer with a graphical desktop environment of any kind, regardless of the system's manufacturer or desktop environment.

If you performed a custom installation of Fedora Core 4 in Chapter 2, "Installing Fedora Core 4," and opted not to install the GNOME or KDE desktop environments (as is often the case with a server-oriented system), the basic set of X Window System applications might be the only applications available to you at the desktop. They are also the only desktop applications available on many older Linux or Unix systems it is therefore important that you be familiar with a few of them in Linux or mixed Linux/Unix environments.

## Using a Desktop Terminal Without GNOME or KDE

If, when you installed Fedora Core 4, you chose to install the X Window System but not GNOME or KDE, the desktop you experience appears somewhat different from Fedora Core 4 desktop shown so far in this book. Furthermore, you don't have a menubar from which to launch a terminal application. Instead, you find yourself in a desktop environment called TWM, using the X Window System's more basic terminal application, xterm.

The TWM environment does have a menu; you can access it by clicking the **root window**—any area of the desktop not covered by an application window. You can launch a new terminal application in TWM at any time using this menu, as shown in Figure 26.4.

You can start the applications in the following sections from the command line in GNOME, KDE, or TWM.

**FIGURE 26.4**
The default X
Window System
desktop is quite
plain; here, the
TWM root menu
is used to
launch a new
xterm terminal
application.

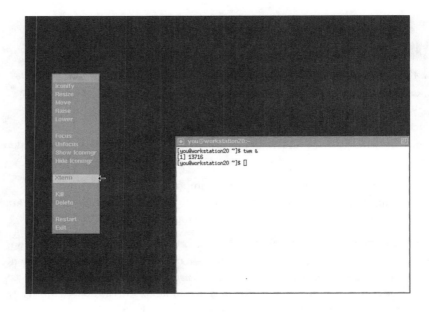

**By the Way**

**Getting to the TWM Environment**

You can also access the TWM environment by logging in using the Failsafe
Terminal session option at the Fedora Core 4 login screen and then entering the
command **twm &** at the single terminal on the failsafe desktop.

## Using X Window System Convenience Applications

The basic X Window System applications include a number of small convenience
applications that, when used together, create a more pleasant user experience.

The xclock application provides a nice-looking desktop clock. Entering **xclock &** at
the command line in a terminal window displays a clock, running the clock application in the background.

The xcalc application provides a functional calculator that can be used to perform
most simple types of calculations. Entering **xcalc &** at the command line in a terminal window displays the calculator, running the calculator application in the
background.

The xload application displays a graph of the workload on your system's processor
over time. On busy systems, this application can provide an indication of how

slowly your system might be responding to incoming network requests. The harder the processor is working, the higher the graph goes. Entering **xload &** at the command line in a terminal window displays the load graph, running the load application in the background.

The xmag application magnifies a small area of the screen by enabling you to click the area you would like enlarged. When you enter **xmag &** at the command line in a terminal window, the mouse pointer changes. Wherever your next mouse click occurs on the display, a 64-by-64 pixel area is magnified and displayed in an application window.

Figure 26.5 shows all these convenience applications being used on the Linux desktop.

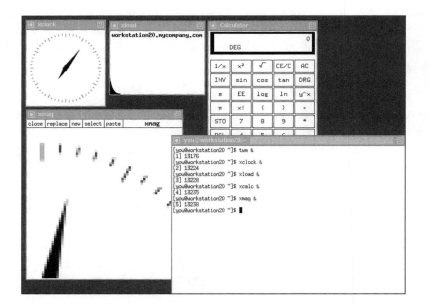

**FIGURE 26.5**
All these X Window System applications were started from the same terminal window.

## Want to Control Remote Applications?

You can control applications started using remote shells using the same job control tools for the local command line that you learned about in Chapter 20, "Creating, Editing, and Saving Text Files."

*By the Way*

# Interacting with the User in Shell Scripts

In Chapter 25, "Harnessing the Power of the Shell," you learned to write shell scripts to perform sequences of commands without user intervention. Sometimes it is also helpful to be able to get user input as a shell script is running—to allow the user of the script to make choices about how tasks will be performed, for example.

The xmessage command can be used in shell scripts to enable the scripts to interact easily with the user via the mouse.

## Using xmessage in Shell Scripts

To use xmessage in your shell scripts, you must call it from within a script by using the -buttons option and two arguments: a comma-separated list of buttons and the message that should be displayed to the user above the buttons. The format looks like this:

```
xmessage -buttons "button1,button2,button3" "My Message"
```

This command causes a dialog box with buttons labeled *button1*, *button2*, and *button3* to appear below the message My Message. For example, the following call to xmessage displays the dialog box shown in Figure 26.6:

```
xmessage -buttons "Yes,No" "Would you like some ice cream?"
```

**FIGURE 26.6**
A dialog box created by calling the xmessage command.

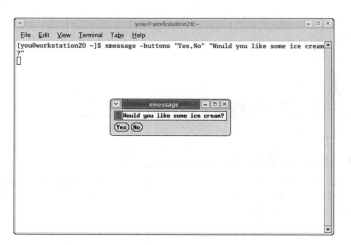

When the user clicks one of the buttons beneath the message, the dialog box disappears and returns a value to the script, which is assigned to the special shell variable $?. If the first button is clicked, the value 101 is assigned to the variable. If the second button is clicked, the value 102 is assigned to the variable, and so on.

## Sample xmessage Script

To illustrate the use of xmessage, let's study some sample scripts. These samples use techniques you learned in Chapter 25, so if you find yourself confused by the explanations, you should review Chapter 25 before continuing.

Suppose you want to create your own replacement for the rm command (used to remove files) that prompts the user with a confirmation dialog box before actually deleting a file. Listing 26.1 shows what a script called myrm, which does just this, might look like. Start an editor, create a file called ~/bin/myrm, and enter the listing. Then let's go over it line by line to see how it works.

**LISTING 26.1**    Sample Script for myrm **Command**

```
1:  #!/bin/sh
2:
3:  xmessage -buttons "Yes,No" "Remove file $1?"
4:  RESULT=$?
5:
6:  if [ $RESULT -eq 101 ]; then
7:      rm "$1"
8:  fi
```

This short shell script performs a simple function, so dissecting it is fairly easy:

▶ Line 1 begins with the standard header for a shell script file. This header is required for a shell script to work.

▶ Line 3 uses xmessage to display a dialog box with Yes and No buttons. The message is simply the words Remove file. This message is followed by the first argument supplied by the user, which is substituted for $1.

▶ Line 4 saves the value of the special variable $?, which contains the exit status of xmessage, to the variable RESULT. If the first button is clicked, the value of RESULT is 101. If the second button is clicked, its value is 102.

▶ Lines 6–8 check to see whether the value of RESULT is 101. If so, it means that the user clicked Yes, so the file is deleted. If not, no action is performed; the script simply reaches its end, so it exits without deleting the file.

To try out this script, use the chmod command to make myrm executable:

```
[you@workstation20 ~]$ chmod u+x ~/bin/myrm
[you@workstation20 ~]$
```

Then try using the script to delete a file like `myfile.tex`. Entering the following command causes the dialog box shown in Figure 26.7 to be displayed:

```
[you@workstation20 ~]$ myrm myfile.tex
```

Clicking the Yes button at this point causes the file to be deleted. Clicking the No button leaves the file intact.

**FIGURE 26.7**
The `myrm` command displays a dialog box asking whether you really want to delete the file you've supplied as an argument.

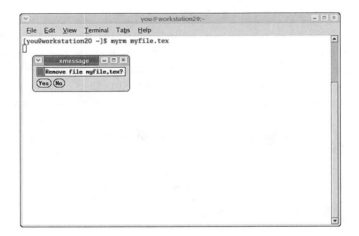

## Second Sample `xmessage` Script

One more example might help illustrate a more dynamic use of the `xmessage` command. Suppose you have a set of LaTeX files in your home directory. If you don't, create some empty LaTeX files now for purposes of illustration using the `touch` command:

```
[you@workstation20 ~]$ touch myfile.tex yourfile.tex oldfile.tex newfile.tex
[you@workstation20 ~]$
```

Now suppose you want to create a shell script that enables you to edit any one of your LaTeX files in an emacs window by typing **texedit** and selecting the name of your file using an xmessage dialog. To create this script, start a text editor window and enter Listing 26.2 as `~/bin/texedit`. Then let's go over it line by line.

**LISTING 26.2**    Sample Script for `texedit` Command

```
1:  #!/bin/sh
2:
3:  xmessage -buttons "$(ls -m *.tex)" "Which LaTeX file?"
4:  RESULT=$?
5:
6:  INDEX=100
```

**LISTING 26.2**  Continued

```
 7:  for TEXFILE in *.tex; do
 8:      INDEX=$(expr $INDEX + 1)
 9:      if [ $RESULT = $INDEX ]; then
10:          emacs $TEXFILE &
11:      fi
12:  done
```

This script is also relatively short, but its operation is somewhat more complex than the script in the first sample:

▶ Line 1 begins with the standard header for a shell script file. Again, the header is required for a shell script to work as expected.

▶ Line 3 uses xmessage and command substitution to display a dialog box with one button listing each .tex file in the current working directory. This is done with a call to the ls command using the -m option, which causes listed files to be separated by commas (see the ls manual page for details).

▶ Line 4 saves the value of the special variable $?, which contains the exit status of xmessage, to the variable RESULT. If the first button is clicked, the value of RESULT is 101. If the second button is clicked, its value is 102.

▶ Line 6 creates a variable that the script uses to count through the buttons one by one. Because clicking the first button results in the value 101, the counter begins at 100.

▶ Lines 7–12 create a for..do loop; the commands between for and done are executed once for each .tex file in the current working directory; each time through, the variable TEXFILE contains the name of a .tex filename in the current directory.

▶ Line 8 adds 1 to the value of INDEX for each time through the loop, meaning that for the first value of TEXFILE, the value of INDEX is 101; when the value of TEXFILE changes the second time through the loop, the value of INDEX changes once more to 102, and so on.

▶ Lines 9–11 watch the value of INDEX. When it is the same as the value of RESULT, meaning that the value of TEXFILE is the same as the button the user clicked, the emacs editor is started using TEXFILE as an argument.

Now let's look at the script in action. After you save the file ~/bin/texedit, remember to use the chmod command to mark it as executable so that you can call it at the command line:

```
[you@workstation20 ~]$ chmod u+x ~/bin/texedit
[you@workstation20 ~]$
```

The dialog box in Figure 26.8 appears after you enter the texedit command at the command prompt:

```
[you@workstation20 ~]$ texedit
```

**FIGURE 26.8**
The xmessage
dialog box
enables the
user to choose
between all the
.tex files in the
current working
directory.

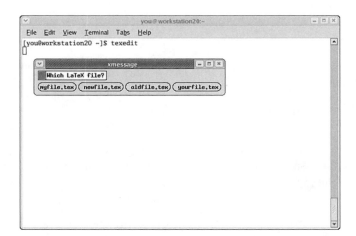

Clicking one of the filename buttons causes the file in question to be loaded into a new emacs editor application window.

# Scripting the File Manager

You can access shell scripts through the file manager and direct them to act upon selected files. To do this, you select files in the file manager and then right-click them to produce a list of shell scripts you've written. From this list, you then choose the scripts that you want to act upon the selected files. In the following sections, again you might need to refer to Chapter 25 if you have trouble following along with the sample scripts.

## Creating and Using File Manager Shell Scripts

To create shell scripts that can be used with the file manager (which is responsible for your desktop and the application windows used to copy, open, or move files), create and save any scripts that you want to the ~/.gnome2/nautilus-scripts directory.

When a script is called from the file manager, the script behaves just as if it had been called from the command line. The file manager passes the names of the selected files to the script as arguments that can then be accessed through the usual shell variables—$1 for the first argument, $2 for the second argument, and so on, or $@ to access the entire list of arguments at once.

## Sample File Manager Shell Script

To illustrate the use of shell scripts with the file manager, let's consider a sample script. Suppose you want to be able to create a backup copy of any file simply by right-clicking the file and selecting a menu option called FileBackup. This menu option would have the effect of creating a copy of the file, with the extension .bak added, in the ~/Backups directory.

Enter the script in Listing 26.3 into a text editor now and save it to ~/.gnome2/ nautilus-scripts. Then let's go through it line by line.

> **By the Way**

---

### If the Script Directory Doesn't Exist

You may find that the ~/.gnome2/nautilus-scripts directory does not yet exist. If this is the case, use the mkdir command to create it before saving the script or use the file manager to create it.

If you need a refresher, you can learn about the mkdir command in Chapter 6, "Working with Files in the Shell," and creating directories using the file manager in Chapter 5, "Working with Files on the Desktop."

---

**LISTING 26.3**    Sample FileBackup Script for Use with Nautilus

```
1:  #!/bin/sh
2:
3:  if [ ! -d ~/Backups ]; then
4:      mkdir ~/Backups
5:  fi
6:
7:  for BACKUPFILE in $@; do
8:      cp $BACKUPFILE ~/Backups/$BACKUPFILE.bak
9:  done
```

This script is reasonably short and reasonably simple as well, but it performs as expected. Here's how it works:

▶ Line 1 provides the standard shell script header.

▶ Lines 3–5 test to see whether the ~/Backups directory exists. If it doesn't, it is created with the mkdir command.

▶ Lines 7–9 are a for..do loop; Line 8 is repeated once for each filename supplied to the script as an argument. Each time through, the variable BACKUPFILE contains the name of a file that has been selected in the file manager for backup.

After you save the script and exit your editor, don't forget to make the script file executable:

```
[you@workstation20 ~]$ chmod u+x ~/.gnome2/nautilus-scripts/FileBackup
```

To test the script, right-click a file in the file manager window and select the Scripts menu. You see the new FileBackup script in the menu, as shown in Figure 26.9.

**FIGURE 26.9**
The new FileBackup script appears in the Scripts menu after it has been marked as executable.

If you select FileBackup from the Scripts menu, the file you right-clicked is copied with a .bak extension to the ~/Backups folder (this folder is created if it doesn't already exist).

Using Nautilus scripts of this sort, you can automate many types of file management functionality from the Linux desktop.

*Did you Know?*

## More Nautilus Scripting on the Internet

For a collection of existing Nautilus scripts and more detailed tutorial information, visit the website http://g-scripts.sourceforge.net/.

# Summary

In this chapter, you learned some less common but still useful and powerful techniques for using the Linux desktop.

First, you learned a little bit more about the Terminal application and how to use the terminal window to start and manage desktop applications as shell jobs.

You learned about the standard set of X Window System applications, which are present on most Unix desktop systems, whether or not environments like GNOME and KDE are available. They include programs such as xterm, xclock, and xcalc.

Finally, you learned to use the xmessage command and the Nautilus file manager to automate tasks using desktop tools while interacting with the user via the mouse.

# Q&A

**Q** *Is there a list of all the graphical applications' names so that I can start them from the command line in a terminal window?*

**A** No, there is no comprehensive list. You can find desktop applications mixed in with the programs in /usr/bin, /usr/local/bin, and /usr/X11R6/bin.

**Q** *When I use the xmessage command, I get an error message or an unexpected result. Why?*

**A** Remember to use the -buttons option and to enclose the comma-separated list of quoted button labels and the quoted message text as arguments.

**Q** *The sample Nautilus script won't work with files that have spaces in the filename. How can I fix this problem?*

**A** In the interest of keeping the script simple for illustrative purposes, we did not use techniques for accommodating filenames with spaces or other special characters. The website http://g-scripts.sourceforge.net/ provides freely copyable script code that enables Nautilus scripts to work with filenames containing spaces and other special characters.

# Workshop

The Workshop is designed to help you anticipate possible questions, review what you've learned, and begin learning how to put your knowledge into practice.

## Quiz

1. How would you start the GNOME text editor and cause it to load the file `~/myfile.tex` from the command line?

2. What command would you use to magnify and more closely inspect very small print in an application on your desktop?

3. How do you know which `xmessage` button was clicked in your shell scripts?

4. What directory contains Nautilus scripts?

## Answers

1. `gedit ~/myfile.tex &`

2. `xmag`

3. After `xmessage` exits, the special variable `$?` contains an exit status of `101` if the first button was clicked, `102` if the second button was clicked, `103` if the third button was clicked, and so on.

4. `~/.gnome2/nautilus-scripts`

## Activities

1. Improve the `FileBackup` script so that it displays a confirmation dialog box before backing up each selected file. The dialog box should display the name of the file and then ask the user to select Yes to back the file up or No to omit the file.

2. Place the new and improved `FileBackup` script in your Nautilus menu.

## CHAPTER 27

# Using Desktop Applications Remotely

## What You'll Learn in This Chapter:

▶ How the X Window System's remote display facility works

▶ How to use the `ssh` command to automate the remote display facility

▶ How to use the remote display facility manually when `ssh` is unavailable

▶ How to start an entire X session on a remote computer

You have learned to make effective use of both the Linux desktop and the Linux command line in many common work situations. In this chapter, you learn to use one of the most powerful features of the Linux/Unix computing paradigm and the X Window System: the ability to display running applications remotely—on the monitor of a separate PC on the network.

If you can master the techniques presented in this chapter, the process of using multiple Linux or Unix machines on your network, particularly for administrative tasks, will become an easy one.

---

**This Is a Networking-Oriented Chapter**

*By the Way*

Because many of the tasks discussed in this chapter occur on two computers simultaneously, illustrations are imperfect in demonstrating just what is going on at times.

Some amount of imagination and familiarity with using computers in networked environments will be helpful to your understanding when illustrations fall short.

---

# Understanding the X Window System Protocol

The Linux desktop environment, the X Window System, functions differently from the desktop environments of other operating systems, such as Microsoft Windows. X Window System applications rely on a network protocol to connect to the display on which they appear instead of drawing to the computer display directly. Figure 27.1 illustrates this concept.

Applications running on various computers

**FIGURE 27.1**
X Window System applications communicate with the desktop using a network protocol instead of drawing directly. Thus, applications need not run on the machine where they are displayed.

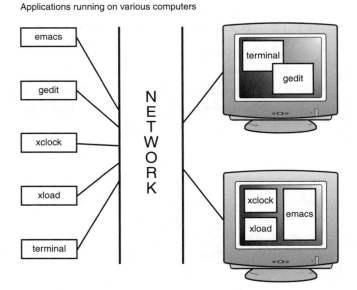

Although the network-oriented nature of the X Window System adds complexity to the desktop environment, it provides a native capability not available in any other operating system's desktop environment. You have the ability to run a program on one machine's processor while displaying the application window on another machine's desktop, automatically using the network for communication between the two. Using this technique, a system administrator working at a Linux computer can start and interact with application windows whose programs are actually running on one or more machines elsewhere on the network.

Simple examples of the uses for the networking capabilities of the X Window System include the following:

▶ Starting `xload` or other monitoring applications on multiple machines around the network but displaying them all on a single computer's desktop. This allows the load or status of a number of different Linux or Unix systems to be monitored graphically from a single location.

▶ Running graphical administration tools for remote systems from a central location. Instead of having to walk from computer to computer, an experienced Linux administrator can manage every Linux or Unix system on the network without ever leaving his or her workstation.

▶ Creating graphical dumb terminals. These computers have little processing power or storage, but instead run only the X Window System and can thus use the storage and processing power of another, more powerful Linux or Unix computer to provide applications and a complete desktop environment.

With the networking capabilities of the X Window System, the sky and your creativity are your only limits.

# Networking X Using the Secure Shell

The secure shell (ssh) command makes it easy to use the remote display facilities of the X Window System, using a command format similar to the one used for general-purpose remote logins. If you've forgotten the general-purpose use of the ssh command, review "Logging In Remotely Using ssh" in Chapter 24, "Using Other Systems Remotely at the Command Line."

---

**Firewall Causing You Trouble?**

If you find that many of the techniques in this chapter don't work for your Red Hat Fedora Core 4 system, see the section titled "Configuring Firewall Security for Remote Display" later in this chapter. There, you learn how to alter the firewalling rules on your Fedora Core 4 system to allow incoming ssh or X connections.

*Did you Know?*

---

## Displaying Single Remote Applications Using ssh

To launch a program on a remote computer, causing the application window for the program to appear on your local Red Hat Fedora 4 system's display, call the ssh command like this:

```
ssh -oForwardX11=yes -l user remotehost program
```

Replace *user* with your login account on the remote system, *remotehost* with the hostname of the remote system, and *program* with the program you want to run. For example, to launch a system load monitor to watch the activity of the processor on a system called `steppenwolf` where you have a login account called `joeuser`, you could enter the `ssh` command as follows:

```
[you@workstation20 ~]$ ssh -oForwardX11=yes -l joeuser steppenwolf
➥/usr/X11R6/bin/xload
joeuser@steppenwolf's password:
```

After you enter your password, the `xload` application appears, monitoring the processor load on the system called `steppenwolf`, as shown in Figure 27.2.

**FIGURE 27.2**
The `xload`
process has
been started
remotely on the
system called
`steppenwolf`,
but its appli-
cation window
appears on
`workstation20`.

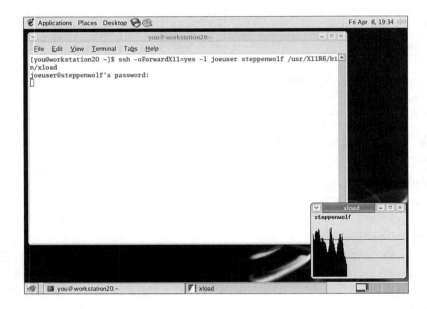

You are not limited to starting noninteractive applications like `xload` this way; you can just as easily remotely interact with programs such as `emacs` or `gedit`.

*By the*
*Way*

## Many Users Can Use the Same Machine at Once

Users new to Linux or Unix often wonder what will happen if they try to run applications on remote systems that are currently in use by other users.

The answer is simple: Everything works as expected, for both users. Because Linux and Unix are multiuser, multitasking, network-oriented operating systems, Linux simply and securely keeps track of which processes and files belong to each user who is currently using the system, whether the user is connected over the network or sitting directly in front of the machine. No user even needs to be aware of others who might be using the same computer system at the same time.

## Displaying Many Remote Applications Locally Using ssh

If you want to start a number of programs on a single remote system and cause each of their application windows to be displayed on your local desktop, you might find that calling ssh over and over again for each program you want to start is a time-consuming process.

In such cases, you will find that it is easier to start a terminal window and log in to the remote system using ssh, as you learned to do in "Logging In Remotely Using ssh" in Chapter 24. After you have a command line on the remote system in your terminal window, use the command line in the terminal to start desktop applications as you normally would from the command line. Each desktop application you launch this way is displayed on your local display, as shown in Figure 27.3.

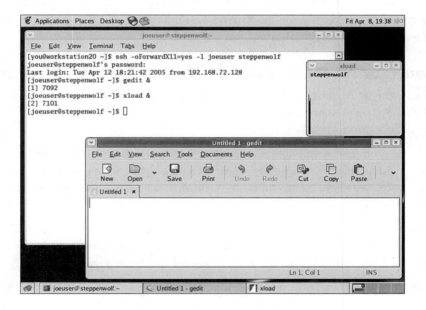

**FIGURE 27.3**
After you log in remotely using ssh, you can start as many applications as you like. Here, gedit and xload have been started.

Notice that you can start your applications in the background using the ampersand (&) or use command-line job control techniques as you would at any shell, even though this particular command line is provided by a remote computer system. For more information on shell job control techniques, refer to "Keeping Your Shell Programs Under Control" in Chapter 20, "Creating, Editing, and Saving Text Files."

## Displaying Local Applications Remotely Using ssh

You can also allow users at Linux desktops on other computers to start programs on your computer, whose application windows will appear on their displays. This is done using the same technique you just learned, performed in reverse order—that is, executing the ssh command on the remote system, listing your Red Hat Fedora 4 system as the host to connect to.

For example, if the user at a computer called workstation10.mycompany.com wanted to start the emacs program on your machine, workstation20, to be displayed on her screen using X's remote display capability, she could execute the following command from her command line:

```
ssh -oForwardX11=yes -l janeuser workstation20 emacs
```

As you can see, the process is symmetrical when using ssh: The system on which the ssh command is executed always displays the application, and the system to which ssh connects actually runs it.

## Configuring Firewall Security for Remote Display

Because the technique we're using in this chapter relies on ssh to manage the X Window System connections, your system must be configured to allow incoming ssh connections for this to take place.

Depending on the firewall options you selected when you installed Red Hat Fedora 4, your system might not currently accept incoming ssh connections. If you find that ssh requests from other systems are refused, you need to enable incoming ssh on your system.

To do this, choose Desktop, System Settings, Security Level to display the firewall configuration tool, as shown in Figure 27.4. Note that if you're not logged on as root, you'll be prompted for a password before the tool is displayed.

To ensure that you can accept incoming X and ssh connections, make sure that the SSH option is checked in the Trusted Services box to indicate that incoming ssh connections are to be allowed.

Check to accept
incoming
ssh connnections

FIGURE 27.4
In the Security
Level
Configuration
tool, you can
enable incoming
ssh connections
so that remote
users can use
remote display.

# Networking X Manually

Whenever possible, you should use the ssh technique already discussed for remote application display because the ssh command performs this task both easily and securely.

If you aren't able to use ssh for some reason and thus can't automate the security policy needs associated with the X Window System's remote display facility, you can use an alternate method—manipulation of the DISPLAY environment variable and xhost security tool—to allow and start remotely displayed applications manually. This can often be the case when you're interacting with older Unix systems in which ssh is not supported or economical.

If you want to run a Linux application on one system and display it on another this way, you must do two things:

▶ Configure the security features on the display system to allow remote applications to open application windows on the screen. You do this using the xhost command. By default, Red Hat Fedora 4 does not allow programs on remote systems to open application windows.

▶ Set the DISPLAY environment variable, which is used by applications to locate and use the graphical display, to point to the graphical display you want applications to use.

## Preparing to Network X Manually

To network X connections manually between Red Hat Fedora 4 systems, you must make one important adjustment to your firewall security configuration. In Red Hat Fedora 4, X does not accept manual remote connections by default. To use X remotely without ssh, you must first change this setting. You can enable incoming X connections by following these steps:

1. Start the tool by choosing Desktop, System Settings, Security Level.

2. In the Other Ports box, enter **6000:tcp** to allow incoming TCP connections on port 6000, which is used by the X Window System.

You are now ready to begin networking X Window System applications manually.

By the Way

### These Steps Are Designed for Red Hat Fedora 4

The steps given to unlock the manual networking capabilities of the X Window System are intended for Red Hat Fedora 4 users. These steps likely will differ in other Linux operating systems or on other Unix platforms. This is one of the reasons many users prefer to simply use ssh to network their X applications: It's much easier!

# Allowing Incoming X Connections with xhost

The xhost command instructs an X Window System desktop to allow other systems to open connections (application windows) for display. Because the host-based security model that makes xhost work is somewhat insecure, you should use xhost to allow incoming connections only if your computer systems are behind a firewall and all users on your network are trusted.

### The xhost Command Can Be Dangerous!

Using the xhost command to enable incoming X connections on a machine that is not behind a dedicated firewall can render your computer vulnerable to attacks, leading to data theft or destruction by malicious Internet users.

To instruct a Linux desktop environment to allow incoming connections via the xhost command, start a terminal application and type the following command:

xhost *hostname* ...

Replace *hostname* with the hostnames of the systems from which application connections should be accepted. For example, to allow programs running on the computer's workstation10 and mailservera to be displayed on the local computer's desktop, enter the following:

```
[you@workstation20 ~]$ xhost workstation10 mailservera
workstation10 being added to access control list
mailservera being added to access control list
[you@workstation20 ~]$
```

Fully qualified domain names and network addresses can also be used with the xhost command:

```
[you@workstation20 ~]$ xhost sunsystem1.yourcompany.com 10.1.24.192
sunsystem1.yourcompany.com being added to access control list
10.1.24.192 being added to access control list
[you@workstation20 ~]$
```

To list those systems currently allowed to connect to the local desktop and create windows on it, enter the xhost command without arguments:

```
[you@workstation20 ~]$ xhost
access control enabled, only authorized clients can connect
INET:workstation10.mycompany.com
INET:mailservera.mycompany.com
INET:sunsystem1.yourcompany.com
INET:10.1.24.192
[you@workstation20 ~]$
```

The listed systems can all open application windows on the local desktop. To remove a system from the list of systems that are allowed to connect to the local desktop, call xhost and place a minus (-) sign in front of the name of the system you would like to remove:

```
[you@workstation20 ~]$ xhost -workstation10.mycompany.com
workstation10.mycompany.com being removed from access control list
[you@workstation20 ~]$
```

# Displaying Local Applications Remotely

When you start a desktop application from the command line, the application decides where it should display its application window by looking at the DISPLAY shell variable. The DISPLAY variable should hold a value of the following format:

*host:0*

For example, if the desktop on the system called newton.mycompany.com has been configured with the xhost command to allow connections from

workstation20.mycompany.com (your system in this example), you can start an
application on workstation20, which shows its application window on newton, by
executing a command line like this one:

```
[you@workstation20 ~]$ DISPLAY=newton.mycompany.com:0 emacs &
[1] 6044
[you@workstation20 ~]$
```

### Access Control Can Be Disabled—But Watch Out!

In some rare cases, completely disabling access control and allowing all systems
to open windows on your display can be helpful. For example, if you're configuring
a local network that is not yet connected to the Internet, you might need to
repeatedly open and close remote applications from a number of different computer systems. Access control can be completely disabled by supplying the plus sign
(+) alone as an argument to xhost:

```
xhost +
```

When you want to reenable access control, once again preventing systems that
are not on the control list from connecting, supply the minus sign (-) alone as an
xhost argument:

```
xhost -
```

You should disable access control only in completely trusted environments—for
example, if your network is not connected to the Internet at all—because disabling access control can represent a major security risk and can lead to attacks,
resulting in data theft or destruction by users outside your network.

This particular command opens an emacs window on the desktop of the computer
newton.mycompany.com on your local network, assuming that the xhost command
has been used on the newton host to allow connections from workstation20. The
emacs program itself uses the processor and memory resources of your workstation
(in this case, workstation20) to run.

### The X Window System Supports Multiple Networked Displays

The :0 at the end of the DISPLAY variable's value indicates that the program
should display its application window on the first display on the remote host.
Because most PCs and workstations have only one display, you won't find yourself
using higher numbers in place of zero very often.

It can get tiresome to have to assign a value to the DISPLAY variable each time you
want to start a new program that displays remotely, particularly if you will be displaying several applications on the same remote display. In cases like this, you can

set the value of DISPLAY and then use the export command to force the value of DISPLAY to be used even when you are starting multiple jobs from the command line:

```
[you@workstation20 ~]$ DISPLAY=newton.mycompany.com:0
[you@workstation20 ~]$ export DISPLAY
[you@workstation20 ~]$
```

After you use export to make the value of DISPLAY apply to all jobs you start from the shell, you no longer need to set the value explicitly to cause an application to display remotely. For example, after you export the value of DISPLAY as shown, the following command starts an emacs window, loads the file myfile.txt, and displays the application window on newton.mycompany.com so that the user sitting in front of that machine can edit myfile.txt:

```
[you@workstation20 ~]$ emacs myfile.txt &
[2] 6078
[you@workstation20 ~]$
```

Remember, after you set and export the value of DISPLAY to point to another workstation, any applications you start are displayed remotely rather than locally. To restore the value of DISPLAY so that applications you start appear on your local display again, set the value of the DISPLAY variable to :0.0:

```
[you@workstation20 ~]$ DISPLAY=:0.0
[you@workstation20 ~]$ export DISPLAY
[you@workstation20 ~]$
```

After you set the value of DISPLAY to :0.0, any applications you start afterward from the command line appear on your local display.

## Displaying Remote Applications Locally

To display remote applications locally, you can use a similar technique. First, ensure that you have used the xhost command to enable incoming connections on the local desktop display, as discussed earlier in "Allowing Incoming X Connections with xhost." Then follow these steps:

1. In a terminal window on your desktop, use the telnet command to log in to the remote system from which you want to start programs that will display locally.

2. After you log in to the remote system with telnet, set and export the DISPLAY variable so that it refers to your local host system.

3. Start your desktop applications as normal; they then appear on your local display.

### Use `telnet` **Only When You Absolutely Have To**

Because the `telnet` command sends passwords across the network without first encrypting them, `telnet` is less secure than `ssh`. Malicious network users can steal passwords used in `telnet` sessions. For this reason, you should use `telnet` only if your network is behind a dedicated firewall, and instead should use the `ssh` techniques, discussed earlier this chapter, whenever possible.

This process is illustrated in the following sequence of commands. Assume that you are working at a system called workstation20.mycompany.com. This sequence starts the emacs application on a remote system called newton and displays its application window on your desktop:

```
[you@workstation20 ~]$ telnet newton
Trying 10.4.26.131...
Connected to newton.
Escape character is '^]'.
SunOS Unix (newton)
login: joeuser
Password:
[joeuser@newton joeuser]$ DISPLAY=workstation20.mycompany.com:0
[joeuser@newton joeuser]$ export DISPLAY
[joeuser@newton joeuser]$ emacs &
[1] 31221
[joeuser@newton joeuser]$
```

After you enter this sequence, the emacs application appears on your local display, running on the system called newton.

# Allowing and Starting Remote X Sessions

Although being able to run individual applications remotely is convenient, sometimes it would be more helpful to run an entire desktop session—beginning with the graphical login screen—from a remote location. This capability can be especially helpful when you're building diskless thin clients or using small computers with minimal Linux installations that need to function as full-fledged workstations.

By changing a setting in the Red Hat Fedora 4 login manager configuration, you can allow remote display of entire desktop sessions, from login through logout. After you make this change, you can launch remote sessions by supplying a special argument to the XFree86 command from a Linux console, or by using the Xvfb command from your desktop.

# Configuring the Login Manager for XDMCP

To allow users to remotely display entire X Window System sessions on a Fedora Core 4 host, you must configure the login manager (the program you see when you first start Red Hat Fedora 4) to allow requests that use the X Display Manager Control Protocol (XDMCP). To do this, start the GNOME Desktop Manager (GDM) Setup tool on the Fedora Core 4 in question by choosing Desktop, System Settings, Login Screen or on any Fedora Core system by typing **gdmsetup** from the command line when logged in as root. Once the tool starts, click the XDMCP tab to display the dialog box shown in Figure 27.5.

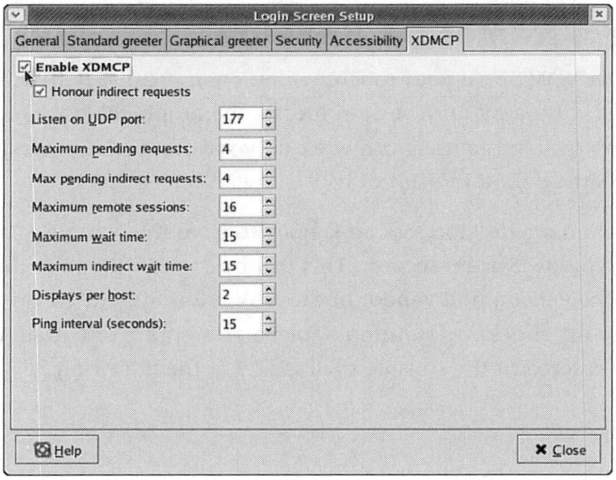

**FIGURE 27.5**
In the GDM Setup tool, check Enable XDMCP to allow other hosts on the network to log in to a desktop session on this host.

On the XDMCP tab, check the first box labeled Enable XDMCP. Then close the dialog box. Choosing this setting enables remote systems to query an entire X Window System session from your computer; your computer displays a login prompt on the remote machine, allowing users to log in and use applications and environments on your machine graphically.

Your firewall must also be properly configured before incoming XDMCP requests are accepted. To do this, start the Security Level Configuration tool as described earlier in this chapter and enter the following additional exceptions into the Other Ports entry box:

```
177:tcp,177:udp
```

This setting allows incoming traffic on port 177, which is the port used by the XDMCP protocol. For more information on using the Security Level Configuration tool to create exceptions for certain network ports, see "Managing the Red Hat Fedora 4 Firewall" in Chapter 30, "Security Basics."

> ### XDMCP Can Also Be a Security Risk
>
> The warning you have become accustomed to also applies here: You should enable incoming XDMCP requests only if your local area network lies behind a dedicated firewall. Allowing incoming XDMCP requests on a machine that is connected directly to the public Internet leaves you vulnerable to attacks, which can result in data loss or theft.

## Querying a Remote X Session

After you enable XDMCP on your machine, remote machines with the X Window System installed can query an X session (access the graphical login prompt on your machine). This way, remote users can work on your machine from login to logout, as if they were sitting right in front of it.

Traditionally, a remote desktop session is queried from the console, not from within an existing X Window System session. This can be done in a number of ways, depending on the version and vendor of the X Window System on the machine. On older Linux or Unix machines running XFree86 version 3.x or earlier, the command that should be entered at the console shell is one of the following:

```
X -query host
Xwrapper -query host
```

Replace *host* with the hostname or IP address of the machine on which an XDMCP session (login prompt) is to be requested. On more recent Linux machines running XFree86 version 4.x or later, including all Fedora Core machines, the command is

```
XFree86 -query host
```

Again, replace *host* with the hostname or IP address of the machine in question. For example, assuming that you have enabled XDMCP on your computer, workstation20, another Red Hat Fedora 4 user on a machine called danscomputer could access your graphical login prompt by entering the following command at the 501console shell:

```
[dan@danscomputer dan]$ XFree86 -query workstation20.mycompany.com
```

After Dan enters this command, the graphical desktop starts on danscomputer and a login prompt is displayed. When Dan logs in, however, he must log in using an account that exists on workstation20, and the desktop environment and

applications that Dan sees are also running on workstation20. In fact, Dan's entire
X Window System session is running on workstation20, even though it is being
displayed on his own monitor.

When you query an entire session this way, none of the other techniques in this
chapter—such as the ssh command or the DISPLAY environment variable—need
to be used; applications are automatically displayed remotely as a part of the
requested session.

# Querying a Remote X Session from the Desktop

On newer Linux and Unix systems, including all systems that run Fedora Core, you
can also start a remote desktop session from your own desktop. This has the effect of
creating a desktop-within-a-desktop: The remote desktop you connect to is displayed
inside an application window on your own desktop. This has several advantages:

▶ The application window for the remote desktop can be minimized or closed
just like any other application window.

▶ You can log in to many remote desktops at the same time, each one of them
appearing in an application window on your own desktop.

▶ Since the remote system only uses an application window on your own desktop, while you are logged in to the remote system, all your own desktop applications are still available to you.

The tool that makes this functionality possible is called the X Virtual Frame Buffer,
or Xvfb for short. To install the Xvfb command on a Fedora Core 4 system, follow
these steps:

1. Choose Desktop, System Tools, Add/Remove Applications to start the Package
Management tool.

2. Click the Details button next to the X Window System software package
group.

3. In the Details view for the X Window System software package group, check
the box next to xorg-x11-Xvfb, as shown in Figure 27.6.

4. Close the Details view; then click Update to install the Xvfb command.

Once the Xvfb command has been installed, you can query a remote desktop login
session by using Xvfb with the following arguments:

```
Xvfb -query remotehost -screen 0 heightxwidthxdepth
```

**FIGURE 27.6**
In the Details
view, check the
box next to
xorg-x11-Xvfb to
install the X
Virtual Frame
Buffer.

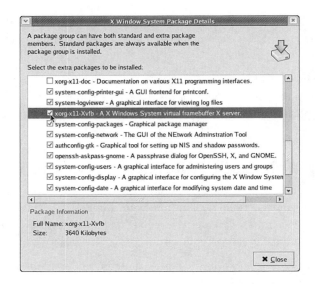

**FIGURE 27.6**
In the Details
view, check the
box next to
xorg-x11-Xvfb to
install the X
Virtual Frame
Buffer.

▶ Replace *remotehost* with the network hostname of the remote system that you want to log in to.

▶ Replace *height* and *width* with the height and width of the desktop that you want; typical sizes include 800×600 or 1024×768, but keep in mind that these should be smaller than the resolution of your own desktop, or the application window will be bigger than your desktop.

▶ Replace *depth* with the color depth you want for the remote desktop session. This should match the display depth of your own desktop. On most modern computers, this will be one of the following: 24, 16, 32, or 8. If a depth of 24 produces an error or inaccurate colors, try the others in succession until you find one that works.

As an example, to start a remote desktop session on a computer called timspc at a desktop resolution of 800×600, enter

```
[you@workstation20 ~]$ Xvfb -query timspc -screen 0 800x600x24
```

Within moments, an 800×600 pixel application window appears on your own desktop, displaying a desktop login prompt for timspc. After entering the username and password for your account on timspc, you are logged in to the desktop of timspc and can use it as if you were sitting physically in front of it.

# Summary

In this chapter, you learned to use one of the unique network capabilities of Unix operating systems to run applications on one machine while displaying their application windows on the graphical desktop of another machine. Specifically, you learned the following:

▶ How to use the ssh command to automate the process of launching remote applications for local display.

▶ How to use the xhost command to control connect permission to the local X Window System display on any Unix or Linux computer. Remember that the ssh method should be used in place of the xhost method whenever possible!

▶ How to use the DISPLAY environment variable in conjunction with the xhost command to start applications locally for remote display.

▶ How to use the telnet command when ssh isn't available in conjunction with xhost and DISPLAY to start applications remotely for local display.

▶ How to enable XDMCP and query entire remote X Window System sessions across the network.

When you master these techniques, your physical location in your network becomes less important because you can access applications of all kinds, whether graphical or text based, on any computer anywhere on your network, from the computer closest to where you are already standing.

# Q&A

**Q** *The X Window System manual page refers to another kind of security called* magic cookie authentication, *which is more secure than the* xhost *command. Why isn't it discussed here?*

**A** The magic cookie method of authentication is indeed more secure than the xhost command method, but it requires the use of several additional commands, as well as the use of a secure means of network communication to transfer the security token—usually ssh. When you use ssh to display applications remotely using the techniques outlined in this chapter, the magic cookie authentication method is automatically used for you anyway. In fact, ssh makes the process still more secure by encrypting all network transmissions. Because the magic cookie process is somewhat difficult to implement by hand and ssh automates it so well with added security to boot, you should simply use ssh whenever you can.

**Q** *Is the remote display facility limited to a one-to-one relationship? That is to say, can I display applications from multiple remote machines on my local display, or can I display local applications on a variety of remote displays simultaneously?*

**A** Yes. There is no limitation on the number of systems that can be involved in remote display connections; it is only required that systems have permission to connect to one another. This permission can be granted using either xhost or ssh, as described.

**Q** *I'm still a little unclear on the basic concept. For example, if I open a file dialog box on a remotely displayed application, which system's files will I see?*

**A** Only the application window itself is displayed remotely; all other aspects of the running program occur on the system where the program was launched. So, if a program running on newton is displayed on workstation20 and a file dialog box is opened, the files on newton appear in the file dialog box, even though the file dialog box itself appears on the display of workstation20. Remote display is simply a way to use a desktop application from a distance, taking advantage of network technology to accomplish this task.

**Q** *Does Fedora Core 4 support VNC? I want to be able to share my desktop with Windows and Mac users.*

**A** Yes. The Xvnc command can be used to start a VNC server on your desktop that remote users can use to access your computer. Consult the Xvnc manual page for more information. The native X11 desktop sharing tools are discussed in this chapter because they provide more functionality to Unix users and are somewhat more network-efficient.

# Workshop

The Workshop is designed to help you anticipate possible questions, review what you've learned, and begin learning how to put your knowledge into practice.

## Quiz

**1.** How would you start the gedit program on a computer called server10, displaying the application on your own desktop, if your login name on server10 is admin36?

2. How would you tell your desktop environment to allow incoming application window connections from a system called robslabmachine.mycompany.com?

3. Without using ssh, what sequence of commands would you enter to start emacs in the background but display its application window on a local system called laptop6.mycompany.com?

4. Why should you use the ssh method of displaying applications remotely rather than the xhost/DISPLAY method whenever possible?

## Answers

1. ssh -oForwardX11=yes -l admin36 server10 gedit

2. xhost robslabmachine.mycompany.com

3. DISPLAY=laptop6.mycompany.com:0
   export DISPLAY
   emacs &

4. Because the ssh method is considerably more secure, using magic cookie authentication and encrypting data and passwords as they are transmitted across the network.

## Activities

1. Use ssh in a terminal window to log in to a remote Linux computer system.

2. From the command line on the remote system, start an emacs window.

3. Use the emacs window to create and save a new text file on the remote system.

# CHAPTER 28

# Command-Line System Administration

## What You'll Learn in This Chapter:

▶ How to list and manage running processes

▶ How to start and stop system and network services

▶ How to create, mount, and unmount file systems by hand

▶ How to add and remove user and group accounts

▶ How to run maintenance, backup, and other tasks at regular intervals

▶ How to shut down or restart the system safely from the command line

System administration is generally a skill with which even casual Linux users must become familiar, simply in the course of day-to-day work. In this chapter, you learn how to perform a number of basic system administration tasks using command-line tools.

Because the tools in this chapter are all carried out at the command line—whether at the console, in a terminal window, or through a remote login—there aren't any figures. However, the examples illustrate the steps involved in each type of task.

### You Don't Have to Remember It All!

The information in this chapter is somewhat dense; it might be difficult to memorize in a single reading. Rather than try to remember it all, think of this chapter as a way to familiarize yourself with the topics and information presented; then you can refer to the text or index in the future, as the need arises.

Be sure to try some of the activities at the end of this chapter to help yourself become comfortable with these topics.

# Using the su Command

You already know that many tasks in Linux can be performed only by the root user. Most of the tasks you perform in this chapter fall into this category. It can often be inconvenient to have to log out and log back in as the root user simply to perform an administration task or two.

Fortunately, Linux provides a command that can be used to temporarily perform tasks as the root user. In its basic form, this command, su, is called without arguments. When you call su, you are prompted for the root password. If you can enter the password correctly, a subshell that is owned by the root user starts, and the shell prompt is displayed. Any commands you enter in the subshell work as though you were logged in as root. After you finish performing administration tasks, enter **exit** to close the subshell and return to the normal user command prompt.

The following lines show a user using the su command to become the root user, issuing a typical administration command to change the password of a user (a command you learn about later in this chapter) and then exiting:

```
[you@workstation20 ~]$ su
Password:
[root@workstation20 you]# passwd janeuser
Changing password for user janeuser
New UNIX password:
Retype new UNIX password:
passwd: all authentication tokens updated successfully
[root@workstation20 you]# exit
[you@workstation20 ~]$
```

*Did you Know?*

---

### Notes About Using the su Command

You know when you are working as the root user on a Fedora Core 4 system because the command prompt ends with a hash mark (#) instead of a dollar sign ($).

Remember to use the su command only when you need to perform an administration task that can't be performed as a normal user. Doing any real work as the root user is a dangerous proposition because Linux does exactly what root says, even if it is harmful to the system itself.

---

# Managing System Processes

Thus far, you haven't had to worry much about which processes were running and what they were called. At most, you've used the jobs command to manage a list of jobs started from a single shell's command line.

Sometimes, however, you need to list and modify running processes on a systemwide basis. Using the command line, you can list all the running processes on a system, kill processes by their process ID number, or reprioritize processes relative to other processes in the system so that you can control processor time allocation on a busy system.

Because normal users can list all processes but have access to *modify* only their own processes, management of systemwide processes is often done as the root user so that all processes can be managed and/or modified.

## Listing Running Processes

The ps command lists processes that are currently running. Because a given Linux system might have a very long list of running processes, and because so much data can be displayed about the properties and resources of each process, the ps command supports a wide range and variety of options to modify its behavior.

The simplest way to call ps is without arguments. Whether called by root or by a normal user, calling the command this way has the effect of listing all the processes owned by the current login with information in several columns:

```
[you@workstation20 ~]$ ps
  PID TTY          TIME CMD
 971  pts/0  00:00:00 bash
 1028 pts/0  00:00:00 ps
[you@workstation20 ~]$
```

This basic ps listing is very small because it includes only those processes owned by the user who has called ps and that were started from the command line. This listing indicates that only two processes have been started by you at the command line: the bash program (the login shell, which provides the command line) and the ps program, which lists itself because it is running, actively displaying the list of processes owned by the user. There are several columns of information in the ps output:

▶ The PID column displays the systemwide process ID number. When you learn to kill or reprioritize processes in the following sections, you use this number in referring to specific processes.

▶ The TTY column displays the system terminal from which the process was started.

▶ The TIME column displays the amount of real time that has been *actively* used by the process since its start. For many processes, these numbers are very small because processes like the shell are typically asleep much of the time waiting for user input, rather than actively calculating or working.

▶ The CMD column displays the command entered to start the process, possibly including (depending on the options supplied to ps) options or arguments supplied by the user on the command line.

The basic ps listing can be helpful when you're logged in as a normal user and simply want to manage your own processes. However, from a system administration perspective, it is often important to get information about all processes currently running on a Linux system or to get extended information about the processes being listed. This way, you can monitor the behavior of multiple users or server processes as the system functions on a day-to-day basis.

By supplying options or arguments to the ps command, you can change the types of processes that are listed and the information that is displayed about each process. The most common and useful ps options are shown in Table 28.1.

**TABLE 28.1    Common Options Used to Alter the Behavior of the ps Command**

| Option | Description |
| --- | --- |
| x | Do not limit process listing to those processes launched from a terminal; include, for example, processes started from a menu or taskbar icon. |
| v | List memory use information in the output |
| a | Display processes launched from a terminal owned by all users, not just by the user issuing the ps command. |
| -e | List all processes—those owned by any user on the system, whether or not they are launched from a terminal. |
| -f | Do a *full* listing of information, including process owner, process parent ID, and start time, among other things. |
| -U *user* | List only processes owned by the user whose login ID is *user*. |
| -G *group* | List only processes owned by the members who belong to the group known as *group*. |
| -H | Use indentation and sorting to show process parent and child relationships visually in the ps output. |

You can mix and match the ps options listed in Table 28.1 on the command line with relative impunity.

Perhaps the two most common ways to call the ps command are with the -e and -f options or with the a and x options, in the following formats:

```
ps -ef
ps ax
```

Both of these commands have similar effects: They display a listing of processes owned by all users, including those processes not launched from a controlling terminal. These two options enable the root user (or any other user, for that matter) to get a quick listing of all running processes on the system.

---

### Where to Learn More

The ps command is quite powerful and flexible, and it's capable of accepting numerous options and displaying a great deal of information about running processes. The ps command is far too involved to explore fully in this chapter. For more information on using ps, consult the ps manual page. For more information on reading manual pages, refer to Chapter 18, "Becoming Familiar with Shell Environments."

A more complete printed reference for ps can be found in *Sams Teach Yourself Unix System Administration in 24 Hours*.

*By the Way*

---

## Adjusting Process Priority

The root user can adjust the priority of any running process upward (less CPU time) or downward (more CPU time) using the renice command and the process ID number of the related process. This way, the administrator can ensure that critical processes on an overloaded system get as much CPU time as possible, sometimes at the expense of other processes. To use the renice command, call it as follows:

```
renice priority pid
```

Replace *priority* with the desired priority, from -20 (highest priority) to +19 (lowest priority). Replace *pid* with the process ID number of the process whose priority you want to change. For example, to maximize the priority of process number 664 while minimizing the priority of process 702, you enter the following:

```
[root@workstation20 you]# renice -20 664
664: old priority 0, new priority -20
[root@workstation20 you]# renice +19 702
702: old priority 0, new priority 19
[root@workstation20 you]#
```

You can see the effects of renice operations in the output of the ps command as well because of the appearance of N (decreased priority) or < (increased priority) in the STAT column, as follows:

```
PID TTY  STAT TIME COMMAND
[...]
 664 ?   S<   0:00 /usr/sbin/sshd
 678 ?   S    0:00 xinetd -stayalive -reuse -pidfile /var/run/xinetd.pid
 702 ?   SN   0:00 sendmail: accepting connections
 712 ?   S    0:00 sendmail: Queue runner@01:00:00 for /var/spool/client
[...]
```

This fragment shows process 664 with a status of S<, which indicates a sleeping process with increased priority relative to other processes. Process 702, on the other hand, shows a status of SN, indicating a sleeping process with decreased priority relative to other processes.

Only the root user can adjust process priority downward (increased priority). Normal users can adjust the priorities of their own processes upward (decreased priority) if they choose.

# Killing Running Processes

Sometimes you need to forcefully kill a running process—for example, if a buggy piece of software has stopped responding, or if a single process has for some reason "run away" and is using vast amounts of CPU time, thus robbing the system of productivity potential.

To kill a running process, use the kill command followed by the process ID number of the process you want to kill. For example, to kill process 702, enter the following:

```
[root@workstation20 you]# kill 702
[root@workstation20 you]#
```

This command sends a signal to process 702 that termination has been requested. Process 702 closes any open files and attempts to exit gracefully. From time to time, you find that even after trying to kill a process, it remains in the process list. Processes that can't be removed with a normal kill must then be terminated with the -KILL argument:

```
[root@workstation20 you]# kill -KILL 702
[root@workstation20 you]#
```

Because the -KILL argument is fairly destructive—it doesn't give a process any chance to close open files or network connections, but rather closes them forcefully as is—you should use it only when other termination attempts fail.

---

### Other Signals and Another Way to Kill

From time to time, you might also see references to the commands `kill -9` and `kill -HUP`.

The `kill -9` command is equivalent to `kill -KILL` and works because signal number 9 is the number used by the system itself to identify the `SIGKILL` signal.

The `kill -HUP` command sends the `SIGHUP` or "hangup" signal to a process. In theory, this signal is supposed to cause a process to restart itself (often to cause recently edited configuration files to be reread). Many server and root-level processes understand this signal, but many user-level processes (for example, a `gedit` or an `emacs` process) either ignore it or treat it like a normal terminate request. The `-HUP` signal is thus best used only when you are very familiar with a process or when the documentation for a particular program suggests it.

Another command, the `killall` command, is sometimes used to kill all processes of a given name, as in the following example:

```
killall emacs
```

The `killall` command can certainly be convenient, but use of this command is *not* recommended, especially on busy systems. Experience over decades of Unix use has demonstrated that it is too easy on a busy system to miskey or to misread the output of `ps` and then, using `killall`, to kill in one single step any number of important processes that shouldn't have been killed!

---

As you expect, the root user is able to terminate or kill any process in the system by process ID, and normal users are able to terminate or kill only processes that they own.

# Managing Running Services

After looking at the lengthy process lists in the preceding sections, you might be wondering just what most of the listed processes actually *are*. Even though Fedora Core 4 is intended to be a desktop-oriented operating system, many of these processes are system and network services of the sort that servers typically offer. In the Unix world, even desktops often need to perform server-oriented tasks such as accepting remote logins or transferring files across the network.

As Linux operates, some of the services it offers are running and others aren't. The default set of services running at any given time is determined by the system's current **runlevel**. A Linux system is always at a specific runlevel; available runlevels are numbered 0 through 6. Each runlevel is associated with a specific list of services, which are started when the system enters the runlevel.

Changes to the list of running services can be made by manipulating the list of services associated with the current runlevel or by changing the default runlevel at which the system operates; both of these tasks are discussed in the following sections.

## Understanding Runlevels

When your Linux system boots, the first process started by the kernel (the core of the operating system) is called init. The init process is responsible for starting all other processes in the system—from the system and network services to the graphical desktop environment. So, how does the init command know what to start?

One primary file, the /etc/inittab file, controls just what init does each time the system starts. A complete description of the format of the /etc/inittab file is beyond the scope of this book, and is better left to an advanced text on system administration. Near the beginning of the /etc/inittab file, however, you see a line that begins with the letters id, something like this one:

```
id:5:initdefault:
```

This line decides the default runlevel of your Fedora Core 4 system. The system in this example has a default runlevel of 5. Recall that seven runlevels are available, numbered 0 through 6. A list of these runlevels and their traditional meanings is shown in Table 28.2.

**TABLE 28.2    The Linux Runlevels and Their Meanings**

| Runlevel | Description |
| --- | --- |
| 0 | Halt. When this is the current runlevel, the system is in the process of shutting down. |
| 1 | Single-user. This runlevel includes little more than a single virtual console running a single command line. Virtually every other service is disabled. This runlevel is usually used for critical system maintenance, such as recovering from hack attacks or repairing disk corruption. |
| 2 | Multiuser, sans file services. This runlevel starts most services but does not enable network file service connections. |
| 3 | Full multiuser. This runlevel starts all enabled services but does not start the X Window System (or, by extension, any Linux desktop environment). Instead, users are able to use virtual consoles only. |
| 4 | User-defined. No conventional definition applies to runlevel 4; it is fully open to user configuration. |

**TABLE 28.2**   Continued

| Runlevel | Description |
| --- | --- |
| 5 | Full multiuser with X. This runlevel starts all enabled services *and* the X Window System and Linux desktop environments. Most Fedora Core 4 users find runlevel 5 to be their default. |
| 6 | Reboot. When this is the current runlevel, the system is in the process of rebooting. |

At any given time, a Linux system is running at a runlevel between 0 and 6. Controlling the list of automatically started services on your Linux system is a matter of setting a default runlevel and then configuring the services associated with that runlevel. You can change the default runlevel at which your system starts by editing the id line in the /etc/inittab file and inserting the runlevel number of your choice. For example, if you want to start with a default runlevel of 3, you edit the line to read as follows:

```
id:3:initdefault:
```

You learn how to control the list of services associated with each runlevel by using the chkconfig command in the next section.

---

### You Can Change Your Runlevel in Midstream

You can change your system's current runlevel without rebooting. This has the effect of changing the list of currently active services as well. To do so, call the init command by hand, supplying the desired runlevel as an argument. For example, to switch to runlevel 3 without rebooting, you type the following:

```
/sbin/init 3
```

After you enter the command, the system takes a few moments to settle down as processes are started and stopped before the system enters runlevel 3, where it remains until you switch again explicitly or reboot.

*Did you Know?*

---

## Selecting Automatically Started Services

In Fedora Core 4, the /sbin/chkconfig command is used at the command line to manage the list of services that are started automatically each time the system starts at a given runlevel. To see a list of available services and the current status of each with respect to each runlevel, call the chkconfig command using the --list option. The output appears in two parts, as shown in the following output fragments:

```
[root@workstation20 you]# /sbin/chkconfig --list
NetworkManager   0:off   1:off   2:off   3:off   4:off   5:off   6:off
acpid            0:off   1:off   2:off   3:on    4:on    5:on    6:off
anacron          0:off   1:off   2:on    3:on    4:on    5:on    6:off
apmd             0:off   1:off   2:on    3:on    4:on    5:on    6:off
atd              0:off   1:off   2:off   3:on    4:on    5:on    6:off
[...]
vncserver        0:off   1:off   2:off   3:off   4:off   5:off   6:off
winbind          0:off   1:off   2:off   3:off   4:off   5:off   6:off
xfs              0:off   1:off   2:on    3:on    4:on    5:on    6:off
ypbind           0:off   1:off   2:off   3:off   4:off   5:off   6:off
yum              0:off   1:off   2:off   3:off   4:off   5:off   6:off
[root@workstation20 you]#
```

*Did you Know?*

**Too Much Information from** chkconfig –list**?**

Remember, you can page the lengthy output of the chkconfig --list command through a pager such as more by using pipes:

/sbin/chkconfig --list ¦ more

There are two components to the output of the chkconfig command:

▶ The first half of the output lists a number of system and network services in the first column; subsequent columns list the on or off status of that service in each runlevel, from 0 through 6.

▶ The second half of the chkconfig output, which is present if you have installed many of the network services discussed in Chapter 33, "Offering Network File Services," or 34, "Offering Web and FTP Service," lists a number of more basic services managed by the xinetd service. Each of the more basic xinetd services is either on or off globally, for all runlevels for which xinetd is active.

A complete listing of, and set of descriptions for, all these services is beyond the scope of this book and better left to a book on Unix-style networking. However, some of the best-known services that can appear in the output of chkconfig are described in Table 28.3.

**TABLE 28.3**   The Most Common Services Manageable by chkconfig

| Service | Description |
| --- | --- |
| httpd | The Apache web server is used to answer incoming http requests to your Linux system. |
| sendmail | The Sendmail SMTP server is used to enable your Linux system to act as a full-fledged SMTP mail server. |

**TABLE 28.3**  Continued

| Service | Description |
| --- | --- |
| nfs | The Network File System service is used to enable your Linux system to act as a file server to other Unix or Linux computer systems. |
| named | The BIND service is used to enable your Linux system to act as a domain name server to other computers on your network. |
| smb | The Samba service is used to enable your Linux system to act as a file server to Windows computer systems. |
| sshd | The Secure Shell service is used to enable your Linux system to provide secure remote logins. |
| telnet | The Telnet service is used to enable your Linux system to provide less secure but more backward-compatible remote logins. |
| vsftpd | The File Transfer Protocol service is used to enable your Linux system to allow incoming File Transfer Protocol (ftp) logins. |

You can globally enable or disable any of the services in Table 28.3 or the services in the chkconfig --list output by calling chkconfig and supplying first the name of the service and then the word on or off as an argument. For example, to completely disable both web service and incoming telnet service, you would enter the following two commands:

```
[root@workstation20 you]# /sbin/chkconfig httpd off
[root@workstation20 you]# /sbin/chkconfig telnet off
[root@workstation20 you]#
```

You can easily check to see whether your changes have taken effect by using the chkconfig --list command again in combination with the grep command to filter the output. For example, to check on the new status of the httpd service, enter the following:

```
[root@workstation20 you]# /sbin/chkconfig --list | grep httpd
httpd           0:off    1:off    2:off    3:off    4:off    5:off    6:off
[root@workstation20 you]#
```

For services not managed by xinetd (those in the first half of the chkconfig listing), you can also enable or disable services on a runlevel-by-runlevel basis by using the --level option, supplying the level to change as the first argument. For example, to reenable web service for runlevel 3 only and verify the result, you enter the following commands:

```
[root@workstation20 you]# /sbin/chkconfig --level 3 httpd on
[root@workstation20 you]# /sbin/chkconfig --list | grep httpd
httpd           0:off    1:off    2:off    3:on     4:off    5:off    6:off
[root@workstation20 you]#
```

---

**Uninstalled Services**

Services that haven't been installed on your system will not be listed in the output of chkconfig. If you find that you want to offer a common network service that hasn't been installed on your system, refer to Chapter 31, "Installing Linux Software."

---

After making changes to your chkconfig configuration, you need to reboot or use the service command in the next section for the changes you've made to your current runlevel to take effect.

# Stopping, Starting, and Restarting Running Services

Sometimes over the course of a network's lifetime, it is helpful to be able to temporarily stop a running service that is normally offered, to temporarily offer a service that is not normally offered, or to restart a running service on your Linux system. Often this is the case when you have changed a configuration file or when a service seems to have become unstable or overloaded.

You do not need to use the chkconfig utility or restart your system to make temporary changes of this sort. You can use the service command to stop, start, or restart running services one by one. To do this, call the service command, supplying the service whose name matches an entry in the chkconfig service list as the first argument and either stop, start, or restart as a second argument.

For example, to start the httpd service when it hasn't already been running, enter the following command:

```
[root@workstation20 you]# /sbin/service httpd start
Starting httpd:                    [ OK ]
[root@workstation20 you]#
```

To stop the service once again, call service with httpd as an argument again, but with stop as the second argument instead:

```
[root@workstation20 you]# /sbin/service httpd stop
Stopping httpd:                    [ OK ]
[root@workstation20 you]#
```

The restart argument is used in the same way to force a running service to restart, usually after you edit its configuration file (to activate new changes) or if the service has encountered a bug and stopped responding or encountered other problems.

The changes you make to the running status of a service this way last only until the system is rebooted; for example, if you call service with httpd start to start your web server but don't have the httpd service enabled via chkconfig, the next time you reboot, the httpd service is not activated automatically.

# Managing File Systems

The ability to manage the configuration and availability of file systems is an important system administration skill, particularly for systems heavily involved in a network's infrastructure. At various times, you might need to configure and add an additional hard drive to a server system or provide system services with access to files on a separate file server. For these types of tasks, you need to know how to create, mount, and unmount file systems.

**Creating** a file system refers to the process by which a hard drive or other storage device is made ready to store files (this process is often called **formatting** in other operating systems). **Mounting** a file system refers to the process of making the contents of a device or network share available to users and processes within the Linux file system. **Unmounting** a file system refers to the process of disconnecting a device or network share and its contents from the Linux file system.

---

**These Sections Assume Knowledge of PC Hardware**

*By the Way*

Much of the rest of the "Managing File Systems" subsections assume that you have some familiarity with PC hardware, such as hard drives, removable storage devices, and SCSI hardware. If this is not the case, you might need to refer to additional sources of information about PC hardware to make use of the information presented here.

---

## Creating File Systems

Before you can mount and use a new or empty storage device like a hard drive, Zip or Jaz disk, or other removable storage device with Linux, you must create a file system on it. For purposes of example, let's build an ext2 file system in this chapter.

---

**Other Tools for Dealing with Linux File Systems**

*By the Way*

If you prefer to use metadata-journaled file systems, such as ext3 or reiserfs, or file systems associated with other operating systems, such as vfat or minix, you need to refer to the fdisk and mkfs commands and man pages instead of using parted. For most Linux users interested in general-purpose data storage, however, the ext2 file system and parted command work well.

---

Two major steps are involved in creating a new `ext2` file system for use with Linux:

**1.** Identify the name of the device where the new file system is to be created.

**2.** Create a partition on the device and format that partition using the desired type of file system, such as a Linux `ext3` file system or a Windows FAT32 file system.

The name of the device where the new file system and partition are to be created depends on the type of device and the type of connection through which the device communicates with your computer system. Most often, the device is connected either through an IDE channel or a SCSI controller.

▶ For IDE devices, the name of the device is `/dev/hda`, `/dev/hdb`, `/dev/hdc`, or `/dev/hdd`, depending on whether the device is connected to the primary master, primary slave, secondary master, or secondary slave channels, respectively.

▶ For SCSI devices, the name of the device is `/dev/sda` through `/dev/sdg` (or higher) depending on two factors—the position of the device in the SCSI ID chain and the number of earlier storage devices present. The first SCSI hard drive or random-writable (that is, not CD-R, CD-RW, or tape) device found is `/dev/sda`, the second is `/dev/sdb`, and so on, regardless of the absolute SCSI ID number.

After you identify the device on which you want to create a new file system for use with Linux, you call `parted` with the device name as an argument followed by the `print` option to display information about the device's size and any existing partitions that might reside on it:

```
[root@workstation20 you]# /sbin/parted /dev/sdb print
Disk geometry for /dev/sdb: 0.000-3992.717 megabytes
Disk label type: msdos
Minor   Start   End       Type      Filesystem Flags
1       0.031   3992.717  primary   FAT
Information: Don't forget to update /etc/fstab, if necessary.
[root@workstation20 ~]$
```

In this particular example, one existing partition of the FAT (Windows) type must be removed before a new partition or file system can be created. The first column indicates that this is partition 1 on the device `/dev/sdb`. To remove it, use `parted` with the `rm` option and the number of the partition to remove as an argument. Then call `parted` with the `print` option to verify that the partition has been removed:

```
[root@workstation20 you]# /sbin/parted /dev/sdb rm 1
[root@workstation20 you]# /sbin/parted /dev/sdb print
```

```
Disk geometry for /dev/sdb: 0.000-3992.717 megabytes
Disk label type: msdos
Minor  Start    End    Type    Filesystem Flags
Information: Don't forget to update /etc/fstab, if necessary.
[root@workstation20 you]#
```

_Did you_
_Know?_

## What If You Get an Unrecognized Disk Label Error?

If you are attempting to create a file system on a brand new disk, the print option of parted might give you an "unrecognized disk label" error. If this is the case, you need to run the following command first and then proceed with the print option and the rest of this section:

```
/sbin/parted /dev/sdb mklabel msdos
```

This command prepares the disk for use on a standard PC computer with Linux; you can then partition and create file systems on the disk as usual.

_Watch_
_Out!_

## Deleting Partitions

When you are deleting partitions, be sure that you do not delete partitions on the wrong device. You don't want to lose valuable files on a device you're already using!

With existing partitions removed, you are free to create new partitions. This is done using the parted command as follows:

```
parted device mkpartfs primary fstype begin end
```

Replace *device* with the device name where you're creating a new file system, *fstype* with either fat (for a Windows file system) or ext2 (for a Linux file system), and *begin* and *end* with the begin and end positions of the new partition, in megabytes.

For example, to create a Linux file system the size of the entire disk shown in the examples thus far, you issue the following parted command:

```
[root@workstation20 you]# /sbin/parted /dev/sdb mkpartfs primary ext2 0 3992.717
[root@workstation20 you]# /sbin/parted /dev/sdb print
Disk geometry for /dev/sdb: 0.000-3992.717 megabytes
Disk label type: msdos
Minor  Start    End    Type    Filesystem Flags
1    0.031  3992.717 primary  ext2
Information: Don't forget to update /etc/fstab, if necessary.
[root@workstation20 you]#
```

You can create up to four partitions on any device using this technique; Linux and Windows partitions can be freely intermixed.

### Don't Make Partitions That Overlap!

You must be sure that you do not cause partitions to overlap. For example, if you create a partition from 0–300MB, your second partition must not begin earlier than 301MB. If you try to cause partitions to overlap, you receive an error message.

File systems you create this way are referred to by appending their partition number to the device name. For example, when you learn to mount file systems in the next section, you mount the first partition on /dev/sdb by referring to /dev/sdb1, the second partition by referring to /dev/sdb2, and so on.

### Creating an ext3 Partition?

When you use parted, you create an ext2 filesystem. This basic Linux filesystem type is fast and very reliable, but is subject in very, very rare circumstances to filesystem corruption caused by brownouts or similar situations in which Linux is suddenly and improperly shut down.

The slower ext3 filesystem is nearly corruption-proof except in cases of hardware failure, and might thus be more appropriate for mission-critical and server environments. To create an ext3 filesystem once you have used parted to create a partition, use the mkfs.ext3 command in conjunction with the full device name of the partition you just created, as discussed earlier. For example, to make an ext3 filesystem on partition number 2 of /dev/sdb, enter

    /sbin/mkfs.ext3 /dev/sdb2

### For More Detailed parted Instructions...

For comprehensive documentation of the parted command, visit the online parted manual, which can be found in the alphabetically sorted online list of GNU manuals at http://www.gnu.org/manual/.

## Mounting and Unmounting File Systems

Whether you want to access a newly created file system, the data on an existing device or file system, or the data on a network share, in the Linux operating system, you must first mount a data storage area before you are able to read from or write to it. Some more common data storage areas, like those on USB keys or CD-ROM drives, are automatically mounted by Fedora Core 4 and appear instantly on the desktop when connected. For those that aren't automatically mounted, however, the following four steps must be performed:

1. You must create or identify a **mountpoint**. This is an empty directory somewhere in your existing Linux file system that you choose and/or create where the contents of the new data storage area will eventually be accessed.

2. You must identify the device name or network source of the data area. If you have just created a file system on a disk device in the previous section and now want to mount it, you use a device name like /dev/hda1 or /dev/sda1. If you are mounting a network file system, this is supplied by your network administrator and is a hostname followed by a path, such as fileserver.mycompany.com:/pub/ storagearea.

3. You must identify the *type* of file system you are mounting. For nearly all Windows file systems, including removable devices such as floppy disks or Zip disks, this is vfat. For Linux file systems, this is usually ext2, ext3, or reiserfs. For networked file systems, this is usually nfs. For CD-ROM devices, this is iso9660, and for DVD devices, it's udf. If in doubt, contact your media provider or network administrator.

4. You must issue a correctly formed mount command to supply all the following information to Linux so that the data or storage area can be available to you.

The format of the mount command is as follows:

```
mount -t fstype [-o options] datasource mountpoint
```

Replace fstype with the type of file system (vfat, ext2, ext3, reiserfs, nfs, iso9660, udf, or other type you have been instructed to use). Replace datasource with the device name (/dev/hda1, /dev/sda1, and so forth) or network path (address:/path). Replace mountpoint with the place in your local file system where this data or this storage area is to appear. The -o options option is not required but can be used to provide additional options, usually one of the following:

▶ -o ro specifies that the file system should be mounted read-only. Any attempts to write to it by anyone (even the root user) will fail. Note that CD-ROM devices are always mounted read-only, whether or not you supply this option.

▶ -o umask=0000 is used with Windows FAT32 file systems to allow *all users* to read and write any data on this device. Use this option with extreme caution; it allows any user to remove any file on the file system in question! This option is generally used on personal Linux computers that dual-boot with Windows, to allow all the Windows files on a mounted Windows hard drive to be accessed by normal user accounts.

Additional options can be found in the man page for the mount command.

To illustrate, if you want to mount the ext2 file system you created on /dev/sdb1 in the previous section to a new directory called /publicspace, you first create /publicspace and then issue the mount command supplying all three as arguments:

```
[root@workstation20 you]# mkdir /publicspace
[root@workstation20 you]# mount -t ext2 /dev/sdb1 /publicspace
[root@workstation20 you]#
```

The contents of the device /dev/sdb1 can now be accessed or modified by reading or writing to files or directories in the /publicspace tree. To verify that this is the case, you can print the list of mounted file systems by entering the mount command without arguments:

```
[root@workstation20 you]# mount
/dev/sda2 on / type ext3 (rw)
none on /proc type proc (rw)
usbdevfs on /proc/bus/usb type usbdevfs (rw)
/dev/sda1 on /boot type ext3 (rw)
none of /dev/pts type devpts (rw,gid=5,mode=620)
none on /dev/shm type tmpfs (rw)
/dev/sdb1 on /publicpsace type ext2 (rw)
[root@workstation20 you]#
```

When the mount command is called without arguments, each line of output contains the device or resource, the mountpoint, the file system type, and any options the device has been mounted with, in that order. Complete documentation for file system types and options can be found in the mount manual page.

You can unmount a mounted file system with the umount command. The umount command simply needs one argument: either the name of the device or resource to unmount, or the name of the mountpoint where the device or resource was mounted. For example, considering the mount commands we've issued in this section, the following two umount commands are equivalent:

```
umount /dev/sdb1
```

```
umount /publicspace
```

After you unmount a device or resource, you can verify that it no longer appears in the mounted file systems list by using the mount or df commands without arguments.

---

**What Is a** Device Is Busy **Error?**

If, while attempting to unmount a file system, you get a device is busy error, it means that some process or some user's current working directory still resides within that file system, or some process is still using a file stored on that file system. Until the user or process changes the current working directory or the open file is closed, you cannot unmount the file system.

---

# Maintaining the /etc/fstab File

The /etc/fstab file is a list of devices and resources, file system types, and mount-points that control which file systems are mounted when the computer starts. This file also lists which file systems are mountable and unmountable by regular users. Each line in the /etc/fstab file represents one mounted or mountable file system, and each line is formatted as follows:

```
device mountpoint fstype option1,option2,.. dump fscklvl
```

Each of the fields in this file is described in Table 28.4.

**TABLE 28.4**   Fields in the /etc/fstab File

| Field | Description |
|---|---|
| device | The name of the device or resource that contains the file system to which this line applies. |
| mountpoint | The place where the file system should be mounted within the local file system tree. |
| fstype | The type of file system, usually vfat (for Windows devices), nfs (for networked file systems), ext2, ext3, reiserfs, iso9660, or udf. |
| options | A comma-separated list of options, as listed in the man page for the mount command. Common options include user and owner, which let normal users mount and unmount the device; noauto, which prevents the device from being automatically mounted at start time; and defaults, which means that no special options are used. |
| dump | A value indicating whether this file system should be backed up by the dump command. This is a relic from Unix days gone by; because the dump command is obsolete as of Linux 2.4, this value should always be set to 0. |

**TABLE 28.4**   Continued

| Field | Description |
|---|---|
| *fscklvl* | For all file systems other than the root file system, this should be set to 2. The root file system should be set to 1. File systems that don't require checking, such as `reiserfs` or `iso9660`, can be set to 0. If in doubt, this field should contain the value 2. |

If you would like to cause a file system such as the one created in the previous section to automatically be mounted when the system starts, add an entry to the bottom of the `/etc/fstab` file containing the device, mountpoint, file system type, and other information. Following the sample file system created in the previous section, you add the following line:

```
/dev/sdb1 /publicspace ext2 defaults 0 2
```

By editing the `/etc/fstab` file, you can cause Linux to automatically mount added storage devices or networked file systems each time you boot. You can also add additional removable storage devices so that users can mount and unmount them as needed.

For further documentation of the `/etc/fstab` file or the options that can be used in it, see the manual pages for `fstab(5)` and `mount`.

# Managing Accounts

Being able to add and remove users and groups is of primary importance to you as a system administrator if you are running a multiuser Linux system or a Linux system on a network to which many people have remote login permission. In Chapter 7, "Understanding File Properties," you learned about users, groups, and permissions. Now you learn how to create the user and group accounts with which permissions work.

The process of adding or deleting users and groups at the command line is an easy one; the tasks at hand are accomplished with the `adduser`, `groupadd`, `userdel`, and `groupdel` commands.

## Adding and Removing User Accounts

Whenever you want to give a new user access to your Linux system with his or her own set of files and login information, you need to add a user account to your system. This is accomplished in two simple steps:

1. Call the adduser command, stored in /usr/sbin, supplying the name of the account you want to create as an argument and, optionally, the -c "Name" option to supply the real name of the user, which is used by email programs.

2. Call the passwd command, supplying the name of the account you just created as an argument, to assign a password to the account.

For example, to create a new account for a user named joe, you call adduser supplying joe as an argument, and then call passwd supplying joe as an argument, entering a password for joe when prompted:

```
[root@workstation20 you]# /usr/sbin/adduser -c "Joe Brady" joe
[root@workstation20 you]# passwd joe
Changing password for user joe.
New UNIX password:
Retype new UNIX password:
passwd: all authentication tokens updated successfully.
[root@workstation20 you]#
```

After you create an account for joe, he can log in using the password that you configured for him. His home directory has been created too: /home/joe.

To delete a user account, simply use the userdel command, which resides in /usr/sbin, supplying the name of the account you want to delete as an argument and, optionally, the -r option if you want to delete the user's home directory. To delete the account for joe that you just created, along with joe's home directory, enter the following:

```
[root@workstation20 you]# /usr/sbin/userdel -r joe
[root@workstation20 you]#
```

Without fanfare, joe's account and his home directory are deleted irrecoverably from the system.

---

**Take Care When Deleting Accounts**

If you want to delete an account but you're not sure which one, you can get a listing of the accounts that exist on your system by displaying the /etc/passwd file, which contains all user accounts with their account numbers, one per line.

*Do not*, however, delete any accounts with user numbers lower than 500 because accounts numbered below 500 belong to system services and might be critical for the proper functioning of Fedora Core 4.

---

*Watch Out!*

# Adding and Removing Groups

Groups enable users to become affiliated with one another, to work collectively on projects, or to access a specific facility or device that nongroup users can't. To create a group, use the groupadd command, stored in /usr/sbin, supplying the name of the group to create as an argument. To create a group called programmers, supply the name as an argument to groupadd as follows:

```
[root@workstation20 you]# /usr/sbin/groupadd programmers
[root@workstation20 you]#
```

The process of deleting groups is similarly easy and is accomplished using the groupdel command, also stored in /usr/sbin. To delete a group, call groupdel and supply the name of the group you want to delete as an argument:

```
[root@workstation20 you]# /usr/sbin/groupdel programmers
[root@workstation20 you]#
```

The group is deleted.

## Administering Groups

Because groups are, by definition, a collection of individual users, they require some maintenance: You must be able to add users to a group or delete users from a group, and to assign group administration privileges to a specific user. All this is accomplished by calling the gpasswd command.

After you create a group, you can give group administration privileges to a regular user by calling the gpasswd command with the -A option, and supplying the name of the user and the name of the group as arguments. For example, to give the user joe administration privileges for the group programmers, you enter the following command:

```
[root@workstation20 you]# gpasswd -A joe programmers
[root@workstation20 you]#
```

The user joe now has administration privileges for the group programmers and can add and delete users, set the password, and clear the password for the group.

To add users, joe issues the gpasswd command with the -a option, supplying the name of the user to add and the name of the group he administers as arguments. For example, if joe adds jane to the group programmers, he enters the following command:

```
[joe@workstation20 joe]$ gpasswd -a jane programmers
[joe@workstation20 joe]$
```

The user jane is now a member of programmers until joe removes her. To remove jane from programmers, joe calls the gpasswd command with the -d option, supplying the user to remove, jane, and the group to remove her from, programmers, as arguments:

```
[joe@workstation20 joe]$ gpasswd -d jane programmers
[joe@workstation20 joe]$
```

For information on additional capabilities offered to the root user by the gpasswd command, including the ability to use group passwords, see the gpasswd manual page.

## Changing Group Membership

For regular users to use their group memberships, they must use the newgrp command. The newgrp command is called with the name of a group as an argument; the user's group identity then changes to that of the specified group if the user is a member of the group. For example, if jane, a member of programmers, wants to access the files belonging to the group programmers, she calls newgrp from her command prompt, supplying programmers as an argument:

```
[jane@workstation20 jane]$ newgrp programmers
[jane@workstation20 jane]$
```

Users can return to their default (that is, login) group identity by issuing the newgrp command without arguments:

```
[jane@workstation20 jane]$ newgrp
[jane@workstation20 jane]$
```

# Using cron to Manage Periodic Jobs

Every Linux and Unix system includes a service called cron that enables users to automatically run specific commands or scripts periodically, according to user-defined timing options. This service offers a range of unique tasks—periodic backups, email status reports, home directory cleanups, and so forth.

There are two levels of cron process lists: the systemwide lists and the per-user lists. The systemwide cron process lists should be used only to manage system-oriented processes; for all personal jobs that need to be periodically run, the per-user cron lists should be used instead.

## Adding Systemwide cron Processes

Systemwide cron processes are most often used for tasks such as periodic backups, log rotation, and system health monitoring. To create a systemwide cron process, you create a shell script that performs the task you want to accomplish and then, using the cp or mv commands, place it into one of several special directories in /etc:

▶ Shell scripts copied to /etc/cron.hourly are run once every hour at one minute past the hour.

▶ Shell scripts copied to /etc/cron.daily are run once every day at 4:02 a.m.

▶ Shell scripts copied to /etc/cron.weekly are run once every week on Sunday at 4:22 a.m.

▶ Shell scripts copied to /etc/cron.monthly are run once every month, on the first day of the month, at 4:42 a.m.

As is the case with all shell scripts you want to run, scripts that you copy to the /etc/cron.* folders must be marked as executable for them to work properly.

**Did you Know?**

> **Monitoring with** anacron
>
> If you are wondering what happens to your daily shell scripts when your computer isn't running at 4:02 a.m., you needn't worry. Fedora Core 4 includes a service called anacron that monitors your cron tasks. When you first boot your Linux system, anacron runs those tasks that missed their last scheduled execution, ensuring that no cron job is ever missed.

## Editing Per-User cron Processes

In addition to the systemwide list of cron tasks, which only the root user has permission to edit (because they reside in the /etc folder), cron provides a special way for individual users to manage a personal list of periodic tasks. This is done with the crontab command. To edit your personal lists of cron tasks, enter the crontab -e command at any command line:

```
[you@workstation20 ~]$ crontab -e
```

The vi editor takes over your terminal or console, pointing toward a special file that cron reads to perform the tasks you request. By editing and saving this file, you can cause cron to call any command or script for you on a periodic basis.

Each line in the file represents a separate task and must be a list of data fields of the following format:

```
min hour mday month wday command
```

The meaning of each of these fields is described in Table 29.5. Each of them is meaningful: cron uses the values of every field on a specific line to construct the time(s) at which a task should be run.

**TABLE 28.5**    Fields in the `crontab` File

| Field | Description and Format |
| --- | --- |
| *min* | The minute (from 0-60) at which this job should be run. Multiple values can be specified by separating them with commas (for example, 0,15,30,45), and a range of values can be specified to cause the job to run every minute in the range (for example, 15-40). Lists and ranges can also be mixed (for example, 0-15,30-45). An asterisk (*) indicates any minute. |
| *hour* | The hour (from 0-24) at which this job should be run. As was the case with *min*, lists, ranges, a combination of the two, or an asterisk may appear in this field. |
| *mday* | The day of the month (from 1-31) on which this job should be run. As was the case with *min*, lists, ranges, a combination of the two, or an asterisk may appear in this field. |
| *month* | The month of the year (from 1-12) in which this job should be run. As was the case with *min*, lists, ranges, a combination of the two, or an asterisk may appear in this field. |
| *wday* | The day of the week (from 0-7, both representing Sunday), on which this job should be run. As was the case with *min*, lists, ranges, a combination of the two, or an asterisk may appear in this field. |

Enter each of your periodic tasks. After you finish, save the file and exit the vi editor; the new list of jobs is read by cron and carried out at the times you specify until the jobs are removed again—meaning when you enter crontab -e and delete them from the file.

Let's examine a few lines from a crontab file for illustration purposes:

```
* * * * * fetchmail
0 15 * * * mcopy ~/database.txt a:
1 0 1 1 * new_year_script
```

The first of these entries calls the fetchmail program described in Chapter 23, "Using the Network at the Command Line," once every minute of every day. In short, this line downloads the user's new mail once per minute.

The second of these entries copies a file called database.txt from the user's home directory to the floppy disk in drive a: every day at 3:00 p.m., presumably for backup purposes.

The final entry runs a shell script called new_year_script every New Year's Day at 12:01 a.m.

# Shutting Down and Restarting

The graphical Fedora Core 4 login screen provides an easy way to shut down or restart your Linux computer system safely. However, sometimes the ability to shut down or restart from the command line is important. For example, if a server system becomes overloaded by a runaway database request or a coordinated web attack, you might want to be able to restart it from a remote location through a `telnet` or `ssh` login.

The `shutdown` command shuts down or restarts a running Linux system from the command line. `shutdown` is typically used in one of the following two ways:

```
shutdown -h time
shutdown -r time
```

Using `shutdown` with the `-h` option halts a running Linux system. Using `shutdown` with the `-r` option restarts a running Linux system. Replace *time* with one of the following:

▶ The word now to indicate that you want to shut down or restart immediately

▶ A time in 24-hour *hh*:*mm* format, where *hh* is the hour and *mm* is the minute at which the system should shut down or restart

▶ An offset in minutes preceded by a plus sign, such as +30, to indicate that the system should shut down or restart after a specific period of time measured in minutes

For example, to immediately reboot a running Linux system, call the `shutdown` command with the `-r` option and the now argument:

```
/sbin/shutdown -r now
```

> ### Always Shut Down Properly
>
> You should always use either the `shutdown` command or the shut down and restart tools at the graphical login prompt to stop or restart your Linux system. Using the power switch or reset button without first shutting down properly can cause data loss.

# Summary

In this chapter, you were given a crash course in Linux and Unix system administration at the command line. Although it's doubtful that you were able to absorb enough of this information to fly without a net, you can refer to parts of this chapter as you need them in the future.

To recount a few highlights in this chapter, you learned about the following:

▶ The su command, which enables you to access the root account to perform administration tasks without having to log out of a user account and log back in as root

▶ The ps, renice, and kill commands, which enable you to list running processes, adjust their priorities, or kill them forcefully

▶ The chkconfig utility, which enables you to edit the list of running services on a per-runlevel basis, and the /etc/inittab file, which determines your default runlevel

▶ The parted command, which enables you to create new partitions and file systems on storage devices

▶ The mount and umount commands, which enable you to mount and unmount file systems for access to their contents, and the /etc/fstab file, which enables you to determine which file systems are automatically mounted at boot time

▶ The adduser, userdel, groupadd, and groupdel commands, which enable you to add users, delete users, add groups, and delete groups, respectively

▶ The gpasswd and newgrp commands, which are used by group administrators and users in the course of group management

▶ The cron system, /etc/cron.* directories, and crontab command, which enable both the root user and normal users to schedule tasks of all kinds for periodic execution

Linux and Unix system administration is a very involved topic, enough to have already merited volume upon volume of published documentation. We at least managed to scratch the surface in this chapter.

For more involved system administration documentation for Linux systems, consult *The Linux System Administrator's Guide*, which can be found at http://www.tldp.org/LDP/sag/ and *Sams Teach Yourself Unix System Administration in 24 Hours.*

# Q&A

**Q.** *When I try to use* `chkconfig` *to enable some services, I get an error message about files not being found. Why?*

**A.** In most cases, you get this message because you have not installed the required software to support the service in question. Refer to Chapter 31 for details on how to install additional Fedora Core 4 Linux software.

**Q.** *I have created a new* `cron` *task, but it doesn't seem to be running. Why?*

**A.** First, if your task is a script, double-check to make sure that it begins with `#!/bin/sh` and is marked as executable. If your changes were made in the `vi` editor, make sure that you saved the file before exiting. Finally, depending on where your script is located, you might need to call it with a full path, such as `/home/you/bin/myscript` instead of just `myscript`.

# Workshop

The Workshop is designed to help you anticipate possible questions, review what you've learned, and begin learning how to put your knowledge into practice.

## Quiz

1. How would you get a listing of *all* currently running processes on a Linux system?

2. How would you forcibly kill, without questions or delay, process number 1340?

3. How would you enable the `httpd` (web) server for runlevel 4?

4. How do you list all file systems on the device `/dev/hdb`, as well as its size?

5. How do you edit the personal list of periodic tasks?

## Answers

1. `ps ax`

   or

   `ps -ef`

2. `kill -KILL 1340`

3. /sbin/chkconfig --level 4 httpd on

4. /sbin/parted /dev/hdb print

5. crontab -e

## Activities

1. Get a list of all of the processes currently running on your system using the ps command and the ax arguments.

2. Use the chkconfig command and the -list option to get a listing of all the services that your Linux system runs at various runlevels.

3. Use the service command and the restart argument to restart one of the services currently running on your Linux system.

4. Add a user account called galileo and assign it a password. Log in to the account to verify that it exists. Then log out and back in as root again and delete the account and its home directory.

5. Use the shutdown command to reboot your system.

# CHAPTER 29

# Desktop System Administration

---

## What You'll Learn in This Chapter:

▶ How to view and manage the list of running processes
▶ How to manage print jobs
▶ How to configure or reconfigure network interfaces
▶ How to start, stop, and manage services
▶ How to add and delete user and group accounts
▶ How to access and browse through the system logs

In this chapter, you learn to perform a number of system administration tasks using the Linux desktop. Although you won't always have access to the desktop environment (often the case if you've installed a server-only configuration), the desktop tools are generally easier to use than their command-line counterparts.

Although most of the tools in this chapter must be run as root to function properly, in most cases you don't actually need to be logged in as root to use them. If you are logged in to your desktop as another user and start one of these tools, you are prompted for the root password; once you enter the password, the tool starts. In some tools, you are prompted for the root password only if you attempt to make a change or perform an operation requiring root privileges.

## Managing System Processes

As you learned in Chapter 28, "Command-Line System Administration," in any running system, it is important to be able to list the running processes, to change the priority at which they execute relative to other processes, and to kill those processes that need to be ended for some reason or other.

At the desktop, all these tasks are accomplished with the System Monitor tool. Open the System Monitor by choosing Applications, System Tools, System Monitor. The System Monitor window appears, open to the Process Listing tab, as shown in Figure 29.1.

**FIGURE 29.1**
The System Monitor tool (maximized here) displays a list of running processes.

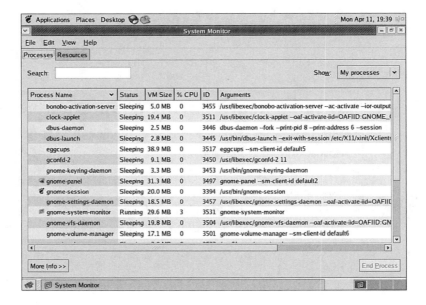

You can use the options in the Process Listing tab to list the processes that are running on your system, change the priority (amount of CPU time) given to running processes, and kill processes you decide should no longer run.

The list of displayed processes is updated on a continuous basis as system conditions evolve and the list of currently running processes changes.

You can change the view options to limit the display to certain types of running programs. That action trims the length of the displayed list and limits the display to only those files you're interested in viewing. To change the view, open the Show drop-down list to the right of the Search box and choose any of these options:

► The All Processes option displays all the processes running on the system, regardless of owner or whether the process is currently active (calculating or executing rather than waiting for data or input).

► The My Processes option displays all the processes owned by the user who started the System Monitor tool.

► The Active Processes option displays all processes that are currently active.

## Adjusting Process Priority

The Process Listing tab in the System Monitor can be used to adjust the priority of any running process upward (less CPU time) or downward (more CPU time). By adjusting the priority, you ensure that critical processes get as much CPU time as possible on an overloaded system, sometimes at the expense of other processes. For example, suppose that you are running a large spreadsheet computation involving many thousands of cells on a Linux computer that is also your small company's web server. Because you want to ensure that customers can access your website as quickly as possible while the spreadsheet computes for several hours, you could adjust the priority of your spreadsheet application upward (less CPU time) so that it uses processing resources only when other tasks—like the web server—don't need them.

To adjust the priority of a running process, select its entry in the Process Name list and then choose Edit, Change Priority. The Change Priority dialog box appears, as shown in Figure 29.2.

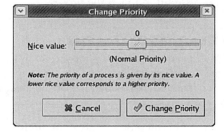

**FIGURE 29.2**
Here, the priority for sendmail is being changed. To increase the priority of the selected process, drag the slider to the left. Drag the slider to the right to decrease the process's priority.

In the Change Priority dialog box, adjust the slider downward toward negative numbers to raise the priority of the process (giving it more CPU time) or toward positive numbers to lower the priority of the process (giving it less CPU time). All user processes have a default priority (also sometimes known as a **nice value**) of 0. After you adjust the priority of the process relative to other running processes, click the Change Priority button to assign the priority and close the dialog box.

## Killing Running Processes

If a running process becomes unresponsive or if you need to stop the process for administrative reasons, you can use the System Monitor tool to end or kill the process. When you end a process, Linux asks the process to exit. Occasionally, a process refuses to do so—sometimes because it is still busy storing information or working, sometimes because it has become unstable. When this situation occurs, you might decide that you want to kill the process, interrupting anything it might be doing and causing it to exit immediately. When you kill a process, any unsaved files opened by the process are lost, and the process does not have a chance to close open network connections gracefully and perform other similar housekeeping tasks before exiting. Thus, it is usually a good idea to try to end a process first, killing it afterward only if absolutely necessary.

To end a process, select it in the Process Name list of the Process Listing tab and click the End Process button at the lower-right corner of the tab. The End Process confirmation dialog box appears.

To confirm that you want to end the process, click the End Process button. The System Monitor tool sends a signal to the process indicating that it is time to quit.

If you find that you can't cause the process to quit using the End Process button, you can force the process to be killed. Select the offending process from the Process Name list and then choose Edit, Kill Process; the Kill Process confirmation dialog box appears. Click the Kill Process button to kill the process.

**Watch Out!**

### Careless Killing Can Lead to Lost Data

You should use the Kill Process option only after you try to kill a process using the End Process button. Forcefully killing a process takes it out of the process table without giving it a chance to close open files or connections.

To confirm that you want to kill the process unconditionally, click the Kill Process button. The process is terminated forcefully and removed from the list of running processes.

**By the Way**

### Killing an Application Doesn't Kill for Good

Ending or killing a running process does not affect your ability to run the same program in the future, nor does it affect other instances of the same application that are also running.

# Managing Running Services

Because Fedora Core 4 is a Unix-style system, your system is busy supplying services most of the time, many of them to you, the desktop user. This is true even if your computer isn't officially acting as a network server. As you work with your system, you might need to enable additional services to meet new work demands, or disable services you no longer need or use. These and other service management tasks are accomplished through the Service Configuration tool. You can use the Service Configuration tool to determine which services begin running when you start up your system at each runlevel (you learned about runlevels in Chapter 28).

## Using the Service Configuration Tool

Using the Service Configuration tool, you can edit the list of services that start each time Linux starts. To start the Service Configuration tool, click Desktop, System Settings, Server Settings, Services. This selection starts the Service Configuration tool, as shown in Figure 29.3.

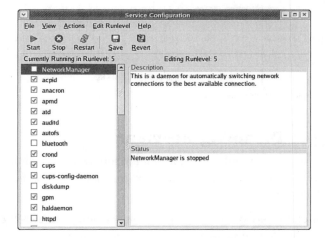

**FIGURE 29.3**
The Service Configuration tool allows you to start, stop, enable, disable, or get information about Linux services.

Whenever running, the Service Configuration tool is set to make changes to one of the three multiuser runlevels 3, 4, or 5. Because you are using the graphical environment, the default behavior is to edit runlevel 5, the runlevel that boots into graphics mode. If you want to edit a runlevel other than 5, you can select another runlevel using the Edit Runlevel menu. For more information on runlevels, what they are, and how they work, refer to Chapter 29.

Notice that the tool shown in Figure 29.3 contains three panels. The panel on the left contains a list of the available services, along with check boxes to enable or disable them. The panels on the right contain descriptions of the services (in the Description box) and status information about running services (in the Status box). Each time you click the name of a service, the description and status information panels are updated to show information about that service, as shown in Figure 29.4.

Service description appears here

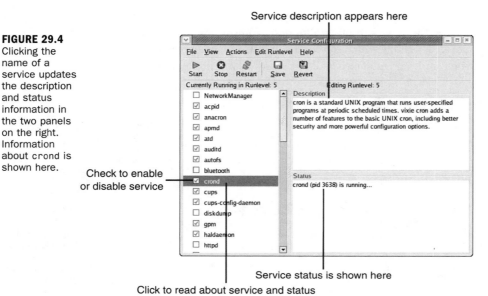

**FIGURE 29.4**
Clicking the name of a service updates the description and status information in the two panels on the right. Information about crond is shown here.

Check to enable or disable service

Click to read about service and status

Service status is shown here

## Enabling or Disabling Services

To enable a service for the runlevel you're editing, simply place a check in the box next to the service you want to enable. The next time Linux starts, that service will be started automatically.

Similarly, to disable a service for the runlevel you're editing, uncheck the box next to the service you want to disable. The next time Linux starts, the service in question will not start.

When you are done editing the list of services that will be active for the selected runlevel, click the Save button to save your changes.

**Watch Out!**

| **Don't Make Changes You Don't Understand!** |
| --- |
| Even though some services might seem from their descriptions to be obscure or potentially unuseful to you, you should take care not to alter the list of running services unless you know for sure that a service needs to be enabled or disabled.<br><br>Enabling many services can increase your exposure to security risks and malicious network activity; disabling some services can render your desktop or file system nonfunctional. |

# Stopping, Starting, and Restarting Services

Sometimes you need to temporarily stop a running service or offer a service that is not normally offered. Or you might need to restart a running service, usually to accommodate changes in the configuration file or to fix a service that is no longer responding. You can change the state of a service by using the Service Configuration tool's Start, Stop, and Restart buttons, located at the left end of the Service Configuration toolbar.

To stop a currently running service, click it in the Service Configuration list of currently running services and then click the Stop button. To start a service that isn't currently running, click it and then click the Start button. Finally, to restart a currently running service, click the service and then click the Restart button.

In each case, if the start, stop, or restart operation fails, you see a notification of failure; otherwise, you see a notification of success, as shown in Figure 29.5.

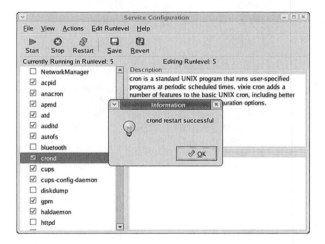

**FIGURE 29.5**
After a successful start, stop, or restart operation, you receive a notification of success.

Often when a start, stop, or restart operation fails, is because the software for the service in question was not installed when you installed Fedora Core 4. If you know this to be the case, refer to Chapter 31, "Installing Linux Software," for details on installing the needed software. Other common causes include incomplete or incorrectly formatted configuration files, or a missing system resource of some kind. When a failure occurs, check the Add/Remove software tool to make sure that the service is installed, and consult the system manual page for the service in question for help in diagnosing the problem. If you're still unsure about the cause, you might find hints in the system logs; refer to "Reading System Logs" later this chapter for details on how to consult them.

# Managing Network Interfaces

In most cases, you need to configure your network interface or interfaces only once—when you install Fedora Core 4. If you add or remove network interface hardware or the configuration of your network changes, however, you might need to make additional changes to your network configuration.

Fedora Core 4 provides a desktop Network Configuration tool to manage and configure your network interfaces. The Network Configuration tool is used to configure such items as address, nameserver, and gateway configuration, as well as the hardware network devices installed on your system. Start the Network Configuration tool by choosing Desktop, System Settings, Network. The Network Configuration tool appears, as shown in Figure 29.6, listing all the network interfaces configured on your system.

**FIGURE 29.6**
Using the
Network
Configuration
tool, you can
configure your
network
interfaces.

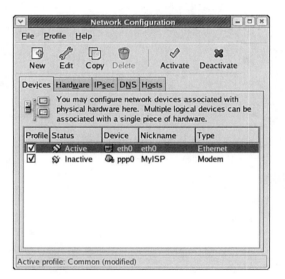

## Editing Static IP or DHCP Properties

To edit the address properties of a particular network interface, select the interface you want to configure in the Network Configuration dialog box and then click the Edit button. A more detailed configuration dialog box is displayed, as shown in Figure 29.7.

To specify that the network device in question should be automatically configured, click the Automatically Obtain IP Address Settings option. Then configure the rest of the automatic configuration options:

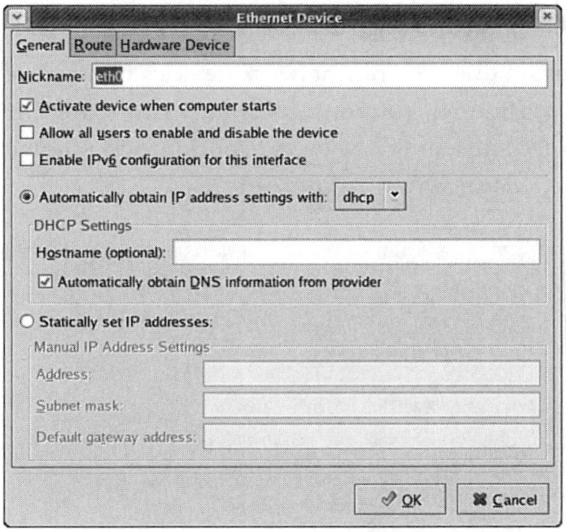

**FIGURE 29.7**
Using the Ethernet Device dialog, you can configure the IP address of the selected Ethernet hardware.

▶ Select a protocol type from the drop-down list. For most networks, the correct automatic configuration type is the default, Dynamic Host Configuration Protocol (DHCP).

▶ If your network is capable of supplying nameserver information, check Automatically Obtain DNS Information from Provider.

▶ If you have been instructed to manually configure your system's hostname, enter your assigned hostname in the Hostname box.

If your network administrator has given you an IP address, netmask, and gateway address for use with your host, you should choose to configure the network interface manually. To do so, click the Statically Set IP Addresses option. Then fill out the remaining fields:

▶ Enter your assigned IP address in the Address box.

▶ Enter your netmask in the Subnet Mask box.

▶ Enter your default gateway in the Default Gateway Address box.

After you configure your network hardware to work properly with your network, click the OK button to accept the settings you selected and dismiss the detailed configuration dialog box.

## Manually Configuring DNS Information

If you have not selected to have your network device's nameserver (DNS) information automatically configured, you must manually configure the DNS information. To do this, click the DNS tab in the Network Configuration dialog box. The DNS options are displayed, as shown in Figure 29.8.

**FIGURE 29.8**
On the DNS tab, you can configure the name service properties for your network hardware.

To configure the basic DNS properties for your network interface, do the following:

▶ Enter your assigned hostname in the Hostname box.

▶ Enter your primary DNS address in the Primary DNS box, your secondary DNS in the Secondary DNS box, and your tertiary DNS (if applicable) in the Tertiary DNS box.

▶ Enter the primary domain name of your network in the DNS Search Path box; this domain is appended to hostnames when a domain name is not specified.

After you configure the DNS properties as desired, choose File, Save. If you configured all the network properties for your hardware correctly, click the Close Window button to close the Network Configuration dialog box.

## Enabling or Disabling Network Interfaces

Sometimes you might need to completely disable a running network device—for example, if you are experiencing a hacking attack or if you need to troubleshoot some aspect of network operation by disconnecting from the network. To disable a network device, click the device in the device list of the main Network Device Control tool (refer to Figure 29.6), and then click the Deactivate button.

To activate a network device that has been deactivated, click the device in the list and then click the Activate button.

After you make all the desired changes to your network equipment, click the Close button to dismiss the Network Device Control tool.

# Managing Accounts

In Chapter 7, "Understanding File Properties," you learned about file ownership and the way file permissions relate to the user and group of each file in the Linux file system. Here, you learn to add and delete user and group accounts using desktop tools.

In Fedora Core 4, you can add and remove users and groups by using the Red Hat User Manager tool. You can start the User Manager tool by choosing Desktop, System Settings, Users and Groups. The User Manager tool opens with the Users tab on top, as shown in Figure 29.9.

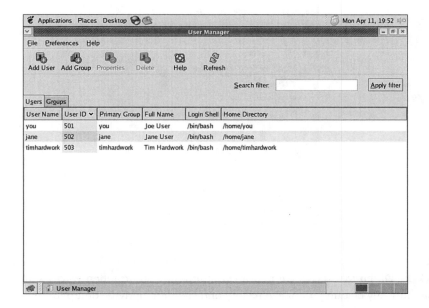

**FIGURE 29.9**
Using the User Manager tool (shown maximized), you can add and remove users and groups.

## Adding and Removing Users

To add a user account in the User Manager, click the Add User button near the top of the window. The Create New User dialog box appears.

To create a new user account, fill out the fields in the top of the Create New User dialog box:

- ▶ Enter the desired login name for the new account into the User Name box.

- ▶ Enter the user's full name into the Full Name box.

- ▶ Enter the desired password for the user into the Password box and then enter it again into the Confirm Password box to verify that it has been typed correctly.

- ▶ Leave the Create Home Directory and Create a Private Group for the User boxes checked, and the Specify User ID Manually box unchecked.

The Create New User dialog, completed to create an account for the new user (named Jack User), is shown in Figure 29.10.

**FIGURE 29.10**
Using the
Create New
User dialog box,
you can enter
the details for a
new account.

After you fill out the entry boxes in the top half of the Create New User dialog box, click the OK button to create a new account using the information you've supplied, automatically creating a home directory and creating a private group for the user in question. The Create New User dialog box disappears, and the new user appears in the Users list in the User Manager.

To delete a user, click the user you want to delete in the Users list and then click the Delete button near the top of the User Manager tool. The user you have selected is then removed from the list of users.

## Adding and Removing Groups

To add or remove groups, click the Groups tab in the User Manager tool. The list of groups is displayed in the tab.

To add a new group, click the Add Group button. The Create New Group dialog box is displayed, as shown in Figure 29.11.

**FIGURE 29.11**
In the Create New Group dialog box, you enter the name of the group you would like to create.

Enter the name of the group you want to create in the Create New Group dialog, leave the Specify Group ID Manually box unchecked, and click the OK button to create the group. The dialog box disappears, and the new group you created appears in the User Manager Groups list.

To delete a group, click the group you want to delete in the Groups list and then click the Delete button in the User Manager toolbar near the top of the window. The group disappears from the list of groups and is removed from the system.

## Editing Group Membership

To edit the list of members in a particular group, select the group whose membership list you would like to edit in the Groups list and then click the Properties button near the top of the User Manager tool. The Group Properties dialog box appears. Click the Group Users tab, and the list of system users is displayed, as shown in Figure 29.12.

Check the boxes next to the users who should be included as members of the group; clear a check box to remove a member. After you finish editing the group membership, click the OK button to accept the updated list of users. The Group

**FIGURE 29.12**
Using the Group
Users tab in
the Group
Properties dia-
log box, you can
edit the list of
members in
a group.

Members column in the Users list is updated to reflect the new list of group members.

After you finish adding or removing users or groups and editing group memberships, choose File, Quit to exit the User Manager.

# Reading System Logs

As a matter of course, Fedora Core 4 maintains a number of system logs to record activity that occurs in various parts of the system. The information in these logs can be especially helpful when you encounter trouble, such as unexpected program crashes or device errors, because Linux generates a log entry for most common problems.

You can read system logs using the System Logs tool. Start the tool by choosing Applications, System Tools, System Logs. To read the messages in a system log, choose a log from the list in the left pane of the window; the messages it contains appear in the right pane (see Figure 29.13).

Messages that could indicate a problem of some kind are marked with attention symbols (yellow icons containing exclamation marks for warnings or red stop-sign-like icons for problems). If you're experiencing trouble, these entries are the first items to check when seeking the source of a problem.

To search for a particular keyword in the currently displayed log, enter the keyword you want to search for in the Filter For entry box and click the Filter button. Only entries containing the keyword you enter are displayed.

When you finish viewing system logs, choose File, Quit to exit the System Logs tool.

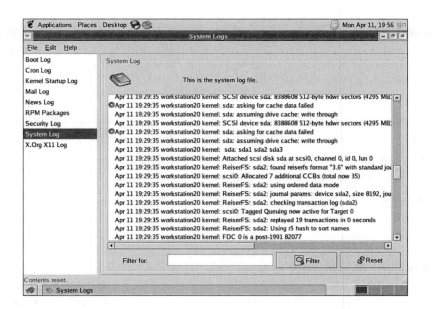

**FIGURE 29.13**
Using the System Logs tool (shown maximized), you can read and search through the various Linux system logs. Here, the contents of the system log are displayed. Use the Filter option to search for a message containing a specific keyword.

# Mounting and Unmounting File Systems

Filesystems for most common removable devices, like USB keys or CD-ROMs, are automatically mounted by Fedora Core 4, and shown on the desktop as an icon.

You can use the User Mount tool to mount and unmount file systems that aren't typically automatically mounted—such as external hard drive file systems or back-up filesystems—according to the entries in the /etc/fstab file discussed in Chapter 28, "Command-Line System Administration." Start the User Mount tool by choosing Desktop, System Tools, Disk Management. The User Mount Tool window is displayed, as shown in Figure 29.14.

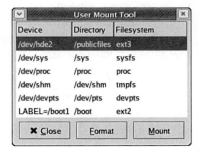

**FIGURE 29.14**
The User Mount Tool window displays a list of all file systems that the current user is allowed to mount, unmount, and/or format.

> **Need a Refresher on Mounting, Unmounting, and** /etc/fstab**?**
>
> For a discussion of the uses for mounting and unmounting file systems and the format and use of the /etc/fstab file, refer to "Managing File Systems" in Chapter 28.

To change the mount status of one of the listed file systems, click its entry in the User Mount Tool window. One of two things happens:

- ▶ If the file system is currently unmounted, the Mount button is displayed; clicking it mounts the file system.

- ▶ If the file system is currently mounted, the Unmount button is displayed; clicking it unmounts the file system.

> **The User Mount Tool is User-specific!**
>
> Unlike the other tools in this chapter, the User Mount Tool is user-specific. It won't ask you for a password if you're not logged in as root; instead, it will simply display a list of the disks that the current user is allowed to mount or unmount. To have access to all disks, you must actually log in to the desktop using the root account, *then* start the User Mount Tool.

## Formatting a Device or Partition

If you have permission to reformat a device or partition, the Format button is activated in the User Mount Tool window. Clicking the Format button for a nonremovable device presents a confirmation dialog box. Because formatting deletes all information stored on a disk, Fedora Core 4 asks you to confirm that you truly want to go forward with the formatting operation.

Formatting takes from a few moments to quite some time, depending on the size of the device, the file system it will contain, and whether a verify pass is performed. During this time, the User Mount Tool window buttons are grayed out. When the format is complete, the buttons are activated again.

After you make all desired changes to the mounted or unmounted states of the available file systems and have formatted devices and partitions as desired, click the Close button to close the User Mount Tool window.

# Summary

In this chapter, you learned to perform a number of common system administration tasks using graphical tools. Specifically, you learned the following:

- ▶ How to use the System Monitor tool to list, reprioritize, and kill running processes

- ▶ How to use the Service Configuration tool to change the list of services that are started each time your computer boots, and to start, stop, and restart running services

- ▶ How to use the Network Device Control tool to manage your network interfaces, including selecting between static and dynamic IP configurations

- ▶ How to use the User Manager tool to add or delete users or groups and to edit group memberships

- ▶ How to use the System Logs tool to view the most recent entries in various Linux logs and to identify potential problem entries

- ▶ How to use the User Mount Tool to mount, unmount, and format file systems as they are listed in the /etc/fstab file

Although the primary vehicle for system administration in Linux remains the command line, the graphical tools described in this chapter can be used to perform the more common system administration tasks you're likely to encounter.

# Q&A

**Q** *Can I create new partitions or change the file system type of existing partitions using the User Mount Tool?*

**A** No. For instructions on creating partitions or changing file system types, refer to "Creating File Systems" in Chapter 28.

**Q** *How do I know the options to select or the data to enter in the Network Device Control tool?*

**A** Information about whether you should use static or dynamic network configuration, as well as details about your IP address, netmask, DNS, and gateway must all be provided by your network administrator or Internet Service Provider. You should be able to obtain your IP address, netmask, name server, and gateway, if needed, from them.

# Workshop

The Workshop is designed to help you anticipate possible questions, review what you've learned, and begin learning how to put your knowledge into practice.

## Quiz

1. Where do you edit group memberships using desktop tools?

2. Should the End Process button or the Kill Process option be used first in the System Monitor tool?

3. In the System Logs tool, how do you know which entries deserve your attention more than others?

## Answers

1. You edit group memberships in the Group Users tab of the Group Properties dialog box in the User Manager tool.

2. Always try the End Process button first. Only in the rare case that it fails to end a process should you use the Kill Process option.

3. The most telling entries are marked with a small red attention icon, which indicates potential problems.

## Activity

1. Spend some time reading your system logs, just to see what your Fedora Core 4 computer has been doing lately.

# CHAPTER 30

# Security Basics

---

## *What You'll Learn in This Chapter:*

▶ How to manage the Fedora Core 4 firewalling configuration

▶ How to use file permissions in new ways to improve system security

▶ How to protect the root account in several ways

▶ How to automatically log out inactive users

In this chapter, you learn to perform some basic security-oriented optimization on your Linux system. Any Fedora Core 4 can be configured in hundreds of flexible ways to maximize security and safety from outside attacks while still permitting you, the user, to finish the work you need to finish. You should follow along with this chapter and understand the settings discussed here if you plan to use your computer on a network for any period of time.

For server systems, you should also take care to read the notes in Chapters 33, "Offering Network File Services," and 34, "Offering Web and FTP Service," about any network services you plan to provide.

### Security Is Not to Be Taken Lightly

If your system is to be an important network server or will be exposed to a large number of users, you should seriously consider studying Linux security in greater depth than can be presented in a single chapter in a book like this one.

Starting points from the Linux Documentation Project include these two online books:

▶ *The Linux Administrator's Security Guide*
http://www.seifried.org/lasg/

▶ *Securing and Optimizing Linux*
http://www.tldp.org/LDP/solrhe/

Fedora Core 4 also includes a system called Security-Enhanced Linux (SELinux), which we don't discuss extensively here, primarily because it can make Linux systems much more difficult to work with. If you're interested in absolute maximum security, however, you should follow the instructions you find in this chapter for enabling SELinux, then visit http://www.nsa.gov/selinux/ for details on configuring and using SELinux.

# Managing the Fedora Core 4 Firewall

If your Fedora Core 4 PC will be connected to a network at any time, whether by Ethernet, modem, or some other technology, the first task in securing your Linux computer should be to shore up your network security at the packet level.

Specifically, you need to be able to tell Linux exactly what kinds of network traffic you expect and want to receive so that Linux can discard all the rest of the network traffic it receives. This configuration is done with the Security Level Configuration tool.

### Redefining the Firewall

More experienced network users may be confused by our use of the term *firewall* here. Traditional firewalls are dedicated embedded computer systems that act as gateways to corporate or private networks. They continually work to filter out harmful network traffic for hundreds or even thousands of users on local subnetworks.

Recently, the term **firewalling** has also been applied by many software companies to the general practice of packet filtering (blocking unwanted network traffic), even when it occurs in software on a single user's PC or workstation. It is this second, more flexible sense of the word *firewall* that we are using in this chapter—software packet filtering to block unwanted network traffic as it enters your computer.

It is possible to use Fedora Core 4 to build a dedicated firewall/gateway system, but uses of this type are beyond the scope of a beginning book like this one; an advanced Linux text or networking guide can provide additional details.

# Using the Security Level Configuration Tool

To start the Security Level Configuration tool on the Linux desktop, choose Desktop, System Settings, Security Level. If you are not logged in as the root user, you'll be prompted for a password. After entering a password, the Security Level Configuration tool included with Fedora Core 4 appears, as shown in Figure 30.1.

**FIGURE 30.1**
Using the Security Level Configuration tool, you can configure the Fedora Core 4 firewalling properties.

The Security Level Configuration tool is easy to use:

▶ Using the Security Level drop-down list, you can enable or disable the Linux firewall. Under most circumstances, your firewall should be enabled at all times.

▶ If you plan to offer any of the services shown in the Trusted Services box, check the box next to the service you want to offer to allow it through your firewall.

▶ If one of your network connections is known to be safe (for example, if it doesn't lead to the Internet and you receive no public traffic from it—if it's purely for a small, local network) then check the Trusted box next to it if you want to allow all network traffic through. Never check the Trusted box for a network port that receives data from the Internet.

For the typical desktop user, the correct settings are to choose Enable Firewall from the Security level drop-down list, to check No Trusted Services, and to check No Trusted Devices.

## Opening Your Firewall to Other Kinds of Traffic

If you provide network services not listed in the Allow Incoming area of the Security Level Configuration tool, you need to enable traffic for these services by entering the details for their network port and protocol types in the Other Ports entry box.

The port and protocol details for each network service are located in the `/etc/services` file, which you can view at the command line by using a pager such as `less` or `more`. A segment of the `/etc/services` file is shown in Listing 30.1.

**LISTING 30.1    A Segment of the `/etc/services` File**

```
pop2          109/tcp     pop-2   postoffice    # POP version 2
pop2          109/udp     pop-2
pop3          110/tcp     pop-3                  # POP version 3
pop3          110/udp     pop-3
sunrpc        111/tcp     portmapper     # RPC 4.0 portmapper TCP
sunrpc        111/udp     portmapper     # RPC 4.0 portmapper UDP
auth          113/tcp     authentication tap ident
auth          113/udp     authentication tap ident
sftp          115/tcp
sftp          115/udp
uucp-path     117/tcp
uucp-path     117/udp
nntp          119/tcp     readnews untp  # USENET News Transfer Protocol
nntp          119/udp     readnews untp  # USENET News Transfer Protocol
```

The first column in the `/etc/services` file lists the service name. Some services are listed on more than one line; these services require more than one port or protocol. The second column in the `/etc/services` file lists the ports and protocols required by each service. For example, the pop3 (Post Office Protocol version 3) network service shown in Listing 31.1 requires the availability of network port 110 using both the tcp and udp protocols.

To enable a service in the Security Level Configuration tool, you must enter each of the required port and protocol pairs mentioned in the `/etc/services` file for the service, separating individual pairs with commas, in the following format:

`port1:proto1,port2:proto2,...`

For example, to enable the Network News Transfer Protocol (nntp) and Post Office Protocol 3 (pop3) services as mentioned in Listing 30.1, you would enter the following text into the Other Ports entry box:

`119:tcp,119:udp,110:tcp,110:udp`

After you configure the properties of your Fedora Core 4 firewall to suit your needs, click OK to save your changes, activate the new firewall settings, and close the Security Level Configuration tool.

## Enabling and Disabling SELinux

You might recall that in Chapter 2, "Installing Fedora Core 4," you were instructed to disable SELinux by default for your Fedora Core 4 computer system.

If you will be using your computer while directly connected to the Internet (rather than through a company network or using a dedicated router for your local network), or if you expect large numbers of untrusted users to have access to your computer system, you should consider enabling SELinux, which provides a very high level of security.

You can choose to turn SELinux on and off by choosing the SELinux tab in the Security Level Configuration tool, as shown in Figure 30.2.

**FIGURE 30.2**
The SELinux tab of the Security Level Configuration tool is used to enable or disable SELinux.

To enable SELinux, check the Enabled box, click OK, and then reboot your Fedora Core 4 system.

Because SELinux is only really needed under particular circumstances (such as those just described), and because it adds significant user-unfriendliness and complexity to Linux, we won't discuss it further in this book. You can learn more about SELinux and its use by visiting the SELinux home page at http://www.nsa.gov/selinux/.

# Understanding Advanced Permissions

In Chapter 7, "Understanding File Properties," you learned the basics of file ownership and permissions in Linux. You also learned to use the chmod command at the command line to change file permissions using the symbols (letters) r, w, and x for read, write, and execute.

The basic set of read, write, and execute permissions and the basic file ownership behavior work well for most situations. However, Linux does provide a way for administrators to change the ownerships of existing files, as well as an additional set of permissions properties for more unique situations, which can provide finer-grained control over the ways in which files and directories behave.

## Changing File Ownership

The chown command can be used to change the user and/or group ownership of an existing file. This capability can be useful if, for example, you want to make a file you created readable to other members of a group of which you are a member. By changing the file's group ownership and permissions, you can make the file read-able by members of the group while remaining secure with regard to other users of the system.

To use the chown command to change ownership for an existing file or directory, call chown as follows:

```
chown user.group file
```

Replace *user* with the name of the user who should be given ownership of the file and *group* with the name of the group that should be given ownership of the file. Replace *file* with the name of the file whose ownership is to be changed. For example, to change the group ownership of a file called myfile.txt to the programmers group, you issue the following command:

```
[you@workstation20 ~]$ chown you.programmers myfile.txt
[you@workstation20 ~]$
```

**By the Way**

### Users Can't Change User Ownership

Normal users can't change user ownership. They can change only group owner-ship—and only to groups of which they are members.

The root user can change both user and group ownerships of any existing user account or group.

## Using chmod **in Numeric Mode**

In Chapter 7, you learned that each file or directory in a Linux system is governed by three sets of read, write, and execute switches. When considered from left to right as they are usually written, these sets of switches belong to the file's owning user, the file's owning group, and everyone else, in that order. For example, the following permissions string represents a normal file that is readable, writable, and executable by everyone:

```
-rwxrwxrwx
```

In the symbolic mode of the chmod command, you use symbols such as u, g, o, r, w, and x arranged in various patterns as arguments to change these permissions. The numeric mode of chmod works somewhat differently. To call chmod in numeric mode, you use the following format:

```
chmod NNN file
```

Each N must be a numeric digit. The first N represents the permissions for the owning user of the file; the second N, for the owning group; and the third N, for everyone else. Each N has a value of zero (0) for no permissions or a single-digit sum created from the values in Table 31.1 to indicate the absolute permissions that are to be assigned.

**TABLE 31.1** Permissions Values for chmod's Numeric Mode

| Value | Meaning |
|---|---|
| 4 | Read permission is granted for this file or directory. |
| 2 | Write permission is granted for this file or directory. |
| 1 | Execute permission is granted for this file or directory. |

For example, to assign full read, write, and execute permissions for all users to a file called myfile.txt, you enter the following:

```
[you@workstation20 ~]$ chmod 777 myfile.txt
[you@workstation20 ~]$
```

Table 30.2 shows a number of additional examples for numeric strings, which can be provided to chmod, and their symbolic meanings.

**TABLE 30.2** Examples of Numeric Values for chmod and Resulting Permissions

| Number | Permissions | Description |
|---|---|---|
| 664 | -rw-rw-r-- | The owning user and owning group can read and write. Other users can only read. |
| 444 | -r--r--r-- | All users anywhere can read. No other permissions are granted. |

**TABLE 30.2**    Continued

| Number | Permissions | Description |
|--------|-------------|-------------|
| 700 | - rwx - - - - - - | The owning user can read, write, and execute. No other permissions are granted. |
| 750 | - rwxr - x - - - | The owning user can read, write, and execute. The owning group can read and execute. No other permissions are granted. |

Although the symbolic mode of chmod is typically preferred by beginners, most longtime Linux or Unix users prefer to use the numeric mode for its simplicity and brevity.

## Understanding Special Permissions

As you use Linux, you will from time to time encounter several additional types of permissions values in the output of long directory listings. Understanding these special permissions is important because they significantly alter the way in which programs or directories behave:

▶ A letter s appearing in a file's user permissions' execute position indicates that when this program is run, it is granted access to files and system resources as though it had been called by its owning user, rather than by the user who actually called it. Files with this permission switch set are called **SUID (Set User ID) executables**.

▶ A letter s appearing in a file's group permissions' execute position indicates that when this program is run, it is granted access to files and system resources as though it had been called by a member of its owning group, rather than by the group of the user who actually called it. Files with this permission switch set are called **SGID (Set Group ID) executables**.

▶ A letter t appearing in the last position of a directory's permissions indicates that users who are allowed to write to this directory are allowed to remove only files or directories for which they are the owning user. This permission switch is known simply as the **sticky bit**.

The SUID and SGID bits are rarely used; the sticky bit is used more often, usually to create a public storage area in which users can create and remove their own files. You can assign the SUID, SGID, and sticky bits to file or directory permissions using chmod's numeric mode by including an extra digit at the beginning of the numeric permissions code supplied to chmod as an argument. The values used in this optional first digit are shown in Table 30.3.

**TABLE 30.3** Codes Used to Assign Special Permissions with chmod

| Value | Meaning |
|-------|---------|
| 4 | Assigns the SUID (Set User ID) property to this executable file |
| 2 | Assigns the SGID (Set Group ID) property to this executable file |
| 1 | Assigns the sticky bit to this directory |

Table 30.4 provides some sample numeric codes for chmod that use special permissions, along with resulting descriptions.

**TABLE 30.4** Special Permissions Examples Using chmod's Numeric Mode

| Number | Permissions | Description |
|--------|-------------|-------------|
| 4754 | -rwsr-xr-- | The owning user can read, write, and execute. The owning group can read and execute. Everyone else can read. When this program is executed, its user permissions behave as though it were called by its owning user. |
| 2754 | -rwxr-sr-- | The owning user can read, write, and execute. The owning group can read and execute. Everyone else can read. When this program is executed, its group permissions behave as though it were called by a member of its owning group. |
| 6554 | -r-sr-sr-- | The owning user can read and execute. The owning group can read and execute. Everyone else can read. When this program is executed, its user permissions behave as though it were called by its owning user, and its group permissions behave as though it were called by a member of its owning group. |
| 1777 | drwxrwxrwt | All users can read, create files in, and delete files from this directory and can make this directory their current working directory. However, users can delete only files that they themselves own. |

To assign the SUID or SGID properties to an executable file, you must be either the owner of the file or a member of the file's owning group, respectively—or the root user. The SUID and SGID properties are rarely used.

> ## Why Are SUID and SGID Important?
>
> An understanding of the SUID and SGID properties is important for Linux security precisely because these properties are so potentially insecure: They allow users to transcend their account identities, which are fundamental to permissions. The SUID and SGID properties have been judiciously limited to a few programs such as su in Fedora Core 4. You should rarely, if ever, assign them yourself.
>
> More importantly, you should be very suspicious of SUID or SGID files that have creation dates well after the date on which you installed Fedora Core 4. You should also be wary of SUID or SGID files that aren't in a binaries directory such as /sbin, /usr/bin, or /usr/sbin.
>
> You can get a listing of all SUID and SGID binaries by using the following two find commands:
>
> ```
> find / -perm +2000
>
> find / -perm +4000
> ```
>
> You should run these commands soon after you install your system and save the output; afterward, you should run them again periodically to check for the emergence of new SUID or SGID files. If such a file appears, use chmod to remove its executable permissions at once and refer to Chapter 35, "Backups, Troubleshooting, and Rescue."

# Protecting the Root Account

The root account is one of the greatest vulnerabilities of Linux and Unix operating systems because the root account is all-powerful: root can create, read, modify, and delete any file in the system or enable or disable any resource or service. Because the root account is so powerful, the default protection for the account—a simple password—should be considered inadequate in most cases.

Fortunately, a relatively simple change to the security surrounding the root account can greatly increase the overall security of your Linux system. The change in question is the use of the wheel group to protect the su command. The wheel group is a special group whose members, by convention, are the only users given access to the su command on most Unix systems.

## Enabling the wheel Group

You already learned that the su command can be called from the command line by a normal user to allow the user to take on the root identity to perform system administration tasks. This capability is convenient, but it is also dangerous: If a malicious user can call su repeatedly, he or she might eventually be able to guess the root password, thereby gaining unrestricted access to the entire system.

---

### SUID and SGID Illustrated

By the Way

The su command provides an excellent illustration of the power and danger of SUID and SGID permissions.

The su command works because, by default, it is owned by the root user and is an SUID executable. This means that when it is called, it behaves as though it were called by the root user—thereby giving the program access to protected resources, such as those needed to change identities. To illustrate, try looking at a long directory listing of the su program:

```
[root@workstatino20 you]# ls -l /bin/su
-rwsr-xr-x  1 root    root    19092 Jul 31 07:34 /bin/su
[root@workstation20 you]#
```

---

By convention and tradition, secured Unix systems use a special group called wheel to identify an elite group of system administrators who have access to the su command. All other users are prevented from calling it. To give the wheel group teeth, you must do two things:

1. Add to the wheel group at least one user who has administration privileges because he or she can call su.

2. Change the group ownership and permissions of the su program to restrict access to members of the wheel group.

## Adding Users to wheel

To add a user to the wheel group at the command line, use the gpasswd command with the -a option, passing the name of the user to add and the group to add the user to (in this case, wheel) as arguments:

```
[root@workstation20 you]# gpasswd -a you wheel
[root@workstation20 you]#
```

---

### Adding Users to wheel

Did you Know?

You can also use the Fedora Core 4 User Manager tool discussed in "Managing Accounts" in Chapter 29, "Desktop System Administration," to add users to the wheel group if you are uncomfortable with command-line tools.

---

If you want to give other users administration privileges, add them to the wheel group now as well. Only members of the wheel group will be able to call su when you are done with the following sections.

## Changing Ownership and Permissions of su

After you add members to the wheel group as desired, change the ownership of the su command from root.root (user root, group root) to root.wheel (user root, group wheel) using the chmod command. Using this command, you can restrict execute permissions to members of the wheel group, removing public execute permissions entirely:

```
[root@workstation20 you]# chown root.wheel /bin/su
[root@workstation20 you]#
```

Now that you have added administrators to the wheel group as desired and changed the ownership of su to root.wheel, assign the following permissions to su:

- ▶ Owner (root) read, write, and SUID execute

- ▶ Group (wheel) read and execute

- ▶ No permissions for nonowner, nongroup members

Using the numeric mode of the chmod command, you can assign these permissions by supplying the numeric code 4750 as an argument to chmod, followed by the file whose permissions you want to change, /bin/su:

```
[root@workstation20 you]# chmod 4750 /bin/su
[root@workstation20 you]# ls -l /bin/su
-rwsr-x---  1 root    wheel     19092 Jul 31 07:34 /bin/su
[root@workstation20 you]#
```

The su command is now protected from all normal users. When users who are not members of the special administrative wheel group try to access the su command, permission is denied:

```
[jane@workstation20 jane]$ su
bash: /bin/su: Permission denied
[jane@workstation20 jane]$
```

# Logging Users Out Automatically

It is not uncommon for a user to log in to her account on a Linux system and to then become preoccupied with some other task or situation, forgetting that she is logged in at all. The user's session then sits inactive for an extended period of time.

Unfortunately, inactive user sessions can represent a serious security risk, especially on systems that allow remote logins. Network connections that are left open this way can eventually be hijacked by malicious users, who then have access to the user's account and, by extension, your system.

Aside from the religious use of `ssh` in place of `telnet` or other remote login commands, this type of risk can most easily be remedied by setting a login timeout—a delay after which a user automatically is logged out if she hasn't pressed a key.

The `TMOUT` variable can be used to cause the default shell to automatically log out the user after a period of inactivity, measured in seconds. For example, setting the value of `TMOUT` to `1800` would log out the user after 1800 seconds, or 30 minutes, of inactivity.

## Setting a Login Timeout

To cause the value of the `TMOUT` variable to automatically be set whenever a user logs in, you must create a file in the `/etc/profile.d` directory, which contains a set of script fragments that are automatically run each time a user logs in. This file should end with `.sh` to indicate that it is for the standard shell and should set the value of the `TMOUT` variable. Use a text editor to create a file called `/etc/profile.d/secure.sh`, which contains only a single line:

```
TMOUT=1800
```

After you save the file and exit the text editor, don't forget to mark it as executable by everyone:

```
[root@workstation20 you]# chmod ugo+x /etc/profile.d/secure.sh
[root@workstation20 you]#
```

Linux also includes a number of alternate shells in addition to the standard shell; advanced Linux or Unix users can use the `chsh` command to select among them for day-to-day command-line work. Two alternate shells provide login timeout functionality; they are called `csh` and `tcsh`. To accommodate these alternate shells, you must create another script fragment. In these, the timeout variable is `autologout`, and the timer value is measured in minutes. Use a text editor to create a file for these shells called `/etc/profile.d/secure.csh`, which contains only the following line:

```
set autologout=30
```

Again, don't forget to mark the file as executable:

```
[root@workstation20 you]# chmod ugo+x /etc/profile.d/secure.csh
[root@workstation20 you]#
```

Account holders who log in using any of the major shells are now logged out after 30 minutes of inactivity.

## Removing Minor Shells

The list of shells from which users of the chsh command can select includes several shells that do not support login timeouts at all. For this reason, these shells should be removed from the list of shells available to users, which is stored in /etc/shells.

The default /etc/shells file is shown in Listing 30.2. The entries for the ash and bsh shells, which do not support login timeouts, can be removed using a text editor to produce the shortened /etc/shells file shown in Listing 30.3.

**LISTING 30.2**    The Original /etc/shells File

```
/bin/sh
/bin/bash
/sbin/nologin
/bin/bash2
/bin/ash
/bin/bsh
/bin/tcsh
/bin/csh
```

**LISTING 30.3**    The Edited /etc/shells File

```
/bin/sh
/bin/bash
/sbin/nologin
/bin/bash2
/bin/tcsh
/bin/csh
```

After you edit the /etc/shells file, users can select only from shells that log them out after a period of inactivity.

# Summary

In this chapter, you learned some simple yet fundamental techniques to help protect your Linux computer system against network attacks, break-ins, and inadvertent security lapses.

First, you learned to use the Security Level Configuration tool to choose a basic level of software firewalling (also known as **packet filtering**) for your Linux system. You then learned to create exceptions to the firewalling rules to allow the types of network traffic you need to allow so that you can provide the services you want to provide. You also learned how to enable and disable SELinux, should you feel that your computer is in a vulnerable enough position to require the extra level of assurance that SELinux offers.

Next, you learned about advanced use of file permissions—including some potentially dangerous types of permissions—and how to locate files that have been assigned them.

Then, you learned to restrict use of the su command, perhaps the most powerful and dangerous command in Linux security, to a special group of users who belong to the privileged wheel account.

Finally, you learned to limit the amount of time a remote login session can remain inactive before the system decides that it's a risky session and terminates it.

Although these security measures are only a beginning—important servers should be fully secured according to a Linux security guide or book and further protected with SELinux—they do represent enough basic security to get you up and running without obvious risks.

# Q&A

**Q** *In Chapter 28, "Command-Line System Administration," I learned about* cron. *Using the* find *commands in this chapter, can I create a* cron *task that automatically searches for new SUID or SGID binaries periodically?*

**A** Yes, this is an ideal use of the cron system and shell scripting, and a good exercise to help you learn the ins and outs of both.

**Q** *I have read other Linux security guides on the Web that recommend securing the* su *command by editing a file in the* /etc/pam.d *directory. What's the difference between implementing* wheel *using permissions and implementing* wheel *using PAM?*

**A** The su command can be used to become any user for whom you have a valid password, not just the root user. The /etc/pam.d method of restricting su access allows only members of wheel to become the root user, but regular users can still use su to become other regular users, provided that they have the correct passwords. The permissions-based method discussed in this chapter puts the su command completely off limits to everyone but members of wheel—a more secure solution altogether, and without major drawbacks because legitimate uses of su by non-wheel members are rare.

# Workshop

The Workshop is designed to help you anticipate possible questions, review what you've learned, and begin learning how to put your knowledge into practice.

## Quiz

1. What file contains the list of network port numbers and protocol types for network services?

2. How would you add the user you to the wheel group?

3. How would you assign the following permissions to a file called myfile.txt using chmod's numeric mode: user read, user write, user execute, group read, group execute—and nothing further?

4. What timeout values would you assign to TMOUT and autologout to cause inactive users to be logged out after an hour?

## Answers

1. /etc/services

2. gpasswd -a you wheel

3. chmod 750 myfile.txt

4. TMOUT=3600
   set autologout=60

## Activities

1. Create a wheel group on your computer and implement the security techniques related to wheel discussed in this chapter.

2. Add users who should have access to the su command to the wheel group.

3. After configuring your system for a login timeout, try logging in remotely and waiting until you are automatically logged out to ensure that the timeout value works.

# CHAPTER 31

# Installing Linux Software

## What You'll Learn in This Chapter:

▶ How to add or remove components of Fedora Core 4
▶ How to install third-party software packages in Fedora Core 4
▶ How to create desktop program launchers

In this chapter, you learn how to install additional software in Fedora Core 4, either from your Fedora Core 4 CD-ROMs or from Internet sites that offer Linux software. As you use Linux more, you'll be able to use these skills to customize the list of software packages that are installed on your computer system, thereby enhancing your workflow considerably.

## Installing and Removing Fedora Core 4 Components

Fedora Core 4 comes on one DVD or several CD-ROMs packed full of software. When you installed Fedora Core 4 on your computer system, however, only some of this software was copied to your hard drive. If you followed the directions in Chapter 2, "Installing Fedora Core 4," you have installed only those software components most commonly used by Fedora Core 4 users who want a Unix-style workstation.

It is likely that at some point while using Fedora Core 4, you will want to revise the list of software components that have been installed on your computer—either by uninstalling software you no longer use to free up space or by installing additional software from the Fedora Core 4 CD-ROMs. Fortunately, Fedora Core 4 includes an easy-to-use desktop tool called the Package Management tool for installing or uninstalling software packages.

A software package is a program or logical collection of several related programs and the data files that they require in order to operate. Packaging software in this way allows a number of files and program components to be installed or uninstalled in one operation.

## Starting the Package Management Tool

To start the Package Management tool on the Linux desktop, you choose Desktop, System Settings, Add/Remove Applications. If you are not logged in as root, you are asked to enter the root password before the Package Management tool starts.

When the Package Management tool is started, it scans the list of software packages already installed on your system so that it can show you a list of already installed packages and offer you the choice to remove one more of them, should you choose to do so. This check can take anywhere from a few moments to several minutes, depending on the speed of your system and the number of packages that are already installed. After the scan is complete, the main Package Management tool window appears, as shown in Figure 31.1.

**FIGURE 31.1**
After the scan of already installed packages is complete, the Package Management tool appears.

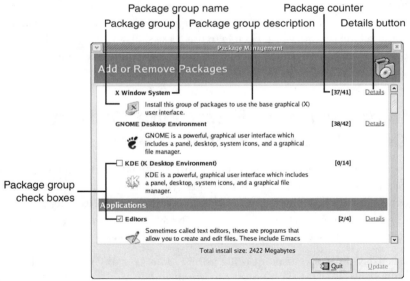

The main display of the Package Management tool gives you a list of available groups of related packages (applications or application components). You can use this list to either add or remove software from each package group. To understand the information presented in the main display, you must be familiar with its components:

▶ Each *package group* is identified by a *package group name* and a *package group description*. Together, these items represent a set or category of related software components that can be installed or removed as a unit. Read the description below the group name to understand how the components are related and what functions they perform.

▶ The *package group check box* is used to specify that a specific package group is either installed or marked for installation (checked) or not installed or marked for removal (not checked). If no check box appears next to a group, the group is installed by default and cannot be removed.

▶ Next to each package group you also see a *package counter*, which shows the number of packages (components) from the software group that are already installed on the system, as well as the total number of packages in the group.

▶ The *Details button* next to package groups that are installed or have been marked for installation is used to select the components from the package group that should be installed.

## Installing and Removing Software in Groups

The check box next to a package group in the Package Management tool indicates its current state. If a box is not checked, no software packages from the package group are installed on your computer, or you have marked the group for removal by unchecking it. If a box is checked, at least one software package from the package group is installed on your computer, or you have marked the group for installation by checking it.

To remove an entire package group, uncheck the box next to the group in the Package Management tool. Any software from the package group that is present on your system is marked for removal, the package counter for the group is updated to reflect this change, and the details button next to the group disappears, as shown in Figure 31.2.

To install a package group, check the box next to the group in the Package Management tool. The package group is marked for installation, and the package counter for the group is updated to show that a number of packages for the group are installed. When checked, some package groups install every component, whereas others install only a default collection of the most popular packages in the group. A details button also appears next to the newly checked group, as shown in Figure 31.3.

**FIGURE 31.2**
Unchecking the box next to a package group marks any installed components from the group for removal.

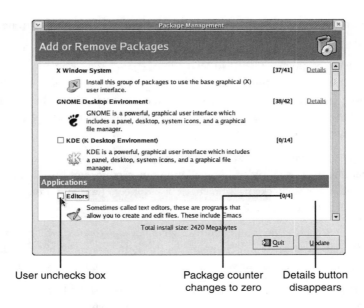

User unchecks box · Package counter changes to zero · Details button disappears

User checks box

**FIGURE 31.3**
Checking the box next to a group marks the default selection of packages in the group for installation.

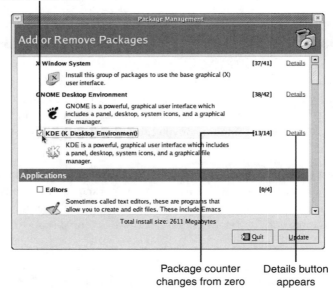

Package counter changes from zero · Details button appears

# Using the Details Dialog Box

The Details button next to each package group provides additional functionality that helps in the following situations:

▶ You may find that you want more fine-grained control over the packages that are installed or uninstalled in a package group.

▶ You may find that a package group's description leaves you unclear on precisely what kinds of software a package group contains.

▶ You may want to customize the list of packages to be installed when you select a group for installation, or you may want to remove only a single package from a package group while leaving the rest of its packages installed.

The Details dialog box opened from the Package Management tool solves each of these problems. The Details dialog box is used to do any one or all of the following:

▶ List every software package in the package group so that you know exactly what will be installed or uninstalled when checking or unchecking a package group.

▶ Alter the default list of packages that are installed when a package group is selected for installation.

▶ Remove packages one by one without removing other packages in an installed package group.

To open the Details dialog box, click the Details button next to an installed package group or a package group you've marked for installation. The Details dialog box is shown in Figure 31.4.

Checking an unchecked package in the Details dialog box marks the package for installation if it is not already installed; unchecking a checked package in the Details dialog box marks the package for deinstallation if it is currently installed.

After you customize the list of packages for the package group to suit your needs, click the Close button to accept the list of packages you've selected for the package group.

**FIGURE 31.4**
The Details dialog box contains a detailed list of packages in a package group, with a check box for each package.

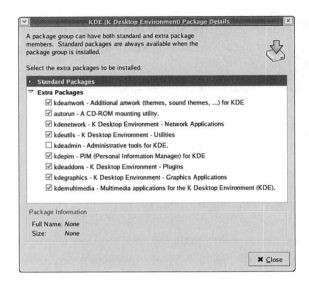

**KDE (K Desktop Environment) Package Details**

A package group can have both standard and extra package members. Standard packages are always available when the package group is installed.

Select the extra packages to be installed:

▸ **Standard Packages**
▽ **Extra Packages**
  ☑ kdeartwork - Additional artwork (themes, sound themes, ...) for KDE
  ☑ autorun - A CD-ROM mounting utility.
  ☑ kdenetwork - K Desktop Environment - Network Applications
  ☑ kdeutils - K Desktop Environment - Utilities
  ☐ kdeadmin - Administrative tools for KDE.
  ☑ kdepim - PIM (Personal Information Manager) for KDE
  ☑ kdeaddons - K Desktop Environment - Plugins
  ☑ kdegraphics - K Desktop Environment - Graphics Applications
  ☑ kdemultimedia - Multimedia applications for the K Desktop Environment (KDE).

Package Information
Full Name: *None*
Size:    *None*

**✕ Close**

---

*By the Way*

## Standard Packages and Extra Packages

The Details dialog boxes for some package groups contain two lists of packages, one labeled Standard Packages (with no check boxes) and one labeled Extra Packages (with check boxes that you can use to install or remove software).

Packages in the Standard Packages list are required packages. If you want to install any package in the group, all the Standard Packages are required; therefore, no check boxes appear next to the Standard Packages (because you can't uninstall them).

Packages in the Extra Packages list are optional. They appear with check boxes that you can use to install or remove the packages by checking or unchecking them, respectively.

## Updating Your System

After you select or deselect package groups and/or individual packages to suit your needs, marking packages for installation or deinstallation in the process, click the Update button at the lower right of the Package Management tool. The tool takes a moment to process the list of installations and deinstallations you've scheduled; a progress bar indicates how much longer the tool needs to finish its survey.

After the Package Management tool determines what is needed for the software you've requested to be installed or uninstalled, it displays a summary of the changes you've requested, as shown in Figure 31.5. If you would like to see a detailed listing of the software packages that will be installed or removed, click the Show Details button; this alters the display to show a more detailed list of packages to be installed or removed.

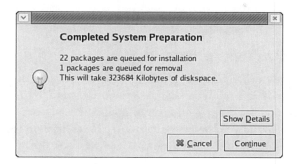

When you are ready to proceed with the changes you've requested, installing packages you've marked for installation and uninstalling packages you've marked for removal, click the Continue button. The Package Management tool proceeds with the installations and removals, showing a progress bar to indicate how much work remains.

If you've selected to install packages, you are asked to insert one or more of your Fedora Core 4 CD-ROMs at some point. When this occurs, insert the requested CD-ROM and click the OK button to continue. After the Package Management tool finishes installing and uninstalling software, it displays a dialog box to indicate that the process has completed. Click the OK button to dismiss the Update Complete dialog box; then click the Quit button in the lower right of the Package Management tool to exit the tool and return to your desktop.

# Using Third-Party Software

If you plan to use Linux software you have downloaded from websites or acquired through third parties, it is likely that the software you want to install will be delivered in Red Hat Package Manager (RPM) files—the type of software package file used by Fedora Core 4.

Every RPM software package contains two major components:

▶ The software program and its components

▶ A list of package **dependencies**—the system components or other software that is needed by the software package you're about to install

If you attempt to install a software package that depends on other software that hasn't yet been installed, Fedora Core 4 attempts to locate and install the additional required software as well. Provided that all necessary dependencies can be met (that each required software component can be located), installing RPM software packages is an easy task.

## Installing Software Packages

To install an RPM software package, locate the icon for the RPM file you'd like to install. Software packages that you have downloaded using the Firefox web browser are usually shown on the desktop and can be double-clicked from there. If you didn't save the download to your desktop but to some other location (such as /home/you, your home directory), browse to the folder using the file manager to locate the program you downloaded.

After you locate the RPM software package file you want to install, double-click its icon to begin the installation process, as shown in Figure 31.6.

**FIGURE 31.6**
Double-click the RPM software package on the desktop or in the file manager to begin the installation process.

If you are not logged in as root, after double-clicking, you are asked to provide the root password before continuing.

Before installing the software items contained in the RPM software package, Fedora Core 4 checks the software package's list of requirements to ensure that all the package's needs can be met by your computer system and by Fedora Core 4. After Fedora Core 4 has evaluated the requirements for the software package in question, it displays a dialog box listing the number of packages that will be added to the system and the disk space the installation will consume. To see a more detailed list of the changes, click the Show Details button to switch to the detailed view. When you are ready to proceed with the installation, click the Continue button.

After you click Continue, the installation of the software package and the packages upon which it depends (if Fedora Core 4 is able to locate them) begins. If Fedora Core 4 is unable to find and install some of the software upon which your package depends, you instead see a dialog box listing the missing dependencies. The next section contains tips for dealing with missing dependencies.

As the installation is being performed, you might be asked to insert one or more of your Fedora Core 4 CD-ROMs so that additional required software can be installed. After all the needed software packages have been installed, a Completed System Preparation dialog box is displayed to confirm that installation completed normally. The software package and any packages upon which it depended have now been installed on your computer system.

Click the OK button to dismiss the confirmation dialog box and return to your Linux desktop.

---

**What Happens When You're Upgrading a Package?**

When you double-click the package for a newer version of a program that has already been installed in your system, the Fedora Core 4 package manager automatically assumes that you want to upgrade the software application in question. For this reason, you don't need to remove an old version before installing a newer one.

*By the Way*

---

# Dealing with Failed Dependencies

In some cases, you might find that when you try to install an RPM software package, Fedora Core 4 is unable to locate the components needed to fulfill the package's dependencies. When this happens, an error message is displayed listing the missing software components, as shown in Figure 31.7.

In cases like this, you can try several remedies to rectify the problem:

▶ If the software you're trying to install comes in multiple, separate RPM files, try changing the order in which you're installing them. First install the packages upon which other packages depend, or rubber-band select all of the packages at the same time, then right-click on any one of the selected files and select Open with "Install Packages" to install them all simultaneously.

▶ Contact the vendor or revisit the website from which your software package came to see whether the additional needed components are available.

▶ Visit the http://www.rpmfind.net website and search for the names of the required packages. A wide variety of commonly needed packages can be downloaded there.

**FIGURE 31.7**
When Fedora Core 4 Linux is unable to find and install needed software packages, a dependency failure results.

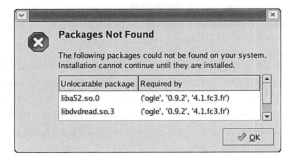

**Packages Not Found**

The following packages could not be found on your system. Installation cannot continue until they are installed.

| Unlocatable package | Required by |
|---|---|
| liba52.so.0 | ('ogle', '0.9.2', '4.1.fc3.fr') |
| libdvdread.so.3 | ('ogle', '0.9.2', '4.1.fc3.fr') |

✔ OK

# Using the rpm Command

The rpm command provides a way for packages to be installed or removed at the command line. It also provides several additional package management options that the desktop tools don't provide.

## Installing RPM Packages with rpm

To install a package using the rpm command at the Linux command line, follow these steps:

1. Make sure you are working as the root user; use the su command if necessary to become root.

2. Make the directory containing the .rpm files you want to install your current working directory.

3. Enter the rpm command with the -i (install) option, supplying the name of the package you want to install as an argument.

For example, assuming that you are working as root and want to install a package called mypackage.rpm, which is in the current directory, you would enter the following:

```
[root@workstation20 you]# rpm -i opera-7.54-20050131.5-shared-qt.i386-en.rpm
[root@workstation20 you]#
```

If there are no problems or errors, the package is installed and no additional messages are displayed. You can then use the software according to the manufacturer or supplier's instructions.

## Upgrading RPM Packages with rpm

If you use the rpm command to attempt to install a package that is already installed, you see an error message like this one:

```
package mypackage is already installed
```

If the package you are trying to install is a vendor-supplied upgrade or a later version of the existing package that is already installed on your system, you can automatically remove the old package and replace it with the new one by using the -U (upgrade) option with the rpm command:

```
[root@workstation20 you]# rpm -U mypackage.rpm
[root@workstation20 you]#
```

Again, if the original package is successfully upgraded (replaced) by the newer package, no additional messages are displayed.

## Dealing with Failed Dependencies Using rpm

When rpm is asked to install a software package that requires software not already installed on your system, an error message like this one is displayed:

```
error: Failed dependencies:
    alsa-lib is needed by ogle-0.9.1-fr3
    libasound.so.2 is needed by ogle-0.9.1-fr3
    libasound.so.2(ALSA_0.9) is needed by ogle-0.9.1-fr3
    libdvdread >= 0.9.4 is needed by ogle-0.9.1-fr3
    libdvdread.so.3 is needed by ogle-0.9.1-fr3
```

Unlike the desktop package installer, the rpm command does not have the capability of automatically asking you to insert your Fedora Core 4 CD-ROMs to install needed packages that are a part of Fedora Core 4. If you are experiencing a dependency failure while trying to install a third party application and need to use the command line installer, you should first check the Fedora Core 4 CD-ROMs to see whether the package(s) you need can be found there. To check each Fedora Core 4 CD-ROM at the command line, follow these steps:

1. Insert the CD-ROM you want to search.

2. Type **mount /mnt/cdrom** to ensure that the CD-ROM is mounted.

3. Type **find /mnt/cdrom -print | grep *dependency***, where *dependency* is the name of the package or software item needed—for example, **find /mnt/cdrom | grep libdvdcss** to search for a package called libdvdcss.

4. If the find command finds and lists any RPM packages by the needed name, type **rpm -i** to install the package(s) that find has found.

5. Type **umount /mnt/cdrom** to unmount the CD-ROM.

6. Repeat these steps for each Fedora Core 4 CD-ROM (you might need to search all of them) and for each package required to fulfill dependencies.

*Did you Know?*

> **Remember How to Use** mount, umount, find, **and** grep**?**
>
> For a refresher on the mount and umount commands, refer to Chapter 28, "Command-Line System Administration."
>
> For a refresher on the find and grep commands, refer to Chapter 19, "Performing Basic Shell Tasks."

If you are unable to find the needed package(s) on the Fedora Core 4 CD-ROMs, refer to the section earlier in this chapter called "Dealing with Failed Dependencies" for more suggestions on resolving failed dependencies.

*By the Way*

> **Trying to Install a Fedora Package?**
>
> If your goal is to install a Fedora package from the CD-ROM at the command line, and you are experiencing dependency failures in that context, use the yum command discussed in Chapter 32, "Keeping Fedora Core Updated" instead of the rpm command discussed here.
>
> The yum command can install many common Fedora (and even some third party) packages for you, and will automatically resolve and download needed dependencies for you.

## Getting Information with rpm

The rpm command can alsoprovide you with various types of information on the software packages that are installed on your system, as well as some information about software packages that are not yet installed.

To get a listing of all software packages currently installed on your system, use the rpm command with the -q (query) and -a (all packages) options. On a typical Linux system, this list is hundreds of lines long, so be sure to save the output to a file or to pipe it to a pager:

```
[root@workstation20 you]# rpm -q -a ¦ more
```

You can also search the list of installed packages to see whether a specific package is installed by piping the output of rpm to the grep command, supplying the name of the package you want to search for as an argument to grep:

```
[root@workstation20 you]# rpm -q -a ¦ grep bash
bash-2.05b-5
[root@workstation20 you]#
```

To learn more about any individual package that is already installed, use the -q (query) and -i (information) options, supplying the name of the package as an argument:

```
[root@workstation20 you]# rpm -q -i bash
Name        : bash                  Relocations: /usr
Version     : 3.0                       Vendor: Red Hat, Inc.
Release     : 29                    Build Date: Wed Mar 2 09:31:15 2005
Install Date: Wed Mar 23 20:51:52 2005  Build Host: porky.build.redhat.com
Group       : System Environment/Shells Source RPM: bash-3.0-29.src.rpm
Size        : 5121307                  License: GPL
Signature   : DSA/SHA1, Tue Mar  8 18:57:41 2005, Key ID da84cbd430c9ecf8
Packager    : Red Hat, Inc. <http://bugzilla.redhat.com/bugzilla>
Summary     : The GNU Bourne Again shell (bash) version 3.0.
Description :
The GNU Bourne Again shell (Bash) is a shell or command language
interpreter that is compatible with the Bourne shell (sh). Bash
incorporates useful features from the Korn shell (ksh) and the C shell
(csh). Most sh scripts can be run by bash without modification. This
package (bash) contains bash version 3.0, which improves POSIX
compliance over previous versions. However, many old shell scripts
will depend upon the behavior of bash 1.14, which is included in the
bash1 package. Bash is the default shell for Red Hat Linux.  It is
popular and powerful, and you'll probably end up using it.
[root@workstation20 you]#
```

Several additional information-gathering functions are available using the rpm command; see the manual page for rpm for details.

## Uninstalling Software with rpm

If you find that you no longer use a piece of software and would like to free up the space it is using, you can also use the rpm command to remove installed software packages. To remove an installed software package using rpm, supply the -e option followed by the name of the package you want to remove as an argument. You do not need to supply version numbers in the package names when removing software packages. Do *not* supply the `.rpm` extension to the filename when you call `rpm -e`:

```
[root@workstation20 you]# rpm -e mypackage
[root@workstation20 you]#
```

If the software package is successfully uninstalled, you see no further output.

Sometimes you encounter dependency problems when attempting to remove a package, as can be seen in this example:

```
[root@workstation20 you]# rpm -e qt
error: Failed dependencies

        libqt-mt.so.3 is needed by (installed) arts-1.1.3-2.2
        libqt-mt.so.3 is needed by (installed) kdelibs-3.1.3-6.2
        libqt-mt.so.3 is needed by (installed) kdebase-3.1.3-5.2
        qt >= 1:3.1.2 is needed by (installed) kdelibs-3.1.3-6.2
        /usr/lib/qt-3.1 is needed by (installed) redhat-artwork-0.73.2-1E
[root@workstation20 you]#
```

When this situation occurs, you have two choices:

▶ Begin by removing the software packages that depend on the package that you want to remove and then remove the package.

▶ Leave the package in place because other installed packages depend on it.

*Watch*
*Out!*

### Don't Remove a Package If You Don't Know What It Is!

Using rpm to prune your Linux installation to save space is not a good idea. Many packages that don't appear in desktop menus are nevertheless important system packages. Removing them might remove functionality from your Linux system.

## Resolving Circular Dependencies

Very rarely when using rpm to install or remove packages, you encounter circular dependencies.

The term **circular dependencies** refers to a situation in which two packages depend on each other, as can be seen in this illustration:

```
[root@workstation20 you]# rpm -i mypackage-a.rpm
error: Failed dependencies:
    mypackage-b is needed by mypackage-a
[root@workstation20 you]# rpm -i mypackage-b.rpm
error: Failed dependencies:
    mypackage-a is needed by mypackage-b
[root@workstation20 you]#
```

When this situation occurs, you can solve the problem by supplying all the packages involved as arguments together:

```
[root@workstation20 you]# rpm -i mypackage-a.rpm mypackage-b.rpm
[root@workstation20 you]#
```

When you supply the packages to rpm simultaneously, rpm is able to resolve all the dependencies, allowing packages with circular dependencies to be installed or removed.

# Using Application Launchers

After you successfully install a desktop application, the first thing you generally want to do is start it. To find out how, consult the documentation that came with your application or the website from which it was downloaded for detailed instructions. Usually, an application is launched using one of two techniques:

- ▶ If the application adds itself to the Applications menu, you navigate to the correct menu item and select it.

- ▶ If the application doesn't add itself to the Applications menu, you must start a terminal and launch the application at the command line.

If you install an application that requires the latter, as is the case with many older applications and many applications from the Unix world, you might find that launching the program from a terminal window is an inconvenience. In cases like this, you can create an application launcher (a clickable icon) on your desktop menubar to streamline the process of launching the application.

## Creating an Application Launcher

To create an application launcher in on the menubar, right-click an empty part of the menubar and choose Add to Panel. The Add to Panel dialog box appears, as shown in Figure 31.8.

Select the first option, Custom Application Launcher, and click Add to display the Create Launcher dialog box shown in Figure 31.9.

On the Basic tab of the Create Launcher dialog box, fill out the entry boxes as follows:

- ▶ Enter a name for your application launcher in the Name entry box. This name should be something brief but descriptive, such as Opera Web Browser or Civilization: Call to Power Game.

▶ Leave the Generic Name entry box blank. This box isn't used for application launchers of this type.

▶ Enter a more general (but still brief) description in the Comment box—for example, Web Browser or Game.

▶ Enter the command you normally enter at the command line to start the application into the Command box.

Select to create new application launcher

**FIGURE 31.8**
The Add to Panel dialog lists a number of options for customizing the menubar.

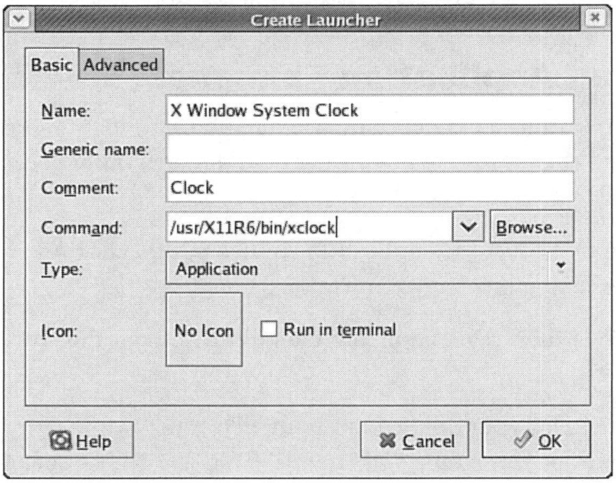

Click Add to proceed

**FIGURE 31.9**
Using the Create Launcher dialog box, you can create an application launcher in the taskbar.

After you fill out all the boxes as needed, click the Icon button to bring up the Browse Icons dialog box, in which you can choose an icon for your launcher, as shown in Figure 31.10.

**FIGURE 31.10**
Browse through the selection of icons provided with Fedora Core 4 and choose one that seems to suit your program.

Select the icon you would like to use for your application launcher by clicking it and then clicking the OK button. The icon dialog box closes. Click the OK button in the Create Launcher dialog box to create your application launcher. Your new launcher appears in the menubar.

From now on, clicking the application launcher icon on the menubar launches your application.

# Summary

In this chapter, you learned how to install and remove software in a number of different contexts:

▶ You learned how to use the Package Management tool to install or remove components of the Fedora Core 4 operating system, to allow your system to adjust as your needs change.

▶ You learned how to use desktop tools to install third-party software, including software that you have downloaded from the Internet.

▶ You learned how to use the command-line rpm tool to install or remove software packages at the command line.

▶ Finally, you learned how to create application launchers for applications you've installed so that you don't have to open a terminal window and enter a command to start them.

By customizing the selection of software on your system and installing third-party software of your own choosing, you can truly make your Linux system your own.

# Q&A

**Q** *I have seen Linux software packages on the Internet that end in* .tar.gz, .tar.bz2, .tgz, *and* .deb. *How do I install these types of software in Fedora Core 4?*

**A** Software packages that end in .deb are for the Debian Linux operating system and operating systems that are based on it; they are not easily usable with Fedora Core 4. Files ending in .tar.gz, .tar.bz2, or .tgz are not software packages; they usually contain application source code that must be built using a C compiler and other command-line tools. Sometimes they also contain the finished programs themselves, but they still lack the dependency information needed to make them true software packages. Instructions for installing software from source code are beyond the scope of this book, but the man pages for tar and gunzip contain enough information to help you access these types of files.

**Q** *I am trying to install a software package that seems to have an endless list of dependencies. I've managed to get packages to resolve some of these dependencies, but each of these new packages has dependencies of its own. What gives?*

**A** This situation often happens when a package you are trying to install was intended for a different version of Fedora Core 4 or for a different Linux operating system that also uses the RPM package format. Usually, a lengthy list of dependencies, which continues to grow with each new package, indicates that the software package you began with will not be easy to install. Try to install the package with yum, discussed in the next chapter. If that fails, try instead to find a version of the software package for Fedora Core 4.

# Workshop

The Workshop is designed to help you anticipate possible questions, review what you've learned, and begin learning how to put your knowledge into practice.

## Quiz

1. How do you install an RPM software package using desktop tools?

2. How do you install an RPM software package at the command line?

3. Why create an application launcher?

## Answers

1. Use the file manager to browse to the directory containing the RPM file; then double-click the file's icon.

2. `rpm -i mypackage.rpm`

3. You create an application launcher so that you don't have to start a terminal and type a command each time you want to launch an application.

## Activities

1. Start the Package Management tool and browse the available software package groups and software packages. If you see some software that you would like to install, do so.

2. Start a terminal and use the `rpm` command to list the packages installed on your system. Use the `rpm` command to find information on a few that you find interesting.

3. Create application launchers for some of the X Window System convenience applications in `/usr/bin/X11`.

# CHAPTER 32

# Keeping Fedora Core 4 Updated

## What You'll Learn in This Chapter:

▶ How to connect to the Red Hat Network
▶ How to select and install updates
▶ How to monitor update activity on the taskbar
▶ How to keep your system up to date from the command line

Software updates are an integral part of modern computing. Most computers in use today are connected to the Internet in one way or another, where new types of attacks and malicious software emerge daily. When you keep your Fedora Core system up to date, you ensure that your computer is protected against this type of activity. Software updates can also improve system stability, which can be crucial if your Fedora Core system provides network services to busy users.

For users of the Fedora Core and Red Hat Enterprise Linux families of operating systems, system update services are provided by the Red Hat Network.

## Introducing the Red Hat Network

The Red Hat Network is a premium service provided by Red Hat to streamline software updates and systems management for customers with an installed base of Red Hat Enterprise Linux or Fedora Core systems.

While working through this book, you may have noticed a slowly flashing red icon near the upper-right of your screen. This icon is the Red Hat Network Alert Notification Tool.

Once configured, it changes color to indicate the status of your Fedora Core 4 system relative to the updates available on the Red Hat Network:

▶ Red means that new updates are available, and you haven't yet installed them.

▶ Blue means that your system is current; all available updates have been installed.

▶ Green means that your computer and the Red Hat Network are currently communicating about the availability of new updates.

Before you can use the Alert Notification Tool, however, it must be configured.

## Configuring the Alert Notification Tool

To configure the Alert Notification Tool for use, right-click its icon and choose Configuration from the context menu, as shown in Figure 32.1. You are greeted by a welcome notice. Click Forward to view the Alert Notification Tool terms of service. If you agree to the terms of service, click Forward again to see the Proxy Configuration page, as shown in Figure 32.2.

**FIGURE 32.1**
Right-click the Alert Notification Tool icon and select Configuration to launch the configuration process.

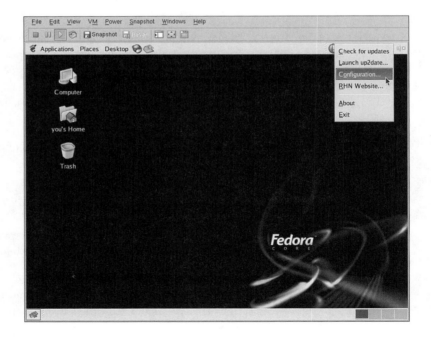

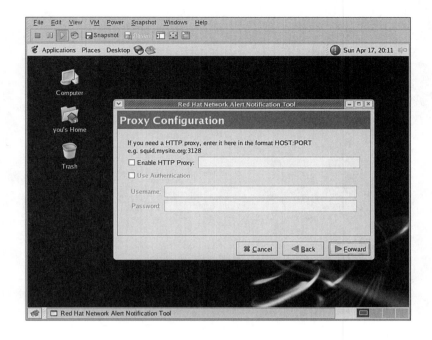

**FIGURE 32.2**
If your company firewall requires the use of a web proxy, enter its details on the Proxy Configuration page.

If you know that your corporate firewall or network requires the use of a World Wide Web proxy server, check the box labeled Enable HTTP Proxy and enter its details now. Most users can simply leave the box unchecked. Click Forward to continue to the Configuration Complete notice, as shown in Figure 32.3. Click Apply to save your changes and activate the tool.

## Using the Alert Notification Tool

After the Alert Notification Tool has been activated, from time to time you see it change to green as it checks for new updates for your Fedora Core 4 system. Whenever new updates are found, the tool's icon flashes red once again. When this occurs, click the icon to show the Alert Notification Tool dialog box, as shown in Figure 32.4.

This dialog box contains three tabs, each of which summarizes a different type of information about updates and your Fedora Core 4 computer:

▶ The Critical Information tab lists update-related information that must be handled immediately or about which you should be aware.

**FIGURE 32.3**
Configuring
the Alert
Notification Tool
really is that
easy. Click
Apply to save
your changes.

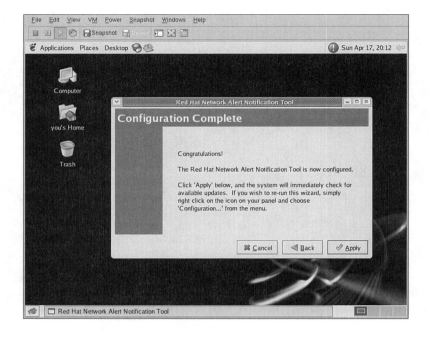

**FIGURE 32.4**
Click the Alert
Notification Tool
icon when it is
flashing red to
show a dialog
box that sum-
marizes critical
information,
updates, and
exclusions.

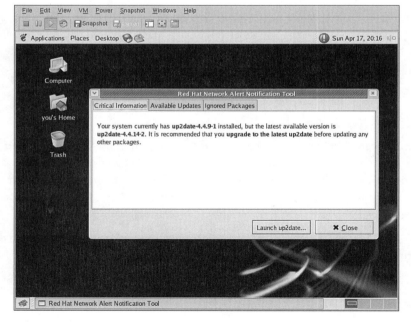

▶ The Available Updates tab, shown in Figure 32.5, lists all the currently available updates that you haven't yet installed.

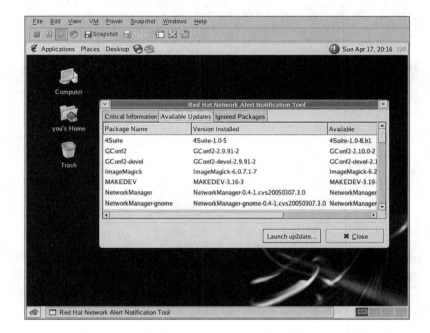

**FIGURE 32.5**
The Available Updates tab shows the updates that you haven't yet installed.

▶ The Ignored Packages tab, shown in Figure 32.6, shows all the packages that are currently flagged to be excluded from system updates; the tab also provides you with tools to edit the list.

After surveying the information displayed in the Alert Notification Tool's summary dialog box, click the Launch up2date button to start the Red Hat Network agent and begin the update process.

The Red Hat Network agent (called up2date) begins by asking you to confirm number of configuration options, as shown in Figure 32.7. When the agent first appears, you are shown the General tab, where you can configure the Red Hat Network agent to work with your web proxy. After you have entered your network's proxy information, or if you don't use a web proxy, click OK to continue.

**FIGURE 32.6**
The Ignored Packages tab shows packages that you have indicated should not be updated.

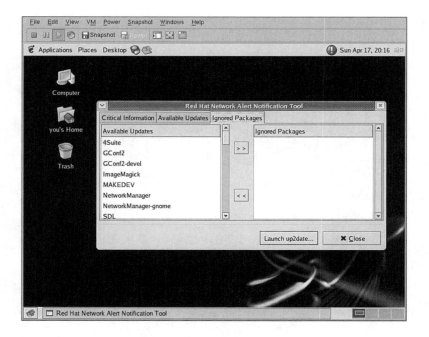

**By the Way**

## What About the Other Two Tabs?

The Retrieval/Installation and Package Exceptions tabs contain options that most users do not need to change and should probably leave as is. Feel free to browse through the tabs, but don't change any settings with one exception:

If you want to be able to undo any updates installed by the Red Hat Network tool, check the Enable RPM Rollbacks option in the Retrieval/Installation tab. Note that checking this option will cause updates to consume up to twice as much storage space.

Once you click OK to accept the configuration shown in the Red Hat Network Configuration dialog box, you are shown the Welcome to Red Hat Network Agent message. Click Forward to display the list of channels that contain updates. Unless you have been instructed by a network administrator or technical support to do otherwise, leave the default selection of channels in place. Click Forward to continue.

The Red Hat Network agent now begins checking the list of packages currently installed on your system. It then checks the availability of packages in your subscribed channels. This process may take several minutes, depending on the speed of your network connection, as you see the names of all the updated packages listed for you, one by one, as shown in Figure 32.8.

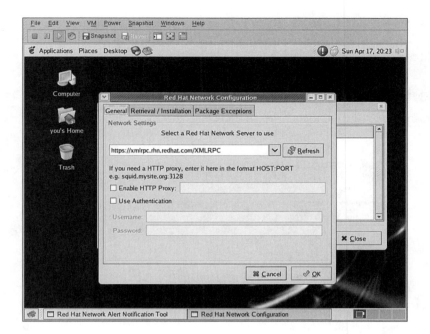

**FIGURE 32.7**
The Red Hat Network agent gives you a chance to confirm its basic configuration. Enter your web proxy information here or just click OK to continue.

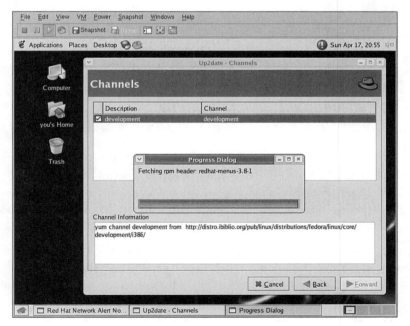

**FIGURE 32.8**
The Red Hat Network agent downloads package information for each of the available updates.

After the Red Hat Network agent has scanned your subscribed channels for updates that can be installed on your Fedora Core 4 system, you're ready to begin selecting and installing updates.

## Selecting and Installing Software Updates

Depending on the set of packages that are currently available as updates, you may now see the Packages Flagged to Be Skipped page, as shown in Figure 32.9.

**FIGURE 32.9**
Some packages are flagged to be skipped. If updates to these packages are available, you're asked whether you want to update them anyway.

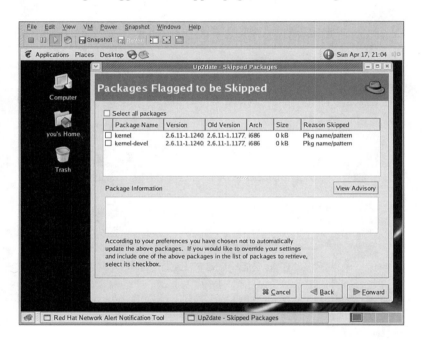

By default, the Linux kernel (the core of the operating system) and a few other related packages are marked to be skipped when you update your Red Hat computer. This is done in the interest of safety, because on rare occasions kernel updates can create unexpected compatibility or stability problems.

If updates are available to these packages, the Red Hat Network agent shows you the Packages Flagged to Be Skipped page to give you the opportunity to install updates to these packages anyway. Most of the time, these updates can be installed without any issues at all. If you are shown the Packages Flagged to Be Skipped page and would like to update the packages in the list, check the box labeled Select All Packages.

In either case, click Forward to continue to the Available Package Updates page, as shown in Figure 32.10.

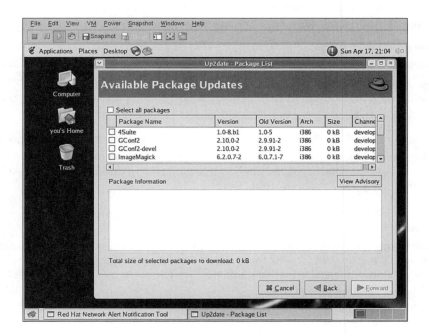

**FIGURE 32.10**
The Red Hat Network agent displays a list of all the available updates. Check the Select All Packages box to mark them all for installation.

If this is the first time you've updated your Fedora Core 4 computer using the Red Hat Network, the list of available updates is likely to be quite long. In most cases, you will want to install all the available updates. To do so, simply check the box labeled Select All Packages.

If know that you want to install only a select group of updates for some reason and have a list of what they are, scroll through the list of packages and place checks next to those packages that you want to be updated.

After you finish marking packages for update, click Forward. The Red Hat Network agent compiles a list of all the updates you've chosen and checks the software dependencies for each package, displaying a progress bar as it works.

If additional packages must be installed to satisfy the dependency requirements of the software updates you've selected, the Red Hat Network agent notifies you that additional packages will be installed, asking you to click Forward to begin installing the updates you selected.

After checking package dependencies (or after you click Forward, in cases in which additional packages were needed), the Red Hat Network agent begins downloading the updates you've selected. Two progress bars indicate the download progress of the current package (upper bar) and the download progress for the entire collection of updates to be installed. Depending on the number and size of packages marked for update, the download stage can take some time.

After the download process is complete, the words All finished appear near the bottom of the application window. Click the Forward button to install the updates that have been downloaded. The installation process, too, can be somewhat time consuming. Once again, you see two progress bars, one for the current package's installation and one for the installation progress of all packages combined.

When installation finishes, you again see the words All finished near the bottom of the application window. Click Forward to display a brief notice that your updates have all been installed; click Finish when this notice is displayed to close the Red Hat Network agent.

*By the Way*

### Reboot Your Computer

Even though the Red Hat Network update agent doesn't necessarily require you to do so, it's a good idea to reboot your Fedora Core 4 system after updates have been installed to be sure that new settings take effect and that there have been no complications in the update.

# Keeping Fedora Core 4 Updated from the Command Line

For users who require a command-line tool for Fedora Core updates (for example, users running a Linux server system who did not install the desktop components of Fedora), there is another software tool that can be used to keep Fedora Core 4 up to date.

The yum command can be used to update a Fedora Core 4 system or install additional Fedora Core 4 software from the command line. Officially, yum is short for Yellowdog Updater Modified, though it may be easier to remember it as being short for Your Update Manager.

## Updating Fedora Core 4 Using yum

It's surprisingly easy to update a Fedora Core 4 system using yum. In most cases, simply supply the update argument to the yum command from a command prompt (you must be logged in as root to do so). The yum command then checks the update server for updates and begins to compile a list of the software that must be updated:

```
[you@workstation20 you]# yum update
Setting up Update Process
Setting up Repos
[...]
```

As yum collects information on the available list of updates and the dependencies for each package, you'll see a great deal of information about software packages and versions scroll by. Eventually, yum will finish its calculations and ask you whether you want to download and install the list of updated components. Answer yes by entering a **Y**:

```
Update: yum.noarch 0:2.3.2-1 - development
Update: zlib.i386 0:1.2.2.2-3 - development
Update: zlib-devel.i386 0:1.2.2.2-3 - development

Performing the following to resolve dependencies:
  Install: libgcj.i386 0:4.0.0-0.42 - development
  Install: libgcrypt-devel.i386 0:1.2.1-1 - development
  Install: libgpg-error-devel.i386 0:1.0-2 - development
  Install: libtool-ltdl.i386 0:1.5.14.multilib2-6 - development
  Install: perl-Compress-Zlib.i386 0:1.34-2 - development
  Install: pm-utils.i386 0:0.01-1 - development
  Install: python-elementtree.i386 0:1.2.6-4 - development
  Install: sqlite-devel.i386 0:3.1.2-3 - development
Total download size: 518 M
Is this ok [y/N]: y
Downloading Packages:
(1/436): apmd-3.2.2-2.i38 100% |====================| 82 kB
(2/436): evolution-2.2.2- 100% |====================| 9.0 MB
(3/436): gnome-pilot-2.0. 100% |====================| 520 kB
```

After confirming that you want yum to download and install the packages, yum will proceed to do so with no further ado. Once your command prompt returns, your system has been updated. Reboot your computer to ensure that all updates take effect.

## Installing Additional Software Using yum

The yum command can also be used as a convenient tool for installing Fedora Core 4 components and their dependencies without having to resort to installing from CD-ROM. For many users with broadband or corporate Internet connections, this is a much easier way to handle the installation of Fedora Core software components. Note that when software components are installed using yum, you gain the added benefit of automatically having installed the latest version of the component in question.

To install software components automatically using yum, just supply the word install and the name of the package that you want to install as arguments to the yum command:

```
[you@workstation20 you]# yum install samba
```

In a process identical to the one you experience when using yum for updates, yum will query the update server for the latest version of the software package and all of its dependencies before asking you whether you want to download and install them.

Once again, answer Y and yum will go to work, downloading and installing the Fedora Core 4 component that you have requested.

# Summary

In this chapter, you learned how to use the Red Hat Network agent and the Red Hat Network Alert Notification Tool to keep your Fedora Core 4 computer system up to date. Specifically, you learned how to

▶ Configure the Fedora Core 4 system to use Red Hat Network

▶ See updates and mark them for installation using the Red Hat Network agent, up2date

▶ Configure the Red Hat Network Alert Notification Tool to provide you with ongoing status information about Red Hat Network updates

▶ See a summary of update data and start the Red Hat Network agent using the Alert Notification Tool

▶ Perform command-line updates and Fedora Core 4 component installations using yum

Using the tools that you have learned about in this chapter, you should be able to keep your Fedora Core 4 system current and safe from malicious network users or unstable applications.

# Q&A

**Q** *I've heard about a tool called* apt-rpm *that sounds similar to* yum. *Is there such a thing, and does it have any advantages?*

**A** The apt-rpm package manager is indeed very similar to yum and does its job similarly well. For most users, and for beginning users in particular, there is little functional difference between the two. Because yum is installed automatically with Fedora Core 4 and apt-rpm must be downloaded separately, we have discussed yum here.

**Q** *What if I don't purchase a subscription to Fedora Core 4 via the Red Hat Network? Am I free to continue to use this software legally without buying a subscription?*

**A** Yes, you can continue to use Fedora Core 4 even if you don't own or purchase a subscription to Fedora Core 4. The End User License Agreement and the GNU General Public License, which detail your rights to this software, can be found in the text files EULA and GPL on the first Fedora Core 4 CD-ROM.

# Workshop

The Workshop is designed to help you anticipate possible questions, review what you've learned, and begin learning how to put your knowledge into practice.

## Quiz

1. How do you install only a limited selection of available updates, rather than all of them at once?

2. What do the colors of the Red Hat Network Alert Notification Tool icon mean?

## Answers

1. In the Red Hat Network agent, up2date, check the boxes next to the individual packages you would like to install on the Available Package Updates page.

2. Blue means that your Fedora Core 4 system is currently up to date. Red means that new updates are currently available. Green means that the Alert Notification Tool is communicating with the Red Hat Network to see whether new updates are available.

## Activities

1. Click the Red Hat Network Alert Notification Tool icon and browse through the list of currently available updates, if there are any.

2. If updates are available for your Fedora Core 4 system, install them now.

# CHAPTER 33

# Offering Network File Services

---

## *What You'll Learn in This Chapter:*

▶ How to share files with Unix and Linux systems using the Network File System (NFS)

▶ How to share files with Windows systems using Samba

In this chapter, you learn how to share files over the network with other Linux, Unix, or Windows hosts. You also learn how to exercise some measure of control over which files are shared with whom.

## Before You Begin

This chapter refers often to topics covered in earlier chapters. If you haven't yet read them or haven't read them recently, consider refamiliarizing yourself with the following topics and chapters before continuing with this chapter:

▶ Using the Package Management tool to install Fedora Core 4 components, covered in Chapter 31, "Installing Linux Software."

▶ Using text editors to make changes to text files, covered in Chapter 5, "Working with Files on the Desktop," and Chapter 20, "Creating, Editing, and Saving Text Files"

▶ Using Fedora Core 4 and Linux system administration tools to enable or disable installed services for a given runlevel, covered in Chapter 28, "Command-Line System Administration," and Chapter 29, "Desktop System Administration"

▶ Managing the Linux firewalling configuration, including the Other ports box in the Security Level Configuration tool, covered in Chapter 30, "Security Basics"

You will find illustrations and examples in this chapter as you make use of these tools, but for in-depth discussion, refer to the chapters listed in the preceding list.

You will find that some network terminology is unavoidable when discussions of network services begin in earnest. If you are completely unfamiliar with Transmission Control Protocol/Internet Protocol (TCP/IP) networking—the type used by Linux, Unix, and most of the Internet—you should consider keeping a TCP/IP reference of some sort handy, to help you with basic concepts and unfamiliar terms. One of the best on the Internet, with links to a number of other helpful resources, can be found in Wikipedia at:

http://en.wikipedia.org/wiki/TCP/IP

# Offering Network File System Service

The Network File System (NFS) is the de facto standard for file system sharing among Linux and Unix computers. Although other Unix standards for file system sharing offer more security-oriented features or provide better network performance, NFS remains the most widely supported file system sharing service in the Unix world.

The NFS Server Configuration tool is not installed by default in Fedora Core 4 unless you chose the Server installation option when you were installing Fedora Core 4 on your computer. Activating your NFS therefore involves the following steps:

1. Install the NFS Server Configuration tool.

2. Configure the list of filesystems that you want to share via NFS using the configuration tool.

3. Configure your firewall to allow NFS traffic through your network interface.

## Installing the NFS Server Configuration tool

To install the NFS Server Configuration tool so that you can configure NFS on your system, follow these steps:

1. Open the Package Management tool by choosing Desktop, System Settings, Add/Remove software from the desktop menubar.

2. Click the Details button next to the Server Configuration Tools package group. In the details view, check the box next to system-config-nfs, as shown in Figure 33.1. Then click the Close button to close the details view and, in the Package Management tool, click the Update button to update your system.

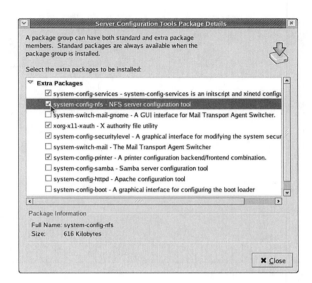

**FIGURE 33.1**
In the Package Management tool's details view for Server Configuration Tools, check the box next to system-config-nfs.

3. When the list of changes is displayed in a confirmation dialog box, click Continue to install the NFS Server Configuration tool on your Fedora Core 4.

4. Log out of your desktop and then log back in again to update the list of applications in your menus.

The NFS Server Configuration tool is now installed on your Fedora Core 4 system and is ready to be used.

## Adding and Configuring NFS Shares

Before you can enable the NFS service, you must configure it so that only the parts of your file system you choose to share are available on the network. You can configure your NFS service in two ways: by using the NFS Server Configuration tool on your desktop or by editing the NFS server configuration files directory with a text editor.

You can start the NFS Server Configuration tool, shown in Figure 33.2, by choosing Desktop, System Settings, Server Settings, NFS from the desktop menubar.

To add an **NFS share** (a directory tree in your file system that other Linux or Unix users can access), choose File, Add Share or click the Add button near the top of the application window. The Add NFS Share dialog box is displayed, as shown in Figure 33.3.

Enter the name of the directory tree you want to share with other users into the Directory entry box. All the directory tree's contents are available to other users via NFS after you share it.

**FIGURE 33.2**
The NFS Server
Configuration
tool is used to
configure your
Fedora Core 4
system for the
Network File
System.

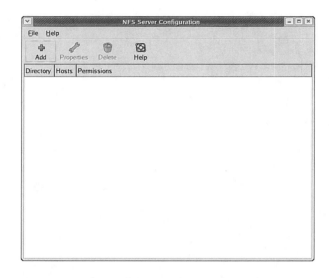

**FIGURE 33.3**
Using the Add
NFS Share
dialog box, you
can add to the
list of file sys-
tem trees that
are available to
network users.

In the Host(s) entry box, you must enter a host or set of hosts on your network that are allowed to use this shared file system. Hosts can be specified in several ways:

▶ To share this directory tree with a single host, enter the host's IP address or name into the box. For example, enter the following:

```
10.2.4.24
```

or

```
workstation10.mycompany.com
```

▶ To share this directory tree with an entire subnetwork, enter the host's IP address, a slash, and then the network mask (you can obtain the network mask from your system administrator). For example, the following entry shares with every machine on the 10.2.4 subnetwork:

```
10.2.4.0/255.255.255.0
```

▶ To share this directory tree with an entire domain or subdomain, use an asterisk (*) as a wildcard (pattern matching) character to indicate the range of hosts you want to share with. For example, the following entry shares with every host on the mycompany.com domain:

```
*.mycompany.com
```

Set the Basic Permissions option to suit your needs. If you want users to be able to read or write to files, select Read/Write; otherwise, select Read-only. Note that Linux file system permissions still apply, even when a directory tree is shared as read/write; users still are prevented from accessing files they don't have permission to access.

After you fill out the Basic tab, click the OK button to dismiss the Add NFS Share dialog box and add the directory tree to the list of shared file systems. The new shared directory tree appears in the list of shared directories in the NFS Server Configuration tool, as shown in Figure 33.4.

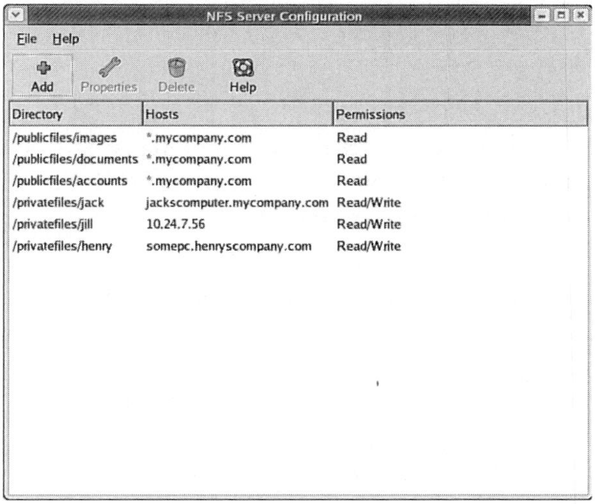

**FIGURE 33.4**
After you enter share details into the Add NFS Share dialog box, the directory tree appears in the NFS Server Configuration tool.

Repeat the process as many times as necessary to add other directory trees you want to share on your network. After your list of shared directory trees is complete, you can close the configuration tool window by clicking on the Close Window button or by choosing File, Quit from the application menu.

## Starting NFS Automatically via the Desktop

To cause the NFS service to start automatically each time your computer is started using the list of shares you created, you must enable NFS in the list of services that are associated with your default runlevel.

To enable NFS, choose Desktop, System Settings, Server Settings, Services to launch the Service Configuration tool. In the Service Configuration tool, ensure that the nfs service is checked, as shown in Figure 33.5.

**FIGURE 33.5**
Using the Service Configuration tool, you can specify that the NFS service should start automatically.

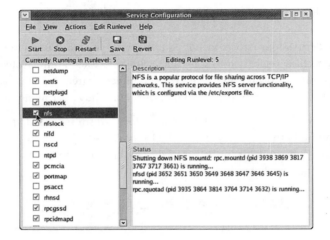

If the nfs service is not checked, check it now to indicate that NFS should be started when your computer starts. After you enable the service, click Save to save your changes. Then choose File, Quit to exit the tool.

## Configuring NFS at the Command Line

The NFS service can also be configured from the command line, if you are more comfortable editing configuration files directly. The NFS service is controlled by the /etc/exports file, which is a text file listing the directory trees to be shared, one per line. To configure your NFS service, simply load the /etc/exports file into your favorite text editor and edit it. The format of each line in the /etc/exports file is as follows:

`/directorytree host(access)`

Replace /directorytree with the directory tree that should be shared, *host* with the host or set of hosts to share using the same format given in the "Adding and Configuring NFS Shares" section earlier this chapter, and *access* with either ro for read-only access or rw for read/write access.

For example, to share /home/you with all the hosts directly in the mycompany.com domain, giving read-only access to the file system, enter the following line into the /etc/exports file:

```
/home/you *.mycompany.com(ro)
```

To also share /publicfiles/august with read/write access to all the machines on the 10.2.4 subnetwork and /tmp with read/write access to a host called barney, enter the following lines into the /etc/exports file:

```
/publicfiles/august 10.2.4.0/255.255.255.0(rw)
/tmp barney.mycompany.com(rw)
```

Enter a line for each directory tree you want to share into the /etc/exports file. When you finish editing the file, save it and exit the text editor.

If you are not already running the NFS service and want to start it immediately based on your new settings, call the service command with the nfs and start arguments:

```
[root@workstation20 you]# /sbin/service nfs start
Starting NFS services:              [ OK ]
Starting NFS quotas:                [ OK ]
Starting NFS daemon:                [ OK ]
Starting NFS mountd:                [ OK ]
[root@workstation20 you]#
```

---

**Use** restart **Instead of** start **for Running Services**

If you are already running the NFS service and want the changes you've made to /etc/exports to take effect, use the restart argument instead of the start argument when calling the nfs script.

*By the Way*

---

As the service command starts the NFS server, you should see four progress messages, each followed by the word OK in brackets. If instead at some point you see FAILED, check your /etc/exports file to make sure that you have formatted it correctly and check your system log for diagnostic information the NFS service is returning. For further help with the format of /etc/exports, see the exports manual page. Consider also consulting your Linux system logs. For details on how to do this, refer to Chapter 29.

# Starting NFS Automatically via the Command Line

You can use the chkconfig command at the command line to cause the NFS service to start automatically each time you start your computer.

To cause NFS to automatically start for a specific runlevel, supply the --level option and the runlevel you want to use with NFS:

```
[root@workstation20 you]# /sbin/chkconfig --level 5 nfs on
[root@workstation20 you]#
```

After you use the chkconfig command to enable NFS, NFS automatically starts each time you boot.

# Allowing NFS Through Your Firewall

Even if you have correctly configured NFS and started the NFS service, you cannot share files with other Linux or Unix users unless you instruct the Linux firewall to allow NFS traffic to be processed.

The mechanism NFS uses to mount shared directory trees is actually quite complex and thus requires both tcp and udp access to ports 111, 369, and 2049. These numbers correspond to the sunrpc, rpc2portmap, and nfs services in the /etc/ services file, respectively.

*By the Way*

> ## What Is All This Network Jargon?
>
> **RPC** stands for **Remote Procedure Call**, **UDP** for **User Datagram Protocol**, and **TCP** for **Transmission Control Protocol**. These standards are all used extensively in Internet networking and Unix operating systems. All three types of communication are essential for the proper functioning of NFS.
>
> For more information on RPC, UDP, TCP, and other networking terms, consult a comprehensive guide to TCP/IP networking.

To allow NFS requests to reach your Linux system, you must lower your firewalling security level to Medium and then create special filtering exceptions for these ports. To do this, start the Security Level Configuration tool by choosing Desktop, System Settings, Security Level. Check the Customize option, and enter the following list of ports into the Other Ports entry box:

```
111:tcp,111:udp,369:tcp,369:udp,2049:tcp,2049:udp
```

If you previously allowed traffic on other ports or for other services using the Security Level Configuration tool, don't forget to enter them again, too: The settings you're entering now *replace* the previous security level settings, not augment them.

After you finish with the Security Level Configuration tool, click the OK button to accept, save, and activate your changes. Remote users should now be able to mount your shared NFS directory trees without problems.

# Offering Windows File Sharing Service

Fedora Core 4 includes software that enables your Linux computer to share files with Windows computers on your network. This software is often referred to by its proper name, Samba, or by the type of high-level protocol it uses—Server Message Blocks, or SMB.

The Windows file server is not installed by default in Fedora Core 4 unless you chose the Server installation option when you were installing Fedora Core 4 on your computer. Activating your Windows file server is therefore a matter of several steps:

1. Install the Windows file server.

2. Use the Samba Server Configuration tool to make Windows shares available to network users.

3. Configure the Windows file server to start automatically each time you boot your computer system.

4. Configure your firewall to allow Windows file sharing requests.

## Installing Windows File Sharing Service

To ensure that the Windows file server is installed or to install it if it hasn't already been installed, follow these steps:

1. Open the Package Management tool by choosing Desktop, System Settings, Add/Remove Applications.

2. Check the box next to the Windows File Server package group, as shown in Figure 33.6. Then click the Update button to update your system.

3. When the list of changes is displayed in a confirmation dialog box, click Continue to install the Windows File Server on your Fedora Core 4 system.

4. Log out of your desktop and then log back in again to update the list of applications in your menus.

The Windows file server and related tools should now be installed on your system and ready for use.

## Starting the Samba Server Configuration Tool

The Samba Server Configuration tool is used to provide Fedora Core 4 with details about which files and directories should be made available to other Windows hosts on your network. To start the Samba Server Configuration tool, choose Desktop,

System Settings, Server Settings, Samba. The Samba Server Configuration tool appears, as shown in Figure 33.7.

**FIGURE 33.6**
In the Package Management tool, check the box next to the Windows File Server package group.

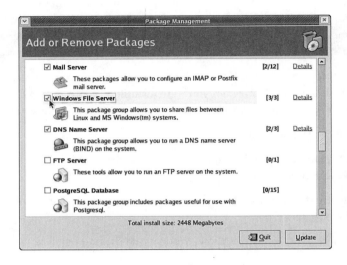

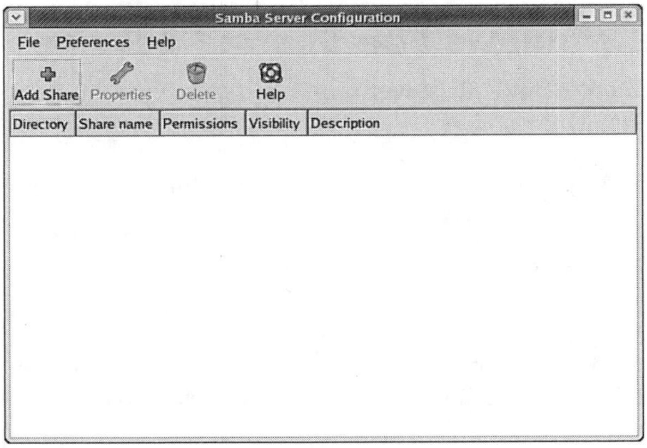

**FIGURE 33.7**
The Samba Server Configuration tool tells Fedora Core 4 which files and directories you want to share.

# Deciding on a Security Model

You can choose to give access to Windows file sharing users in two ways for a given shared folder or set of files:

▶ Complete, public access. After you share a file or directory, it is available to everyone on your network.

▶ Per-user access. After creating a list of users who should have access to Windows file sharing on your Fedora Core 4 computer, you give access to shared files or directories on a per-user basis, drawing from this list.

You can use a combination of these two paradigms, giving complete public access to some shared files or directories, while restricting other shared files or folders to a select list of users.

## Creating a Samba User List

To limit access to shared files or directories on a per-user basis, you must create and maintain a list of Samba users on your Fedora Core 4 system. To edit the list of Samba users, choose Preferences, Samba Users from the Samba Server Configuration tool's menu bar. The Samba Users dialog box is displayed, as shown in Figure 33.8.

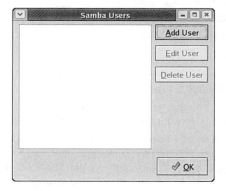

**FIGURE 33.8**
Using the Samba Users dialog box, you can maintain the list of users given access to Samba shares.

To add a new user to this list of users, click the Add User button on the right side of the dialog box. Another dialog box, labeled Create New Samba User, is displayed, as shown in Figure 33.9.

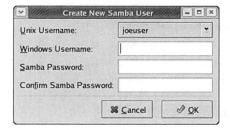

**FIGURE 33.9**
Using the Create New Samba User dialog box, you can create a new Samba user, linking a Fedora Core 4 user account to a remote Windows system account.

Follow these steps to fill out the fields in the Create New Samba User dialog box:

1. In the Unix Username drop-down list, select the name of the local (Fedora Core 4) user who will be gaining access to this computer's files across the Windows network.

2.  In the Windows Username text entry box, enter the user's account name on the Windows network or on the remote Windows host.

3.  In the Samba Password text entry box, enter the user's Windows network or Windows host password.

4.  Reenter the password in the Confirm Samba Password box to be sure that you've typed it correctly.

5.  Click OK to save your changes and add the user to the list of Samba users.

Repeat these steps for each Fedora Core 4 user who needs to be given access to Fedora Core 4 files while using remote Windows computers. After you finish editing the user list, click OK to close the Samba Users dialog box and save your changes.

*By the Way*

> ### Editing and Deleting Samba Users
>
> You may have noticed two other buttons in the Samba Users dialog box. These buttons do exactly what you would expect them to do, based on their labels.
>
> The Edit User button is used to edit settings for the user who is currently selected in the list. When you click Edit User, a dialog box identical to the Create New Samba User dialog box appears, with settings already filled out for the user in question. Edit them as necessary and click OK to save your changes.
>
> The Delete User button is used to remove the user who is currently selected from the Samba users list. The deleted user loses all Windows networking privileges to your Fedora Core 4 computer, except for shared files or directories that are marked as public.

## Creating Windows Shares

Windows networking makes files and directories available in units known as shares. To create a new share that will be made available from your Fedora Core 4 system, choose File, Add Share or click the Add button near the top of the Samba Server Configuration tool window. The Create Samba Share dialog box is displayed, as shown in Figure 33.10.

To add a share in the Create Samba Share dialog box, follow these steps:

1.  Enter the path (folder or directory tree) that you want to share in the Directory text entry box.

2.  Enter the name of the share in the Share box. This is the name of the icon under which the directory will appear when others browse your computer. For

example, some appropriate share names might be HardDrive, PublicFiles, or Graphics.

**FIGURE 33.10**
The Create Samba Share dialog box helps you to create new shares that will be made available from your Fedora Core 4 computer.

3. Enter a brief human-readable description of this share in the Description box.

4. Check the Writable box if you want to grant both read and write permission to other hosts on the network, or leave it unchecked if the directory should be shared for reading only.

5. Check the Visible box if you want the share to show up in other users' file managers when they browse your computer. Leave it unchecked if remote users should have to request the share by name to see it.

6. Click the Access tab in the Create Samba Share dialog box.

7. If you want to make the share public (accessible to everyone on the network), select Allow Access to Everyone. Otherwise, select Only Allow Access to Specific Users and then place checks in the boxes next to the names of users who should be allowed to access this share on the network, as shown in Figure 33.11.

**FIGURE 33.11**
To limit share access to a specific group of users, select Only Allow Access to Specific Users; then check the boxes by their names.

8. Click OK to save the share you have created.

*By the Way*

---

## Permissions Matter When Files Are Shared

Even if a user or group of users is given read-only or read/write permission for a share, Linux file system permissions are still in charge. The remote user's ability to read from or write to a shared file or directory is limited by the permissions given to that user by the Linux file system. For more information on file system permissions, refer to Chapter 7, "Understanding File Properties."

---

Repeat this process for each share that you need to create. After you finish creating all the shares you need, choose File, Quit or click the Close button near the upper right of the application window to save your changes.

## Starting and Autostarting Windows File Service

To start the Windows file server from your desktop after you configure it, choose Desktop, Server Settings, Services to display the Service Configuration tool. Select the smb service; then click the Start button near the top of the application window, as shown in Figure 33.12.

**FIGURE 33.12**
To start Windows file sharing, select the smb service and click Start. To cause the service to start each time Fedora Core 4 starts, check the box next to smb.

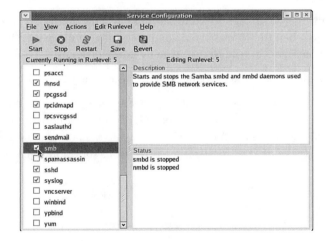

To cause Windows file sharing to start each time Fedora Core 4 starts, check the box next to the smb service, then click Save, and then choose File, Quit to exit the Services Configuration tool.

From the command line, you can start Windows file sharing by using the `service` command you learned about in Chapter 28:

```
[root@workstation20 you]$ /sbin/service smb start
[root@workstation20 you]$
```

You can configure the Windows file server to start automatically for your default runlevel by using the chkconfig command at the command line along with the --level option, supplying smb and the word on as arguments:

```
[root@workstation20 you]# /sbin/chkconfig --level 5 smb on
[root@workstation20 you]#
```

## Allowing Windows File Service Through Your Firewall

Although your Windows file server is now fully configured and running, users on your network cannot access your Windows shares until you tell the firewall to allow Windows file service traffic.

To enable Windows file service traffic, start the Security Level Configuration tool by choosing Desktop, System Settings, Security Level. Configure your firewall as usual but enter the following additional ports into the Other Ports entry box at the bottom of the tool:

```
137:tcp,137:udp,138:tcp,138:udp,139:tcp,139:udp
```

Once again, be sure to enter these ports as well as any other special ports you configured for your firewall because each time you run the Security Level Configuration tool, it replaces the previous settings instead of augmenting them. After you configure your firewall, click the OK button to save and activate your firewall settings and close the Security Level Configuration tool.

# Summary

In this chapter, you learned how to configure a Fedora Core 4 computer to act as a file server for other Linux or Unix computers, as well as for Windows computers on your network.

To enable your Network File System (NFS) service, you learned to do the following:

▶ Install the NFS Configuration tool to easily add and configure NFS exports

▶ Add NFS shares, either by using the NFS Server Configuration tool or by editing the /etc/exports file directly

▶ Configure the NFS server to start automatically each time you boot Linux, either by using the Service Configuration tool or the chkconfig command

▶ Edit your packet filtering configuration to allow NFS network traffic

To enable your Windows file sharing service, you learned to do the following:

▶ Install the Windows File Server package group

▶ Use the Samba Server Configuration tool to create and edit a user list and a share list

▶ Configure the Samba server to start automatically each time you boot Linux, either by using the Service Configuration tool or the `chkconfig` command

▶ Edit your packet filtering configuration to allow Windows networking traffic

Using the techniques you learned in this chapter, you should now be able to efficiently and naturally exchange files with nearly any computer on your network.

This chapter presented enough information to get you up and running. However, if you plan to run a high-volume or high-profile file server, you should seriously consider consulting more advanced documentation for these services and for Linux network security. One of the favorite sources of documentation in the Linux world is *The Linux Documentation Project* at http://www.tldp.org.

# Q&A

**Q** *How do I access NFS shares from another Linux or Unix system?*

**A** As explained in Chapter 29, you can mount a remote file system on a Linux or Unix computer using the following command:

```
mount -t nfs host:/tree /mnt/point
```

Replace *host* with the hostname of the server, */tree* with the shared directory tree, and */mnt/point* with the mountpoint on the local system where you want the shared files to appear. For example, to mount the /publicfiles directory on a host called mack on the local directory /network/publicfiles, you enter the following:

```
mount -t nfs mack:/publicfiles /network/publicfiles
```

**Q** *Can I also use Samba to share my printers with other Windows machines?*

**A** Yes, but because of driver issues related to printing in Windows, the process can at times be rather complex, and is therefore beyond the scope of a beginning-level book like this one. Consult the online Samba documentation at http://www.samba.org for details on printing with Samba.

**Q** *Can I use Linux to serve files to Mac OS computers?*

**A** Yes. Mac OS X includes the capability of sharing files using either Windows file sharing or NFS; you can choose to use whichever method you prefer. Consult your Mac OS X documentation for details on mounting NFS or Windows shares in Mac OS.

# Workshop

The Workshop is designed to help you anticipate possible questions, review what you've learned, and begin learning how to put your knowledge into practice.

## Quiz

1. What does the /etc/exports file do?

2. What general security level must be used for NFS to function properly?

3. What happens if you create a public, read/write share that points to a directory that is marked read-only by its Linux permissions?

## Answers

1. The /etc/exports file contains a list of the NFS shares offered by your computer system.

2. To offer NFS services, you must use the Medium security level and accept ports 111, 369, and 2049.

3. Because Linux file ownership and permissions supercede any Samba configuration, no remote user will be able to write to a read/write share that is marked read-only by its Linux permissions.

# CHAPTER 34

# Offering Web and FTP Service

## What You'll Learn in This Chapter:

▶ How to install and enable the Apache web server
▶ How to provide basic content using the web server
▶ How to configure the FTP service to allow logins and home directory access
▶ How to enable anonymous FTP logins

In this chapter, you learn how to configure your Fedora Core 4 computer system to act as a web server or an FTP server. These services represent the most visible uses of the Internet, beyond simple email. Together, they can turn your Linux computer into a capable Internet server platform.

## Before You Begin

This chapter refers often to topics covered in earlier chapters. If you haven't yet read them or haven't read them recently, consider refamiliarizing yourself with the following topics and chapters before continuing:

▶ Using the Package Management tool to install Fedora Core 4 components, covered in Chapter 31, "Installing Linux Software."

▶ Using text editors to make changes to plaintext files, covered in Chapter 5, "Working with Files on the Desktop," and Chapter 20, "Creating, Editing, and Saving Text Files"

▶ Using Fedora Core 4 and Linux system administration tools to enable or disable installed services for a given runlevel, covered in Chapter 28, "Command-Line System Administration," and Chapter 29, "Desktop System Administration"

▶ Managing the Linux firewalling configuration, including the Other Ports box in the Security Level Configuration tool, covered in Chapter 30, "Security Basics"

You will find illustrations and examples in this chapter as you use these tools, but for in-depth discussion, refer to the chapters listed in the preceding list.

As we've said already, you will find that some network terminology is unavoidable when discussions of network services begin in earnest. If you are completely unfamiliar with Transmission Control Protocol/Internet Protocol (TCP/IP) networking—the type used by Linux, Unix, and most of the Internet—you should consider keeping a TCP/IP reference of some sort handy, to help you with basic concepts and unfamiliar terms.

# Running a Web Server

Using Linux, you can configure your computer to act as a web **server**—a computer that delivers web content to web browsers running on computers around your network or around the Internet at large.

The web server software included with Fedora Core 4 is the single most popular web server platform in use today and is known as the Apache web server. To use your Fedora Core 4 system as a web server with existing web content, you must complete the following tasks:

1. Install the Apache web server by installing the web server software group

2. Install the tools used to configure the Apache web server by checking system-config-httpd in the Server Configuration Tools software group

3. Configure Linux to automatically start the Apache web server each time Linux starts

4. Configure your Linux firewall to allow traffic related to web requests

## Installing Apache

You can install the Apache web server using the Package Management tool. Start this tool by choosing Desktop, System Settings, Add/Remove Applications. In the Package Management tool, scroll down to the Servers category and check the box next to the Web Server package group, as shown in Figure 34.1. Then click the Update button to install the new software.

Before you use the Apache web server, you should also install the Apache Configuration tool, so that you can make more involved changes to Apache's configuration if you choose to do so. You can do this in the software configuration tool by following these steps:

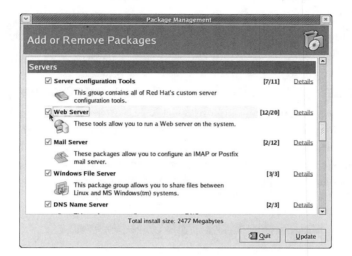

1. Click the Details button next to the Server Configuration Tools software group in the Package Management tool, as shown in Figure 34.2.

2. Check the box next to the system-config-httpd software package.

3. Click Close to close the Details view, then click Update to install the software on your system.

4. Log out of your desktop, then log back in again to update your desktop menus.

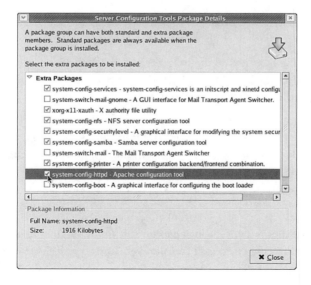

The Apache web server and a user-friendly tool to configure it are now installed on your computer system and ready for use. In fact, for many users, no additional Apache configuration is required at all!

## Configuring Apache to Start Automatically

To use your Fedora Core 4 computer as a web server after you have installed the Apache web server software, you must configure Apache to start automatically each time you start Linux. To configure Apache to start automatically using desktop tools, choose Desktop, System Settings, Server Settings, Services to start the Service Configuration tool. Check the box next to the httpd service, as shown in Figure 34.3.

**FIGURE 34.3**
Use the Service Configuration tool to configure the Apache web server to start each time Linux starts.

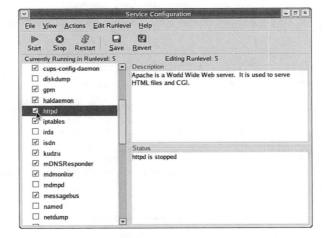

After you check the box next to the httpd service, click the Save button to save your changes. Next, click the Start button to start the httpd service now. Then choose File, Quit to exit the Service Configuration tool.

If you prefer to use command-line tools, you can use the chkconfig command to configure the Apache web server to start automatically each time Linux starts at your default runlevel. Call the chkconfig command, supplying httpd and the word on as arguments:

```
[root@workstation20 you]# /sbin/chkconfig --level 5 httpd on
[root@workstation20 you]#
```

You have now configured your web server to start automatically when Linux starts, but if you've just installed it, it isn't running yet. To start it, either reboot Linux or call the `service` command, supplying `httpd` and the word `start` as arguments to cause the server to start now:

```
[root@workstation20 you]# /sbin/service httpd start
Starting httpd:                    [ OK ]
[root@workstation20 you]#
```

## Allowing Web Requests Through Your Firewall

Now you have the Apache web server running, but before it can answer web requests from machines on your network or from the Internet at large, you must configure your firewall to allow web requests. To do this, start the Security Level Configuration tool by choosing Desktop, System Settings, Security Level.

Ensure that the security level is set to Enable Firewall, then check the WWW (HTTP) option in the Trusted Services area of the tool, as shown in Figure 34.4. Click OK to save your changes.

**FIGURE 34.4**
Check the WWW (HTTP) box in the Security Level Configuration tool to allow web requests through your firewall.

## Using the Apache Web Server

After a reboot, or after starting Apache using the Service Configuration tool, your web server is up and running and allowing requests from the outside world. The default Apache configuration is adequate and correct for most users—no need for additional up-front configuration when starting out. The properties of the web server in its default configuration are as follows:

▶ Your web content goes in the /var/www/html directory tree. Note that any files your web server should deliver must be set to have publicly (all users) readable permissions.

▶ The contact email address, which is displayed to visitors when errors occur, is root@*hostname*, where *hostname* is your computer's hostname.

▶ The default index files, which will be loaded for any visited directory, are index.php, index.html, index.htm, and index.shtml, in that order.

▶ Your Common Gateway Interface (CGI) /cgi-bin/ scripts should be placed in the /var/www/cgi-bin directory.

▶ Secure Sockets Layer (SSL) https:// connections are supported.

Because your web server is already online if you've followed the steps outlined thus far in this chapter, you can begin copying your content to or creating your content in /var/www/html; any files you place there from now on will be instantly available to the world.

## Enabling Home Directory Websites

If your Linux computer system serves a number of users, you might want to give each user the opportunity to host his or her own home page. Although you can do this while still keeping all content in the /var/www/html directory tree, it is certainly not convenient, and of course it's not a good idea to give multiple users write access to system directories.

The Apache web server has the capability of giving each user on a Linux system her own HTML content directory, by default in /home/*user*/public_html. Visitors can then load the index page at /home/*user*/public_html/index.html by constructing a URL using the hostname of your web server followed by a slash (/), a tilde (~), another slash, and the name of the user whose home page should be loaded, as follows:

```
http://host.mycompany.com/~jane/
```

For example, this URL loads the file index.html stored in the /home/jane/ public_html directory.

To enable this functionality in Apache, you must edit the web server configuration file, /etc/httpd/conf/httpd.conf. Load the file into your favorite text editor and search for the text shown in Listing 34.1.

**LISTING 34.1**    Text to Change to Enable Home Pages

```
<IfModule mod_userdir.c>
  #
  # UserDir is disabled by default since it can confirm the presence
  # of a username on the system (depending on home directory
  # permissions).
  #
  UserDir disable
```

Notice the text UserDir disable. If user home directories are to be enabled, you must change this line to read UserDir public_html, as shown in Listing 34.2.

**LISTING 34.2**    Text Changed to Enable Home Pages

```
<IfModule mod_userdir.c>
  #
  # UserDir is disabled by default since it can confirm the presence
  # of a username on the system (depending on home directory
  # permissions).
  #
  UserDir public_html
```

Then save the httpd.conf file and exit. To cause the changes to take effect, restart your web server using either the Service Configuration tool you used earlier or using the service command, supplying httpd and restart as arguments:

```
[root@workstation20 you]# /sbin/service httpd restart
Stopping httpd:                    [ OK ]
Starting httpd:                    [ OK ]
[root@workstation20 you]#
```

---

**You Can Restart a Web Server Gracefully**

*Did you Know?*

On a busy web server, you should use the graceful argument instead of the restart argument to restart the web server:

```
    /sbin/service httpd graceful
```

When a web server is restarted using the graceful argument, it might not restart and update its configuration immediately; instead, it processes all pending requests before restarting, to make sure that everyone who has requested to view your website is able to do so.

---

Before a user's public_html directory can be used, the permissions for the user's home directory, the ~/public_html directory, and the contents of the ~/public_html directory must be correctly configured:

▶ Using chmod in numeric mode, you must set the user's home directory to 711— user read, write, and execute; group execute; and other (public) execute.

▶ Using chmod in numeric mode, you must set the user's ~/public_html directory and all subdirectories to 755—user read, write, and execute; group read and execute; and public read and execute.

▶ Using chmod in numeric mode, you must set all the content files in the user's ~/public_html directory tree, such as HTML files and images, to 644—user read and write, group read, and public read.

---

### Don't Change a User's File Permissions Without Asking

If you're administering a system with many users, always warn users before changing the permissions of any files or directories in their home directory. Using administration privileges to change users' file or directory permissions without first warning them of which files and directories will be changed might make public files that were intended to remain private or endanger the files in other ways! By warning users first of the changes that will be made to their home directory, you give them a chance to move critical files or directories to other areas, or to ask you, the administrator, not to make the change in the first place.

---

If permissions are incorrectly set or if a user does not have a public_html directory, visitors who try to load a user's home page get an error message saying that the page in question is Forbidden.

## Introducing the Apache Configuration Tool

The default configuration of the Apache web server is sufficient to provide access to basic public web content. The default configuration may not be appropriate, however, when business interests or large amounts of content are at stake. You can use the Apache Configuration tool to configure many of the options related to the Apache web server and its level of security and performance while operating.

To start the Apache Configuration tool, choose Desktop, System Settings, Server Settings, HTTP; the Apache Configuration tool is displayed, as shown in Figure 34.5.

The Apache configuration tool contains four basic tabs—Main, Virtual Hosts, Server, and Performance Tuning—that function as follows:

▶ The Main tab contains general systemwide configuration options, including the fully qualified domain name of your web server, the email address of the administrator, and the set of Ethernet addresses on which your web server will listen for incoming requests.

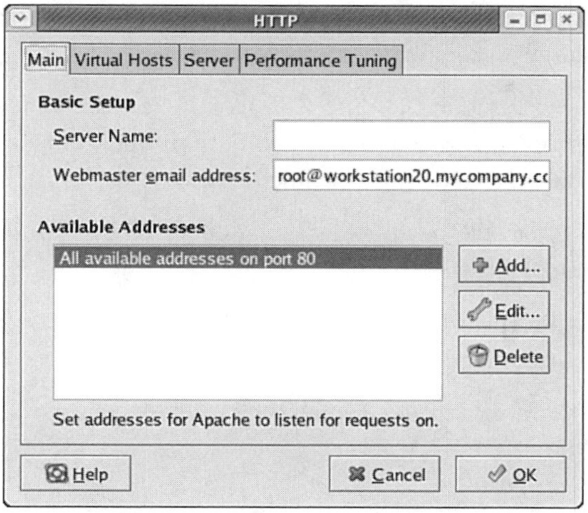

FIGURE 34.5
The Apache
Configuration
tool provides a
graphical inter-
face for config-
uring the
Apache web
server.

▶ The Virtual Hosts tab enables you to configure the default host (most commonly used for small web servers) or a number of user-definable virtual hosts,
such as are commonly used by ISPs or larger companies.

▶ The Server tab enables you to configure some basic housekeeping properties,
such as the directory in which Apache will write machine-readable error information if it crashes, and the user and group identities under which Apache
should run. As a general rule, changing these options is not a good idea.

▶ The Performance Tuning tab enables you to fine-tune your Apache installation for the amount of traffic you expect to receive. It includes options such
as the maximum number of connections Apache will manage at one time
before it begins turning down requests for web content.

The two most important tabs are the Virtual Hosts tab, where most security control
occurs and where multiple hosts are managed if you are running a larger server,
and the Performance Tuning tab, which enables you to adjust Apache's workload to
suit your computer system hardware and the set of scripts (if any) you'll be using on
your website.

## Basic Apache Security

As you run your web server on a day-to-day basis, you will likely want to be able to
control which Internet users can view which parts of your website. Some areas of a
site are meant for public consumption, and other parts are intended for certain

viewers only. You can control viewership of your site by filtering web requests based on the Internet addresses from which viewers originate.

You can filter requests through the Virtual Hosts tab. Because we're covering only the basics in this chapter, let's assume that you are running only a single web host that provides you with basic web server functionality.

To control which visitors will be able to see files delivered by your default virtual host, follow these steps:

1. Click the Virtual Hosts tab and then click the Edit Default Settings button to display the Virtual Host Properties dialog box.

2. Click the Performance tab to display the Directory configuration pane, as shown in Figure 34.6.

**FIGURE 34.6**
In the Directories item of the Virtual Host Properties dialog box, you can configure directories on your website to have specific security features.

By default, only one directory, the root directory (/) appears in the list, meaning that all of the directories on your web server share the same set of security properties. If you wish to specify different per-directory security measures, you can add new directory trees to the list by clicking the Add button; you can then give different directories different access properties.

For now, simply highlight the root directory and click the Edit button to display the Directory Options dialog box, as shown in Figure 34.7.

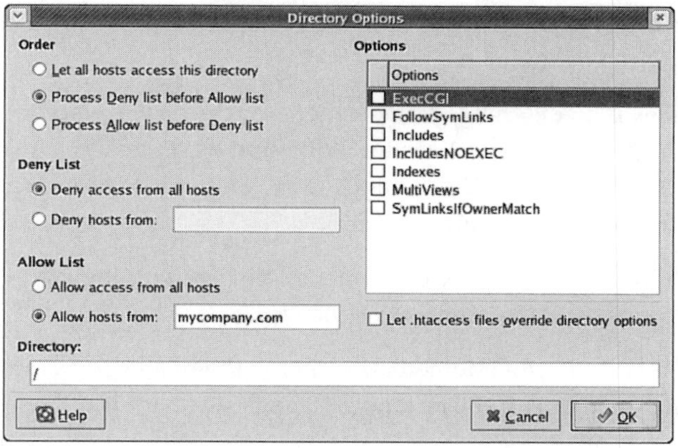

**FIGURE 34.7**
Using the Directory Options dialog box, you can give specific security properties to directories within your web content directory tree.

Several settings on the left side of the Directory Options dialog box are related to access control based on the IP address or domain name of connecting hosts. These settings are configured as follows:

▶ If you want all visitors to be able to access this directory, check Let All Hosts Access This Directory. If you want to restrict access only to certain hosts, choose either Process Deny List before Allow List or Process Allow List before Deny List (you'll create lists of denied or allowed hosts in a moment).

▶ The Deny List and Allow List options are used in conjunction with the previously discussed option to create rules (and, if you so desire, exceptions) about which hosts should or shouldn't be able to access content stored in the directory in question. You can enter hosts as IP numbers, partial IP numbers, or partial domains. The configuration shown in Figure 34.7 would allow only hosts in the domain mycompany.com to access content in the root directory and its children.

In the Options list box, you can choose from a number of options to enable or disable certain capabilities for the specified directory. Select or deselect check boxes to control the following capabilities:

▶ If the ExecCGI box is checked, scripts requested from files in this directory will be called. If it is not checked, they won't.

▶ If the FollowSymLinks box is checked, symbolic links in this directory that point to other files or directories will be followed and used. If it is not checked, they will be ignored.

▶ If the Includes box is checked, server-side includes in content files will be honored. If it is not checked, they will be ignored.

▶ If the IncludesNOEXEC box is checked, requests in server-side includes to use #exec will not be honored.

▶ If the Indexes box is checked, the contents of the directory (a directory index) will be displayed to the web visitor requesting the index if no index file is present in the directory. If it is not checked, attempts to visit directories without an index file will return an error.

▶ If the Multiview box is checked, content-negotiated multiviews will be allowed. If it is not checked, they will not be allowed.

▶ If the SymLinksIfOwnerMatch box is checked, symbolic links in the directory will be followed only if the destination file or directory has the same owner as the symbolic link itself.

**Don't Change Options Lightly**

Do not check any option box unless you know for sure that you need the capability it provides. Each of these options represents additional vulnerability that could conceivably be exploited by a malicious web user.

Near the bottom of the dialog, you'll also find a check box labeled Let .htaccess Override Directory Options. If this box is checked and Apache finds a file called .htaccess in the directory in question, configuration directives in the .htaccess file will override the configuration you've specified in the configuration tool.

When you finish configuring the host security options for the directory in question, click the OK button to save your changes and return to the Virtual Host Properties dialog box's Directory pane. If you want to configure additional security properties for other directories within your web content tree, click the Add button to bring the Directory Options dialog box back up. In the Directory box of the Directory Options dialog box, enter the name of the directory to which these options should apply and then set the options for that directory just as you did for your root content directory.

When you finish making changes to your Apache configuration, click OK in the Virtual Host Properties dialog box and click OK in the Apache Configuration tool to exit and save your changes.

## Additional Apache Configuration Information

The Apache web server can also be configured using your favorite text editor. To do this, edit the files stored in /etc/httpd/conf and /etc/httpd/conf.d. These files are large and fairly involved, however, so you shouldn't venture into editor-based configuration unless you have an Apache reference volume handy.

Because the Apache web server is a relatively complex application, further Apache configuration is beyond the scope of a beginning-level book like this one. A great deal of in-depth documentation for Apache can be found on the main Apache website, at http://httpd.apache.org/docs-2.0/.

# Running a File Transfer Protocol Server

The File Transfer Protocol (FTP) service allows users to download files from—and in some cases upload files to—your Linux system using special programs called **FTP clients**, or in some cases using a standard web browser.

To offer FTP service on your Linux computer, you must do the following:

- ▶ Install the vsftpd service on your computer
- ▶ Configure Linux to automatically start the vsftpd service when you start your computer
- ▶ Configure your Linux firewall to allow traffic related to FTP requests

## Installing vsftpd

You can install the vsftpd FTP server using the Package Management tool. Start this tool by choosing Desktop, System Settings, Add/Remove Applications. In the Package Management tool, scroll down to the Servers category and check the box next to the FTP Server package group, as shown in Figure 34.8. Then click the Update button to install the new  software.

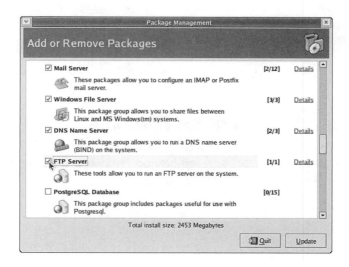

**FIGURE 34.8**
Use the Package Management tool to install the vsftpd FTP server that comes with Fedora Core 4.

## Enabling or Disabling FTP

To configure Fedora Core 4 to start the `vsftpd` server each time you start your computer, choose Desktop, System Settings, Server Settings, Services to start the Service Configuration tool. Check the box next to the `vsftpd` service, as shown in Figure 34.9.

**FIGURE 34.9**
Using the Service Configuration tool, you can configure Fedora Core 4 to start vsftpd server as needed whenever you start your computer.

After you check the box next to the `vsftpd` service, click the Save button to save your changes. Be sure to click the Start button first if you want to run `vsftpd` right away.

If you prefer to use command-line tools, you can use the `chkconfig` command to configure Fedora Core 4 to automatically start the `vsftpd` server:

```
[root@workstation20 you]# /sbin/chkconfig --level 5 gssftp on
[root@workstation20 you]#
```

You have now configured your Fedora Core 4 computer to accept incoming FTP connections.

## Allowing FTP Through Your Firewall

Before incoming FTP requests can be received, you must configure your Linux firewall to allow FTP-related traffic. To do this, choose Desktop, System Settings, Security Level to start the Security Level Configuration tool.

In the standard Security Level Configuration tool, check the box next to FTP in the Trusted Services area.

Be sure also that the Enable Firewall option is selected from the Security level drop-down list.

# Controlling FTP Access

The FTP server normally allows users to log in with their account and password information, thereby gaining full read and write access to your system—limited only by file system permissions—just as if they were accessing files directly. If certain users have no valid need to access their files remotely via FTP, you should disable FTP logins for their accounts as a precautionary measure.

The /etc/ftpusers file contains a list of login accounts, one per line, that are not allowed to log in to FTP using their account. To shut off FTP access for a specific user on your system, use your favorite text editor to add a line to /etc/ftpusers containing only the name of the account. For example, to prevent you from logging in via ftp, add the following line to /etc/ftpusers:

you

The user you is no longer allowed to log in to FTP via his account.

# Using or Disabling Anonymous FTP

File Transfer Protocol is a special kind of service that allows connecting users to log in as the user ftp or the user anonymous without supplying a password, to access a set of files you have provided for public download. Anonymous FTP is commonly used to distribute large software or media files to the general public via the Internet.

By default, the Fedora Core 4 FTP server is configured to allow anonymous logins. The files that users will be able to download when they log in anonymously are those stored in /var/ftp.

There is no reason to allow anonymous logins, however, if you don't plan to distribute files publicly via FTP. If this is the case for you, you should disable anonymous FTP. You can do this simply by editing the /etc/ftpusers file and adding the user ftp to the end of the file.

---

**Be Careful with Anonymous FTP**                                    *Watch Out!*

Anonymous FTP is a service with a relatively poor security history. To avoid data loss or theft, it is recommended that Linux and Unix beginners or users without a dedicated and properly configured FTP host not run anonymous FTP servers.

If you do plan to offer anonymous FTP, you *must* take care to remove write permission from all directories in /var/ftp and write and execute permission from all files in /var/ftp.

---

# Summary

In this chapter, you learned to install and use the Apache web server and FTP server, which come with Fedora Core 4. Specifically, you learned the following:

▶ How to install and start the Apache web server

▶ How to allow web requests through your firewall

▶ Where to place your HTML content so that Apache can deliver it to users who request it

▶ How to enable the `vsftpd` server for FTP service

▶ How to control the list of users who can log in to FTP

# Q&A

**Q.** *When I try to load my web pages (or the web pages of one of my users), I get a `403 Forbidden` error. How can I fix this problem?*

**A.** Any content that Apache delivers to the outside world must be set to be readable by everyone so that the account under which Apache runs will be able to read it. Also refer back to the special list of permissions required for users' home directories in the "Enabling Home Directory Websites" section.

**Q.** *I've added a user to the `/etc/ftpusers` file, but she can't log in via FTP. Why?*

**A.** Counterintuitively, the `/etc/ftpusers` file is a list of users who are *forbidden* from using FTP, not a list of users who are *allowed* to use FTP. Remove the user from `/etc/ftpusers`, and she should be able to log in.

# Workshop

The Workshop is designed to help you anticipate possible questions, review what you've learned, and begin learning how to put your knowledge into practice.

## Quiz

1. Where should your system's web content be stored?

2. Where should your individual users' web content be stored if you are offering home pages to your users?

3. How do you disable anonymous FTP logins?

## Answers

1. `/var/www/html`

2. `~/public_html`

3. Add the user `ftp` to the end of the `/etc/ftpusers` file.

## Activities

1. Enable the Apache web server and post some HTML content at the main index.

2. Enable public web directories for users and create a personal home page for yourself.

# CHAPTER 35

# Backups, Troubleshooting, and Rescue

---

## What You'll Learn in This Chapter:

▶ How to back up your data, either on magnetic tape or removable media
▶ How to automate backups using shell scripts and the `cron` service
▶ How to restore data that you have previously backed up
▶ How to recognize signs of trouble and what to do about it
▶ How to use the Fedora Core 4 `rescue` system

In this last chapter, you learn how to deal with some of the tedious chores of computing life: making backups of your valuable data, restoring from these backups, and knowing just when to do either. Although discussions of backing up or restoring data and performing rescue operations often get lost in the shuffle of more immediately useful topics, you should pay as much—or perhaps more—attention to this chapter as you have to all the rest. This book is 35 chapters long, and working through it may seem to take days or even weeks—but it can take much longer than that to re-create months' or years' worth of data that was lost because you didn't maintain regular backups.

## Backing Up and Restoring Your Data

By the time you have used Linux for a few months, you will have built a collection of important files of various kinds—important spreadsheets, documents in progress, web content, or any number of other types of files. What an annoyance—or worse—it would be to lose them!

Modern hard drives are remarkably reliable, especially when compared to the storage devices used by early computers. However, for every handful of users who have never lost an important file due to circumstance or hardware failure, there is at least one user who has seen hours and hours of work lost in the void. Users who suffer data loss inevitably regret not having made backups of their data.

A number of common types of backup media are in widespread use today, but they all fit into one of three major categories:

▶ Hot-pluggable drives, like USB or IEEE1394 (FireWire) hard drives or storage keys. These devices have a fixed amount of storage and can be accessed like a hard drive or floppy drive. Back up files by copying them to the external drive or key and then store it in a safe place.

▶ Tape drives, such as 8mm or 4mm DAT drives or DLT cartridge streamers. These devices typically have very large storage capacities, which must be accessed in a single, extended read or write (stream) operation, rather than a file at a time.

▶ Removable disk drives, such as Zip, Jaz, Orb, DVD-RAM, magneto-optical, or LS-120. These devices act like a cross between a floppy drive and a hard drive: They are removable and easily (randomly) accessible like floppy drives but hold much more data than can fit on a single floppy disk. If you have many gigabytes of data, though, watch out: Making a backup copy of every file on a full 80 gigabyte hard drive can take more 100 CD-R disks or more than 300 Zip disks.

▶ CD-R and DVD-R drives, which can be written to only once (or in some cases, several times) and which must also be written in a single, extended write operation using special software tools. If you need to use a CD-R or DVD-R drive in Linux, see the manual pages for `mkisofs` and `cdrecord`, or refer to Chapter 15, "Playing and Recording Sound and Music" for details on burning files to CDs or DVDs using the file manager.

If your Linux computer is acting as a personal workstation or small server, most of the files you want to save will be documents—OpenOffice.org files, World Wide Web content, LaTeX source files, or similar things that you have invested your time and effort in creating. These types of files don't take up much space and are relatively easy to back up simply by copying them to your backup medium.

If you need to back up a larger amount of data or a large number of files, a tool specially designed for backing up large amounts of data, like the `tar` command, can be extremely helpful.

Both of these techniques are discussed in the sections that follow.

# Backing Up to Disk or Removable Media

In Chapter 15, "Playing and Recording Sound and Music," you learned how to copy files onto CD-ROM discs. USB keys and Zip, Jaz, or other removable magnetic storage devices are also ideal backup media for small-to-medium amounts of data. They are more convenient than CD-ROMs because they can be accessed in the same way as the rest of your Linux file system, though they generally hold slightly less.

Backing up files or entire directory trees to removable disk devices from your desktop is simple. Just insert the disk into its drive or the USB key into your USB port and, if the Fedora Core 4 desktop supports it, an icon will appear for the device, as shown in Figure 35.1.

**FIGURE 35.1**
Icons for compatible removable storage devices appear automatically when the device or disk is inserted. Double-click to open a file manager window.

Icon for USB storage device appears after device is inserted

Copy files into USB storage device window to back up

Double-click a removable device's desktop icon to open a file manager window into which you can copy important files—from your desktop, your home directory, or anywhere else—for safe-keeping.

To access devices that aren't automatically shown on your desktop you'll need to use the mount and cp commands. Access the device and store backup files by following these three steps:

**1.** Use the mount command to mount the removable disk device so that you can copy files to it.

2. Use the cp command to copy individual files or the cp command with the -R option to copy entire directory trees to the removable disk, or use the file manager to copy files and directories you want to back up.

3. Unmount the removable disk and file it away for safekeeping.

### If You Find Yourself Lost in This Section

The information in this section refers to material covered in earlier chapters.

The mount command—and how to use it with common SCSI and IDE devices—was discussed in Chapter 28, "Command-Line System Administration."

The cp and mkdir commands were discussed in several places in Chapter 6, "Working with Files in the Shell."

The process of copying files and directories using the file manager was discussed in several places in Chapter 5, "Working with Files on the Desktop."

Additional information can also be found in the mount, cp, and mkdir manual pages.

To illustrate, let's step through a sample backup session at the command line. For this example, assume that you are using a common removable slide-in, slide-out hard disk drive, connected as the master device on your secondary IDE channel. The disk you're using is formatted as a single Windows volume, meaning that it has just one partition of the type that Windows creates by default.

Your first order of business is to mount the disk. First, make a mountpoint where your files will appear by using the mkdir command. By convention, mountpoints for removable devices reside in the /mnt directory:

```
[you@workstation20 you]# mkdir /mnt/removable
[you@workstation20 you]#
```

Now, mount the disk so that you can copy files to it. Because it was formatted for Windows, the correct file system type to supply to the mount command is vfat (consult the manual page for mount for more details on various filesystem types):

```
[you@workstation20 you]# mount -t vfat /dev/hdc1 /mnt/removable
[you@workstation20 you]#
```

Now that your disk has been mounted, you can begin to copy files to it using the cp command. Let's assume that you want to copy the file /var/www/mypage.html and the entire contents of your home directory to the disk. You can use the cp command with the -R argument to copy entire directory trees. To do this, simply supply a list of files and directory trees you want to copy as arguments, listing the destination directory as your final argument. If you want to see the files listed as they are copied, use the -v (verbose) argument:

```
[root@workstation20 you]# cp -R -v /var/www/mypage.html /home/you /mnt/removable
'/var/www/mypage.html' -> '/mnt/removable/mypage.html'
'/home/you/myfile.txt' -> '/mnt/removable/you/myfile.txt'
'/home/you/document-1.tex' -> '/mnt/removable/you/document-1.tex'
'/home/you/document-2.tex' -> '/mnt/removable/you/document-2.tex'
'/home/you/old/budget-jan.sxw' -> '/mnt/removable/you/old/budget-jan.sxw'
'/home/you/old/budget-feb.sxw' -> '/mnt/removable/you/old/budget-feb.sxw'
[root@workstation20 you]#
```

You can see by the output of the cp command that your files have been copied to the /mnt/removable directory, which is the place where your removable disk is mounted. Now that your files have been backed up, unmount your removable disk:

```
[root@workstation20 you]# umount /mnt/removable
[root@workstation20 you]#
```

The next time you shut down, remove the slide-out hard disk and file it away for safekeeping, or until the next time you want to save files offline. Your files have now been backed up.

## Creating Magnetic Tape Backups with tar

Backups to disk devices are relatively easy to perform. However, depending on the format of your disks—they are generally formatted for Windows—there is a good chance that any permissions and ownership information connected with your files will not be preserved when you back them up with the cp command.

Furthermore, the cp command can't be used to copy files to magnetic tape devices, which often used for backing up larger amounts of data or backing up data on frequent basis, simply because magnetic tape is available in sizes that far exceed anything single removable disks can offer and because magnetic tape is generally less expensive, past a certain size threshold, than other types of storage.

The aforementioned problems can be solved by using the tar (Tape ARchive) command, which can communicate with magnetic tape drives and can also be used to save the permissions of files you back up on Windows-formatted media. The tar command must be used entirely from the command line; it has no graphical equivalent. To create a backup with the tar command, call tar in the following format:

```
tar -c -v -f dest /path1 [/path2 ...]
```

The required -c option tells tar that you want to *create* a backup. The optional -v option causes tar to display the name of each file as it is backed up.

Replace *dest* with the device or file that should hold the backed-up data. Table 35.1 lists some common magnetic tape devices; *dest* can also simply be the name of a file, however, as is the case if you are backing up to a mounted removable disk device.

Replace */path1* with the directory tree that `tar` should back up, the optional */path2* with the second directory tree `tar` should back up, and so on.

**TABLE 35.1** Common Magnetic Tape Device Names

| Device | Description |
| --- | --- |
| /dev/st0 | First SCSI magnetic tape device |
| /dev/st1 | Second SCSI magnetic tape device |
| /dev/ht0 | First IDE magnetic tape device |
| /dev/ht1 | Second IDE magnetic tape device |

# Backing Up with `tar` Examples

Given what you've just learned about using the `tar` command, let's step through some examples for purposes of illustration.

To back up the /home directory tree (which backs up all user home directories) to the first SCSI tape device, listing each file as it is being processed, you use the following command:

```
tar -c -v -f /dev/st0 /home
```

To back up the files in /var/www/html and /var/www/cgi-bin to the first IDE tape device, listing each file as it is being processed, you use the following command:

```
tar -c -v -f /dev/ht0 /var/www/html /var/www/cgi-bin
```

To back up the /home, /var/www, and /var/ftp directory trees to a backup file called backup-oct52004.tar, which is to be stored on a removable disk mounted on /mnt/opticaldisk—without bothering to list the files as they are stored—you use the following command:

```
tar -c -f /mnt/opticaldisk/backup-oct52004.tar /home /var/www /var/ftp
```

Because `tar` is a relatively quick command that does little processing of your files, you will find that the speed of your backups is limited only by the speed of your storage device or streaming tape device.

---

### Creating a List of Your Backup Files

If you want to create a list or index of the files you're backing up, use the `-v` option and then save `tar`'s output to a file, like this:

```
tar -c -v -f /dev/st0 /home > filelist.txt
```

---

### Compressing Critical Backup Data

If you have read the `tar` manual page and found the compress (`-z`) option, you might be tempted to use it for your tape backups.

Don't.

When you use the `tar` compress option, `tar` doesn't compress files individually; it compresses the entire *stream* of files as they are written out. This is great, unless your backup media develops an error.

If `tar` finds a read error when restoring from an uncompressed backup, `tar` can often recover, losing only the file in which the error occurred. When `tar` finds a read error when restoring from a compressed backup, *all the files in the backup are lost*.

You should thus *never* use the compress (`-z`) option for creating critical backups.

Most modern tape drives (4mm, 8mm, and DLT) compress your data as it is written anyway, so using `-z` generally produces little in the way of space savings.

---

## Restoring `tar` Backups

To restore files from a backup with the `tar` command, call `tar` in the following format:

```
tar -x -v -f source [pattern ...]
```

The required `-x` option tells `tar` that you want to *extract* (restore from) a backup. The optional `-v` option causes `tar` to display the name of each file as it is restored.

Replace *source* with the device or file that should hold the backed-up data. Refer to Table 36.1 for some common magnetic tape devices; and once again, *source* can also be the name of a backup file rather than a device.

If you don't supply a *pattern*, `tar` restores every file stored on the streaming tape device or in the backup file. Sometimes, however, you want to restore only a single file or small list of files. When this is the case, replace *pattern* with a list of quote-enclosed filenames you want to restore, or patterns you want to use to select which files are to be restored.

**Be Careful When You Restore a** `tar` **Backup**

When you restore a `tar` backup, any existing files to which you have write permission will be overwritten by the files being restored. For this reason, you should always be sure to see whether any existing files will be overwritten before starting a restore.

Note that when you restore using `tar`, the files in the backup are restored *relative to your current working directory*. This means that if you backed up the /var/www directory tree using `tar` and now want to restore the files to /var/www, you must first make the root directory (/) your current working directory using the cd command. If, for example, you try to restore the backup while /home/you is your current working directory, the restored files will end up in /home/you/var/www.

## Restoring `tar` Backups Examples

Using what you've just learned about the `tar` command, let's step through a few restoration examples to illustrate.

To restore all the files on the magnetic tape in the first SCSI tape drive, listing each file as it is restored, use the following command:

```
tar -x -v -f /dev/st0
```

To restore only the files from the /var/www tree stored on the magnetic tape in the second IDE tape drive, listing each file as it is restored, use the following command:

```
tar -x -v -f /dev/ht1 "var/www/*"
```

To silently (without listing) restore only the plaintext (.txt) files from the /home/you directory stored on the magnetic tape in the second SCSI tape drive, use the following command:

```
tar -x -f /dev/st1 "home/you/*.txt"
```

Silent backups or restores of this kind are often useful when you're writing scripts because you often want to keep output from shell scripts to a minimum.

To silently restore all the files from the `tar` backup file called backup-oct52004.tar stored on the removable disk mounted on the /mnt/opticaldisk directory, use the following command:

```
tar -x -f /mnt/opticaldisk/backup-oct52004.tar
```

Using `tar`'s backup and restore capabilities, you can preserve any file on your system that you want to save and restore it later if something should happen to it.

> **Restoring from** `tar` **Can Be Slow**
>
> If you are restoring only one or two particular files from a large backup, you might find that the `tar` command takes some time to complete. The reason is that `tar` must read through every file in a backup, regardless of whether you chose to restore every file.

**By the Way**

## Testing and Listing Backups

Sometimes you want to verify the integrity of a magnetic tape, to make sure that the files on it can still be restored. You can accomplish this by calling `tar` using the -t option:

```
tar -t -f source
```

Replace *source* with the name of the device containing the magnetic tape or the name of the `tar` file that you want to test. If there are any errors in the backup (meaning that some of the files stored in it can't be restored), an error message is displayed. If `tar` reads the entire tape or the entire backup file and then exits silently, the backup is problem free.

To create an index of an existing backup tape or file, save the output of the `tar` command to a file.

For example, to save a list of the contents of the tape in the first SCSI tape drive to the file `tape1contents.txt`, use the following command:

```
tar -t -f /dev/st0 > tape1contents.txt
```

If, while you're testing a backup, `tar` reports errors, you should throw away the media immediately and begin backing up to a new tape or disk because `tar` errors usually indicate aging or failing magnetic media.

> **Magnetic Media Is Not Archive Material!**
>
> Although media verification does have its place, you shouldn't use it as a way to store information on magnetic media for **archival** (long-term preservation) purposes.
>
> Magnetic media of all kinds should be considered useful only for short-term backup purposes because it will gradually degrade over time.

**Watch Out!**

## Automating `tar` Backups

One of the biggest advantages of `tar`'s command-line nature is the fact that it can easily be used in scripts or called using the `cron` service. This makes automating a single backup or a series of backups very easy to do: You just use your favorite text editor to create shell scripts that use the tar command, as outlined in previous sections, and then call those shell scripts using cron.

### More on cron and Shell Scripting

The cron service, which is used to schedule tasks to be carried out repeatedly at specific intervals, was discussed in "Using cron to Manage Periodic Jobs" in Chapter 28, "Command-Line System Administration."

Shell scripting was discussed in Chapter 25, "Harnessing the Power of the Shell."

Let's step through a detailed example for illustration purposes. Suppose that your computer system has two tape drives in it: one SCSI tape drive and one IDE tape drive. You are the system administrator and are responsible for backups, so you create the following backup policy:

▶ Every morning at 2:30 a.m., you back up the entire /home directory tree, which contains all your users' files, to the tape in the SCSI tape drive, verifying the contents of the tape afterward and saving any error messages displayed during verification in a file called /var/log/NightlyErrors.txt.

▶ Once a week at 5:00 p.m. on Sunday afternoon, you back up the contents of the /var/www tree to the tape in the IDE tape drive, verifying the contents of the tape afterward and saving any error messages displayed during verification in a file called /var/log/WeeklyErrors.txt.

While logged in as root, using vi (or emacs, if you prefer), you create a script called system-backup, as shown in Listing 35.1; then you copy it to ~/bin and mark it as executable.

### LISTING 35.1    The system-backup Script You Create As Administrator

```
#!/bin/sh

if [ "$1" = nightly ]; then
  tar -c -f /dev/st0 /home
  tar -t -f /dev/st0 2> /var/log/NightlyErrors.txt
fi

if [ "$1" = weekly ]; then
  tar -c -f /dev/ht0 /var/www
  tar -t -f /dev/ht0 2> /var/log/WeeklyErrors.txt
fi
```

When called with the `nightly` argument, the `system-backup` script shown in Listing 35.1 backs up the `/home` directory tree to tape drive `/dev/st0` and then tests the archive for integrity, making a log file in the process. When called with the `weekly` argument, it backs up the `/var/www` directory tree to tape drive `/dev/ht0` and then tests that archive, again making a log file in the process.

After you create the script, you issue the `crontab -e` command to edit the `root` user's list of periodic jobs. In the special `cron` control file, you enter the following lines:

```
30 2 * * * ~/bin/system-backup nightly
0 17 * * * ~/bin/system-backup weekly
```

After entering these lines, you save and exit. Your backup regimen is now in place; you need to remember only to load or switch tapes as necessary. Linux, `cron`, and `tar` take care of the rest, and any errors encountered are saved as `/var/log/backup.daily` and `/var/log/backup.weekly`. Remember to check these logs often to make sure that your backups are being completed without media errors!

Your own backup automation techniques using `cron`, shell scripts, and `tar` can, of course, be much more complex and nuanced than these; you are limited only by your imagination and your ability to master shell scripting.

# Dealing with Catastrophic Failures

Most anyone who has worked with computers for any length of time knows that sometimes our worst fears come true: A computer system suffers a failure of some kind, which prevents it from even starting properly any longer.

Although Linux is a very stable operating system, if you use it long enough, you are still likely to encounter a situation at some point in which Linux is unable to start properly, even though your computer can at least be powered on and your hard drive appears to be functioning.

Red Hat has provided a special tool called `rescue` that can be used to try to salvage some of your data in situations like this.

## Starting `rescue`

To start the `rescue` tool, insert your Fedora Core 4 install DVD or CD-ROM and allow it to boot your system. At the `boot:` prompt at the Fedora Core 4 title screen, type the phrase **linux rescue** as shown in Figure 35.2, then press Enter.

**FIGURE 35.2**
Type the phrase
linux rescue
when booting
your Fedora
Core 4 install
CD to start the
rescue system.

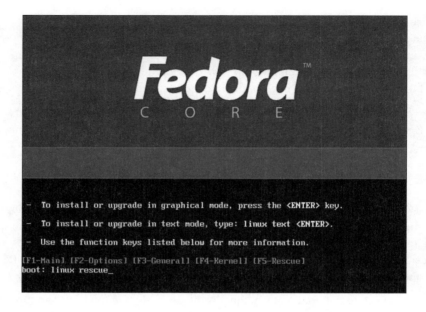

**FIGURE 35.2**
Type the phrase
linux rescue
when booting
your Fedora
Core 4 install
CD to start the
rescue system.

*Did you*
*Know?*

## For Users Without Bootable DVD or CD-ROM Drives

If your computer doesn't have bootable DVD or CD-ROM capability, you need to use the installation floppy disks that you created near the end of Chapter 1, "Preparing to Install Fedora Core 4."

You soon see several preliminary dialog boxes that will help the Fedora Core 4 rescue mode to configure itself for use:

▶ When you are asked to select your native language, use your up- and down-arrow keys to select your native language; then press Enter.

▶ When you are asked to select your keyboard layout, use your up- and down-arrow keys to select the type of international keyboard you are using; then press Enter. If you are unsure about the type of keyboard you are using, simply press Enter to accept the default selection, which is the correct one for most users.

▶ When you are asked whether you want to set up networking, as shown in Figure 35.3, use your Tab key to select the No option and press Enter, unless you absolutely need networking enabled to restore your system and you are prepared (and knowledgeable enough) to use command-line networking tools covered in earlier chapters.

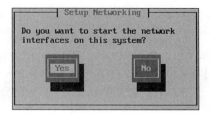

After answering each dialog box appropriately, you see the Rescue dialog box, as shown in Figure 35.4.

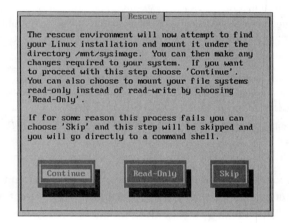

The dialog box offers to have rescue try to find and mount the file systems that make up your Linux installation. Use the Tab key here to select the Read-Only option and then press Enter, thereby allowing rescue to try to access your data while ensuring that it won't be damaged any further. After rescue finds your Linux file system, it displays a message telling you that the file system has been mounted on /mnt/sysimage.

Press Enter to go to a Linux command prompt, where you are able to try to salvage your data, a process explored in the next section.

## Attempting File System Repairs

If rescue is able to find and mount your Linux file system, you can try to use a technique that often restores nonbooting Linux systems to full functionality: the file system check. The e2fsck command can be used to thoroughly check your Linux file system for structural problems and attempt to repair them.

To use e2fsck in rescue, you call it with the -f option (to force a full file system check) and supply the name of the device you want to check as an argument. There is, however, one catch: e2fsck must never be run on mounted file systems. Therefore, to test your file systems using e2fsck in rescue, follow the steps outlined next.

**By the Way**

### When Nothing Is Found by rescue

If you receive a message saying that rescue was unable to find or unable to mount your Linux file system, there is little more that you can do to salvage any current data stored in your Linux file system.

Simply reset your system (starting with the install CD) and reinstall Linux. Then restore data from whatever backups you do have using the instructions earlier in this chapter.

**By the Way**

### More on Using Pipes at the Command Line

You learned about data pipes and the grep command in Chapter 19, "Performing Basic Shell Tasks."

First, enter the mount command without arguments to list the mounted file systems; pipe the output of mount to the grep command and search for the text sysimage. This gives you a list of the devices that make your Linux file system because, as rescue told you, all your Linux file system is mounted under /mnt/sysimage.

```
sh-3.00# mount ¦ grep sysimage
/dev/sda2 on /mnt/sysimage type ext3 (ro)
/dev/sda1 on /mnt/sysimage/boot type ext3 (ro)
/dev/proc on /mnt/sysimage/proc type proc (ro,nodiratime)
/dev/sys on /mnt/sysimage/sys type sysfs (ro)
/dev on /mnt/sysimage/dev type sh-3.00#
```

Ignore lines that begin with /dev/proc, /dev/sys, and /dev (the last three lines). They are virtual file systems, and no real devices are connected to them. Pay attention only to volumes of type ext3, ext2, or reiserfs. In this case, the Linux file system is stored on two devices: /dev/sda1 and /dev/sda2. Before using the e2fsck utility, you must unmount all these file systems. To do this, issue umount for each file system in the list, beginning at the bottom and moving upward:

```
sh-3.00# umount /mnt/sysimage/proc
sh-3.00# umount /mnt/sysimage/sys
sh-3.00# umount /mnt/sysimage/boot
sh-3.00# umount /mnt/sysimage
sh-3.00#
```

Your Linux file system has now been unmounted, and you can proceed to check each device by using the e2fsck command, supplying the -f option followed by the device name for the device you want to check each time through. For example, to start with /dev/sda1, you enter

```
sh-3.00# e2fsck -f /dev/sda1
e2fsck 1.36 (05-Feb-2005)
Pass 1: Checking inodes, blocks and sizes
[...]
/: 76751/434592 files (0.2% non-contiguous), 346776/867510 blocks
sh-3.00#
```

The output e2fsck produces varies depending on the type and number of problems (if any) that e2fsck finds on the device. If you are asked any questions by e2fsck, press Enter to accept the default choice. The guts of the Linux file system are beyond the scope of a book like this one, and perhaps more importantly, choices *other than* the default choice are almost *never* the correct choice for the best chance at full repair. When e2fsck finishes checking a device, it prints a brief, somewhat cryptic summary of the number of files, noncontiguous files, and used blocks on the system.

After you check all your devices, enter **exit** at the command prompt to exit rescue and reboot your system. If you are now able to boot normally into Fedora Core 4, your problem has been solved.

## Salvaging Files

If you are able to start rescue mode, rescue is able to find your Linux file system, you are able to run file system checks using e2fsck, and yet your system *still* doesn't start normally, there is likely nothing left to do but try to save any current files in your Linux file system before reinstalling Fedora Core 4. Although a Linux expert might still have been able to repair the system, more advanced types of repairs are beyond the scope of a book like this one and are generally beyond the reach of Linux beginners.

Restart Fedora Core 4's rescue in the same way you did before. After your file systems have been mounted on /mnt/sysimage again, you can proceed to use the backup techniques described in "Backing Up and Restoring Your Data" earlier in this chapter to save any current files you might want to save from your file system tree; commands such as mount, cp, and tar are all available to you in rescue. Remember, however, to adjust for the fact that your file system is now mounted on /mnt/sysimage. For example, to back up what is normally your /home tree to a SCSI tape drive using the tar command, you would now have to enter the following:

```
tar -c -f /dev/st0 /mnt/sysimage/home
```

Similarly, a file called `myimportantfile.txt` that normally resided in your home directory at `/home/you` would now be accessed as `/mnt/sysimage/home/you/myimportantfile.txt`.

After you save the files you want to save from your Linux file system, exit rescue mode, reinstall Linux following the directions in Part I of this book, and then restore your important data from the backups you've just made.

# Recognizing Other Critical Problems

Sometimes it's obvious that you need to go into "emergency mode" and try to preserve your data and rescue your system—for example, if you suffer a complete hard drive failure or if you are unable to boot Linux at all. There are, however, two times when it is desirable to preemptively take drastic action to save your system even though your system still appears to be mostly functional:

▶ Situations in which your hard drive is displaying symptoms of file system corruption or approaching failure

▶ Situations in which you can determine that your Linux system might have fallen victim to network hacking or Trojan horse or worm programs

Left unchecked, either of these situations can lead to eventual unexpected downtime, data loss, or even data theft. The following sections detail how to spot these types of situations and what to do should they occur.

## Recognizing File System Trouble

**File system corruption** occurs when the organization of the data on your hard drive is unexpectedly damaged, thereby causing Linux to begin to lose track of where some files begin or end, or of which files contain what data. After your file system becomes corrupt, continued access to the disk usually *increases* the spread of file system corruption, thereby endangering and potentially damaging still more files with every passing minute.

A few telltale signs indicate that you are likely beginning to experience file system corruption:

▶ You begin to encounter files that contain **garbage**, a mishmash of nonsensical data that doesn't represent the content that you were expecting a file to have—the content that you remember actually *storing* in the file in the first place.

▶ You begin to encounter directory problems—filenames containing garbage, spontaneously appearing or disappearing files, files or directories that can't be removed or edited even when permissions would seem to indicate that such things should be possible.

▶ You find files that, when accessed, seem to crash your computer system or the program you're using every time, without fail, in the same way.

▶ You begin to lose files or directories entirely, even though you have not deleted them; they're just suddenly gone.

If you believe that you are experiencing file system corruption, follow the steps earlier in this chapter in the "Dealing with Catastrophic Failures" section to start the rescue tool and perform checks on your file systems using e2fsck. Doing this should repair the corruption that has occurred on your file system and make it safe for use again—although any data that was corrupted is lost forever.

---

### Hard drives can tell you when they're sick

*Did you Know?*

Many hard drives in modern computers are capable of reporting on their status, and telling you when they're sick. Linux includes a command, smartctl, that can ask a hard drive to test itself and report on its health. To test a hard drive, type the following as root:

```
/usr/sbin/smartctl -t long /dev/device
```

Remember to replace /dev/device with the actual device in question, for example /dev/hda for the first IDE hard drive in the system. The smartctl command will tell you how long the test will take, and will then disappear into the background and run the test. Once the listed amount of time has elapsed, run the following command as root:

```
/usr/sbin/smartctl -a /dev/device
```

Again, remember to replace /dev/device with the actual device. This command will generate lots of output, but only the last few lines are important. If the Status column for the test you just ran shows Completed without error, then your hard drive is fine. If it reports any kind of error or failure instead, back your hard drive up and replace it immediately!

If you want to learn more about smartctl, read its manual page using the man command.

---

If e2fsck is unable to find any problems in your Linux file systems, whatever symptoms you are experiencing are not due to file system corruption. In some cases, they might be due to malicious activity (we deal with this topic in the next section); in other cases, they might simply represent an aspect of the normal functioning of the Linux operating system that is unfamiliar to you.

> ### Data Corruption Is Usually a Warning of Things to Come!
>
> If you are experiencing repeated bouts of file system corruption, you find that your system often hangs with the hard drive activity light on, or you begin to find log entries that refer to I/O errors or missing sectors on one of the devices used by your Linux file system, you are likely going to experience a catastrophic hard drive failure in the near future.
>
> You should back up your data immediately and replace your hard drive to avoid unexpected downtime and/or data loss!

## Recognizing Malicious Network Activity

There is one other type of critical problem that some unfortunate Linux users no doubt experience—particularly those who are connected to busy networks or directly to the Internet. Linux systems are often targeted by hackers or other types of malicious network users. The reason is that most Linux systems on networks are not just PCs, but are typically servers—configured to accept incoming requests while providing important services to many users.

In general, Linux should be very good at repelling attacks, especially if you have properly configured your firewall as described in Chapter 30, "Security Basics." However, from time to time, it is inevitable that some attacks are successful. Recognizing the symptoms of having been successfully attacked can help you avoid extensive amounts of data loss or unwilling participation in Internet crimes. As long as your Linux system is connected to a network, you should stay vigilant in watching for all the following:

▶ Newly appearing SUID/SGID files, which indicate that someone is trying to access or has already accessed root-level functionality on your system. For more information on SUID/SGID special permissions, refer to "Understanding Special Permissions" in Chapter 30.

▶ The appearance of new accounts in the /etc/passwd file or new groups in the /etc/group file that you did not create.

▶ System log records of users remotely logging in using accounts that don't seem to exist or that you did not create.

▶ Unexplained heavy network traffic that doesn't appear to be connected to any service you're running, or unfamiliar processes in the output of the ps command that always eventually return even after you kill them repeatedly.

▶ Any of the previously mentioned issues combined with symptoms of file system corruption—disappearing files, undeletable files, or unreadable files or directories in spite of correct permissions, and so on.

If you find yourself experiencing any of these symptoms, your system has likely been compromised. Unfortunately, this counts as a catastrophic failure. When a computer system is compromised by a malicious network user, he usually replaces many of the operating system components with modified components, which allow them to steal your data, use your computer in attacks on other computers, or perform other unwanted behavior.

If you think your system has been compromised, you should *immediately* shut down your computer system to prevent further unknown malicious activity. Boot into rescue as described in "Dealing with Catastrophic Failures" earlier in this chapter, taking care not to enable networking. Save your important data files *only* (no programs or applications; they might have been replaced by harmful dupes) using the techniques described in "Backing Up and Restoring Your Data" earlier in this chapter. Then reinstall Fedora Core 4 from scratch as described in Part I of this book and restore your data from the backups you made.

After your Linux system is running again, review Chapter 30, "Security Basics," and implement the techniques described there. Afterward, refer to Chapter 32, "Keeping Fedora Core Updated," to ensure that all of the latest updates and security measures have been installed on your system.

# Summary

In this chapter, you gained the final set of administrative tools and skills needed for you to become a safe and happy longtime Linux user. Specifically, you learned the following:

▶ How to back up and restore your important data files using removable disk media and simple copying

▶ How to back up and restore your important data files to magnetic tape or to special backup files using the tar command

▶ How to try to rescue a system that has experienced a catastrophic failure of some sort and no longer boots correctly

▶ How to salvage files from a broken system if you are unable to rescue it

▶ How to recognize other situations in which data salvage and subsequent reinstallation and restoration might be apropos, including situations caused by file system corruption and malicious network activity

Congratulations! You've survived all 35 chapters. You've learned how to install and configure Linux to work on your computer system, you've mastered a basic set of applications and techniques at the Linux command line, you've learned how to make efficient use of Linux desktop applications, and you've learned how to perform most basic administration tasks in Linux.

Although you might not feel like a guru yet, keep working at it and you will eventually become one. Experiment, read manual pages, and consult the documentation at http://www.tldp.org often. In time, you will find that you can make Linux work for you on your terms, efficiently and reliably.

When you are ready to become a guru, consider consulting the *Red Hat Linux Unleashed* series of books, also by Sams. The information in this series applies to all Red Hat operating systems, including Fedora Core and other members of the Red Hat Linux and Fedora Core family of operating systems.

# Q&A

**Q.** *I have a magnetic tape device, but it isn't connected to a SCSI controller or an IDE controller. How can I access it?*

**A.** Although Linux does include drivers for many older tape devices, there are so many of them—and they behave in so many different ways—that use of such devices in Linux is best left to the pros. Consider upgrading to an industry-standard SCSI or IDE streamer instead; the newer drives are much more reliable, and using them with Linux and the tar command is relatively easy.

**Q.** *Can I back up my entire system, rather than just my data files, using* tar?

**A.** Yes, you can back up every directory tree but /proc using the tar command. Restoring from a systemwide backup of this sort is a matter of booting restore, using parted and mount (both of which you've learned about) to create and mount a new file system, and then streaming the data back on to the hard drive with tar. Beware, however—if you have experienced hacking activity, any compromised files might also be restored in such an operation. It is usually therefore a better idea to back up data files only.

**Q.** *I have experienced file system corruption several times, but each time,* rescue *and* e2fsck *are able to repair the problem. Why should I buy a new hard drive?*

**A** Because repeated bouts of file system corruption indicate that your hard drive is *losing data* that has been stored there. Aside from the fact that some of your data is disappearing forever, it is very likely that a hard drive that is losing data will fail completely in short order. Try running the `smartctl` test described earlier to be sure.

# Workshop

The Workshop is designed to help you anticipate possible questions, review what you've learned, and begin learning how to put your knowledge into practice.

## Quiz

1. What command would you use to back up the /var/www, /var/logs, and /home directory trees to the only IDE tape drive on a Linux computer system?

2. How do you start the Fedora Core 4 rescue tool?

3. What command is used to perform file system checks of the Linux ext2 and ext3 file systems?

4. Finding garbage in your files is a symptom of what type of critical problem?

## Answers

1. `tar -c -f /dev/ht0 /var/www /var/logs /home`

2. Boot from your install media (floppy or CD-ROM) and enter the text **linux rescue** at the boot: prompt.

3. `e2fsck`

4. File system corruption

## Activities

1. Design and implement a backup regimen for your data—either an automatic one using shell scripts and cron or simply a manual one that you decide to abide by faithfully.

2. Try booting into the rescue tool just to test it and become familiar with the process.

3. Use the tar command to store a few files of your choosing in a backup file and then restore them to another directory.

# Appendixes

# APPENDIX A

# Installer Troubleshooting

In general, the Fedora Core 4 installer is a reasonably foolproof tool, which does a good job of installing Linux. However, to enjoy the benefits it provides, you must first be able to start it. This appendix deals with two subjects related to the Fedora Core 4 installer:

▶ The installer's failure to find hard drive or CD-ROM drive devices to install to or from, respectively

▶ The use of the text-based installer when your graphics hardware isn't supported by the default installer

## Loading Modules at Install Time

In some cases—most notably when either your hard drive or CD-ROM drive is connected to your computer via a SCSI controller—Fedora Core 4 cannot start the installer right away because either it isn't able to find your CD-ROM drive or it isn't able to find your hard drive. This situation occurs because none of the drivers in the installer's default driver list is able to communicate with your hardware. In this case, the installer asks about the nature of your hardware and then asks you to select a driver, as shown in Figures A.1 through A.3.

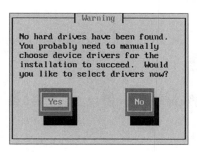

**FIGURE A.1**
The installer can't find a hard drive.

**FIGURE A.2**
The installer
asks whether
you would like
to load drivers
manually.

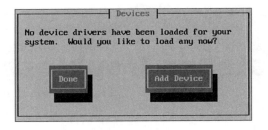

**FIGURE A.3**
The installer
asks you to
choose the driv-
er for the con-
troller to which
your hard drive
is connected.

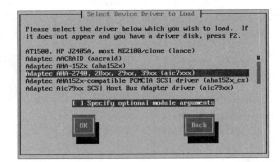

When you are given a list of driver modules, scroll up and down through the list until the one that matches your hardware is highlighted. Then press Tab until the word OK is highlighted, and the driver will be loaded.

Generally, if you can't find the module in a list, you can press your F2 key to search from an additional list of modules. After you press F2, a message box appears, asking you to insert the driver floppy disk you learned to make in Chapter 1, "Preparing to Install Fedora Core 4"; insert the disk and press Enter. An alternate list of drivers is displayed.

After you select the correct driver, the Fedora Core 4 installer finds your hardware, and the installation process proceeds as outlined in Chapter 2, "Installing Fedora Core 4."

# Using Module Parameters: A Last Resort

If a module fails to load, you do not get an error message, but the installer asks again how to locate the missing piece of hardware and continues to offer you the same list of drivers. If you are sure about the type of hardware you possess and yet your driver is failing to load, you might need to supply extra information to the driver to get it to load correctly. Unfortunately, the list of values needed by each driv-er can be found only in the source code of the Linux kernel itself or from the driver's author (or manufacturer). You can download the source code of the Linux kernel from the anonymous FTP site ftp.kernel.org. Because navigating the Linux kernel source requires some experience in dealing with programming in the C language, module parameters are best used by experienced users or those with previous Linux experience.

To supply parameters to a module, use the Tab key to highlight the Specify Optional Module Arguments option and then press the spacebar to select it; an asterisk appears in the selection box, as shown in Figure A.4.

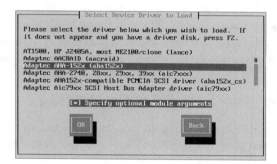

**FIGURE A.4**
If the driver doesn't load the first time, try again, but choose to specify module arguments.

When you attempt to load a driver after selecting that you want to specify module arguments, the Enter Module Parameters screen is displayed before the driver is loaded. In this screen, you can enter various types of configuration data, as shown in Figure A.5.

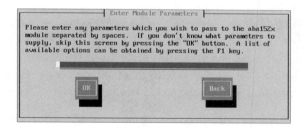

**FIGURE A.5**
You can configure the device driver in the Enter Module Parameters screen if you are familiar with your hardware.

The set of options that can be configured varies from device to device, but generally some indication is provided for how to proceed, though it might at first seem obtuse. The Enter Module Parameters screen displays anywhere from one to several input lines, each of which accepts additional information about the module or driver. For example, some SCSI drivers might ask you to supply an input/output base address (ioport), interrupt request line (irq), and host adapter SCSI ID (host scsiid) in a specific format. Follow the cues given on the Enter Module Parameters screen to enter the information for your hardware.

In some cases, the module's request for information is more explicit: A module might ask only for an IRQ, a base address, or a revision level for your hardware. If in doubt, feel free to experiment with values to try to get your hardware working. Obviously, you must be reasonably familiar with PC hardware in general, with your own hardware in particular, and with the conventions in use in Linux and the C programming language to be able to configure module parameters effectively during the install process. Regrettably, every driver is different, so the information you must provide and the format in which it should be provided varies from driver to driver (and from manufacturer to manufacturer, if you have manufacturer-supplied driver disks for Fedora Core 4 or for Fedora Core 4). Try to follow the visual cues and supplied values for each driver as guidelines. In the end, it is nearly always easier for inexperienced users to replace an undetected hardware item than to try to load a driver manually in this fashion.

# Using the Text Mode Installer

Some computers are not capable of running the standard Fedora Core 4 installer that uses graphics and your mouse. When this is true, one of two things happens:

▶ The Fedora Core 4 installer detects that your computer is not compatible with its graphics mode, and the text mode installer starts instead, automatically.

▶ Your computer crashes, displays the installer screens incorrectly, or otherwise prevents you through abnormal circumstances from completing the install process as it is shown in Chapter 2.

If the latter is true in your case, you need to force the text mode installer to start preemptively so that the graphical installer is never started. To do this, boot from your Fedora Core 4 install media and enter the phrase **linux text** at the boot: prompt. This causes the Fedora Core 4 installer to bypass the graphics mode entirely and begin the text mode installer after the media check, as shown in Figure A.6.

Fortunately, the text mode installer functions almost identically to the default installer discussed in Chapter 2. The program flow and offered choices and options are the same; only the appearance is different. You should therefore be able to navigate the text mode installer using Chapter 2 as a guide, provided that you keep the following in mind:

▶ Highlighted text (red letters on a gray background) serves the same purpose as the mouse in the default installer; any highlighted text is currently being "pointed at."

▶ The Enter key serves the same purpose as your mouse button would in the default installer; pressing the Enter key chooses the currently highlighted (pointed at) option.

▶ Pressing the Tab key repeatedly is like moving the mouse—each time you press the Tab key, the highlight moves to the next choice on the screen. When offered a choice, press Tab until the highlight points to the option you want to select; then press your Enter key to select it.

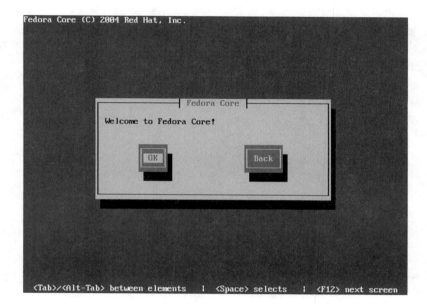

**FIGURE A.6**
The text mode installer doesn't use graphics and doesn't use your mouse; it relies on your keyboard exclusively.

The fact that you are forced to use the text mode indicates a greater chance that Fedora Core 4 is not compatible with your display hardware. You might find that after you finish the text mode installer, Fedora Core 4's graphical mode doesn't work when you boot your system. If this is the case, you might want to consider upgrading your graphics hardware to be compatible with Fedora Core 4. After you have done so, I hope you'll attempt to install Fedora Core 4 again!

# Installing from Network Volumes or Hard Drives

Although this book has been largely concerned with the use of Fedora Core 4 on a single desktop computer, installed from the included CD-ROM media, it's also possible to manage Fedora Core 4 installations for larger numbers of computers. For example, if you plan to install Fedora Core 4 on a large number of networked computer systems, having to insert and remove CDs throughout the install for each computer in question can be time-consuming.

For these and other kinds of situations, Fedora Core 4 provides for several alternate install methods, aside from the basic CD-ROM install. To enable installation from sources other than CD-ROM, enter the words **linux askmethod** at the prompt when first booting your install media.

The installer boots into text mode, and you are asked to select a language and keyboard layout (see the details earlier in this appendix for text mode navigation hints). After selecting a language and keyboard layout, you see a dialog box asking you to select an installation source, as shown in Figure A.8.

**FIGURE A.7**
After booting with linux askmethod, you are asked to select an installation source.

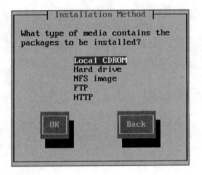

Each option is slightly different in the way it works, but all of them eventually lead to the text mode installer described earlier:

▶ Select Local CD-ROM to continue to install from the currently inserted CD-ROM, rather than one of the alternate sources.

▶ Select Hard Drive if you have previously copied the entire contents of the Fedora Core 4 CD-ROMs into a single directory tree on your hard drive and want to use those files as your source media.

▶ Select NFS Image if the contents of the Fedora Core 4 CD-ROMs can be accessed on some other computer via Network File Service (NFS); you are then asked to provide network details about the remote machine so that the NFS volume can be mounted.

▶ Select FTP if you want to install from contents of the Fedora Core 4 CD-ROMs that are stored on a remote machine and available via File Transfer Protocol (FTP); you are then asked for the remote machine's address, the path to the archive, and login information.

▶ Select HTTP if you want to install from contents of the Fedora Core 4 CD-ROMs that are stored on a remote machine and available via its web server; you are then asked for a remote URL and login information.

Complete details about these alternate installation methods are beyond the scope of a book like this one. For most readers, the correct installation method remains the CD-ROMs that are included with this book, as outlined in Chapter 2.

# APPENDIX B

# Adding Windows Compatibility to Linux

Though Fedora Core 4 ships with a large variety of productivity and development applications, many Linux users find themselves wanting or needing to run Windows applications in Linux. Although running such applications was hard to achieve in the early days of Linux, the past several years have seen an explosion in Windows compatibility software for Linux.

## Windows Compatibility Overview

The three popular Windows-compatibility solutions for Linux users can be summarized, in brief, as follows:

▶ CrossOver Office provides the best user experience, Linux integration, and speed, but for a limited set of applications—Internet Explorer, Microsoft Office, Adobe Photoshop, and Lotus Notes being the most important.

▶ VMware Workstation is more difficult to install, requires more system resources (disk space, memory, and processor time), but also provides additional flexibility: It can be used to run applications from a number of different operating systems on your Linux desktop, and it can also be used to create several independent, virtual, networkable PCs from a single computer system.

▶ Netraverse Win4Lin represents a kind of compromise between these two; it is nearly as fast as CrossOver Office but doesn't suffer from CrossOver Office's limited set of applications. On the other hand, Win4Lin still requires that you install a complete Windows operating system and use all your Windows programs from within a single application window, as does VMware, on both counts.

The remainder of this appendix discusses these three Windows compatibility solutions for Linux in more detail.

The retail versions of all three of these software packages include documentation and RPM installers compatible with Fedora Core 4's software installation tools (which you learn about in Chapter 31, "Installing Linux Software").

**By the Way**

## This Software is Not Part of Fedora Core

All the software products discussed in this chapter are third-party products. This means that they are not included on your Fedora Core 4 DVD, nor are they supported by the Fedora Project or Red Hat, Inc. Instead, you must purchase the software in question from one of the following vendors:

CodeWeavers—http://www.codeweavers.com

VMware—http://www.vmware.com

Netraverse—http://www.netraverse.com

Every software product discussed in this chapter is available in RPM format. This means that after purchasing them and reading the included documentation for each product, you can install them using the techniques you learn in Chapter 31.

In-depth details on starting and using each software product are provided by the vendor; this appendix is intended only as an overview.

# Codeweavers CrossOver Office

CrossOver Office is unique among the three Windows compatibility solutions discussed in this chapter in that it comes closest to allowing you to run Windows applications natively—in their own application windows, with transparent access to the Linux file system, your home

**By the Way**

You can learn more about or purchase CrossOver Office by visiting the CodeWeavers website at http://www.codeweavers.com.

## CrossOver Office: Architecture and Capabilities

CrossOver Office is built using the open-source WINE (which stands for Wine Is Not an Emulator) project. WINE is a reimplementation of the Windows API for Linux, meaning that as it matures, it will gradually form the basis for complete or near-complete Windows compatibility, without the need to actually run an instance of the Windows operating system.

Because WINE is currently only partially complete, it is not yet able to run all Windows applications successfully. However, the authors of WINE and CrossOver Office have focused on major applications first, so current versions of CrossOver Office can run the latest versions of many of the most essential or commonly needed Windows applications at native speeds in Linux. These applications include

- ▶ Microsoft Internet Explorer
- ▶ Microsoft Office
- ▶ Windows Media Player
- ▶ Adobe Photoshop
- ▶ Lotus Notes

# VMware Workstation

VMware Workstation is unique among the three Windows compatibility solutions discussed in this chapter in that it provides the tools necessary to run applications from a whole variety of operating systems in Fedora Core 4, including

- ▶ Microsoft Windows (all versions)
- ▶ Microsoft MS-DOS
- ▶ Other Unix systems
- ▶ Novell NetWare
- ▶ Various other PC-compatible operating systems

Although the interface isn't as intuitive or clean as the CrossOver Office interface, VMware provides a much more powerful solution for developers and system administrators who need extensive compatibility with a variety of applications, or who need to run several virtual computers inside a single real computer.

> You can learn more about or purchase VMware Workstation by visiting the VMware website at http://www.vmware.com.

**By the Way**

## VMware: Architecture and Capabilities

VMware achieves its extensive compatibility by behaving like a virtual (imaginary) computer system that is separate from your Fedora Core 4 computer—even though technically VMware is an application that is running inside your Fedora Core 4 computer. To do this, VMware opens an application window on your Linux desktop that will function as the display (screen) of this virtual computer. Your CD-ROM drive, printer, and network connection act as the CD-ROM drive, printer, and network connections for the virtual computer as well. A section of your hard drive (contained in a large file) is given to this virtual computer and acts as its hard drive.

Such a virtual computer, whose screen is an application window on your desktop, looks and functions very much like a separate real computer to most programs. For this reason, you can install any supported operating system and applications on its (imaginary) hard drive—Windows and windows applications if needed, FreeBSD and FreeBSD applications if needed, or even QNX and QNX applications if that's what your needs call for. These operating systems and applications then run in the application window on your Linux desktop that acts as the virtual computer's display.

One important side effect of this architecture should be noted: You can start as many VMware application windows as you like; each one can be a separate virtual computer with its own virtual hard drive and its own network address. For this reason, one Fedora Core 4 machine running VMware, with one network cable plugged into its network jack, can appear to be 10 or even 20 independent computers on your network, running a variety of operating systems and applications.

One final benefit bears mentioning here: If you are running Microsoft Windows and Windows applications using VMware Workstation, you don't need to worry about Windows crashes. If Microsoft Windows or any of its applications crash, only the virtual computer is affected and its application window closes. Fedora Core 4 continues to operate without any ill effects, healthy and unaffected by the Windows crash. The same holds true for any operating system running in the virtual machine.

# Netraverse Win4Lin

Netraverse Win4Lin is the third Windows compatibility option covered in this appendix, and it represents a kind of middle ground between the previous two. Like VMware, Win4Lin runs an entire Windows operating system in a virtual computer. Like CrossOver Office, on the other hand, Win4Lin shares your Fedora Core 4 file system instead of using a virtual hard drive. Win4Lin is also a light user of processor and memory resources, like CrossOver Office (and unlike VMware).

You can learn more about or purchase Win4Lin by visiting the Netraverse website at http://www.netraverse.com.

## Win4Lin: Architecture and Capabilities

Based on a Windows-on-Unix technology that was originally sold as MERGE for UnixWare, Win4Lin actually does merge, in some ways, Windows and Linux.

Instead of creating a true virtual computer with imaginary hardware, as VMware Workstation does, Win4Lin allows certain versions of Microsoft Windows to run in Linux using a clever trick: Win4Lin replaces the Windows standard drivers for sound cards, graphics hardware, hard drives, and the like, with drivers that interface to Linux's own drivers for the same devices.

This clever architecture allows Win4Lin to avoid the overhead that VMware Workstation incurs in creating imaginary hardware like sound cards and SCSI controllers that are actually compatible with real hardware of the same ilk. On the other hand, it means that Win4Lin is limited to running Windows operating systems; it doesn't support other operating systems such as QNX or FreeBSD, even if they are PC compatible.

In fact, Win4Lin is limited to running just the following versions of Microsoft Windows (and, by extension, applications compatible with them):

▶ Microsoft Windows 95

▶ Microsoft Windows 98

▶ Microsoft Windows Me

Notably absent from this list are versions of Microsoft Windows that are based on Windows NT technology, including Windows NT 3.5, Windows NT 4.0, Windows 2000, and Windows XP. However, the vast majority of Windows applications remain compatible with Windows 95, 98, and Me, and thus function properly in Win4Lin.

# Index

**partitions**